T0187329

Get the eBooks FREE!

(PDF, ePub, Kindle, and liveBook all included)

We believe that once you buy a book from us, you should be able to read it in any format we have available. To get electronic versions of this book at no additional cost to you, purchase and then register this book at the Manning website.

Go to https://www.manning.com/freebook and follow the instructions to complete your pBook registration.

That's it!
Thanks from Manning!

ASP.NET Core in Action

ASP.NET
Core in Action

ANDREW LOCK

MANNING
SHELTER ISLAND

For online information and ordering of this and other Manning books, please visit
www.manning.com. The publisher offers discounts on this book when ordered in quantity.
For more information, please contact

    Special Sales Department
    Manning Publications Co.
    20 Baldwin Road
    PO Box 761
    Shelter Island, NY 11964
    Email: orders@manning.com

Manning Publications Co.
20 Baldwin Road
PO Box 761
Shelter Island, NY 11964

Development editor: Marina Michaels
Technical development editor: Kris Athi
Review editor: Ivan Martinović
Project manager: David Novak
Copyeditor: Safis Editing
Proofreader: Elizabeth Martin
Technical proofreader: Tanya Wilke
Typesetter: Dottie Marsico
Cover designer: Marija Tudor

ISBN 9781617294617
Printed and bound by CPI Group (UK) Ltd, Croydon, CR0 4YY

brief contents

contents

preface

ASP.NET has a long history—Microsoft released the first version in 2002 as part of the original .NET Framework 1.0. Since then, it's been through multiple iterations, each version bringing added features and extensibility. But each iteration was built on the same underlying framework provided by System.Web.dll. This library is a part of the .NET Framework, and so comes pre-installed in all versions of Windows.

This brings mixed blessings. On the one hand, the ASP.NET 4.X framework is a reliable, battle-tested platform for building modern applications on Windows. On the other hand, it's also limited by this reliance—changes to the underlying System .Web.dll are far-reaching and, consequently, slow to roll out. It also fundamentally excludes the many developers building on and deploying to Linux or macOS.

When I first began looking into ASP.NET Core, I was one of those developers. A Windows user at heart, I was issued with a Mac by my employer, and so was stuck working on a virtual machine all day. ASP.NET Core promised to change all that, allowing me to develop natively on both my Windows machine and Mac.

I was relatively late to the party in many respects, only taking an active interest just before the time of the RC2 release of ASP.NET Core. By that point, there had already been eight (!) beta releases, many of which contained significant breaking changes; by not diving in fully until RC2, I was spared the pain of dodgy tooling and changing APIs.

What I saw really impressed me. ASP.NET Core let developers leverage their existing knowledge of the .NET framework, and of ASP.NET MVC applications in particular, while baking-in current best practices like dependency injection, strongly typed configuration, and logging. On top of that, you could build and deploy cross-platform. I was sold.

This book came about largely due to my approach to learning about ASP.NET Core. Rather than simply reading documentation and blog posts, I decided to try something new and start writing about what I learned. Each week, I would dedicate some time to exploring a new aspect of ASP.NET Core, and I'd write a blog post about it. When the possibility of writing a book came about, I jumped at the chance—another excuse to dive further into the framework!

Since I started this book, a lot has changed, both with the book and ASP.NET Core. The first major release of the framework, in June 2016, still had many rough edges; the tooling experience in particular. But with the release of ASP.NET Core 2.0 in August 2017, the framework has really come into its own. I think ASP.NET Core 2.0 is a no-brainer for most people, so the book has evolved from targeting version 1.0 when I first started, to targeting 2.0 now. I describe the major differences between the versions in the book where appropriate, but I strongly encourage you to use ASP.NET Core 2.0 when you have the choice.

This book covers everything you need to get started with ASP.NET Core, whether you're completely new to web development or an existing ASP.NET developer. It focuses very much on the framework itself, so I don't go into details about client-side frameworks such as Angular and React, or technologies like Docker. Personally, I find it a joy to work with ASP.NET Core apps compared to apps using the previous version of ASP.NET, and I hope that passion comes through in this book!

acknowledgments

While there's only one name on the cover of this book, a plethora of people contributed to both its writing and production. In this section, I'd like to thank everyone who has encouraged me, contributed, and put up with me for the past year.

First, and most important, I'd like to thank my girlfriend, Becky. Your continual support and encouragement means the world to me and has kept me going through such a busy time. You've taken the brunt of my stress and pressure and I'm eternally grateful. I love you always.

I'd also like to thank my whole family for their support—in particular, my parents, Jan and Bob, for putting up with my ranting and supplying me with coffee when holed up working on my visits back home. To my sister, Amanda, thanks for your always upbeat chats, and to Kathy and Jon, thanks for all the words of encouragement.

On a professional level, I'd like to thank Manning for giving me this opportunity. Brian Sawyer "discovered" me and encouraged me to submit a proposal for what eventually became this book. Dan Maharry initiated the project as my development editor and helped craft the approach for the book and its target audience. Those first few months and rewrites were hard work, but the book is better for it. Dan passed the baton to Marina Michaels, who served as development editor for the remainder of the book. With a keen eye and daunting efficiency, Marina was instrumental in getting this book to the finish line.

Kris Athi read through numerous drafts and provided invaluable feedback. Tanya Wilke was the technical proofer, coming on board at the last minute with a grueling schedule to meet.

To everyone at Manning who helped get this book published, heartfelt thanks. Thanks to all of the MEAP reviewers for their comments, which helped improve the book in innumerable ways: Adam Bell, Andy Kirsch, Björn Nordblom, Emanuele Origgi, George Onofrei, Jason Pike, Joel Clermont, Jonathan Wood, Jose Diaz, Ken Muse, Ludvig Gislason, Mark Elston, Mark Harris, Matthew Groves, Nicolas Paez, Pasquale Zirpoli, Richard Michaels, Ronald E Lease, and Wayne Mather. A special thanks to Dave Harney for his meticulous comments in the forums.

I would have never been in the position to write this book if it weren't for the excellent content produced by the .NET community and those I follow on Twitter. In particular, thanks to Jon Galloway for regularly featuring my blog on the ASP.NET community standup.

David Pine and Mike Brind were instrumental in my achieving the Microsoft Valued Professional (MVP). MVPs themselves, I thank them both for their hard work in the community.

Thanks to Chris Hayford for giving me my first ASP.NET job while I was still finishing my PhD and for giving me my first chance to explore ASP.NET Core.

Finally, thanks to Mick Delany for the chance to really put ASP.NET Core through its paces, and for giving me the time to work on this book.

about this book

This book is about the ASP.NET Core framework, what it is, and how you can use it to build web applications. While some of this content is already available online, it's scattered around the internet in disparate documents and blog posts. This book guides you through building your first applications, introducing additional complexity as you cement previous concepts.

I present each topic using relatively short examples, rather than building on a single example application throughout the book. There are merits to both approaches, but I wanted to ensure the focus remained on the specific topics being taught, without the mental overhead of navigating an increasingly large project.

By the end of the book, you should have a solid understanding of how to build apps with ASP.NET Core, its strengths and weaknesses, and how to leverage its features to build apps securely. While I don't spend a lot of time on application architecture, I do make sure to point out best practices, especially where I only superficially cover architecture in the name of brevity.

Who should read this book

This book is for C# developers who are interested in learning a cross-platform web framework. It doesn't assume you have any experience building web applications; you may be a mobile or desktop developer, for example, though previous experience with ASP.NET or another web framework is undoubtedly beneficial.

Other than a working knowledge of C# and .NET, I assume some knowledge of common object-oriented practices and a basic understanding of relational databases in general. To avoid the scope of the book ballooning, I assume a passing familiarity with HTML and CSS, and of JavaScript's place as a client-side scripting language. You don't need to know any JavaScript or CSS frameworks for this book, though ASP.NET Core works well with both if that is your forte.

Web frameworks naturally touch on a wide range of topics, from the database and network, to visual design and client-side scripting. I provide as much context as possible, but where the subject matter is too great, I include links to sites and books where you can learn more.

How this book is organized

This book is divided into three parts, twenty chapters, and two appendices. Ideally, you'll read the book cover to cover and then use it as a reference, but I realize that won't suit everyone. While I use small sample apps to demonstrate a topic, some chapters build on the work of previous ones, so the content will make more sense when read sequentially.

I strongly suggest reading the chapters in part 1 in sequence, as each chapter builds on topics introduced in the previous chapters. Part 2 is best read sequentially, though most of the chapters are independent if you wish to jump around. You can read the chapters in part 3 out of order, though I recommend only doing so after you've covered parts 1 and 2.

Part 1 provides a general introduction to ASP.NET Core and the overall architecture of a web application built using the framework. Once we have covered the basics, we dive into the Model-View-Controller (MVC) architecture, which makes up the bulk of most ASP.NET Core web applications.

- Chapter 1 introduces ASP.NET Core and its place in the web development landscape. It discusses when you should and shouldn't use ASP.NET Core, the basics of web requests in ASP.NET Core, and the options available for a development environment.
- Chapter 2 walks through all the components of a basic ASP.NET Core application, discussing their roles and how they combine to generate a response to a web request.
- Chapter 3 describes the middleware pipeline, the main application pipeline in ASP.NET Core. It defines how incoming requests are processed and how a response should be generated.
- Chapter 4 gives an overview of the MVC middleware component. This large component is responsible for managing the pages and APIs in your application, and for generating responses to web requests.
- Chapter 5 describes the MVC routing system. Routing is the process of mapping incoming request URLs to a specific class and method, which executes to generate a response.
- Chapter 6 looks at model binding, the process of mapping form data and URL parameters passed in a request to concrete C# objects.

- Chapter 7 shows how to generate HTML web pages using the Razor template language.
- Chapter 8 builds on chapter 7 by introducing Tag Helpers, which can greatly reduce the amount of code required to build forms and web pages.
- Chapter 9 describes how to use the MVC middleware to build APIs that can be called by client-side apps.

Part 2 covers important topics related to building fully featured web applications, once you've understood the basics.

- Chapter 10 describes how to use ASP.NET Core's built-in dependency injection container to configure your application's services.
- Chapter 11 discusses how to read settings and secrets in ASP.NET Core, and how to map them to strongly typed objects.
- Chapter 12 introduces Entity Framework Core for saving data into a relational database.
- Chapter 13 builds on the topics in part 1 by introducing the MVC filter pipeline.
- Chapter 14 describes how to add user profiles and authentication to your application using ASP.NET Core Identity.
- Chapter 15 builds on the previous chapter by introducing authorization for users, so you can restrict which pages a signed-in user can access.
- Chapter 16 looks at how to publish your app, how to configure your app for a production environment, and how to optimize your client-side assets.

The four chapters that make up part 3 cover important, cross-cutting aspects of ASP.NET Core development.

- Chapter 17 shows how to configure logging in your application, and how to write log messages to multiple locations.
- Chapter 18 explores some of the security considerations you should take into account when developing your application, including how to configure your application for HTTPS.
- Chapter 19 describes how to build and use a variety of custom components, including custom middleware, custom Tag Helpers, and custom validation attributes.
- Chapter 20 shows how to test an ASP.NET Core application with the xUnit testing framework. It covers both unit tests and integration tests using the Test Host.

The two appendices provide supplementary information. Appendix A provides some background to .NET Core and .NET Standard, how they fit in the .NET landscape, and how you should use them in your apps. Appendix B contains a number of links that I've found useful in learning about ASP.NET Core.

About the code

Source code is provided for all chapters except chapters 1 and 5. You can view the source code for each chapter in my GitHub repository at https://github.com/ andrewlock/asp-dot-net-core-in-action. A ZIP file containing all the source code is also available from the publisher's website at https://www.manning.com/books/asp-dot-net-core-in-action.

All the code examples in this book use ASP.NET Core 2.0 and were built using both Visual Studio and Visual Studio Code. Equivalent examples for ASP.NET Core 1.x are available for chapters 3–13 in the source code but are not referenced in the book itself. To build and run the examples, you'll need to install the .NET Core SDK, as described in chapter 1.

The source code is formatted in a `fixed-width font like this` to separate it from ordinary text. Sometimes code is also **in bold** to highlight code that has changed from previous steps in the chapter, such as when a new feature adds to an existing line of code.

In many cases, the original source code has been reformatted; we've added line breaks and reworked indentation to accommodate the available page space in the book. In rare cases, even this was not enough, and listings include line-continuation markers (➥). Additionally, comments in the source code have often been removed from the listings when the code is described in the text. Code annotations accompany many of the listings, highlighting important concepts.

Book forum

Purchase of *ASP.NET Core in Action* includes free access to a private web forum run by Manning Publications where you can make comments about the book, ask technical questions, and receive help from the author and from other users. To access the forum, go to https://forums.manning.com/forums/asp-dot-net-core-in-action. You can also learn more about Manning's forums and the rules of conduct at https://forums .manning.com/forums/about.

Manning's commitment to our readers is to provide a venue where a meaningful dialogue between individual readers and between readers and the author can take place. It is not a commitment to any specific amount of participation on the part of the author, whose contribution to the forum remains voluntary (and unpaid). We suggest you try asking the author some challenging questions lest his interest stray! The forum and the archives of previous discussions will be accessible from the publisher's website as long as the book is in print.

about the author

ANDREW LOCK graduated with an engineering degree from Cambridge University, specializing in software engineering, and went on to obtain a PhD in digital image processing. He has been developing professionally using .NET for the last seven years, using a wide range of technologies, including WinForms, ASP.NET WebForms, ASP.NET MVC, and ASP.NET Web Pages. His focus is currently on the new ASP.NET Core framework, exploring its capabilities and deploying several new applications. Andrew has a very active blog at https://andrewlock.net, dedicated to ASP.NET Core. It's frequently featured in the community spotlight by the ASP.NET team at Microsoft, on the .NET blog, and in the weekly community stand-ups, and recently earned him the Microsoft Valued Profossional (MVP) award.

about the cover illustration

The caption for the illustration on the cover of *ASP.NET Core in Action* is "The Captain Pasha. Kapudan pasha, admiral of the Turkish navy." The Kapudan Pasha was the highest military rank of the Ottoman Navy from 1567 until 1867 when the post was abolished and replaced with the Naval Minister. The illustration is taken from a collection of costumes of the Ottoman Empire published on January 1, 1802, by William Miller of Old Bond Street, London. The title page is missing from the collection and we have been unable to track it down to date. The book's table of contents identifies the figures in both English and French, and each illustration bears the names of two artists who worked on it, both of whom would no doubt be surprised to find their art gracing the front cover of a computer programming book ... two hundred years later.

The collection was purchased by a Manning editor at an antiquarian flea market in the "Garage" on West 26th Street in Manhattan. The seller was an American based in Ankara, Turkey, and the transaction took place just as he was packing up his stand for the day. The Manning editor didn't have on his person the substantial amount of cash that was required for the purchase, and a credit card and check were both politely turned down. With the seller flying back to Ankara that evening, the situation was getting hopeless. What was the solution? It turned out to be nothing more than an old-fashioned verbal agreement sealed with a handshake. The seller simply proposed that the money be transferred to him by wire, and the editor walked out with the bank information on a piece of paper and the portfolio of images under his arm. Needless to say, we transferred the funds the next day, and we remain grateful and impressed by this unknown person's trust in one of us.

We at Manning celebrate the inventiveness, the initiative, and, yes, the fun of the computer business with book covers based on the rich diversity of regional life of two centuries ago, brought back to life by the pictures from this collection.

Part 1

Getting started with MVC

Web applications are everywhere these days, from social media web apps and news sites, to the apps on your phone. Behind the scenes, there is almost always a server running a web application or web API. Web applications are expected to be infinitely scalable, deployed to the cloud, and highly performant. Getting started can be overwhelming at the best of times and doing so with such high expectations can be even more of a challenge.

The good news for you as readers is that ASP.NET Core was designed to meet those requirements. Whether you need a simple website, a complex e-commerce web app, or a distributed web of microservices, you can use your knowledge of ASP.NET Core to build lean web apps that fit your needs. ASP.NET Core lets you build and run web apps on Windows, Linux, or macOS. It's highly modular, so you only use the components you need, keeping your app as compact and performant as possible.

In part 1, you'll go from a standing start all the way to building your first web applications and APIs. Chapter 1 gives a high-level overview of ASP.NET Core, which you'll find especially useful if you're new to web development in general. You'll get your first glimpse of a full ASP.NET Core application in chapter 2, in which we look at each component of the app in turn and see how they work together to generate a response.

Chapter 3 looks in detail at the middleware pipeline, which defines how incoming web requests are processed and how a response is generated. We take a detailed look at one specific piece of middleware, the MVC middleware, in chapters 4 through 6. This is the main component used to generate responses in ASP.NET Core apps, so we examine the behavior of the middleware itself, routing, and model binding. In Chapters 7 and 8, we look at how to build a UI for your application using the Razor syntax and Tag Helpers, so that users can navigate and interact with your app. Finally, in chapter 9, we explore specific features of ASP.NET Core that let you build web APIs, and how that differs from building UI-based applications.

There's a lot of content in part 1, but by the end, you'll be well on your way to building simple applications with ASP.NET Core. Inevitably, I gloss over some of the more complex configuration aspects of the framework, but you should get a good understanding of the MVC middleware and how you can use it to build dynamic web apps. In later parts of this book, we'll dive deeper into the framework, where you'll learn how to configure your application and add extra features, such as user profiles.

Getting started with ASP.NET Core

This chapter covers

- What is ASP.NET Core?
- How ASP.NET Core works
- Choosing between .NET Core and .NET Framework
- Preparing your development environment

Choosing to learn and develop with a new framework is a big investment, so it's important to establish early on whether it's right for you. In this chapter, I'll provide some background about ASP.NET Core, what it is, how it works, and why you should consider it for building your web applications.

If you're new to .NET development, this chapter will help you to choose a development platform for your future apps. For existing .NET developers, I'll also provide guidance on whether now is the right time to consider moving your focus to .NET Core, and the advantages ASP.NET Core can bring over previous versions of ASP.NET.

By the end of this chapter, you should have a good idea of the model you intend to follow, and the tools you'll need to get started—so without further ado, let's dive in!

1.1   *An introduction to ASP.NET Core*

ASP.NET Core is the latest evolution of Microsoft's popular ASP.NET web framework, released in June 2016. Recent versions of ASP.NET have seen many incremental updates, focusing on high developer productivity and prioritizing backwards compatibility. ASP.NET Core bucks that trend by making significant architectural changes that rethink the way the web framework is designed and built.

ASP.NET Core owes a lot to its ASP.NET heritage and many features have been carried forward from before, but ASP.NET Core is a new framework. The whole technology stack has been rewritten, including both the web framework and the underlying platform.

At the heart of the changes is the philosophy that ASP.NET should be able to hold its head high when measured against other modern frameworks, but that existing .NET developers should continue to be left with a sense of familiarity.

1.1.1   *Using a web framework*

If you're new to web development, it can be daunting moving into an area with so many buzzwords and a plethora of ever-changing products. You may be wondering if they're all necessary—how hard can it be to return a file from a server?

Well, it's perfectly possible to build a static web application without the use of a web framework, but its capabilities will be limited. As soon as you want to provide any kind of security or dynamism, you'll likely run into difficulties, and the original simplicity that enticed you will fade before your eyes!

Just as you may have used desktop or mobile development frameworks for building native applications, ASP.NET Core makes writing web applications faster, easier, and more secure. It contains libraries for common things like

- Creating dynamically changing web pages
- Letting users log in to your web app
- Letting users use their Facebook account to log in to your web app using OAuth
- Providing a common structure to build maintainable applications
- Reading configuration files
- Serving image files
- Logging calls to your web app

The key to any modern web application is the ability to generate dynamic web pages. A *dynamic web page* displays different data depending on the current logged-in user, for example, or it could display content submitted by users. Without a dynamic framework, it wouldn't be possible to log in to websites or to have any sort of personalized data displayed on a page. In short, websites like Amazon, eBay, and Stack Overflow (seen in figure 1.1) wouldn't be possible.

Hopefully, it's clear that using a web framework is a sensible idea for building high-quality web applications. But why choose ASP.NET Core? If you're a C# developer, or even if you're new to the platform, you've likely heard of, if not used, the previous version of ASP.NET—so why not use that instead?

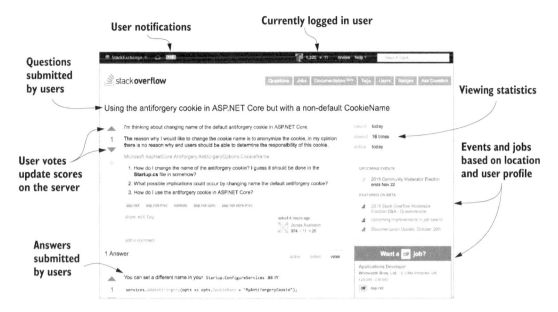

Figure 1.1   The Stack Overflow website (http://stackoverflow.com) is built using ASP.NET and is almost entirely dynamic content.

1.1.2   The benefits and limitations of ASP.NET

To understand *why* Microsoft decided to build a new framework, it's important to understand the benefits and limitations of the existing ASP.NET web framework.

The first version of ASP.NET was released in 2002 as part of .NET Framework 1.0, in response to the then conventional scripting environments of classic ASP and PHP. ASP.NET Web Forms allowed developers to rapidly create web applications using a graphical designer and a simple event model that mirrored desktop application-building techniques.

The ASP.NET framework allowed developers to quickly create new applications, but over time, the web development ecosystem changed. It became apparent that ASP.NET Web Forms suffered from many issues, especially when building larger applications. In particular, a lack of testability, a complex stateful model, and limited influence over the generated HTML (making client-side development difficult) led developers to evaluate other options.

In response, Microsoft released the first version of ASP.NET MVC in 2009, based on the Model-View-Controller pattern, a common web design pattern used in other frameworks such as Ruby on Rails, Django, and Java Spring. This framework allowed you to separate UI elements from application logic, made testing easier, and provided tighter control over the HTML-generation process.

ASP.NET MVC has been through four more iterations since its first release, but they have all been built on the same underlying framework provided by the System .Web.dll file. This library is part of .NET Framework, so it comes pre-installed with all versions of Windows. It contains all the core code that ASP.NET uses when you build a web application.

This dependency brings both advantages and disadvantages. On the one hand, the ASP.NET framework is a reliable, battle-tested platform that's a great choice for building modern applications on Windows. It provides a wide range of features, which have seen many years in production, and is well known by virtually all Windows web developers.

On the other hand, this reliance is limiting—changes to the underlying System .Web.dll are far-reaching and, consequently, slow to roll out. This limits the extent to which ASP.NET is free to evolve and results in release cycles only happening every few years. There's also an explicit coupling with the Windows web host, Internet Information Service (IIS), which precludes its use on non-Windows platforms.

In recent years, many web developers have started looking at cross-platform web frameworks that can run on Windows, as well as Linux and macOS. Microsoft felt the time had come to create a framework that was no longer tied to its Windows legacy, thus ASP.NET Core was born.

1.1.3 *What is ASP.NET Core?*

The development of ASP.NET Core was motivated by the desire to create a web framework with four main goals:

- To be run and developed cross-platform
- To have a modular architecture for easier maintenance
- To be developed completely as open source software
- To be applicable to current trends in web development, such as client-side applications and deploying to cloud environments

In order to achieve all these goals, Microsoft needed a platform that could provide underlying libraries for creating basic objects such as lists and dictionaries, and performing, for example, simple file operations. Up to this point, ASP.NET development had always been focused, and dependent, on the Windows-only .NET Framework. For ASP.NET Core, Microsoft created a lightweight platform that runs on Windows, Linux, and macOS called .NET Core, as shown in figure 1.2.

.NET Core shares many of the same APIs as .NET Framework, but it's smaller and currently only implements a subset of the features .NET Framework provides, with the goal of providing a simpler implementation and programming model. It's a completely new platform, rather than a fork of .NET Framework, though it uses similar code for many of its APIs.

With .NET Core alone, it's possible to build console applications that run cross-platform. Microsoft created ASP.NET Core to be an additional layer on top of console applications, such that converting to a web application involves adding and composing libraries, as shown in figure 1.3.

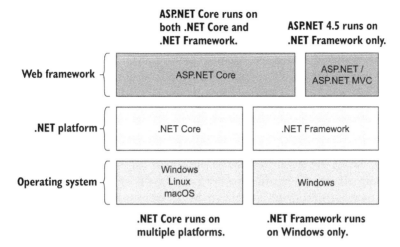

Web framework — ASP.NET Core runs on both .NET Core and .NET Framework.
ASP.NET 4.5 runs on .NET Framework only.

Web framework — ASP.NET Core | ASP.NET / ASP.NET MVC

.NET platform — .NET Core | .NET Framework

Operating system — Windows Linux macOS | Windows

.NET Core runs on multiple platforms. | .NET Framework runs on Windows only.

Figure 1.2   The relationship between ASP.NET Core, ASP.NET, .NET Core, and .NET Framework. ASP.NET Core runs on both .NET Framework and .NET Core, so it can run cross-platform. Conversely, ASP.NET runs on .NET Framework only, so is tied to the Windows OS.

You write a .NET Core console app that starts up an instance of an **ASP.NET Core** web server.

Microsoft provides, by default, a cross-platform web server called Kestrel.

Your web application logic is run by Kestrel. You'll use various libraries to enable features such as logging and HTML generation as required.

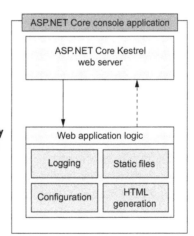

ASP.NET Core console application

ASP.NET Core Kestrel web server

Web application logic

Logging | Static files

Configuration | HTML generation

Figure 1.3   The ASP.NET Core application model. The .NET Core platform provides a base console application model for running command-line apps. Adding a web server library converts this into an ASP.NET Core web app. Additional features, such as configuration and logging, are added by way of additional libraries.

By adding an ASP.NET Core web server to your .NET Core app, your application can run as a web application. ASP.NET Core is composed of many small libraries that you can choose from to provide your application with different features. You'll rarely need all the libraries available to you and you only add what you need. Some of the libraries are common and will appear in virtually every application you create, such as the ones for reading configuration files or performing logging. Other libraries build on top of these base capabilities to provide application-specific functionality, such as third-party logging-in via Facebook or Google.

Most of the libraries you'll use in ASP.NET Core can be found on GitHub, in the Microsoft ASP.NET Core organization repositories at https://github.com/aspnet. You can find the core libraries here, such as the Kestrel web server and logging libraries, as well as many more peripheral libraries, such as the third-party authentication libraries.

All ASP.NET Core applications will follow a similar design for basic configuration, as suggested by the common libraries, but in general the framework is flexible, leaving you free to create your own code conventions. These common libraries, the extension libraries that build on them, and the design conventions they promote make up the somewhat nebulous term ASP.NET Core.

1.2   When to choose ASP.NET Core

Hopefully, you now have a general grasp of what ASP.NET Core is and how it was designed. But the question remains: should you use it? Microsoft will be heavily promoting ASP.NET Core as its web framework of choice for the foreseeable future, but switching to or learning a new web stack is a big ask for any developer or company. This section describes some of the highlights of ASP.NET Core and gives advice on the sort of applications you should build with it, as well as the sort of applications you should avoid.

1.2.1   What type of applications can you build?

ASP.NET Core provides a generalized web framework that can be used on a variety of applications. It can most obviously be used for building rich, dynamic websites, whether they're e-commerce sites, content-based sites, or large n-tier applications—much the same as the previous version of ASP.NET.

Currently, there's a comparatively limited number of third-party libraries available for building these types of complex applications, but there are many under active development. Many developers are working to port their libraries to work with ASP.NET Core—it will take time for more to become available. For example, the open source content management system (CMS), Orchard[1] (figure 1.4), is currently available as a beta version of Orchard Core, running on ASP.NET Core and .NET Core.

Traditional, server-side-rendered web applications are the bread and butter of ASP.NET development, both with the previous version of ASP.NET and ASP.NET

---

[1] The Orchard project (www.orchardproject.net/). Source code at https://github.com/OrchardCMS/.

Figure 1.4   The ASP.NET Community Blogs website (https://weblogs.asp.net) is built using the Orchard CMS. Orchard 2 is available as a beta version for ASP.NET Core development.

Core. Additionally, single-page applications (SPAs), which use a client-side framework that commonly talks to a REST server, are easy to create with ASP.NET Core. Whether you're using Angular, Ember, React, or some other client-side framework, it's easy to create an ASP.NET Core application to act as the server-side API.

> **DEFINITION**   *REST* stands for REpresentational State Transfer. RESTful applications typically use lightweight and stateless HTTP calls to read, post (create/update), and delete data.

ASP.NET Core isn't restricted to creating RESTful services. It's easy to create a web service or remote procedure call (RPC)-style service for your application, depending on your requirements, as shown in figure 1.5. In the simplest case, your application might expose only a single endpoint, narrowing its scope to become a microservice. ASP.NET Core is perfectly designed for building simple services thanks to its cross-platform support and lightweight design.

You should consider multiple factors when choosing a platform, not all of which are technical. One example is the level of support you can expect to receive from its creators. For some organizations, this can be one of the main obstacles to adopting open source software. Luckily, Microsoft has pledged to provide full support for each

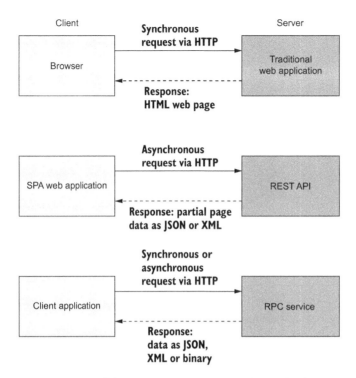

Figure 1.5   ASP.NET Core can act as the server-side application for a variety of different clients: it can serve HTML pages for traditional web applications, it can act as a REST API for client-side SPA applications, or it can act as an ad-hoc RPC service for client applications.

major and minor point release of the ASP.NET Core framework for three years[2]. And as all development takes place in the open, you can sometimes get answers to your questions from the general community, as well as Microsoft directly.

When deciding whether to use ASP.NET Core, you have two primary dimensions to consider: whether you're already a .NET developer, and whether you're creating a new application or looking to convert an existing one.

1.2.2   *If you're new to .NET development*

If you're new to .NET development and are considering ASP.NET Core, then welcome! Microsoft is pushing ASP.NET Core as an attractive option for web development beginners, but taking .NET cross-platform means it's competing with many other frameworks on their own turf. ASP.NET Core has many selling points when compared to other cross-platform web frameworks:

- It's a modern, high-performance, open source web framework.
- It uses familiar design patterns and paradigms.

---

[2] View the support policy at www.microsoft.com/net/core/support.

- C# is a great language (or you can use VB.NET or F# if you prefer).
- You can build and run on any platform.

ASP.NET Core is a re-imagining of the ASP.NET framework, built with modern software design principles on top of the new .NET Core platform. Although new in one sense, .NET Core has drawn significantly from the mature, stable, and reliable .NET Framework, which has been used for well over a decade. You can rest easy knowing that by choosing ASP.NET Core and .NET Core, you'll be getting a dependable platform as well as a fully-featured web framework.

Many of the web frameworks available today use similar, well-established design patterns, and ASP.NET Core is no different. For example, Ruby on Rails is known for its use of the Model-View-Controller (MVC) pattern; Node.js is known for the way it processes requests using small discrete modules (called a pipeline); and dependency injection is found in a wide variety of frameworks. If these techniques are familiar to you, you should find it easy to transfer them across to ASP.NET Core; if they're new to you, then you can look forward to using industry best practices!

> **NOTE** You'll encounter MVC in chapter 4, a pipeline in chapter 3, and dependency injection in chapter 10.

The primary language of .NET development, and ASP.NET Core in particular, is C#. This language has a huge following, and for good reason! As an object-oriented C-based language, it provides a sense of familiarity to those used to C, Java, and many other languages. In addition, it has many powerful features, such as Language Integrated Query (LINQ), closures, and asynchronous programming constructs. The C# language is also designed in the open on GitHub, as is Microsoft's C# compiler, code-named Roslyn.[3]

> **NOTE** I will use C# throughout this book and will highlight some of the newer features it provides, but I won't be teaching the language from scratch. If you want to learn C#, I recommend *C# in Depth* by Jon Skeet (Manning, 2008).

One of the major selling points of ASP.NET Core and .NET Core is the ability to develop and run on any platform. Whether you're using a Mac, Windows, or Linux, you can run the same ASP.NET Core apps and develop across multiple environments. As a Linux user, a wide range of distributions are supported (RHEL, Ubuntu, Debian, CentOS, Fedora, and openSUSE, to name a few), so you can be confident your operating system of choice will be a viable option. Work is even underway to enable ASP.NET Core to run on the tiny Alpine distribution, for truly compact deployments to containers.

---

[3] The C# language and .NET Compiler Platform GitHub source code repository can be found at https://github.com/dotnet/roslyn.

Built with containers in mind

Traditionally, web applications were deployed directly to a server, or more recently, to a virtual machine. Virtual machines allow operating systems to be installed in a layer of virtual hardware, abstracting away the underlying hardware. This has several advantages over direct installation, such as easy maintenance, deployment, and recovery. Unfortunately, they're also heavy both in terms of file size and resource use.

This is where containers come in. Containers are far more lightweight and don't have the overhead of virtual machines. They're built in a series of layers and don't require you to boot a new operating system when starting a new one. That means they're quick to start and are great for quick provisioning. Containers, and Docker in particular, are quickly becoming the go-to platform for building large, scalable systems.

Containers have never been a particularly attractive option for ASP.NET applications, but with ASP.NET Core, .NET Core, and Docker for Windows, that's all changing. A lightweight ASP.NET Core application running on the cross-platform .NET Core framework is perfect for thin container deployments. You can learn more about your deployment options in chapter 16.

As well as running on each platform, one of the selling points of .NET is the ability to write and compile only once. Your application is compiled to Intermediate Language (IL) code, which is a platform-independent format. If a target system has the .NET Core platform installed, then you can run compiled IL from any platform. That means you can, for example, develop on a Mac or a Windows machine and deploy *the exact same files* to your production Linux machines. This compile-once, run-anywhere promise has finally been realized with ASP.NET Core and .NET Core.

1.2.3   *If you're a .NET Framework developer creating a new application*

If you're currently a .NET developer, then the choice of whether to invest in ASP.NET Core for new applications is a question of timing. Microsoft has pledged to provide continued support for the older ASP.NET framework, but it's clear their focus is primarily on the newer ASP.NET Core framework. In the long term then, if you want to take advantage of new features and capabilities, it's likely that ASP.NET Core will be the route to take.

Whether ASP.NET Core is right for you largely depends on your requirements and your comfort with using products that are early in their lifecycle. The main benefits over the previous ASP.NET framework are

- Cross-platform development and deployment
- A focus on performance as a feature
- A simplified hosting model
- Regular releases with a shorter release cycle
- Open source
- Modular features

As a .NET developer, if you aren't using any Windows-specific constructs, such as the Registry, then the ability to build and deploy applications cross-platform opens the door to a whole new avenue of applications: take advantage of cheaper Linux VM hosting in the cloud, use Docker containers for repeatable continuous integration, or write .NET code on your Mac without needing to run a Windows virtual machine. ASP.NET Core, in combination with .NET Core, makes all of this possible.

It's important to be aware of the limitations of cross-platform applications—not all the .NET Framework APIs are available in .NET Core. It's likely that most of the APIs you need will make their way to .NET Core over time, but it's an important point to be aware of. See the "Choosing a platform for ASP.NET Core" section later in this chapter to determine if cross-platform is a viable option for your application.

NOTE With the release of .NET Core 2.0 in August 2017, the number of APIs available dramatically increased, more than doubling the API surface area.

The hosting model for the previous ASP.NET framework was a relatively complex one, relying on Windows IIS to provide the web server hosting. In a cross-platform environment, this kind of symbiotic relationship isn't possible, so an alternative hosting model has been adopted, one which separates web applications from the underlying host. This opportunity has led to the development of Kestrel: a fast, cross-platform HTTP server on which ASP.NET Core can run.

Instead of the previous design, whereby IIS calls into specific points of your application, ASP.NET Core applications are console applications that self-host a web server and handle requests directly, as shown in figure 1.6. This hosting model is conceptually much simpler and allows you to test and debug your applications from the command line, though it doesn't remove the need to run IIS (or equivalent) in production, as you'll see in section 1.3.

Changing the hosting model to use a built-in HTTP web server has created another opportunity. Performance has been somewhat of a sore point for ASP.NET applications in the past. It's certainly possible to build high-performing applications—Stack Overflow (http://stackoverflow.com) is testament to that—but the web framework itself isn't designed with performance as a priority, so it can end up being somewhat of an obstacle.

To be competitive cross-platform, the ASP.NET team have focused on making the Kestrel HTTP server as fast as possible. TechEmpower (www.techempower.com/benchmarks) has been running benchmarks on a whole range of web frameworks from various languages for several years now. In Round 13 of the plain text benchmarks, TechEmpower announced that ASP.NET Core with Kestrel was the fastest mainstream full-stack web framework, in the top ten of all frameworks![4]

---

[4] As always in web development, technology is in a constant state of flux, so these benchmarks will evolve over time. Although ASP.NET Core may not maintain its top ten slot, you can be sure that performance is one of the key focal points of the ASP.NET Core team.

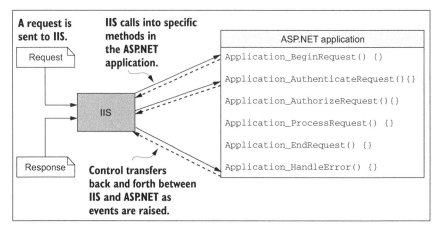

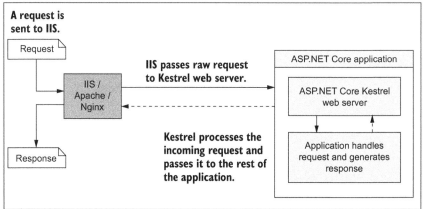

Figure 1.6   **The difference between hosting models in ASP.NET (top) and ASP.NET Core (bottom). With the previous version of ASP.NET, IIS is tightly coupled with the application. The hosting model in ASP.NET Core is simpler; IIS hands off the request to a self-hosted web server in the ASP.NET Core application and receives the response, but has no deeper knowledge of the application.**

Web servers: naming things is hard

One of the difficult aspects of programing for the web is the confusing array of often conflicting terminology. For example, if you've used IIS in the past, you may have described it as a web server, or possibly a web host. Conversely, if you've ever built an application using Node.js, you may have also referred to that application as a web server. Alternatively, you may have called the physical machine on which your application runs a web server!

Similarly, you may have built an application for the internet and called it a website or a web application, probably somewhat arbitrarily based on the level of dynamism it displayed.

In this book, when I say "web server" in the context of ASP.NET Core, I am referring to the HTTP server that runs as part of your ASP.NET Core application. By default, this is the Kestrel web server, but that's not a requirement. It would be possible to write a replacement web server and substitute if for Kestrel if you desired.

The web server is responsible for receiving HTTP requests and generating responses. In the previous version of ASP.NET, IIS took this role, but in ASP.NET Core, Kestrel is the web server.

I will only use the term web application to describe ASP.NET Core applications in this book, regardless of whether they contain only static content or are completely dynamic. Either way, they're applications that are accessed via the web, so that name seems the most appropriate!

Many of the performance improvements made to Kestrel did not come from the ASP.NET team themselves, but from contributors to the open source project on GitHub.[5] Developing in the open means you typically see fixes and features make their way to production faster than you would for the previous version of ASP.NET, which was dependent on .NET Framework and, as such, had long release cycles.

In contrast, ASP.NET Core is completely decoupled from the underlying .NET platform. The entire web framework is implemented as NuGet packages, independent of the underlying platform on which it builds.

> **NOTE** NuGet is a package manager for .NET that enables importing libraries into your projects. It's equivalent to Ruby Gems, npm for JavaScript, or Maven for Java.

To enable this, ASP.NET Core was designed to be highly modular, with as little coupling to other features as possible. This modularity lends itself to a pay-for-play approach to dependencies, where you start from a bare-bones application and only add the additional libraries you require, as opposed to the kitchen-sink approach of previous ASP.NET applications. Even MVC is an optional package! But don't worry, this approach doesn't mean that ASP.NET Core is lacking in features; it means you need to opt in to them. Some of the key infrastructure improvements include

- Middleware "pipeline" for defining your application's behavior
- Built-in support for dependency injection
- Combined UI (MVC) and API (Web API) infrastructure
- Highly extensible configuration system
- Scalable for cloud platforms by default using asynchronous programming

---

[5] The Kestrel HTTP server GitHub project can be found at https://github.com/aspnet/KestrelHttpServer.

Each of these features was possible in the previous version of ASP.NET but required a fair amount of additional work to set up. With ASP.NET Core, they're all there, ready, and waiting to be connected!

Microsoft fully supports ASP.NET Core, so if you have a new system you want to build, then there's no significant reason not to. The largest obstacle you're likely to come across is a third-party library holding you back, either because they only support older ASP.NET features, or they haven't been converted to work with .NET Core yet.

Hopefully, this section has whetted your appetite with some of the many reasons to use ASP.NET Core for building new applications. But if you're an existing ASP.NET developer considering whether to convert an existing ASP.NET application to ASP.NET Core, that's another question entirely.

1.2.4   *Converting an existing ASP.NET application to ASP.NET Core*

In contrast with new applications, an existing application is presumably already providing value, so there should always be a tangible benefit to performing what may amount to a significant rewrite in converting from ASP.NET to ASP.NET Core. The advantages of adopting ASP.NET Core are much the same as for new applications: cross-platform deployment, modular features, and a focus on performance. Determining whether or not the benefits are sufficient will depend largely on the particulars of your application, but there are some characteristics that are clear indicators *against* conversion:

- Your application uses ASP.NET Web Forms
- Your application is built using WCF or SignalR
- Your application is large, with many "advanced" MVC features

If you have an ASP.NET Web Forms application, then attempting to convert it to ASP.NET Core isn't advisable. Web Forms is inextricably tied to System.Web.dll, and as such will likely never be available in ASP.NET Core. Converting an application to ASP.NET Core would effectively involve rewriting the application from scratch, not only shifting frameworks but also shifting design paradigms. A better approach would be to slowly introduce Web API concepts and try to reduce the reliance on legacy Web Forms constructs such as ViewData. You can find many resources online to help you with this approach, in particular, the www.asp.net/web-api website.

Similarly, if your application makes heavy use of SignalR, then now may not be the time to consider an upgrade. ASP.NET Core SignalR is under active development but has only been released in alpha form at the time of writing. It also has some significant architectural changes compared to the previous version, which you should take into account.

Windows Communication Foundation (WCF) is currently not supported either, but it's possible to consume WCF services by jumping through some slightly obscure hoops. Currently, there's no way to host a WCF service from an ASP.NET Core application, so if you need the features WCF provides and can't use a more conventional REST service, then ASP.NET Core is probably best avoided.

If your application was complex and made use of the previous MVC or Web API extensibility points or message handlers, then porting your application to ASP.NET Core could be complex. ASP.NET Core is built with many similar features to the previous version of ASP.NET MVC, but the underlying architecture is different. Several of the previous features don't have direct replacements, and so will require rethinking.

The larger the application, the greater the difficulty you're likely to have converting your application to ASP.NET Core. Microsoft itself suggests that porting an application from ASP.NET MVC to ASP.NET Core is at least as big a rewrite as porting from ASP.NET Web Forms to ASP.NET MVC. If that doesn't scare you, then nothing will!

So, when *should* you port an application to ASP.NET Core? As I've already mentioned, the best opportunity for getting started is on small, green-field, new projects instead of existing applications. That said, if the application in question is small, with little custom behavior, then porting *might* be a viable option. Small implies reduced risk and probably reduced complexity. If your application consists primarily of MVC or Web API controllers and associated Razor views, then moving to ASP.NET Core may be feasible.

1.3 How does ASP.NET Core work?

By now, you should have a good idea of what ASP.NET Core is and the sort of applications you should use it for. In this section, you'll see how an application built with ASP.NET Core works, from the user requesting a URL, to a page being displayed on the browser. To get there, first you'll see how an HTTP request works for any web server, and then you'll see how ASP.NET Core extends the process to create dynamic web pages.

1.3.1 How does an HTTP web request work?

As you know, ASP.NET Core is a framework for building web applications that serve data from a server. One of the most common scenarios for web developers is building a web app that you can view in a web browser. The high-level process you can expect from any web server is shown in figure 1.7.

The process begins when a user navigates to a website or types a URL in their browser. The URL or web address consists of a *hostname* and a *path* to some resource on the web app. Navigating to the address in your browser sends a request from the user's computer to the server on which the web app is hosted, using the HTTP protocol.

> **DEFINITION** The *hostname* of a website uniquely identifies its location on the internet by mapping via the Domain Name Service (DNS) to an IP Address. Examples include microsoft.com, www.google.co.uk, and facebook.com.

The request passes through the internet, potentially to the other side of the world, until it finally makes its way to the server associated with the given hostname on which the web app is running. The request is potentially received and rebroadcast at multiple routers along the way, but it's only when it reaches the server associated with the hostname that the request is processed.

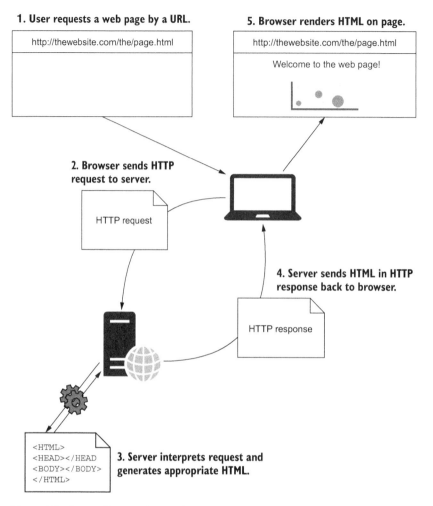

1. User requests a web page by a URL.

http://thewebsite.com/the/page.html

5. Browser renders HTML on page.

http://thewebsite.com/the/page.html

Welcome to the web page!

2. Browser sends HTTP request to server.

HTTP request

4. Server sends HTML in HTTP response back to browser.

HTTP response

```
<HTML>
<HEAD></HEAD
<BODY></BODY>
</HTML>
```

3. Server interprets request and generates appropriate HTML.

Figure 1.7   Requesting a web page. The user starts by requesting a web page, which causes an HTTP request to be sent to the server. The server interprets the request, generates the necessary HTML, and sends it back in an HTTP response. The browser can then display the web page.

Once the server receives the request, it will check that it makes sense, and if it does, will generate an HTTP response. Depending on the request, this response could be a web page, an image, a JavaScript file, or a simple acknowledgment. For this example, I'll assume the user has reached the homepage of a web app, and so the server responds with some HTML. The HTML is added to the HTTP response, which is then sent back across the internet to the browser that made the request.

As soon as the user's browser begins receiving the HTTP response, it can start displaying content on the screen, but the HTML page may also reference other pages and links on the server. To display the complete web page, instead of a static, colorless, raw HTML file, the browser must repeat the request process, fetching every referenced file. HTML, images, CSS for styling, and JavaScript files for extra behavior are all fetched using the exact same HTTP request process.

Pretty much all interactions that take place on the internet are a facade over this same basic process. A basic web page may only require a few simple requests to fully render, whereas a modern, large web page may take hundreds. The Amazon.com homepage (www.amazon.com), for example, currently makes 298 requests, including 6 CSS files, 14 JavaScript files, and 245 image files!

Now you have a feel for the process, let's see how ASP.NET Core dynamically generates the response on the server.

1.3.2 How does ASP.NET Core process a request?

When you build a web application with ASP.NET Core, browsers will still be using the same HTTP protocol as before to communicate with your application. ASP.NET Core itself encompasses everything that takes place on the server to handle a request, including verifying the request is valid, handling login details, and generating HTML.

Just as with the generic web page example, the request process starts when a user's browser sends an HTTP request to the server, as shown in figure 1.8. A reverse-proxy server captures the request, before passing it to your application. In Windows, the reverse-proxy server will typically be IIS, and on Linux or macOS it might be NGINX or Apache.

> **DEFINITION** A *reverse proxy* is software responsible for receiving requests and forwarding them to the appropriate web server. The reverse proxy is exposed directly to the internet, whereas the underlying web server is exposed only to the proxy. This setup has several benefits, primarily security and performance for the web servers.

The request is forwarded from the reverse proxy to your ASP.NET Core application. Every ASP.NET Core application has a built-in web server, Kestrel by default, which is responsible for receiving raw requests and constructing an internal representation of the data, an HttpContext object, which can be used by the rest of the application.

From this representation, your application should have all the details it needs to create an appropriate response to the request. It can use the details stored in Http-Context to generate an appropriate response, which may be to generate some HTML, to return an "access denied" message, or to send an email, all depending on your application's requirements.

Once the application has finished processing the request, it will return the response to the web server. The ASP.NET Core web server will convert the representation into a raw HTTP response and send it back to the reverse proxy, which will forward it to the user's browser.

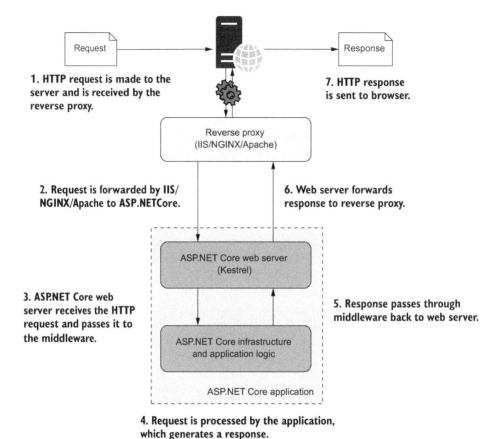

1. HTTP request is made to the server and is received by the reverse proxy.

7. HTTP response is sent to browser.

Reverse proxy
(IIS/NGINX/Apache)

2. Request is forwarded by IIS/NGINX/Apache to ASP.NETCore.

6. Web server forwards response to reverse proxy.

ASP.NET Core web server
(Kestrel)

3. ASP.NET Core web server receives the HTTP request and passes it to the middleware.

5. Response passes through middleware back to web server.

ASP.NET Core infrastructure and application logic

ASP.NET Core application

4. Request is processed by the application, which generates a response.

Figure 1.8   How an ASP.NET Core application processes a request. A request is received from a browser at the reverse proxy, which passes the request to the ASP.NET Core application, which runs a self-hosted web server. The web server processes the request and passes it to the body of the application, which generates a response and returns it to the web server. The web server relays this to the reverse proxy, which sends the response to the browser.

To the user, this process appears to be the same as for the generic HTTP request shown in figure 1.7—the user sent an HTTP request and received an HTTP response. All the differences are server-side, within our application.

You may be thinking that having a reverse proxy *and* a web server is somewhat redundant. Why not have one or the other? Well, one of the benefits is the decoupling of your application from the underlying operating system. The same ASP.NET Core web server, Kestrel, can be cross-platform and used behind a variety of proxies without putting any constraints on a particular implementation. Alternatively, if you wrote a new ASP.NET Core web server, you could use that in place of Kestrel without needing to change anything else about your application.

Another benefit of a reverse proxy is that it can be hardened against potential threats from the public internet. They're often responsible for additional aspects, such as restarting a process that has crashed. Kestrel can stay as a simple HTTP server without having to worry about these extra features when it's used behind a reverse proxy. Think of it as a simple separation of concerns: Kestrel is concerned with generating HTTP responses; a reverse proxy is concerned with handling the connection to the internet.

You've seen how requests and responses find their way to and from an ASP.NET Core application, but I haven't yet touched on how the response is generated. In part 1 of this book, we'll look at the components that make up a typical ASP.NET Core application and how they all fit together. A lot goes into generating a response in ASP.NET Core, typically all within a fraction of a second, but over the course of the book we'll step through an application slowly, covering each of the components in detail.

Before we dive in, you need to choose an underlying platform for your first ASP.NET Core application and set up a development environment in which to build it.

1.4   *Choosing a platform for ASP.NET Core*

ASP.NET Core was developed along with .NET Core and is often mentioned in the same breath, so it can be easy to forget that ASP.NET Core is platform-agnostic. You can build and run an ASP.NET Core application on both .NET Core or .NET Framework. The same features will be available in both cases, so why would you choose one over the over? Which route is right for you depends on both your history and the application you're looking to build, so in this section I've highlighted some advantages and disadvantages to consider.

1.4.1   *Advantages of using .NET Framework*

One of the most significant advantages of the full .NET framework is its maturity—it has been developed for 16 years, has been battle-hardened, and extensively deployed. For some, this maturity will be a significant deciding factor. It will already be installed on your servers and building an ASP.NET Core on top involves (relatively) little risk to your existing environment.

For others, particularly existing ASP.NET developers, the cross-platform and container-friendly .NET Core won't hold any appeal. These developers will, by necessity, be used to deploying to Windows servers, and it's perfectly reasonable to want to continue to do so, while still taking advantage of all ASP.NET Core has to offer.

The biggest reason to stick with the full .NET Framework when .NET Core was first released was because you needed to make use of Windows-specific features, such as the Registry or Directory Services. Microsoft have since released a compatibility pack[6] that makes these APIs available in .NET Core, but they're only available when running .NET Core on Windows, not on Linux or macOS. If you know your app relies on many Windows-only features, then .NET Framework may be the easiest option.

---

[6] The Windows Compatibility Pack is designed to help port code from .NET Framework to .NET Core. See http://mng.bz/50hu.

WARNING If you choose to run on .NET Framework only, you won't be able to easily run your application cross-platform.

One advantage of using .NET Framework is that it has the greatest library support, in the form of NuGet packages. Library authors are being encouraged to make their libraries work identically on both .NET Framework and .NET Core by targeting .NET Standard, but that transition is a slow process.

.NET Standard[7] defines the APIs that are available on a given .NET platform. It's made up of multiple versions (for example, 1.1 and 1.2), each of which adds additional APIs compared to previous versions. Think of it as an "interface" for various .NET frameworks; the frameworks (such as .NET Core, .NET Framework, and Mono) all "implement" a version of .NET Standard.

TIP You can create a new type of library that targets .NET Standard instead of targeting a specific framework. That allows you to use your library across multiple platforms, including .NET Core and .NET Framework. See appendix A for further details.

.NET Standard 2.0 vastly increases the number of APIs available to libraries that target it, covering almost the same area as .NET Framework 4.6.1. At the time of writing, 56% of packages on NuGet.org target the full framework rather than .NET Standard, so if your application currently relies on one of those packages, you'll have to choose .NET Framework for your ASP.NET Core application.

TIP .NET Standard 2.0 contains a compatibility shim that allows you to reference .NET Framework 4.6.1 libraries from a .NET Standard library. For details, see http://mng.bz/jH8Y and appendix A.

1.4.2 *Advantages of using .NET Core*

If you're considering ASP.NET Core for a project, the chances are you're also interested in the associated features .NET Core brings, such as the cross-platform capabilities. If that's the case, then those features are obvious reasons to choose .NET Core as the underlying platform to use with ASP.NET Core.

The open source nature of .NET Core development can be a big deciding factor for some people. Open source development means you can clearly see how features and bugs are being addressed. If there's a particular feature you feel strongly about or a bug that's plaguing you, you can always submit a pull-request and see your code in the .NET Core platform!

Related to this, and the highly modular design of .NET Core, it's likely that the platform will see a faster release cycle than other platforms. Updates to .NET Framework require a massive amount of regression testing to ensure there are no subtle interactions that could break old applications. In contrast, installations of .NET Core are

---

[7] The .NET Standard GitHub repository can be found at https://github.com/dotnet/standard/blob/master/docs/faq.md.

independent of one another, so you can install multiple versions of .NET Core side-by-side. .NET Core also follows semantic versioning (SemVer), so you can be sure that your old applications won't be affected by installing a new version of the framework.

> **WARNING** Be aware that the faster release cycle generally means larger changes between .NET Core versions when you update your apps. For example, upgrading from .NET Core 1.0 to 2.0 is a significant and potentially breaking change.

Which platform you choose will depend on your use case. The full .NET Framework is still supported, and is being actively developed, but it's clear the focus of Microsoft is with .NET Core right now. If you're starting a new application from scratch and the libraries you require have been updated to use .NET Standard, then .NET Core seems to make the most logical choice for the future.

One final option is to multitarget your application, allowing it to run on both .NET Core and .NET Framework. This requires a little more effort to set up and maintain in terms of dependency wrangling, but it's a viable option if you're going to need to run in both environments. In this book, I'm going to be targeting the .NET Core platform, but all the examples should work equally with .NET Framework without any modification.

Once you've selected a platform for your ASP.NET Core applications, it's time to prepare your development environment—the last step before you build your first ASP.NET Core application!

1.5 *Preparing your development environment*

For .NET developers in a Windows-centric world, Visual Studio was pretty much a developer requirement in the past. But with .NET Core and ASP.NET Core going cross-platform, that's no longer the case.

All of ASP.NET Core (creating new projects, building, testing, and publishing) can be run from the command line for any supported operating system. All you need is the .NET Core SDK and tooling, which provides the .NET Command Line Interface (CLI). Alternatively, if you're on Windows, and not comfortable with the command line, you can still use File > New Project in Visual Studio to dive straight in. With ASP.NET Core, it's all about choice!

In a similar vein, you can now get a great editing experience outside of Visual Studio thanks to the OmniSharp project.[8] This is a set of libraries and editor plugins that provide code suggestions and autocomplete (IntelliSense) across a wide range of editors and operating systems. How you setup your environment will likely depend on which operating system you're using and what you're used to.

Remember that, if you're using .NET Core, the operating system you choose for development has no bearing on the final systems you can run on—whether you

---

[8] Information about the OmniSharp project can be found at www.omnisharp.net. Source code can be found at https://github.com/omnisharp.

choose Windows, macOS, or Linux for development, you can deploy to any supported system.

1.5.1   *If you're a Windows user*

For a long time, Windows has been the best system for building .NET applications, and with the availability of Visual Studio that's still the case.

Visual Studio (figure 1.9) is a full-featured integrated development environment (IDE), which provides one of the best all-around experiences for developing ASP.NET Core applications. Luckily, the Visual Studio Community edition is now free for open source, students, and small teams of developers! Visual studio comes loaded with a whole host of templates for building new projects, debugging, and publishing, without ever needing to touch a command prompt.

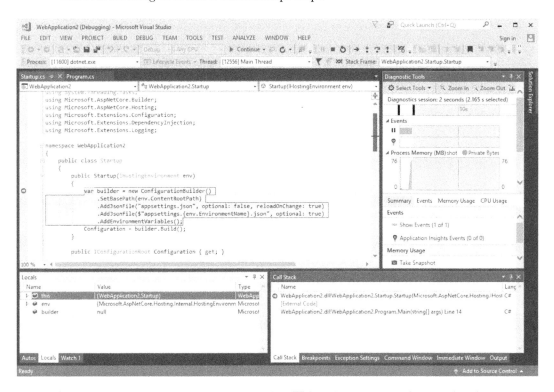

Figure 1.9   Visual Studio provides the most complete ASP.NET Core development environment for Windows users.

Sometimes, though, you don't want a full-fledged IDE. Maybe you want to quickly view or edit a file, or you don't like the sometimes unpredictable performance of Visual Studio. In those cases, a simple editor may be all you want or need, and Visual Studio Code is a great choice. Visual Studio Code (figure 1.10) is an open source, lightweight editor that provides editing, IntelliSense, and debugging for a wide range of languages, including C# and ASP.NET Core.

```
                            Startup.cs - live.asp.net

EXPLORER                C# Startup.cs ●                                                    ⊡ ...

▲ OPEN EDITORS           2    // Licensed under the Apache License, Version 2.0. See License.txt in the project root for lice
  ● C# Startup.cs src/live.asp.net    3
▲ LIVE.ASP.NET           4    using System.Security.Claims;
                         5    using live.asp.net.Formatters;
  ▲ ▨ live.asp.net       6    using live.asp.net.Services;
    ▷ ▨ Controllers      7    using Microsoft.AspNetCore.Authentication.Cookies;
    ▷ ▨ Formatters       8    using Microsoft.AspNetCore.Builder;
    ▷ ▨ Models           9    using Microsoft.AspNetCore.Hosting;
    ▷ ▨ Properties       10   using Microsoft.AspNetCore.Http;
    ▷ ▨ Services         11   using Microsoft.Extensions.Configuration;
    ▷ ▨ TagHelpers       12   using Microsoft.Extensions.DependencyInjection;
    ▷ ▨ ViewModels       13   using Microsoft.Extensions.Logging;
    ▷ ▨ Views            14   using Microsoft.IdentityModel.Protocols.OpenIdConnect;
    ▷ ▨ wwwroot          15
      C# AppSettings.cs  16   namespace live.asp.net
      appsettings.json   17   {
      appsettings.Productio... 18     public class Startup
    ▨ gulpfile.js        19     {
      live.asp.net.xproj  20        public Startup(IHostingEnvironment env)
    ▨ package.json       21        {
      C# Program.cs       22            var builder = new ConfigurationBuilder()
      project.json        23                .SetBasePath(env.ContentRootPath)
      project.lock.json   24                .AddJsonFile("appsettings.json")
      C# Startup.cs        25                .AddJsonFile($"appsettings.{env.EnvironmentName}.json", optional: true);
      ⚙ web.config        26                ⊙ Add
    ◇ .gitattributes      27            if (env.IsD ⊙ AddApplicationInsightsSettings
    ◇ .gitignore          28            {          ⊙ AddEnvironmentVariables   IConfigurationBuilder AddEnvir...
      CONTRIBUTING.md     29                builder ⊙ Adds an Microsoft.Extensions.Configuration.IConfigurationProvider ... ⊙
      global.json         30                builder ⊙ AddInMemoryCollection
      LICENSE.txt         31            }           ⊙ AddJsonFile
    ▨ live.asp.net.sln    32                        ⊙ AddUserSecrets
      ⚙ NuGet.Config      33                builder.Add|
                          34
                          35                Configuration = builder.Build();
                          36            }
                          37
                          38            public IConfigurationRoot Configuration { get; set; }
                          39
 ◇ dev ○ ⊗1 ▲0 ❶3                              Ln 33, Col 24   Spaces: 4   UTF-8 with BOM   LF   C#   ▨ live.asp.net.sln  ☺
```

Figure 1.10 Visual Studio Code provides cross-platform IntelliSense and debugging.

Whether you install Visual Studio or another editor, such as Visual Studio Code, you'll need to install the .NET Core tooling to start building ASP.NET Core apps. You can either download it from the ASP.NET website (https://get.asp.net) or select the .NET Core cross-platform development workload during Visual Studio 2017 installation.

1.5.2   *If you're a Linux or macOS user*

As a Linux or macOS user, you have a whole host of choices. OmniSharp has plugins for most popular editors, such as Vim, Emacs, Sublime, Atom, and Brackets, not to mention the cross-platform Visual Studio Code. Install the appropriate plugin to your favorite and you'll be writing C# in no time.

Again, you'll need to install the .NET Core SDK from the ASP.NET website (https://get.asp.net) to begin .NET Core and ASP.NET Core development. This will give you the .NET Core runtime and the .NET CLI to start building ASP.NET Core applications.

The .NET CLI contains everything you need to get started, including several project templates. You don't get a huge number to choose from by default, but you can

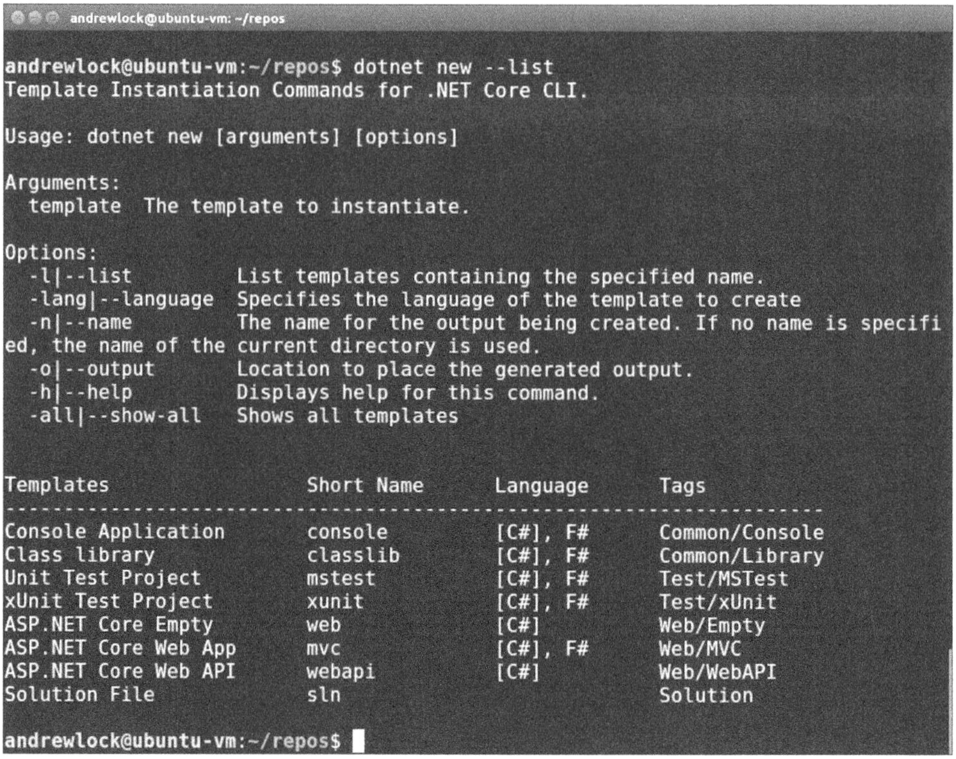

Figure 1.11   The .NET CLI includes several templates by default, as shown here. You can also install additional templates or create your own.

install new ones from GitHub or NuGet if you want more variety. You can easily create applications from the predefined templates to quick-start your development, as shown in figure 1.11.

In addition, in May 2017, Microsoft released Visual Studio for Mac. With VS for Mac you can build cross ASP.NET Core apps, using a similar editor experience to Visual Studio, but on an app designed natively for macOS. VS for Mac is still young, but if you're a macOS user, then it's a great choice and will no doubt see many updates.

In this book, I'll be using Visual Studio for most of the examples, but you'll be able to follow along using any of the tools I've mentioned. The rest of the book assumes you've successfully installed .NET Core and an editor on your computer.

You've reached the end of this chapter; whether you're new to .NET or an existing .NET developer, there's a lot to take in—frameworks, platforms, .NET Framework (which is a platform!). But take heart: you now have all the background you need and, hopefully, a development environment to start building applications using ASP.NET Core.

In the next chapter, you'll create your first application from a template and run it. We'll walk through each of the main components that make up your application and see how they all work together to render a web page.

Summary

- ASP.NET Core is a new web framework built with modern software architecture practices and modularization as its focus.
- It's best used for new, "green-field" projects with few external dependencies.
- Existing technologies such as WCF and SignalR can't currently be used with ASP.NET Core, but work is underway to integrate them.
- Fetching a web page involves sending an HTTP request and receiving an HTTP response.
- ASP.NET Core allows dynamically building responses to a given request.
- An ASP.NET Core application contains a web server, which serves as the entry-point for a request.
- ASP.NET Core apps are protected from the internet by a reverse-proxy server, which forwards requests to the application.
- ASP.NET Core can run on both .NET Framework and .NET Core. If you need Windows-specific features such as the Windows Registry, you should use .NET Framework, but you won't be able to run cross-platform. Otherwise, choose .NET Core for the greatest reach and hosting options.
- The OmniSharp project provides C# editing plugins for many popular editors, including the cross-platform Visual Studio Code editor.
- On Windows, Visual Studio provides the most complete all-in-one ASP.NET Core development experience, but development using the command line and an editor is as easy as on other platforms.

Your first application

This chapter covers

- Creating your first ASP.NET Core web application
- Running your application
- Understanding the components of your application

After reading chapter 1, you should have a general idea of how ASP.NET Core applications work and when you should use them. You should have also set up a development environment to start building applications. In this chapter, you'll dive right in by creating your first web app. You'll get to kick the tires and poke around a little to get a feel for how it works, and in later chapters, I'll show how you go about customizing and building your own applications.

As you work through this chapter, you should begin to get a grasp of the various components that make up an ASP.NET Core application, as well as an understanding of the general application-building process. Most applications you create will start from a similar *template*, so it's a good idea to get familiar with the setup as soon as possible.

DEFINITION A *template* provides the basic code required to build an application. You can use a template as the starting point for building your own apps.

I'll start by showing how to create a basic ASP.NET Core application using one of the Visual Studio templates. If you're using other tooling, such as the .NET CLI, then you'll have similar templates available. I use Visual Studio 2017 and ASP.NET Core 2.0 in this chapter, but I also provide tips for working with the .NET CLI.

TIP You can view the application code for this chapter in the GitHub repository for the book at https://github.com/andrewlock/asp-dot-net-core-in-action.

Once you've created your application, I'll show you how to restore all the necessary dependencies, compile your application, and run it to see the HTML output. The application will be simple in some respects—it will only have three different pages—but it'll be a fully configured ASP.NET Core application.

Having run your application, the next step is to understand what's going on! We'll take a journey through all the major parts of an ASP.NET Core application, looking at how to configure the web server, the middleware pipeline, and HTML generation, among other things. We won't go into detail at this stage, but you'll get a feel for how they all work together to create a complete application.

We'll begin by looking at the plethora of files created when you start a new project and learn how a typical ASP.NET Core application is laid out. In particular, I'll focus on the Program.cs and Startup.cs files. Virtually the entire configuration of your application takes place in these two files, so it's good to get to grips with what they are for and how they're used. You'll see how to define the middleware pipeline for your application, and how you can customize it.

Finally, you'll see how the app generates HTML in response to a request, looking at each of the components that make up the MVC middleware. You'll see how it controls what code is run in response to a request, and how to define the HTML that should be returned for a particular request.

At this stage, don't worry if you find parts of the project confusing or complicated; you'll be exploring each section in detail as you move through the book. By the end of the chapter, you should have a basic understanding of how ASP.NET Core applications are put together, right from when your application is first run to when a response is generated. Before we begin though, we'll review how ASP.NET Core applications handle requests.

2.1 A brief overview of an ASP.NET Core application

In chapter 1, I described how a browser makes an HTTP request to a server and receives a response, which it uses to render HTML on the page. ASP.NET Core allows you to dynamically generate that HTML depending on the particulars of the request so that you can, for example, display different data depending on the current logged-in user.

Say you want to create a web app to display information about your company. You could create a simple ASP.NET Core app to achieve this, especially if you might later want to add dynamic features to your app. Figure 2.1 shows how the application would handle a request for a page in your application.

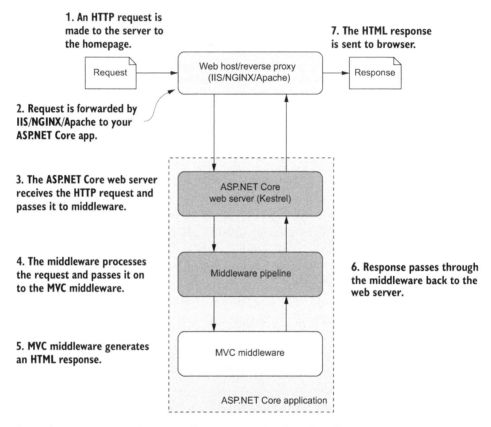

1. An HTTP request is made to the server to the homepage.

7. The HTML response is sent to browser.

Request

Web host/reverse proxy (IIS/NGINX/Apache)

Response

2. Request is forwarded by IIS/NGINX/Apache to your ASP.NET Core app.

3. The ASP.NET Core web server receives the HTTP request and passes it to middleware.

ASP.NET Core web server (Kestrel)

4. The middleware processes the request and passes it on to the MVC middleware.

Middleware pipeline

6. Response passes through the middleware back to the web server.

5. MVC middleware generates an HTML response.

MVC middleware

ASP.NET Core application

Figure 2.1 An overview of an ASP.NET Core application. The ASP.NET Core application contains a number of blocks that process an incoming request from the browser. Every request passes to the middleware pipeline. It potentially modifies it, then passes it to the MVC middleware at the end of the pipeline to generate a response. The response passes back through the middleware, to the server, and finally, out to the browser.

Much of this diagram should be familiar to you from figure 1.8 in chapter 1; the request and response, the reverse proxy, and the ASP.NET Core web server are all still there, but you'll notice that I've expanded the ASP.NET Core application itself to show the middleware pipeline and the MVC middleware. This is the main custom part of your app that goes into generating the response from a request.

The first port of call after the reverse proxy forwards a request is the ASP.NET Core web server, which is the default cross-platform Kestrel server. Kestrel takes the raw incoming request and uses it to generate an `HttpContext` object the rest of the application can use.

> **The HttpContext object**
>
> The `HttpContext` constructed by the ASP.NET Core web server is used by the application as a sort of storage box for a single request. Anything that's specific to this particular request and the subsequent response can be associated with it and stored in it. This could include properties of the request, request-specific services, data that's been loaded, or errors that have occurred. The web server fills the initial `Http-Context` with details of the original HTTP request and other configuration details and passes it on to the rest of the application.

NOTE Kestrel isn't the only HTTP server available in ASP.NET Core, but it's the most performant and is cross-platform. I'll only refer to Kestrel throughout the book. The main alternative, HTTP.sys, only runs on Windows and can't be used with IIS.[1]

Kestrel is responsible for receiving the request data and constructing a C# representation of the request, but it doesn't attempt to handle the request directly. For that, Kestrel hands the `HttpContext` to the middleware pipeline found in every ASP.NET Core application. This is a series of components that processes the incoming request to perform common operations such as logging, handling exceptions, or serving static files.

NOTE You'll learn about the middleware pipeline in detail in the next chapter.

After the middleware pipeline comes the MVC block. This is responsible for generating the HTML that makes up the pages of a typical ASP.NET Core web app. It's also typically where you find most of the business logic of your app, by calling out to various services in response to the data contained in the original request. Not every app needs an MVC block, but it's typically how you'll build most apps that display HTML to a user.

NOTE I'll cover MVC controllers in chapter 4 and generating HTML in chapters 7 and 8.

---

[1] If you want to learn more about HTTP.sys, the documentation describes the server and how to use it: https://docs.microsoft.com/en-us/aspnet/core/fundamentals/servers/httpsys.

Most ASP.NET Core applications follow this basic architecture, and the example in this chapter is no different. First, you'll see how to create and run your application, then we'll look at how the code corresponds to the outline in figure 2.1. Without further ado, let's create an application!

2.2 Creating your first ASP.NET Core application

You can start building applications with ASP.NET Core in many different ways, depending on the tools and operating system you're using. Each set of tools will have slightly different templates, but they have many similarities. The example used throughout this chapter is based on a Visual Studio 2017 template, but you can easily follow along with templates from the .NET CLI or Visual Studio for Mac.

REMINDER   This chapter uses Visual Studio 2017 and ASP.NET Core 2.0.

Getting an application up and running typically follows four basic steps, which we'll work through in this chapter:

1 *Generate*—Create the base application from a template to get started.
2 *Restore*—Restore all the packages and dependencies to the local project folder using NuGet.
3 *Build*—Compile the application and generate all the necessary assets.
4 *Run*—Run the compiled application.

2.2.1 Using a template to get started

Using a template can quickly get you up and running with an application, automatically configuring many of the fundamental pieces for you. Both Visual Studio and the .NET CLI come with a number of standard templates for building web applications, console applications, and class libraries. To create your first web application, open Visual Studio and perform the following steps:

1 Choose File > New > Project.
2 From the Templates node on the left, choose .NET Core, and then select ASP.NET Core Web Application.
3 Enter a Name, Location, and a solution name (optional) and click OK, as shown in figure 2.2.
4 On the following screen (figure 2.3):
   ▪ Select ASP.NET Core 2.0. The generated application will target ASP.NET Core 2.0.
   ▪ Select Web Application (Model-View-Controller). This ensures you create a traditional web application that generates HTML and is designed to be viewed by users in a web browser directly. The other web application template uses the

Choose .NET Core
from templates menu.

Select ASP.NET Core
Web Application.

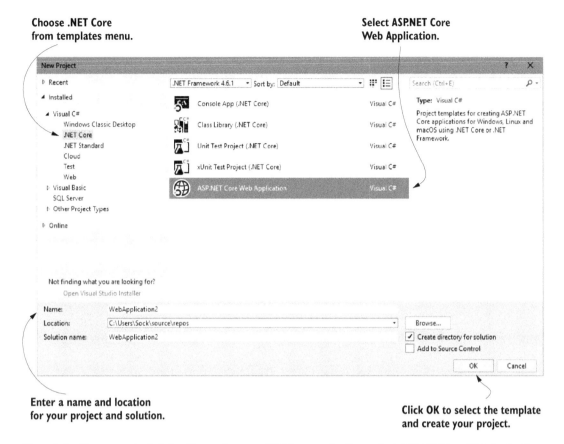

Enter a name and location
for your project and solution.

Click OK to select the template
and create your project.

Figure 2.2 The new project dialog. To create a new .NET Core application, select ASP.NET Core Web Application from the .NET Core templates. Enter a name, location, and a solution name (optional) and click OK.

new Razor Pages[2] functionality of ASP.NET Core 2.0. The Web API template generates an application that returns data in a format that can be consumed by single-page applications (SPAs) and APIs. The Angular, React.js, and React.js and Redux templates create applications for specific SPAs.

- Ensure No Authentication is specified. You'll learn how to add users to your app in chapter 14.
- Ensure Enable Docker Support is unchecked.
- Click OK.

_____

[2] Razor Pages is a page-based alternative framework to the traditional MVC approach. It was introduced in ASP .NET Core 2.0. You can read about it here: https://docs.microsoft.com/en-us/aspnet/core/mvc/razor-pages/.

Select ASP.NET Core 2.0.

**Select Web Application
(Model-View-Controller).**

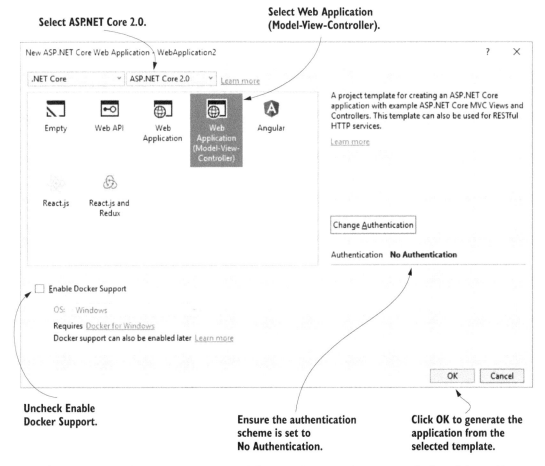

**Uncheck Enable
Docker Support.**

**Ensure the authentication
scheme is set to
No Authentication.**

**Click OK to generate the
application from the
selected template.**

Figure 2.3   The web application template screen. This screen follows on from the New Project dialog and lets you customize the template that will generate your application. For this starter project, you'll create an MVC web application without authentication.

5 Wait for Visual Studio to generate the application from the template. Once Visual Studio has finished generating the application, you'll be presented with an introductory page about ASP.NET Core, and you should be able to see that Visual Studio has created and added a number of files to your project, as shown in figure 2.4.

NOTE If you're developing using the .NET CLI, you can create a similar application by running `dotnet new mvc -o WebApplication2` from the command line. The `-o` argument ensures the CLI creates the template in a subfolder called WebApplication2.

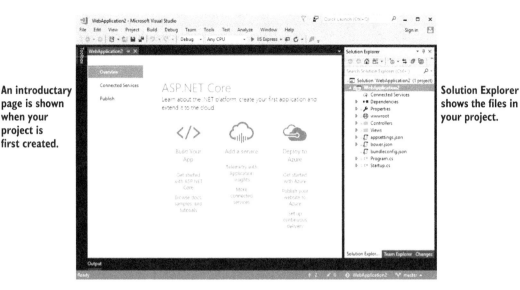

An introductory page is shown when your project is first created.

Solution Explorer shows the files in your project.

Figure 2.4   Visual Studio after creating a new ASP.NET Core application from a template.

2.2.2   *Building the application*

At this point, you have most of the files necessary to run your application, but you've got two steps left. First, you need to ensure all the dependencies used by your project are copied to your local directory, and second, you need to compile your application so that it can be run.

The first of these steps isn't strictly necessary, as both Visual Studio and the .NET CLI automatically restore packages when they first create your project, but it's good to know what's going on. In earlier versions of the .NET CLI, before 2.0, you needed to manually restore packages using `dotnet restore`.

You can compile your application by choosing Build > Build Solution, by using the shortcut Ctrl+Shift+B, or by running `dotnet build` from the command line. If you build from Visual Studio, the output window that shows the progress of the build, and assuming everything is hunky dory, will compile your application, ready for running. You can also run the `dotnet build` console commands from the Package Manager Console in Visual Studio.

> **TIP**   Visual Studio and the .NET CLI tools will automatically build your application when you run it if they detect that a file has changed, so you generally won't need to explicitly perform this step yourself.

NuGet packages and the .NET Core command line interface

One of the foundational components of .NET Core cross-platform development is the .NET Core command line interface (CLI). This provides a number of basic commands for creating, building, and running .NET Core applications. Visual Studio effectively calls these automatically, but you can also invoke them directly from the command line if you're using a different editor. The most common commands during development are

- dotnet restore
- dotnet build
- dotnet run

Each of these commands should be run inside your project folder and will act on that project alone.

All ASP.NET Core applications have dependencies on a number of different external libraries, which are managed through the NuGet package manager. These dependencies are listed in the project, but the files of the libraries themselves aren't included. Before you can build and run your application, you need to ensure there are local copies of each dependency in your project folder. The first command, dotnet restore, will ensure your application's NuGet dependencies are copied to your project folder. With the 2.0 version of the .NET CLI, you no longer need to explicitly run this command; later commands will implicitly restore packages for you, if necessary.

ASP.NET Core projects list their dependencies in the project's csproj file. This is an XML file that lists each dependency as a PackageReference node. When you run dotnet restore, it uses this file to establish which NuGet packages to download and copy to your project folder. Any dependencies listed are available for use in your application.

You can compile your application using dotnet build. This will check for any errors in your application and, if there are no issues, will produce an output that can be run using dotnet run.

Each command contains a number of switches that can modify its behavior. To see the full list of available commands, run

```
dotnet --help
```

or to see the options available for a particular command, new for example, run

```
dotnet new --help
```

2.3   *Running the web application*

You're ready to run your first application and there are a number of different ways to go about it. In Visual Studio, you can either click the green arrow on the toolbar next to IIS Express, or press the F5 shortcut. Visual Studio will automatically open a web browser window for you with the appropriate URL and, after a second or two, you should be presented with your brand new application, as shown in figure 2.5. Alternatively, you can run the application from the command line with the .NET CLI tools using dotnet run and open the URL in a web browser manually, using the address provided on the command line.

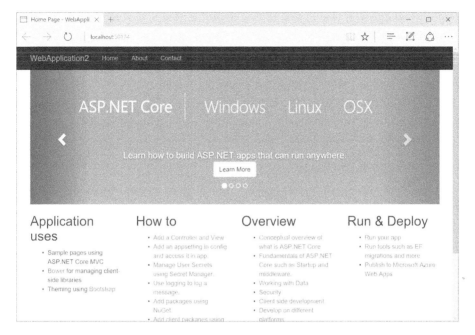

Figure 2.5   The homepage of your new **ASP.NET Core application**

By default, this page shows a variety of links to external resources and a big banner carousel at the top of the page, which scrolls through several images. At the top of the page are three links: Home, About, and Contact. The Home link is the page you're currently on. Clicking About or Contact will take you to a new page, as shown in figure 2.6. As you'll see shortly, you'll use MVC in your application to define these three pages and to build the HTML they display.

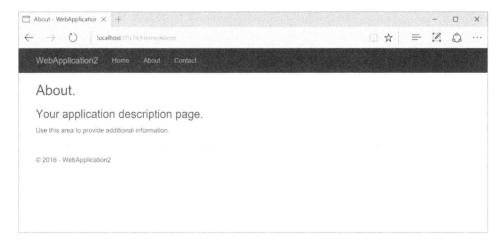

Figure 2.6   The About page of your application. You can navigate between the three pages of the application using the Home, About, and Contact links in the application's header. The app generates the content of the pages using MVC.

At this point, you need to notice a couple of things. First, the header containing the links and the application title "WebApplication2" is the same on all three pages. Second, the title of the page, as shown in the tab of the browser, changes to match the current page. You'll see how to achieve these features in chapter 7, when we discuss the rendering of HTML using Razor templates.

There isn't any more to the user experience of the application at this stage. Click around a little and, once you're happy with the behavior of the application, roll up your sleeves—it's time to look at some code!

2.4   Understanding the project layout

When you're new to a framework, creating an application from a template like this can be a mixed blessing. On the one hand, you can get an application up and running quickly, with little input required on your part. Conversely, the number of files can sometimes be overwhelming, leaving you scratching your head working out where to start. The basic web application template doesn't contain a huge number of files and folders, as shown in figure 2.7, but I'll run through the major ones to get you oriented.

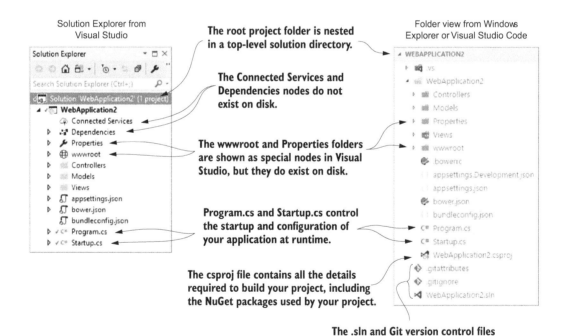

Figure 2.7   The Solution Explorer and folder on disk for a new ASP.NET Core application. The Solution Explorer also displays the Connected Services and Dependencies nodes, which list the NuGet and client-side dependencies, though the folders themselves don't exist on disk.

The first thing to notice is that the main project, WebApplication2, is nested in a top-level directory with the name of the solution, also WebApplication2 in this case. Within this top-level folder, you'll also find the solution (.sln) file for use by Visual Studio and files related to Git version control,[3] though these are hidden in Visual Studio's Solution Explorer view.

> **NOTE** Visual Studio uses the concept of a solution to work with multiple projects. The example solution only consists of a single project, which is listed in the .sln file.

Inside the solution folder, you'll find your project folder, which in turn contains five subfolders—Models, Controllers, Views, Properties, and wwwroot. Models, Controllers, and Views (unsurprisingly) contain the MVC Model, Controller, and View files you'll use to build your application. The Properties folder contains a single file, launchSettings.json, which controls how Visual Studio will run and debug the application. The wwwroot folder is special, in that it's the only folder in your application that browsers are allowed to directly access when browsing your web app. You can store your CSS, JavaScript, images, or static HTML files in here and browsers will be able to access them. They won't be able to access any file that lives outside of wwwroot.

Although the wwwroot and Properties folders exist on disk, you can see that Solution Explorer shows them as special nodes, out of alphabetical order, near the top of your project. You've got two more special nodes in the project, Dependencies and Connected Services, but they don't have a corresponding folder on disk. Instead, they show a collection of all the dependencies, such as NuGet packages, client-side dependencies, and remote services that the project relies on.

In the root of your project folder, you'll find several JSON files, such as appsettings .json, bundleconfig.json, and bower.json. These provide various configuration settings, some of which are used at runtime, and others which are used to build your app at compile time.

> **NOTE** Bower is a client-side asset management system for obtaining CSS and JavaScript libraries. Bower is no longer supported, and so the ASP.NET team are exploring alternatives to fulfill this role. The bower.json file will likely be removed from the default templates and replaced in ASP.NET Core 2.1.

The most important file in your project is WebApplication2.csproj, as it describes how to build your project. Visual Studio doesn't explicitly show the csproj file in Solution Explorer, but you can edit it if you right-click the project name and choose Edit WebApplication2.csproj. We'll have a closer look at this file in the next section.

---

[3] The Git files will only be added if you select Create new Git repository from the New Project dialog. You don't have to use Git, but I strongly recommend using some sort of version control when you build applications. If you're somewhat familiar with Git, but still find it a bit daunting, and a rebase terrifying, I highly recommend reading http://think-like-a-git.net/. It helped me achieve Git enlightenment.

Finally, Visual Studio shows two C# files in the project folder—Program.cs and Startup.cs. In sections 2.6 and 2.7, you'll see how these fundamental classes are responsible for configuring and running your application.

2.5 *The csproj project file: defining your dependencies*

The csproj file is the project file for .NET applications and contains the details required for the .NET tooling to build your project. It defines the type of project being built (web app, console app, or library), which platform the project targets (.NET Core, .NET Framework 4.5, Mono, and so on), and which NuGet packages the project depends on.

The project file has been a mainstay of .NET applications, but in ASP.NET Core it has had a facelift to make it easier to read and edit. These changes include:

- *No GUIDs*—Previously, Global Unique Identifiers (GUIDs) were used for many things, now they're rarely used in the project file.
- *Implicit file includes*—Previously, every file in the project had to be listed in the csproj file for it to be included in the build. Now, files are automatically compiled.
- *No paths to NuGet package dlls*—Previously, you had to include the path to the dll files contained in NuGet packages in the csproj, as well as listing the dependencies in a packages.xml file. Now, you can reference the NuGet package directly in your csproj, and don't need to specify the path on disk.

All of these changes combine to make the project file far more compact than you'll be used to from previous .NET projects. The following listing shows the entire csproj file for your sample app.

> **Listing 2.1 The csproj project file, showing SDK, target framework, and references**

The SDK attribute specifies the type of project you're building.

```
<Project Sdk="Microsoft.NET.Sdk.Web">
```

```
  <PropertyGroup>
    <TargetFramework>netcoreapp2.0</TargetFramework>
  </PropertyGroup>
```
The TargetFramework is the framework you'll run on, in this case, .NET Core 2.0.

```
  <ItemGroup>
    <PackageReference Include="Microsoft.AspNetCore.All"
      Version="2.0.0" />
  </ItemGroup>
```
You reference NuGet packages with the PackageReference element.

```
  <ItemGroup>
    <DotNetCliToolReference Version="2.0.0"
      Include="Microsoft.VisualStudio.Web.CodeGeneration.Tools" />
  </ItemGroup>
```
Additional tools used by Visual Studio to generate controllers and views at design time

```
</Project>
```

For simple applications, you probably won't need to change the project file much. The `Sdk` attribute on the `Project` element includes default settings that describe how to build your project, whereas the `TargetFramework` element describes the framework your application will run on. For .NET Core 2.0 projects, this will have the `netcoreapp2.0` value; if you're running on the full .NET Framework, 4.6.1, this would be `net461`.

> **TIP** With the new csproj style, Visual Studio users can right-click a project in Solution Explorer and choose Edit <projectname>.csproj, without having to close the project first.

The most common changes you'll make to the project file are to add additional NuGet packages using the `PackageReference` element. By default, your app references a single NuGet package, Microsoft.AspNetCore.All. This is a *metapackage* that includes all of the packages associated with ASP.NET Core 2.0. It's only available when you're targeting .NET Core, but it means you don't have to reference each individual ASP.NET Core package.

> **DEFINITION** A *metapackage* is a NuGet package that contains no code, referencing one or more other NuGet packages instead. By adding the metapackage to your app, you can conveniently and implicitly add all of the packages it references. In ASP.NET Core 2.1, the Microsoft.AspNetCore.App metapackage package is referenced by default instead. You can read about the difference between the App and All metapackages at https://github.com/aspnet/Announcements/issues/287.

As well as NuGet package references, you can add command-line tools to your project file. The default template includes a tool used under the covers by Visual Studio for code generation. You'll see how to add new tools in chapter 12.

The simplified project file format is much easier to edit by hand than previous versions, which is great if you're developing cross-platform. But if you're using Visual Studio, don't feel like you have to take this route. You can still use the GUI to add project references, exclude files, manage NuGet packages, and so on. Visual Studio will update the project file itself, as it always has.

> **TIP** For further details on the changes to the csproj format, see the documentation at https://docs.microsoft.com/en-us/dotnet/core/tools/csproj.

The project file defines everything Visual Studio and the .NET CLI need to build your app. Everything, that is, except the code! In the next section, we'll take a look at the entry point for your ASP.NET Core application—the Program.cs class.

2.6 *The Program class: building a web host*

All ASP.NET Core applications start in the same way as .NET Console applications—with a Program.cs file. This file contains a `static void Main` function, which is a standard characteristic of console apps. This method must exist and is called whenever you start your web application. In ASP.NET Core applications, it's used to build and run an `IWebHost` instance, as shown in the following listing, which shows the default Program.cs file. The `IWebHost` is the core of your ASP.NET Core application, containing the application configuration and the Kestrel server that listens for requests and sends responses.

Listing 2.2   The default Program.cs configures and runs an `IWebHost`

```
public class Program
{
    public static void Main(string[] args)
    {
        BuildWebHost(args)          ◄——————  Create an IWebHost using
            .Run();      ◄————————————————    the BuildWebHost method.
    }

    public static IWebHost BuildWebHost(string[] args) =>
        WebHost.CreateDefaultBuilder(args)   ◄———————
            .UseStartup<Startup>()    ◄————————
            .Build();    ——►
    }
```

Run the IWebHost, start listening for requests and generating responses.

Create a WebHostBuilder using the default configuration.

The Startup class defines most of your application's configuration.

Build and return an instance of IWebHost from the WebHostBuilder.

The `Main` function contains all the basic initialization code required to create a web server and to start listening for requests. It uses a `WebHostBuilder`, created by the call to `CreateDefaultBuilder`, to define how the `IWebHost` is configured, before instantiating the `IWebHost` with a call to `Build()`.

> **NOTE**   You'll find this pattern of using a builder object to configure a complex object repeated throughout the ASP.NET Core framework. It's a useful technique for allowing users to configure an object, delaying its creation until all configuration has finished. It's one of the patterns described in the "Gang of Four" book, *Design Patterns: Elements of Reusable Object-Oriented Software* (Addison Wesley, 1994).

Much of your app's configuration takes place in the `WebHostBuilder` created by the call to `CreateDefaultBuilder`, but it delegates some responsibility to a separate class, `Startup`. The `Startup` class referenced in the generic `UseStartup<>` method is where you configure your app's services and define your middleware pipeline. In section 2.7, we'll spend a while delving into this crucial class.

At this point, you may be wondering why you need two classes for configuration: `Program` and `Startup`. Why not include all of your app's configuration in one class or the other?

Figure 2.8 shows the typical split of configuration components between `Program` and `Startup`. Generally speaking, `Program` is where you configure the infrastructure of your application, such as the HTTP server, integration with IIS, and configuration sources. In contrast, `Startup` is where you define which components and features your application uses, and the middleware pipeline for your app.

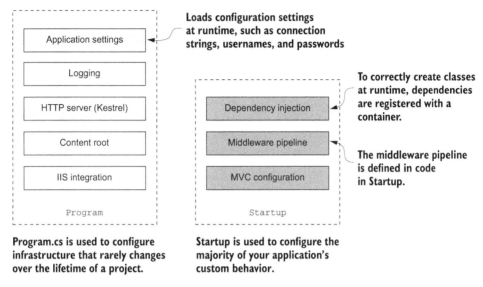

Program.cs is used to configure infrastructure that rarely changes over the lifetime of a project.

Startup is used to configure the majority of your application's custom behavior.

Figure 2.8   The difference in configuration scope for `Program` and `Startup`. `Program` is concerned with infrastructure configuration that will typically remain stable throughout the lifetime of the project. In contrast, you'll often modify `Startup` to add new features and to update application behavior.

The `Program` class for two different ASP.NET Core applications will generally be similar, but the `Startup` classes will often differ significantly (though they generally follow a similar pattern, as you'll see shortly). You'll rarely find that you need to modify `Program` as your application grows, whereas you'll normally update `Startup` whenever you add additional features. For example, if you add a new NuGet dependency to your project, you'll normally need to update `Startup` to make use of it.

The `Program` class is where a lot of app configuration takes place, but in the default templates this is hidden inside the `CreateDefaultBuilder` method. The `Create-DefaultBuilder` method is a static helper method, introduced in ASP.NET Core 2.0, to simplify the bootstrapping of your app by creating a `WebHostBuilder` with some common configuration. In chapter 11, we'll peek inside this method and explore the configuration system, but for now, it's enough to keep figure 2.8 in mind, and to be aware that you can completely change the `IWebHost` configuration if you need to.

Once the configuration of the `WebHostBuilder` is complete, the call to `Build` produces the `IWebHost` instance, but the application still isn't handling HTTP requests yet. It's the call to `Run` that starts the HTTP server listening. At this point, your application is fully operational and can respond to its first request from a remote browser.

2.7   *The Startup class: configuring your application*

As you've seen, Program is responsible for configuring a lot of the infrastructure for your app, but you configure some of your app's behavior in Startup. The Startup class is responsible for configuring two main aspects of your application:

- *Service registration*—Any classes that your application depends on for providing functionality—both those used by the framework and those specific to your application—must be registered so that they can be correctly instantiated at runtime.
- *Middleware and MVC*—How your application handles and responds to requests.

You configure each of these aspects in its own method in Startup, service registration in ConfigureServices, and middleware configuration in Configure. A typical outline of Startup is shown in the following listing.

> Listing 2.3   An outline of Startup.cs showing how each aspect is configured

```
public class Startup
{
    public void ConfigureServices(IServiceCollection services)      ◁┐
    {                                            Configure services by registering
        // method details                        services with the IServiceCollection.
    }

    public void Configure(IApplicationBuilder app)      ◁────
    {                                       Configure the middleware pipeline
        // method details                    for handling HTTP requests.
    }
}
```

The WebHostBuilder created in Program calls ConfigureServices and then Configure, as shown in figure 2.9. Each call configures a different part of your application, making it available for subsequent method calls. Any services registered in the Configure-Services method are available to the Configure method. Once configuration is complete, an IWebHost is created by calling Build() on the WebHostBuilder.

An interesting point about the Startup class is that it doesn't implement an interface as such. Instead, the methods are invoked by using *reflection* to find methods with the predefined names of Configure and ConfigureServices. This makes the class more flexible and enables you to modify the signature of the method to accept additional parameters that are fulfilled automatically. I'll cover how this works in detail in chapter 10, for now it's enough to know that anything that's configured in ConfigureServices can be accessed by the Configure method.

> **DEFINITION**   *Reflection* in .NET allows you to obtain information about types in your application at runtime. You can use reflection to create instances of classes at runtime, and to invoke and access them.

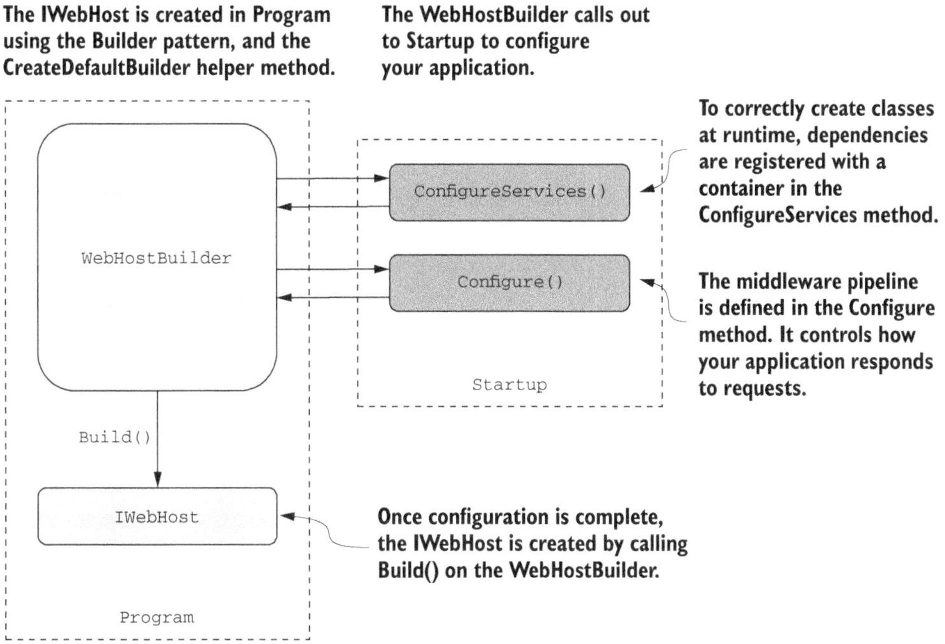

The IWebHost is created in Program using the Builder pattern, and the CreateDefaultBuilder helper method.

The WebHostBuilder calls out to Startup to configure your application.

To correctly create classes at runtime, dependencies are registered with a container in the ConfigureServices method.

The middleware pipeline is defined in the Configure method. It controls how your application responds to requests.

Once configuration is complete, the IWebHost is created by calling Build() on the WebHostBuilder.

Figure 2.9   The `WebHostBuilder` is created in Program.cs and calls methods on `Startup` to configure the application's services and middleware pipeline. Once configuration is complete, the `IWebHost` is created by calling `Build()` on the `WebHostBuilder`.

Given how fundamental the `Startup` class is to ASP.NET Core applications, the rest of section 2.7 walks you through both `ConfigureServices` and `Configure`, to give you a taste of how they're used. I won't explain them in detail (we have the rest of the book for that!), but you should keep in mind how they follow on from each other and how they contribute to the application configuration as a whole.

2.7.1   Adding and configuring services

ASP.NET Core uses small, modular components for each distinct feature. This allows individual features to evolve separately, with only a loose coupling to others, and is generally considered good design practice. The downside to this approach is that it places the burden on the consumer of a feature to correctly instantiate it. Within your application, these modular components are exposed as one or more *services* that are used by the application.

> **DEFINITION**   Within the context of ASP.Net Core, *service* refers to any class that provides functionality to an application and could be classes exposed by a library or code you've written for your application.

For example, in an e-commerce app, you might have a `TaxCalculator` that calculates the tax due on a particular product, taking into account the user's location in the world. Or you might have a `ShippingCostService` that calculates the cost of shipping to a user's location. A third service, `OrderTotalCalculatorService`, might use both of these services to work out the total price the user must pay for an order. Each service provides a small piece of independent functionality, but you can combine them to create a complete application. This is known as the *single responsibility principle.*

> **DEFINITION** The *single responsibility principle* (SRP) states that every class should be responsible for only a single piece of functionality—it should only need to change if that required functionality changes. It's one of the five main design principles promoted by Robert C. Martin in *Agile Software Development, Principles, Patterns, and Practices* (Pearson, 2011).

The `OrderTotalCalculatorService` needs access to an instance of `ShippingCostService` and `TaxCalculator`. A naïve approach to this problem is to use the `new` keyword and create an instance of a service whenever you need it. Unfortunately, this tightly couples your code to the specific implementation you're using and can completely undo all the good work achieved by modularizing the features in the first place. In some cases, it may break the SRP by making you perform initialization code as well as using the service you created.

One solution to this problem is to make it somebody else's problem. When writing a service, you can declare your dependencies and let another class fill those dependencies for you. Your service can then focus on the functionality for which it was designed, instead of trying to work out how to build its dependencies.

This technique is called dependency injection or the inversion of control (IoC) principle and is a well-recognized *design pattern* that is used extensively.

> **DEFINITION** *Design patterns* are solutions to common software design problems.

Typically, you'll register the dependencies of your application into a "container," which can then be used to create any service. This is true for both your own custom application services and the framework services used by ASP.NET Core. You must register each service with the container before it can be used in your application.

> **NOTE** I'll describe the dependency inversion principle and the IoC container used in ASP.NET Core in detail in chapter 10.

In an ASP.NET Core application, this registration is performed in the `Configure-Services` method. Whenever you use a new ASP.NET Core feature in your application, you'll need to come back to this method and add in the necessary services. This is not as arduous as it sounds, as shown here, taken from the example application.

Listing 2.4 **`Startup.ConfigureServices`: adding services to the IoC container**

```
public class Startup
{
    // This method gets called by the runtime.
    // Use this method to add services to the container.
```

```
    public void ConfigureServices(IServiceCollection services)
    {
        // Add framework services.
        services.AddMvc();
    }
}
```

You may be surprised that a complete MVC application only includes a single call to add the necessary services, but the AddMvc() method is an extension method that encapsulates all the code required to set up the MVC services. Behind the scenes, it adds various Razor services for rendering HTML, formatter services, routing services, and many more!

As well as registering framework-related services, this method is where you'd register any custom services you have in your application, such as the example TaxCalculator discussed previously. The IServiceCollection is a list of every known service that your application will need to use. By adding a new service to it, you ensure that whenever a class declares a dependency on your service, the IoC container knows how to provide it.

With your services all configured, it's time to move on to the final configuration step, defining how your application responds to HTTP requests.

2.7.2 *Defining how requests are handled with middleware*

So far, in the WebHostBuilder and Startup class, you've defined the infrastructure of the application and registered your services with the IoC container. In the final configuration method of Startup, Configure, you define the middleware pipeline for the application, which is what defines the app's behavior. Here's the Configure method for the template application.

Listing 2.5 **Startup.Configure: defining the middleware pipeline**

```
public class Startup                            The IApplicationBuilder is used
{                                               to build the middleware pipeline.
    public void Configure(
        IApplicationBuilder app,       ◁──┐    Other services can be
        IHostingEnvironment env)       ◁──┘    accepted as parameters.
    {
        if (env.IsDevelopment())           ◁────────────────────    Different
        {                                                           behavior when
            app.UseDeveloperExceptionPage();   ◁──┐                 in development
            app.UseBrowserLink();                 │                 or production
        }                                      Only runs in a
        else                                   development environment
        {
            app.UseExceptionHandler("/Home/Error");   ◁──┐
        }                                                 Only runs in a
                                                          production environment
        app.UseStaticFiles();   ◁──┐
Adds the                           │
   MVC                          Adds the static file middleware
middleware └─▷ app.UseMvc(routes =>
               {
```

```
        routes.MapRoute(
            name: "default",
            template: "{controller=Home}/{action=Index}/{id?}");
    });
    }
}
```

As I described previously, middleware consists of small components that execute in sequence when the application receives an HTTP request. They can perform a whole host of functions, such as logging, identifying the current user for a request, serving static files, and handling errors.

The `IApplicationBuilder` that's passed to the `Configure` method is used to define the order in which middleware executes. The order of the calls in this method is important, as the order they're added to the builder in is the order they'll execute in the final pipeline. Middleware can only use objects created by previous middleware in the pipeline—it can't access objects created by later middleware. If you're performing authorization in middleware to restrict the users that may access your application, you must ensure it comes *after* the authentication middleware that identifies the current user.

> **WARNING** It's important that you consider the order of middleware when adding it to the pipeline. Middleware can only use objects created by earlier middleware in the pipeline.

You should also note that an `IHostingEnvironment` parameter is used to provide different behavior when you're in a development environment. When you're running in development (when `EnvironmentName` is set to `"Development"`), the `Configure` method adds one piece of exception-handling middleware to the pipeline; in production, it adds a different one.

The `IHostingEnvironment` object contains details about the current environment, as determined by the `WebHostBuilder` in `Program`. It exposes a number of properties:

- `ContentRootPath`—Location of the working directory for the app, typically the folder in which the application is running
- `WebRootPath`—Location of the wwwroot folder that contains static files
- `EnvironmentName`—Whether the current environment is a development or production environment

`IHostingEnvironment` is already set by the time `Startup` is invoked; you can't change these values using the application settings in `Startup`. `EnvironmentName` is typically set externally by using an environment variable when your application starts.

> **NOTE** You'll learn about hosting environments and how to change the current environment in chapter 11.

In development, `DeveloperExceptionPageMiddleware` (added by the `UseDeveloper-ExceptionPage()` call) ensures that, if your application throws an exception that isn't caught, you'll be presented with as much information as possible in the browser to diagnose the problem, as shown in figure 2.10. It's akin to the "yellow screen of death" in the previous version of ASP.NET, but this time it's white, not yellow!

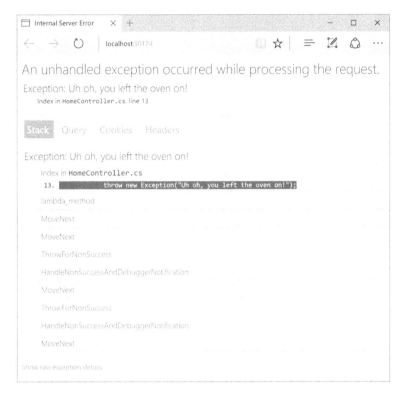

Figure 2.10   The developer exception page contains many different sources of information to help you diagnose a problem, including the exception stack trace and details about the request that generated the exception.

> **NOTE**   The default templates also add `BrowserLinkMiddleware` in development, which reloads your browser when it detects changes in your project. But I personally find this unreliable, so tend to remove it from my projects.

When you're running in a production environment, exposing this amount of data to users would be a big security risk. Instead, `ExceptionHandlerMiddleware` is registered so that, if users encounter an exception in your method, they will be presented with a friendly error page that doesn't reveal the source of the problems. If you run the default template in production mode and trigger an error, then you'll be presented with the message shown in figure 2.11 instead. Obviously, you'd need to update this page to be more visually appealing and more user-friendly, but at least it doesn't reveal the inner workings of your application!

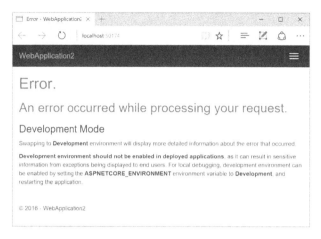

Figure 2.11   The default exception-handling page. In contrast to the developer exception page, this doesn't reveal any details about your application to users. In reality, you'd update the message to something more user-friendly.

The next piece of middleware added to the pipeline is `StaticFileMiddleware`, using this statement:

```
app.UseStaticFiles();
```

This middleware is responsible for handling requests for static files such as CSS files, JavaScript files, and images. When a request arrives at the middleware, it checks to see if the request is for an existing file. If it is, then the middleware returns the file. If not, the request is ignored and the next piece of middleware can attempt to handle the request. Figure 2.12 shows how the request is processed when a static file is requested. When the static-file middleware handles a request, other middleware that comes later in the pipeline, such as the MVC middleware, won't be called at all.

Which brings us to the final and most substantial piece of middleware in the pipeline: the MVC middleware. It's responsible for interpreting the request to determine which method to invoke, for reading parameters from the request, and for generating the final HTML. Despite that, the only configuration required, aside from adding the middleware to the pipeline, is to define a *route* that will be used to map requests to a handler. For each request, the MVC middleware uses this route to determine the appropriate controller and action method on the controller to invoke, and hence, which HTML to generate.

Phew! You've finally finished configuring your application with all the settings, services, and middleware it needs. Configuring your application touches on a wide range of different topics that we'll delve into further throughout the book, so don't worry if you don't fully understand all the steps yet.

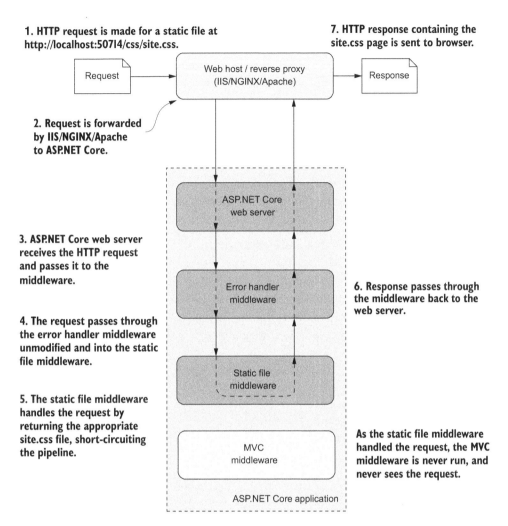

1. HTTP request is made for a static file at http://localhost:50714/css/site.css.

7. HTTP response containing the site.css page is sent to browser.

2. Request is forwarded by IIS/NGINX/Apache to ASP.NET Core.

3. ASP.NET Core web server receives the HTTP request and passes it to the middleware.

4. The request passes through the error handler middleware unmodified and into the static file middleware.

5. The static file middleware handles the request by returning the appropriate site.css file, short-circuiting the pipeline.

6. Response passes through the middleware back to the web server.

As the static file middleware handled the request, the MVC middleware is never run, and never sees the request.

Figure 2.12　An overview of a request for a static file at /css/site.css for an ASP.NET Core application. The request passes through the middleware pipeline until it's handled by the static file middleware. This returns the requested CSS file as the response, which passes back to the web server. The MVC middleware is never invoked and never sees the request.

Once the application is configured, it can start handling requests. But *how* does it handle them? I've already touched on StaticFileMiddleware, which will serve the image and CSS files to the user, but what about the requests that require an HTML response? In the rest of this chapter, I'll give you a glimpse into the MVC middleware and how it generates HTML.

2.8   *MVC middleware and the home controller*

When an ASP.NET Core application receives a request, it progresses through the middleware pipeline until a middleware component can handle it, as you saw in figure 2.12. Normally, the final piece of middleware in a pipeline is the MVC middleware. This middleware will attempt to match a request's path to a configured route, which defines which controller and *action* method to invoke. A path is the remainder of the request URL, once the domain has been removed. For example, for a request to www.microsoft.com/account/manage, the path is /account/manage.

> **DEFINITION**   An *action* is a method that runs in response to a request. A controller is a class that contains a number of action methods that can be logically grouped.

Once the middleware has selected a controller and action for a given request, the appropriate class will be instantiated and the action method invoked. Controllers are ordinary classes, though they often inherit from the Controller base class to provide access to a number of helper methods, as shown in the following listing. Similarly, there's nothing special about action methods, other than that they typically return an IActionResult, which contains instructions for handling the request.

Listing 2.6   The HomeController—an MVC controller

```
public class HomeController : Controller
{
    public IActionResult Index()
    {
        return View();
    }

    public IActionResult About()
    {
        ViewData["Message"] =
            "Your application description page.";

        return View();
    }

    public IActionResult Contact()
    {
        ViewData["Message"] = "Your contact page.";

        return View();
    }

    public IActionResult Error()
    {
```

MVC controllers can inherit from a helper base class but don't have to.

Action methods typically return a ViewResult by calling the View() helper method.

Data can be passed to a view using the ViewData dictionary.

If not specified, the name of the view is taken from the name of the action method.

Data can be passed to a view using the ViewData dictionary.

```
        return View(new ErrorViewModel
        {
            RequestId = Activity.Current?.Id ??
                HttpContext.TraceIdentifier
        });
    }
}
```

Data can also be passed to a view using a view model.

This example shows the `HomeController`, which exposes four different action methods. You may remember from figures 2.5 and 2.6 that the application contains three links: Home, About, and Contact. These links correspond to the `Index`, `About`, and `Contact` action methods. `ExceptionMiddlewareHandler` calls the remaining action method, `Error`, when an error occurs in production.

Each method calls the `View` function that's defined on the `Controller` base class. This method creates a `ViewResult` object, which implements `IActionResult`. By returning a `ViewResult`, the action is asking the MVC middleware to invoke a view to generate the HTML for a response. The name of the view is taken from the name of the action. So, in the case of the first action method, the view will be called `Index`.

> **NOTE** Action methods can use `async` and `await` if you need to use asynchronous programming.[4] In that case, the return value would be `Task<IAction-Result>`.

As well as returning a `ViewResult`, the `About` and `Contact` action methods also set a value in the `ViewData` dictionary. This dictionary only lasts for the duration of the request and can be used to send arbitrary values to the view, which it can use when generating the HTML response.

The `Error` method uses a different approach to pass data from the controller to the view. A dedicated class, a *view model*, is created and passed to the `View()` method with data to display in the view.

> **DEFINITION** A *view model* is a simple object that contains data required by the view to render a UI.

The action methods shown in listing 2.6 and discussed in paragraphs that follow are simple, and you may be wondering why they're worth having. If all they do is return a view to generate, then why do we need controllers at all?

The key thing to remember here is that you now have a framework for performing arbitrarily complex functions in response to a request. You could easily update the action methods to load data from the database, send an email, add a product to a basket, or create an order—all in response to a simple HTTP request. This extensibility is where a lot of the power in MVC lies.

---

[4] For guidance on asynchronous programming, when to use it, and how to use the `async` and `await` keywords, see https://docs.microsoft.com/en-us/dotnet/csharp/async.

The other important point is that you've separated the execution of these methods from the generation of the HTML, as shown in figure 2.13. If the logic changes and you need to add behavior to an action, you don't need to touch the HTML generation code, so you're less likely to introduce bugs. Conversely, if you need to change the UI slightly, change the color of the title for example, then your action method logic is safe.

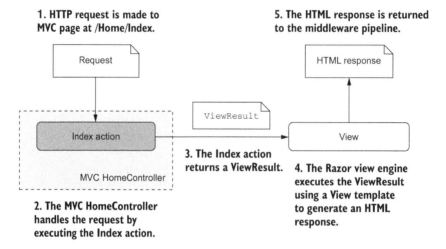

1. HTTP request is made to MVC page at /Home/Index.

Request

2. The MVC HomeController handles the request by executing the Index action.

Index action

MVC HomeController

3. The Index action returns a ViewResult.

ViewResult

5. The HTML response is returned to the middleware pipeline.

HTML response

4. The Razor view engine executes the ViewResult using a View template to generate an HTML response.

View

Figure 2.13   The execution of an MVC controller in response to a request. The `HomeController` handles a request to /Home/Index by executing the `Index` action. This generates a `ViewResult` that contains data that a view uses to generate the HTML response. The execution of the action is independent of the HTML generation, so you can modify one without affecting the other.

With this in mind, all that's left to demonstrate is how to generate the HTML that you send to the client.

2.9   *Generating HTML with Razor template views*

When an action method returns a `ViewResult`, it's signaling to the MVC middleware that it should find a Razor template and generate the appropriate view. In the example, the action method doesn't specify the name of the view to find, so the middleware attempts to find an appropriate file by using naming conventions, as shown in figure 2.14.

Razor view templates are stored in cshtml files (a portmanteau of cs and html) within the Views folder of your project. Generally, they're named according to their associated actions, and reside in subfolders corresponding to the name of the controller. When a controller returns a `ViewResult`, the Razor engine attempts to locate the appropriate view template, as illustrated in figure 2.15. For example, considering the `HomeController` you've already seen, the view template for the `About` action method can be found at Views\Home\About.cshtml, relative to the base project path.

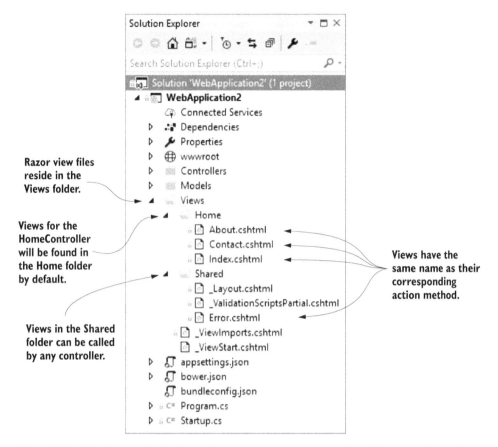

Figure 2.14 View files are located at runtime based on naming conventions. Razor view files reside in a folder based on the name of the associated MVC controller and are named with the name of the action method that requested it. Views in the Shared folder can be used by any controller.

If the MVC middleware can't find a view with the appropriate name in the expected location, it will search in one other location. The Shared folder contains views that any controller can access. For example, the previous `HomeController` contains an `Error` action method, but there's no corresponding cshtml template in the Views\Home folder. In the Views\Shared folder, however, there's an appropriately named view, so the template can be found and rendered without error.

> **TIP** You can modify all of these conventions, including the algorithm shown in figure 2.15, during initial configuration. In fact, you can replace the whole Razor templating engine if required, but that's beyond the scope of this book.

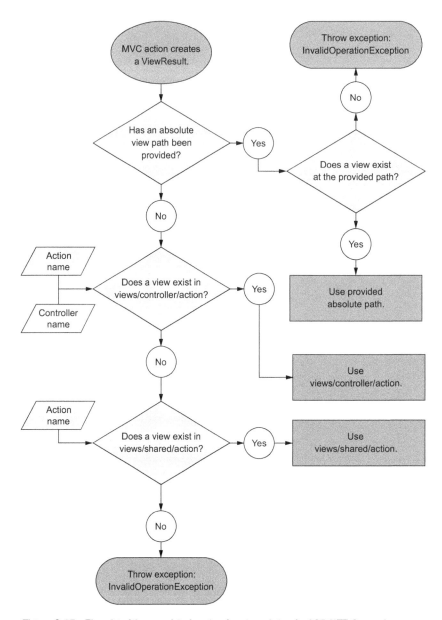

Figure 2.15   The algorithm used to locate view templates in ASP.NET Core when an
action creates a `ViewResult`. If the `ViewResult` has been created using a specific
path to a view, and a view exists at the path, then the view will be used. If not, the
controller name and action name will be used to try and find the view. If that doesn't
exist, the Shared folder and action name will be used. If no view exists at any of the
locations, an `InvalidOperationException` will be thrown.

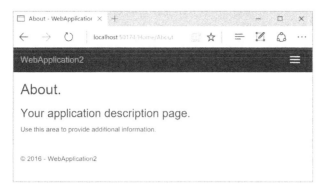

Figure 2.16   Rendering a Razor template to HTML. The About action is invoked and returns a `ViewResult`. The MVC middleware searches for the appropriate Razor template and executes it to generate the HTML displayed in the browser.

Once the template has been located, it can be executed. Figure 2.16 shows the result of executing the `About` action method and rendering the associated Razor template.

The following listing shows the contents of the About.cshtml file. You can see that the file consists of a combination of some standalone C# code, some standalone HTML, and some points where you're writing C# values in the HTML.

Listing 2.7   A simple Razor template—About.cshtml

```
@{
    ViewData["Title"] = "About";        ⊲──┐  C# code that doesn't write to
}                                              the response
```

```
<h2>@ViewData["Title"]</h2>        |  HTML with dynamic C# values
<h3>@ViewData["Message"]</h3>      |  written to the response
```

```
<p>Use this area to provide additional information.</p>    ⊲──┐ Standalone,
                                                                static HTML
```

This file, although small, demonstrates three features of Razor that you can use when building your templates. The simplest and most obvious point is that standalone, static HTML is always valid in a template and will be rendered as is in the response.

Second, you can write ordinary C# code in Razor templates by using this construct

```
@{ /* C# code here */ }
```

Any code between the curly braces will be executed but won't be written to the response. In the listing you're setting the title of the page by writing a key to the `View-Data` dictionary, but you aren't writing anything to the response at this point:

```
@{
    ViewData["Title"] = "About";
}
```

Another feature shown in this template is dynamically writing C# variables to the HTML stream using the @ symbol. This ability to combine dynamic and static markup is what gives Razor templates their power. In the example, you're fetching the `"Title"` and `"Message"` values from the `ViewData` dictionary and writing the values to the response inside the <h2> and <h3> tags, respectively:

```
<h2>@ViewData["Title"]</h2>
<h3>@ViewData["Message"]</h3>
```

You may also remember that you previously set the value of the `"Message"` key in the About action method, which you're now retrieving and writing to the response. This is one of the ways to pass data from an action method to a view—we'll discuss others in chapter 7.

At this point, you might be a little confused by the template from the listing when compared to the output shown in figure 2.16. The title and the message values appear in both the listing and figure, but some parts of the final web page don't appear in the template. How can that be?

Razor has the concept of *layouts*, which are base templates that define the common elements of your application, such as headers and footers. These layouts define a writeable section in which they will render the action method template, such as the code in listing 2.7. The HTML of the layout combines with the action method template to produce the final HTML that's sent to the browser. This prevents you having to duplicate code for the header and footer in every page and means that, if you need to tweak something, you'll only need to do it in one place.

NOTE   I'll cover Razor templates, including layouts, in detail in chapter 7.

And there you have it, a complete ASP.NET Core MVC application! Before I move on, we'll take one last look at how our application handles a request. Figure 2.17 shows a request to the /Home/About path being handled by the sample application. You've seen everything here already, so the process of handling a request should be familiar. It shows how the request passes through the middleware pipeline before being handled by the MVC middleware. A view is used to generate the HTML response, which passes back through the middleware to the ASP.NET Core web server, before being sent to the user's browser.

It's been a pretty intense trip, but you now have a good overview of how an entire application is configured and how it handles a request using MVC. In the next chapter, you'll take a closer look at the middleware pipeline that exists in all ASP.NET Core applications. You'll learn how it's composed, how you can use it to add functionality to your application, and how you can use it to create simple HTTP services.

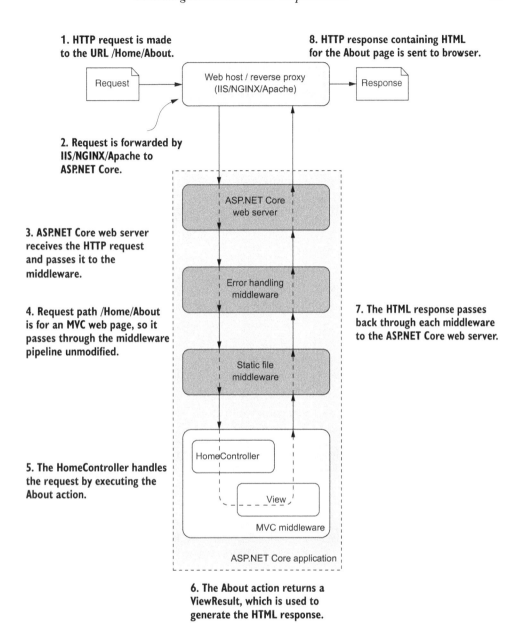

1. HTTP request is made to the URL /Home/About.

8. HTTP response containing HTML for the About page is sent to browser.

2. Request is forwarded by IIS/NGINX/Apache to ASP.NET Core.

3. ASP.NET Core web server receives the HTTP request and passes it to the middleware.

4. Request path /Home/About is for an MVC web page, so it passes through the middleware pipeline unmodified.

7. The HTML response passes back through each middleware to the ASP.NET Core web server.

5. The HomeController handles the request by executing the About action.

6. The About action returns a ViewResult, which is used to generate the HTML response.

Figure 2.17 An overview of a request to the /Home/About page for the sample ASP.NET Core application. The request is received by the reverse proxy and passed to the ASP.NET Core web server. It then passes through the middleware pipeline unchanged, until it's handled by the MVC middleware. The MVC middleware generates an HTML response by executing a view template. The response passes back through the middleware, to the server, and finally, out to the browser.

Summary

- The csproj file contains details of how to build your project, including which NuGet packages it depends on. It's used by Visual Studio and the .NET CLI to build your application.

- Restoring the NuGet packages for an ASP.NET Core application downloads all your project's dependencies so it can be built and run.

- Program.cs defines the `static void Main` entry point for your application. This function is run when your app starts, the same as for console applications.

- Program.cs is where you build an `IWebHost` instance, using a `WebHostBuilder`. The helper method, `WebHost.CreateDefaultBuilder()` can be used to create a `WebHostBuilder` that uses the Kestrel HTTP server, loads configuration settings, sets up logging, and adds IIS integration if necessary. Calling `Build()` creates the `IWebHost` instance.

- You can start the web server and begin accepting HTTP requests by calling `Run` on the `IWebHost`.

- `Startup` is responsible for service configuration and defining the middleware pipeline.

- All services, both framework and custom application services, must be registered in the call to `ConfigureServices` in order to be accessed later in your application.

- Middleware is added to the application pipeline with `IApplicationBuilder`. Middleware defines how your application responds to requests.

- The order in which middleware is registered defines the final order of the middleware pipeline for the application. Typically, `MvcMiddleware` is the last middleware in the pipeline. Earlier middleware, such as `StaticFileMiddleware`, will attempt to handle the request first. If the request is handled, `MvcMiddleware` will never receive the request.

- An MVC controller consists of a group of actions that can be invoked in response to a request, based on the request URL. An action can return a `ViewResult`, which will cause a Razor view to be executed and HTML to be generated.

- Razor cshtml files are located, by convention, in a folder corresponding to the associated controller, and are named the same as their associated action.

- Razor templates can contain standalone C#, standalone HTML, and dynamic HTML generated from C# values. By combining all three, you can build highly dynamic applications.

- Razor layouts define common elements of a web page, such as headers and footers. They let you extract this code into a single file, so you don't have to duplicate it across every Razor template.

Handling requests with the middleware pipeline

This chapter covers

- What middleware is
- Serving static files using middleware
- Adding functionality using middleware
- Combining middleware to form a pipeline
- Handling exceptions and errors with middleware

In the previous chapter, you had a whistle-stop tour of a complete ASP.NET Core application to see how the components come together to create a web application. In this chapter, we focus in on one small subsection: the middleware pipeline.

The middleware pipeline is one of the most important parts of configuration for defining how your application behaves and how it responds to requests. Understanding how to build and compose middleware is key to adding functionality to your applications.

In this chapter, you'll learn what middleware is and how to use it to create a pipeline. You'll see how you can chain multiple middleware components together, with each component adding a discrete piece of functionality. The examples in this chapter are limited to using existing middleware components, showing how to arrange them in the correct way for your application. In chapter 19, you'll learn how to build your own middleware components and incorporate them into the pipeline.

We'll begin by looking at the concept of middleware, all the things you can achieve with it, and how a middleware component often maps to a "cross-cutting concern." These are the functions of an application that cut across multiple different layers. Logging, error handling, and security are classic cross-cutting concerns that are all required by many different parts of your application. As all requests pass through the middleware pipeline, it's the preferred location to configure and handle these aspects.

In section 3.2, I'll explain how you can compose individual middleware components into a pipeline. You'll start out small, with a web app that only displays a holding page. From there, you'll learn how to build a simple static-file server that returns requested files from a folder on disk.

Next, you'll move on to a more complex pipeline containing multiple middleware. You'll use this example to explore the importance of ordering in the middleware pipeline and to see how requests are handled when your pipeline contains more than one middleware.

In section 3.3, you'll learn how you can use middleware to deal with an important aspect of any application: error handling. Errors are a fact of life for all applications, so it's important that you account for them when building your app. As well as ensuring that your application doesn't break when an exception is thrown or an error occurs, it's important that users of your application are informed about what went wrong in a user-friendly way.

You can handle errors in a number of different ways, but as one of the classic cross-cutting concerns, middleware is well placed to provide the required functionality. In section 3.3, I'll show how you can use middleware to handle exceptions and errors using existing middleware provided by Microsoft. In particular, you'll learn about three different components:

- `DeveloperExceptionPageMiddleware`—Provides quick error feedback when building an application
- `ExceptionHandlerMiddleware`—Provides a user-friendly generic error page in production
- `StatusCodePagesMiddleware`—Converts raw error status codes into user-friendly error pages

By combining these pieces of middleware, you can ensure that any errors that do occur in your application won't leak security details and won't break your app. On top of that, they will leave users in a better position to move on from the error, giving them as friendly an experience as possible.

You won't see how to build your own middleware in this chapter—instead, you'll see that you can go a long way using that provided as part of ASP.NET Core. Once you understand the middleware pipeline and its behavior, it will be much easier to understand when and why custom middleware is required. With that in mind, let's dive in!

3.1 What is middleware?

The word *middleware* is used in a variety of contexts in software development and IT, but it's not a particularly descriptive word—what is middleware?

In ASP.NET Core, middleware is C# classes that can handle an HTTP request or response. Middleware can

- Handle an incoming HTTP *request* by generating an HTTP *response*.
- Process an incoming HTTP *request*, modify it, and pass it on to another piece of middleware.
- Process an outgoing HTTP *response*, modify it, and pass it on to either another piece of middleware, or the ASP.NET Core web server.

You can use middleware in a multitude of ways in your own applications. For example, a piece of logging middleware might note when a request arrived and then pass it on to another piece of middleware. Meanwhile, an image-resizing middleware component might spot an incoming request for an image with a specified size, generate the requested image, and send it back to the user without passing it on.

The most important piece of middleware in most ASP.NET Core applications is the `MvcMiddleware` class. This class normally generates all your HTML pages and API responses and is the focus of most of this book. Like the image-resizing middleware, it typically receives a request, generates a response, and then sends it back to the user, as shown in figure 3.1.

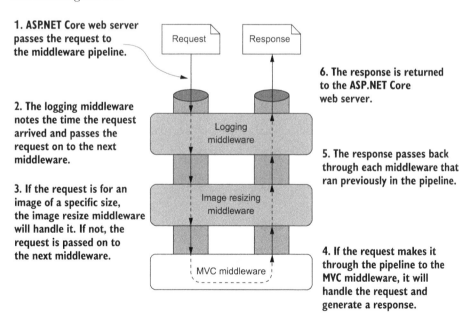

Figure 3.1 Example of a middleware pipeline. Each middleware handles the request and passes it on to the next middleware in the pipeline. After a middleware generates a response, it passes it back through the pipeline. When it reaches the ASP.NET Core web server, the response is sent to the user's browser.

DEFINITION This arrangement, where a piece of middleware can call another piece of middleware, which in turn can call another, and so on, is referred to as a *pipeline.* You can think of each piece of middleware as a section of pipe— when you connect all the sections, a request flows through one piece and into the next.

One of the most common use cases for middleware is for the cross-cutting concerns of your application. These aspects of your application need to occur with every request, regardless of the specific path in the request or the resource requested. These include things like

- Logging each request
- Adding standard security headers to the response
- Associating a request with the relevant user
- Setting the language for the current request

In each of these examples, the middleware would receive a request, modify it, and then pass the request on to the next piece of middleware in the pipeline. Subsequent middleware could use the details added by the earlier middleware to handle the request in some way. For example, in figure 3.2, the authentication middleware associates the request with a user. The authorization middleware uses this detail to verify whether the user has permission to make that specific request to the application or not.

If the user has permission, the authorization middleware will pass the request on to the MVC middleware to allow it to generate a response. If the user doesn't have

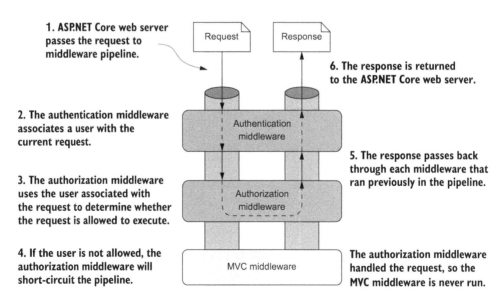

Figure 3.2 Example of a middleware component modifying the request for use later in the pipeline. Middleware can also short-circuit the pipeline, returning a response before the request reaches later middleware.

permission, the authorization middleware can short-circuit the pipeline, generating a response directly. It returns the response to the previous middleware before the MVC middleware has even seen the request.

A key point to glean from this is that the pipeline is *bidirectional*. The request passes through the pipeline in one direction until a piece of middleware generates a response, at which point the response passes *back* through the pipeline, passing through each piece of middleware for a *second* time, until it gets back to the first piece of middleware. Finally, this first/last piece of middleware will pass the response back to the ASP.NET Core web server.

The HttpContext object

We mentioned the HttpContext in chapter 2, and it's sitting behind the scenes here too. The ASP.NET Core web server constructs an HttpContext, which the ASP.NET Core application uses as a sort of storage box for a single request. Anything that's specific to this particular request and the subsequent response can be associated with and stored in it. This could include properties of the request, request-specific services, data that's been loaded, or errors that have occurred. The web server fills the initial HttpContext with details of the original HTTP request and other configuration details and passes it on to the rest of the application.

All middleware has access to the HttpContext for a request. It can use this, for example, to determine whether the request contained any user credentials, which page the request was attempting to access, and to fetch any posted data. It can then use these details to determine how to handle the request.

Once the application has finished processing the request, it will update the Http-Context with an appropriate response and return it through the middleware pipeline to the web server. The ASP.NET Core web server will then convert the representation into a raw HTTP response and send it back to the reverse proxy, which will forward it to the user's browser.

As you saw in chapter 2, you define the middleware pipeline in code as part of your initial application configuration in Startup. You can tailor the middleware pipeline specifically to your needs—simple apps may need only a short pipeline, whereas large apps with a variety of features may use much more middleware. Middleware is the fundamental source of behavior in your application—ultimately, the middleware pipeline is responsible for responding to any HTTP requests it receives.

Requests are passed to the middleware pipeline as HttpContext objects. As you saw in chapter 2, the ASP.NET Core web server builds an HttpContext object from an incoming request, which passes up and down the middleware pipeline. When you're using existing middleware to build a pipeline, this is a detail you'll rarely have to deal with. But, as you'll see in the final section of this chapter, its presence behind the scenes provides a route to exerting extra control over your middleware pipeline.

> **Middleware vs. HTTP modules and HTTP handlers**
>
> In the previous version of ASP.NET, the concept of a middleware pipeline isn't used. Instead, we have HTTP modules and HTTP handlers.
>
> An *HTTP handler* is a process that runs in response to a request and generates the response. For example, the ASP.NET page handler runs in response to requests for .aspx pages. Alternatively, you could write a custom handler that returns resized images when an image is requested.
>
> *HTTP modules* handle the cross-cutting concerns of applications, such as security, logging, or session management. They run in response to the lifecycle events that a request progresses through when it's received by the server. Examples of events include `BeginRequest`, `AcquireRequestState`, and `PostAcquireRequestState`.
>
> This approach works, but it's sometimes tricky to reason about which modules will run at which points. Implementing a module requires a relatively detailed understanding of the state of the request at each individual lifecycle event.
>
> The middleware pipeline makes understanding your application far simpler. The pipeline is completely defined in code, specifying which components should run, and in which order.

That's pretty much all there is to the concept of middleware. In the next section, I'll discuss ways you can combine middleware components to create an application, and how to use middleware to separate the concerns of your application.

3.2 *Combining middleware in a pipeline*

Generally speaking, each middleware component has a single primary concern. It will handle one aspect of a request only. Logging middleware will only deal with logging the request, authentication middleware is only concerned with identifying the current user, and static-file middleware is only concerned with returning static files (when requested).

Each of these concerns is highly focused, which makes the components themselves small and easy to reason about. It also gives your app added flexibility; adding a static-file middleware doesn't mean you're forced into having image-resizing behavior or authentication. Each of these features is an additional piece of middleware.

To build a complete application, you compose multiple middleware components together into a pipeline, as shown in the previous section. Each middleware has access to the original request, plus any changes made by previous middleware in the pipeline. Once a response has been generated, each middleware can inspect and/or modify the response as it passes back through the pipeline, before it's sent to the user. This allows you to build complex application behaviors from small, focused components.

In the rest of this section, you'll see how to create a middleware pipeline by composing small components together. Using standard middleware components, you'll learn to create a holding page and to serve static files from a folder on disk. Finally, you'll take another look at the default middleware pipeline you built previously, in chapter 2, and decompose it to understand why it's built like it is.

3.2.1 *Simple pipeline scenario 1: a holding page*

For your first app, and your first middleware pipeline, you'll learn how to create an app consisting of a holding page. This can be useful when you're first setting up your application, to ensure it's processing requests without errors.

> **TIP** Remember, you can view the application code for this book in the GitHub repository at https://github.com/andrewlock/asp-dot-net-core-in-action.

In previous chapters, I've mentioned that the ASP.NET Core framework is composed of many small, individual libraries. You typically add a piece of middleware by referencing a package in your application's csproj project file and configuring the middleware in the `Configure` method of your `Startup` class. Microsoft ships a few standard middleware components with ASP.NET Core for you to choose from, though you can obviously also use third-party components from NuGet and GitHub, or you can build your own custom middleware.

> **NOTE** I'll discuss building custom middleware in chapter 19.

Unfortunately, there isn't a definitive list of Microsoft middleware available anywhere. With a bit of searching on https://nuget.org you can often find middleware with the functionality you need. Alternatively, the ASP.NET Core GitHub repositories (https://github.com/aspnet) contain source code for all the Microsoft middleware. Regretabbly they're split across multiple different repositories, so hunting them down can be a bit of a chore. For example, the StaticFiles repository unsurprisingly contains the `StaticFileMiddleware`, whereas the Security repository contains a variety of middleware for performing both authentication and authorization.

In this section, you'll see how to create one of the simplest middleware pipelines, consisting of `WelcomePageMiddleware` only. `WelcomePageMiddleware` is designed to quickly provide a sample page when you're first developing an application, as you can see in figure 3.3. You wouldn't use it in a production app, but it's a single, self-contained middleware component you can use to ensure your application is running correctly.

> **TIP** `WelcomePageMiddleware` is contained in the Microsoft.AspNetCore .Diagnostics NuGet package, which most new project templates include by default as part of the Microsoft.AspNetCore.All metapackage. The metapackage includes all of the packages in ASP.NET Core, so you won't need to include other packages if the metapackage is referenced.[1] If the metapackage isn't included, you'll need to add the package using the `PackageReference` element in your csproj file.

Even though this application is simple, the exact same process occurs when it receives an HTTP request, as shown in figure 3.4.

---

[1] For a description of the benefits of the Microsoft.AspNetCore.All metapackage and how it works, see my blog post at http://mng.bz/bSw8.

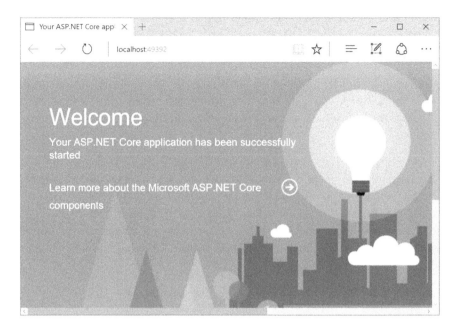

Figure 3.3   The Welcome page middleware response. Every request to the application, at any path, will return the same Welcome page response.

The request passes to the ASP.NET Core web server, which builds a representation of the request and passes it to the middleware pipeline. As it's the first (only!) middleware in the pipeline, WelcomePageMiddleware receives the request and must decide how to handle it. The middleware responds by generating an HTML response, no matter what request it receives. This response passes back to the ASP.NET Core web server, which forwards it on to the user to display in their browser.

As with all ASP.NET Core applications, you define the middleware pipeline in the Configure method of Startup by adding middleware to an IApplicationBuilder object. To create your first middleware pipeline, consisting of a single middleware component, you can add the middleware.

Listing 3.1   Startup for a Welcome page middleware pipeline

```
using Microsoft.AspNetCore.Builder;

namespace WebApplication3
{
    public class Startup        ⟵──┐  The Startup class is very simple
    {                                  for this basic application.
        public void Configure(IApplicationBuilder app)   ⟵──  The Configure
        {                                                       method is used to
            app.UseWelcomePage();   ⟵──                         define the
        }                                                       middleware pipeline.
    }                     The only middleware
}                          in the pipeline
```

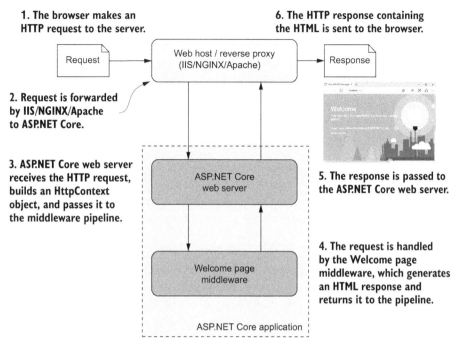

1. The browser makes an HTTP request to the server.

6. The HTTP response containing the HTML is sent to the browser.

2. Request is forwarded by IIS/NGINX/Apache to ASP.NET Core.

3. ASP.NET Core web server receives the HTTP request, builds an HttpContext object, and passes it to the middleware pipeline.

5. The response is passed to the ASP.NET Core web server.

4. The request is handled by the Welcome page middleware, which generates an HTML response and returns it to the pipeline.

Figure 3.4 `WelcomePageMiddleware` handles a request. The request passes from the reverse proxy to the ASP.NET Core web server and, finally, to the middleware pipeline, which generates an HTML response.

As you can see, the Startup for this application is very simple. The application has no configuration and no services, so Startup doesn't have a constructor or a ConfigureServices method. The only required method is Configure, in which you call UseWelcomePage.

You build the middleware pipeline in ASP.NET Core by calling methods on IApplicationBuilder, but this interface doesn't define methods like UseWelcomePage itself. Instead, these are *extension* methods, defined in each middleware's NuGet package.

Using extension methods allows these packages to effectively add functionality to the IApplicationBuilder class, while keeping their functionality isolated from it. Under the hood, the methods are typically calling *another* extension method to add the middleware to the pipeline. For example, behind the scenes, the UseWelcomePage method adds the WelcomePageMiddleware to the pipeline using

```
UseMiddleware<WelcomePageMiddleware>();
```

This convention of creating an extension method for each piece of middleware and starting the method name with Use is designed to improve discoverability when adding middleware to your application. You still have to remember to reference the appropriate NuGet package in your csproj project file before the extension methods will become available!

Calling the `UseWelcomePage` method adds `WelcomePageMiddleware` as the next middleware in the pipeline. Although you're only using a single middleware component here, it's important to remember that the order in which you make calls to `IApplicationBuilder` in `Configure` defines the order that the middleware will run in the pipeline.

> **WARNING** Always take care when adding middleware to the pipeline and consider the order in which it will run. A component can't access data created by later middleware if it comes before it in the pipeline.

This is the most basic of applications, returning the same response no matter which URL you navigate to, but it shows how easy it is to define your application behavior using middleware. Now we'll make things a little more interesting and return a different response when you make requests to different paths.

3.2.2 *Simple pipeline scenario 2: Handling static files*

In this section, I'll show how to create one of the simplest middleware pipelines you can use for a full application: a static file application.

Most web applications, including those with dynamic content, serve a number of pages using static files. Images, JavaScript, and CSS stylesheets are normally saved to disk during development and are served up when requested, normally as part of a full HTML page request.

For now, you'll use `StaticFileMiddleware` to create an application that only serves static files from the wwwroot folder when requested, as shown in figure 3.5. In this example, a static HTML file called Example.html exists in the wwwroot folder. When you request the file using the /Example.html path, it's loaded and returned as the response to the request.

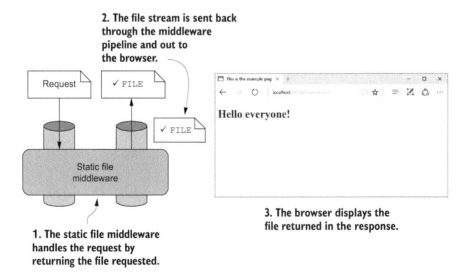

Figure 3.5   Serving a static HTML file using the static file middleware

If the user requests a file that doesn't exist in the wwwroot folder, for example Missing.html, then the static file middleware won't serve a file. Instead, a 404 HTTP error code response will be sent to the user's browser, which will show its default "File Not Found" page, as shown in figure 3.6.

> **NOTE** How this page looks will depend on your browser. In some browsers, for example Internet Explorer (IE), you might see a completely blank page.

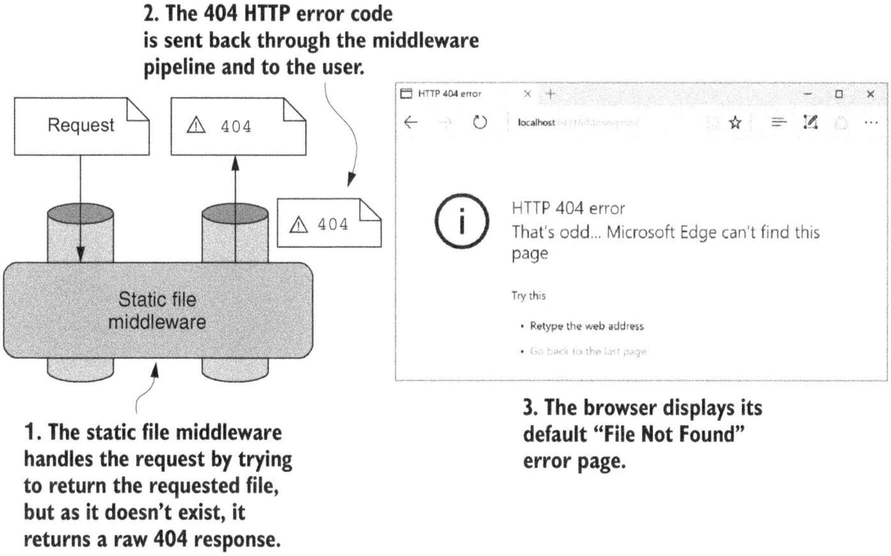

2. The 404 HTTP error code is sent back through the middleware pipeline and to the user.

1. The static file middleware handles the request by trying to return the requested file, but as it doesn't exist, it returns a raw 404 response.

3. The browser displays its default "File Not Found" error page.

Figure 3.6 Returning a 404 to the browser when a file doesn't exist. The requested file did not exist in the wwwroot folder, so the ASP.NET Core application returned a 404 response. The browser, Microsoft Edge in this case, will then show the user a default "File Not Found" error.

Building the middleware pipeline for this application is easy, consisting of a single piece of middleware, `StaticFileMiddleware`, as you can see in the following listing. You don't need any services, so configuring the middleware pipeline in `Configure` with `UseStaticFiles` is all that's required.

Listing 3.2 Startup for a static file middleware pipeline

```
using Microsoft.AspNetCore.Builder;

namespace WebApplication3
{
    public class Startup
    {
        public void Configure(IApplicationBuilder app)
        {
            app.UseStaticFiles();
        }
    }
}
```

The Startup class is very simple for this basic static file application.

The Configure method is used to define the middleware pipeline.

The only middleware in the pipeline

> **TIP**   Remember, you can view the application code for this book in the GitHub repository at https://github.com/andrewlock/asp-dot-net-core-in-action.

When the application receives a request, the ASP.NET Core web server handles it and passes it to the middleware pipeline. `StaticFileMiddleware` receives the request and determines whether or not it can handle it. If the requested file exists, the middleware handles the request and returns the file as the response, as shown in figure 3.7.

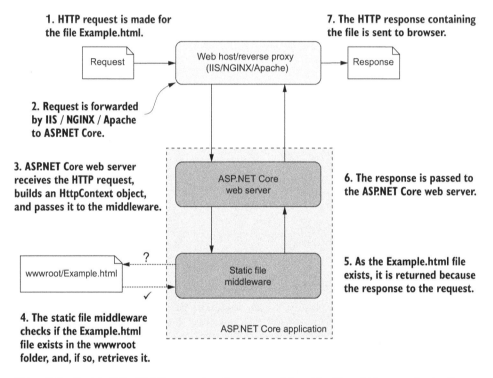

Figure 3.7 `StaticFileMiddleware` **handles a request for a file. The middleware checks the wwwroot folder to see if the requested Example.html file exists. The file exists, so the middleware retrieves it and returns it as the response to the web server and, ultimately, out to the browser.**

If the file doesn't exist, then the request effectively passes *through* the static file middleware unchanged. But wait, you only added one piece of middleware, right? Surely you can't pass the request through to the next middleware if there *isn't* another one?

Luckily, ASP.NET Core effectively adds an automatic "dummy" piece of middleware to the end of the pipeline. This middleware always returns a 404 response if it's called.

> **TIP**   Remember, if no middleware generates a response for a request, the pipeline will automatically return a simple 404 error response to the browser.

HTTP response status codes

Every HTTP response contains a *status code* and, optionally, a *reason phrase* describing the status code. Status codes are fundamental to the HTTP protocol and are a standardized way of indicating common results. A 200 response, for example, means the request was successfully answered, whereas a 404 response indicates that the resource requested couldn't be found.

Status codes are always three digits long and are grouped into five different classes, based on the first digit:

- *1xx*—Information. Not often used, provides a general acknowledgment.
- *2xx*—Success. The request was successfully handled and processed.
- *3xx*—Redirection. The browser must follow the provided link, to allow the user to log in, for example.
- *4xx*—Client error. There was a problem with the request. For example, the request sent invalid data, or the user isn't authorized to perform the request.
- *5xx*—Server error. There was a problem on the server that caused the request to fail.

These status codes typically drive the behavior of a user's browser. For example, the browser will handle a 301 response automatically, by redirecting to the provided new link and making a second request, all without the user's interaction.

Error codes are found in the 4xx and 5xx classes. Common codes include a 404 response when a file couldn't be found, a 400 error when a client sends invalid data (an invalid email address for example), and a 500 error when an error occurs on the server. HTTP responses for error codes may or may not include a response body, which is content to display when the client receives the response.

This basic ASP.NET Core application allows you to easily see the behavior of the ASP.NET Core middleware pipeline and the static file middleware in particular, but it's unlikely your applications will be as simple as this. It's more likely that static files will form one part of your middleware pipeline. In the next section, we'll look at how to combine multiple middleware, looking at a simple MVC application.

3.2.3 *Simple pipeline scenario 3: An MVC web application*

By this point, you, I hope, have a decent grasp of the middleware pipeline, insofar as understanding that it defines your application's behavior. In this section, you'll see how to combine multiple middleware to form a pipeline, using a number of standard middleware components. As before, this is performed in the `Configure` method of `Startup` by adding middleware to an `IApplicationBuilder` object.

You'll begin by creating a basic middleware pipeline that you'd find in a typical ASP.NET Core MVC template and then extend it by adding middleware. The output when you navigate to the homepage of the application is shown in figure 3.8—identical to the sample application shown in chapter 2.

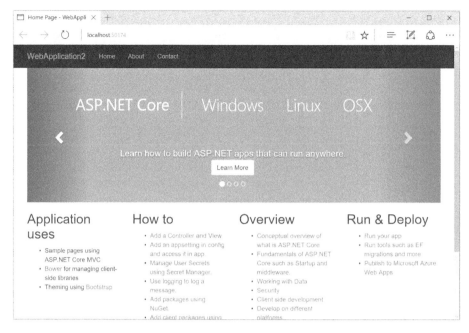

Figure 3.8   A simple MVC application. The application uses only three pieces of middleware: an MVC middleware to serve the HTML, a static file middleware to serve the image files, and an exception handler middleware to capture any errors.

As you can see in the figure, creating this simple application requires only three pieces of middleware: MVC middleware to generate the HTML, static file middleware to serve the image files from the wwwroot folder, and an exception handler middleware to handle any errors that might occur. The configuration of the middleware pipeline for the application occurs in the Configure method of Startup, as always, and is shown in the following listing. As well as the middleware configuration, this also shows the call to AddMvc() in ConfigureServices, which is required when using MVC middleware. You'll learn more about service configuration in chapter 10.

Listing 3.3   A basic middleware pipeline for an MVC application

```
public class Startup
{
    public class ConfigureServices(IServiceCollection services
    {
        services.AddMvc();
    }

    public void Configure(IApplicationBuilder app)
    {
        app.UseExceptionHandler("/Home/Error");

        app.UseStaticFiles();

        app.UseMvc(routes =>
```

```
        {
            routes.MapRoute(
                name: "default",
                template: "{controller=Home}/{action=Index}/{id?}");
        });
    }
}
```

The addition of middleware to `IApplicationBuilder` to form the pipeline should be familiar to you now, but there are a couple of points worth noting in this example. First, all of the methods for adding middleware start with `Use`. As I mentioned earlier, this is thanks to the convention of using extension methods to extend the functionality of `IApplicationBuilder`; by prefixing the methods with `Use` they should be easier to discover.

Another important point about this listing is the order of the `Use` methods in the `Configure` method. The order in which you add the middleware to the `IApplication-Builder` object is the same order in which they're added to the pipeline. This creates a pipeline similar to that shown in figure 3.9.

The exception handler middleware is called first, which passes the request on to the static file middleware. The static file handler will generate a response if the request corresponds to a file, otherwise it will pass the request on to the MVC middleware.

The impact of ordering can most obviously be seen when you have two pieces of middleware that are both listening for the same path. For example, the MVC middleware in the example pipeline currently responds to a request to the homepage of the application (with the `"/"` path) by generating the HTML response shown in figure 3.9.

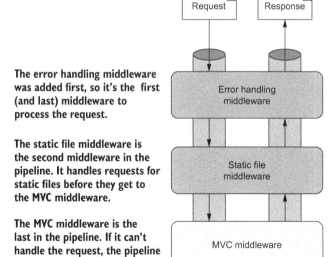

The error handling middleware was added first, so it's the first (and last) middleware to process the request.

The static file middleware is the second middleware in the pipeline. It handles requests for static files before they get to the MVC middleware.

The MVC middleware is the last in the pipeline. If it can't handle the request, the pipeline returns a 404 reponse.

Figure 3.9   The middleware pipeline for the example application in listing 3.3. The order in which you add the middleware to `IApplicationBuilder` defines the order of the middleware in the pipeline.

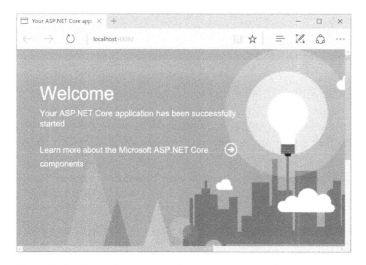

Figure 3.10 **The Welcome page middleware response. The Welcome page middleware comes before the MVC middleware, so a request to the homepage returns the Welcome page middleware instead of the MVC response.**

Figure 3.10 shows what happens if you reintroduce a piece of middleware you saw previously, WelcomePageMiddleware, and configure it to respond to the "/" path as well. As you saw in section 3.2.1, WelcomePageMiddleware is designed to return a fixed HTML response, so you wouldn't use it in a production app, but it illustrates the point nicely. In the following listing, it's added to the start of the middleware pipeline and configured to respond only to the "/" path.

Listing 3.4 Adding `WelcomePageMiddleware` to the pipeline

```
public class Startup
{
    public class ConfigureServices(IServiceCollection services
    {
        services.AddMvc();
    }
    public void Configure(IApplicationBuilder app)
    {
        app.UseWelcomePage("/");

        app.UseExceptionHandler("/Home/Error");

        app.UseStaticFiles();

        app.UseMvc(routes =>
        {
            routes.MapRoute(
                name: "default",
                template: "{controller=Home}/{action=Index}/{id?}");
        });
    }
}
```

WelcomePageMiddleware handles all requests to the "/" path and returns a sample HTML response.

Requests to "/" will never reach the MVC middleware.

Even though you know the MVC middleware can also handle the "/" path, Welcome-PageMiddleware is earlier in the pipeline, so it returns a response when it receives the request to "/", short-circuiting the pipeline, as shown in figure 3.11. None of the other middleware in the pipeline runs for the request, so none has an opportunity to generate a response.

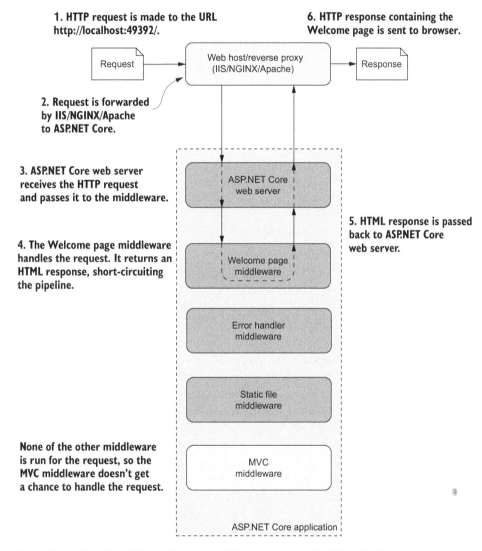

Figure 3.11 Overview of the application handling a request to the "/" path. The welcome page middleware is first in the middleware pipeline, so it receives the request before any other middleware. It generates an HTML response, short-circuiting the pipeline. No other middleware runs for the request.

If you moved `WelcomePageMiddleware` to the end of the pipeline, after the call to `Use-Mvc`, then you'd have the opposite situation. Any requests to `"/"` would be handled by the MVC middleware and you'd never see the Welcome page.

> **TIP** You should always consider the order of middleware when adding to the `Configure` method. Middleware added earlier in the pipeline will run (and potentially return a response) before middleware added later.

All of the examples shown so far attempt to handle an incoming request and generate a response, but it's important to remember that the middleware pipeline is bi-directional. Each middleware component gets an opportunity to handle both the incoming request and the outgoing response. The order of middleware is most important for those components that create or modify the outgoing response.

In the previous example, I included `ExceptionHandlerMiddleware` at the start of the application's middleware pipeline, but it didn't seem to do anything. Error handling middleware characteristically ignores the incoming request as it arrives in the pipeline, and instead inspects the outgoing response, only modifying it when an error has occurred. In the next section, I'll detail the types of error handling middleware that are available to use with your application and when to use them.

3.3   *Handling errors using middleware*

Errors are a fact of life when developing applications. Even if you write perfect code, as soon as you release and deploy your application, users will find a way to break it, whether by accident or intentionally! The important thing is that your application handles these errors gracefully, providing a suitable response to the user, and doesn't cause your whole application to fail.

The design philosophy for ASP.NET Core is that every feature is opt-in. So, as error handling is a feature, you need to explicitly enable it in your application. Many different types of errors could occur in your application and there are many different ways to handle them, but in this section I'll focus on two: exceptions and error status codes.

Exceptions typically occur whenever you find an unexpected circumstance. A typical (and highly frustrating) exception you'll no doubt have experienced before is `NullReferenceException`, which is thrown when you attempt to access an object that hasn't been initialized. If an exception occurs in a middleware component, it propagates up the pipeline, as shown in figure 3.12. If the pipeline doesn't handle the exception, the web server will return a 500 status code back to the user.

In some situations, an error won't cause an exception. Instead, middleware might generate an error status code. One such case you've already seen is when a requested path isn't handled. In that situation, the pipeline will return a 404 error, which results in a generic, unfriendly page being shown to the user, as you saw in figure 3.6. Although this behavior is "correct," it doesn't provide a great experience for users of your application.

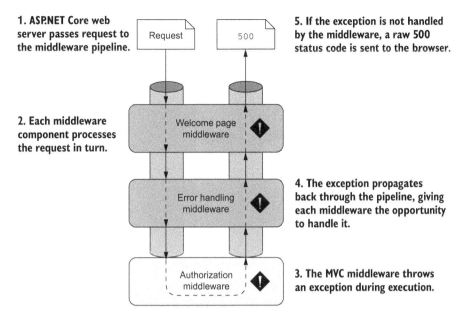

1. ASP.NET Core web server passes request to the middleware pipeline.

5. If the exception is not handled by the middleware, a raw 500 status code is sent to the browser.

Request

500

2. Each middleware component processes the request in turn.

Welcome page middleware

4. The exception propagates back through the pipeline, giving each middleware the opportunity to handle it.

Error handling middleware

Authorization middleware

3. The MVC middleware throws an exception during execution.

Figure 3.12   An exception in the MVC middleware propagates through the pipeline. If the exception isn't caught by middleware earlier in the pipeline, then a 500 "Server error" status code will be sent to the user's browser.

Error handling middleware attempts to address these problems by modifying the response before the app returns it to the user. Typically, error handling middleware either returns details of the error that occurred or it returns a generic, but friendly, HTML page to the user. You should always place error handling middleware early in the middleware pipeline to ensure it will catch any errors generated in subsequent middleware, as shown in figure 3.13. Any responses generated by middleware earlier in the pipeline than the error handling middleware can't be intercepted.

The remainder of this section shows several types of error handling middleware that are available for use in your application. You can use any of them by referencing either the Microsoft.AspNetCore.All or the Microsoft.AspNetCore.Diagnostics NuGet packages in your project's csproj file.

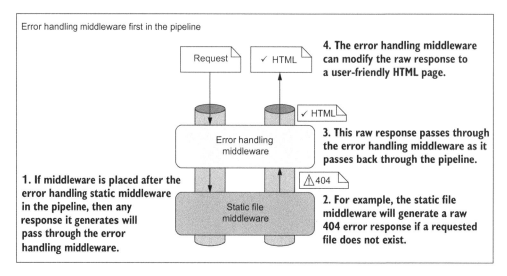

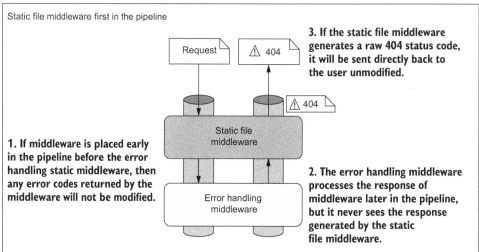

Figure 3.13   Error handling middleware should be placed early in the pipeline to catch raw status code errors. In the first case, the error handling middleware is placed before the static file middleware, so it can replace raw status code errors with a user-friendly error page. In the second case, the error handling middleware is placed after the static file middleware, so raw error status codes can't be modified.

3.3.1   *Viewing exceptions in development: DeveloperExceptionPage*

When you're developing an application, you typically want access to as much information as possible when an error occurs somewhere in your app. For that reason, Microsoft provides `DeveloperExceptionPageMiddleware`, which can be added to your middleware pipeline using

```
app.UseDeveloperExceptionPage();
```

When an exception is thrown and propagates up the pipeline to this middleware, it will be captured. The middleware then generates a friendly HTML page, which it returns with a 500 status code to the user, as shown in figure 3.14. This page contains a variety of details about the request and the exception, including the exception stack trace, the source code at the line the exception occurred, and details of the request, such as any cookies or headers that had been sent.

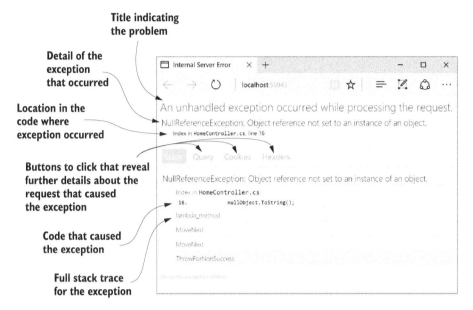

Figure 3.14   The developer exception page shows details about the exception when it occurs during the process of a request. The location in the code that caused the exception, the source code line itself, and the stack trace are all shown by default. You can also click the Query, Cookies, or Headers buttons to reveal further details about the request that caused the exception.

Having these details available when an error occurs is invaluable for debugging a problem, but they also represent a security risk if used incorrectly. You should never return more details about your application to users than absolutely necessary, so you should only ever use `DeveloperExceptionPage` when developing your application. The clue is in the name!

> **WARNING**   Never use the developer exception page when running in production. Doing so is a security risk as it could publicly reveal details about your application's code, making you an easy target for attackers.

If the developer exception page isn't appropriate for production use, what should you use instead? Luckily, there's another general-purpose error handling middleware you *can* use in production, one that you've already seen and used: `ExceptionHandler-Middleware`.

3.3.2   *Handling exceptions in production: ExceptionHandlerMiddleware*

The developer exception page is handy when developing your applications, but you shouldn't use it in production as it can leak information about your app to potential attackers. You still want to catch errors though, otherwise users will see unfriendly error pages or blank pages, depending on the browser they're using.

You can solve this problem by using ExceptionHandlerMiddleware. If an error occurs in your application, the user will be presented with a custom error page that's consistent with the rest of the application, but that only provides the necessary details about the error. For example, a custom error page, such as the one shown in figure 3.15, can keep the look and feel of the application by using the same header, displaying the currently logged-in user, and only displaying an appropriate message to the user instead of the full details of the exception.

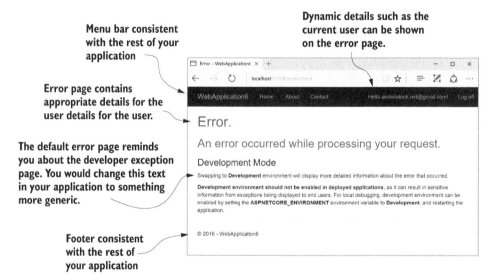

Figure 3.15   A custom error page created by `ExceptionHandlerMiddleware`**. The custom error page can keep the same look and feel as the rest of the application by reusing elements such as the header and footer. More importantly, you can easily control the error details displayed to users.**

If you were to peek at the Configure method of almost any ASP.NET Core application, you'd almost certainly find the developer exception page used in combination with ExceptionHandlerMiddleware, in a similar manner to that shown here.

Listing 3.5   Configuring exception handling for development and production

```
public void Configure(IApplicationBuilder app, IHostingEnvironment env)
{
    if (env.IsDevelopment())        ◁── Configure a different pipeline
    {                                    when running in development.
```

```
    app.UseDeveloperExceptionPage();
}
else
{
    app.UseExceptionHandler("/home/error");
}

// additional middleware configuration
}
```

> The developer exception page should only be used when running in development mode.

> When in production, ExceptionHandlerMiddleware is added to the pipeline.

As well as demonstrating how to add ExceptionHandlerMiddleware to your middleware pipeline, this listing shows that it's perfectly acceptable to configure different middleware pipelines depending on the environment when the application starts up. You could also vary your pipeline based on other values, such as settings loaded from configuration.

> **NOTE** You'll see how to use configuration values to customize the middleware pipeline in chapter 11.

When adding ExceptionHandlerMiddleware to your application, you'll typically provide a path to the custom error page that will be displayed to the user. In the example listing, you used an error handling path of /home/error:

```
app.UseExceptionHandler("/home/error");
```

ExceptionHandlerMiddleware will invoke this path after it captures an exception, in order to generate the final response. The ability to dynamically generate a response is a key feature of ExceptionHandlerMiddleware—it allows you to re-execute a middleware pipeline in order to generate the response sent to the user.

Figure 3.16 shows what happens when ExceptionHandlerMiddleware handles an exception. It shows the flow of events when the MVC middleware generates an exception when a request is made to the /home path. The final response returns an error status code but also provides an HTML response to display to the user, using the /error path.

The sequence of events when an exception occurs somewhere in the middleware pipeline after ExceptionHandlerMiddleware is as follows:

1 A piece of middleware throws an exception.
2 ExceptionHandlerMiddleware catches the exception.
3 Any partial response that has been defined is cleared.
4 The middleware overwrites the request path with the provided error handling path.
5 The middleware sends the request back down the pipeline, as though the original request had been for the error handling path.
6 The middleware pipeline generates a new response as normal.
7 When the response gets back to ExceptionHandlerMiddleware, it modifies the status code to a 500 error and continues to pass the response up the pipeline to the web server.

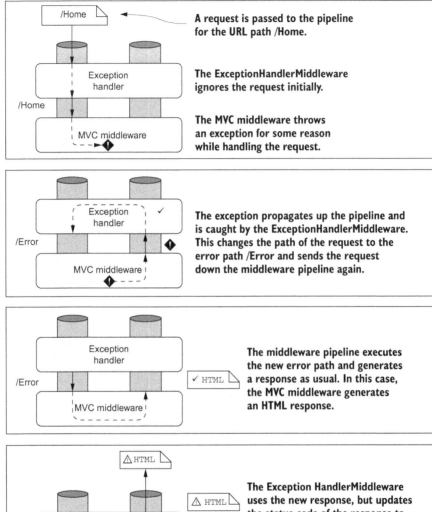

A request is passed to the pipeline for the URL path /Home.

The ExceptionHandlerMiddleware ignores the request initially.

The MVC middleware throws an exception for some reason while handling the request.

The exception propagates up the pipeline and is caught by the ExceptionHandlerMiddleware. This changes the path of the request to the error path /Error and sends the request down the middleware pipeline again.

The middleware pipeline executes the new error path and generates a response as usual. In this case, the MVC middleware generates an HTML response.

The Exception HandlerMiddleware uses the new response, but updates the status code of the response to a 500 status code. This indicates to the browser that an error occurred, but the user sees a friendly web page indicating something went wrong.

Figure 3.16 `ExceptionHandlerMiddleware` handling an exception to generate an HTML response. A request to the /Home path generates an exception, which is handled by the middleware. The pipeline is re-executed using the /Error path to generate the HTML response.

The main advantage that re-executing the pipeline brings is the ability to have your error messages integrated into your normal site layout, as shown in figure 3.15. It's certainly possible to return a fixed response when an error occurs, but you wouldn't be able to have a menu bar with dynamically generated links or display the current user's name in the menu. By re-executing the pipeline, you can ensure that all the dynamic areas of your application are correctly integrated, as if the page was a standard page of your site.

> **NOTE** You don't need to do anything other than add `ExceptionHandler-Middleware` to your application and configure a valid error handling path to enable re-executing the pipeline. The middleware will catch the exception and re-execute the pipeline for you. Subsequent middleware will treat the re-execution as a new request, but previous middleware in the pipeline won't be aware anything unusual happened.

Re-executing the middleware pipeline is a great way to keep consistency in your web application for error pages, but there are some gotchas to be aware of. First, middleware can only modify a response generated further down the pipeline if the response hasn't yet been sent to the client. This can be a problem if, for example, an error occurs while ASP.NET Core is sending a static file to a client. In that case, where bytes have already begun to be sent to the client, the error handling middleware won't be able to run, as it can't reset the response. Generally speaking, there's not a lot you can do about this issue, but it's something to be aware of.

A more common problem occurs when the error handling path throws an error during the re-execution of the pipeline. Imagine there's a bug in the code that generates the menu at the top of the page:

1 When the user reaches your homepage, the code for generating the menu bar throws an exception.
2 The exception propagates up the middleware pipeline.
3 When reached, `ExceptionHandlerMiddleware` captures it and the pipe is re-executed using the error handling path.
4 When the error page executes, it attempts to generate the menu bar for your app, which again throws an exception.
5 The exception propagates up the middleware pipeline.
6 `ExceptionHandlerMiddleware` has already tried to intercept a request, so it will let the error propagate all the way to the top of the middleware pipeline.
7 The web server returns a raw 500 error, as though there was no error handling middleware at all.

Thanks to this problem, it's often good practice to make your error handling pages as simple as possible, to reduce the possibility of errors occurring.

WARNING   If your error handling path generates an error, the user will see a generic browser error. It's often better to use a static error page that will always work, rather than a dynamic page that risks throwing more errors.

`ExceptionHandlerMiddleware` and `DeveloperExceptionPageMiddleware` are great for catching exceptions in your application, but exceptions aren't the only sort of errors you'll encounter. In some cases, your middleware pipeline will return an HTTP error status code in the response. It's important to handle both exceptions and error status codes to provide a coherent user experience.

3.3.3   *Handling other errors: StatusCodePagesMiddleware*

Your application can return a wide range of HTTP status codes that indicate some sort of error state. You've already seen that a 500 "server error" is sent when an exception occurs and isn't handled and that a 404 "file not found" error is sent when a URL isn't handled by any middleware. 404 errors, in particular, are common, often occurring when a user enters an invalid URL.

TIP   As well as indicating a completely unhandled URL, 404 errors are often used to indicate that a specific requested object was not found. For example, a request for the details of a product with an ID of 23 might return a 404 if no such product exists.

Without handling these status codes, users will see a generic error page, such as in figure 3.17, which may leave many confused and thinking your application is broken. A better approach would be to handle these error codes and return an error page that's in keeping with the rest of your application or, at the very least, doesn't make your application look broken.

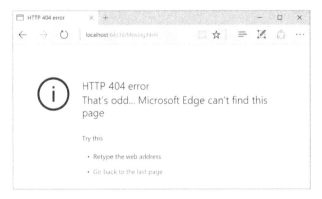

Figure 3.17   A generic browser error page. If the middleware pipeline can't handle a request, it will return a 404 error to the user. The message is of limited usefulness to users and may leave many confused or thinking your web application is broken.

Microsoft provides `StatusCodePagesMiddleware` for handling this use case in the Microsoft.AspNetCore.Diagnostics package. As with all error handling middleware, you should add it early in your middleware pipeline, as it will only handle errors generated by later middleware components.

You can use the middleware a number of different ways in your application. The simplest approach is to add the middleware to your pipeline without any additional configuration, using

```
app.UseStatusCodePages();
```

With this method, the middleware will intercept any response that has an HTTP Status code that starts with 4xx or 5xx and has no response body. For the simplest case, where you don't provide any additional configuration, the middleware will add a plain text response body, indicating the type and name of the response, as shown in figure 3.18. This is arguably worse than the generic method at this point, but it is a starting point for providing a more consistent experience to users!

Figure 3.18 Status code error pages for a 404 error. You generally won't use this version of the middleware in production as it doesn't provide a great user experience, but it demonstrates that the error codes are being correctly intercepted.

A more typical approach to using `StatusCodePageMiddleware` in production is to re-execute the pipeline when an error is captured, using a similar technique to `ExceptionHandlerMiddleware`. This allows you to have dynamic error pages that fit with the rest of your application. To use this technique, replace the call to `UseStatus-CodePages` with the following extension method

```
app.UseStatusCodePagesWithReExecute("/error/{0}");
```

This extension method configures `StatusCodePageMiddleware` to re-execute the pipeline whenever a 4xx or 5xx response code is found, using the provided error handling path. This is similar to the way `ExceptionHandlerMiddleware` re-executes the pipeline, as shown in figure 3.19.

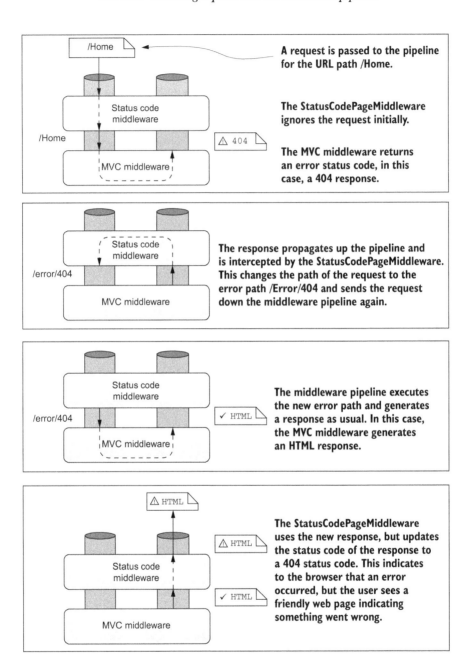

Figure 3.19 `StatusCodePagesMiddleware` re-executing the pipeline to generate an HTML body for a 404 response. A request to the /Home path returns a 404 response, which is handled by the status code middleware. The pipeline is re-executed using the /error/404 path to generate the HTML response.

Note that the error handling path "/error/{0}" contains a format string token, {0}. When the path is re-executed, the middleware will replace this token with the status code number. For example, a 404 error would re-execute the /error/404 path. The handler for the path (typically an MVC route) has access to the status code and can optionally tailor the response, depending on the status code. You can choose any error handling path, as long as your application knows how to handle it.

NOTE You'll learn about MVC routing in chapter 5.

With this approach in place, you can create different error pages for different error codes, such as the 404-specific error page shown in figure 3.20. This technique ensures your error pages are consistent with the rest of your application, including any dynamically generated content, while also allowing you to tailor the message for common errors.

WARNING As before, when re-executing the pipeline, you must be careful your error handling path doesn't generate any errors.

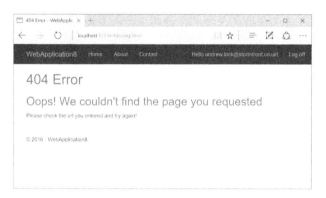

Figure 3.20   An error status code page for a missing file. When an error code is detected (in this case, a 404 error), the middleware pipeline is re-executed to generate the response. This allows dynamic portions of your web page to remain consistent on error pages.

You can use StatusCodePagesMiddleware in combination with other exception handling middleware by adding both to the pipeline. StatusCodePagesMiddleware will only modify the response if no response body has been written. So if another component, for example ExceptionHandlerMiddleware, returns a message body along with an error code, it won't be modified.

NOTE StatusCodePageMiddleware has additional overloads that let you execute custom middleware when an error occurs, instead of re-executing an MVC path.

Error handling is essential when developing any web application; errors happen and you need to handle them gracefully. But depending on your application, you may not always need error handling middleware, and sometimes you may need to disable it for a single request.

3.3.4   *Disabling error handling middleware for Web APIs*

ASP.NET Core isn't only great for creating user-facing web applications, it's also great for creating HTTP services that can be accessed either from another server application, or from a user's browser when running a client-side single-page application. In both of these cases, you probably won't be returning HTML to the client, but rather XML or JSON.

In that situation, if an error occurs, you probably don't want to be sending back a big HTML page saying, "Oops, something went wrong." Returning an HTML page to an application that's expecting JSON could easily break it unexpectedly. Instead, the HTTP 500 status code is more descriptive and useful to a consuming application.

Luckily, this is the default behavior when you don't add error-handling middleware to your application. In the simplest case, where your whole application serves as an API to another application, you could probably get away without any error handling middleware. In reality, you may want to make sure you log the errors using middleware, but you certainly don't need to change the response body in that case.

But what if you have an ASP.NET Core application that takes on both roles—it serves HTML to users using standard MVC controllers and acts as an API in other cases? You'll probably want to ensure your error handling middleware only modifies the requests to HTML endpoints and leaves the API requests to be returned as status codes only.

`StatusCodePagesMiddleware` supports being disabled for a given request. When the middleware runs as part of the middleware pipeline, it adds a *feature* to the collection of features on the `HttpContext` object called `IStatusCodePagesFeature`.

> **DEFINITION**   *Features* define which capabilities the ASP.NET Core web server provides. Each feature is represented as an interface in the `Features` collection property on `HttpContext`. Middleware is free to add or replace features in the collection as part of the request, thereby extending the features available to an application.

You may remember that the ASP.NET Core web server builds an `HttpContext` object representing a request, which passes up and down the middleware pipeline. By adding a feature to the `HttpContext` collection, `StatusCodePagesMiddleware` broadcasts its presence to the rest of the application. This allows other parts of the application to disable `StatusCodePagesMiddleware` if required. For example, a Web API controller could disable the feature if it doesn't want to have error responses replaced with HTML pages, as shown in the following listing.

Listing 3.6 Disabling `StatusCodePagesMiddleware` in a web API controller

```
public class ValuesController : Controller
{
    public string Index()
    {
        var statusCodePagesFeature = HttpContext.Features
            .Get<IStatusCodePagesFeature>();
        if (statusCodePagesFeature != null)
        {
            statusCodePagesFeature.Enabled = false;
        }

        return StatusCode(500);
    }
}
```

Try to get
IStatusCodePagesFeature
from the HttpContext.

Disable the feature
for this request.

Return a 500 error code—it
will pass through
StatusCodePagesMiddleware
untouched.

If StatusCodePagesMiddleware hasn't
been added, the feature will be null.

When the `Index` method in this API controller is hit, it will attempt to retrieve `IStatusCodePagesFeature` from the feature collection on `HttpContext`. If `Status-CodePagesMiddleware` has already run in the request pipeline, then you'll be able to set `Enabled = false`. If it hasn't run, then the feature will be null, so you need to remember to check that before using the variable.

The final call to `return StatusCode(500)` will return an HTTP 500 status code to the client. Ordinarily, `StatusCodePagesMiddleware` would intercept the response and replace it with a friendly HTML page, but in this case the raw status code is sent as it is, without a response body.

That brings us to the end of middleware in ASP.NET Core for now. You've seen how to use and compose middleware to form a pipeline, as well as how to handle errors in your application. This will get you a long way when you start building your first ASP.NET Core applications. Later, you'll learn how to build your own custom middleware, as well as how to perform complex operations on the middleware pipeline, such as forking it in response to specific requests.

In the next chapter, you'll learn about the MVC design pattern and how it applies to ASP.NET Core. You've already seen several examples of MVC controllers but I'll expand on how and when you can make use of them in your application, both for building dynamic web applications and for Web APIs.

Summary

- Middleware has a similar role to HTTP modules and handlers in ASP.NET but is more easily reasoned about.
- Middleware is composed in a pipeline, with the output of one middleware passing to the input of the next.

- The middleware pipeline is two-way: requests pass through each middleware on the way in and responses pass back through in the reverse order on the way out.

- Middleware can short-circuit the pipeline by handling a request and returning a response, or it can pass the request on to the next middleware in the pipeline.

- Middleware can modify a request by adding data to, or changing, the `Http-Context` object.

- If an earlier middleware short-circuits the pipeline, not all middleware will execute for all requests.

- If a request isn't handled, the middleware pipeline will return a 404 status code.

- The order in which middleware is added to `IApplicationBuilder` defines the order in which middleware will execute in the pipeline.

- The middleware pipeline can be re-executed, as long as a response's headers haven't been sent.

- When added to a middleware pipeline, `StaticFileMiddleware` will serve any requested files found in the wwwroot folder of your application.

- `DeveloperExceptionPageMiddleware` provides a lot of information about errors when developing an application but should never be used in production.

- `ExceptionHandlerMiddleware` lets you provide user-friendly custom error handling messages when an exception occurs in the pipeline.

- `StatusCodePagesMiddleware` lets you provide user-friendly custom error handling messages when the pipeline returns a raw error response status code.

- `StatusCodePagesMiddleware` can be disabled by accessing the `Features` property on `HttpContext`.

- Microsoft provides some common middleware and there are many third-party options available on NuGet and GitHub.

Creating web pages
with MVC controllers

4

This chapter covers

- Introducing the Model-View-Controller (MVC) design pattern
- Using MVC in ASP.NET Core
- Creating MVC controllers for serving web pages

In chapter 3, you learned about the middleware pipeline, which defines how an ASP.NET Core application responds to a request. Each piece of middleware can modify or handle an incoming request, before passing the request to the next middleware in the pipeline.

In ASP.NET Core web applications, the final piece of middleware in the pipeline will normally be MvcMiddleware. This is typically where you write the bulk of your application logic, by calling various other classes in your app. It also serves as the main entry point for users to interact with your app. It typically takes one of two forms:

- *An HTML web application, designed for direct use by users.* If the application is consumed directly by users, as in a traditional web application, then the

`MvcMiddleware` is responsible for generating the web pages that the user interacts with. It handles requests for URLs, it receives data posted using forms, and it generates the HTML that users use to view and navigate your app.

- *An API designed for consumption by another machine or in code.* The other main possibility for a web application is to serve as an API, to backend server processes, to a mobile app, or to a client framework for building single page applications (SPAs). The same `MvcMiddleware` can fulfill this role by serving data in machine-readable formats such as JSON or XML, instead of the human-focused HTML output.

In this chapter, you'll learn how ASP.NET Core uses the `MvcMiddleware` to serve these two requirements. You'll start by looking at the Model-View-Controller (MVC) design pattern to see the benefits that can be achieved through its use and learn why it's been adopted by so many web frameworks as a model for building maintainable applications.

Next, you'll learn how the MVC design pattern applies specifically to ASP.NET Core. The MVC pattern is a broad concept that can be applied in a variety of situations, but the use case in ASP.NET Core is specifically as a UI abstraction. You'll see how to add the `MvcMiddleware` to your application, as well as how to customize it for your needs.

Once you've installed the middleware in your app, I'll show how to create your first MVC controllers. You'll learn how to define action methods to execute when your application receives a request and how to generate a result that can be used to create an HTTP response to return. For traditional MVC web applications, this will be a `ViewResult` that can generate HTML.

I won't cover how to create Web APIs in this chapter. Web APIs still use the `Mvc-Middleware` but they're used in a slightly different way. Instead of returning web pages that are directly displayed on a user's browser, they return data formatted for consumption in code. Web APIs are often used for providing data to mobile and web applications, or to other server applications. But they still follow the same general MVC pattern. You'll see how to create a Web API in chapter 9.

> **NOTE** This chapter is the first of several on MVC in ASP.NET Core and the `MvcMiddleware`. As I've already mentioned, this middleware is often responsible for handling all the business logic and UI code for your application, so, perhaps unsurprisingly, it's large and somewhat complicated. The next five chapters all deal with a different aspect of the MVC pattern that makes up the MVC middleware.

In this chapter, I'll try to prepare you for each of the upcoming topics, but you may find that some of the behavior feels a bit like magic at this stage. Try not to become too concerned with exactly how all the pieces tie together; focus on the specific concepts being addressed. It should all become clear as we cover the associated details in the remainder of this first part of the book.

4.1 An introduction to MVC

Depending on your background in software development, you may have previously come across the MVC pattern in some form. In web development, MVC is a common paradigm and is used in frameworks such as Django, Rails, and Spring MVC. But as it's such a broad concept, you can find MVC in everything from mobile apps to rich-client desktop applications. Hopefully that is indicative of the benefits the pattern can bring if used correctly!

In this section, I'll look at the MVC pattern in general, how it applies to ASP.NET Core, and how to add the `MvcMiddleware` to your application. By the end of this section you should have a good understanding of the benefits of this approach and how to get started.

4.1.1 The MVC design pattern

The MVC design pattern is a common pattern for designing apps that have UIs. The original MVC pattern has many different interpretations, each of which focuses on a slightly different aspect of the pattern. For example, the original MVC design pattern was specified with rich-client graphical user interface (GUI) apps in mind, rather than web applications, and so uses terminology and paradigms associated with a GUI environment. Fundamentally, though, the pattern aims to separate the management and manipulation of data from its visual representation.

Before I dive too far into the design pattern itself, let's consider a typical request. Imagine a user of your application requests a page that displays a to-do list. What happens when the `MvcMiddleware` gets this request? Figure 4.1 shows how the MVC pattern is used to handle different aspects of that single page request, all of which combine to generate the final response.

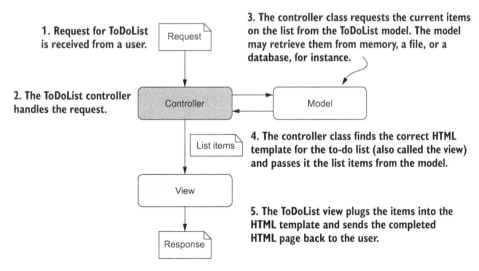

1. Request for ToDoList is received from a user.

2. The ToDoList controller handles the request.

3. The controller class requests the current items on the list from the ToDoList model. The model may retrieve them from memory, a file, or a database, for instance.

4. The controller class finds the correct HTML template for the to-do list (also called the view) and passes it the list items from the model.

5. The ToDoList view plugs the items into the HTML template and sends the completed HTML page back to the user.

Figure 4.1   Requesting a to-do list page for an MVC application. A different component handles each aspect of the request.

In general, three components make up the MVC design pattern:

- *Model*—The data that needs to be displayed, the state of the application.
- *View*—The template that displays the data provided by the model.
- *Controller*—Updates the model and selects the appropriate view.

Each component in an MVC application is responsible for a single aspect of the overall system that, when combined, can be used to generate a UI. The to-do list example considers MVC in terms of a web application, but a request could also be equivalent to the click of a button in a desktop GUI application.

In general, the order of events when an application responds to a user interaction or request is as follows:

1. The controller receives the request.
2. Depending on the request, the controller either fetches the requested data from the application model, or it updates the data that makes up the model.
3. The controller selects a view to display and passes the model to it.
4. The view uses the data contained in the model to generate the UI.

When we describe MVC in this format, the controller serves as the entry point for the interaction. The user communicates with the controller to instigate an interaction. In web applications, this interaction takes the form of an HTTP request, so when a request to a URL is received, the controller handles it.

Depending on the nature of the request, the controller may take a variety of actions, but the key point is that the actions are undertaken using the model. The model here contains all the business logic for the application, so it's able to provide requested data or perform actions.

> **NOTE** In this description of MVC, the model is considered to be a complex beast, containing all the logic for how to perform an action, as well as any internal state.

Consider a request to view a product page for an e-commerce application, for example. The controller would receive the request and would know how to contact some product service that's part of the application model. This might fetch the details of the requested product from a database and return them to the controller.

Alternatively, imagine the controller receives a request to add a product to the user's shopping cart. The controller would receive the request, and most likely invoke a method on the model to request that the product be added. The model would then update its internal representation of the user's cart, by adding, for example, a new row to a database table holding the user's data.

After the model has been updated, the controller needs to select a way to display the data. One of the advantages of using the MVC design pattern is that the model representing the data is decoupled from the final representation of that data, called the view.

This separation creates the possibility for the controller to choose to display the model using a different view, based on where the original request originated, as shown in figure 4.2. If the request came from a standard web application, then the controller can display an HTML view. If the request came from another application, then the controller can choose to return the model in a format the application understands, such as JSON or XML.

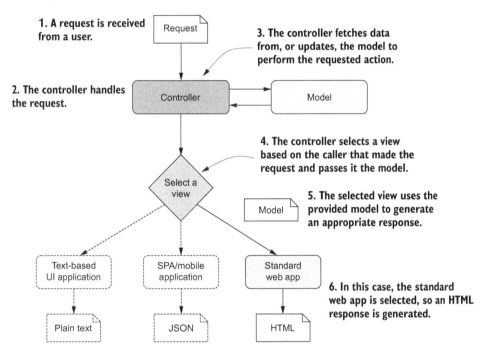

Figure 4.2   Selecting a different view using MVC depending on the caller. The final representation of the model, created by the view, is independent of the controller and business logic.

The other advantage of the model being independent of the view is that it improves testability. UI code is classically hard to test, as it's dependent on the environment—anyone who has written UI tests simulating a user clicking buttons and typing in forms knows that it's typically fragile. By keeping the model independent of the view, you can ensure the model stays easily testable, without any dependencies on UI constructs. As the model often contains your application's business logic, this is clearly a good thing!

Once the controller has selected a view, it passes the model to it. The view can use the data passed to it to generate an appropriate UI, an HTML web page, or a simple JSON object. The view is only responsible for generating the final representation.

This is all there is to the MVC design pattern in relation to web applications. Much of the confusion related to MVC seems to stem from slightly different uses of the term for slightly different frameworks and types of application. In the next section, I'll show

how the ASP.NET Core framework uses the MVC pattern, along with more examples of the pattern in action.

4.1.2   MVC in ASP.NET Core

As you've seen in previous chapters, ASP.NET Core implements MVC using a single piece of middleware, which is normally placed at the end of the middleware pipeline, as shown in figure 4.3. Once a request has been processed by each middleware (and assuming none of them handle the request and short-circuit the pipeline), it will be received by the MVC middleware.

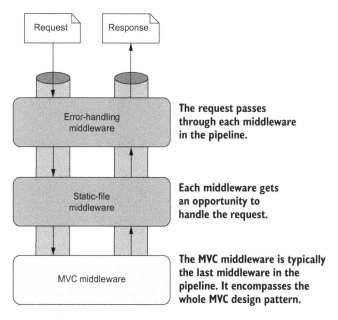

Figure 4.3   The middleware pipeline.

Middleware often handles cross-cutting concerns or narrowly defined requests, such as requests for files. For requirements that fall outside of these functions, or that have many external dependencies, a more robust framework is required. The MvcMiddleware in ASP.NET Core can provide this framework, allowing interaction with your application's core business logic, and the generation of a UI. It handles everything from mapping the request to an appropriate controller to generating the HTML or API response.

In the traditional description of the MVC design pattern, there's only a single type of model, which holds all the non-UI data and behavior. The controller updates this model as appropriate and then passes it to the view, which uses it to generate a UI. This simple, three-component pattern may be sufficient for some basic applications, but for more complex applications, it often doesn't scale.

When not to use the MvcMiddleware

Typically, you'll use `MvcMiddleware` to write most of your application logic for an app. You'll use it to define the APIs and pages in your application, and to define how they interface with your business logic. The `MvcMiddleware` is an extensive framework (as you'll see over the next six chapters) that provides a great deal of functionality to help build your apps quickly and efficiently. But it's not suited to *every* app.

Providing so much functionality necessarily comes with a certain degree of performance overhead. For typical apps, the productivity gains from using MVC strongly outweigh any performance impact. But if you're building small, lightweight apps for the cloud, then you might consider using custom middleware directly (see chapter 19). You might want to also consider *Microservices in .NET Core* by Christian Horsdal Gammelgaard (Manning, 2017).

Alternatively, if you're building an app with real-time functionality, you'll probably want to consider using WebSockets instead of traditional HTTP requests. The WebSockets protocol allows high-performance two-way communication between a server and a client, but they make some things more complicated. You can use WebSockets with ASP.NET Core, but you'll need to handle things such as connection dropouts, server scaling issues, and old browsers yourself. For details, see the documentation at http://mng.bz/Ol13. SignalR Core is in preview at the time of writing (https://github .com/aspnet/SignalR), but will handle some of these considerations for you, so it's worth investigating.

One of the problems when discussing MVC is the vague and ambiguous terms that it uses, such as "controller" and "model." Model, in particular, is such an overloaded term that it's often difficult to be sure exactly what it refers to—is it an object, a collection of objects, an abstract concept? Even ASP.NET Core uses the word "model" to describe several related, but different, components, as you'll see shortly.

DIRECTING A REQUEST TO A CONTROLLER AND BUILDING A BINDING MODEL

The first step when the `MvcMiddleware` receives a request is routing the request to an appropriate controller. Let's think about another page in your to-do application. On this page, you're displaying a list of items marked with a given category, assigned to a particular user. If you're looking at the list of items assigned to the user "Andrew" with a category of "Simple," you'd make a request to the `/todo/list/Simple/Andrew` URL.

Routing takes the path of the request, `/todo/list/Simple/Andrew`, and maps it against a preregistered list of patterns. These patterns match a path to a single controller class and action method. You'll learn more about routing in the next chapter.

> **DEFINITION** An *action* (or *action method*) is a method that runs in response to a request. A *controller* is a class that contains a number of logically grouped action methods.

Once an action method is selected, the *binding model* (if applicable) is generated, based on the incoming request and the method parameters required by the action method, as shown in figure 4.4. A binding model is normally a standard class, with properties that map to the requested data. We'll look at binding models in detail in chapter 6.

> **DEFINITION**   A *binding model* is an object that acts as a "container" for the data provided in a request that's required by an action method.

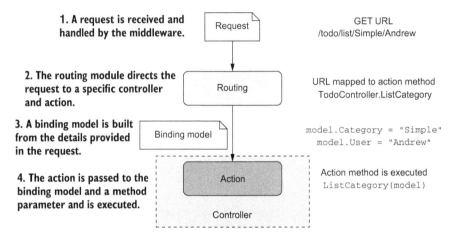

1. A request is received and handled by the middleware.

Request

GET URL
/todo/list/Simple/Andrew

2. The routing module directs the request to a specific controller and action.

Routing

URL mapped to action method
TodoController.ListCategory

3. A binding model is built from the details provided in the request.

Binding model

model.Category = "Simple"
model.User = "Andrew"

4. The action is passed to the binding model and a method parameter and is executed.

Action

Controller

Action method is executed
ListCategory(model)

Figure 4.4   Routing a request to a controller and building a binding model. A request to the /todo/list/Simple/Andrew URL results in the ListCategory action being executed, passing in a populated binding model.

In this case, the binding model contains two properties: Category, which is "bound" to the "Simple" value, and the User property, which is bound to the "Andrew" value. These values are provided in the request URL's path and are used to populate a binding model of the TodoModel type.

This binding model corresponds to the method parameter of the ListCategory action method. This binding model is passed to the action method when it executes, so it can be used to decide how to respond. For this example, the action method uses it to decide which to-do items to display on the page.

EXECUTING AN ACTION USING THE APPLICATION MODEL

The role of an action method in the controller is to *coordinate* the generation of a response to the request it's handling. That means it should perform only a limited number of actions. In particular, it should

- Validate that the data contained in the binding model provided is valid for the request.
- Invoke the appropriate actions on the application model.
- Select an appropriate response to generate based on the response from the application model.

2. The action method calls into services that make up the application model. This might use the domain model to calculate the price of the product, for example.

1. The action uses the category and user provided in the binding model to determine which method to invoke in the application model.

3. The services load the details of the product from the database and return them to the action model.

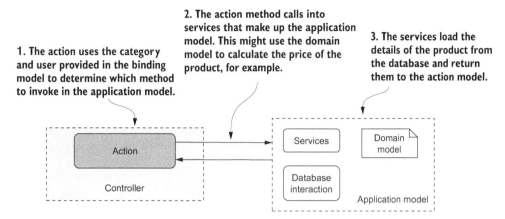

Figure 4.5 When executed, an action will invoke the appropriate methods in the application model.

Figure 4.5 shows the action method invoking an appropriate method on the application model. Here, you can see that the application model is a somewhat abstract concept that encapsulates the remaining non-UI part of your application. It contains the *domain model*, a number of services, and the database interaction.

> **DEFINITION**   The *domain model* encapsulates complex business logic in a series of classes that don't depend on any infrastructure and can be easily tested.

The action method typically calls into a single point in the application model. In our example of viewing a product page, the application model might use a variety of services to check whether the user is allowed to view the product, to calculate the display price for the product, to load the details from the database, or to load a picture of the product from a file.

Assuming the request is valid, the application model will return the required details to the action method. It's then up to the action method to choose a response to generate.

GENERATING A RESPONSE USING A VIEW MODEL

Once the action method has called out to the application model that contains the application business logic, it's time to generate a response. A *view model* captures the details necessary for the view to generate a response.

> **DEFINITION**   A *view model* is a simple object that contains data required by the view to render a UI. It's typically some transformation of the data contained in the application model, plus extra information required to render the page, for example the page's title.

The action method selects an appropriate view template and passes the view model to it. Each view is designed to work with a particular view model, which it uses to generate

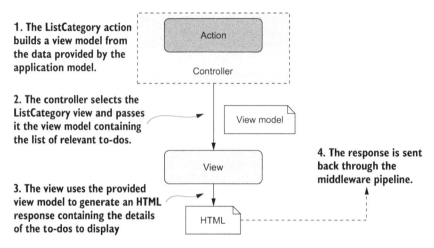

1. The ListCategory action builds a view model from the data provided by the application model.

2. The controller selects the ListCategory view and passes it the view model containing the list of relevant to-dos.

3. The view uses the provided view model to generate an HTML response containing the details of the to-dos to display

4. The response is sent back through the middleware pipeline.

Figure 4.6   **The action method builds a view model, selects which view to use to generate the response, and passes it the view model. It's the view that generates the response.**

the final HTML response. Finally, this is sent back through the middleware pipeline and out to the user's browser, as shown in figure 4.6.

It's important to note that although the action method selects *which view* to display, it doesn't select *what is generated*. It's the view itself that decides what the content of the response will be.

PUTTING IT ALL TOGETHER: A COMPLETE MVC REQUEST

Now that you've seen each of the steps that goes into handling a request in ASP.NET Core using MVC, let's put it all together from request to response. Figure 4.7 shows how all of the steps combine to handle the request to display the list of to-dos for user "Andrew" and the "Simple" category. The traditional MVC pattern is still visible in ASP.NET Core, made up of the action/controller, the view, and the application model.

By now, you might be thinking this whole process seems rather convoluted—so many steps to display some HTML! Why not allow the application model to create the view directly, rather than having to go on a dance back and forth with the controller/action method?

The key benefit throughout this process is the *separation of concerns*:

- The view is responsible only for taking some data and generating HTML.
- The application model is responsible only for executing the required business logic.
- The controller is responsible only for validating the incoming request and selecting the appropriate view to display, based on the output of the application model.

By having clearly defined boundaries, it's easier to update and test each of the components without depending on any of the others. If your UI logic changes, you won't necessarily have to modify any of your business logic classes, so you're less likely to introduce errors in unexpected places.

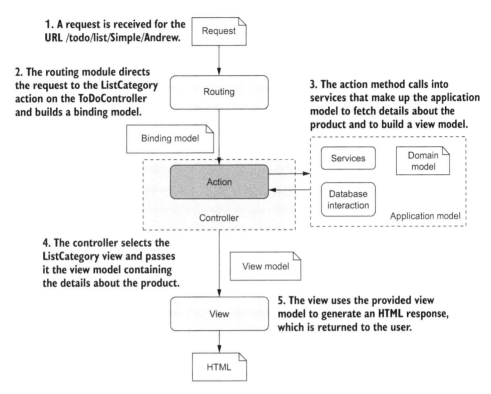

Figure 4.7   A complete MVC request for the list of to-dos in the "Simple" category for user "Andrew"

The dangers of tight coupling

Generally speaking, it's a good idea to reduce coupling between logically separate parts of your application as much as possible. This makes it easier to update your application without causing adverse effects or requiring modifications in seemingly unrelated areas. Applying the MVC pattern is one way to help with this goal.

As an example of when coupling rears its head, I remember a case a few years ago when I was working on a small web app. In our haste, we had not properly decoupled our business logic from our HTML generation code, but initially there were no obvious problems—the code worked, so we shipped it!

A few months later, someone new started working on the app, and immediately "helped" by renaming an innocuous spelling error in a class in the business layer. Unfortunately, the names of those classes had been used to generate our HTML code, so renaming the class caused the whole website to break in users' browsers! Suffice it to say, we made a concerted effort to apply the MVC pattern after that, and ensure we had a proper separation of concerns.

The examples shown in this chapter demonstrate the vast majority of the MVC middleware functionality. It has additional features, such as the filter pipeline, that I'll cover later (chapter 13), and I'll discuss binding models in greater depth in chapter 6, but the overall behavior of the system is the same.

Similarly, in chapter 9, I'll discuss how the MVC design pattern applies when you're generating machine-readable responses using Web API controllers. The process is, for all intents and purposes, identical, with the exception of the final result generated.

In the next section, you'll see how to add the MVC middleware to your application. Most templates in Visual Studio and the .NET CLI will include the MVC middleware by default, but you'll see how to add it to an existing application and explore the various options available.

4.1.3   *Adding the MvcMiddleware to your application*

The MVC middleware is a foundational aspect of all but the simplest ASP.NET Core applications, so virtually all templates include it configured by default. But to make sure you're comfortable with adding MVC to an existing project, I'll show how to start with a basic empty application and add the MVC middleware to it from scratch.

The result of your efforts won't be exciting yet. We'll display "Hello World" on a web page, but it'll show how simple it is to convert an ASP.NET Core application to use MVC. It also emphasizes the pluggable nature of ASP.NET Core—if you don't need the functionality provided by the MVC middleware, then you don't have to include it. Here's how you add the `MvcMiddleware` to your application:

1 In Visual Studio 2017, choose File > New > Project.
2 From the New Project dialog, choose .NET Core, then select ASP.NET Core Web Application.
3 Enter a Name, Location, and optionally a solution name, and click OK.
4 Create a basic template without MVC by selecting the Empty Project template in Visual Studio, as shown in figure 4.8. You can create a similar empty project using the .NET CLI with the `dotnet new web` command.

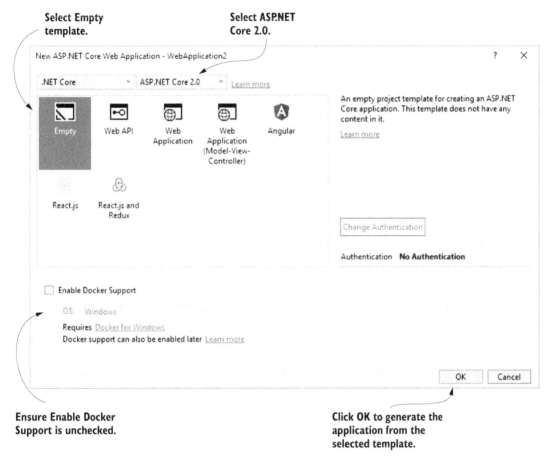

Select Empty template.

Select ASP.NET Core 2.0.

Ensure Enable Docker Support is unchecked.

Click OK to generate the application from the selected template.

Figure 4.8   Creating an empty ASP.NET Core template. The empty template will create a simple ASP.NET Core application that contains a small middleware pipeline, but not the `MvcMiddleware`.

5   Edit your project file by right-clicking the project and selecting Edit *Project*
    .csproj, where *Project* is the name of your project, as shown in figure 4.9.

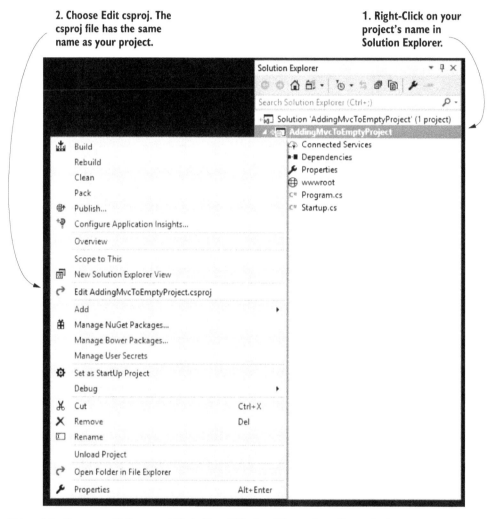

**Figure 4.9   You can edit the csproj file in Visual Studio while you have the project open.
Alternatively, edit the csproj file directly in a text editor.**

6 The default ASP.NET Core 2.0 template references the Microsoft.AspNetCore
  .All metapackage in its csproj file:

```
<PackageReference Include="Microsoft.AspNetCore.All" Version="2.0.0" />
```

This includes all of the packages in ASP.NET Core, so you won't need to reference any others.[1] If you're targeting the full .NET Framework instead of .NET
Core, you can't use the metapackage, so you'll need to add the Microsoft.Asp-
NetCore.Mvc package to your project explicitly. You can add NuGet packages
using the graphical NuGet Package Manager in Visual Studio by editing the
csproj file to include the package, or by running the following command from
the project folder (not the solution folder):

```
dotnet add package Microsoft.AspNetCore.Mvc
```

This adds a `<PackageReference>` element to your project's csproj file:

```
<PackageReference Include="Microsoft.AspNetCore.Mvc" Version="2.0.0" />
```

7 Add the necessary MVC services (in bold) in your Startup.cs file's `Configure-
  Services` method:

```
public void ConfigureServices(IServiceCollection services)
{
    services.AddMvc();
}
```

8 Add the `MvcMiddleware` to the end of your middleware pipeline with the `Use-
  Mvc` extension method (in bold). For simplicity, remove any other middleware
  from the `Configure` method of Startup.cs for now:

```
public void Configure(IApplicationBuilder app, IHostingEnvironment env)
{
    app.UseMvc(routes =>
    {
        routes.MapRoute(
            name: "default",
            template: "{controller=Home}/{action=Index}/{id?}");
    });
}
```

9 Right-click your project in Solution Explorer and choose Add > Class, as shown
  in figure 4.10.

---

[1] In ASP.NET Core 2.1, a different metapackage, Microsoft.AspNetCore.App, is referenced, which includes
slightly fewer packages than the All metapackage. See https://github.com/aspnet/Announcements/issues/
287 for details.

2. Click Add to open the Add submenu.

1. Right-click on your project name to bring up the context menu.

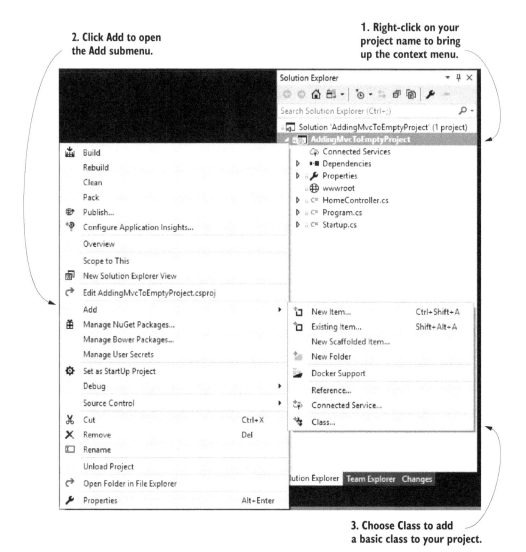

3. Choose Class to add a basic class to your project.

Figure 4.10   Adding a new class to your project

10   In the dialog box, name your class HomeController and click OK, as shown in figure 4.11.

11   Add an action called Index (in bold) to the generated class:

```
public class HomeController
{
    public string Index()
    {
        return "Hello world!";
    }
}
```

Leave Class selected.

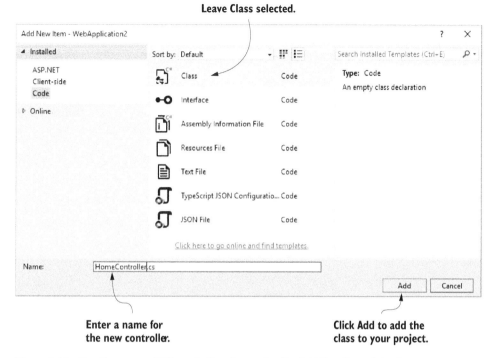

Figure 4.11 Creating a new MVC controller class using the Add New Item dialog box

Once you've completed all these steps, you should be able to restore, build, and run your application.

> **NOTE** You can run your project by pressing F5 from within Visual Studio (or by calling `dotnet run` at the command line from the project folder). This will restore any referenced NuGet packages, build your project, and start your application. Visual Studio will automatically open a browser window to access your application's homepage.

When you make a request to the `"/"` path, the application invokes the `Index` method on `HomeController` due to the way you configured routing in the call to `UseMvc`. Don't worry about this for now; we'll go into it in detail in the next chapter.

This returns the `"Hello world!"` string value, which is rendered in the browser as plain text. You're returning data rather than a view here, so it's more of a Web API controller, but you could've created a `ViewResult` to render HTML instead.

You access the MVC functionality by adding the Microsoft.AspNetCore.Mvc package (or more commonly the Microsoft.AspNetCore.All metapackage) to your project. The `MvcMiddleware` relies on a number of internal services to perform its function, which must be registered during application startup. This is achieved with the call to `AddMvc` in the `ConfigureServices` method of Startup.cs. Without this, you'll get exceptions at runtime when the `MvcMiddleware` is invoked, reminding you that the call is required.

The call to UseMvc in Configure registers the MvcMiddleware itself in the middleware pipeline. As part of this call, the routes that are used to map URL paths to controllers and actions are registered. We used the default convention here, but you can easily customize these to match your requirements.

NOTE   I'll cover routing in detail in the next chapter.

As you might expect, the MvcMiddleware comes with a large number of options for configuring how it behaves in your application. This can be useful when the default conventions and configuration don't meet your requirements. You can modify these options by passing a configuration function to the AddMvc call that adds the MVC services. This listing shows how you could use this method to customize the maximum number of validation errors that the MVC middleware can handle.

Listing 4.1   Configuring MVC options in Startup.cs

```
public void ConfigureServices(IServiceCollection services)
{
    services.AddMvc(options =>          ◁────────────────────────        AddMvc has an
    {                                                                    overload that
        options.MaxModelValidationErrors = 100;      ◁──────────        takes a lambda
    });                                                                  function.
}                              A number of properties are
                               available to customize the
                               MvcMiddleware behavior.
```

You can replace many parts of the MVC middleware internals this way, thanks to the extensible design of the middleware. You won't often need to touch the MVC options, but it's nice to be able to customize them when the need arises.

Customizing the MVC middleware internals

As I've hinted, the MvcMiddleware exposes a large amount of its internal configuration through the AddMvc method, as shown in the following figure. The options object contains many different properties that you can use to extend and modify the default behavior of the middleware.

Some of the customizations options available when configuring the MvcMiddleware

> By manipulating these options, you can control things such as how data is read from the request, how the data should be validated, and how the output data is formatted. You can even modify the way actions function across your whole application. For details on the options available, see the API reference on https://docs.microsoft.com.

The final part of adding MVC to your application is creating the controllers that are invoked when a request arises. But what makes a class act as a controller?

4.1.4   What makes a controller a controller?

Controllers in ASP.NET Core are classes that contain a logical grouping of action methods. How you define them is largely up to you, but there are a number of conventions used by the runtime to identify controllers.

Convention over configuration

Convention over configuration is a sometimes-controversial approach to building applications, in which a framework makes certain assumptions about the structure or naming of your code. Conforming to these assumptions reduces the amount of boilerplate code a developer must write to configure a project—you typically only need to specify the cases where your requirements don't match the assumptions.

Imagine you have a number of provider classes that can load different types of files. At runtime, you want to be able to let the user select a file and you'd automatically select the correct provider. To do this, you could explicitly register all the providers in some sort of central configuration service, or you could use a convention to rely on the runtime to "find" your classes and do the wiring up for you. Typically, in .NET, this is achieved by using reflection to search through all the types in an assembly and find those with a particular name, that derive from a base class, or that contain specific named methods.

ASP.NET Core takes this approach in a number of cases, perhaps most notably with the `Startup` class, whose configuration methods are "discovered" at runtime, rather than by explicitly implementing an interface.

This approach can sometimes result in an almost magical effect of things working for no apparent reason, which some people find confusing. It can occasionally make debugging problems tricky due to the additional level of indirection at play. On the other hand, using conventions can result in terser code, as there's no explicit wiring-up necessary, and can provide additional flexibility, for example by allowing the signature of the methods in your `Startup` class to vary.

MVC or Web API controllers are discovered and used by the `MvcMiddleware` as long as they are instantiable (they have a public constructor, aren't static, and aren't abstract) and either:

- Have a name ending in "Controller," for example `HomeController`

- Inherit from the `Controller` or `ControllerBase` class (or a class that inherits from these)

The `MvcMiddleware` will identify any class that meets these requirements at runtime and make it available to handle requests as required. Although not required, the Microsoft.AspNetCore.Mvc package provides a base class, `Controller`, that your controllers can inherit from. It's often a good idea to use this class given that it contains a number of helper methods for returning results, as you'll see later in this chapter.

> **TIP** If you're building a Web API, you can also inherit from `ControllerBase`. This includes many of the same helper methods, but no helpers for creating views.

Another common convention is to place all your controller files in a Controllers subfolder in your project, as shown in figure 4.12. This can be useful for organizing some projects, but it isn't required for the `MvcMiddleware` to discover them. You're free to place your controller files anywhere you like in your project folder.

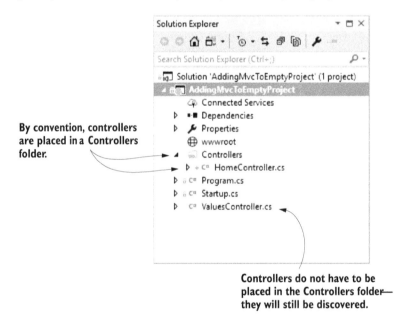

By convention, controllers are placed in a Controllers folder.

Controllers do not have to be placed in the Controllers folder—they will still be discovered.

Figure 4.12   Controller location conventions in ASP.NET Core. MVC applications often place controllers in a Controllers subfolder, but they can be located anywhere in your project—the `MvcMiddleware` will still identify and make them available to handle requests.

Based on these requirements, it's possible to come up with a variety of naming conventions and hierarchies for your controllers, all of which will be discovered at runtime. In general, it's far better to stick to the common convention of naming your controllers by ending them with Controller, and optionally inheriting from the `Controller` base class.

Listing 4.2 Common conventions for defining controllers

```
public class HomeController: Controller        ◁─┐  Suffix your controller
{                                                 │  names with Controller
    public ViewResult Index()
    {
        return View();    ◁─────────┐  Inheriting from the Controller
    }                               │  base class allows access to
}                                   │  utility methods like View().

public class ValuesController        ◁──┐
{                                        │  If you're not using the
    public string Get()                  │  utility methods in your
    {                                    │  controller, you don't need
        return "Hello world!";           │  to inherit from Controller.
    }
}
```

It's worth noting that although these examples have (implicit) parameterless constructors, it's perfectly acceptable to have dependencies in your constructor. In fact, this is one of the preferred mechanisms for accessing other classes and services from your controllers. By requiring them to be passed during the construction of the controller, you explicitly define the dependencies of your controller, which, among other things, makes testing easier. The dependency injection container will automatically populate any required dependencies when the controller is created.

NOTE See chapter 10 for details about configuring, and using, dependency injection.

The controllers you've seen so far all contain a single action method, which will be invoked when handling a request. In the next section, I'll look at action methods, how to define them, how to invoke them, and how to use them to return views.

4.2 MVC controllers and action methods

In the first section of this chapter, I described the MVC design pattern and how it relates to ASP.NET Core. In the design pattern, the controller receives a request and is the entry point for UI generation. In ASP.NET Core, the entry point is an action method that resides in a controller. An *action, or action method*, is a method that runs in response to a request.

MVC controllers can contain any number of action methods. Controllers provide a mechanism to logically group actions and so apply a common set of rules to them. For example, it's simple to require a user to be logged in when accessing any action method on a given controller by applying an attribute to the controller; you don't need to apply the attribute to every individual action method.

NOTE You'll see how to apply authorization requirements to your actions and controllers in chapter 15.

Any public method on a controller acts as an action method, and so can be invoked by a client (assuming the routing configuration allows it). The responsibility of an action method is generally threefold:

- Confirm the incoming request is valid.
- Invoke the appropriate business logic corresponding to the incoming request.
- Choose the appropriate *kind* of response to return.

An action doesn't need to perform all of these actions, but at the very least it must choose the kind of response to return. For a traditional MVC application that's returning HTML to a browser, action methods will typically return either a `ViewResult` that the `MvcMiddleware` will use to generate an HTML response, or a `RedirectResult`, which indicates the user should be redirected to a different page in your application. In Web API applications, action methods often return a variety of different results, as you'll see in chapter 9.

It's important to realize that an action method doesn't generate a response directly; it selects the *type* of response and prepares the data for it. For example, returning a `ViewResult` doesn't generate any HTML at that point, it indicates which view template to use and the view model it will have access to. This is in keeping with the MVC design pattern in which it's the *view* that generates the response, not the *controller*.

> **TIP** The action method is responsible for choosing what sort of response to send; the *view engine* in the `MvcMiddleware` uses the action result to generate the response.

It's also worth bearing in mind that action methods should generally not be performing business logic directly. Instead, they should call appropriate services in the application model to handle requests. If an action method receives a request to add a product to a user's cart, it shouldn't directly manipulate the database or recalculate cart totals, for example. Instead, it should make a call to another class to handle the details. This approach of separating concerns ensures your code stays testable and manageable as it grows.

4.2.1 *Accepting parameters to action methods*

Some requests made to action methods will require additional values with details about the request. If the request is for a search page, the request might contain details of the search term and the page number they're looking at. If the request is posting a form to your application, for example a user logging in with their username and password, then those values must be contained in the request. In other cases, there will be no such values, such as when a user requests the homepage for your application.

The request may contain additional values from a variety of different sources. They could be part of the URL, the query string, headers, or in the body of the request itself. The middleware will extract values from each of these sources and convert them into .NET types.

If an action method definition has method arguments, the additional values in the request are used to create the required parameters. If the action has no arguments, then the additional values will go unused. The method arguments can be simple types, such as strings and integers, or they can be a complex type, as shown here.

Listing 4.3 Example action methods

The SearchService is provided to the HomeController for use in action methods.

```
public class HomeController: Controller
{
    private SearchService _searchService;
    public HomeController(SearchService searchService)
    {
        _searchService = searchService;
    }

    public ViewResult Index()
    {
        return View();
    }

    public IActionResult Search(SearchModel searchModel)
    {
        if(ModelState.IsValid)
        {
            var viewModel = _searchService.Search(searchModel);
            return View(viewModel);
        }
        return Redirect("/")
    }
}
```

An action without parameters requires no additional values in the request.

The method doesn't need to check if the model is valid, it just returns a response.

The action method requires the request to have values for the properties in SearchModel.

If the model was not valid, the method indicates the user should be redirected to the path "/".

If the model is valid, a view model is created and passed to the view.

In this example, the Index action method doesn't require any parameters, and the method is simple—it returns a view to the user. The Search action method, conversely, accepts a SearchModel object. This could contain multiple different properties that are obtained from the request and are set on the model in a process called *model binding*. The SearchModel object is often described as a *binding model*.

NOTE I'll discuss model binding in detail in chapter 6.

When an action method accepts parameters, it should always check that the model provided is valid using ModelState.IsValid. The ModelState property is exposed when you inherit from the base Controller or ControllerBase class and can be used to check that the method parameters are valid. You'll see how the process works in chapter 6 when you learn about validation.

Once an action establishes that the method parameters provided to an action are valid, it can execute the appropriate business logic and handle the request. In the case of the `Search` action, this involves calling the provided `SearchService` to obtain a view model. This view model is then returned in a `ViewResult` by calling the base method

```
return View(viewModel);
```

If the model wasn't valid, then you don't have any results to display! In this example, the action returns a `RedirectResult` using the `Redirect` helper method. When executed, this result will send a 302 redirect response to the user, which will cause their browser to navigate to the homepage.

Note that the `Index` method returns a `ViewResult` in the method signature, whereas the `Search` method returns an `IActionResult`. This is required in the `Search` method in order to allow the C# to compile (as the `View` and `Redirect` helper methods return different types of values), but it doesn't change the final behavior of the methods. You could just as easily have returned an `IActionResult` in the `Index` method and the behavior would be identical.

> **TIP**   If you're returning more than one type of result from an action method, you'll need to ensure your method returns an `IActionResult`.

4.2.2   *Using ActionResult*

In the previous section, I emphasized that action methods only decide *what* to generate, and don't perform the generation of the response. It's the `IActionResult` returned by an action method which, when executed by the `MvcMiddleware` using the view engine, will generate the response.

This approach is key to following the MVC design pattern. It separates the decision of what sort of response to send from the generation of the response. This allows you to easily test your action method logic to confirm the right sort of response is sent for a given output. You can then separately test that a given `IActionResult` generates the expected HTML, for example.

ASP.NET Core has many different types of `IActionResult`:

- `ViewResult`—Generates an HTML view.
- `RedirectResult`—Sends a 302 HTTP redirect response to automatically send a user to a specified URL.
- `RedirectToRouteResult`—Sends a 302 HTTP redirect response to automatically send a user to another page, where the URL is defined using routing.
- `FileResult`—Returns a file as the response.
- `ContentResult`—Returns a provided string as the response.
- `StatusCodeResult`—Sends a raw HTTP status code as the response, optionally with associated response body content.
- `NotFoundResult`—Sends a raw 404 HTTP status code as the response.

Each of these, when executed by the `MvcMiddleware`, will generate a response to send back through the middleware pipeline and out to the user.

VIEWRESULT AND REDIRECTRESULT

When you're building a traditional web application and generating HTML, most of the time you'll be using the `ViewResult`, which generates an HTML response using Razor (by default). We'll look at how this happens in detail in chapter 7.

You'll also commonly use the various redirect-based results to send the user to a new web page. For example, when you place an order on an e-commerce website you typically navigate through multiple pages, as shown in figure 4.13. The web application sends HTTP redirects whenever it needs you to move to a different page, such as when a user submits a form. Your browser automatically follows the redirect requests, creating a seamless flow through the checkout process.

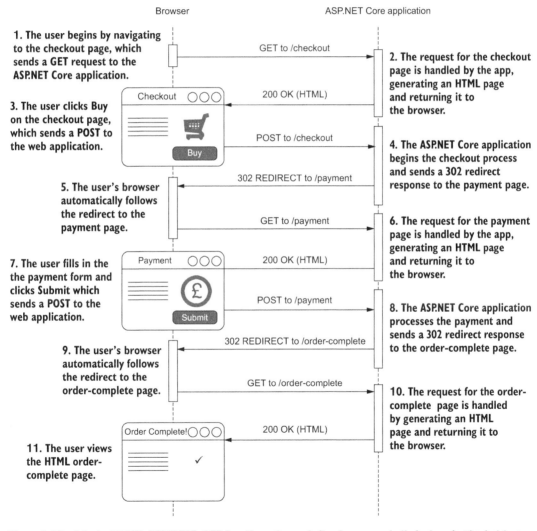

Figure 4.13   A typical POST, REDIRECT, GET flow through a website. A user sends their shopping basket to a checkout page, which validates its contents and redirects to a payment page without the user having to manually change the URL.

NotFoundResult and StatusCodeResult

As well as HTML and redirect responses, you'll occasionally need to send specific HTTP status codes. If you request a page for viewing a product on an e-commerce application, and that product doesn't exist, a 404 HTTP status code is returned to the browser and you'll typically see a "Not found" web page. The MvcMiddleware can achieve this behavior by returning a NotFoundResult, which will return a raw 404 HTTP status code. You could achieve a similar result using the StatusCodeResult and setting the status code returned explicitly to 404.

Note that the NotFoundResult doesn't generate any HTML; it only generates a raw 404 status code and returns it through the middleware pipeline. But, as discussed in the previous chapter, you can use the StatusCodePagesMiddleware to intercept this raw 404 status code after it's been generated and provide a user-friendly HTML response for it.

Creating ActionResult classes using helper methods

ActionResult classes can be created and returned using the normal new syntax of C#:

```
return new ViewResult()
```

If your controller inherits from the base Controller class, then you can also use a number of helper methods for generating an appropriate response. It's common to use the View method to generate an appropriate ViewResult, the Redirect method to generate a RedirectResponse, or the NotFound method to generate a NotFoundResult.

> **TIP** Most ActionResult classes have a helper method on the base Controller class. They're typically named Type, and the result generated is called Type-Result. For example, the Content method returns a ContentResult instance.

As discussed earlier, the act of *returning* an IActionResult doesn't immediately generate the response—it's the *execution* of an IActionResult by the MvcMiddleware, which occurs outside the action method. After producing the response, the MvcMiddleware returns it to the middleware pipeline. From there, it passes through all the registered middleware in the pipeline, before the ASP.NET Core web server finally sends it to the user.

By now, you should have an overall understanding of the MVC design pattern and how it relates to ASP.NET Core. The action methods on a controller are invoked in response to given requests and are used to select the type of response to generate by returning an IActionResult.

In traditional web apps, the MvcMiddleware generates HTML web pages. These can be served to a user who's browsing your app with a web browser, as you'd see with a traditional website. It's also possible to use the MvcMiddleware to send data in a machine-readable format, such as JSON, by returning data directly from action methods, as you'll see in chapter 9. Controllers handle both of these use cases, the only tangible difference being the data they return. These are typically known as MVC and Web API controllers, respectively.

It's important to remember that the whole MVC infrastructure in ASP.NET Core is a piece of middleware that runs as part of the middleware pipeline, as you saw in the previous chapter. Any response generated, whether a `ViewResult` or a `Redirect-Result`, will pass back through the middleware pipeline, giving a potential opportunity for middleware to modify the response before the web server sends it to the user.

An aspect I've only vaguely touched on is how the `MvcMiddleware` decides which action method to invoke for a given request. This process is handled by the routing infrastructure and is a key part of MVC in ASP.NET Core. In the next chapter, you'll see how to define routes, how to add constraints to your routes, and how they deconstruct URLs to match a single action and controller.

Summary

- MVC allows for a separation of concerns between the business logic of your application, the data that's passed around, and the display of data in a response.
- Controllers contain a logical grouping of action methods.
- ASP.NET Core controllers inherit from either the `Controller` or `Controller-Base` class or have a name that ends in controller.
- Action *methods* decide what sort of response to generate; action *results* handle the generation.
- Action methods should generally delegate to services to handle the business logic required by a request, instead of performing the changes themselves. This ensures a clean separation of concerns that aids testing and improves application structure.
- Action methods can have parameters whose values are taken from properties of the incoming request.
- When building a traditional web application, you'll generally use a `ViewResult` to generate an HTML response.
- You can send users to a new URL using a `RedirectResult`.
- The `Controller` base class exposes many helper methods for creating an `ActionResult`.
- The MVC and Web API infrastructure is unified in ASP.NET Core. The only thing that differentiates a traditional MVC controller from a Web API controller is the data it returns. MVC controllers normally return a `ViewResult`, whereas Web API controllers typically return data or a `StatusCodeResult`.

Mapping URLs to methods using conventional routing

This chapter covers

- Mapping URLs to action methods using conventions
- Using constraints and default values to match URLs
- Generating URLs from route parameters

In chapter 4, you learned about the MVC design pattern, and how ASP.NET Core uses it to generate the UI for an application. Whether you're building a traditional HTML web application or creating a Web API for a mobile application, you can use the MvcMiddleware to generate a response. This is typically placed at the end of the middleware pipeline and handles requests after all the other middleware in the pipeline have executed.

In ASP.NET Core, you build MVC applications by creating controller classes that contain action methods. An action method executes in response to an appropriate request. It's responsible for invoking the required business logic in the application model and determining what type of result to return. That might be a ViewResult indicating the template to use for HTML generation, a RedirectResult to forward the user to another URL, a StatusCodeResult if you're writing a Web API, and so on.

Although not explicitly part of the classic MVC design pattern, one crucial part of the MVC pattern in ASP.NET Core is selecting the correct action method to invoke in response to a given request, as shown in figure 5.1. This process is called *routing* and is the focus of this chapter.

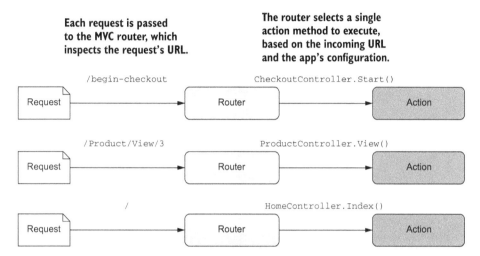

Each request is passed to the MVC router, which inspects the request's URL.

The router selects a single action method to execute, based on the incoming URL and the app's configuration.

Figure 5.1   The router is responsible for mapping incoming requests to an action method that will be executed to handle the request.

This chapter begins by identifying the need for routing, why it's useful, and the advantages it has over traditional layout-based mapping. You'll see several examples of routing techniques, and the separation routing can bring between the layout of your code and the URLs you expose.

The bulk of this chapter focuses on how to define your routes so that the correct action method executes in response to a request to a URL. I'll show how to build powerful route templates and give you a taste of the available options.

In section 5.5, I'll describe how to use the routing system to *generate* URLs, which you can use to create links and redirect requests for your application. One of the benefits of using a routing system is that it decouples your action methods from the underlying URLs that are used to execute them. This allows you to change the URLs your app uses by tweaking the routing system, leaving your action methods untouched. Using URL generation lets you avoid littering your code with hardcoded URLs like /Product/View/3, and instead lets you generate them at runtime, based on the current routing system.

By the end of this chapter, you should have a much clearer understanding of how an ASP.NET Core application works. You can think of routing as the glue that ties the middleware pipeline to the MVC design strategy used by the MvcMiddleware. With middleware, MVC, and routing under your belt, you'll be writing web apps in no time!

5.1   *What is routing?*

In chapter 3, you saw that an ASP.NET Core application contains a middleware pipeline, which defines the behavior of your application. Middleware is well suited to handling both cross-cutting concerns, such as logging and error handling, and narrowly focused requests, such as requests for images and CSS files.

To handle more complex application logic, you'll typically use the `MvcMiddleware` at the end of your middleware pipeline, as you saw in chapter 4. This can handle an appropriate request by invoking a method, known as an action method, and using the result to generate a response.

One aspect that I glossed over was how to select an action to execute when you receive a request. What makes a request "appropriate" for a given action? The process of mapping a request to a given handler is called *routing*.

> **DEFINITION**   *Routing* in ASP.NET Core is the process of mapping an incoming HTTP request to a specific handler. In MVC, the handler is an action method.

When you use the `MvcMiddleware` in your application, you configure a *router* to map any incoming requests to the MVC route handler. This takes in a URL and deconstructs it to determine which controller and action method it corresponds to. A simple routing pattern, for example, might determine that the `/product/view` URL maps to the `View` action on the `ProductController`, as shown in figure 5.2.

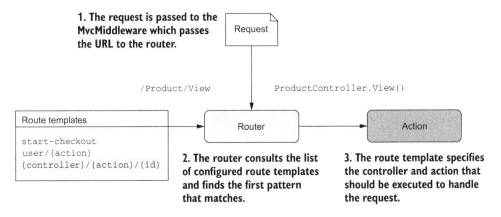

Figure 5.2   The router compares the request URL against a list of configured route templates to determine which action method to execute.

You can define many different routing patterns, each of which can set how a number of different URLs map to a variety of action methods. You can also have multiple patterns that all point to the same action method from different URLs. Alternatively, you could have a pattern that would only match a single URL, and maps to a single specific action.

Why use routing?

The first version of ASP.NET MVC introduced routing, back when ASP.NET Web Forms was the de facto Microsoft web framework. Routing was introduced as a way to decouple the URLs exposed by an application from the handlers that would generate the response.

Before routing, URLs typically mapped to a physical file on disk that would handle a request. For example, a request to the `/product.aspx` URL would map to a product.aspx file that would reside in the root folder of the application. This file would contain the logic and HTML generation code required to service the request. This had the advantage of being simple to reason about, and it was easy to see all the URLs your application exposed by viewing the project directory structure.

Unfortunately, this approach has several issues. One common problem is the renaming of files. If you needed to rename a file—maybe the filename had a typo in it—you were intrinsically changing the public URLs exposed to your users. Any previous links to the page would be broken, including any URLs within your own application that pointed to that page.

Another common complaint is the "ugly" URLs that are often required. The typical method of passing variable data when not using routing is to pass it in the query string, resulting in URLs such as `/product.aspx?id=3`. Compare this to equivalents using routing such as `/product/3` or `/product/apple-tv`, and hopefully the advantage here is clear. You can still use query string parameters in addition to routing, but your application doesn't have to use them to allow variable segments in the URL.

Fundamentally, routing enables you to explicitly define the URLs used to navigate your application, without tying you to a particular file layout or structure for your application. There are conventions that you'll generally use in your application to make defining the URLs easier, but you're free to vary the two independently if required.

In the `MvcMiddleware`, the outcome of successfully routing a request will be a single selected action and its associated controller. The middleware will then use this action to generate an appropriate response.

Exactly what your URLs will look like and the action methods they map to will obviously be specific to your application, but you'll see a number of typical conventions used. These can be applied to any number of applications, as many web apps follow a similar design.

In this chapter, imagine you've been asked to build an online currency converter for a bank. The application will have traditional pages like a homepage and a contact page, but the meat of the website will be a series of pages for viewing the exchange rates of different currencies, and for converting from one exchange rate to the next.

As you're going to be trying to attract as much traffic as possible to your web app, it's important that the URLs you use are easy to understand and make sense to both the customer and search engines. We're going to start with simple examples, and as we make our way through the chapter, we'll explore ways to improve the URLs your app exposes.

As a starter, you might choose to expose the URLs shown in table 5.1, which would map to the associated actions.

Table 5.1   Possible URLs and action method mappings for the customer section of a web application

Exposed URL	Maps to action method	Notes
`/currencies`	`CurrenciesController.List()`	Shows the list of all currencies you support
`/rates/view/1`	`RatesController.View(id)`	Shows the exchange rate for the currency with `id=1`
`/rates/edit/4`	`RatesController.Edit(id)`	Shows the form for editing the exchange rate of the currency with `id=4`
`/orders/customer/3`	`OrdersController.Customer(id)`	Shows all the previous orders for customer with `id=1`

I hope you can see that the URLs are all quite similar in structure—this is a common convention but is completely customizable, as you'll see later. The first segment of the URL maps to the name of the selected controller, and the second segment maps to the name of the action (except in the case of `List`, which was not explicitly specified). Additionally, the `id` for the action method has been automatically assigned from the URL.

This approach to creating URLs, where you directly infer the controller and action method from the segments of the URL is called *convention-based*. This approach is often used when building traditional HTML web applications using MVC, as it makes the structure easy to reason about for users and gives *hackable URLs*.

> **DEFINITION**   *Hackable URLs* refer to the ability to guess the URL for an action you want to perform, based on previous URLs you've seen. For example, based on the URLs in table 5.1, you might expect that the URL to view order number 4 would be `/orders/view/4`. This property is generally seen as desirable when building web applications.

The ability to set default values for URL segments when they aren't explicitly provided can be useful for allowing multiple URLs that point to the same action method. You saw it in table 5.1, where the `List` action was inferred from the `/currencies` URL. A common convention used by default in most ASP.NET Core MVC applications is that the homepage of your application is invoked using the `HomeController.Index()` action method. With the default conventions, any of the following URL paths will invoke this action:

- `/`
- `/home`
- `/home/index`

These conventions make building web applications simpler to reason about and maintain, as it's easy to infer which controller and action will be called.

> **TIP** Where possible, it's often a good idea to stick close to the default routing conventions. This will make your app easier to maintain in the long run, especially for other people looking at your code.

Depending on your requirements, a purely convention-based approach may not be sufficient to provide the URLs you need. What if you want a specific nonstandard URL for your checkout page, or you're only told the required URL after you've already built the controllers? In table 5.1, the `/currencies` URL is used to execute the `CurrenciesController.List` action; what if you want to change this so the action executes when you navigate to the `/view-currencies` URL instead?

Luckily, the routing system is sufficiently flexible that you can easily create URLs that map to arbitrary action methods. Here are two examples:

- `/start-checkout`—Could map to `CheckoutController.BillingAddress()`
- `/view/rates`—Could map to `RatesController.Index()`

Another use case for judicious use of routing is to make URLs more user friendly. This can be useful on sites where having a readable URL is important for search engine optimization, such as e-commerce sites, public websites, or blogs.

Take another look at table 5.1. The URL to view the current exchange rate for a currency was `/rates/view/1`. This would work fine, but it doesn't tell users much—which currency will this show? Will it be a historical view or the current rate?

Luckily, with routing it's easy to modify your exposed URLs without having to change your controllers and actions at all. Depending on your routing configuration, you could easily set the URL pointing to the `RatesController.View` action method to any of the following:

- `/rates/view/1`
- `/rates/USD`
- `/current-exchange-rate-for-USD`

I know which of these I'd most like to see in the URL bar of my browser, and which link I'd be most likely to click! I hope these examples have provided a glimpse of the benefits of setting up sensible routes for your application. In the next section, you'll see how to define your routes in ASP.NET Core, and we'll look at setting up the routing for the currency converter application in more detail.

5.2 Routing to MVC controllers and actions

Routing is a key part of the MVC design pattern in ASP.NET Core, as it connects the incoming request to a specific controller action. Note that this only happens if the request reaches the `MvcMiddleware` in the middleware pipeline. The request could be short-circuited before reaching the `MvcMiddleware`, either due to a previous middleware handling the request and generating a response (such as the `StaticFileMiddleware`, for example) or a previous middleware generating an error. In these two cases, the `Mvc-Middleware` won't run, and so no routing will occur.

If the request does make it to the `MvcMiddleware`, then the first step is to route the request to the required action method. You have two different ways to define these mappings in your application:

- Using global, conventional routing
- Using attribute routing

The convention-based routes are defined globally for your application. You can use convention-based routes to map all of the controllers and actions in your application, as long as your code conforms to the conventions you define. This provides a succinct and terse way to expose your action methods at easily understood URLs. Traditional HTML-based MVC web applications typically use this approach to routing.

You can also use attribute-based routes to tie a given URL to a specific action method by placing `[Route]` attributes on the action methods themselves. This provides a lot more flexibility as you can explicitly define what a URL for a given action method should be. This approach is more verbose than the convention-based approach, as it requires applying attributes to every action method in your application. Despite this, the additional flexibility it provides can often be useful, especially when building Web APIs.

Whichever technique you use, you'll define your expected URLs using *route templates*. These define the pattern of the URL you're expecting, with placeholders for parts that may vary.

> **DEFINITION** *Route templates* define the structure of known URLs in your application. They're strings with placeholders for variables that can contain optional values and map to controllers and actions.

A single route template can match a number of different URLs. The `/product/index` and `/product` URLs would both be matched by the `product/{action=index}` route template, for example, and the `/customer/1` and `/customer/2` URLs would both be matched by the `customer/{id}` route template. The route template syntax is powerful and contains many different features that are controlled by splitting a URL into multiple *segments*.

> **DEFINITION** A *segment* is a small contiguous section of a URL. It's separated from other URL segments by at least one character, often by the / character. Routing involves matching the segments of a URL to a route template.

For a single-route template, you can define

- Specific, expected strings
- Variable segments of the URL
- Optional segments of a URL
- Default values when an optional segment isn't provided
- Constraints on segments of a URL, for example, ensuring that it's numeric

Your application will often define a number of different route templates, perhaps defining different conventions for different sections of your application or providing more hackable URLs for certain important pages. You'll see how to define multiple conventional routes in the next section.

A typical conventional route will contain placeholders for different segments of a URL, where the controller and action are often inferred from the incoming URL. For example, the `{controller}/{action}` single route template would map both of the following URLs to their corresponding actions:

- `/customer/list`—To the `CustomerController.List()` action
- `/product/view`—To the `ProductsController.View()` action

These route templates are global, so you define them in Startup.cs when adding the `MvcMiddleware` to your pipeline, as you'll see in the next section. When routing an incoming URL, the middleware uses the full collection of defined conventional routes and attempts to determine the appropriate controller and action they correspond to.

For each request, the `MvcMiddleware` determines the action to execute by following the process set out in figure 5.3. For each defined route template, the router attempts to split the request's URL into segments corresponding to the template.

If the URL pattern matches, the router infers the controller and action from the URL. If this points to a valid action method, then routing is complete and the action method is executed. If the route template doesn't match the URL, or the specified controller-action pair doesn't exist, then the router moves on to the next defined template and attempts to match that, until no more routes are left.

If none of the route templates match the incoming URL, then the `MvcMiddleware` is unable to handle the request, so the request will continue along the middleware pipeline. As the `MvcMiddleware` is typically the last middleware in the pipeline, this normally means a 404 response will be generated.

The alternative to this conventional approach, in which routes are defined globally for your application, is to define the specific URL that a given action maps to. Conceptually, this is kind of the reverse approach; instead of taking a URL and working out which action it maps to, you take an action and generate the URL it maps to. When a request arrives, the middleware checks if it corresponds to any of these URLs.

As this approach is tied so closely to the action methods themselves, it's implemented using attributes placed on the action methods themselves, and hence is termed attribute routing.

You're free to combine both conventional and attribute routing in your applications. Typically, you'll use conventional routing for your MVC controllers serving HTML and attribute routing for your Web API controllers, where the ability to precisely control an action's associated route template can be useful.

> **TIP**   Use conventional routing for controllers returning HTML and attribute routing for Web API controllers where possible.

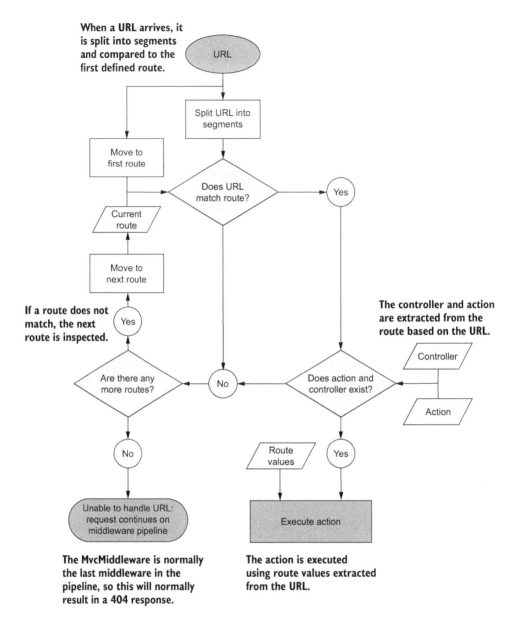

When a URL arrives, it is split into segments and compared to the first defined route.

If a route does not match, the next route is inspected.

The controller and action are extracted from the route based on the URL.

The MvcMiddleware is normally the last middleware in the pipeline, so this will normally result in a 404 response.

The action is executed using route values extracted from the URL.

Figure 5.3   Flow chart showing how the MvcMiddleware matches a URL against multiple routes to determine which action method to execute

In the next section, you'll learn how to define and use conventional routing in your application, but many of the concepts described apply equally when you're using attribute routing. I'll cover attribute routing and how it interacts with conventional routing in chapter 9, when I discuss building a Web API.

5.3 Routing using conventions

You configure conventional routing when you add the `MvcMiddleware` to your middleware pipeline with the `UseMvc` method. You've added this middleware several times so far in this book, so the following listing should look familiar.

Listing 5.1 Configuring the `MvcMiddleware` in the middleware pipeline

```
public class Startup
{
    public void ConfigureServices(IServiceCollection services)
    {
        services.AddMvc();
    }

    public void Configure(IApplicationBuilder app)
    {
        app.UseMvc(routes =>
        {
            routes.MapRoute(
                name: "default",
                template: "{controller=Home}/{action=Index}/{id?}");
        });
    }
}
```

When you call `UseMvc`, you also provide a lambda that defines all of the global conventional routes for your application. Each call to `MapRoute` on the provided instance of `IRouteBuilder` configures a new conventional route.

In the listing you can see you've added the default route template. This is a typical default added by most MVC project templates. It was created with a `name` so that it can be referenced from other parts of your program (as you'll see later in the section on URL generation), and a `template`, which is the route template used to match against URLs.

The route template itself has a rich syntax that splits a URL into a number of segments. In the next section, you'll learn about this syntax and see how it can be used to match a variety of URLs.

This example only lists a single route so all the URLs in this application would have to conform to the same general structure. To add more variety, and handle more specific requirements, it's perfectly acceptable to configure multiple global convention-based routes.

For the currency converter application, imagine a requirement exists to be able to view details about a particular currency (which country uses it and so on) by navigating to a URL that contains the currency code, such as `/currency/USD` or `/currency/GBP`.

In listing 5.2, you'll add an additional route for viewing currencies by name. When requests are made to the required URLs, this route will match and execute the `CurrenciesController.View()` action method.

Listing 5.2   Adding multiple routes to the `MvcMiddleware`

```
public class Startup
{
    public void ConfigureServices(IServiceCollection services)
    {
        services.AddMvc();
    }

    public void Configure(IApplicationBuilder app)
    {
        app.UseMvc(routes =>
        {
            routes.MapRoute(
                name: "currency_by_code",
                template: "currency/{code}",
                defaults: new { controller="Currencies", action="View" });
            routes.MapRoute(
                name: "default",
                template: "{controller=Home}/{action=Index}/{id?}");
        });
    }
}
```

> The name of the route can be used during **URL** generation, as you'll see later.

> The route template defines the structure of the URL to match.

> **NOTE** You may see these hardcoded route templates and be tempted to make them dynamic by loading them from a configuration file or similar. Although possible, this is generally unnecessary—the routes are intimately tied to both your app's structure and its public API, so hardcoding the values here is the norm.

The order in which you add the routes to the `IRouteBuilder` defines the order against which the routing infrastructure will attempt to match an incoming request. It will attempt to match the first route configured, and only if that isn't a match will it look at subsequent routes.

> **NOTE** It's important to consider the order of your conventional routes. You should list the most specific routes first, in order of decreasing specificity, until you get to the most broad/general route.

Figure 5.4 shows the consequence of not ordering your routes correctly. A set of route templates has been defined in a social networking application:

- `Photos/{action}/{id?}`—Routes to actions on `PhotoController` with the `{id}` ID
- `{controller}/{action}`—Default convention, will route to many actions
- `Person/{name}/View`—Routes to `PersonController`. `View()`, to view the detailed profile of the user with the `{name}` name

Notice the ordering here—you've added the default conventional router *before* the custom route for viewing the detailed profile information of a user.

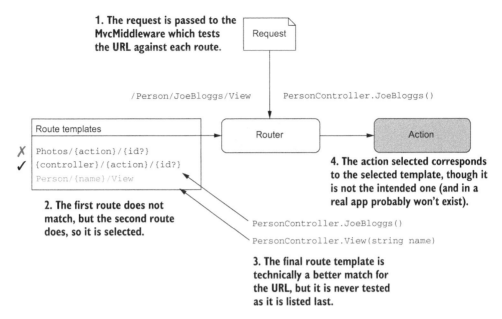

1. The request is passed to the MvcMiddleware which tests the URL against each route.

Request

`/Person/JoeBloggs/View`   `PersonController.JoeBloggs()`

Route templates   Router   Action

✗ `Photos/{action}/{id?}`
✓ `{controller}/{action}/{id?}`
   `Person/{name}/View`

4. The action selected corresponds to the selected template, though it is not the intended one (and in a real app probably won't exist).

2. The first route does not match, but the second route does, so it is selected.

`PersonController.JoeBloggs()`
`PersonController.View(string name)`

3. The final route template is technically a better match for the URL, but it is never tested as it is listed last.

Figure 5.4   The order in which conventional routes are configured in your application controls the order in which they're matched to a URL during routing.

Imagine your app receives a request to the `/Person/JoeBloggs/View` URL. This incoming URL is a perfect match for the final route, but because the route preceding it is more general, the final route is never tested. Consequently, the `JoeBloggs()` action method is executed instead of the method you might expect, `View(string name)`, with `name = "JoeBloggs"`. To fix this problem, you can swap the order of the last two routes. This is obviously a somewhat contrived example—it's unlikely you'll have an action method called `JoeBloggs`!—but hopefully the principle is clear.

Every conventional route must define the controller and action to run when a URL matches the route. This can be done either using the route template syntax, in which the controller and action name are taken directly from the URL, or by using default values, as you'll see in the next section.

5.3.1   *Understanding route templates*

When you define a route during the configuration of the `MvcMiddleware`, you specify a route template that defines the URL pattern the route will match. The route template has a rich, flexible syntax, but a simple example is shown in figure 5.5.

A router parses a route template by splitting it into a number of segments. A segment is typically separated by the `/` character, but it can be any valid character. Each segment is either

- *A literal value*—For example, `api` in figure 5.5
- *A route parameter*—For example, `{controller}` and `{action}` in figure 5.5

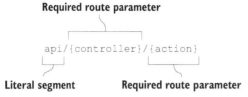

Figure 5.5   A simple route template showing a literal segment and required route parameters

Literal values must be matched exactly (ignoring case) by the request URL. If you need to match a particular URL exactly, you can use a template consisting only of literals.

Imagine your boss tells you the currency converter app must have a contact page, which should be at the `/about/contact` URL. You could achieve this using the `about/contact` route template. This route template consists of only literal values, and so would only match this single URL. None of the following URLs would match this route template:

- `/about`
- `/about-us/contact`
- `/about/contact/email`

> **WARNING**   Note that although the URL paths start with a `/` character when a request is made to your application, the route templates don't! If you include the `/` character, you'll get an error at runtime when routing runs.

Literal segments are often more useful when used in conjunction with route parameters. Route parameters are sections of a URL that may vary but still be a match for the template. Route parameters are defined by giving them a name, and placing them in braces, such as `{controller}` or `{action}`. When used in this way, parameters are still required, so there must be a segment in the request URL that they correspond to, but the value can vary.

This ability to vary gives you great flexibility. For example, you could use the simple `{controller}/{action}` route template in the currency converter application to map the following request URLs:

- `/currencies/list`—Where `controller=currencies` and `action=list`
- `/rates/view`—Where `controller=rates` and `action=view`

But note that this template would *not* map the following URLs:

- `/currencies/`—No action parameter specified
- `/rates/view/USD`—Extra URL segment not found in route template

The literal segment and route parameters are the two cornerstones of the ASP.NET Core router. With these two concepts, it's possible to build all manner of URLs for your application.

When a route template defines a route parameter, and the route matches a URL, the value associated with the parameter is captured and stored in a dictionary of values associated with the request. These *route values* typically drive other behavior in the MvcMiddleware, such as model binding.

> **DEFINITION** *Route values* are the values extracted from a URL based on a given route template. Each route parameter in a template will have an associated route value and is stored as a string pair in a dictionary. They can be used during model binding, as you'll see in chapter 6.

The most important use of route parameters in conventional routing is for determining the controller and action that a route is associated with. Specifically, a conventional route *must* specify the {controller} and {action} route parameters so that the router can map the URL to an action to execute. It does this by first attempting to find a controller in your application named the same as the controller route value, which has an action with the same name as the action route value (ignoring case sensitivity).

> **WARNING** The controller and action route values *must* be able to be calculated for every route template so that the router knows which action to look for.

As well as the basic features of literals and variable route parameter segments, route templates can use a number of additional features to build more powerful conventions, and hence more varied URLs. These can let you have optional URL segments, can provide default values when a segment isn't specified, or can place additional constraints on the value that's valid for a given route parameter. The next section takes a look at some of these, and ways you can apply them.

5.3.2 *Using optional and default values*

In the previous section, you saw a simple route template, with a literal segment and two required routing parameters. In figure 5.6, you can see a more complex route that uses a number of additional features.

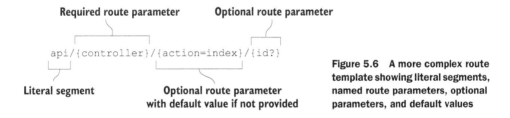

Figure 5.6 A more complex route template showing literal segments, named route parameters, optional parameters, and default values

The literal api segment and the required {controller} parameter are the same as you saw in figure 5.5. The {action} parameter looks similar, but it has a default value specified for it, index. If the URL doesn't contain a segment corresponding to the action parameter, then the router will use the index value instead.

The final segment of figure 5.6, {id?}, defines an optional route parameter called id. This segment of the URL is optional—if present, the router will capture the value for the id parameter; if it isn't there, then it won't create a route value for id.

You can specify any number of route parameters in your templates, and these values will be available to you when it comes to model binding. Remember that only the {controller} and {action} parameters are compulsory, and that the router uses only these values to decide which action to execute.

> **NOTE** The router uses only the {controller} and {action} parameters to determine which action to execute. Model binding can use any other route parameter values, but these don't affect action selection.

The complex route template of figure 5.6 allows you to match a greater variety of URLs by making some parameters optional and providing a default for action. Table 5.2 shows some of the possible URLs this template would match, and the corresponding route values the router would create.

Table 5.2   URLs that would match the template of figure 5.6 and their corresponding route values

URL	Route values
api/product/view/3	controller=product, action=view, id = 3
api/product/view	controller=product, action=view
api/product	controller=product, action=index
api/customer/list	controller=customer, action=list
api/order	controller=order, action=index
api/order/edit/O-123	controller=order, action=edit, id = O-123

Note that there's no way to specify a value for the optional id parameter without also specifying the action and controller parameters. You can't put an optional parameter before a required parameter, as there would be no way of specifying the required parameter only. Imagine your route template had an optional controller parameter:

```
{controller?}/{action}
```

Now try to think of a URL that would specify the action parameter, but not the controller. It can't be done!

Using default values allows you to have multiple ways to call the same URL, which may be desirable in some cases. Remember the default MVC route template from listing 5.1?

```
{controller=Home}/{action=Index}/{id?}
```

The meaning of this template should be a little more obvious now. It uses default values for the {controller} and {action} parameters, which means multiple URLs can get you to the homepage of the application (typically the action HomeController .Index()):

- /
- /Home
- /Home/Index

Each of these URLs will execute the same action, as they will all match the default route template.

By using default values and optional constraints, you can start to add some more interesting URLs to your currency converter application. For example, you could add a route to view currencies, where if you don't specify a currency it assumes USD using

```
{controller}/{currency=USD}/{action=view}
```

I've added two default values here, so you could map any of the following URLs:

- `/rates`—`controller=rates, action=view, currency=USD`
- `/rates/GBP`—`controller=rates, action=view, currency=GBP`
- `/rates/USD/edit`—`controller=rates, action=edit, currency=USD`
- `/currencies`—`controller=currencies, action=view, currency=USD`

Adding default values allows you to use shorter and more memorable URLs in your application for common URLs, but still have the flexibility to match a variety of other routes.

5.3.3 *Adding additional constraints to route parameters*

By defining whether a route parameter is required or optional, and whether it has a default value, you can match a broad range of URLs with a pretty terse template syntax. Unfortunately, in some cases this can end up being a little *too* broad. Routing only matches URL segments to route parameters, it doesn't know anything about the data that you're expecting those route parameters to contain. Considering the `{controller=Home}/{action=Index}/{id?}` default template, the following URLs would all match:

- `/Home/Edit/test`
- `/Home/Edit/123`
- `/1/2/3`

These URLs are all perfectly valid given the template's syntax, but some might cause problems for your application. It might surprise you initially that all of those URLs also match the currency route template you defined at the end of the last section:

```
{controller}/{currency=USD}/{action=view}
```

These URLs all have three segments, and so the router happily assigns route values and matches the template when you probably don't want it to!

- `/Home/Edit/test`—`controller=Home, currency=Edit, action=test`
- `/Home/Edit/123`—`controller=Home, currency=Edit, action=123`
- `/1/2/3`—`controller=1, currency=2, action=3`

Typically, the router passes route values other than `controller` and `action` as parameters to action methods through a process called model binding (which we'll discuss in detail in the next chapter). For example, an action method with the `public`

IActionResult Edit(int id) signature would obtain the id parameter from the id route value. If the id route parameter ends up assigned a noninteger value from the URL, then you'll get an exception when it's bound to the integer id action method parameter.

To avoid this problem, it's possible to add additional *constraints* to a route template that must be satisfied for a URL to be considered a match. Constraints can be defined in a route template for a given route parameter using : (a colon). For example, {id:int} would add the IntRouteConstraint to the id parameter. For a given URL to be considered a match, the value assigned to the id route value must be convertible to an integer.

You can apply a large number of route constraints to route templates to ensure that route values are convertible to appropriate types. You can also check more advanced constraints, for example, that an integer value has a particular minimum value, or that a string value has a maximum length. Table 5.3 describes a number of the possible constraints available, but you can find a more complete list online at http://mng.bz/U11Q.

Table 5.3 A few route constraints and their behavior when applied

Constraint	Example	Match examples	Description
int	{qty:int}	123, -123, 0	Matches any integer
Guid	{id:guid}	d071b70c-a812-4b54-87d2-7769528e2814	Matches any Guid
decimal	{cost:decimal}	29.99, 52, -1.01	Matches any decimal value
min(value)	{age:min(18)}	18, 20	Matches integer values of 18 or greater
length(value)	{name:length(6)}	andrew,123456	Matches string values with a length of 6
optional int	{qty:int?}	123, -123, 0, null	Optionally matches any integer
optional int max(value)	{qty:int:max(10)?}	3, -123, 0, null	Optionally matches any integer of 10 or less

> **TIP** As you can see from table 5.3, you can also combine multiple constraints; place a colon between them or use an optional mark (?) at the end.

Using constraints allows you to narrow down the URLs that a given route template will match. Figure 5.7 shows an enhanced version of the flow chart shown in figure 5.3. After the router matches a URL to a route template, it interrogates the constraints to check that they're all valid. If they are, then the router will continue to attempt to find an appropriate action method. If the constraints aren't valid, then the router will check the next defined route template instead.

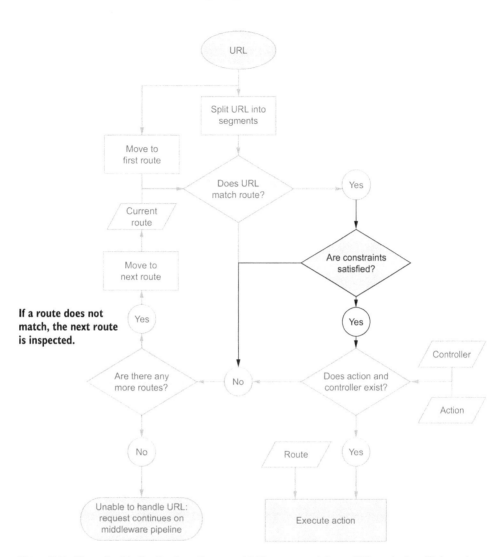

Figure 5.7 Flow chart indicating how the `MvcMiddleware` matches a URL against multiple routes to determine the action method to execute when a route template uses constraints

WARNING Don't use route constraints to validate general input, for example to check that an email address is valid. Doing so will result in 404 "Page not found" errors, which will be confusing for the user.

You can use a simple constraint on the currency converter route to ensure that the currency route parameter only matches strings of length 3 using a simple length constraint:

```
{controller}/{currency=USD:length(3)}/{action=view}
```

Although not foolproof, this should help ensure the router only maps appropriate URLs to this route.

5.3.4   *Defining default values and constraints using anonymous objects*

All of the examples shown in this section on route templates have defined default values and route constraints inline as part of the route template, using the {action= view} and {id:int} syntax.

It's also possible to specify constraints and defaults separately when creating your routes, by using different overloads of MapRoute and anonymous objects. For example, the definition of your currency converter route template, in which constraints and defaults are defined inline, looks like the following at the moment:

```
routes.MapRoute(
        name: "default",
        template: "{controller}/}/{currency=USD:length(3)}/{action=view}");
```

This same route could also be defined using an alternative overload of MapRoute.

Listing 5.3   Defining route constraints and default values using anonymous types

```
routes.MapRoute(
        name: "default",
        template: "{controller}/{currency}/{action}",      Required. The raw route
                                                            template, without
        defaults: new {                                    defaults or constraints
            currency="USD",            Optional. The default values to
            action="View"             use when a parameter is missing
        },
        constraints: new {                       Optional. Constraints
            currency = new LengthRouteConstraint(3)   to apply to route
        });                                      parameters
```

The inline approach to specifying constraints is normally sufficient for most route templates and is generally preferable for readability. But some route templates can't be defined using the inline approach, and you must use the anonymous type approach.

You might not want users to have to specify "currencies" at the start of the URL (for example, /currencies/USD), so that the router knows which controller to use. You can use anonymous objects to avoid this by removing controller from the template and specifying a default value for it.

Listing 5.4   Using anonymous types to set default values of missing parameters

```
routes.MapRoute(
        name: "currencies",
        template: "{currency}/{action}",      The controller parameter is set as
        defaults: new {                       required, but can't be changed as it's
            controller=currencies,           no longer in the template.
            currency="USD",
            action="View"
        },
```

```
constraints: new {
    currency = new LengthRouteConstraint(3)
});
```

Another common case is when you want to have a highly customized URL for a particularly important action method. You might want the `/checkout` URL to point to the `PaymentController.StartProcess()` action method. You could define a route to perform this mapping in a number of ways, one of which is shown here.

Listing 5.5 Using anonymous types to set the default values of missing parameters

```
routes.MapRoute(
    name: "start_checkout",              The template will match a
    template: "checkout",                single URL only: /checkout.
    defaults: new { controller="Payment", action="StartProcess" });

                                          The controller and
                                          action must be defined.
```

As we've already discussed, you must always define the `controller` and `action` route parameters for a given route, so the middleware can work out which action to execute. By using the `defaults` anonymous type, you can ensure the route is valid without having to include the name of the controller or the action in your template definition or URL.

We're coming to the end of our look at conventional route templates, but before we move on there's one more type of parameter to think about, the catch-all parameter.

5.3.5 Matching arbitrary URLs with the catch-all parameter

You've already seen how route templates take URL segments and attempt to match them to parameters or literal strings. These segments normally split around the slash character, `/`, so the route parameters themselves won't contain a slash. What do you do if you need them to, or you don't know how many segments you're going to have?

Going back to the currency converter application—you've already defined a route template that will match the `/USD/view` URL and will execute the action to view the USD currency. But what if you also want the URL to contain all the currencies to show exchange rates for? Here are some examples:

- `/USD/convert/GBP`—Show USD currency with exchange rates to GBP
- `/USD/convert/GBP/EUR`—Show USD currency with exchange rates to GBP and EUR
- `/USD/convert/GBP/EUR/CAD`—Show USD with rates for GBP, EUR, and CAD

If you want to support showing any number of currencies, then you need a way of capturing everything shown after the `convert` segment. Listing 5.6 shows how you can capture all these segments in a single parameter called `others` by using a catch-all parameter.

```
routes.MapRoute(
        name: "convert_currencies",
        template:
    "{currency}/convert/{*others}",
        defaults: new { controller="currencies", action="View" });
```

> The template consists of a parameter for currency, a literal segment, and a catch-all parameter.

> The template doesn't specify controller or action; you must define them here.

Catch-all parameters can be declared using an asterisk inside the parameter definition, like {*others}. This will match the remaining unmatched portion of a URL, including any slashes or other characters that aren't part of earlier parameters. They can also match an empty string. For the USD/convert/GBP/EUR URL, the value of others would be "GBP/EUR".

In the listing, I've specified a fixed literal segment, "convert", so that part of the URL isn't included in the catch-all title parameter. I've used the anonymous type approach again for specifying the controller and action parameters.

An important point to bear in mind with catch-all parameters is that they're greedy, and more general than most other routes. This can result in a catch-all route intercepting a URL intended for a more specific route. To get around this, define the catch-all route after the more specific routes.

> **TIP**   Take particular care when ordering catch-all routes. They will capture the whole unmatched portion of a URL. Counteract greedy routes by defining them later in your Startup.Configure method.

Convention-based routing is normally the standard approach taken when creating an HTML-based web application. Conventional routing generally makes your application's controller structure easy to understand and browse, which is mirrored in the URL surface for the application. Conveniently, they're also succinct to define, with a single route definition serving for many different controllers and action methods.

Sometimes however, and especially when building a Web API, you might find yourself creating more and more route templates that map to a single action. In those cases, attribute routing may be a better approach. I'll show how to use attribute routing in chapter 9.

5.4   *Handling multiple matching actions for a route*

Whether you're using conventional routing or attribute routing, you'll often find that you want to match a single URL to two different action methods. One of the most common situations is when you're submitting a form.

In standard web application forms, a browser makes an HTTP GET request to a page to fetch the initial form from the server and display it to the user. A user might request the login page for a website using /Account/Login. The user then fills in the form, and submits the data using an HTTP POST request to the same URL.

Up to this point, I've said that the router uses only the URL to determine the selected controller and action, and that only a single action may be executed. If that's the case, how can this possibly work?! Well, without further work, it won't. The Mvc-Middleware would throw an exception when the URL is requested saying "Multiple actions matched."

Luckily, ASP.NET Core provides a number of attributes you can use to pick a winning action method, when the router would normally end up selecting multiple actions. Listing 5.7 shows an AccountController with the two action methods you want to disambiguate. It's typical for the two corresponding methods to have the same name, where the POST action takes additional parameters corresponding to the form values entered by the user.

Listing 5.7   Selecting an action using the HttpPostAttribute

```
public class AccountController : Controller
{                                              As the method has no Http attribute,
    public IActionResult Login()       ◁───    it can match GET or POST requests.
    {
        /* method implementation*/             Indicates the method is a match
    }                                          for POST requests only.

    [HttpPost]                         ◁────
    public IActionResult Login(string username, string password)   ◁────────
    {
        /* method implementation*/             The method names are identical,
    }                                          hence both methods match the
}                                              same /Account/Login URL.
```

In order to select one action over the other for a given request, you've decorated the second method with an HttpPostAttribute. This limits the type of requests an action can match. In this case, the [HttpPost] attribute indicates that the second Login method is a match for POST requests only, and not any other HTTP methods.

For the initial GET request, there's now only one method that's a match—the first action in the controller—so this action executes to generate the response. The user can then enter their details, press submit, and send a POST request.

Now, both methods can still handle POST requests—the first method can handle any HTTP method and the second method can handle only POST requests. But an action method with an IActionContraint attribute "trumps" an action method without one. The second action method "wins" the contest and executes in response to the POST request. All the common HTTP methods, such as GET, POST, PUT, and DELETE, have IActionContraint HTTP methods.

NOTE   Use types of IActionConstraint, such as [HttpPost] and [HttpGet], to provide precedence to one action method over another where they would match the same URL.

That brings us to the end of the discussion of mapping URLs to action methods when the MvcMiddleware receives a request. One of the most important things to keep in mind when configuring your routing is to stick to a logical set of URLs. Doing so will make it easier for you, as well as your clients, to reason about which action a URL will execute.

Mapping URLs to actions is only half of the responsibilities of the routing system. It's also used to *generate* URLs so that you can easily reference your actions from other parts of your application.

5.5   *Generating URLs from route parameters*

One of the by-products of using the routing infrastructure in ASP.NET Core is that your URLs can be somewhat fluid. If you rename a controller and you're using convention-based routing, then the URLs associated with the actions will also change. For example, renaming the `List` action to `Index` on the `CurrencyController` would cause the URL for the action to change from `/Currency/List` to `/Currency/Index`.

Trying to manually manage these links within your app would be a recipe for heartache, broken links, and 404s. If your URLs were hardcoded, then you'd have to remember to do a find-and-replace with every rename!

Luckily, you can use the routing infrastructure to generate appropriate URLs dynamically at runtime instead, freeing you from the burden. Conceptually, this is almost an exact reverse of the process of mapping a URL to an action method, as shown in figure 5.8. Instead of taking a URL, finding the first route satisfied and splitting it into route values, the router takes in the route values and finds the first route it can use to build a URL with them.

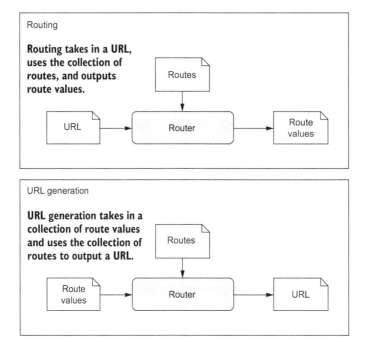

Figure 5.8   A comparison between routing and URL generation. Routing takes in a URL and generates route values, but URL generation uses a route value to generate a URL.

5.5.1 Generating URLs based on an action name

You might need to generate URLs in a number of places in your application, and one common location is in your controllers. The following listing shows how you could generate a link to the view page for a currency, using the `Url` helper from the `Controller` base class.

Listing 5.8 Generating a URL using `IUrlHelper` and the action name

```
public class CurrencyController : Controller        ◁──┐  Deriving from Controller gives
{                                                         access to the Url property.
    public IActionResult Index()
    {
        var url = Url.Action("View", "Currency", new { code = "USD" });  ◁──┐
        return Content($${"The URL is {url}");  ◁──┐
    }
    public IActionResult View(string code)  ◁─┐
    {
        /* method implementation*/
    }                              The URL generated
}                                  will route to the
                                   View action method.
```

Deriving from Controller gives access to the Url property.

You provide the controller and action name, along with any additional route values.

The URL generated will route to the View action method.

With the default convention, this will return "The URL is /Currency/View/USD".

The `Url` property is an instance of `IUrlHelper` that allows you to easily generate URLs for your application by referencing other action methods. It exposes an `Action` method to which you pass the name of the action method, the name of the controller, and any additional route data. The helper will then generate a URL based on the collection of registered conventional routes.

> **TIP** Instead of using strings for the name of the action method, use the C# 6 `nameof` operator to make the value refactor-safe, for example, `nameof(View)`.

The `IUrlHelper` has a number of different overloads of the `Action` method, some of which don't require you to specify all the routing values. If you're routing to an action in the same controller, you can omit the controller name when generating the URL. The helper uses *ambient values* from the current request and overrides these with any specific values you provide.

> **DEFINITION** Ambient values are the route values for the current request. They always include `controller` and `action` but can also include any additional route values set when the action was initially located using routing.

In listing 5.8, as well as providing the controller and action name, I passed in an anonymous object, `new { code = "USD" }`. This object provides additional route values when generating the URL, in this case setting the `code` parameter to `"USD"`. The `IUrlHelper` will use these values when finding the correct route to use for generation. It will pick the first route for which it has all the required route parameters.

If a selected route explicitly includes the defined route value in its definition, such as in the `"{controller}/{action}/{code}"` route template, then the route value will be used in the URL path, such as in the example, `/currency/view/GBP`.

If a route doesn't contain the route value explicitly, such as in the `"{controller}/{action}"` template, then the route value is appended as additional data as part of the *query string*, for example `/currency/view?code=GBP`.

> **DEFINITION**   The *query string* is part of a URL that contains additional data that doesn't fit in the path. It isn't used by the routing infrastructure for identifying which action to execute, but can be used for model binding, as you'll see in chapter 6.

Generating URLs based on the action you want to execute is convenient, and the usual approach taken in most cases. Unfortunately, sometimes the nature of conventional routing means that generating the correct URL based on route parameters can be tricky. This is often the case when you have multiple conventional routes that overlap in the URLs they cover. In these cases, routing based on a specific route's name can sometimes be easier.

5.5.2   Generating URLs based on a route name

The `IUrlHelper` class exposes the `RouteUrl` method for generating URLs based on a specific named route. This takes the name of a route and uses the provided route values to generate a URL specifically for that route. For example, if you had defined the name `"view_currency"` when declaring the routes in Startup.cs

```
routes.MapRoute(
      name: "view_currency",
      template: "{controller=currency}/{action=view}/{code}");
```

then you could use this during URL generation.

Listing 5.9   Generating a URL using a named route

```
public class CurrencyController : Controller
{
    public IActionResult Index()
    {
        var url = Url.RouteUrl("view_currency", new { code = "GBP" });

        return Content("The URL is {url}");
    }

    public IActionResult View (string code)
    {
        /* method implementation*/
    }
}
```

You provide the name of the route to use, along with any additional route values.

This will use the specified route, returning "The URL is /Currency/View/GBP".

The URL generated will route to the View action method.

Using named routes can sometimes simplify the process of generating URLs, as it avoids issues introduced by overlapping URLs in your route templates. The URL generation process uses your defined list of routes in order to determine which URL to generate—if the route you need is at the end of registered routes, then referencing it by name can often be easier.

5.5.3 Generating URLs with ActionResults

Generating a URL from within your controllers is less common than you might think—it's more usual to generate a URL as part of the action result returned by an action method. This is normally the case when you want to redirect a user's browser to a particular action or route. Conceptually, it's the same as generating a URL using the Url property and sending the URL back as a redirect response to the user.

Listing 5.13 shows two ways to generate URLs from an ActionResult. The RedirectToAction method takes in action and controller names, as well as route parameters, and generates a URL in the same way as the Url.Action method. Similarly, the RedirectToRoute is equivalent to Url.RouteUrl.

> **Listing 5.10   Generating redirect URLs from an `ActionResult`**

```
public class CurrencyController : Controller
{
    public IActionResult RedirectingToAnActionMethod()
    {
        return RedirectToAction("View", "Currency", new { id = 5 });
    }

    public IActionResult RedirectingToARoute()
    {
        return RedirectToRoute("view_currency", new { code = "GBP" });
    }

    public IActionResult RedirectingToAnActionInTheSameController()
    {
        return RedirectToAction("Index");
    }

    public IActionResult Index()
    {
        /* method implementation */
    }
}
```

The RedirectToRoute method generates a RedirectToRouteResult with the generated URL.

Only the action name is specified, so the current controller will be used to generate the URL.

The RedirectToAction method generates a RedirectToActionResult with the generated URL.

As with the IUrlHelper, you can use a number of different overloads to generate the correct URL. The listing shows an example of providing the action name to the RedirectToAction method. This will use the ambient value of the controller parameter, `"Currency"` in this case, when generating URLs. Consequently, it will create a URL pointing to the `CurrencyController.Index` action.

As well as generating URLs from your controllers, you'll find you need to generate URLs when building HTML in your views. This is necessary in order to provide navigation links in your web application. You'll see how to achieve this when we look at Razor Tag Helpers in chapter 8, but the approach is nearly the same as you've already seen here.

Congratulations, you've made it all the way through this detailed discussion on routing! Routing is one of those topics that people often get stuck on when they come to building an application, which can be frustrating. You'll revisit the other approach to routing, attribute routing, when I describe how to create Web APIs in chapter 9, but rest assured, you've already covered all the tricky details in this chapter!

The most important thing to focus on is keeping your routes simple. If you do, then you'll find it much easier to reason about the URLs in your application and avoid giving yourself a headache trying to work out why the wrong action methods are executing!

In chapter 6, we'll dive into the M of MVC—the various models of ASP.NET Core. You'll see how the route values generated during routing are bound to your action method parameters, and perhaps more importantly, how to validate the values you're provided.

Summary

- Routing is the process of mapping an incoming request URL to an action method that will execute to generate a response.

- Route templates define the structure of known URLs in your application. They're strings with placeholders for variables that can contain optional values and map to controllers and actions.

- Routes can be defined either globally using conventional routing or can be mapped explicitly to an action using attribute routing.

- An application can have many different routes. The router will attempt to find the first route where the route template matches the incoming URL.

- It's important to consider the order of your conventional routes. You should list the most specific routes first, in order of decreasing specificity, until you get to the most broad/general route.

- Route parameters are variable values extracted from a request's URL.

- Route parameters can be optional and can have default values used when they're missing.

- Route parameters can have constraints that restrict the possible values allowed. If a route parameter doesn't match its constraints, the route isn't considered a match.

- The `controller` and `action` route values *must* be able to be calculated for every route template. They can either be matched from the URL or using default values.
- Don't use route constraints as general input validators. Use them to disambiguate between two similar routes.
- Use a catch-all parameter to capture the remainder of a URL into a route value.
- The `[HttpPost]` and `[HttpGet]` attributes allow choosing between actions based on the request's HTTP method when two actions correspond to the same URL.
- You can use the routing infrastructure to generate internal URLs for your application.
- The `IUrlHelper` can be used to generate URLs as a string based on an action name or on the name of a specific route.
- You can use the `RedirectToAction` and `RedirectToRoute` methods to generate URLs while also generating a redirect response.

The binding model: retrieving and validating user input

This chapter covers

- Using request values to create a binding model
- Customizing the model binding process
- Validating user input using `DataAnnotations` attributes

In chapter 5, I showed you how to define a route with parameters—perhaps for the day in a calendar or the unique ID for a product page. But say a user requests a given product page—what then? Similarly, what if the request includes data from a form, to change the name of the product, for example? How do you handle that request and access the values the user provided?

In the first half of this chapter, we'll look at using a *binding model* to retrieve those parameters from the request so that you can use them in your action methods. You'll see how to take the data posted in the form or in the URL and *bind* them to C# objects. These objects are passed to your action methods as method parameters so you can do something useful with them—return the correct diary entry or change a product's name, for instance.

Once your code is executing in an action method, you might be forgiven for thinking that you can happily use the binding model without any further thought. Hold on now, where did that data come from? From a user—you know they can't be trusted! The second half of the chapter focuses on how to make sure that the values provided by the user are valid and make sense for your app.

You can think of the binding model as the *input* model to an action method, taking the user's raw HTTP request and making it available to your code by populating a "plain old CLR object" (POCO). Once your action method has run, you're all set up to use the *output* models in ASP.NET Core's implementation of MVC—the view models and API models. These are used to generate a response to the user's request. We'll cover them in chapters 7 and 9.

Before we go any further, let's recap the MVC design pattern and how binding models fit into ASP.NET Core.

6.1 Understanding the M in MVC

MVC is all about the separation of concerns. The premise is that by isolating each aspect of your application to focus on a single responsibility, it reduces the interdependencies in your system. This makes it easier to make changes without affecting other parts of your application.

The classic MVC design pattern has three independent components:

- *Controller*—Calls methods on the model and selects a view.
- *View*—Displays a representation of data that makes up the model.
- *Model*—The data to display and the methods for updating itself.

In this representation, there's only one model, which represents all the business logic for the application as well as how to update and modify its internal state. ASP.NET Core has multiple models, which takes the single responsibility principle one step further than some views of MVC.

In chapter 4, we looked at an example of a to-do list application that can show all the to-do items for a given category and username. With this application, you make a request to a URL that's routed using `todo/list/{category}/{username}`. This will then return a response showing all the relevant to-do items, as shown in figure 6.1.

The application uses the same MVC constructs you've already seen, such as routing to an action method, as well as a number of different *models*. Figure 6.2 shows how a request to this application maps to the MVC design pattern and how it generates the final response, including additional details around the model binding and validation of the request.

ASP.NET Core MVC has a number of different models, most of which are POCOs, and the application model, which is more of a concept around a collection of services.

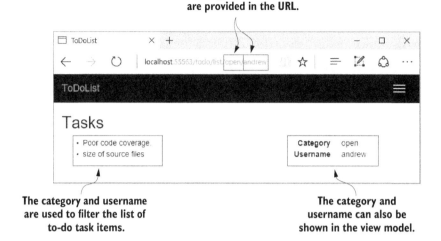

**The category and username
are provided in the URL.**

**The category and username
are used to filter the list of
to-do task items.**

**The category and
username can also be
shown in the view model.**

**Figure 6.1   A basic to-do list application that displays to-do list items. A user can filter
the list of items by changing the** `category` **and** `username` **parameters in the URL.**

Each of the models in ASP.NET Core MVC is responsible for handling a different aspect of the overall request:

- *Binding model*—This includes information that's explicitly provided by the user when making a request, as well as additional contextual data. This includes things like route parameters parsed from the URL, the query string, and form or JSON data in the request body. The binding model itself is one or more .NET objects that you define. They're passed to a controller's action method as parameters when it's executed.

  For this example, the binding model would include the name of the category, `open`, and the username, `Andrew`. The `MvcMiddleware` inspects the binding model before the action method executes to check whether the provided values are valid, though the method will execute even if they're not.

- *Application model*—This is typically a whole group of different services and classes—anything needed to perform some sort of business action in your application. It may include the domain model (which represents the thing your app is trying to describe) and database models (which represent the data stored in a database), as well as any other additional services.

  In the to-do list application, the application model would contain the complete list of to-do items, probably stored in a database, and would know how to find only those to-do items in the `open` category assigned to `Andrew`.

  Modeling your domain is a huge topic, with many different possible approaches, so it's outside the scope of this book, but we'll touch briefly on creating database models in chapter 11.

- *View model*—This contains the data needed by the view to generate a response, such as the list of to-dos in the open category assigned to Andrew. It often also contains extra data, such as the total number of to-dos in all categories.
- *API model*—A variation on the view model, in which the whole model represents the data to return. Web API controllers use this to generate the final response to return to the caller, normally in the form of a JSON or XML response. You'll see how to create and use API models in chapter 9.

The main difference between API models and view models is that API models contain only the data to return, whereas view models often contain

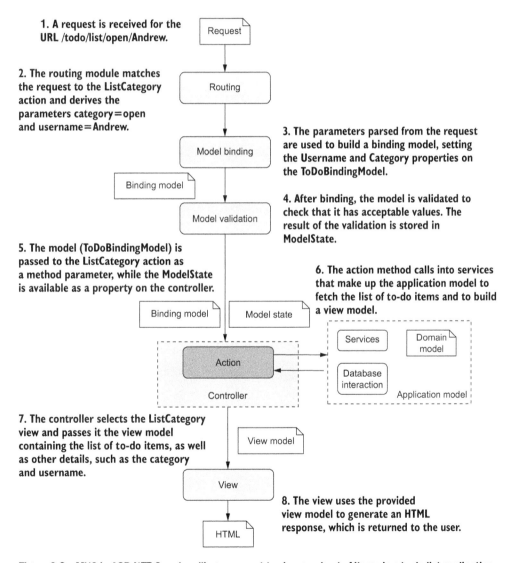

Figure 6.2   **MVC in ASP.NET Core handling a request to view a subset of items in a to-do list application**

additional information related to generating the view. You define both types of model, and both can be POCOs.

These four types of models make up the bulk of any MVC application, handling the input, business logic, and output of each controller action. Imagine you have an e-commerce application that allows users to search for clothes by sending requests to the URL `/search/{query}` URL, where `{query}` holds their search term:

- *Binding model*—Would take the `{query}` route parameter from the URL and any values posted in the request body (maybe a sort order, or number of items to show), and bind them to a C# class, which acts as a throwaway data transport class. This would be passed as a method parameter to the action method when it's invoked.
- *Application model*—The services and classes that perform the logic. When invoked by the action method, this would load all the clothes that match the query, applying the necessary sorting and filters, and return the results back to the controller.
- *View model*—The values provided by the application model would be added to the view model, along with other metadata, such as the total number of items available, or whether the user can currently check out.

The important point about all these models is that their responsibilities are well-defined and distinct. Keeping them separate and avoiding reuse helps to ensure your application stays agile and easy to update.

Now that you've been properly introduced to the various models in ASP.NET Core MVC, it's time to focus on how to use them. This chapter looks at the binding models that are built from incoming requests—how are they created, and where do the values come from?

6.2 *From request to model: making the request useful*

By now, you should be familiar with the `MvcMiddleware` handling a request by executing an action method on a controller. You've also already seen a number of action methods, such as

```
public IActionResult EditProduct(ProductModel product)
```

Action methods are normal C# methods (there's nothing particularly special about them), so the ASP.NET Core framework needs to be able to call them in the usual way. When action methods accept parameters as part of their method signature, such as the preceding `product`, the framework needs a way to generate those objects. Where exactly do they come from, and how are they created?

I've already hinted that in most cases, these values come from the request itself. But the HTTP request that the server receives is a series of strings—how does the `MvcMiddleware` turn that into a .NET object? This is where *model binding* comes in.

DEFINITION   *Model binding* extracts values from a request and uses them to create .NET objects that are passed as method parameters to the action being executed.

The model binder is responsible for looking through the request that comes in and finding values to use. It then creates objects of the appropriate type and assigns these values to your model in a process called *binding*. These objects are then provided to your action methods as method parameters.

  This binding is a one-way population of an object from the request, not the two-way data-binding that desktop or mobile development sometimes uses.

NOTE   Some method parameters can also be created using dependency injection, instead of from the request. For more details on dependency injection, see chapter 10.

The `MvcMiddleware` can automatically populate your binding models for you using properties of the request, such as the URL they used, any headers sent in the HTTP request, any data explicitly POSTed in the request body, and so on. These models are then passed to your action methods as method parameters.

  By default, MVC will use three different *binding sources* when creating your binding models. It will look through each of these in order and will take the first value it finds (if any) that matches the name of the parameter:

- *Form values*—Sent in the body of an HTTP request when a form is sent to the server using a POST.
- *Route values*—Obtained from URL segments or through default values after matching a route.
- *Query string values*—Passed at the end of the URL, not used during routing.

The model binding process is shown in figure 6.3. The model binder checks each binding source to see if it contains a value that could be set on the model. Alternatively, the model can also choose the specific source the value should come from, as you'll see later in this section. Once each property is bound, the model is validated and is passed to the action method to execute it. You'll learn about the validation process in the second half of this chapter.

  Figure 6.4 shows an example of a request creating the `ProductModel` method argument using model binding for the initial example, the `EditProduct` action method:

```
public IActionResult EditProduct(ProductModel product)
```

The `Id` property has been bound from a URL route parameter, but the `Name` and `SellPrice` have been bound from the request body. The big advantage of using model binding is that you don't have to write the code to parse requests and map the data yourself. This sort of code is typically repetitive and error-prone, so using the built-in conventional approach lets you focus on the important aspects of your application: the business requirements.

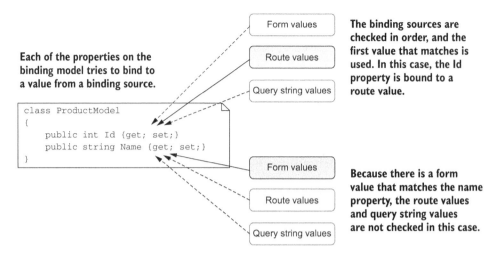

Each of the properties on the binding model tries to bind to a value from a binding source.

The binding sources are checked in order, and the first value that matches is used. In this case, the Id property is bound to a route value.

Because there is a form value that matches the name property, the route values and query string values are not checked in this case.

Form values

Route values

Query string values

```
class ProductModel
{
    public int Id {get; set;}
    public string Name {get; set;}
}
```

Form values

Route values

Query string values

Figure 6.3   Model binding involves mapping values from binding sources, which correspond to different parts of a request.

TIP   Model binding is great for reducing repetitive code. Take advantage of it whenever possible and you'll rarely find yourself having to access the Request object directly.

If you need to, the capabilities are there to let you completely customize the way model binding works, but it's relatively rare that you'll find yourself needing to dig too deep into this. For the vast majority of cases it works as is, as you'll see in the remainder of this section.

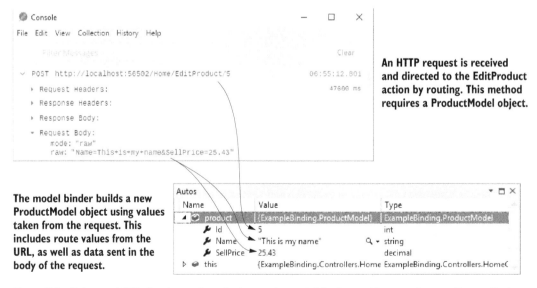

An HTTP request is received and directed to the EditProduct action by routing. This method requires a ProductModel object.

The model binder builds a new ProductModel object using values taken from the request. This includes route values from the URL, as well as data sent in the body of the request.

Figure 6.4   Using model binding to create an instance of a model that's used to execute an action method

6.2.1 Binding simple types

You'll start your journey into model binding by considering a simple action method. The next listing shows a simple calculator action method that takes one number as a method parameter and squares it by multiplying it by itself.

Listing 6.1 An action method accepting a simple parameter

```
public CalculatorController : Controller
{                                                    The method parameter
    public IActionResult Square(int value)  ◁─────── is the binding model.
    {
        var result = value * value;    ◁─────────────┐  A more complex example
                                                      │  would do this work in an
        var viewModel = new ResultViewModel(result);  │  external service, in the
        return View(viewModel);                       │  application model.
    }
}                                                     │
                    The result is passed to the view to
                   generate a response using a view model.
```

In the last chapter, you learned about routing and how this selects which action method to execute. The number of route templates that would match the action method you've defined is endless, but use the following simple template:

```
{controller}/{action}/{value}
```

When a client requests a URL, for example `/Calculator/Square/5`, the `MvcMiddleware` uses routing to parse it for route parameters. With the preceding template, this would produce the following route values:

- `controller=Calculator`
- `action=Square`
- `value=5`

The router only uses the controller and action parameters for routing, but all the values are stored in a collection as name-value pairs. The router will look for the `Calculator-Controller.Square` action method, it will find the method defined in the previous listing and will then attempt to execute it.

This action method contains a single parameter—an integer called `value`—which is your binding model. When the `MvcMiddleware` executes this action method, it will spot the expected parameter, flick through the route values associated with the request, and find the `value=5` pair. It can then bind the `value` parameter to this route value and execute the method. The action method itself doesn't care about where this value came from; it goes along its merry way, creating a view model and returning a `ViewResult`.

The key thing to appreciate is that you didn't have to write any extra code to try to extract the `value` from the URL when the method executed. All you needed to do was create a method parameter with the right name and let model binding do its magic.

Route values aren't the only values the model binder can use to create your action method parameters. As you saw previously, MVC will look through three default *binding sources* to find a match for your action parameters:

- Form values
- Route values
- Query string values

Each of these binding sources store values as name-value pairs. If none of the binding sources contain the required value, then the method parameter receives a new instance of the type instead. The exact value the method parameter will have in this case depends on the type of the variable:

- For value types, the value will be `default(T)`. For an `int` parameter this would be `0`, and for a `bool` it would be `false`.
- For reference types, the type is created using the default constructor. For custom types like `ProductModel`, that will create a new object. For nullable types like `int?` or `bool?`, the value will be `null`.
- For string types, the value will be `null`.

WARNING   It's important to consider the behavior of your action method if model binding fails to bind your method parameters. If none of the binding sources contain the value, the value passed to the method could be `null`, or have an unexpected default value.

Listing 6.1 shows how to bind a single method parameter. Let's take the next logical step and look at how you'd bind multiple method parameters.

In the previous chapter, we looked at configuring routing while building a currency converter application. As the next step in your development, your boss asks you to create a method in which the user provides a value in one currency and you must convert it to another. You first create an action method that accepts the three values you need, as shown next, and configure a specific route template using `"{currencyIn}/{currencyOut}"`.

> **Listing 6.2   An action method accepting multiple binding parameters**

```
public ConverterController
{
    public IActionResult ConvertCurrency(
        string currencyIn,
        string currencyOut,
        int qty)
    {
        /* method implementation */
    }
}
```

As you can see, there are three different parameters to bind. The question is, where will the values come from and what will they be set to? The answer is, it depends! Table 6.1

shows a whole variety of possibilities. All these examples use the same route and action method, but depending on the data sent, different values can be bound from what you might expect, as the available binding sources offer conflicting values.

Table 6.1 Binding request data to action method parameters from two binding sources

URL (route values)	HTTP body data (form values)	Parameter values bound

`/GBP/USD`		`currencyIn=GBP,`
		`currencyOut=USD`
		`qty=0`

`/GBP/USD?currencyIn=CAD`	`QTY=50`	`currencyIn=GBP,`
		`currencyOut=USD`
		`qty=50`

`/GBP/USD?qty=100`	`qty=50`	`currencyIn=GBP,`
		`currencyOut=USD`
		`qty=50`

`/GBP/USD?qty=100`	`currencyIn=CAD&`
	`currencyOut=EUR&`
	`qty=50`
		`currencyIn=CAD,`
		`currencyOut=EUR`
		`qty=50`

For each example, be sure you understand why the bound values have the values that they do. In the first example, the `qty` value isn't found in the form data, in the route values, or in the query string, so it has the default value of `0`. In each of the other examples, the request contains one or more duplicated values; in these cases, it's important to bear in mind the order in which the model binder consults the binding sources. By default, form values will take precedence over other binding sources, including route values!

> **NOTE** The default model binder isn't case sensitive, so a binding value of `QTY=50` will happily bind to the `qty` parameter.

Although this may seem a little overwhelming, it's relatively unusual to be binding from all these different sources at once. It's more common to have your values all come from the request body as form values, maybe with an ID from URL route values. This scenario serves as more of a cautionary tale about the knots you can twist yourself into if you're not sure how things work under the hood!

In these examples, you happily bound the `qty` integer property to incoming values, but as I mentioned earlier, the values stored in binding sources are all strings. What types can you convert a string to? The model binder will convert pretty much any primitive .NET type such as `int`, `float`, `decimal` (and `string` obviously), plus anything that has a `TypeConverter`.[1] There are a few other special cases that can be converted from a string, such as `Type`, but thinking of it as primitives only will get you a long way there!

---

[1] TypeConverters can be found in the System.ComponentModel.TypeConverter package. You can view the source code at http://mng.bz/CShQ.

6.2.2   Binding complex types

If it seems like only being able to bind simple primitive types is a bit limiting, then you're right! Luckily, that's not the case for the model binder. Although it can only convert strings *directly* to those primitive types, it's also able to bind complex types by traversing any properties your binding model exposes.

In case this doesn't make you happy straight off the bat, let's look at how you'd have to bind your actions if simple types were your only option. Imagine a user of your currency converter application has reached a checkout page and is going to exchange some currency. Great! All you need now is to collect their name, email, and phone number. Unfortunately, your action method would have to look something like this:

```
public IActionResult Checkout(string firstName, string lastName, string
    phoneNumber, string email)
```

Yuck! Four parameters might not seem that bad right now, but what happens when the requirements change and you need to collect other details? The method signature will keep growing. The model binder will bind the values quite happily, but it's not exactly clean code.

SIMPLIFYING METHOD PARAMETERS BY BINDING TO COMPLEX OBJECTS

A common pattern when you have many method parameters is to extract a class that encapsulates the data the method requires. If extra parameters need to be added, you can add a new property to this class. This class becomes your binding model and might look something like this.

> **Listing 6.3   A binding model for capturing a user's details**

```
public UserBindingModel
{
    public string FirstName { get; set; }
    public string LastName { get; set; }
    public string Email { get; set; }
    public string PhoneNumber { get; set; }
}
```

With this model, you can now update your action's method signature to

```
public IActionResult Checkout(UserBindingModel model)
```

Functionally, the model binder treats this new complex type a little differently. Rather than looking for parameters with a value that matches the parameter name (model), it attempts to create a new instance of the model using new UserBindingModel().

> **NOTE**   You don't have to use custom classes for your methods; it depends on your requirements. If your action method needs only a single integer, then it makes more sense to bind to the simple parameter.

Next, the model binder loops through all the properties your model exposes, such as FirstName and LastName. For each of these properties, it consults the collection of binding sources and attempts to find a name-value pair that matches. If it finds one, it sets the value on the property and moves on to the next.

> **TIP** Although the name of the model isn't necessary in this example, the model binder will also look for properties prefixed with the name of the model, such as `model.FirstName` and `model.LastName`. This can be useful if you have multiple complex arguments to an action method, as it ensures the correct properties are bound on each type.

Once all the properties that can be bound on the binding model are set, the model is passed to the action method, which is executed as usual. The behavior from this point is identical to when you have lots of individual parameters—you'll end up with the same values set on your binding model—the code is cleaner and easier to work with.

> **TIP** For a class to be model-bound, it must have a default public constructor. You can only bind properties which are public and settable.

With this technique you can bind complex hierarchical models, whose properties are themselves complex models. As long as each property exposes a type that can be model-bound, the binder can traverse it with ease.

BINDING COLLECTIONS AND DICTIONARIES

As well as ordinary custom classes and primitives, you can bind to collections, lists, and dictionaries. Imagine you had a page in which a user selected all the currencies they were interested in; you'd display the rates for all those selected, as shown in figure 6.5.

To achieve this, you could create an action method that accepted a `List<string>` type such as

```
IActionResult ShowRates(List<string> currencies);
```

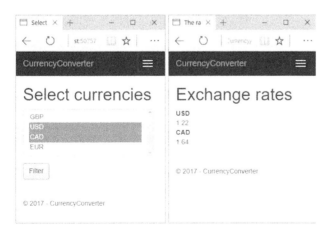

Figure 6.5   The select list in the currency converter application will send a list of selected currencies to the application. Model binding can bind the selected currencies and customize the view for the user to show the equivalent cost in the selected currencies.

You could then POST data to this method by providing values in a number of different formats:

- `currencies[index]`—Where `currencies` is the name of the parameter to bind and `index` is the index of the item to bind, for example, `currencies[0]=GBR&currencies[1]=USD`.
- `[index]`—If there's only a single list, you can omit the name of the parameter, for example, `[0]=GBR&[1]=USD`.
- `currencies`—Alternatively, you can omit the `index` and send `currencies` as the key value for every value, for example, `currencies=GBR&currencies=USD`.

The key values can come from route values and query values, but it's far more common to POST them in a form. Dictionaries can use similar binding, where the dictionary key replaces the index both where the parameter is named and where it's omitted.

If this all seems a bit confusing, don't feel too alarmed. If you're building a traditional web application, and using Razor views to generate HTML, then it will take care of most of the naming for you. As you'll see in chapter 8, the view will ensure that any form data you POST will be generated in the correct format.

BINDING FILE UPLOADS WITH IFORMFILE

A common feature of many websites is the ability to upload files. This could be a relatively infrequent activity, for example if a user uploads a profile picture for their Stack Overflow profile, or it may be integral to the application, like uploading photos to Facebook.

Letting users upload files to your application

Uploading files to websites is a pretty common activity, but you should carefully consider whether your application needs that ability. Whenever files can be uploaded by users the road is fraught with danger.

You should be careful to treat the incoming files as potentially malicious, don't trust the filename provided, take care of large files being uploaded, and don't allow the files to be executed on your server.

Files also raise questions as to where the data should be stored—should they go in a database, in the filesystem, or some other storage? None of these questions has a straightforward answer and you should think hard about the implications of choosing one over the other. Better yet, if you can avoid it, don't let users upload files!

ASP.NET Core supports uploading files by exposing the `IFormFile` interface. You can use this interface as a method parameter to your action method and it will be populated with the details of the file upload:

```
public IActionResult UploadFile(IFormFile file);
```

You can also use an `IEnumerable<IFormFile>` if your action method accepts multiple files:

```
public IActionResult UploadFiles(IEnumerable<IFormFile> file);
```

The `IFormFile` object exposes several properties and utility methods for reading the contents of the uploaded file, some of which are shown here:

```
public interface IFormFile
{
    string ContentType { get; }
    long Length { get; }
    string FileName { get; }
    Stream OpenReadStream();
}
```

As you can see, this interface exposes a `FileName` property, which returns the filename that the file was uploaded with. But you know not to trust users, right? You should never use the filename directly in your code—always generate a new filename for the file before you save it anywhere.

> **WARNING** Never use posted filenames in your code. Users can use them to attack your website and access files they shouldn't be able to.

The `IFormFile` approach is fine if users are only going to be uploading small files. When your method accepts an `IFormFile` instance, the whole content of the file is buffered in memory and on disk before you receive it. You can then use the `Open-ReadStream` method to read the data out.

If users post large files to your website, you may find you start to run out of space in memory or on disk, as it buffers each of the files. In that case, you may need to stream the files directly to avoid saving all the data at once. Unfortunately, unlike the model binding approach, streaming large files can be complex and error-prone, so it's outside the scope of this book. For details, see the documentation at http://mng.bz/SH7X.

> **TIP** Don't use the `IFormFile` interface to handle large file uploads as you may see performance issues.

For the vast majority of your action methods, the default configuration of model binding for simple and complex types works perfectly well, but you may find some situations where you need to take a bit more control. Luckily, that's perfectly possible, and you can completely override the process if necessary by replacing the `ModelBinders` used in the guts of the `MvcMiddleware`.

It's rare to need that level of customization—a far more common requirement is to be able to specify which binding source to use to bind an action method parameter.

6.2.3   *Choosing a binding source*

As you've already seen, by default the ASP.NET Core model binder will attempt to bind all action method parameters from three different binding sources: form data, route data, and the query string.

Occasionally, you may find it necessary to specifically declare which binding source to bind to, but in other cases, these three sources won't be sufficient. The most common scenarios are when you want to bind a method parameter to a request header value, or when the body of a request contains JSON-formatted data that you want to bind to a parameter. In these cases, you can decorate your action method parameters (or binding model class properties) with attributes that say where to bind from, as shown here.

Listing 6.4   Choosing a binding source for model binding

```
public class PhotosController
{                                          The userId will be bound from an
    public IActionResult TagPhotosWithUser(   HTTP header in the request.
        [FromHeader] string userId,    ◁───┘
        [FromBody] List<Photo> photos)  ◁───
    {                                          The list of photos will be bound to
        /* method implementation */            the body of the request, typically
    }                                          in JSON format.
}
```

In this example, an action method updates a collection of photos with a user. You've got method parameters for the ID of the user to tag in the photos, userId, and a list of Photo objects to tag, photos.

Rather than binding these action methods using the standard binding sources, you've added attributes to each parameter, indicating the binding source to use. The [FromHeader] attribute has been applied to the userId parameter. This tells the model binder to bind the value to an HTTP request header value called userId.

You're also binding a list of photos to the body of the HTTP request by using the [FromBody] attribute. This will read JSON from the body of the request and will bind it to the List<Photo> method parameter.

> **WARNING**   Developers familiar with the previous version of ASP.NET should take note that the [FromBody] attribute is explicitly required when binding to JSON requests. This differs from previous ASP.NET behavior, in which no attribute was required.[2]

You aren't limited to binding JSON data from the request body—you can use other formats too, depending on which InputFormatters you configure the MvcMiddleware

---

[2] ASP.NET Core 2.1 introduces the [ApiController] attribute, which allows you to add model binding conventions designed for Web API controllers. This means [FromBody] is automatically used for complex parameters. For details see http://mng.bz/FYH1.

to use. By default, only a JSON input formatter is configured. You'll see how to add an XML formatter in chapter 9, when I discuss Web APIs.

You can use a few different attributes to override the defaults and to specify a binding source for each method parameter:

- [FromHeader]—Bind to a header value
- [FromQuery]—Bind to a query string value
- [FromRoute]—Bind to route parameters
- [FromForm]—Bind to form data posted in the body of the request
- [FromBody]—Bind to the request's body content

You can apply each of these to any number of method parameters, as you saw in listing 6.4, with the exception of the [FromBody] attribute—only one parameter may be decorated with the [FromBody] attribute. Also, as form data is sent in the body of a request, the [FromBody] and [FromForm] attributes are effectively mutually exclusive.

> **TIP** Only one parameter may use the [FromBody] attribute. This attribute will consume the incoming request as HTTP request bodies can only be safely read once.

As well as these attributes for specifying binding sources, there are a few other attributes for customizing the binding process even further:

- [BindNever]—The model binder will skip this parameter completely.[3]
- [BindRequired]—If the parameter was not provided, or was empty, the binder will add a validation error.
- [FromServices]—Used to indicate the parameter should be provided using dependency injection (see chapter 10 for details).

In addition, you've got the [ModelBinder] attribute, which puts you into "God mode" with respect to model binding. With this attribute, you can specify the exact binding source, override the name of the parameter to bind to, and specify the type of binding to perform. It'll be rare that you need this one, but when you do, at least it's there!

By combining all these attributes, you should find you're able to configure the model binder to bind to pretty much any data your action method wants to receive. If you're building a traditional web app, then you'll probably find you rarely need to use them; the defaults should work well for you in most cases.

This brings us to the end of this section on model binding. If all has gone well, you should have a populated binding model, and the middleware can execute the action method. It's time to handle the request, right? Nothing to worry about?

Not so fast! How do you know that the data you received was valid? That you haven't been sent malicious data attempting a SQL injection attack, or a phone number full of letters?

---

[3] You can use the [BindNever] attribute to prevent mass assignment, as discussed in this post: http://mng.bz/QvfG.

The binder is relatively blindly assigning values sent in a request, which you're happily going to plug into your own methods? What's to stop nefarious little Jimmy from sending malicious values to your application?

Except for basic safeguards, there's nothing stopping him, which is why it's important that you always validate the input coming in. ASP.NET Core provides a way to do this in a declarative manner out of the box, which is the focus of the second half of this chapter.

6.3 Handling user input with model validation

Validation in general is a pretty big topic, and one that you'll need to consider in every app you build. ASP.NET Core makes it relatively easy to add validation to your applications by making it an integral part of the framework.

6.3.1 The need for validation

Data can come from many different sources in your web application—you could load it from files, read it from a database, or you could accept values that a user typed into a form in requests. Although you might be inclined to trust that the data already on your server is valid (though this is sometimes a dangerous assumption!), you definitely shouldn't trust the data sent as part of a request.

Validation occurs in the MvcMiddleware after model binding, but before the action executes, as you saw in figure 6.2. Figure 6.6 shows a more compact view of where model validation fits in this process, demonstrating how a request to a checkout page that requests a user's personal details is bound and validated.

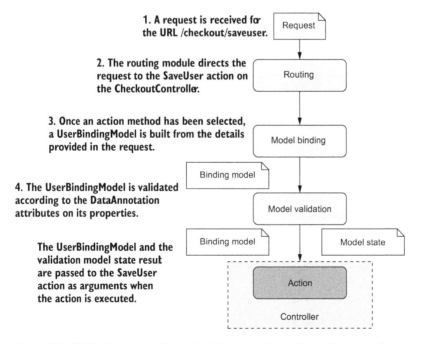

Figure 6.6   Validation occurs after model binding but before the action method executes. The action executes whether or not validation is successful.

You should always validate data provided by users before you use it in your methods. You have no idea what the browser may have sent you. The classic example of "little Bobby Tables" (https://xkcd.com/327/) highlights the need to always validate any data sent by a user.

The need for validation isn't only to check for security threats, though; it's also needed to check for nonmalicious errors, such as:

- Data should be formatted correctly (email fields have a valid email format).
- Numbers might need to be in a particular range (you can't buy -1 copies of this book!).
- Some values may be required but others are optional (name may be required for a profile but phone number is optional).
- Values must conform to your business requirements (you can't convert a currency to itself, it needs to be converted to a difference currency).

It might seem like some of these can be dealt with easily enough in the browser—for example, if a user is selecting a currency to convert to, don't let them pick the same currency; and we've all seen the "please enter a valid email address" messages.

Unfortunately, although this *client-side validation* is useful for users, as it gives them instant feedback, you can never rely on it, as it will always be possible to bypass these browser protections. It's always necessary to validate the data as it arrives at your web application, using *server-side validation.*

> **WARNING**   In your application, always validate user input on the server side.

If that feels a little redundant, like you'll be duplicating logic and code, then I'm afraid you're right. It's one of the unfortunate aspects of web development; the duplication is a necessary evil. Thankfully, ASP.NET Core provides several features to try to reduce this burden.

If you had to write this validation code fresh for every app, it would be tedious and likely error-prone. Luckily, you can simplify your validation code significantly using a set of attributes provided by .NET Core and the .NET Framework.

6.3.2 *Using DataAnnotations attributes for validation*

Validation attributes, or more precisely `DataAnnotations` attributes, allow you to specify rules that the properties in your model should conform to. They provide *metadata* about your model by describing the *sort* of data the model should contain, as opposed to the data itself.

> **DEFINITION**   *Metadata* describes other data, specifying the rules and characteristics the data should adhere to.

You can apply `DataAnnotations` attributes directly to your binding models to indicate the type of data that's acceptable. This allows you to, for example, check that required fields have been provided, that numbers are in the correct range, and that email fields are valid email addresses.

As an example, let's consider the checkout page for your currency converter application. You need to collect details about the user before you can continue, so you ask them to provide their name, email and, optionally, a phone number. The following listing shows the `UserBindingModel` decorated with validation attributes that represent the validation rules for the model. This expands on the example you saw in listing 6.3.

Listing 6.5   Adding `DataAnnotations` to a binding model to provide metadata

Values marked Required must be provided.

```
Public class UserBindingModel
{
    [Required]
    [StringLength(100)]        The StringLengthAttribute sets the
    [Display(Name = "Your name")]   maximum length for the property.
    public string FirstName { get; set; }

    [Required]
    [StringLength(100)]        The StringLengthAttribute sets the
    [Display(Name = "Last name")]   maximum length for the property.
    public string LastName { get; set; }

    [Required]                 Validates the value of Email
    [EmailAddress]             is a valid email address
    public string Email { get; set; }

    [Phone]
    [Display(Name = "Phone number")]
    public string PhoneNumber { get; set; }
}
```

Customizes the name used to describe the property

Suddenly your binding model contains a whole wealth of information where previously it was pretty sparse on details. For example, you've specified that the `FirstName` property should always be provided, that it should have a maximum length of 100 characters, and that when it's referred to (in error messages, for example) it should be called `"Your name"` instead of `"FirstName"`.

The great thing about these attributes is that they clearly declare the *expected* state of the model. By looking at these attributes, you know what the properties will/should contain. They also provide hooks for the ASP.NET Core framework to validate that the data set on the model during model binding is valid, as you'll see shortly.

You've got a plethora of attributes to choose from when applying `DataAnnotations` to your models. I've listed some of the common ones here, but you can find more in the `System.ComponentModel.DataAnnotations` namespace. For a more complete list, I recommend using IntelliSense in Visual Studio/Visual Studio Code, or you can always look at the source code directly on GitHub (http://mng.bz/7N7s).

- `[CreditCard]`—Validates that a property has a valid credit card format
- `[EmailAddress]`—Validates that a property has a valid email address format

- `[StringLength(max)]`—Validates that a string has at most the `max` amount of characters
- `[MinLength(min)]`—Validates that a collection has at least the `min` amount of items
- `[Phone]`—Validates that a property has a valid phone number format
- `[Range(min, max)]`—Validates that a property has a value between `min` and `max`
- `[RegularExpression(regex)]`—Validates that a property conforms to the `regex` regular expression pattern
- `[Url]`—Validates that a property has a valid URL format
- `[Required]`—Indicates the property that must be provided
- `[Compare]`—Allows you to confirm that two properties have the same value (for example, `Email` and `ConfirmEmail`)

WARNING The `[EmailAddress]` and other attributes only validate that the *format* of the value is correct. They don't validate that the email address exists.

The `DataAnnotations` attributes aren't a new feature—they have been part of the .NET Framework since version 3.5—and their usage in ASP.NET Core is almost the same as in the previous version of ASP.NET.

They're also used for other purposes, in addition to validation. Entity Framework Core (among others) uses `DataAnnotations` to define the types of column and rule to use when creating database tables from C# classes. You can read more about Entity Framework Core in chapter 12, and in Jon P Smith's *Entity Framework Core in Action* (Manning, 2018).

If the `DataAnnotation` attributes provided out of the box don't cover everything you need, then it's also possible to write custom attributes by deriving from the base `ValidationAttribute`. You'll see how to create a custom attribute for your currency converter application in chapter 19.

Alternatively, if you're not a fan of the attribute-based approach, the `MvcMiddleware` is flexible enough that you can replace the validation infrastructure with your preferred technique. For example, you could use the popular FluentValidation library (https://github.com/JeremySkinner/FluentValidation) in place of the `Data-Annotations` attributes if you prefer.

TIP `DataAnnotations` are good for input validation of properties in isolation, but not so good for validating business rules. You'll most likely need to perform this validation outside the `DataAnnotations` framework.

Whichever validation approach you use, it's important to remember that these techniques don't protect your application by themselves. The `MvcMiddleware` will ensure the validation occurs, but it doesn't automatically do anything if validation fails. In the next section, we'll look at how to check the validation result on the server and handle the case where validation has failed.

6.3.3   *Validating on the server for safety*

Validation of the binding model occurs before the action executes, but note that the action *always* executes, whether the validation failed or succeeded. It's the responsibility of the action method to handle the result of the validation.

> **NOTE**   Validation happens automatically but handling validation failures is the responsibility of the action method.

The MvcMiddleware stores the output of the validation attempt in a property on the ControllerBase base class called ModelState. This object is a ModelStateDictionary, which contains a list of all the validation errors that occurred after model binding, as well as some utility properties for working with it.

As an example, listing 6.6 shows the SaveUser action method being invoked with the UserBindingModel shown in the previous section. This action doesn't do anything with the data currently, but the pattern of checking ModelState early in the method is the key takeaway here.

Listing 6.6   Checking model state to view the validation result

Deriving from Controller makes
the ModelState property available.

The model parameter
contains the model-
bound data.

```
public class CheckoutController : Controller
{
    public IActionResult SaveUser(UserBindingModel model)
    {
        if(!ModelState.IsValid)
        {
            return View(model);
        }

        /* Save to the database, update user, return success *
        return RedirectToAction("Success");
    }
}
```

If there were
validation errors,
IsValid will be false.

Validation failed, so redisplay the form
with errors, and finish the method early.

Validation passed, so
it's safe to use the data
provided in model.

If the ModelState indicates an error occurred, the method immediately calls the View helper method, passing in the model. This will return a ViewResult that will ultimately generate HTML to return to the user, as you saw in chapter 4. By passing in the model, the view can repopulate the values the user provided in the form when it's displayed, as shown in figure 6.7. Also, helpful messages to the user can be added using the validation errors in the ModelState.

If the request is successful, the action method returns a RedirectToAction result that will redirect the user to the Success action on the CheckoutController. This pattern of returning a redirect response after a successful POST is called the POST-REDIRECT-GET pattern.

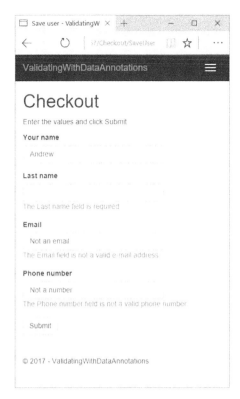

Figure 6.7 When validation fails, you can redisplay the form to display `ModelState` **validation errors to the user. Note the "Your name" field has no associated validation errors, unlike the other fields.**

NOTE The error messages displayed on the form are the default values for each validation attribute. You can customize the message by setting the `ErrorMessage` property on any of the validation attributes. For example, you could customize a `[Required]` attribute using `[Required(ErrorMessage=` `"Required")]`.

POST-REDIRECT-GET

The POST-REDIRECT-GET design pattern is a web development pattern that prevents users from accidently submitting the same form multiple times. Users typically submit a form using the standard browser POST mechanism, sending data to the server. This is the normal way by which you might take a payment, for example.

If a server takes the naive approach and responds with a 200 OK response and some HTML to display, then the user will still be on the same URL. If the user refreshes their browser, they will be making an *additional* POST to the server, potentially making another payment! Browsers have some mechanisms to avoid this, such as in the following figure, but the user experience isn't desirable.

(continued)

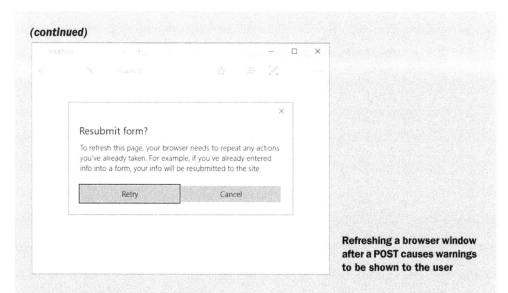

Refreshing a browser window after a POST causes warnings to be shown to the user

The POST-REDIRECT-GET pattern says that in response to a successful POST, you should return a REDIRECT response to a new URL, which will be followed by the browser making a GET to the URL. If the user refreshes their browser now, then they'll be refreshing the final GET call. No additional POST is made, so no additional payments or side effects should occur.

This pattern is easy to achieve in ASP.NET Core MVC applications using the pattern shown in listing 6.6. By returning a `RedirectToActionResult` after a successful POST, your application will be safe if the user refreshes the page in their browser.

You might be wondering why validation isn't handled automatically—if validation has occurred, and you have the result, why does the action method get executed at all? Isn't there a risk that you might forget to check the validation result?

This is true, and in some cases the best thing is to make the generation of the validation check and response automatic—this is often the case for Web APIs, and can be made automatic using filters, which we'll cover in chapters 9 and 13.

For traditional web apps however, you typically still want to generate an HTML response, even when validation failed. This allows the user to see the problem, and potentially correct it. This is often harder to make automatic, especially as the view model you use to generate your view and the binding model that's validated are often different classes.

By including the `IsValid` check explicitly in your action methods, it's easier to control what happens when other validation fails. If the user tries to update a product, then you won't know whether the requested product ID exists as part of the `Data-Annotations` validation, only whether the ID has the correct format. By moving the validation to the action method, you can treat data and business rule validation failures similarly.

You might find you need to load additional data into the view model before you can regenerate the view—a list of available currencies, for example. That all becomes simpler and more explicit with the `IsValid` pattern.

I hope I've hammered home how important it is to validate user input in ASP.NET Core, but just in case: VALIDATE! There, we're good. Having said that, *just* performing validation on the server can leave users with a slightly poor experience. How many times have you filled out a form online, submitted it, gone to get a snack, and come back to find out you mistyped something and have to redo it. Wouldn't it be nicer to have that feedback immediately?

6.3.4 *Validating on the client for user experience*

You can add client-side validation to your application in a couple of different ways. HTML5 has several built-in validation behaviors that many browsers will use. If you display an email address field on a page and use the "email" HMTL input type, then the browser will automatically stop you from submitting an invalid format, as shown in figure 6.8.

Figure 6.8   By default, modern browsers will automatically validate fields of the email type before a form is submitted.

Your application doesn't control this validation, it's built into modern HTML5 browsers.[4] The alternative approach is to perform client-side validation by running Java-Script on the page and checking the values the user has entered before submitting the form. This is the default approach used in ASP.NET Core MVC when you're building a traditional web application.

I'll go into detail on how to generate the client-side validation helpers in the next chapter, where you'll see the `DataAnnotations` attributes come to the fore once again. By decorating a view model with these attributes, you provide the necessary metadata to the Razor engine for it to generate the appropriate HTML.

With this approach, the user sees any errors with their form immediately, even before the request is sent to the server, as shown in figure 6.9. This gives a much shorter feedback cycle, providing a much better user experience.

If you're building an SPA, then the onus is on the client-side framework to validate the data on the client side before posting it to the Web API. The Web API will still validate the data when it arrives at the server, but the client-side framework is responsible for providing the smooth user experience.

---

[4] HTML5 constraint validation support varies by browser. For details on the available constraints, see http://mng.bz/daX3.

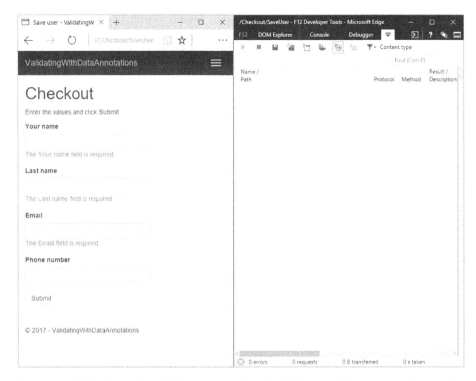

Figure 6.9   With client-side validation, clicking Submit will trigger validation to be shown in the browser before the request is sent to the server. As shown in the right-hand pane, no request is sent.

When you use the Razor templating engine to generate your HTML, you get much of this validation for free. It automatically configures the validation for the built-in attributes without requiring any additional work. Unfortunately, if you've used custom ValidationAttributes, then these will only run on the server by default; you need to do some wiring up of the attribute to make it work on the client side too. Despite this, custom validation attributes can be useful for handling common scenarios in your application, as you'll see in chapter 19.

That concludes this look at the binding models of MVC. You saw how the ASP.NET Core framework uses model binding to simplify the process of extracting values from a request and turning them into normal .NET objects you can quickly work with. The most important aspect of this chapter is the focus on validation—this is a common concern for all web applications, and the use of DataAnnotations can make it easy to add validation to your models.

In the next chapter, we continue our journey through MVC by looking at how to create views. In particular, you'll learn how to generate HTML in response to a request using the Razor templating engine.

Summary

- ASP.NET Core MVC has three distinct models, each responsible for a different aspect of a request. The binding model encapsulates data sent as part of a request, the application model represents the state of the application, and the view model contains data used by the view to generate a response.

- Model binding extracts values from a request and uses them to create .NET objects to pass as method parameters to the action being executed.

- By default, there are three binding sources: POSTed form values, route values, and the query string. The binder will interrogate these in order when trying to bind an action method parameter.

- When binding values to parameters, the names of the parameters aren't case sensitive.

- You can bind to simple method parameter types or to the properties of complex types.

- To bind complex types, they must have a default constructor and public, settable properties.

- Simple types must be convertible to strings to be bound automatically, for example numbers, dates, and Boolean values.

- Collections and dictionaries can be bound using the `[index]=value` and `[key]=value` syntax, respectively.

- You can customize the binding source for an action parameter using `[From*]` attributes applied to the method, such as `[FromHeader]` and `[FromBody]`. These can be used to bind to nondefault binding sources, such as headers or JSON body content.

- In contrast to the previous version of ASP.NET, the `[FromBody]` attribute is required when binding JSON properties (previously it was not required).

- Validation is necessary to check for security threats. Check that data is formatted correctly, confirm it conforms to expected values and that it meets your business rules.

- ASP.NET Core provides `DataAnnotations` attributes to allow you to declaratively define the expected values.

- Validation occurs automatically after model binding, but you must manually check the result of the validation and act accordingly in your action method by interrogating the `ModelState` property.

- Client-side validation provides a better user experience than server-side validation alone, but you should always use server-side validation.

- Client-side validation uses JavaScript and attributes applied to your HTML elements to validate form values.

Rendering HTML using Razor views

This chapter covers

- Creating views to display HTML to a user
- Using C# and the Razor markup syntax to generate HTML dynamically
- Reusing common code with layouts and partial views

In the previous four chapters, I've covered a whole cross-section of MVC, including the MVC design pattern itself, controllers and actions, routing, and binding models. This chapter shows how to create your views—the UI to your application. For desktop apps, that might be WinForms or WPF. For Web APIs, that might be a non-visual view, such as a JSON or XML response, which is subsequently used to generate HTML in the client's browser. For traditional web applications, the UI is the HTML, CSS, and JavaScript that's delivered to the user's browser directly, and that they interact with.

In ASP.NET Core, views are normally created using the *Razor* markup syntax (sometimes described as a templating language), which uses a mixture of HTML and C# to generate the final result. This chapter covers some of the features of Razor and how to use it to build the view templates for your application.

Generally speaking, users will have two sorts of interactions with your app: they read data that your app displays, and they send data or commands back to it. The Razor language contains a number of constructs that make it simple to build both types of applications.

When displaying data, you can use the Razor language to easily combine static HTML with values from your view model. Razor can use C# as a control mechanism, so adding conditional elements and loops is simple, something you couldn't achieve with HTML alone.

The normal approach to sending data to web applications is with HTML forms. Virtually every dynamic app you build will use forms; some applications will be pretty much nothing *but* forms! ASP.NET Core and the Razor templating language include a number of helpers that make generating HTML forms easy, called *Tag Helpers*.

> **NOTE** You'll get a brief glimpse of Tag Helpers in the next section, but I'll explore them in detail in the next chapter.

In this chapter, we'll be focusing primarily on displaying data and generating HTML using Razor, rather than creating forms. You'll see how to render values from your view model to the HTML, and how to use C# to control the generated output. Finally, you'll learn how to extract the common elements of your views into sub-views called *layouts* and *partial views*, and how to compose them to create the final HTML page.

7.1 Views: rendering the user interface in MVC

As you know from earlier chapters on the MVC design pattern, it's the job of the controller and action method to choose which view to return to the client. For example, if you're developing a to-do list application, imagine a request to view a particular to-do item, as shown in figure 7.1.

A typical request follows the steps shown in figure 7.1:

1 The request is received by Kestrel and uses routing to determine the action to invoke—the `ViewToDo` method on `ToDoController`.

2 The model binder uses the request to build the action method's binding model, as you saw in the last chapter. This is passed to the action method as a method parameter when it's executed. The action method checks that you have passed a valid `id` for the to-do item, making the request valid.

3 Assuming all looks good, the action method calls out to the various services that make up the application model. This might load the details about the to-do from a database, or from the filesystem, returning them to the controller. As part of this process, either the application model or the controller itself generates a *view model*.

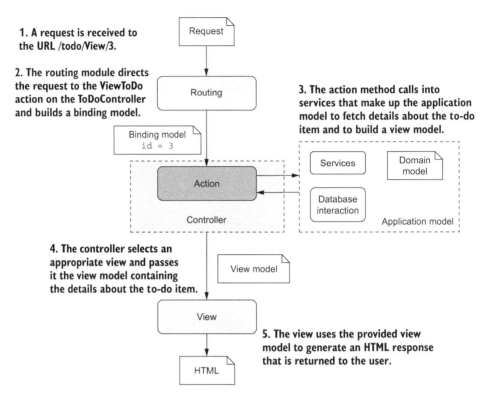

1. A request is received to the URL /todo/View/3.

2. The routing module directs the request to the ViewToDo action on the ToDoController and builds a binding model.

Request

Routing

Binding model
id = 3

3. The action method calls into services that make up the application model to fetch details about the to-do item and to build a view model.

Action

Services

Domain model

Database interaction

Controller

Application model

4. The controller selects an appropriate view and passes it the view model containing the details about the to-do item.

View model

View

5. The view uses the provided view model to generate an HTML response that is returned to the user.

HTML

Figure 7.1 Handling a request for a to-do list item using ASP.NET Core MVC

The view model is a custom class, typically a POCO, that contains all the data required to render a view. In this example, it contains details about the to-do itself, but it might also contain other data: how many to-dos you have left, whether you have any to-dos scheduled for today, your username, and so on, anything that controls how to generate the end UI for the request.

4   The final task for the action method is to choose a view template to render. In most cases, an action method will only need to render a single type of template, but there are situations when you might like to render a different one depending on the data you get back from the application model. For example, you may have one template for to-do items that contain a list of tasks, and a different template when the to-do item contains a picture, as in figure 7.2.

5   The selected view template uses the view model to generate the final response, and returns it back to the user via the middleware pipeline.

A common thread throughout this discussion of MVC is the separation of concerns it brings, and this is no different when it comes to your views. It would be easy enough to directly generate the HTML in your application model or in your controller actions, but instead you'll delegate that responsibility to a single component, the view.

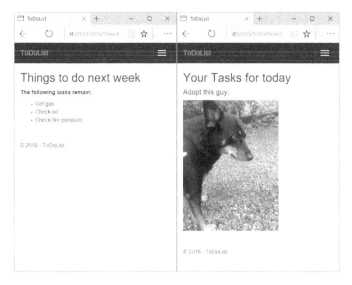

Figure 7.2   The controller is responsible for selecting the appropriate template to render the view model. For example, a list of to-do items can be displayed using a different template to a to-do item consisting of a picture.

But even more than that, you'll also separate the *data* required to build the view from the *process* of building it, by using a view model. The view model should contain all the dynamic data needed by the view to generate the final output.

An action method selects a template and requests that a view be rendered by returning a `ViewResult` object that contains the view model. You saw this type in chapter 4, but we'll look closer at how you they're typically used in the following sections.

When a `ViewResult` executes, it locates the requested Razor template and executes the content. The use of C# in the template means you can dynamically generate the final HTML sent to the browser. This allows you to, for example, display the name of the current user in the page, hide links the current user doesn't have access to, or render a button for every item in a list.

Imagine your boss asks you to add a page to your application that displays a list of the application's users. You should also be able to view a user from the page, or create a new one, as shown in figure 7.3.

With Razor templates, generating this sort of dynamic content is simple. For example, the following listing shows the template that could be used to generate the interface in figure 7.3. It combines standard HTML with C# statements, and uses Tag Helpers to generate the form elements.

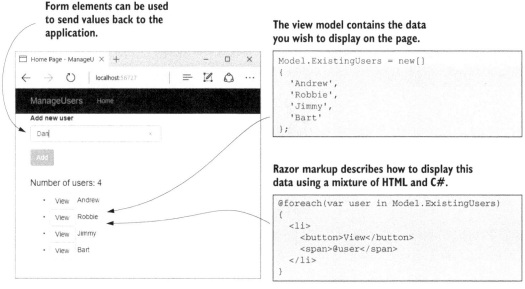

Form elements can be used to send values back to the application.

The view model contains the data you wish to display on the page.

```
Model.ExistingUsers = new[]
{
    'Andrew',
    'Robbie',
    'Jimmy',
    'Bart'
};
```

Razor markup describes how to display this data using a mixture of HTML and C#.

```
@foreach(var user in Model.ExistingUsers)
{
    <li>
        <button>View</button>
        <span>@user</span>
    </li>
}
```

By combining the data in your view model with the Razor markup, HTML can be generated dynamically, instead of being fixed at compile time.

Figure 7.3   The use of C# in Razor lets you easily generate dynamic HTML that varies at runtime.

Listing 7.1   A Razor template to list users and a form for adding a new user

```
@model IndexViewModel

<div class="row">
<div class="col-md-12">                    Normal HTML is sent to
<form asp-action="Index">                  the browser unchanged.
    <div class="form-group">
        <label asp-for="NewUser"></label>            Tag Helpers attach to
        <input class="form-control" asp-for="NewUser" />   HTML elements to
        <span asp-validation-for="NewUser"></span>        create forms.
    </div>
    <div class="form-group">
        <button type="submit"
            class="btn btn-success">Add</button>
    </div>
</form>
</div>
</div>
                                           Values can be written
                                           from C# objects to
                                           the HTML.
<h4>Number of users: @Model.ExistingUsers.Count</h4>
<div class="row">
<div class="col-md-12">
<ul>                                       C# constructs like for
    @foreach (var user in Model.ExistingUsers)   loops can be used in Razor.
```

```
    {
        <li>
            <a class="btn btn-default"
                asp-action="ViewUser"
                asp-route-userName="@user">View</a>
            <span>@user</span>
        </li>
    }
</ul>
</div>
</div>
```

> Tag Helpers can also be used outside of forms to help in other HTML generation.

This example demonstrates a variety of Razor features. There's a mixture of HTML that's written unmodified to the response output, and various C# constructs that are used to dynamically generate HTML. In addition, you can see a number of Tag Helpers. These look like normal HTML attributes that start asp-, but they're part of the Razor language. They can customize the HTML element they're attached to, changing how it's rendered. They make building HTML forms much simpler than they would be otherwise. Don't worry if this template is a bit overwhelming at the moment; we'll break it all down as you progress through this chapter and the next.

You add Razor templates to your project as cshtml files. They're sometimes copied directly to the server when you deploy your application and are compiled at runtime by your application. If you modify one of these files, then your app will automatically recompile it on the fly. If you don't need that capability and would rather take the one-time performance hit at compile time, then you can also precompile these files when you build your app. Precompilation is the default in ASP.NET Core 2.0.

> **NOTE** Like most things in ASP.NET Core, it's possible to swap out the Razor templating engine and replace it with your own server-side rendering engine. You can't replace Razor with a client-side framework like AngularJS or React. If you want to take this approach, you'd use Web APIs instead. I'll discuss Web APIs in detail in chapter 9.

In the next section, you'll learn how to choose a view template to invoke from your controller and how to pass your view model to it to build the HTML response.

7.2 Creating Razor views

With ASP.NET Core, whenever you need to display an HTML response to the user, you should use a view to generate it. Although it's possible to directly return a `string` from your action methods that would be rendered as HTML in the browser, this approach doesn't adhere to the MVC separation of concerns and will quickly leave you tearing your hair out.

> **NOTE** Some middleware, such as the `WelcomePageMiddleware` you saw in chapter 3, may generate HTML responses without using a view, which can make sense in some situations. But your MVC controllers should always generate HTML using views.

This chapter focuses on the final part of the ASP.NET Core MVC pattern, the view generation. Figure 7.4 shows a zoomed-in view of this process, right after the action has invoked the application model and received some data back.

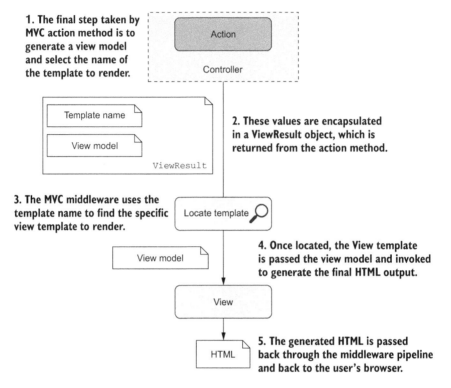

1. The final step taken by MVC action method is to generate a view model and select the name of the template to render.

Action

Controller

Template name

View model

ViewResult

2. These values are encapsulated in a ViewResult object, which is returned from the action method.

3. The MVC middleware uses the template name to find the specific view template to render.

Locate template

4. Once located, the View template is passed the view model and invoked to generate the final HTML output.

View model

View

HTML

5. The generated HTML is passed back through the middleware pipeline and back to the user's browser.

Figure 7.4   The process of generating HTML from an MVC controller using a view

Some of this figure should be familiar—it's similar to the lower half of figure 7.1. It shows that the action method uses a `ViewResult` object to indicate that a view should be created. This `ViewResult` contains the view model and the name of the view template to render.

At this point, the control flow passes back to the MVC middleware, which uses a series of heuristics (as you'll see shortly) to locate the view, based on the template name provided. Once a template has been located, the Razor engine passes it the view model from the `ViewResult` and invokes it to generate the final HTML.

You saw how to create controllers in chapter 4, and in this section, you'll see how to create views and `ViewResult` objects and how to specify the template to render. You can add a new view template to your application in Visual Studio by right-clicking in your application in Solution Explorer and choosing Add > New Item, and selecting MVC View Page from the dialog, as shown in figure 7.5. If you aren't using Visual Studio, create a blank new file with the cshtml file extension.

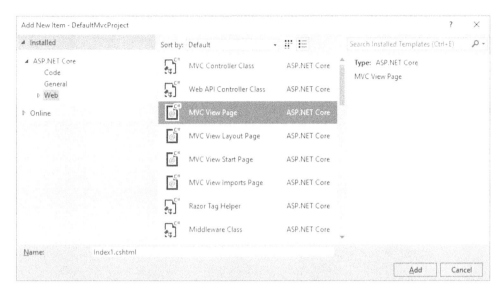

Figure 7.5   The Add New Item dialog. Choosing MVC View Page will add a new Razor template view file to your application.

With your view template created, you now need to invoke it. In the remainder of this section you'll see how to create a `ViewResult` and provide it a view model so that your view can render the data it contains.

7.2.1   Selecting a view from a controller

In most cases, you won't create a `ViewResult` directly in your action methods. Instead, you'll use one of the `View` helper methods on the `Controller` base class. These helper methods simplify passing in a view model and selecting an action method, but there's nothing magic about them—all they do is simplify creating `ViewResult` objects.

In the simplest case, you can call the `View` method without any arguments, as shown next. This helper method returns a `ViewResult` that will use conventions to find the view template to render.

Listing 7.2   Returning `ViewResult` from an action method using default conventions

```
public class HomeController : Controller
{
    public IActionResult Index()
    {
        return View();
    }
}
```

> Inheriting from the **Controller** base class makes the **View** helper methods available.

> The **View** helper method returns a **ViewResult**.

In this example, the `View` helper method returns a `ViewResult` without specifying the name of a template to run. Instead, the name of the template to use is based on the name of the action method. Given that the controller is called `HomeController` and the method is called `Index`, by default the Razor template engine will look for a template at the Views/Home/Index.cshtml location.

This is another case of using conventions in MVC to reduce the amount of boilerplate you have to write. As always, the conventions are optional. You can also explicitly pass the name of the template to run as a `string` to the `View` method. For example, if the `Index` method instead returned `View("ListView");`, then the templating engine would look for a template called ListView.cshtml instead. You can even specify the complete path to the view file, relative to your application's root folder, such as `View ("Views/global.cshtml");`,which would look for the template at the Views/global .chtml location.

> **NOTE** When specifying the absolute path to a view, you must include both the top-level Views folder and the cshtml file extension in the path.

Figure 7.6 shows the complete process used by the default Razor templating engine to try to locate the correct View template to execute. It's possible for more than one template to be eligible, for example if an Index.chstml file exists in both the Home and Shared folders. In a manner analogous to routing, the engine will use the first template it finds.

You may find it tempting to be explicit by default and provide the name of the view file you want to render in your controller; if so, I'd encourage you to fight that urge. You'll have a much simpler time if you embrace the conventions as they are and go with the flow. That extends to anyone else who looks at your code; if you stick to the standard conventions, then there'll be a comforting familiarity when they look at your app. That can only be a good thing!

Now you know where to place your view templates, and how to direct the templating engine to them. It's about time to take a closer look at a template, so you can see what you're working with!

7.2.2 *Introducing Razor templates*

Razor templates contain a mixture of HTML and C# code interspersed with one another. The HTML markup lets you easily describe exactly what should be sent to the browser, whereas the C# code can be used to dynamically change what is rendered. For example, the listing 7.3 shows an example of Razor rendering a list of strings, representing to-do items.

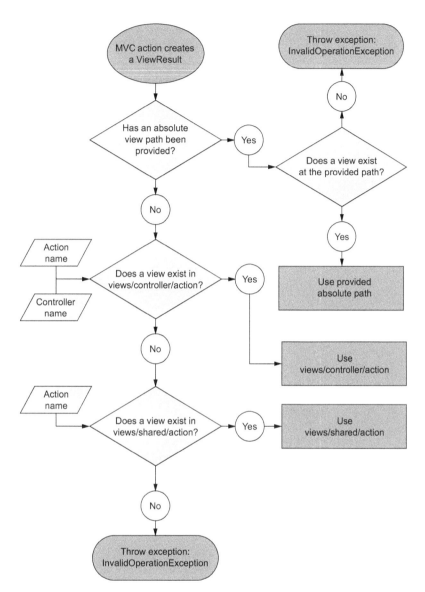

Figure 7.6 A flow chart describing how the Razor templating engine locates the correct view template to execute

```
@{
    var tasks = new List<string>
        { "Buy milk", "Buy eggs", "Buy bread" };
}
```

Arbitrary C# can be executed in a template. Variables remain in scope throughout the page.

```
<h1>Tasks to complete</h1>
<ul>
@for(var i=0; i< tasks.Count; i++)
{
  var task = tasks[i];
  <li>@i - @task</li>
}
</ul>
```

◁── Standard HTML markup will be
rendered to the output unchanged.

Mixing C# and HTML
allows you to dynamically
create HTML at runtime.

The pure HTML sections in this template are the angle brackets. The Razor engine copies this HTML directly to the output, unchanged, as though you were writing a normal HTML file.

As well as HTML, you can also see a number of C# statements in there. The advantage of being able to, for example, use a `for` loop rather than having to explicitly write out each `<li>` element should be self-evident. I'll dive a little deeper into more of the C# features of Razor in the next section. When rendered, this template would produce the HTML shown here.

Listing 7.4   HTML output produced by rendering a Razor template

```
<h1>Tasks to complete</h1>
<ul>
  <li>0 - Buy milk</li>
  <li>1 - Buy eggs</li>
  <li>2 - Buy bread</li>
</ul>
```

HTML from the Razor template is
written directly to the output.

The <li> elements are generated
dynamically based on the data.

◁── HTML from the Razor template is
written directly to the output.

As you can see, the final output of a Razor template after it's been rendered is simple HTML. There's nothing complicated left, just straight markup that can be sent to the browser and rendered. Figure 7.7 shows how a browser would render it.

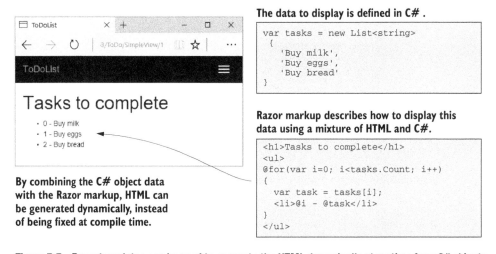

The data to display is defined in C# .

```
var tasks = new List<string>
  {
    'Buy milk',
    'Buy eggs',
    'Buy bread'
  }
```

Razor markup describes how to display this
data using a mixture of HTML and C#.

```
<h1>Tasks to complete</h1>
<ul>
@for(var i=0; i<tasks.Count; i++)
{
  var task = tasks[i];
  <li>@i - @task</li>
}
</ul>
```

By combining the C# object data
with the Razor markup, HTML can
be generated dynamically, instead
of being fixed at compile time.

Figure 7.7   Razor templates can be used to generate the HTML dynamically at runtime from C# objects.

In this example, I hardcoded the list values for simplicity—there was no dynamic data provided. This is often the case on simple action methods like you might have on your homepage—you need to display an almost static page. For the rest of your application, it will be far more common to have some sort of data you need to display, encapsulated by a view model.

7.2.3 *Passing data to views*

In ASP.NET Core, you have a number of ways of passing data from an action method in a controller to a view. Which approach is best will depend on the data you're trying to pass through, but in general you should use the mechanisms in the following order:

- *View model*—The view model should be used to encapsulate any data that needs to be displayed, which is specific to that view. It's a strongly typed class that can be any sort of object you like. The view model is available in the view when it's rendered, as you'll see shortly.
- ViewData—This is a dictionary of objects with string keys that can be used to pass arbitrary data from the controller to the view.
- ViewBag—A version of the ViewData that uses C# dynamic objects instead of string keys. It's a wrapper around the ViewData object, so you can use it in place of ViewData if you prefer dynamic to Dictionary. I'll only refer to ViewData in this book, as they're almost the same thing.
- HttpContext—Technically the HttpContext object is available in both the controller and view, so you *could* use it to transfer data between them. But don't—there's no need for it with the other methods and abstractions available to you.

Far and away the best approach for passing data from a controller to a view is to use a view model. There's nothing special about a view model; it's a custom class that you create to hold the data you require.

> **NOTE** Many frameworks have the concept of a data context for binding UI components. The view model is a similar concept, in that it contains values to display in the UI, but the binding is only one-directional; the view model provides values to the UI, and once the UI is built and sent as a response, the view model is destroyed.

You can make a view model available by passing it to the View helper method from your controller, as shown in the following listing. In this example, I've created a ToDoItemViewModel to hold the values I want to display in the view—the Title and its Tasks.

Listing 7.5 Passing a view model to a view for a controller

```
public class ToDoController : Controller        ⟵─┐  Inheriting from the Controller-based
{                                                  │  class provides the helper View methods
    public IActionResult ViewTodo(int id)
    {
```

```
        var viewModel = new ToDoItemViewModel
        {
            Title = "Tasks for today",
            Tasks = new List<string>{
            {
                "Get fuel",
                "Check oil",
                "Check tyre pressure"
            }
        };

        return View(viewModel);
    }
}
```

**Building a view model: this would
normally call out to a database or
filesystem to load the data.**

⟵ **Creates a ViewResult that looks for a view
called ViewTodo, and passes it the viewModel**

By passing it to the `View` method, the `viewModel` instance will be available in the template, allowing you to access the values it contains from the view template. All that's required is to add an `@model` *directive* at the top of your template so that it knows the `Type` of the view model it should expect:

`@model ToDoItemViewModel`

> **DEFINITION**   A *directive* is a statement in a Razor file that changes the way the template is parsed or compiled. Another common directive is the `@using newNamespace` directive, which would make objects in the `newNamespace` namespace available.

Once you've added this directive, you can access any of the data on the `todoModel` you provided, using the `Model` property. For example, to display the `Title` property from the `ToDoItemViewModel`, you'd use `<h1>@Model.Title</h1>`. This would render the string provided on the original `viewModel` object, producing the `<h1>Tasks  for today</h1>` HTML.

> **TIP**   Note that the `@model` directive should be at the top of your view, and has a lowercase `m`. The `Model` property can be accessed anywhere in the view and has an uppercase `M`.

In the vast majority of cases, using a view model is the way to go; it's the standard mechanism for passing data between the controller and the view. But in some circumstances, a view model may not be the best fit. This is often the case when you want to pass data between view layouts (you'll see how this works in the last section of this chapter).

A common example is the title of the page. You need to provide a title for every page, so you *could* create a base class with a `Title` property and make all your view models inherit from it. But that's a little cumbersome, so a common approach for this situation is to use the `ViewData` collection to pass data around.

In fact, the standard MVC templates use this approach by default rather than using view models by setting values in the `ViewData` dictionary from within the action methods:

```
public IActionResult Contact()
{
    ViewData["Message"] = "Your contact page.";
```

```
    return View();
}
```

They're then displayed in the template using

```
<h3>@ViewData["Message"]</h3>
```

> **NOTE** Personally, I don't agree with the default approach in the templates—the message being presented is integral to the page, so it should probably be part of a view model.

You can also set values on the `ViewData` dictionary from within the view itself:

```
@{
    ViewData["Title"] = "About";
}
<h2>@ViewData["Title"].</h2>
```

This template sets the value of the `"Title"` key in the `ViewData` dictionary to `"About"` and then fetches the key to render in the template. This might seem superfluous, but as the `ViewData` dictionary is shared throughout the request, it makes the title of the page available in layouts, as you'll see later. When rendered, this would produce the following output:

```
<h2>About.</h2>
```

> **TIP** Create a set of global, static constants for any `ViewData` keys, and reference those instead of typing `"Title"` repeatedly. You'll get IntelliSense for the values, they'll be refactor-safe, and you'll avoid hard-to-spot typos.

As I mentioned previously, there are other mechanisms besides view models and `ViewData` that you can use to pass data around, but these two are the only ones I use personally, as you can do everything you need with them.

You've had a small taste of the power available to you in Razor templates, but in the next section, I'd like to dive a little deeper into some of the available C# capabilities.

7.3 Creating dynamic web pages with Razor

You might be glad to know that pretty much anything you can do in C# is possible in Razor syntax. Under the covers, the cshtml files are compiled into normal C# code (with `string` for the raw HTML sections), so whatever weird and wonderful behavior you need can be created.

Having said that, just because you *can* do something doesn't mean you *should*. You'll find it much easier to work with, and maintain, your files if you keep them as simple as possible. This is true of pretty much all programming, but I find especially so with Razor templates.

This section covers some of the more common C# constructs you can use. If you find you need to achieve something a more exotic, refer to the Razor syntax documentation at https://docs.microsoft.com/en-us/aspnet/core/mvc/views/razor.

7.3.1   *Using C# in Razor templates*

One of the most common requirements when working with Razor templates is to render a value you've calculated in C# to the HTML. For example, you might want to print the current year to use with a copyright statement in your HTML, to give

```
<p>Copyright 2018 ©</p>
```

or you might want to print the result of a calculation, for example

```
<p>The sum of 1 and 2 is <i>3</i><p>
```

You can do this in two ways, depending on the exact C# code you need to execute. If the code is a single statement, then you can use the @ symbol to indicate you want to write the result to the HTML output, as shown in figure 7.8. You've already seen this used to write out values from the view model or from `ViewData`.

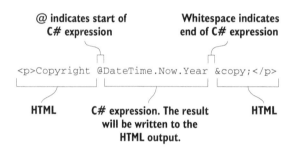

Figure 7.8   Writing the result of a C# expression to HTML. The @ symbol indicates where the C# code begins and the expression ends at the end of the statement, in this case at the space.

If the C# you want to execute is something that *needs* a space, then you need to use parentheses to demarcate the C#, as shown in figure 7.9.

Figure 7.9   When a C# expression contains whitespace, you must wrap it in parentheses using `@()` so the Razor engine knows where the C# stops and HTML begins.

These two approaches, in which C# is evaluated and written directly to the HTML output, are called *Razor expressions*. Sometimes you want to execute some C#, but you don't need to output the values. I used this technique when we were setting values in `ViewData`:

```
@{
    ViewData["Title"] = "About";
}
```

This example demonstrates a *Razor code block*, which is normal C# code, identified by the @{} structure. Nothing is written to the HTML output here, it's all compiled as though you'd written it in any other normal C# file.

> **TIP** When you execute code within code blocks, it must be valid C#, so you need to add semicolons. Conversely, when you're writing values directly to the response using Razor expressions, you don't need them. If your output HTML breaks unexpectedly, keep an eye out for missing or rogue extra semicolons!

Razor expressions are one of the most common ways of writing data from your view model to the HTML output. You'll see the other approach, using Tag Helpers, in the next chapter. Razor's capabilities extend far further than this, however, as you'll see in the next section where you'll learn how to include traditional C# structures in your templates.

7.3.2 *Adding loops and conditionals to Razor templates*

One of the biggest advantages of using Razor templates over static HTML is the ability to dynamically generate the output. Being able to write values from your view model to the HTML using Razor expressions is a key part of that, but another common use is loops and conditionals. With these, you could hide sections of the UI, or produce HTML for every item in a list, for example.

Loops and conditionals include constructs such as if and for loops, and using them in Razor templates is almost identical to C#, but you need to prefix their usage with the @ symbol. In case you're not getting the hang of Razor yet, when in doubt, throw in another @!

One of the big advantages of Razor in the context of ASP.NET Core is that it uses languages you're already familiar with: C# and HTML. There's no need to learn a whole new set of primitives for some other templating language: it's the same if, foreach, and while constructs you already know. And when you don't need them, you're writing raw HTML, so you can see exactly what the user will be getting in their browser.

In listing 7.6 , I've applied a number of these different techniques in the template for displaying a to-do item. You can see the @model directive indicates I've provided a ToDoItemViewModel view model, which is used to generate the final HTML. The view model has a bool IsComplete property, as well as a List<string> property called Tasks, which contains any outstanding tasks.

Listing 7.6 Razor template for rendering a `ToDoItemViewModel`

```
@model ToDoItemViewModel      ◁─── The @model directive indicates
<div>                              the type of view model in Model.
    @if (Model.IsComplete)
    {
        <strong>Well done, you're all done!</strong>    The if control structure
    }                                                   checks the value of the
    else                                                view model's IsComplete
    {                                                   property at runtime.
```

```
        <strong>The following tasks remain:</strong>
        <ul>
            @foreach (var task in Model.Tasks)          ◁─┐   The foreach structure
            {                                             │   will generate the <li>
                <li>@task</li>          ◁─┐               │   elements once for each
            }                            │                │   task in Tasks.
        </ul>            A razor expression is
    }                    used to write the task
</div>                   to the HTML output.
```

This code definitely lives up to the promise of mixing C# and HTML! There are traditional C# control structures, like `if` and `foreach`, that you'd expect in any normal program, interspersed with the HTML markup that I want to send to the browser. As you can see, the `@` symbol is used to indicate when I'm starting a control statement, but I generally let the Razor template infer when I'm switching back and forth between HTML and C#.

The template shows how to generate dynamic HTML at runtime, depending on the exact data provided. If the view model has outstanding `Tasks`, then the HTML will generate a list item for each task, producing output something like that shown in figure 7.10.

The data to display is defined in the model.

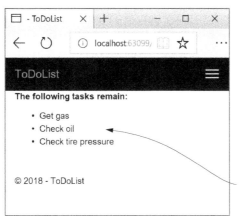

```
Model.IsComplete = false;
Model.Tasks = new List<string>
{
    "Get gas",
    "Check oil",
    "Check tire pressure"
};
```

Razor markup can include C# constructs such as if statements and for loops.

```
@if (Model.IsComplete)
{
    <p>Well done, you're all done!</p>
} else {
    <p>The following tasks remain:</p>
    <ul>
    @foreach(var task in Model.Tasks)
    {
        <li>@task</li>
    }
    </ul>
}
```

Only the relevant if block is rendered to the HTML, and the content within a foreach loop is rendered once for every item.

Figure 7.10   The Razor template generates a `<li>` item for each remaining task, depending on the view model passed to the view at runtime.

IntelliSense and tooling support

The mixture of C# and HTML might seem hard to read in the book, and that's a reasonable complaint. It's also another valid argument for trying to keep your Razor templates as simple as possible.

Luckily, if you're using Visual Studio or Visual Studio Code, then the tooling can help somewhat. As you can see in this figure, the C# portions of the code are shaded to help distinguish them from the surrounding HTML.

```
ToDoList                                    _  □  ✕

View.cshtml  ⊕ ✕
        @model ToDoItemViewModel

  <p>
        @if (Model.IsComplete)
        {
            <strong>Well done, you're all done!</strong>
        } else {
            <strong>The following tasks remain:</strong>
            <ul>
            @foreach (var task in Model.Tasks)
            {
                <li>@task</li>
            }
            </ul>
        }
  </p>
```

Visual Studio shades the C# regions of code and highlights @ symbols where C# transitions to HTML. This makes the Razor templates easier to read.

Although the ability to use loops and conditionals is powerful—they're one of the advantages of Razor over static HTML—they also add to the complexity of your view. Try to limit the amount of logic in your views to make them as easy to understand and maintain as possible.

A common trope of the ASP.NET Core team is that they try to ensure you "fall into the pit of success" when building an application. This refers to the idea that, by default, the *easiest* way to do something should be the *correct* way of doing it. This is a great philosophy, as it means you shouldn't get burned by, for example, security problems if you follow the standard approaches. Occasionally, however, you may need to step beyond the safety rails; a common use case is when you need to render some HTML contained in a C# object to the output, as you'll see in the next section.

7.3.3 Rendering HTML with Raw

In the previous example, I rendered the list of tasks to HTML by writing the string task using the @task Razor expression. But what if the task variable contains HTML you want to display, so instead of "Check oil" it contains "Check oil"? If you use a Razor expression to output this as you did previously, then you might hope to get this:

```
<li><strong>Check oil</strong></li>
```

But that's not the case. The HTML generated comes out like this:

```
<li>&lt;strong&gt;Check oil&lt;/strong&gt;</li>
```

Hmm, looks odd, right? What's happened here? Why did the template not write your variable to the HTML, like it has in previous examples? If you look at how a browser displays this HTML, like in figure 7.11, then hopefully it makes more sense.

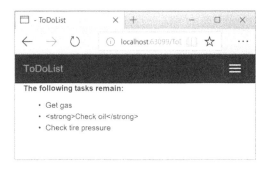

Figure 7.11 The second item, <strong>Check oil<strong> has been HTML-encoded, so the <strong> elements are visible to the user as part of the task.

Razor templates encode C# expressions before they're written to the output stream. This is primarily for security reasons; writing out arbitrary strings to your HTML could allow users to inject malicious data and JavaScript into your website. Consequently, the C# variables you print in your Razor template get written as HTML-encoded values.

In some cases, you might need to directly write out HTML contained in a string to the response. If you find yourself in this situation, first, stop. Do you *really* need to do this? If the values you're writing have been entered by a user, or were created based on values provided by users, then there's a serious risk of creating a security hole in your website.

If you *really* need to write the variable out to the HTML stream, then you can do so using the Html property on the view page and calling the Raw method:

```
<li>@Html.Raw(task)</li>
```

With this approach, the string in task will be directly written to the output stream, producing the HTML you originally wanted, <li><strong>Check oil</strong></li>, which renders as shown in figure 7.12.

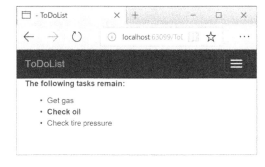

Figure 7.12 The second item, "<strong>Check oil<strong>" has been output using Html.Raw(), so it hasn't been HTML encoded. The <strong> elements result in the second item being shown in bold instead.

WARNING Using `Html.Raw` on user input creates a security risk that users could use to inject malicious code into your website. Avoid using `Html.Raw` if possible!

The C# constructs shown in this section can be useful, but they can make your templates harder to read. It's generally easier to understand the intention of Razor templates that are predominantly HTML markup rather than C#.

In the previous version of ASP.NET, these constructs, and in particular the `Html` helper property, were the standard way to generate dynamic markup. You can still use this approach in ASP.NET Core by using the various `HtmlHelper`[1] methods on the `Html` property, but these have largely been superseded by a cleaner technique: Tag Helpers.

NOTE I'll discuss Tag Helpers, and how to use them to build HTML forms, in the next chapter.

Tag Helpers are a useful feature that's new to Razor in ASP.NET Core, but a number of other features have been carried through from the previous version of ASP.NET. In the final section of this chapter, you'll see how you can create nested Razor templates and use partial views to reduce the amount of duplication in your views.

7.4 Layouts, partial views, and _ViewStart

Every HTML document has a certain number of elements that are required: `<html>`, `<head>`, and `<body>`. As well, there are often common sections that are repeated on every page of your application, such as the header and footer, as shown in figure 7.13. Each page on your application will also probably reference the same CSS and Java-Script files.

All of these different elements add up to a maintenance nightmare. If you had to manually include these in every view, then making any changes would be a laborious, error-prone process. Instead, Razor lets you extract these common elements into *layouts*.

DEFINITION A *layout* in Razor is a template that includes common code. It can't be rendered directly, but it can be rendered in conjunction with normal Razor views.

By extracting your common markup into layouts, you can reduce the duplication in your app. This makes changes easier, makes your views easier to manage and maintain, and is generally good practice! In this section, you'll see how to create a layout and reference it from your normal Razor views.

---

[1] HTML Helpers are almost obsolete, though they're still available if you prefer to use them.

**Header common to every
page in the app**

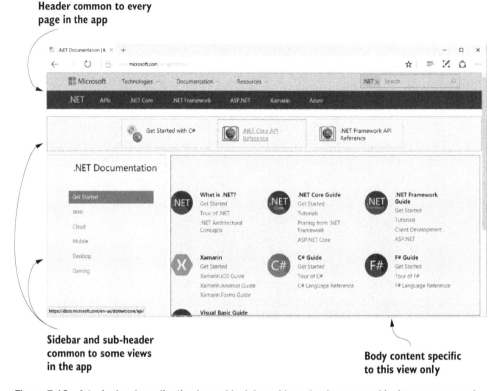

**Sidebar and sub-header
common to some views
in the app**

**Body content specific
to this view only**

Figure 7.13   A typical web application has a block-based layout, where some blocks are common to every page of your application. The header block will likely be identical across your whole application, but the sub-header and sidebar are probably identical for all the pages in one section. The body content will differ for every page in your application.

7.4.1   *Using layouts for shared markup*

Layout files are, for the most part, normal Razor templates that contain markup common to more than one page. An ASP.NET Core app can have multiple layouts, and layouts can reference other layouts. A common use for this is to have different layouts for different sections of your application. For example, an e-commerce website might use a three-column view for most pages, but a single-column layout when you come to the checkout pages, as shown in figure 7.14.

You'll often use layouts across many different action methods, so they're typically placed in the Views/Shared folder. You can name them anything you like, but there's a common convention to use _Layout.cshtml as the filename for the base layout in your application. This is the default name used by the MVC templates in Visual Studio and the .NET CLI.

TIP   A common convention is to prefix your layout files with an underscore (_) to distinguish them from standard Razor templates in your Views folder.

Three-column layout   Single-column layout

Figure 7.14   The https://manning.com website uses different layouts for different parts of the web application. The product pages use a three-column layout, but the cart page uses a single-column layout.

A layout file looks similar to a normal Razor template, with one exception: every layout must call the @RenderBody() function. This tells the templating engine where to insert the content from the child views. A simple layout is shown in the following listing. Typically, your application will reference all your CSS and JavaScript files in the layout, as well as include all the common elements such as headers and footers, but this example includes pretty much the bare minimum HTML.

Listing 7.7   A basic Layout.cshtml file calling `RenderBody`

```
<!DOCTYPE html>
<html>
<head>
    <meta charset="utf-8" />
    <title>@ViewData["Title"]</title>
    <link rel="stylesheet" href="~/css/site.css" />
</head>
<body>
    @RenderBody()
</body>
</html>
```

ViewData is the standard mechanism for passing data to a layout from a view.

Elements common to every page, such as your CSS, are typically found in the layout.

Tells the templating engine where to insert the child view's content

As you can see, the layout file includes the required elements, such as <html> and <head>, as well as elements you need on every page, such as <title> and <link>. This example also shows the benefit of storing the page title in ViewData; the layout can render it in the <title> element so that it shows in the browser's tab, as shown in figure 7.15.

Figure 7.15   The contents of the `<title>` element is used to name the tab in the user's browser, in this case Home Page.

Views can specify a layout file to use by setting the `Layout` property inside a Razor code block.

Listing 7.8   Setting the `Layout` property from a view

```
@{
    Layout = "_Layout";
    ViewData["Title"] = "Home Page";
}
<h1>@ViewData["Title"]</h1>
<p>This is the home page</p>
```

Set the layout for the page to _Layout.cshtml.

ViewData is a convenient way of passing data from a view to the layout.

The content in the view to render inside the layout

Any contents in the view will be rendered inside the layout, where the call to `@Render-Body()` occurs. Combining the two previous listings will result in the following HTML being generated and sent to the user.

Listing 7.9   Rendered output from combining a view with its layout

```
<!DOCTYPE html>
<html>
<head>
    <meta charset="utf-8" />
    <title>Home Page</title>
    <link rel="stylesheet" href="/css/site.css" />
</head>
<body>
    <h1>Home Page</h1>
    <p>This is the home page</p>
</body>
<html>
```

ViewData set in the view is used to render the layout.

The RenderBody call renders the contents of the view.

Judicious use of layouts can be extremely useful in reducing the duplication on a page. By default, layouts only provide a single location where you can render content from the view, at the call to `@RenderBody`. In cases where this is too restrictive, you can render content using *sections*.

7.4.2   *Overriding parent layouts using sections*

A common requirement when you start using multiple layouts in your application is to be able to render content from child views in more than one place in your layout. Consider the case of a layout that uses two columns. The view needs a mechanism for saying "render *this* content in the *left* column" and "render this *other* content in the *right* column". This is achieved using *sections*.

> **NOTE** Remember, all of the features outlined in this chapter are specific to Razor, which is a server-side rendering engine. If you're using a client-side SPA framework to build your application, you'll likely handle these requirements in other ways, either within the client code or by making multiple requests to a Web API endpoint.

Sections provide a way of organizing where view elements should be placed within a layout. They're defined in the view using an `@section` definition, as shown in the following listing, which defines the HTML content for a sidebar separate from the main content, in a section called `Sidebar`. The `@section` can be placed anywhere in the file, top or bottom, wherever is convenient.

Listing 7.10   Defining a section in a view template

```
@{
    Layout = "_TwoColumn";                  All content inside the braces
}                                           is part of the Sidebar section,
                                            not the main body content.
@section Sidebar {
    <p>This is the sidebar content</p>
}                                           Any content not inside an
                                            @section will be rendered
<p>This is the main content </p>            by the @RenderBody call.
```

The section is rendered in the parent layout with a call to `@RenderSection()`. This will render the content contained in the child section into the layout. Sections can be either required or optional. If they're required, then a view *must* declare the given `@section`; if they're optional then they can be omitted, and the layout will skip it. Skipped sections won't appear in the rendered HTML. This listing shows a layout that has a required section called `Sidebar`, and an optional section called `Scripts`.

Listing 7.11   Rendering a section in a layout file, _TwoColumn.cshtml

```
@{
    Layout = "_Layout";              This layout is nested
}                                    inside a layout itself.
<div class="main-content">
    @RenderBody()                    Renders all the content from a
</div>                               view that isn't part of a section
<div class="side-bar">
    @RenderSection("Sidebar", required: true)     Renders the Sidebar section; if
</div>                                            the Sidebar section isn't defined
                                                  in the view, throws an error
@RenderSection("Scripts", required: false)

                                     Renders the Scripts section;
                                     if the Scripts section isn't
                                     defined in the view, ignore it.
```

TIP   It's common to have an optional section called Scripts in your layout pages. This can be used to render additional JavaScript that's required by some views, but that isn't needed on every view. A common example is the jQuery Unobtrusive Validation scripts for client-side validation. If a view requires the scripts, it adds the appropriate @section Scripts to the Razor markup.

You may notice that the previous listing defines a Layout property, even though it's a layout itself, not a view. This is perfectly acceptable, and lets you create nested hierarchies of layouts, as shown in figure 7.16.

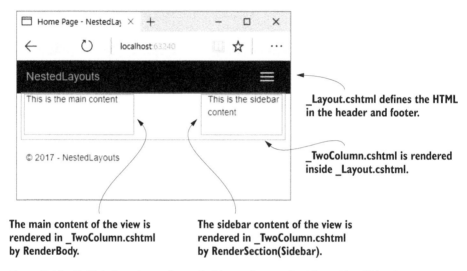

_Layout.cshtml defines the HTML in the header and footer.

_TwoColumn.cshtml is rendered inside _Layout.cshtml.

The main content of the view is rendered in _TwoColumn.cshtml by RenderBody.

The sidebar content of the view is rendered in _TwoColumn.cshtml by RenderSection(Sidebar).

Figure 7.16   Multiple layouts can be nested to create complex hierarchies. This allows you to keep the elements common to all views in your base layout and extract layout common to multiple views into sub-layouts.

Layout files and sections provide a lot of flexibility to build sophisticated UIs, but one of their most important uses is in reducing the duplication of code in your application. They're perfect for avoiding duplication of content that you'd need to write for every view. But what about those times when you find you want to reuse part of a view somewhere else? For those cases, you have partial views.

7.4.3   *Using partial views to encapsulate markup*

Partial views are exactly what they sound like—they're part of a view. They provide a means of breaking up a larger view into smaller, reusable chunks. This can be useful for both reducing the complexity in a large view by splitting it into multiple partial views, or for allowing you to reuse part of a view inside another.

Most web frameworks that use server-side rendering have this capability—Ruby on Rails has partial views, Django has inclusion tags, and Zend has partials. All of these work in the same way, extracting common code into small, reusable templates. Even client-side templating engines such as Mustache and Handlebars used by client-side frameworks like AngularJs and Ember have similar "partial view" concepts.

Consider a to-do list application. You might find you have an action method that displays a single to-do with a given id using a view called ViewToDo.cshtml. Later on, you create a new action method that displays the five most recent to-do items using a view called RecentToDos.cshtml. Instead of copying and pasting the code from one view to the other, you could create a partial view, called _ToDo.cshtml.

Listing 7.12 Partial view _ToDo.cshtml for displaying a `ToDoItemViewModel`

```
@model ToDoItemViewModel          ◁──────────    Partial views can use a view
                                                 model, just like normal views.
<h2>@Model.Title</h2>
<ul>
    @foreach (var task in Model.Tasks)    The content of the partial
    {                                      view, which previously existed
        <li>@task</li>                     in the ViewToDo.cshtml file
    }
</ul>
```

Both the ViewToDo.cshtml and RecentToDos.cshtml views can now render the _ToDo .cshtml partial view. Partial views are rendered using the `@await Html.PartialAsync` method and can be passed a view model to render. For example, the RecentToDos.cshtml view could achieve this using

```
@model List<ToDoItemViewModel>

@foreach(var todo in Model)
{
    @await Html.PartialAsync("_ToDo", todo)
}
```

You can call the partial in a number of other ways, such as `Html.Partial` and `Html.RenderPartial`, but `Html.PartialAsync` is recommended.[2]

> **NOTE** Like layouts, partial views are typically named with a leading underscore.

The Razor code contained in a partial view is almost identical to a standard view. The main difference is the fact that partial views are typically called from other views rather than as the result of an action method. The only other difference is that partial views don't run _ViewStart.cshtml when they execute, which you'll see shortly.

---

[2] You should use the asynchronous partial methods to render partials where possible, as the synchronous methods can lead to subtle performance issues.

Child actions in ASP.NET Core

In the previous version of ASP.NET MVC, there was the concept of a *child action*. This was an action method that could be invoked *from inside a view*. This was the main mechanism for rendering discrete sections of a complex layout that had nothing to do with the main action method. For example, a child action method might render the shopping cart on an e-commerce site.

This approach meant you didn't have to pollute every page's view model with the view model items required to render the shopping cart, but it fundamentally broke the MVC design pattern, by referencing controllers from a view.

In ASP.NET Core, child actions are no more. View components have replaced them. These are conceptually quite similar in that they allow both the execution of arbitrary code and the rendering of HTML, but they don't directly invoke controller actions. You can think of them as a more powerful partial view that you should use anywhere a partial view needs to contain significant code or business logic. You'll see how to build a small view component in chapter 19.

Partial views aren't the only way to reduce duplication in your view templates. Razor also allows you to pull common elements such as namespace declarations and layout configuration into centralized files. In the final section of this chapter, you'll see how to wield these files to clean up your templates.

7.4.4   *Running code on every view with _ViewStart and _ViewImports*

Due to the nature of views, you'll inevitably find yourself writing certain things repeatedly. If all of your views use the same layout, then adding the following code to the top of every page feels a little redundant:

```
@{
    Layout = "_Layout";
}
```

Similarly, if you've declared your view models in a different namespace to your app's default, for example the WebApplication1.Models namespace, then having to add @using WebApplication1.Models to the top of the page can get to be a chore. Thankfully, ASP.NET Core includes two mechanisms for handling these common tasks: _ViewImports.cshtml and _ViewStart.cshtml.

IMPORTING COMMON DIRECTIVES WITH _VIEWIMPORTS

The _ViewImports.cshtml file contains directives that will be inserted at the top of every view. This includes things like the @using and @model statements that you've already seen—basically any Razor directive. To avoid adding a using statement to every view, you can include it in here instead.

Listing 7.13 A typical _ViewImports.cshtml file importing additional namespaces

```
@using WebApplication1          ◁──────── The default namespace of your application
@using WebApplication1.Models   ◁─────── Add this directive to avoid placing in every view
@addTagHelper *, Microsoft.AspNetCore.Mvc.TagHelpers  ◁──┐ Makes Tag Helpers
                                                          │ available in your views
```

The _ViewImports.cshtml file can be placed in any folder, and it will apply to all views and sub-folders in that folder. Typically, it's placed in the root Views folder so that it applies to every view in your app.

It's important to note that you should *only* put Razor directives in _ViewImports .cshtml—you can't put any old C# in there. As you can see in the previous listing, this is limited to things like @using or the @addTagHelper directive that you'll learn about in the next chapter. If you want to run some arbitrary C# at the start of every view in your application, for example to set the Layout property, then you should use the _ViewStart.cshtml file instead.

RUNNING CODE FOR EVERY VIEW WITH _VIEWSTART

You can easily run common code at the start of every view by adding a _ViewStart file to the Views folder in your application. This file can contain any Razor code, but it's typically used to set the Layout for all the views in your application, as shown in the following listing. You can then omit the Layout statement from all views that use the default layout. If a view needs to use a nondefault layout then you can override it by setting the value in the view itself.

Listing 7.14 A typical _ViewStart.cshtml file setting the default layout

```
@{
    Layout = "_Layout";
}
```

Any code in the _ViewStart.cshtml file runs before the view executes. Note that _ViewStart.cshtml only runs for full views—it doesn't run for layouts or partials views. Also, note that the names for these special Razor files are enforced rather than conventions.

> **WARNING** You must use the names _ViewStart.cshtml and _ViewImports .cshtml for the Razor engine to locate and execute them correctly. To apply them to all your app's views, add them to the root of the Views folder, not to the Shared subfolder.

If you only want to run _ViewStart.cshtml or _ViewImports.cshtml for some of your views, you can include additional _ViewStart.cshtml or _ViewImports.cshtml files in a controller-related subfolder. The controller-specific files will run after the root Views folder files.

Partial views, layouts, and AJAX

This chapter describes using Razor to render full HTML pages server-side, which are then sent to the user's browser in traditional web apps. A common alternative approach when building web apps is to use a JavaScript client-side framework to build a Single Page Application (SPA), which renders the HTML client-side in the browser.

One of the technologies SPAs typically use is AJAX (Asychronous JavaScript and XML), in which the browser sends requests to your ASP.NET Core app without reloading a whole new page. It's also possible to use AJAX requests with apps that use server-side rendering. To do so, you'd use JavaScript to request an update for part of a page.

If you want to use AJAX with an app that uses Razor, you should consider making extensive use of partial views. You can then expose these via additional actions. Using AJAX can reduce the overall amount of data that needs to be sent back and forth between the browser and your app, and it can make your app feel smoother and more responsive, as it requires fewer full-page loads. But using AJAX with Razor can add complexity, especially for larger apps. If you foresee yourself making extensive use of AJAX to build a highly dynamic web app, you might want to consider using Web API controllers and a client-side framework (see chapter 9) instead.

That concludes our first look at rendering HTML using the Razor templating engine. You saw how to select a view, pass a view model to it, and render the data to the HTML. Finally, you saw how to build complex layouts and reduce duplication in your views using partial views.

In the next chapter, you'll learn about Tag Helpers and how to use them to build HTML forms, a staple of modern web applications. Tag Helpers are one of the biggest improvements to Razor in ASP.NET Core, so getting to grips with them will make editing your views an overall more pleasant experience!

Summary

- In MVC, views are responsible for generating the UI for your application.
- Razor is a templating language that allows you to generate dynamic HTML using a mixture of HTML and C#.
- HTML forms are the standard approach for sending data from the browser to the server. You can use Tag Helpers to easily generate these forms.
- By convention, views are named the same as the action that invokes them, and reside either in a folder with the same name as the action method's controller or in the Shared folder.
- Controllers can override the default view template by passing the template name when returning a `ViewResult` using the `View` helper method on the `Controller` base class.

- Controllers can pass strongly typed data to a view using a view model. To access the properties on the view model, the view should declare the model type using the `@model` directive.
- Controllers can pass key-value pairs to the view using the `ViewData` dictionary.
- Razor expressions render C# values to the HTML output using `@` or `@()`. You don't need to include a semicolon after the statement when using Razor expressions.
- Razor code blocks, defined using `@{}`, execute C# without outputting HTML. The C# in Razor code blocks must be complete statements, so it must include semicolons.
- Loops and conditionals can be used to easily generate dynamic HTML in templates, but it's a good idea to limit the number of `if` statements in particular, to keep your views easy to read.
- If you need to render a `string` as raw HTML you can use `Html.Raw`, but do so sparingly—rendering raw user input can create a security vulnerability in your application.
- Tag Helpers allow you to bind your data model to HTML elements, making it easier to generate dynamic HTML while staying editor friendly.
- You can place HTML common to multiple views in a layout. The layout will render any content from the child view at the location `@RenderBody` is called.
- Encapsulate commonly used snippets of Razor code in a partial view. A partial view can be rendered using `@await Html.PartialAsync()`.
- _ViewImports.cshtml can be used to include common directives, such as `@using` statements, in every view.
- _ViewStart.cshtml is called before the execution of each main view and can be used to execute code common to all views, such as a default layout page. It doesn't execute for layouts or partial views.
- _ViewImports.cshtml and _ViewStart.cshtml are hierarchical—files in the root folder execute first, followed by files in controller-specific view folders.

Building forms
with Tag Helpers

This chapter covers

- Building forms easily with Tag Helpers
- Generating URLs with the Anchor Tag Helper
- Using Tag Helpers to add functionality to Razor

In chapter 7, you learned about Razor templates and how to use them to generate the views for your MVC application. By mixing HTML and C#, you can create dynamic applications that can display different data based on the request, the logged-in user, or any other data you can access.

Displaying dynamic data is an important aspect of many web applications, but it's typically only one half of the story. As well as displaying data to the user, you often need the user to be able to submit data *back* to your application. You can use data to customize the view, or to update the application model by saving it to a database, for example. For traditional web applications, this data is usually submitted using an HTML form.

In chapter 6, you learned about model binding, which is how you *accept* the data sent by a user in a request and convert it into a C# object that you can use in your action methods. You also learned about validation, and how important it is to validate the data sent in a request. You used `DataAnnotations` to define the rules associated with your models, as well as other associated metadata like the display name for a property.

The final aspect we haven't yet looked at is how to *build* the HTML forms that users use to send this data in a request. Forms are one of the key ways users will interact with your application in the browser, so it's important they're both correctly defined for your application and also user friendly. ASP.NET Core provides a feature to achieve this, called *Tag Helpers.*

Tag Helpers are new to ASP.NET Core. They're Razor components that you can use to customize the HTML generated in your templates. Tag Helpers can be added to an otherwise standard HTML element, such as an `<input>`, to customize its attributes based on your view model, saving you from having to write boilerplate code. They can also be standalone elements and can be used to generate completely customized HTML.

> **NOTE** Remember, Razor, and therefore Tag Helpers, are for server-side HTML rendering. You can't use Tag Helpers directly in frontend frameworks like Angular or React.

If you've used the previous version of ASP.NET, then Tag Helpers may sound reminiscent of HTML Helpers, which could also be used to generate HTML based on your view model. Tag Helpers are the logical successor to HTML Helpers, as they provide a more streamlined syntax than the previous, C#-focused helpers. HTML Helpers are still available in ASP.NET Core, so if you're converting some old templates to ASP.NET Core, or want to, you can use them in your templates, but I won't be covering them in this book.

In this chapter, you'll primarily learn how to use Tag Helpers when building forms. They simplify the process of generating correct element names and IDs so that model binding can occur seamlessly when the form is sent back to your application. To put them into context, you're going to carry on building the currency converter application that you've seen in previous chapters. You'll add the ability to submit currency exchange requests to it, validate the data, and redisplay errors on the form using Tag Helpers to do the leg work for you, as shown in figure 8.1.

As you develop the application, you'll meet the most common Tag Helpers you'll encounter when working with forms. You'll also see how you can use Tag Helpers to simplify other common tasks, such as generating links, conditionally displaying data in your application, and ensuring users see the latest version of an image file when they refresh their browser.

To start, I'll talk a little about why you need Tag Helpers when Razor can already generate any HTML you like by combining C# and HTML in a file.

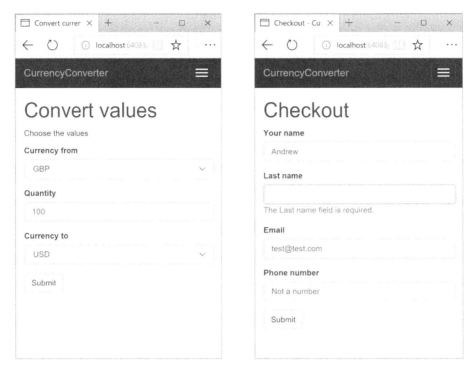

Figure 8.1   The currency converter application forms, built using Tag Helpers. The labels, dropdowns, input elements, and validation messages are all generated using Tag Helpers.

8.1   *Catering to editors with Tag Helpers*

One of the common complaints about the mixture of C# and HTML in Razor templates is that you can't easily use standard HTML editing tools with them; all the @ and {} symbols in the C# code tend to confuse the editors. Reading the templates can be similarly difficult for people; switching paradigms between C# and HTML can be a bit jarring sometimes.

This arguably wasn't such a problem when Visual Studio was the only supported way to build ASP.NET websites, as it could obviously understand the templates without any issues, and helpfully colorize the editor. But with ASP.NET Core going cross-platform, the desire to play nicely with other editors reared its head again.

This was one of the biggest motivations for Tag Helpers. They integrate seamlessly into the standard HTML syntax by adding what look to be attributes, typically starting with asp-*. They're most often used to generate HTML forms, as shown in the following listing. This listing shows a view from the first iteration of the currency converter application, in which you choose the currencies to convert and the quantity.

Listing 8.1   User registration form using Tag Helpers

Use @model to describe the view model type for Tag Helpers.

Tag Helpers on Forms are used to generate the action URL.

```
@model CurrencyConverterModel

<form asp-action="Convert" asp-controller="Currency">
    <div class="form-group">
        <label asp-for="CurrencyFrom"></label>
        <input class="form-control" asp-for="CurrencyFrom" />
        <span asp-validation-for="CurrencyFrom"></span>
    </div>
    <div class="form-group">
        <label asp-for="Quantity"></label>
        <input class="form-control" asp-for="Quantity" />
        <span asp-validation-for="Quantity"></span>
    </div>
    <div class="form-group">
        <label asp-for="CurrencyTo"></label>
        <input class="form-control" asp-for="CurrencyTo" />
        <span asp-validation-for="CurrencyTo"></span>
    </div>
    <button type="submit" class="btn btn-default">Submit</button>
</form>
```

Validation messages are written to a span using Tag Helpers.

Validation messages are written to a span using Tag Helpers.

Validation messages are written to a span using Tag Helpers.

asp-for on Labels generates the caption for labels based on the view model.

asp-for on Inputs generate the correct type, value, and validation attributes for the model.

At first glance, you might not even spot the Tag Helpers, they blend in so well with the HTML! This makes it easy to edit the files with any standard HTML text editor. But don't be concerned that you've sacrificed readability in Visual Studio—as you can see in figure 8.2, elements with Tag Helpers are clearly distinguishable from the standard HTML <div> element and the standard HTML class attribute on the <input> element. The C# properties of the view model being referenced (CurrencyFrom, in this case) are also still shaded, as with other C# code in Razor files. And of course, you get IntelliSense, as you'd expect.

```
<form asp-action="Convert">
    <div class="form-group">
        <label asp-for="CurrencyFrom"></label>
        <input class="form-control" asp-for="CurrencyFrom" />
        <span asp-validation-for="CurrencyFrom"></span>
    </div>
    <div class="form-group">
        <label asp-for="Qu"></label>
        <input class="fo  Quantity        sp-for="Quantity" />
        <span asp-valida       ntity"></span>
    </div>
```

Figure 8.2   In Visual Studio, Tag Helpers are distinguishable from normal elements by being bold and a different color, C# is shaded, and IntelliSense is available.

TIP   Visual Studio 2017 currently doesn't have native IntelliSense support for the asp-* Tag Helpers themselves, though it will be enabled in an update. In the meantime, install the Razor Language Services extension.[1] Unfortunately, IntelliSense for Tag Helpers isn't available in Visual Studio Code.

Tag Helpers are extra attributes on standard HTML elements (or new elements entirely) that work by modifying the HTML element they're attached to. They let you easily integrate your server-side values, such as those in your view model, with the generated HTML.

Notice that listing 8.1 didn't specify the captions to display in the labels. Instead, you declaratively used asp-for="CurrencyFrom" to say, "for this <label>, use the Currency-From property to work out what caption to use." Similarly, for the <input> elements, Tag Helpers are used to

- Automatically populate the values from the view model
- Choose the correct input type to display (for example, a number input for the Quantity property)
- Display any validation errors, as shown in figure 8.3[2]

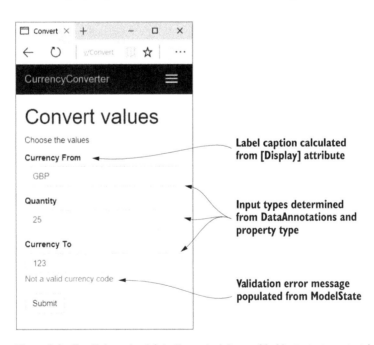

Figure 8.3   Tag Helpers hook into the metadata provided by DataAnnotations, as well as the property types themselves. The Validation Tag Helper can even populate error messages based on the ModelState, as you saw in the last chapter on validation.

---

[1]   You can install Visual Studio extensions by clicking Tools > Extensions and Updates, or by viewing on the Visual Studio Marketplace at http://mng.bz/LcNX.

[2]   To learn more about the internals of Tag Helpers, read the documentation at http://mng.bz/Idb0.

Tag Helpers can perform a variety of functions by modifying the HTML elements they're applied to. This chapter introduces a number of the common Tag Helpers and how to use them, but it's not an exhaustive list. I don't cover all of the helpers that come out of the box in ASP.NET Core (there are more coming with every release!), and you can easily create your own, as you'll see in chapter 18. Alternatively, you could use those published by others on NuGet or GitHub.[3] As with all of ASP.NET Core, Microsoft is developing Tag Helpers in the open on GitHub, so you can always take a look at the source to see how they're implemented.

> **WebForms flashbacks**
>
> For those who remember ASP.NET back in the day of WebForms, before the advent of the MVC pattern for web development, Tag Helpers may be triggering your PTSD. Although the `asp-` prefix is somewhat reminiscent of ASP.NET Web Server control definitions, never fear—the two are different beasts.
>
> Web Server controls were directly added to a page's backing C# class, and had a broad scope that could modify seemingly unrelated parts of the page. Coupled with that, they had a complex lifecycle that was hard to understand and debug when things weren't working. The perils of trying to work with that level of complexity haven't been forgotten, and Tag Helpers aren't the same.
>
> Tag Helpers don't have a lifecycle—they participate in the rendering of the element to which they're attached, and that's it. They can modify the HTML element they're attached to, but they can't modify anything else on your page, making them conceptually much simpler. An additional capability they bring is the ability to have multiple Tag Helpers acting on a single element—something Web Server controls couldn't easily achieve.
>
> Overall, if you're writing Razor templates, you'll have a much more enjoyable experience if you embrace Tag Helpers as integral to its syntax. They bring a lot of benefits without obvious downsides, and your cross-platform-editor friends will thank you!

8.2 Creating forms using Tag Helpers

The Tag Helpers for working with forms are some of the most useful and are the ones you'll probably use most often. You can use them to generate HTML markup based on properties of your view model, creating the correct `id` and `name` attributes and setting the `value` of the element to the model property's value (among other things). This capability significantly reduces the amount of markup you need to write manually.

Imagine you're building the checkout page for the currency converter application, and you need to capture the user's details on the checkout page. In chapter 6, you built a `UserBindingModel` binding model (shown in listing 8.2), added `DataAnnotation`

---

[3] I've published a few custom Tag Helpers on GitHub at http://mng.bz/FYH1

attributes for validation, and saw how to model bind it in your action method. In this chapter, you'll see how to create the view for it, using the `UserBindingModel` as a view model.

> **WARNING** For simplicity, I'm using the same object for both my binding model and view model, but in practice you should use two separate objects to avoid mass-assignment attacks on your app.[4]

Listing 8.2 `UserBindingModel` for creating a user on a checkout page

```
public class UserBindingModel
{
    [Required]
    [StringLength(100, ErrorMessage = "Maximum length is {1}")]
    [Display(Name = "Your name")]
    public string FirstName { get; set; }

    [Required]
    [StringLength(100, ErrorMessage = "Maximum length is {1}")]
    [Display(Name = "Last name")]
    public string LastName { get; set; }

    [Required]
    [EmailAddress]
    public string Email { get; set; }

    [Phone(ErrorMessage = "Not a valid phone number.")]
    [Display(Name = "Phone number")]
    public string PhoneNumber { get; set; }
}
```

The `UserBindingModel` is decorated with a number of `DataAnnotations` attributes. In the previous chapter, you saw that these attributes are used during model validation when your binding model is bound, before the action method is executed. These attributes are *also* used by the Razor templating language to provide the metadata required to generate the correct HTML when you use Tag Helpers.

With the help of the `UserBindingModel`, Tag Helpers, and a little HTML, you can create a Razor view that lets the user enter their details, as shown in figure 8.4.

The Razor template to generate this page is shown in listing 8.3. This code uses a variety of tag helpers, including

- A Form Tag Helper on the `<form>` element
- Label Tag Helpers on the `<label>`
- Input Tag Helpers on the `<input>`
- Validation Message Tag Helpers on `<span>` validation elements for each property in the `UserBindingModel`

---

[4] You can read about techniques for working with separate binding and view models at http://mng.bz/QvfG.

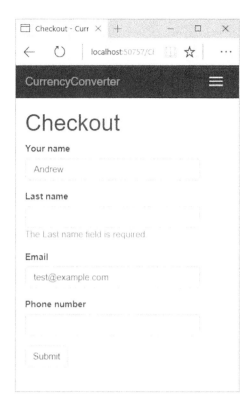

Figure 8.4 The checkout page for an application. The HTML is generated based on a `UserBindingModel`, using Tag Helpers to render the required element values, input types, and validation messages.

Listing 8.3 Razor template for binding to `UserBindingModel` on the checkout page

```
@model UserBindingModel                ◁──────────
@{
    ViewData["Title"] = "Checkout";
}
<h1>@ViewData["Title"]</h1>

<form asp-action="Index" asp-controller="Checkout">     ◁───
    <div class="form-group">
        <label asp-for="FirstName"></label>      ◁──────
        <input class="form-control" asp-for="FirstName" />
        <span asp-validation-for="FirstName"></span>
    </div>
    <div class="form-group">
        <label asp-for="LastName"></label>
        <input class="form-control" asp-for="LastName" />
        <span asp-validation-for="LastName"></span>
    </div>
    <div class="form-group">
        <label asp-for="Email"></label>
        <input class="form-control" asp-for="Email" />     ◁───
        <span asp-validation-for="Email"></span>
    </div>
```

The @model directive describes the view model for the page.

Form Tag Helpers use routing to determine the URL the form will be posted to.

The Label Tag Helper uses DataAnnotations on a property to determine the caption to display.

The Input Tag Helper uses DataAnnotations to determine the type of input to generate.

```
    <div class="form-group">
        <label asp-for="PhoneNumber"></label>
        <input class="form-control" asp-for="PhoneNumber" />
        <span asp-validation-for="PhoneNumber"></span>      ◁─────────┐
    </div>                                                             │
    <button type="submit" class="btn btn-default">Submit</button>     │
</form>                                                                │
```

The Validation Tag Helper displays error messages associated with the given property.

You can see the HTML markup that this template produces in listing 8.4. This Razor markup and the resulting HTML produces the results you saw in figure 8.4. You can see that each of the HTML elements with a Tag Helper have been customized in the output: the <form> element has an `action` attribute, the <input> elements have an `id` and `name` based on the name of the referenced property, and both the <input> and <span> have `data-*` elements for validation.

Listing 8.4   HTML generated by the Razor template on the checkout page

```
<form action="/Checkout" method="post">
  <div class="form-group">
    <label for="FirstName">Your name</label>
    <input class="form-control" type="text"
      id="FirstName" name="FirstName" value=""
      data-val="true" data-val-length-max="100"
      data-val-length="Maximum length is 100."
      data-val-required="The Your name field is required." />
    <span class="field-validation-valid"
      data-valmsg-for="FirstName" data-valmsg-replace="true"></span>
  </div>
  <div class="form-group">
    <label for="LastName">Last name</label>
    <input class="form-control" type="text"
      id="LastName" name="LastName" value=""
      data-val="true" data-val-length-max="100"
      data-val-length="Maximum length is 100."
      data-val-required="The Last name field is required." />
    <span class="field-validation-valid"
      data-valmsg-for="LastName" data-valmsg-replace="true"></span>
  </div>
  <div class="form-group">
    <label for="Email">Email</label>
    <input class="form-control" type="email"
      id="Email" name="Email" value=""
      data-val="true" data-val-length-max="100"
      data-val-email="The Email field is not a valid e-mail address."
      data-val-required="The Email field is required." />
    <span class="field-validation-valid"
      data-valmsg-for="Email" data-valmsg-replace="true"></span>
  </div>
  <div class="form-group">
    <label for="PhoneNumber">Phone number</label>
    <input class="form-control" type="tel"
      id="PhoneNumber" name="PhoneNumber" value=""
```

```
        data-val="true" data-val-length-max="100"
        data-val-phone="Not a valid phone number." />
      <span class="field-validation-valid"
        data-valmsg-for="PhoneNumber" data-valmsg-replace="true"></span>
    </div>
    <button type="submit" class="btn btn-default">Submit</button>
    <input name="__RequestVerificationToken" type="hidden"
      value="CfDJ8PkYhAINFx1JmYUVIDWbpPyy_TRUNCATED" />
</form>
```

Wow, that's a lot of markup! If you're new to working with HTML, this might all seem a little overwhelming, but the important thing to notice is that *you didn't have to write most of it*! The Tag Helpers took care of the vast majority of the plumbing for you. That's basically Tag Helpers in a nutshell; they simplify the fiddly mechanics of building HTML forms, leaving you to concentrate on the overall design of your application instead of writing boilerplate markup.

> **NOTE** If you're using Razor to build your views, Tag Helpers will make your life easier, but they're entirely optional. You're free to write raw HTML without them, or to use the previous HTML Helpers.

Tag Helpers simplify and abstract the process of HTML generation, but they generally try to do so without getting in your way. If you need the final generated HTML to have a particular attribute, then you can add it to your markup. You can see that in the previous listings where class attributes are defined on `<input>` elements, such as `<input class="form-control" asp-for="FirstName" />`, they pass untouched through from Razor to the HTML output.

> **TIP** This is different from the way HTML Helpers worked in the previous version of ASP.NET; they often required jumping through hoops to set attributes in the generated markup.

Even better than this, you can also set attributes that are normally generated by a Tag Helper, like the `type` attribute on an `<input>` element. For example, if the `Favorite-Color` property on your view model was a `string`, then by default, Tag Helpers would generate an `<input>` element with `type="text"`. Updating your markup to use the HTML5 `color` picker type is trivial; set the `type` in the markup:

```
<input type="color" asp-for="FavoriteColor" />
```

> **TIP** HTML5 adds a huge number of features, including lots of form elements that you may not have come across before, such as `range` inputs and `color` pickers. We're not going to cover them in this book, but you can read about them on the Mozilla Developer Network website at http://mng.bz/qOc1.

In this section, you'll build the currency calculator Razor templates from scratch, adding Tag Helpers as you find you need them. You'll probably find you use most of the common form Tag Helpers in every application you build, even if it's on a simple login page.

8.2.1 *The Form Tag Helper*

The first thing you need to start building your HTML form is, unsurprisingly, the `<form>` element. In the previous example, the `<form>` element was augmented with two Tag Helper attributes: `asp-action` and `asp-controller`:

```
<form asp-action="Index" asp-controller="Checkout">
```

This resulted in the addition of `action` and `method` attributes to the final HTML, indicating the URL that the form should be sent to when submitted:

```
<form action="/Checkout" method="post">
```

Setting the `asp-action` and `asp-controller` attributes allows you to specify the action method in your application that the form will be posted to when it's submitted. The `asp-action` and `asp-controller` attributes are added by a `FormTagHelper`. This Tag Helper uses the values provided to generate a URL for the `action` attribute using the URL generation features of routing that I described at the end of chapter 5.

> **NOTE** Tag Helpers can make multiple attributes available on an element. Think of them like properties on a Tag Helper configuration object. Adding a single asp- attribute activates the Tag Helper on the element. Adding additional attributes lets you override further default values of its implementation.

The Form Tag Helper makes a number of other attributes available on the `<form>` element that you can use to customize the generated URL. You've already seen the `asp-action` and `asp-controller` attributes for setting the `controller` and `action` route parameters. Hopefully you'll remember from chapter 5 that you can set other route parameters too, all of which will be used to generate the final URL. For example, the default route template looks something like `{controller}/{action}/{id?}`.

As you can see, there's an optional `id` route parameter that will be used during URL generation. How can you set this value for use during URL generation?

The Form Tag Helper defines an `asp-route-*` wildcard attribute that you can use to set arbitrary route parameters. Set the * in the attribute to the route parameter name. For the example, to set the `id` route parameter, you'd set the `asp-route-id` value, so

```
<form asp-action="View" asp-controller="Product" asp-route-id="5">
```

would generate the following markup, using the default route template to generate the URL:

```
<form action="/Product/View/5" method="post">
```

You can add as many asp-route-* attributes as necessary to your <form> to generate the correct action URL, but sometimes that's still not enough. In chapter 5, I described using a route name when generating URLs as being another option. You can achieve this with the Form Tag Helper by using the asp-route attribute.

> **NOTE** Use the asp-route attribute to specify the route *name* to use, and the asp-route-* attributes to specify the route *parameters* to use during URL generation.

Imagine you're building a social networking application, and you've defined a custom route called view_posts for viewing the posts of a user with a given username:

```
routes.MapRoute(
      name: "view_posts",
      template: "{username}/posts",
      defaults: new {controller="User", action="ViewPosts");
```

You can ensure the URL generated for a <form> uses this route by employing the following combination of asp-route and asp-route-username, where the current username is stored in the Username property on the view model.

```
<form asp-route="view_posts" asp-route-username="@Model.Username">
```

> **TIP** You can use values from your view model (and C# in general) in Tag Helpers like you would in normal Razor. See chapter 7 for details.

The main job of the Form Tag Helper is to generate the action attribute, but it performs one additional, important function: generating a hidden <input> field needed to prevent *cross-site request forgery* (CSRF) attacks.

> **DEFINITION** *Cross-site request forgery* (CSRF) attacks are a website exploit that can be used to execute actions on your website by an unrelated malicious website. You'll learn about them in detail in chapter 18.

You can see the generated hidden <input> at the bottom of the generated <form> in listing 8.4; it's named __RequestVerificationToken and contains a seemingly random string of characters. This field won't protect you on its own, but I'll describe in chapter 18 how it's used to protect your website. The Form Tag Helper generates it by default, so generally speaking you won't need to worry about it, but if you need to disable it, you can do so by adding asp-antiforgery="false" to your <form> element.

The Form Tag Helper is obviously useful for generating the action URL, but it's time to move on to more interesting elements, those that you can see in your browser!

8.2.2 *The Label Tag Helper*

Every <input> field in your currency converter application needs to have an associated label so the user knows what the <input> is for. You could easily create those yourself, manually typing the name of the field and setting the for attribute as appropriate, but luckily there's a Tag Helper to do that for us.

The Label Tag Helper is used to generate the caption (the visible text) and the `for` attribute for a `<label>` element, based on the properties in the view model. It's used by providing the name of the property in the `asp-for` attribute:

```
<label asp-for="FirstName"></label>
```

The Label Tag Helper uses the `[Display]` DataAnnotations attribute that you saw in chapter 6 to determine the appropriate value to display. If the property you're generating a label for doesn't have a `[Display]` attribute, the Label Tag Helper will use the name of the property instead. So, for the model

```
public class UserBindingModel
{
    [Display(Name = "Your name")]
    public string FirstName { get; set; }

    public string Email { get; set; }
}
```

in which the `FirstName` property has an `[Display]` attribute, but the `Email` property doesn't; the following Razor

```
<label asp-for="FirstName"></label>
<label asp-for="Email"></label>
```

would generate the HTML

```
<label for="FirstName">Your Name</label>
<label for="Email">Email</label>
```

The caption text inside the `<label>` element uses the value set in the [Display] attribute, or the property name in the case of the `Email` property. Also note that the `for` attribute has been generated with the name of the property. This is a key bonus of using Tag Helpers—it hooks in with the element IDs generated by other Tag Helpers, as you'll see shortly.

> **NOTE** The `for` attribute is important for accessibility. It specifies the ID of the element to which the label refers.

As is typical with Tag Helpers, the Label Tag Helper won't override values you set yourself. If, for example, you don't want to use the caption generated by the helper, you could insert your own manually. The following code

```
<label asp-for="Email">Please enter your Email</label>
```

would generate the HTML

```
<label for="Email">Please enter your Email</label>
```

As ever, you'll generally have an easier time with maintenance if you stick to the standard conventions and don't override values like this, but the option is there. Right, next up is a biggie: the Input and Textarea Tag Helpers.

8.2.3 *The Input and Textarea Tag Helpers*

Now you're getting into the meat of your form—the `<input>` elements that handle user input. Given that there's such a wide array of possible input types, there's a variety of different ways they can be displayed in the browser. For example, Boolean values are typically represented by a `checkbox` type `<input>` element, whereas integer values would use a `number` type `<input>` element, and a date would use the `date` type, shown in figure 8.5.

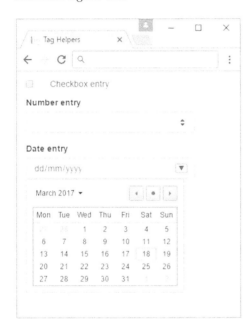

Figure 8.5   Various input element types. The exact way in which each type is displayed varies by browser.

To handle this diversity, the Input Tag Helper is one of the most powerful Tag Helpers. It uses information based on both the type of the property (`bool`, `string`, `int`, and so on) and any `DataAnnotations` attributes applied to it (`[EmailAddress]` and `[Phone]`, among others) to determine the type of the `input` element to generate. The `DataAnnotations` are also used to add `data-val-*` client-side validation attributes to the generated HTML.

Consider the `Email` property from listing 8.2 that was decorated with the `[Email-Address]` attribute. Adding an `<input>` is as simple as using the `asp-for` attribute:

```
<input asp-for="Email" />
```

The property is a `string`, so ordinarily, the Input Tag Helper would generate an `<input>` with `type="text"`. But the addition of the `[EmailAddress]` attribute provides additional metadata about the property. Consequently, the Tag Helper generates an HTML5 `<input>` with `type="email"`:

```
<input type="email" id="Email" name="Email"
    value="test@example.com" data-val="true"
    data-val-email="The Email Address field is not a valid e-mail address."
    data-val-required="The Email Address field is required."
    />
```

You can take a whole host of things away from this example. First, the id and name attributes of the HTML element have been generated from the name of the property. These are the same as the value referenced by the Label Tag Helper in its for attribute.

Also, the initial value of the field has been set to the value currently stored in the property ("test@example.com", in this case). The type of the element has also been set to the HTML5 email type, instead of using the default text type.

Perhaps the most striking addition is the swath of data-val-* attributes. These can be used by client-side JavaScript libraries such as jQuery to provide client-side validation of your DataAnnotations constraints. Client-side validation provides instant feedback to users when the values they enter are invalid, providing a smoother user experience than can be achieved with server-side validation alone, as I described in chapter 6.

Client-side validation

In order to enable client-side validation in your application, you need to add more jQuery libraries to your HTML pages. In particular, you need to include the jQuery, jQuery-validation, and jQuery-validation-unobtrusive JavaScript libraries. You can do this in a number of ways, but the simplest is to include the script files at the bottom of your view using

```
<script src="https://ajax.aspnetcdn.com/ajax/jquery/jquery-2.2.0.
    min.js"></script>
<script src="https://ajax.aspnetcdn.com/ajax/jquery.validate/1.14.0/
    jquery.validate.min.js"></script>
<script src="https://ajax.aspnetcdn.com/ajax/jquery.validation.unobtrusive/
    3.2.6/jquery.validate.unobtrusive.min.js"></script>
```

The default MVC templates include these scripts for you, in a handy partial template that you can add to your page in a Scripts section. If you're using the default layout and need to add client-side validation to your view, add the following section somewhere on your view:

```
@section Scripts{
    @Html.Partial("_ValidationScriptsPartial")
}
```

This will ensure the appropriate scripts are added using a best-practice approach, by serving from a content delivery network (CDN) for speed and using your application as a fallback if there are network issues.

The Input Tag Helper tries to pick the most appropriate template for a given property based on `DataAnnotation` attributes or the type of the property. Whether this generates the exact `<input>` type you need may depend, to an extent, on your application. As always, you can override the generated `type` by adding your own `type` attribute to the Razor. Table 8.1 shows how some of the common data types are mapped to `<input>` types, and how the data types themselves can be specified.

Table 8.1 Common data types, how to specify them, and the input element type they map to

Data type	How it's specified	Input element type
byte, int, short, long, uint	Property type	number
decimal, double, float	Property type	text
string	Property type, `[DataType(DataType.Text)]` attribute	text
HiddenInput	`[HiddenInput]` attribute	hidden
Password	`[Password]` attribute	password
PhoneAttribute	`[Phone]` attribute	tel
EmailAddress	`[EmailAddress]` attribute	email
Url	`[Url]` attribute	url
Date	DateTime property type, `[DataType(DataType.Date)]` attribute	date

The Input Tag Helper has one additional attribute that can be used to customize the way data is displayed: `asp-format`. HTML forms are entirely string-based, so when the value of an `<input>` is set, the Input Tag Helper must take the value stored in the property and convert it to a `string`. Under the covers, this performs a `string` `.Format()` on the property's value, passing in a format string.

The Input Tag Helper uses a default format string for each different data type, but with the `asp-format` attribute, you can set the specific format string to use. For example, you could ensure a `decimal` property, Dec, is formatted to three decimal places with the following code:

```
<input asp-for="Dec" asp-format="0.000" />
```

If the Dec property had a value of 1.2, this would generate HTML similar to

```
<input type="text" id="Dec" name="Dec" value="1.200">
```

NOTE   You may be surprised that `decimal` and `double` types are rendered as `text` fields and not as `number` fields. This is due to a number of technical reasons, predominantly related to the way some cultures render numbers with commas and spaces. Rendering as text avoids errors that would only appear in certain browser-culture combinations.

In addition to the Input Tag Helper, ASP.NET Core provides the Textarea Tag Helper. This works in a similar way, using the `asp-for` attribute, but is attached to a `<textarea>` element instead:

```
<textarea asp-for="Multiline"></textarea>
```

This would generate HTML similar to the following. Note that the property value is rendered inside the Tag, and `data-val-*` validation elements are attached as usual:

```
<textarea data-val="true" id="Multiline" name="Multiline"
    data-val-length="Maximum length 200." data-val-length-max="200"
    data-val-required="The Multiline field is required." >This is some text,
I'm going to display it
in a text area</textarea>
```

Hopefully, this section has hammered home how much typing Tag Helpers can cut down on, especially when using them in conjunction with `DataAnnotations` for generating validation attributes. But this is more than reducing the number of keystrokes required; Tag Helpers ensure that the markup generated is *correct*, and has the correct `name`, `id`, and format to automatically bind your binding models when they're sent to the server.

   With `<form>`, `<label>`, and `<input>` under your belt, you're able to build the majority of your currency converter forms. Before we look at displaying validation messages, there's one element I'd like to take a look at: the `<select>`, or drop-down, input.

8.2.4   *The Select Tag Helper*

As well as `<input>` fields, a common element you'll see on web forms is the `<select>` element, or dropdowns and list boxes. Your currency converter application, for example, could use a `<select>` element to let you pick which currency to convert from a list.

   By default, this element shows a list of items and lets you select one, but there are a number of variations, as shown in figure 8.6. As well as the normal select box, you could show a list box, add multiselection, and display your list items in groups.

   To use `<select>` elements in your Razor code, you'll need to include two properties in your view model: one property for the list of options to display and one to hold the value (or values) selected. For example, listing 8.5 shows the view model used to create the three left-most select lists you saw in figure 8.6. Displaying groups requires a slightly different setup, as you'll see shortly.

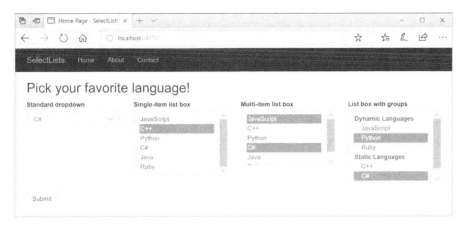

Figure 8.6 Some of the many ways to display `<select>` elements using the Select Tag Helper.

Listing 8.5 View model for displaying select element dropdowns and list boxes

```
public class SelectListsViewModel
{
    public string SelectedValue1 { get; set; }
    public string SelectedValue2 { get; set; }

    public IEnumerable<string> MultiValues { get; set; }

    public IEnumerable<SelectListItem> Items { get; set; }
        = new List<SelectListItem>
    {
        new SelectListItem{Value= "csharp", Text="C#"},
        new SelectListItem{Value= "python", Text= "Python"},
        new SelectListItem{Value= "cpp", Text="C++"},
        new SelectListItem{Value= "java", Text="Java"},
        new SelectListItem{Value= "js", Text="JavaScript"},
        new SelectListItem{Value= "ruby", Text="Ruby"},
    };
}
```

These properties will hold the values selected by the single-selection select boxes.

To create a multiselect list box, use an IEnumerable< >.

The list of items to display in the select boxes

This listing demonstrates a number of aspects of working with `<select>` lists:

- `SelectedValue1`/`SelectedValue2`—Used to hold the values selected by the user. They're model-bound to the selected values and used to preselect the correct item when rendering the form.
- `MultiValues`—Used to hold the selected values for a multiselect list. It's an `IEnumerable`, so it can hold more than one selection per `<select>` element.
- `Items`—Provides the list of options to display in the `<select>` elements. Note that the element type must be `SelectListItem`, which exposes the `Value` and `Text` properties, to work with the Select Tag Helper.

> **NOTE** The Select Tag Helper only works with `SelectListItem` elements. That means you'll normally have to convert from an application-specific list set of items (for example, a `List<string>` or `List<MyClass>`) to the UI-centric `List<SelectListItem>`. But hey, that's why we have view models!

The Select Tag Helper exposes the `asp-for` and `asp-items` attributes that you can add to `<select>` elements. As for the Input Tag Helper, the `asp-for` attribute specifies the property in your view model to bind to. The `asp-items` attribute is provided the `IEnumerable<SelectListItem>` to display the available `<option>`.

> **TIP** It's common to want to display a list of `enum` options in a `<select>` list. This is so common that ASP.NET Core ships with a helper for generating a `SelectListItem` for any enum. If you have an enum of the `TEnum` type, you can generate the available options in your View using `asp-items="Html .GetEnumSelectList<TEnum>()"`.

The following listing shows how to display a drop-down list, a single-selection list box, and a multiselection list box. It uses the view model from the previous listing, binding each `<select>` list to a different property, but reusing the same `Items` list for all of them.

Listing 8.6   Razor template to display a select element in three different ways

```
@model SelectListsViewModel

<select asp-for="SelectedValue1"
    asp-items="Model.Items"></select>

<select asp-for="SelectedValue2"
    asp-items="Model.Items"
    size="@Model.Items.Count()"></select>

<select asp-for="MultiValues"
    asp-items="Model.Items"></select>
```

Creates a standard drop-down select list by binding to a standard property in asp-for

Creates a single-select list box by providing the standard HTML size attribute

Creates a multiselect list box by binding to an IEnumerable property in asp-for

Hopefully, you can see that the Razor for generating a drop-down `<select>` list is almost identical to the Razor for generating a multiselect `<select>` list. The Select Tag Helper takes care of adding the `multiple` HTML attribute to the generated output, if the property it's binding to is an `IEnumerable`.

> **WARNING** The `asp-for` attribute *must not* include the `Model.` prefix. The `asp-items` attribute, on the other hand, *must* include it if referencing a property on the view model. The `asp-items` attribute can also reference other C# items, such as objects stored in `ViewData`, but using the view model is the best approach.

You've seen how to bind three different types of select list so far, but the one I haven't yet covered from figure 8.6 is how to display groups in your list boxes using `<optgroup>`

elements. Luckily, nothing needs to change in your Razor code, you just have to update how you define your `SelectListItems`.

The `SelectListItem` object defines a `Group` property that specifies the `Select-ListGroup` the item belongs to. The following listing shows how you could create two groups and assign each list item to either a "dynamic" or "static" group, using a view model similar to that shown in listing 8.5. The final list item, C#, isn't assigned to a group, so it will be displayed as normal, outside of the grouping.

Listing 8.7   Adding `Groups` to `SelectListItems` to create `optgroup` elements

```
public class SelectListsViewModel
{
    public IEnumerable<string> SelectedValues { get; set; }     ⟵ Initializes the list
    public IEnumerable<SelectListItem> Items { get; set; }         items in the
                                                                   constructor
    public SelectListsViewModel()     ⟵
    {
        var dynamic = new SelectListGroup { Name = "Dynamic" };
        var stat = new SelectListGroup { Name = "Static" };

        ItemsWithGroups = new List<SelectListItem>
        {                                          Creates single instance
          new SelectListItem {                     of each group to pass to
            Value= "js",                               SelectListItems
            Text="Javascript",
            Group = dynamic     ⟵
          },
            new SelectListItem {
            Value= "cpp",                  Sets the appropriate
            Text="C++",                    group for each
            Group = stat       ⟵          SelectListItem
          },
            new SelectListItem {
            Value= "python",
            Text="Python",
            Group = dynamic    ⟵
          },
            new SelectListItem {           If a SelectListItem doesn't
            Value= "csharp",               have a Group, it won't be
            Text="C#",                     added to an optgroup.
          },

        }
    }
}
```

With this in place, the Select Tag Helper will generate `<optgroup>` elements as necessary when rendering the Razor to HTML. The preceding view model would be rendered to HTML as

```
<select id="SelectedValues" name="SelectedValues" multiple="multiple">
    <optgroup label="Dynamic">
        <option value="js">JavaScript</option>
        <option value="python">Python</option>
```

```
    </optgroup>
    <optgroup label="Static Languages">
        <option value="cpp">C++</option>
    </optgroup>
    <option value="csharp">C#</option>
</select>
```

Another common requirement when working with <select> elements is to include an option in the list that indicates "no value selected," as shown in figure 8.7. Without this extra option, the default <select> dropdown will always have a value and default to the first item in the list.

Figure 8.7 Without a "no selection" option, the <select> element will always have a value. This may not be the behavior you desire if you don't want an <option> to be selected by default.

You can achieve this in one of two ways: you could either add the "not selected" option to the available SelectListItems, or you could manually add the option to the Razor, for example by using

```
<select asp-for="Model.SelectedValue" asp-items="Model.Items">
    <option Value = "">**Not selected**</option>
</select>
```

This will add an extra <option> at the top of your <select> element, with a blank Value attribute, allowing you to provide a "no selection" option for the user.

> **TIP** Adding a "no selection" option to a <select> element is so common, you might want to create a partial view to encapsulate this logic, as you saw in the previous chapter. I'll leave it as an exercise for the reader, but you'd need to create a common interface as the view model for your partial view.

With the Input Tag Helper and Select Tag Helper under your belt, you should be able to create most of the forms that you'll need. You have all the pieces you need to create the currency converter application now, with one exception.

Remember, whenever you accept input from a user, you should always validate the data. The Validation Tag Helpers provide a way to display model validation errors to the user on your form, without having to write a lot of boilerplate markup.

8.2.5 *The Validation Message and Validation Summary Tag Helpers*

In section 8.2.3 you saw that the Input Tag Helper generates the necessary `data-val-*` validation attributes on form input elements themselves. But you also need somewhere to display the validation messages. This can be achieved for each property in your view model using the Validation Message Tag Helper applied to a `<span>` by using the `asp-validation-for` attribute:

```
<span asp-validation-for="Email"></span>
```

When an error occurs during client-side validation, the appropriate error message for the referenced property will be displayed in the `<span>`, as shown in figure 8.8. This `<span>` element will also be used to show appropriate validation messages if server-side validation fails, and the form is being redisplayed.

Figure 8.8   Validation messages can be shown in an associated `<span>` by using the Validation Message Tag Helper.

Any errors associated with the `Email` property stored in `ModelState` will be rendered in the element body, and the element will have appropriate attributes to hook into jQuery validation:

```
<span class="field-validation-valid" data-valmsg-for="Email"
  data-valmsg-replace="true">The Email Address field is required.</span>
```

The validation error shown in the element will be replaced when the user updates the `Email` `<input>` field and client-side validation is performed.

> **NOTE** For further details on model validation, see chapter 6.

As well as displaying validation messages for individual properties, you can also display a summary of all the validation messages in a `<div>` by using the Validation Summary Tag Helper, shown in figure 8.9. This renders a `<ul>` containing a list of the `ModelState` errors.

The Validation Summary Tag Helper is applied to a `<div>` using the `asp-validation-summary` attribute and providing a `ValidationSummary` enum value, such as

```
<div asp-validation-summary="All"></div>
```

The `ValidationSummary` enum controls which values are displayed, and has three possible values:

- `None`—Don't display a summary. (I don't know why you'd use this.)
- `ModelOnly`—Only display errors that are *not* associated with a property.
- `All`—Display errors either associated with a property or with the model.

The Validation Summary Tag Helper is particularly useful if you have errors associated with your view model that aren't specific to a property. These can be added to the model state by using a blank key, as shown in listing 8.8. In this example, the property validation

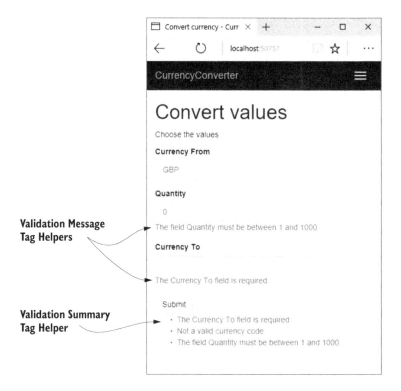

Figure 8.9   Form showing validation errors. The Validation Message Tag Helper is applied to `<span>`, close to the associated input. The Validation Summary Tag Helper is applied to a `<div>`, normally at the top or bottom of the form.

passed, but we provide additional model-level validation that we aren't trying to convert a currency to itself.

Listing 8.8   Adding model-level validation errors to the `ModelState`

```
public class CurrencyController : Controller
{
    [HttpPost]
    public IActionResult Convert(
        CurrencyConverterModel model)
    {
        if(model.CurrencyFrom == model.CurrencyTo)        ◁──  Can't convert
        {                                                       currency to itself
            ModelState.AddModelError(
                string.Empty,                                  Adds model-level error
                "Cannot convert currency to itself");          by using empty key

        }

        if (!ModelState.IsValid)                               If there are any property-
        {                                                      level or model-level errors,
            return View(model);                                display them.
        }
```

```
                //store the valid values somewhere etc
                return RedirectToAction("Index", "Checkout");
        }
}
```

Without the Validation Summary Tag Helper, the model-level error would still be added if the user used the same currency twice, and the form would be redisplayed. Unfortunately, there would have been no visual cue to the user indicating why the form did not submit—obviously that's a problem! By adding the Validation Summary Tag Helper, the model-level errors are shown to the user so they can correct the problem, as shown in figure 8.10.

> **NOTE** For simplicity, I added the validation check to the controller action. A better approach might be to create a custom validation attribute to achieve this instead. That way, your controller stays lean and sticks to the single responsibility principle. You'll see how to achieve this in chapter 19.

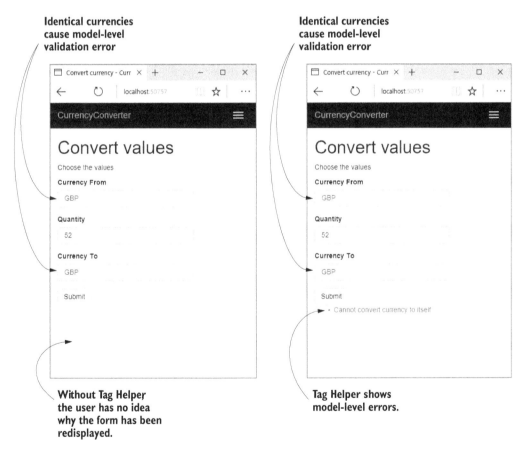

Figure 8.10 Model-level errors are only displayed by the Validation Summary Tag Helper. Without one, users won't have any indication that there were errors on the form, and so won't be able to correct them.

This section has covered most of the common Tag Helpers available for working with forms, including all the pieces you need to build the currency converter forms. They should also be enough to get you going on your own applications, building out your Razor views using your view models. But forms aren't the only area in which Tag Helpers are useful; they're generally applicable any time you need to mix server-side logic with HTML generation.

One such example is generating links to other pages in your application using routing-based URL generation. Given that routing is designed to be fluid as you refactor your application, keeping track of the exact URLs the links should point to would be a bit of a maintenance nightmare if you had to do it "by hand." As you might expect, there's a Tag Helper for that: the Anchor Tag Helper.

8.3   *Generating links with the Anchor Tag Helper*

At the end of chapter 5, I showed how you could generate URLs for links to other pages in your application from inside your controllers and by using `ActionResults`. Views are the other common place where you often need to link to other actions in your application, normally by way of an `<a>` element with an `href` attribute pointing to the appropriate URL.

The Anchor Tag Helper can be used to generate the URL for a given action using routing. Conceptually, this is almost identical to the way the Form Tag Helper generates the `action` URL, as you saw in section 8.2.1. For the most part, using the Anchor Tag Helper is identical too; you provide `asp-controller` and `asp-action` attributes, along with `asp-route-*` attributes as necessary. The default MVC templates use the Anchor Tag Helper to generate the links shown in the navigation bar using the code.

> **Listing 8.9   Using the Anchor Tag Helper to generate URLs in _Layout.cshtml**

```
<ul class="nav navbar-nav">
    <li><a asp-area="" asp-controller="Home"
       asp-action="Index">Home</a></li>
    <li><a asp-area="" asp-controller="Home"
       asp-action="About">About</a></li>
    <li><a asp-area="" asp-controller="Home"
       asp-action="Contact">Contact</a></li>
</ul>
```

As you can see, each `<a>` element has an `asp-action` and `asp-controller` attribute. These use the routing system to generate an appropriate URL for the `<a>`, resulting in the following markup:

```
<ul class="nav navbar-nav">
    <li><a href="/">Home</a></li>
    <li><a href="/Home/About">About</a></li>
    <li><a href="/Home/Contact">Contact</a></li>
</ul>
```

The URLs use default values where possible, so the `Index` action on the `HomeController` generates the simple `"/"` URL instead of `"/Home/Index"`.

If you need more control over the URL generated, the Anchor Tag Helper exposes a number of additional properties you can set, which will be used during URL generation. The most commonly used are

- `asp-action`—Sets the action route parameter.
- `asp-controller`—Sets the controller route parameter.
- `asp-area`—Sets the area route parameter to use. Areas can be used to provide an additional layer of organization to your application.[5]
- `asp-host`—If set, the link will point to the provided host and will generate an absolute URL instead of a relative URL.
- `asp-protocol`—Sets whether to generate an http or https link. If set, it will generate an absolute URL instead of a relative URL.
- `asp-route`—Uses the named route to generate the URL.
- `asp-route-*`—Sets the route parameters to use during generation. Can be added multiple times for different route parameters.

By using the Anchor Tag Helper and its attributes, you generate your URLs using the routing system as described in chapter 5, ensuring that you won't break your application if you rename something. This reduces the duplication in your code by removing the hardcoded URLs you'd otherwise need to embed in all your views.

If you find yourself writing repetitive code in your markup, chances are someone has written a Tag Helper to help with it. The Append Version Tag Helper in the following section is a great example of using Tag Helpers to reduce the amount of fiddly code required.

8.4 *Cache-busting with the Append Version Tag Helper*

A common problem with web development, both when developing and when an application goes into production, is ensuring that browsers are all using the latest files. For performance reasons, browsers often cache files locally and reuse them for subsequent requests, rather than calling your application every time a file is requested.

Normally, this is great—most of the static assets in your site rarely change, so caching them significantly reduces the burden on your server. Think of an image of your company logo—how often does that change? If every page shows your logo, then caching the image in the browser makes a lot of sense.

But what happens if it *does* change? You want to make sure users get the updated assets as soon as they're available. A more critical requirement might be if the JavaScript files associated with your site change. If users end up using cached versions of

---

[5] I won't cover areas in this book. They're an optional aspect of MVC that are often only used on large projects. You can read about them here: http://mng.bz/3X64.

your JavaScript then they might see strange errors, or your application might appear broken to them.

This conundrum is a common one in web development, and one of the most common ways for handling it is to use a *cache-busting query string*.

> **DEFINITION**   A cache-busting query string adds a query parameter to a URL, such as ?v=1. Browsers will cache the response and use it for subsequent requests to the URL. When the resource changes, the query string is also changed, for example to ?v=2. Browsers will see this is a request for a new resource, and will make a fresh request.

The biggest problem with this approach is that it requires you to update a URL every time an image, CSS, or JavaScript file changes. This is a manual step that requires updating every place the resource is referenced, so it's inevitable that mistakes are made. Tag Helpers to the rescue! When you add a <script>, <img>, or <link> element to your application, you can use Tag Helpers to automatically generate a cache-busting query string:

```
<script src="~/js/site.js" asp-append-version="true"></script>
```

The asp-append-version attribute will load the file being referenced and generate a unique hash based on its contents. This is then appended as a unique query string to the resource URL:

```
<script src="/js/site.js?v=EWaMeWsJBYWmL2g_KkgXZQ5nPe"></script>
```

As this value is a hash of the file contents, it will remain unchanged as long as the file isn't modified, so the file will be cached in users' browsers. But if the file is modified, then the hash of the contents will change and so will the query string. This ensures browsers are always served the most up-to-date files for your application without your having to worry about manually updating every URL whenever you change a file.

The default MVC templates in Visual Studio and the .NET CLI make use of Tag Helpers for both forms and cache busting. They also use Tag Helpers to conditionally render different markup depending on the current environment using a technique you haven't seen yet, where the Tag Helper is declared as a completely separate element.

8.5   *Using conditional markup with the Environment Tag Helper*

In many cases, you want to render different HTML in your Razor templates depending if your website is running in a development or production environment. For example, in development, you typically want your JavaScript and CSS assets to be verbose and easy to read, but in production you'd process these files to make them as small as possible. Another example might be the desire to apply a banner to the application when it's running in a testing environment, which is removed when you move to production, shown in figure 8.11.

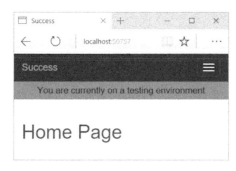

Figure 8.11 The warning banner will be shown whenever you're running in a testing environment, to make it easy to distinguish from production.

> **NOTE** You'll learn about configuring your application for multiple environments in chapter 11.

You've already seen how to use C# to add `if` statements to your markup, so it would be perfectly possible to use this technique to add an extra `div` to your markup when the current environment has a given value. If we assume that the `env` variable contains the current environment, then you could use something like

```
@if(env == "Testing" || env == "Staging")
{
    <div class="warning">You are currently on a testing environment</div>
}
```

There's nothing wrong with this, but a better approach would be to use the Tag Helper paradigm to keep your markup clean and easy to read. Luckily, ASP.NET Core comes with the `EnvironmentTagHelper`, which can be used to achieve the same result in a slightly clearer way:

```
<environment include="Testing,Staging">
    <div class="warning">You are currently on a testing environment</div>
</environment>
```

This Tag Helper is a little different from the others you've seen before. Instead of augmenting an existing HTML element using an `asp-` attribute, *the whole element* is the Tag Helper. This Tag Helper is completely responsible for generating the markup, and it uses an attribute to configure it.

Functionally, this Tag Helper is identical to the C# markup (although for now I've glossed over how the `env` variable could be found), but it's more declarative in its function than the C# alternative. You're obviously free to use either approach, but personally I like the HTML-like nature of Tag Helpers. Either way, the `EnvironmentTagHelper` is used in the default MVC templates, so at least you'll know what it's up to now!

We've reached the end of this chapter on Tag Helpers, and with it, our first look at building traditional web applications that display HTML to users. In the last part of the book, we'll revisit Razor templates, and you'll learn how to build custom components like custom Tag Helpers and View Components. For now, you have everything you need to build complex Razor layouts—the custom components can help tidy up your code down the line.

This chapter, along with the previous four, has been a whistle-stop tour of how to build MVC applications with ASP.NET Core. You now have the basic building blocks to start making simple ASP.NET Core applications. In the second part of this book, I'll show you some of the additional features you'll need to understand to build complete applications. But before we get to that, I'll take a chapter to discuss building Web APIs.

I've mentioned the Web API approach previously, in which your application serves data using the MVC framework, but instead of returning user-friendly HTML, it returns machine-friendly JSON or XML. In the next chapter, you'll see why and how to build a Web API, take a look at an alternative routing system designed for APIs, and learn how to generate JSON responses to requests.

Summary

- Tag Helpers let you bind your data model to HTML elements, making it easier to generate dynamic HTML while remaining editor friendly.

- As with Razor in general, Tag Helpers are for server-side rendering of HTML only. You can't use them directly in frontend frameworks, such as Angular or React.

- Tag Helpers can be standalone elements or can attach to existing HTML using attributes.

- Tag Helpers can customize the elements they're attached to, add additional attributes, and customize how they're rendered to HTML. This can greatly reduce the amount of markup you need to write.

- Tag Helpers can expose multiple attributes on a single element.

- You can add the `asp-action` and `asp-controller` attributes to the `<form>` element to set the `action` URL using the URL generation feature of the MVC middleware's router.

- You specify route values to use during routing with the Form Tag Helper using `asp-route-*` attributes.

- The Form Tag Helper also generates a hidden field that you can use to prevent CSRF attacks.

- You can attach the Label Tag Helper to a `<label>` using `asp-for`. It generates an appropriate `for` attribute and caption based on the `[Display]` DataAnnotations attribute and the view model property name.

- The Input Tag Helper sets the `type` attribute of an `<input>` element to the appropriate value based on a bound property's `Type` and any DataAnnotations applied to it. It also generates the `data-val-*` attributes required for client-side validation.

- To enable client-side validation, you must add the necessary JavaScript files to your view for jQuery validation and unobtrusive validation.

- The Select Tag Helper can generate drop-down `<select>` elements as well as list boxes, using the `asp-for` and `asp-items` attributes.

- To generate a multiselect `<select>` element, bind the element to an `IEnumerable` property on the view model.

- The items supplied in `asp-for` must be an `IEnumerable<SelectListItem>`.

- You can generate an `IEnumerable<SelectListItem>` for an enum `TEnum` using the `Html.GetEnumSelectList<TEnum>()` helper method.

- The Select Tag Helper will generate `<optgroup>` elements if the items supplied in `asp-for` have an associated `SelectListGroup` on the `Group` property.

- Any extra additional `<option>` elements added to the Razor markup will be passed through to the final HTML. You can use these additional elements to easily add a "no selection" option to the `<select>` element.

- The Validation Message Tag Helper is used to render the client- and server-side validation error messages for a given property. Use the `asp-validation-for` attribute to attach the Validation Message Tag Helper to a `<span>`.

- The Validation Summary Tag Helper is used to display validation errors for the model, as well as for individual properties. Use the `asp-validation-summary` attribute to attach the Validation Summary Tag Helper to a `<div>`.

- You can generate `<a>` URLs using the Anchor Tag Helper. This Helper uses routing to generate the `href` URL using `asp-action`, `asp-controller`, and `asp-route-*` attributes.

- You can add the `asp-append-version` attribute to `<link>`, `<script>`, and `<img>` elements to provide cache-busting capabilities based on the file's contents.

- You can use the Environment Tag Helper to conditionally render different HTML based on the app's current execution environment.

Creating a Web API
for mobile and client
applications using MVC

This chapter covers

- Creating a Web API controller to return JSON to clients
- Using attribute routing to customize your URLs
- Generating a response using content negotiation
- Enabling XML formatting

In the previous five chapters, you've worked through each layer of a traditional ASP.NET Core MVC application, using Razor views to render HTML to the browser. In this chapter, you'll see a slightly different take on an MVC application. We'll explore Web APIs, which serve as the backend for client-side SPAs and mobile apps.

You can apply much of what you've learned to Web APIs; they use the same MVC design pattern, and the concepts of routing, model binding, and validation all carry through. The differentiation from traditional web applications is entirely in the *view* part of MVC. Instead of returning HTML, they return data as JSON or XML, which client applications use to control their behavior or update the UI.

In this chapter, you'll learn how to define controllers and actions and see how similar they are to the controllers you already know. You'll learn how to create an API model to return data and HTTP status codes in response to a request, in a way that client apps can understand.

The subsequent section looks at an alternative approach to routing often used with Web APIs, called *attribute routing*. This approach uses the same route templates concept from chapter 5 but applies them to your action methods in a way that's more suited to the customization needs of Web API applications.

You'll also learn how to format the API models returned by your action methods using content negotiation, to ensure you generate a response that the calling client can understand. As part of this, you'll learn how to add support for additional format types, such as XML, so that you can both generate XML responses and receive XML data POSTed to your app.

One of the great aspects of ASP.NET Core is the variety of applications you can create with it. The ability to easily build a generalized HTTP Web API presents the possibility of using ASP.NET Core in a greater range of situations than can be achieved with traditional web apps alone. But should *you* build a Web API and why? In the first section of this chapter, I'll go over some of the reasons why you might or might not want to create a Web API.

9.1 What is a Web API and when should you use one?

Traditional web applications handle requests by returning HTML to the user, which is displayed in a web browser. You can easily build applications of this nature using `Mvc-Middleware` to generate HTML with Razor templates, as you've seen in recent chapters. This approach is common and well understood, but the modern application developer also has a number of other possibilities to consider, as shown in figure 9.1.

Client-side single-page applications (SPAs) have become popular in recent years with the development of frameworks such as Angular, React, and Ember. These frameworks use JavaScript that runs in a user's web browser to generate the HTML they see and interact with. The server sends this initial JavaScript to the browser when the user first reaches the app. The user's browser loads the JavaScript and initializes the SPA, before loading any application data from the server.

Once the SPA is loaded, communication with a server still occurs over HTTP, but instead of sending HTML directly to the browser in response to requests, the server-side application sends data (normally in a format such as JSON or XML) to the client-side application. The SPA then parses the data and generates the appropriate HTML to show to a user, as shown in figure 9.2. The server-side application endpoint that the client communicates with is sometimes called a *Web API*.

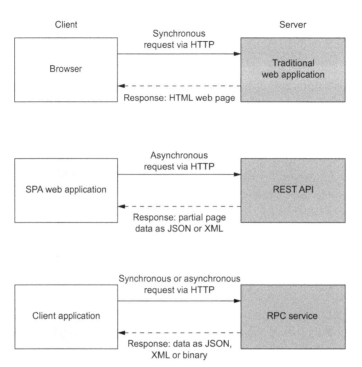

Figure 9.1 Modern developers have to consider a number of different consumers of their applications. As well as traditional users with web browsers, these could be SPAs, mobile applications, or other apps.

DEFINITION   A *Web API* exposes a number of URLs that can be used to access or change data on a server. It's typically accessed using HTTP.

These days, mobile applications are common and are, from the server application's point of view, similar to client-side SPAs. A mobile application will typically communicate with a server application using an HTTP Web API, receiving data in a common format, such as JSON, just like an SPA. It then modifies the application's UI depending on the data it receives.

One final use case for a Web API is where your application is designed to be partially or solely consumed by other services. Imagine you've built a web application to send emails. By creating a Web API, you can allow other application developers to use your email service by sending you an email address and a message. Virtually all languages and platforms have access to an HTTP library they could use to access your service from code.

This is all there is to a Web API. It exposes a number of endpoints (URLs) that client applications can send requests to and retrieve data from. These are used to power the behavior of the client apps, as well as to provide all the data they need to display the correct interface to a user.

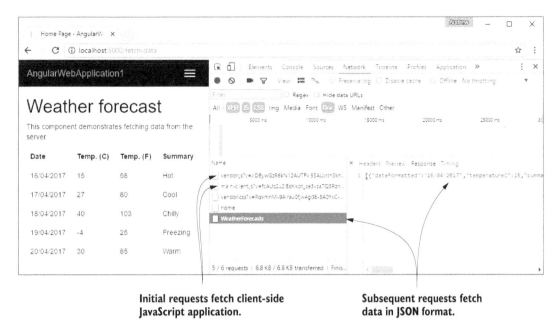

Initial requests fetch client-side JavaScript application.

Subsequent requests fetch data in JSON format.

Figure 9.2 A sample client-side SPA using Angular. The initial requests load the SPA JavaScript into the browser, and subsequent requests fetch data from a Web API, formatted as JSON.

Whether you need or want to create a Web API for your ASP.NET Core application depends on the type of application you want to build. If you're familiar with client-side frameworks, will need to develop a mobile application, or already have an SPA build-pipeline configured, then you'll most likely want to add Web APIs for them to be able to access your application.

One of the selling points of using a Web API is that it can serve as a generalized backend for all of your applications. For example, you could start by building a client-side application that uses a Web API. Later, you could add a mobile app that uses the same Web API, with little or no modification required to your ASP.NET Core code.

If you're new to web development, have no need to call your application from outside a web browser, or don't want/need the effort involved in configuring a client-side application, then you probably won't need Web APIs initially. You can stick to generating your UI using Razor and will no doubt be highly productive!

> **NOTE** Although there has definitely been a shift toward client-side frameworks, server-side rendering using Razor is still relevant. Which approach you choose will depend largely on your preference for building HTML applications in the traditional manner versus using JavaScript on the client.

Having said that, adding Web APIs to your application isn't something you have to worry about ahead of time. Adding them later is simple, so you can always ignore them initially and add them in as the need arises. In many cases, this will be the best approach.

SPAs with ASP.NET Core

The cross-platform and lightweight design of ASP.NET Core means it lends itself well to acting as a backend for your SPA framework of choice. Given the focus of this book and the broad scope of SPAs in general, I won't be looking at Angular, React, or other SPAs here. Instead, I suggest checking out the resources appropriate to your chosen SPA. Books are available from Manning for all the common client-side frameworks:

- React in Action by Mark Tielens Thomas (Manning, 2018) https://livebook .manning.com/#!/book/react-in-action/.
- Angular in Action by Jeremy Wilken (Manning, 2018) https://livebook.manning .com/#!/book/angular-in-action/.
- Vue.js in Action by Erik Hanchett with Benjamin Listwon (Manning, 2018) https://livebook.manning.com/#!/book/vue-js-in-action/.

If you want to get started using ASP.NET Core with an SPA, Microsoft provides a number of templates you can install for use with the .NET CLI. See https://docs .microsoft.com/en-us/ aspnet/core/spa/ for details. Additionally, these use Microsoft JavaScriptServices to provide features such as server-side pre-rendering and hot-module replacement. See http://mng.bz/O4bd for details on integrating JavaScript-Services into your own apps.

Once you've established that you need a Web API for your application, creating one is easy, as it's built into ASP.NET Core. In the next section, you'll see how to create a Web API controller in an existing MVC application.

9.2   *Creating your first Web API Controller*

The MVC design pattern is sometimes only thought of in relation to applications that directly render their UI, like the Razor views you've seen in previous chapters. In ASP.NET Core, the MVC pattern applies equally well when building a Web API; but the view part of MVC involves generating a *machine*-friendly response rather than a *user*-friendly response.

As a parallel to this, you create Web API controllers in ASP.NET Core in the very same way you create traditional MVC controllers. The only thing that differentiates them from a code perspective is the type of data they return—MVC controllers typically return a `ViewResult`; Web API controllers generally return raw .NET objects from the action methods, or an `IActionResult` such as `StatusCodeResult`, as you saw in chapter 4.

> **NOTE** This is different from the previous version of ASP.NET, where the MVC and Web API stacks were completely independent. ASP.NET Core unifies the two stacks into a single approach, which makes using both in a project painless!

To give you an initial taste of what you're working with, figure 9.3 shows the result of calling a Web API endpoint from your browser. Instead of a friendly HTML UI, you receive data that can be easily consumed in code. In this example, the Web API returns a list of `string` fruit names as JSON when you request the URL /Fruit/Index.

> **TIP** Web APIs are normally accessed from code by SPAs or mobile apps, but by accessing the URL in your web browser directly, you can view the data the API is returning.

Figure 9.3   Testing a Web API by accessing the URL in the browser. A GET request is made to the /Fruit/Index URL, which returns a List<string> that has been JSON-encoded into an array of strings.

Listing 9.1 shows the code that was used to create the Web API demonstrated in figure 9.3. This is obviously a trivial example, but it highlights the similarity to traditional MVC controllers. You can add a Web API controller to your project in exactly the same way as you saw in chapter 4, using the New Item dialog in Visual Studio, or by creating a new .cs file when you use the .NET CLI or another IDE.

Listing 9.1   A simple Web API controller

```
public class FruitController : Controller       ◁─────  The Web API controller
{                                                        inherits from the Controller
    List<string> _fruit = new List<string>               base class, as per conventions
    {
        "Pear",                                          The data returned would
        "Lemon",                                         typically be fetched from the
        "Peach"                                          application model in a real app.
    };

    public IEnumerable<string> Index()      ◁─────  The controller exposes a
    {                                               single action method, Index,
        return _fruit;                              which returns the list of fruit.
    }
}
```

There's nothing particularly special about this controller; it returns a list of strings when the action method executes. The only real difference from the equivalent MVC controller in this case is the return type of the action. Instead of returning a `View-Result` or an `IActionResult`, it directly returns the list of strings.

When you return data directly from an action method, you're providing the *API model* for the request. The client will receive this data. It's formatted into an appropriate response, in this case a JSON representation of the list, and sent back to the browser with a 200 (OK) status code.

> **TIP**   ASP.NET Core will format returned data as JSON by default. You'll see how to format the returned data in other ways later in this chapter.

The URL at which a Web API controller is exposed is handled in the same way as for traditional MVC controllers—using routing. The routing module directs a request to a particular controller and action, which is then invoked and returns a result. This result is then used to generate an appropriate response.

Web API controllers don't have to return data directly. You're free to return an `IActionResult` instead, and often this is required. Depending on the desired behavior of your API, you may sometimes want to return data, and other times you may want to return a raw HTTP status code, indicating whether the request was successful. If an API call is made requesting details of a product that does not exist, you might want to return a 404 (Not Found) status code, as you'll see shortly.[1]

Although the primary goal of a Web API is to return data, typically only the most trivial of cases will be able to return data directly from the action method in the manner you've seen. For example, if the request represented a command, such as "Delete the user with ID 9," then there might not *be* any data to return, other than a success/failure status code.

Listing 9.2 shows an example of a case where you'd want to return an `IAction-Result` instead of returning the data directly. It shows another method on the same `FruitController` as before. This method exposes a way for clients to fetch a specific fruit by an `id`, which we'll assume is its index in the list of _fruit you defined in the previous listing. Model binding is used to set the value of the `id` parameter from the request.

Listing 9.2   A Web API action returning `IActionResult` to handle error conditions

```
public IActionResult View(int id)          ◁──────────────    The action method returns an
{                                                              IActionResult as it can no longer
    if (id >= 0 && id < _fruit.Count)      ◁──────────        always return List<string>.
    {
        return Ok(_fruit[id]);    ◁────────                   An element can only be
    }                                                         returned if the id value is a
    return NotFound();    ◁────────────                       valid _fruit element index.
}
```

Using Ok to return data will format the data passed to it and send a 200 status code.

NotFound returns a NotFoundResult, which will send a 404 status code.

---

[1]   ASP.NET Core 2.1 introduces `IActionResult<T>`, which can simplify generating OpenAPI specifications for your Controllers. See http://mng.bz/FYH1 for details.

In the successful path for the action method, the id parameter has a value greater than zero and less than the number of elements in _fruit. When that's true, the value of the element can be returned to the caller. This is achieved by creating an OkResult, using the Ok helper method[1] on the Controller base class. This generates a 200 status code and returns the element in the response body, as shown in figure 9.4, as if you had returned the _fruit[id] object from the method directly.

Figure 9.4 Returning data using the Ok helper method. The Ok method uses the data passed to it to create the response body, then sets the status code to 200.

If the id is outside the bounds of the _fruit list, then the method calls NotFound to create a NotFoundResult. When executed, this method generates a raw 404 HTTP status code response, which will show the default "not found" page for your browser, as shown in figure 9.5. The fact that you're returning two different types depending on the code path taken means that you must mark the action method as returning an IActionResult in order to make the code compile.

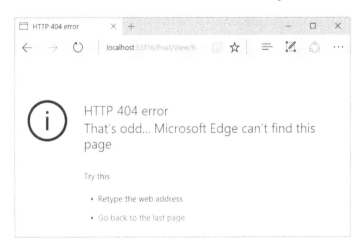

Figure 9.5 A request that generates a raw 404 response without any content, as is typical for a Web API, will show the default "not found" page in a browser.

---

[1] Some people get uneasy when they see the phrase "helper method," but there's nothing magic about the Controller helpers—they're shorthand for creating a new IActionResult of a given type. You don't have to take my word for it though, you can always view the source code for the base class on GitHub at http://mng.bz/NZDt.

You're free to return any type of IActionResult from your Web API controllers, but you'll commonly return StatusCodeResult instances, which return a specific status code with or without associated data. NotFoundResult and OkResult both derive from StatusCodeResult, for example. Another commonly used response is a 400 (bad request), which is normally returned when the data provided in the request fails validation. This can be generated using a BadRequestResult, often using the Bad-Request helper method.

> **TIP**   You learned about various IActionResults in chapter 4. BadRequest-Result, OkResult, and NotFoundResult all inherit from StatusCodeResult, and set the appropriate status code for their type (200, 404, and 400, respectively). Using these wrapper classes makes the intention of your code clearer than relying on other developers to understand the significance of the various status code numbers.

Once you've returned an IActionResult (or other object) from your controller, it's serialized to an appropriate response. This works in several ways, depending on

- The formatters that your app supports
- The data you return from your method
- The data formats the requesting client can handle

You'll learn more about formatters and serializing data at the end of this chapter, but before we go any further, it's worth zooming out a little, and exploring the parallels between traditional MVC applications and Web API endpoints. The two are similar, so it's important to establish the patterns that they share and where they differ.

9.3   *Applying the MVC design pattern to a Web API*

In the previous version of ASP.NET, Microsoft commandeered the generic term "Web API" to create the ASP.NET Web API framework. This framework, as you might expect, was used to create HTTP endpoints that could return formatted JSON or XML in response to requests.

The ASP.NET Web API framework was completely separate from the MVC framework, even though it used similar objects and paradigms. The underlying web stacks for them were completely different beasts and couldn't interoperate.

In ASP.NET Core, that has all changed. You now have a single framework, unified in MvcMiddleware, which you can use to build both traditional web applications and Web APIs. The names MVC and Web API are often still used to differentiate between the different ways the MvcMiddleware can be applied, but there are few differences in the framework itself. You've already seen this yourself; the Web API FruitController you created in the last section derived from the same Controller base class as the examples you've seen in previous chapters.

Consequently, even if you're building an application that consists entirely of Web APIs, using no server-side rendering of HTML with Razor templates, the MVC design pattern still applies. Whether you're building traditional web applications or Web APIs, you can structure your application virtually identically.

After five chapters of it, you're, I hope, nice and familiar with how ASP.NET Core handles an MVC request. But just in case you're not, figure 9.6 shows how `Mvc-Middleware` handles a typical request after passing through the middleware pipeline. This example shows how a request to view the available fruit on a traditional grocery store website might look.

The router routes the request to view all the fruit listed in the `apples` category to the `View` action method on the `FruitController`. The middleware then constructs a binding model, validates it, and passes it to the action. The action method interacts with the application model by calling into services, talking to a database, and returning the necessary data to the action.

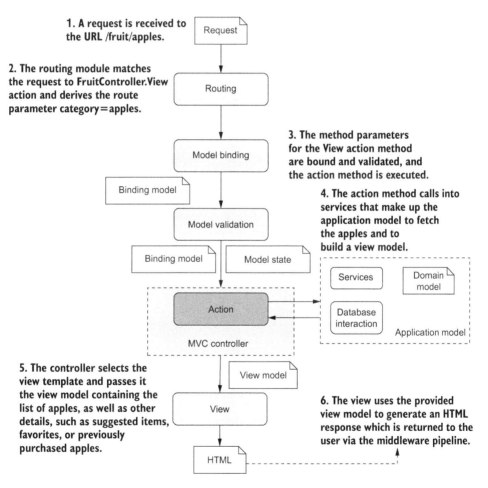

Figure 9.6 Handling a request to a traditional MVC application, in which the view generates an HTML response that's sent back to the user.

Finally, the action method selects a View to render, creates a view model, and executes the view to generate the HTML response. The `MvcMiddleware` returns the response to the middleware pipeline and back to the user's browser.

How would this change if the request came from a client-side or mobile application? If you want to serve machine-readable JSON instead of HTML, how does the MVC process change? As shown in figure 9.7, the answer is "very little." This shows how a Web API endpoint handles a similar request.

As before, routing handles the request by selecting a controller and action to invoke. You'll normally use a slightly different routing system when building a Web API, as you'll see later, but that's completely optional. You can use the same conventional routing as with traditional MVC apps if you prefer.

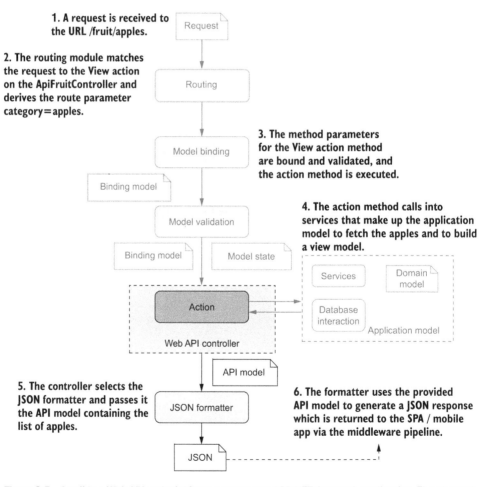

Figure 9.7   A call to a Web API endpoint in an e-commerce ASP.NET Core web application. The ghosted portion of the diagram is identical to figure 9.6.

In this example, routing directs the request to a controller described as a Web API controller, but there's nothing special about this class compared to the MVC controller from figure 9.6. The only difference is that the Web API controller will return data in a machine-readable format, rather than as HTML.

> **TIP** In ASP.NET Core, there's no difference between MVC controllers and Web API controllers. The naming refers only to the difference in the data returned by their methods and the purpose for which they're used.[1]

After routing comes model binding, in which the binder creates a binding model and populates it with values from the request, exactly as in the MVC request. Validation occurs in the same way.

The action executes in the same way as for the MVC controller, by interacting with the application model—the very same application model as is used by the MVC controller. This is an important point; by separating the behavior of your app into an application model, instead of incorporating it into the controllers themselves, you're able to reuse the business logic of your application.

After the application model has returned the data necessary to service the request—the fruit objects in the `apples` category—you see the first difference to the traditional HTML app. Instead of building a *view model*, the action method creates an *API model*. This is analogous to the view model used previously, but rather than containing data used to generate an HTML view, it contains the data that will be sent back in the response.

> **DEFINITION** *View models* contain both *data* required to build a response and *metadata* about how to build the response. API Models only contain the data to be returned in the response.

When we looked at the traditional MVC app, we used the view model in conjunction with a Razor view template to build the final response. With the Web API app, we use the API model in conjunction with a *formatter*. A formatter, as the name suggests, serializes the API model into a machine-readable response, such as JSON or XML. The formatter forms the "V" in the Web API version of MVC, by choosing an appropriate representation for the data to return.

Finally, as with the traditional web app, the generated response is then sent back through the middleware pipeline, passing through each of the configured middleware components, and back to the original caller.

Hopefully, the parallels between traditional web applications and Web APIs are clear; the majority of behavior is identical, only the response varies. Everything from when the request comes in to the interaction with the application model is similar between the paradigms.

---

[1] ASP.NET Core 2.1 introduces the `[ApiController]` attribute. You can use this attribute to opt-in to specific Web API conventions. To learn more about this attribute, see http://mng.bz/FYH1.

Some of the minor differences are down to convention in how Web APIs are used rather than hard and fast rules. These differences aren't specific to Web APIs—you're free to use them with MVC controllers too. You'll tend to use them with Web APIs, primarily due to the differing use cases for traditional MVC apps and Web API apps.

The first of these differences relates to the routing infrastructure and how the router selects action methods for execution based on an incoming request. You've already seen that MVC controllers typically use *conventional* routing, which selects an action method based on a handful of globally defined route templates. In contrast, Web API controllers tend to use *attribute* routing, where each action method is tied directly to one or more specific URLs.

9.4   *Attribute routing: taking fine-grained control of your URLs*

Chapter 5 described the conventional routing scheme, used by default in most traditional web applications. This involves defining a number of global *routes* that `Mvc-Middleware` compares to an incoming request's URL. A route consists of a name, a *route template*, and, optionally, *defaults* and *constraints* to control whether the middleware considers a given request URL to be a match for the route. This listing shows an example of adding the MVC middleware to an application using the default MVC route.

> **Listing 9.3   Defining conventional routing when configuring `MvcMiddleware`**

```
public class Startup
{
    public void ConfigureServices(IServiceCollection services)
    {
        services.AddMvc();
    }

    public void Configure(IApplicationBuilder app)
    {
        app.UseMvc(routes =>
        {
            routes.MapRoute(
                name: "default",
                template: "{controller=Home}/{action=Index}/{id?}");
        });
    }
}
```

With the configuration shown in the listing, the routes are global; they're applied to every request and they can select any action on a controller to be executed, depending on the incoming URL. These routes are terse and defined in one place, so they're often a good choice to use for your MVC applications. Where they fall down is when you need more control over the exact URLs you expose.

When building a Web API application, you sometimes find you want, or need, to make minor changes to the URL a particular action exposes. These URLs form the public API of your application, so it's important that they're easy to consume. Imagine you have a commonly called action on the `CategoriesController` that returns a list of all the current categories on your e-commerce site that contain available products:

```
public IActionResult ListAllCurrentCategoriesWithProducts();
```

Using conventional routing, that would map to an excessively long URL, `/Categories/ListAllCurrentCategoriesWithProducts`. The team decides to shorten it to `/CurrentCategories`, so users can easily understand which section of your app they're in.

With conventional routing you'd need to add a new, highly specific, route in the global configuration, to handle this outlier method. Over time, you might add other similarly specific routes, giving the potential for clashes and breaking other routes in your application. Conventional routing is not as useful when you need to have this level of fine-grained control over your routes.

Instead, a more common approach is to use *attribute routing* for your Web APIs. Attribute routing, as the name suggests, involves applying attributes to your action methods to specify the URL that they should match.

Listing 9.4   Attribute routing example

```
public class HomeController: Controller
{
    [Route("")]                          ◁───────    The Index action will be
    public IActionResult Index()                     executed when the "/"
    {                                                URL is requested.
        /* method implementation*/
    }

    [Route("contact")]                   ◁───────    The Contact action will be
    public IActionResult Contact()                   executed when the
    {                                                "/home/contact" URL is
        /* method implementation*/                   requested.
    }

}
```

By applying [Route] attributes to your controller, you bypass conventional routing for that action method. Each [Route] attribute defines a specific URL that corresponds to the associated action method. In the example provided, the "/" URL maps directly to the Index method and the "/contact" URL maps to the Contact method.

> **TIP**   If you use [Route] attributes on all your action methods, then you don't need to set up any conventional routes when you call UseMvc() in Startup.Configure().

Conceptually, attribute routing takes the opposite approach to conventional routing. The MVC-style conventional routing looks at the incoming URL, checks it against your route templates to fill in the blanks for the controller and action, and then checks to see if the requested controller and action exist in your application.

Attribute routing, on the other hand, starts by looking for all the controllers and action methods in your application that have [Route] attributes. It uses these to calculate the URL that needs to be called to invoke a given action, building a dictionary where the key is the URL and the value is the action method. When a request arrives, the router can check if the key is in the dictionary—if it is, then it knows which action to execute, if it isn't, then the action isn't attribute-routed.

Attribute routing maps URLs to a specific action method, but a single action method can still have multiple URLs. Each URL must be declared with its own Route-Attribute, as shown in this listing, which shows the skeleton of the Web API for a car-racing game.

Listing 9.5   Attribute routing with multiple attributes

```
public class CarController
{
    [Route("car/start")]                       The Start method will be
    [Route("car/ignition")]                    executed when any of these
    [Route("start-car")]                       URLs are reached.
    public IActionResult Start()       ◄─┐
    {                                     The name of the action
        /* method implementation*/        method has no effect on
    }                                      the RouteAttribute or URL.

                                           The RouteAttributes can
    [Route("car/speed/{speed}")]           contain route parameters, in
    [Route("set-speed/{speed}")]           this case speed.
    public IActionResult SetCarSpeed(int speed)
    {
        /* method implementation*/
    }
}
```

The listing shows two different action methods, both of which can be accessed from multiple URLs. For example, the Start method will be executed when any of the following URLS are requested:

- /car/start
- /car/ignition
- /start-car

These URLs are completely independent of the controller and action method names; only the value in the RouteAttribute matters.

> **NOTE**   The controller and action name have no bearing on the URLs or route templates when RouteAttributes are used.

The templates used by the route attributes are standard route templates, the same as you used in chapter 5. You can use literal segments and you're free to define route parameters that will extract values from the URL, as shown by the SetCarSpeed method in the previous listing. That method defines two route templates, both of which define a route parameter, {speed}.

> **TIP** I've used multiple [Route] attributes on each action in this example, but it's best practice to expose your action at a single URL. This will make your API easier to understand and consume by other applications.

Route parameters are handled in the very same way as for conventional routing—they represent a segment of the URL that can vary. The only difference with attribute routing is that the controller and action name are already known, so you're not allowed to use the {controller} and {action} parameters—these are already set to the controller and action that corresponds to the decorated action method.

As before, when defining conventional routes, the route parameters in your RouteAttribute templates can

- Be optional
- Have default values
- Use route constraints

For example, you could update the SetCarSpeed method in the previous listing to constrain {speed} to an integer and to default to 20 like so:

```
[Route("car/speed/{speed=20:int}")]
[Route("set-speed/{speed=20:int}")]
public IActionResult SetCarSpeed(int speed)
```

It's also possible to give your route attributes a name by providing one to RouteAttribute, for example:

```
[Route("set-speed/{speed}", Name = "set_speed")]
public IActionResult SetCarSpeed(int speed)
```

Route names are optional, and aren't used when matching URLs, but they can be useful for URL generation. You saw in chapter 5 how to create URLs in your action methods using the Url helper and the RedirectToRoute method, and how to use them with Tag Helpers in chapter 8. Although you may only have half a dozen conventional routes, you effectively have a route for every attribute-routed action method that has been given a name. Each route name must be unique in the application, so be sure to keep track of them if you do use them!

If you managed to get your head around routing in chapter 5, then attribute routing shouldn't hold any dangers for you. You're writing a custom route template for every action method in your application. When combining both conventional and attribute routing in your application, you need to bear in mind how these two approaches interact and what it means for your URLs.

9.4.1 *Ordering of conventional and attribute routes*

In chapter 5, you saw that the order in which you define conventional routes in Startup.cs controls the order in which those routes are checked when MvcMiddleware receives a request. A route template defined earlier will be tested first, so gets first dibs on handling the request. Because of that, it's important to define the *most specific* routes first, and the *most general* routes at the end.

With attribute routing, ordering doesn't happen in quite the same way. On startup, MvcMiddleware scans your app using reflection and locates all the routes applied using RouteAttributes. It then *automatically* orders the routes from most specific to least specific, as though you had defined the routes in the most optimum way.

Having said that, RouteAttributes *do* have an Order property. You can use this to explicitly ensure a particular route attribute match is attempted before other routes, but I'd strongly advise against using it. Doing so adds another layer of complexity that you need to manage and could be indicative of excessive complexity in the URLs your application exposes.

> **WARNING** If you find yourself relying on a route order, then your URLs are probably confusing. This will make it difficult for clients to consume your API. Instead of using the Order property, look at ways to reduce the overlap between your routes.

What does ordering routes in the most optimum way look like? Well, it obviously depends on your application, and if you've defined your [Route] attributes using a confusing URL space, then there may not be a truly optimum order. In those cases, falling back to route naming can sometimes be an easier solution than trying to coerce the correct order.

An aspect I haven't touched on yet is what happens when you have an application with both conventional and attribute routing. For example, the standard conventional routing for the Index action method

```
public class HomeController
{
    [Route("view")]
    public IActionResult Index() { }
}
```

would suggest that the /home/index URL would invoke the action. On the other hand, attribute routing suggests the /view URL would invoke the action. Who wins? Either? Both?

Well, applying attribute routing to an action means that it can *never* be matched using conventional routing. Even though the action theoretically matches the /home/index route, the conventional router can't even see it, so it will never match.

You're free to use both conventional routing and attribute routing in a single application, but you need to bear this conflict between the two approaches in mind. Even if a convention seems like it should match a particular action, the presence of an attribute route will mean the action won't be matched by the convention.

> **TIP** Attribute routing on an action (or a controller, as you'll see) will make the action unreachable by conventional routing.

This fact lends credence to the convention of sticking to conventional routing for traditional MVC controllers that return HTML using Razor templates and using attribute routing for your Web API controllers. Doing so will make your life a lot simpler and can help avoid conflicts if you're consistent with your naming.[1]

> **TIP** Use conventional routing for MVC controllers, and attribute routing for Web API controllers. Adding a prefix such as `"api"` to your Web API route templates helps to separate the Web API URL space from the MVC URL space.

One thing you might begin noticing when you start using attribute routing is how much more verbose it is than conventional routing. Where with conventional routing you had only a handful of routes, you now have one for every single action method!

This is largely a symptom of the greater control attribute routing provides, but there are a few features available to make your life a little easier. In particular, combining route attributes and token replacement can help reduce duplication in your code.

9.4.2 *Combining route attributes to keep your route templates DRY*

Adding route attributes to all of your API controllers can get a bit tedious, especially if you're mostly following conventions where your routes have a standard prefix such as `"api"` or the controller name. Generally, you'll want to ensure you don't repeat yourself (DRY) when it comes to these strings. The following listing shows two action methods with a number of [Route] attributes. (This is for demonstration purposes only. Stick to one per action if you can!)

Listing 9.6 Duplication in `RouteAttribute` templates

```
public class CarController
{
    [Route("api/car/start")]
    [Route("api/car/ignition")]
    [Route("/start-car")]
    public IActionResult Start()
    {
        /* method implementation*/
    }

    [Route("api/car/speed/{speed}")]
    [Route("/set-speed/{speed}")]
    public IActionResult SetCarSpeed(int speed)
    {
        /* method implementation*/
    }
}
```

---

[1] ASP.NET Core 2.1 introduces the [ApiController] attribute. Applying this attribute to your controller means it must only use [Route] attributes; it will never match conventional routes.

There's quite a lot of duplication here—you're adding `"api/car"` to most of your routes. Presumably, if you decided to change this to `"api/vehicles"`, you'd have to go through each attribute and update it. Code like that is asking for a typo to creep in!

To alleviate this pain, it's also possible to apply `RouteAttributes` to controllers, in addition to action methods. When a controller and an action method both have a route attribute, the overall route template for the method is calculated by combining the two templates.

Listing 9.7 Combining `RouteAttribute` templates

```
[Route("api/car")]
public class CarController
{
    [Route("start")]              Combines to give
    [Route("ignition")]           the "api/car/start"      Combines to give
    [Route("/start-car")]         template                 the "api/car/ignition"
    public IActionResult Start()                            template
    {
                                  Does not combine as
        /* method implementation*/ starts with /, gives the
    }                             "start-car" template

    [Route("speed/{speed}")]                    Combines to give the
    [Route("/set-speed/{speed}")]               " api/car/speed/{speed}"
    public IActionResult SetCarSpeed(int speed) template
    {
                                                Does not combine as starts
        /* method implementation*/              with /, gives the "set-
    }                                           speed/{speed}" template
}
```

Combining attributes in this way can reduce some of the duplication in your route templates and makes it easier to add or change the prefixes (such as switching `"car"` to `"vehicle"`) for multiple action methods. To ignore the `RouteAttribute` on the controller and create an absolute route template, start your action method route template with a slash (`/`).

You can combine multiple `RouteAttribute` on controllers too, if you use inheritance. If all your controllers inherit from a base class, you can use this approach to add a global prefix to all your attribute routes.

Listing 9.8 Using a base class to add a global prefix to `RouteAttribute` templates

```
[Route("api")]                                    The BaseController defines
public class BaseController : Controller { }      the "api" global prefix

[Route("car")]                                    The CarController inherits the
public class CarController : BaseController        RouteAttribute from the BaseController
{                                                  and adds its own prefix
    [Route("start")]
    [Route("ignition")]                 Combines all attributes    Combines all attributes
}                                       to give the                to give the
                                        "api/car/ignition" template "api/car/start" template
```

```
[Route("/start-car")]          ⟵          Does not combine with base
public IActionResult Start()                attributes as it starts with /, so
{                                           remains as "start-car"
    /* method implementation*/
}
}
```

As you can see, the [Route] attribute from the "most-base" controller is used first, followed by the action controller, and finally, the action method, combining to give a single route for the action method. Once again, specifying a leading "/" to the route will prevent route combination and will use only the final [Route] attribute to define the route. This has reduced a lot of the duplication, but you can do one better by using token replacement.

9.4.3 Using token replacement to reduce duplication in attribute routing

The ability to combine attribute routes is handy, but you're still left with some duplication if you're prefixing your routes with the name of the controller, or your route templates use the action name. Luckily, you can simplify even further!

Attribute routes support the automatic replacement of the [action] and [controller] tokens in your attribute routes. These will be replaced with the name of the action and the controller (without the "Controller" suffix), respectively. The tokens are replaced after all attributes have been combined, so this is useful when you have controller inheritance hierarchies. This listing shows how you can simplify the previous route attribute hierarchy.

> **Listing 9.9   Token replacement in RouteAttributes**

```
[Route("api/[controller]")]          ⟵          Token replacement happens
public abstract class BaseController { }          last, so [controller] is replaced
                                                  with "car" not "base"
public class CarController : BaseController
{
    [Route("[action]")]          ⟵          Combines and replaces
    [Route("ignition")]          ⟵          tokens to give the
    [Route("/start-car")]                     "api/car/start" template
    public IActionResult Start()
    {                                Combines and replaces
        /* method implementation*/   tokens to give the
    }                                "api/car/ignition" template
}
```
Does not combine with base attributes as it starts with /, so remains as "start-car"

The router will also replace tokens in the Name property of RouteAttributes, which can make generating unique route names easier. If you use a RouteAttribute on a base controller with a tokenized name

```
[Route("api/[controller]", Name = "[controller]_[action]")]
```

then a unique route name will be generated for each action. You need to be careful if you have multiple `RouteAttributes` applied to a single action, as in the previous listing, as then the route names will no longer be unique!

> **TIP**   Avoid using multiple `[Route]` attributes on your Web API action methods. Having multiple URLs invoke the same action can be confusing for consumers of your app and complicates routing.

We've covered pretty much everything there is to know about attribute routing now, with one exception: handling different HTTP request types like `GET` and `POST`.

9.4.4   *Handling multiple matching actions with attribute routing*

In chapter 5, you saw that you could discriminate between two action methods that match the same URL by using HTTP verb attributes such as `[HttpPost]`. With Web API controllers, the need to distinguish between identical URLs becomes more prevalent, due to their typical design.

Imagine you're building an API to manage your calendar. You want to be able to list and create appointments. Well, a traditional HTTP REST service might define the following URLs and HTTP verbs to achieve this:

- `GET /appointments`—List all your appointments
- `POST /appointments`—Create a new appointment

Note that these two endpoints define the same URL, only the HTTP verb differs. This is common when building Web APIs and, luckily, is easy to model in ASP.NET Core. As with conventional routing, you use attributes such as `[HttpPost]` to define the HTTP verb an action method corresponds to.

> **Listing 9.10   Using HTTP verb attributes with attribute routing**

```
public class AppointmentController
{
    [HttpGet("/appointments")]
    public IActionResult ListAppointments()        Only executed in response
    {                                              to GET /appointments
        /* method implementation */
    }


    [HttpPost("/appointments")]
    public IActionResult CreateAppointment()       Only executed in response
    {                                              to POST /appointments
        /* method implementation */
    }
}
```

These HTTP verb attributes are the same ones you saw used in chapter 5 with conventional routing, but in this case, they also contain the route template themselves. `[HttpGet("/appointments")]` effectively combines `[Route("/appointments")]` and

[HttpGet] into a more compact representation. For that reason, this is the preferred approach for defining your attribute routes.

> **TIP** Define routes using attributes such as [HttpGet], [HttpPost], and [HttpDelete]. This makes the action methods more specific and easier to reason about.

And with that, you'll probably be glad to hear we're finished with routing for Web APIs and, in fact, for the whole book! With the route template details you have in chapter 5 and in this section, you have everything you need to customize the URLs in your application, whether you're using conventional routes or attribute routing.

Conceptually, people often find attribute routing a bit easier to grok, as you're normally mapping a URL one-to-one with an action method. Although having the freedom to define the exact URL for a particular action method is useful, try not to get too power-crazed; always try to think about the users and clients consuming your API. Having a simple and well-defined set of URLs for your application should be your main goal.

With routing checked off the list, it's time to consider the next step in an MVC request—model binding—and how you can customize it for Web APIs. The process is identical for both MVC and Web API, but Web APIs often run into an additional requirement, especially when interoperating with legacy systems—the ability to post XML to a Web API action method. By default, this isn't possible but, luckily, enabling it is easy.

9.5 Enabling additional input formatters: binding to XML data

In chapter 6, I introduced model binding as a way of mapping an incoming request to the method parameters of an action. After the router selects an action method, the model binder is responsible for taking the data posted in a request and mapping it to the method parameters of the action method.

In particular, you saw that by using the [FromBody] attribute on a method parameter, you could bind a parameter to the body of a request.

These days, with mobile applications and SPAs becoming increasingly popular, the vast majority of data posted to Web APIs is JSON. The default model binder supports this out of the box, so all that's required to have the JSON data bound to your method parameter is to add the [FromBody] attribute.[1]

There was a time, however, when XML was king. It's still used for configuration (good old MSBuild and .csproj files) and many communication protocols (SOAP, RSS). Consequently, it's quite likely you'll need to be able to accept XML data to a Web API action at some point.

---

[1] ASP.NET Core 2.1 introduces the [ApiController] attribute. If you decorate your Web API controller with this attribute, you don't need to decorate your binding models with [FromBody]. The MVC middleware will infer that complex types should be bound using [FromBody] automatically.

By default, `MvcMiddleware` only accepts `POST` data in JSON format. In order to be able to accept XML data and have it bind automatically to your models, you'll need additional services.

Customizable by default

The ability to customize each aspect of ASP.NET Core is one of the features that sets it apart from the previous version of ASP.NET. ASP.NET Core configures the vast majority of its internal components using one of two mechanisms—dependency injection or by configuring an `Options` object when you add the service to your application, as you'll see in chapters 10 (dependency injection) and 11 (`Options` object).

As an adjunct to this, much of ASP.NET Core starts from the assumption that you want *nothing* in your application, and lets you add in the things you need. This means you can easily create small, stripped-back web applications, when compared to the monolithic System.Web-based previous version of ASP.NET. Your application has *only* the features you need.

In counterpoint to this, this philosophy means you'll run into many more situations where the default settings won't fit your requirements. Luckily, the ability to easily customize all the components of ASP.NET Core means you'll normally be able to add additional features without too much difficulty.

Before you dig into how to add the formatters, it's worth considering what happens if you try to send XML to an ASP.NET Core application that you haven't yet configured to accept it.

In this example, I've created a simple Web API Controller that parses an object form the request body and returns a 200 OK response:

```
[HttpPost]
public IActionResult Add([FromBody] Car car)
{
    return Ok();
}
```

Figure 9.8 shows a screenshot of Postman (www.getpostman.com), which you can use to create requests for testing your application. I created a request with XML in the body and `POST`ed it to the preceding action. As you can see, the application returns a 415 response code, which means "Unsupported Media Type", indicating that `Mvc-Middleware` was unable to parse the XML in the body of the request.

Clients include the `content-type` header as part of `POST` requests to tell the server what sort of data it's sending. In this case, the request is sent with a `content-type` of `text/xml`. When the request arrives, it checks this header and looks for an *input formatter* that can deserialize the request.

> **TIP** The input formatter is selected based on the `content-type` header of the request.

A request is sent to the web API with
a content-type of text/xml.

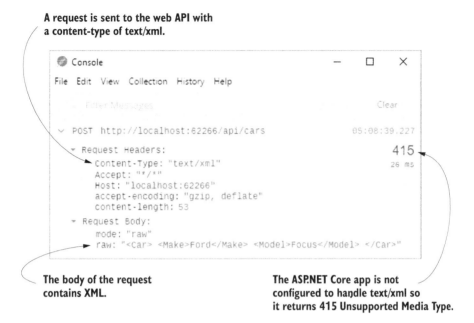

The body of the request
contains XML.

The ASP.NET Core app is not
configured to handle text/xml so
it returns 415 Unsupported Media Type.

**Figure 9.8   When an application can't handle the format of the data sent to a Web API action,
it returns a 415 Unsupported Media Type response.**

You've already seen what happens when you make a request with a `content-type` your app can't deserialize. ASP.NET Core doesn't include an XML input formatter by default when you add MVC to your project, but you can add a NuGet package to provide the functionality.

1   If you're not using the ASP.NET Core 2.0 metapackage, add `<PackageReference>` for the Microsoft.AspNetCore.Mvc.Formatters.Xml package to your csproj file:

```
<PackageReference Include="Microsoft.AspNetCore.Mvc.Formatters.Xml"
    Version="2.0.0" />
```

You can add the preceding line directly, use the Visual Studio package manager, or run the following command from inside your project's folder:

```
dotnet add package Microsoft.AspNetCore.Mvc.Formatters.Xml
```

2   Update the `ConfigureServices` method in Startup to add the formatters to MVC

```
public void ConfigureServices(IServiceCollection services)
{
    services.AddMvc()
            .AddXmlSerializerFormatters();
}
```

That's it! That simple change registers the XML input formatter with `MvcMiddleware`. Whenever your app receives a request with a `content-type` of `text/xml` or `application/`

A request is sent to the
web API with a content-type
of text/xml.

The body of the request
contains XML.

The XML formatter package has been
added, so the request is accepted,
and the action method returns
a 200 OK response.

Figure 9.9   Once the XML formatters have been configured, the application can parse the
`text/xml` content-type and returns a 200 OK response code.

xml, the input formatter will handle it, parse the request, and allow the model binder
to bind your data, so the application can return a 200 response, shown in figure 9.9.

Accepting XML is a common requirement and, luckily, it's easy to enable in your
Web API (and MVC) controllers with the XML formatters package. Similarly, you
often need to customize the format of the data returned by your Web API controllers—whether that's JSON, XML, or a different, custom format. In the next section,
you'll see how you can control this both at the application level and for individual
action methods.

9.6   *Generating a response from a model*

This brings us to the final section in this chapter: formatting a response. You've seen
how to tweak your application for a Web API using attribute routing and adding different input formatters, but the *output* formatting is where Web APIs differ from traditional MVC controllers.

Consider this scenario: You've created a Web API action method for returning a
list of cars you've owned, as in the following listing. It invokes a method on your application model, which hands back the list of data to the controller. Now you need to format the response and return it to the caller.

Listing 9.11   A Web API controller to return a list of cars

```
public class CarsController : Controller        The action is executed with
{                                               a request to GET /api/cars.
    [HttpGet("api/cars")]              ◄─────┐
    public IEnumerable<string> ListCars()  ◄─────────────┐  The API Model containing
    {                                                     │  the data is an
        return new string[]                               │  IEnumerable<string>.
            { "Nissan Micra", "FordFocus" };              │
                                                     This data would normally be
    }                                                fetched from the application model.
}
```

You've already seen that it's possible to return data directly from an action method, in which case, the middleware formats it and returns the formatted data to the caller. But how does the middleware know which format to use? After all, you could serialize it as JSON, as XML, even with a simple `ToString()` call.

The process of determining the format of data to send to clients is known generally as *content negotiation* (conneg). At a high level, the client sends a header indicating the types of content it can understand—the `Accept` header—and the server picks one of these, formats the response, and sends a `content-type` header in the response, indicating which it chose.

The accept and content-type headers

The `accept` header is sent by a client as part of a request to indicate the type of content that the client can handle. It consists of a number of MIME types,[a] with optional weightings (from 0 to 1) to indicate which type would be preferred. For example, the `application/json,text/xml;q=0.9,text/plain;q=0.6` header indicates that the client can accept JSON, XML, and plain text, with weightings of 1.0, 0.9, and 0.6, respectively. JSON has a weighting of 1.0, as no explicit weighting was provided. The weightings can be used during content negotiation to choose an optimal representation for both parties.

The `content-type` header describes the data sent in a request or response. It contains the MIME type of the data, with an optional character encoding. For example, the `application/json; charset=utf-8` header would indicate that the body of the request or response is JSON, encoded using UTF-8.

---

[a] For more on MIME types see http://mng.bz/D3UB.

You're not forced into only sending a `content-type` the client expects and, in some cases, you may not even be *able* to handle the types it requests. What if a request stipulates it can only accept Excel spreadsheets? It's unlikely you'd support that, even if that's the only `content-type` the request contains!

When you return an API model from an action method, whether directly (as in the previous listing) or via an `OkResult` or other `StatusCodeResult`, ASP.NET Core will

A request is sent to the
web API with an accept
header type of text/xml.

The ASP.NET Core app is not configured
to return text/xml, so it returns JSON by
default instead.

Figure 9.10   Even though the request was made with an `Accept` header of `text/xml`,
the response returned was JSON, as the server was not configured to return XML.

always return *something*. If it can't honor any of the types stipulated in the `Accept`
header, it will fall back to returning JSON by default. Figure 9.10 shows that even
though XML was requested, `MvcMiddleware` formatted the response as JSON.

> **NOTE**   In the previous version of ASP.NET, objects were serialized to JSON
> using PascalCase, where properties start with a capital. In ASP.NET Core,
> objects are serialized using camelCase by default, where properties start with a
> lowercase letter.

Whichever way the data is sent, it's serialized by an `IOutputFormatter` implementation. ASP.NET Core ships with a limited number of output formatters out of the box,
but as always, it's easy to add additional ones, or change the way the defaults work.

9.6.1   *Customizing the default formatters: adding XML support*

As with most of ASP.NET Core, the Web API formatters are completely customizable.
By default, only formatters for plain text (`text/plain`), HTML (`text/html`), and
JSON (`application/json`) are configured.

Given the common use case of SPAs and mobile applications, this will get you a long way. But as you saw in section 9.5, you often need to be able to return data in another format, such as XML.

You've already seen how to add XML output-formatting support—it's the same process as adding input-formatter support in section 9.5! Technically, you can add the output and input formatters independently, but it's unlikely you'll need one and not the other. Not many clients are going to send you JSON but demand an XML response!

As you saw in section 9.5, add the Microsoft.AspNetCore.Mvc.Formatters.Xml package, and update the call to AddMvc() to add the output formatters:

```
services.AddMvc()
    .AddXmlSerializerFormatters();
```

With this simple change, the middleware can now format responses as XML. Running the same request as shown in figure 9.10 with XML support enabled means the app will respect the text/xml accept header. The formatter serializes the string array to XML, as shown in figure 9.11, instead of the JSON returned previously.

A request is sent to the web API with an accept header type of text/xml.

With the XML formatters added, the accept header can be honored, so text/xml is returned instead of the default JSON response.

Figure 9.11   With the XML output formatters added, the `text/xml` `Accept` **header is respected and the response can be serialized to XML.**

This is an example of content negotiation, where the client has specified what formats it can handle and the server selects one of those, based on what it can produce. This approach is part of the HTTP protocol, but there are some quirks to be aware of when relying on it in ASP.NET Core. You won't often run into these, but if you're not aware of them when they hit you, they could have you scratching your head for hours!

9.6.2 Choosing a response format with content negotiation

Content negotiation is where a client says which types of data it can accept using the `accept` header and the server picks the best one it can handle. Generally speaking, this works as you'd hope: the server formats the data using a type the client can understand.

The ASP.NET Core implementation has some special cases that are worth bearing in mind:

- By default, the middleware will only return `application/json`, `text/plain` and `text/html` MIME types. You can add additional `IOutputFormatters` to make other types available, as you saw in the previous section for `text/xml`.
- By default, if you return `null` as your API model, whether from an action method, or by passing `null` in `StatusCodeResult`, the middleware will return a `204 No Content` response.
- When you return a `string` as your API model, if no `Accept` header is set, the middleware will format the response as `text/plain`.
- When you use any other class as your API model and there's either no `Accept` header or none of the supported formats were requested, the first formatter that can generate a response will be used (typically JSON by default).
- If the middleware detects that the request is probably from a browser (the `accept` header contains `*/*`), then it will not use conneg. Instead, it will format the response as though no accept header was provided, using the default formatter (typically JSON).

These defaults are relatively sane, but they can certainly bite you if you're not aware of them. The last point in particular, where the response to a request from a browser is virtually always formatted as JSON has certainly caught me out when trying to test XML requests locally!

As you should expect by now, all of these rules are configurable; you can easily change the default behavior in your application if it doesn't fit your requirements. In chapter 4, I showed how to customize MVC by modifying the maximum number of validation errors in your application. The following listing shows a similar approach, in which you can force the middleware to respect the browser's `Accept` header when adding the MVC services in Startup.cs.

Listing 9.12 Customizing MVC to respect the browser Accept header in Web APIs

```
public void ConfigureServices(IServiceCollection services)
{
    services.AddMvc(options =>
    {
        options.RespectBrowserAcceptHeader = true;
    });
}
```

AddMvc has an overload that takes a lambda function

False by default, a number of other properties are also available to be set

In most cases, conneg should work well for you out of the box, whether you're building a SPA or a mobile application. In some cases, you may find you need to bypass the usual conneg mechanisms for certain actions, and there are a number of ways to achieve this, but I won't cover them in this book as I've found I rarely need to use them. For details, see the documentation at http://mng.bz/tnu9.

That brings us to the end of this chapter on Web APIs and, with it, part 1 of this book! It's been a pretty intense tour of ASP.NET Core, with a heavy focus on the MVC middleware. By making it this far, you now have all the knowledge you need to start building simple MVC applications using Razor view templates, or to create a Web API server for your SPA or mobile app.

In part 2, you'll get into some juicy topics, in which you'll learn the details needed to build complete apps, like adding users to your application, saving data to a database, and how to deploy your application.

In chapter 10, we'll look at dependency injection in ASP.NET Core and how it helps create loosely coupled applications. You'll learn how to register the ASP.NET Core framework services with a container and set up your own classes as dependency-injected services. Finally, you'll see how to replace the built-in container with a third-party alternative.

Summary

- A Web API exposes a number of methods or endpoints that can be used to access or change data on a server. It's typically accessed using HTTP.
- Web API action methods can return data directly or can use IActionResult to generate an arbitrary response.
- Web APIs follow the same MVC design pattern as traditional web applications. The formatters which generate the final response form the view.
- Unlike the previous version of ASP.NET, there's no difference between MVC controllers and Web API controllers in ASP.NET Core. The naming refers only to the difference in the data returned by their methods and the purpose for which they're used.
- The data returned by a Web API action is called an API model. It contains the data the middleware will serialize and send back to the client. This differs from

view models, as view models contain both data and metadata about how to generate the response.

- Attribute routing is an alternative way of defining the routes in your application by applying `RouteAttributes` to your action methods. Web API controllers often use this approach, as it allows tighter control over the URL generated for each action method.

- The controller and action name have no bearing on the URLs or route templates when you use attribute routing.

- Route attributes applied to a controller combine with attributes on action methods to form the final template. These are also combined with attributes on inherited base classes.

- If an action or controller uses attribute routing, it can no longer be reached via conventional routing.

- Use the `"[controller]"` and `"[action]"` tokens in your route templates to reduce repetition. They'll be replaced with the current controller and action name.

- The `[HttpPost]` and `[HttpGet]` attributes allow choosing between actions based on the request's HTTP method when two actions correspond to the same URL.

- You can model bind requests sent in the XML format using the Microsoft .AspNetCore.Mvc.Formatters.Xml package. Add the XML formatters by calling `services.AddMvc().AddXmlSerializerFormatters()` in your Startup class. This will also enable XML responses.

- By default, ASP.NET Core will format the API model returned from a Web API controller as JSON.

- If you return more than one type of result from an action method, the method signature must return `IActionResult`.

- In contrast to the previous version of ASP.NET, JSON data is serialized using camelCase rather than PascalCase.

- Content negotiation occurs when the client specifies the type of data it can handle and the server chooses a return format based on this.

- By default, ASP.NET Core can return `text/plain`, `text/html`, and `application/json`, but you can add additional formatters.

- Content negotiation isn't used when the accept header contains `*/*`, such as in most browsers. You can disable this option by modifying the `RespectBrowserAcceptHeader` option when adding MVC services in Startup.cs.

Part 2

Building complete applications

W e covered a lot of ground in part 1. You saw how an ASP.NET Core application is composed of middleware and we focused heavily on the MVC middleware. You saw how to use it to build traditional server-side-rendered apps using Razor and how to build web APIs for mobile and client-side apps.

In part 2, we dive deeper into the framework and look at a variety of components that you'll inevitably need to build more complex apps. By the end of this part, you'll be able to build dynamic applications, customized to specific users, that can be deployed to multiple environments, each with a different configuration.

ASP.NET Core uses dependency injection (DI) throughout its libraries, so it's important that you understand how this design pattern works. In chapter 10, I introduce DI, why it is used, and how to configure the services in your applications to use DI.

Chapter 11 looks at the ASP.NET Core configuration system, which lets you pass configuration values to your app from a range of sources—JSON files, environment variables, and many more. You'll learn how to configure your app to use different values depending on the environment in which it is running, and how to bind strongly typed objects to your configuration to help reduce runtime errors.

Most web applications require some sort of data storage, so in chapter 12, I introduce Entity Framework Core (EF Core). This is a new, cross-platform library that makes it easier to connect your app to a database. EF Core is worthy of a book in and of itself, so I only provide a brief introduction. I show you how to create a database and how to insert, update, and query simple data.

In chapters 13 through 15, we look at how to build more complex applications. You'll see how you can add ASP.NET Core Identity to your apps so that users can log in and enjoy a customized experience. You'll learn how to protect your app using authorization to ensure only certain users can access certain action methods, and you'll see how to refactor your app to extract common code out of your action methods in filters.

In the final chapter of this part, I cover the steps required to make an app live, including how to publish your app to IIS, how to configure the URLs your app listens on, and how to optimize your client-side assets for improved performance.

Service configuration with dependency injection

This chapter covers

- Understanding the benefits of dependency injection
- How ASP.NET Core uses dependency injection
- Configuring your services to work with dependency injection
- Choosing the correct lifetime for your services

In part 1 of this book, you saw the bare bones of how to build applications with ASP.NET Core. You learned how to compose middleware to create your application and how to use the MVC pattern to build traditional web applications and web APIs. This gave you the tools to start building simple applications.

In this chapter, you'll see how to use *dependency injection* (DI) in your ASP.NET Core applications. DI is a design pattern that helps you develop loosely coupled code. ASP.NET Core uses the pattern extensively, both internally in the framework and in the applications you build, so you'll need to use it in all but the most trivial of applications.

You may have heard of DI before, and possibly even used it in your own applications. If so, this chapter shouldn't hold many surprises for you. If you haven't used DI before, never fear, I'll make sure you're up to speed by the time the chapter is done!

This chapter will start by introducing DI in general, the principles it drives, and why you should care about it. You'll see how ASP.NET Core has embraced DI throughout its implementation and why you should do the same when writing your own applications.

Once you have a solid understanding of the concept, you'll see how to apply DI to your own classes. You'll learn how to configure your app so that the ASP.NET Core framework can create your classes for you, removing the pain of having to create new objects manually in your code. Toward the end of the chapter, you'll learn how to control how long your objects are used for and some of the pitfalls to be aware of when you come to write your own applications.

In chapter 19, we'll revisit some of the more advanced ways to use DI, including how to wire up a third-party DI container. For now though, let's get back to basics: what is DI and why should you care about it?

10.1 Introduction to dependency injection

The ASP.NET Core framework has been designed from the ground up to be modular and to adhere to "good" software engineering practices. As with anything in software, what is considered best practice varies over time, but for object-oriented programming, the SOLID[1] principles have stood the test of time.

On that basis, ASP.NET Core has *dependency injection* (sometimes called *dependency inversion*, *DI*, or *inversion of control*[2]) baked in to the heart of the framework. Whether or not you want to use it within your own application code, the framework libraries themselves depend on it as a concept.

This section aims to give you a basic understanding of what dependency injection is, why you should care about it, and how ASP.NET Core uses it. The topic itself extends far beyond the reach of this single chapter. If you want a deeper background, I highly recommend checking out Martin Fowler's articles online.[3]

> **TIP** For a more directly applicable read with many examples in C#, I recommend picking up *Dependency Injection in .NET* by Steven van Deursen and Mark Seemann (Manning, 2017).

---

[1] SOLID is a mnemonic for Single responsibility, Open-closed, Liskov substitution, Interface segregation, and Dependency inversion: https://en.wikipedia.org/wiki/SOLID_(object-oriented_design).

[2] Although related, dependency injection and dependency inversion are two different things. I cover both in a general sense in this chapter, but for a good explanation of the differences, see this post by Derick Bailey: http://mng.bz/vU7N.

[3] Martin Fowler's website at https://martinfowler.com is a gold mine of best-practice goodness. One of the most applicable articles to this chapter can be found at www.martinfowler.com/articles/injection.html.

I'll begin this section by starting with a common scenario: a class in your application depends on a different class, which in turn depends on another. You'll see how dependency injection can help alleviate this chaining of dependencies for you and provide a number of extra benefits.

10.1.1 Understanding the benefits of dependency injection

When you first started programming, the chances are you didn't immediately use a DI framework. That's not surprising, or even a bad thing; DI adds a certain amount of extra wiring that's not warranted in simple applications or when you're getting started. But when things start to get more complex, DI comes into its own as a great tool to help keep that complexity in check.

Let's consider a simple example, written without any sort of DI. Imagine a user has registered on your web app and you want to send them an email. This listing shows how you might approach this initially.

Listing 10.1 Sending an email without DI when there are no dependencies

```
public class UserController : Controller          The action method
{                                                 is called when a
    public IActionResult RegisterUser(string username)   new user is created.

    {
        var emailSender = new EmailSender();       Creates a new instance
        emailSender.SendEmail(username);           of EmailSender
        return View();
    }                                              Uses the new instance
}                                                  to send the email
```

In this example, the `RegisterUser` action on `UserController` executes when a new user registers on your app. This creates a new instance of an `EmailSender` class, and calls `SendEmail()` to send the email. The `EmailSender` class is the one that does the sending of the email. For the purposes of this example, you can imagine it will look something like this:

```
public class EmailSender
{
    public void SendEmail(string username)
    {
        Console.WriteLine($"Email sent to {username}!");
    }
}
```

`Console.Writeline` will perform the sending of the email.

> **NOTE** Although I'm using sending email as a simple example, in practice you might want to move this code out of your `Controller` classes entirely. This sort of task is well suited to using message queues and a background process, but that's outside the scope of this book.

If the EmailSender class is as simple as the previous example and it has no dependencies, then you might not see any need to adopt a different approach to creating objects. And to an extent, you'd be right. But what if you later update your implementation of EmailSender so that it doesn't implement the whole email-sending logic itself?

In practice, EmailSender would need to do a number of things to send an email. It would need to

- Create an email message
- Configure the settings of the email server
- Send the email to the email server

Doing all of that in one class would go against the single responsibility principle (SRP), so you'd likely end up with EmailSender depending on other services. Figure 10.1 shows how this web of dependencies might look. UserController wants to send an email using EmailSender, but in order to do so, it also needs to create the MessageFactory, NetworkClient, and EmailServerSettings objects that EmailSender depends on.

Each class has a number of dependencies, so the "root" class, in this case User-Controller, needs to know how to create every class it depends on, as well as every class its *dependencies* depend on. This is sometimes called the *dependency graph*.

DEFINITION   The *dependency graph* is the set of objects that must be created in order to create a specific requested "root" object.

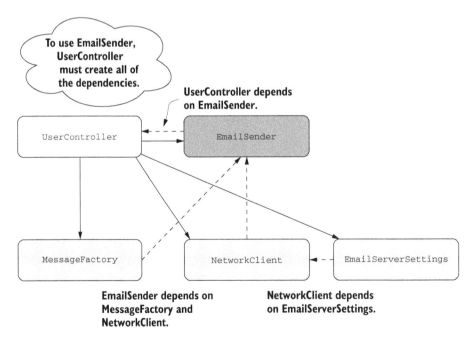

Figure 10.1   Dependency diagram without dependency injection. UserController indirectly depends on all the other classes; it also creates them all.

EmailSender depends on the MessageFactory and NetworkClient objects, so they're provided via the constructor, as shown here.

Listing 10.2　A service with multiple dependencies

```
public class EmailSender                                    The EmailSender now depends
{                                                           on two other classes.
    private readonly NetworkClient _client;
    private readonly MessageFactory _factory;

    public EmailSender(MessageFactory factory, NetworkClient client)
    {
        _factory = factory;                                      Instances of the
        _client = client;                                 dependencies are provided
    }                                                          in the constructor.

    public void SendEmail(string username)            The EmailSender coordinates
    {                                                 the dependencies to create
        var email = _factory.Create(username);        and send an email.
        _client.SendEmail(email);
        Console.WriteLine($"Email sent to {username}!");
    }
}
```

On top of that, the NetworkClient class that EmailSender depends on also has a dependency on an EmailServerSettings object:

```
public class NetworkClient
{
    private readonly EmailServerSettings _settings;
    public NetworkClient(EmailServerSettings settings)
    {
        _settings = settings;
    }
}
```

This might feel a little contrived, but it's common to find this sort of chain of dependencies. In fact, if you *don't* have this in your code, it's probably a sign that your classes are too big and aren't following the single responsibility principle.

So, how does this affect the code in UserController? The following listing shows how you now have to send an email, if you stick to new-ing up objects in the controller.

Listing 10.3　Sending email without DI when you manually create dependencies

```
public IActionResult RegisterUser(string username)
{                                                        To create EmailSender, you also have
    var emailSender = new EmailSender(                   to create all of its dependencies.
        new MessageFactory(),           ◁─── You need a new MessageFactory.
        new NetworkClient(
            new EmailServerSettings
            (                                You're already two layers
                host: "smtp.server.com",     deep, but there could
                port: 25                     feasibly be more.
            ))
```

The NetworkClient also has dependencies.

```
        );
    emailSender.SendEmail(username);
    return View();
}
```

◁─┐ **Finally, you can**
   send the email.

This is turning into some gnarly code. Improving the design of `EmailSender` to separate out the different responsibilities has made calling it from `UserController` a real chore. This code has a number of issues, among them:

- *Not obeying the single responsibility principle*—Our code is now responsible for both *creating* an `EmailSender` object and *using* it to send an email.
- *Considerable ceremony*—Of the 11 lines of code in the `RegisterUser` method, only the last two are doing anything useful. This makes it harder to read and harder to understand the intent of the method.
- *Tied to the implementation*—If you decide to refactor `EmailSender` and add another dependency, you'd need to update every place it's used.

`UserController` has an *implicit* dependency on the `EmailSender` class, as it manually creates the object itself as part of the `RegisterUser` method. The only way to know that `UserController` uses `EmailSender` is to look at its source code. In contrast, `EmailSender` has *explicit* dependencies on `NetworkClient` and `MessageFactory`, which must be provided in the constructor. Similarly, `NetworkClient` has an *explicit* dependency on the `EmailServerSettings` class.

> **TIP**   Generally speaking, any dependencies in your code should be explicit, not implicit. Implicit dependencies are hard to reason about and difficult to test, so you should avoid them wherever you can. DI is useful for guiding you along this path.

Dependency injection aims to solve the problem of building a dependency graph by *inverting* the chain of dependencies. Instead of the `UserController` creating its dependencies manually, deep inside the implementation details of the code, an already-created instance of `EmailSender` is injected via the constructor.

Now, obviously *something* needs to create the object, so the code to do that has to live somewhere. The service responsible for creating an object is called a *DI container* or an *IoC container*, as shown in figure 10.2.

> **DEFINITION**   The *DI container* or *IoC container* is responsible for creating instances of services. It knows how to construct an instance of a service by creating all of its dependencies and passing these to the constructor. I'll refer to it as a DI container throughout this book.

The term dependency injection is often used interchangeably with *inversion of control* (IoC). IoC describes the way that the control of how `EmailSender` is created has been reversed: instead of the `UserController` controlling how to create an instance, it's provided one instead.

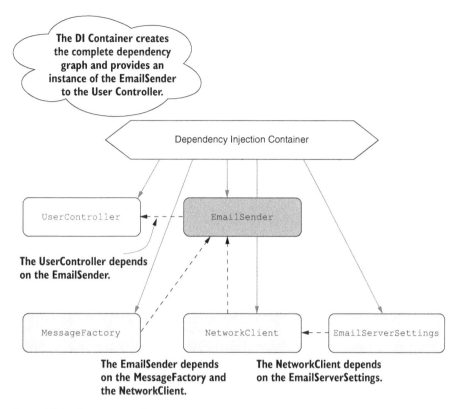

Figure 10.2 Dependency diagram using dependency injection. `UserController`
indrectly depends on all the other classes but doesn't need to know how to create them.
`UserController` declares that it requires `EmailSender` and the container provides it.

NOTE There are many existing DI containers available for .NET: Autofac,
StructureMap, Unity, Ninject, Simple Injector . . . The list goes on! In chapter 19, you'll see how to replace the default ASP.NET Core container with one
of these alternatives.

The advantage of adopting this pattern becomes apparent when you see how much it
simplifies using dependencies. The following listing shows how `UserController`
would look if you used DI to create `EmailSender` instead of doing it manually. All of
the new cruft has gone and you can focus purely on what the controller is doing—calling `EmailSender` and returning a `View`.

Listing 10.4   Sending an email using DI to inject dependencies

```
public class UserController : Controller
{
    private readonly EmailSender _emailSender;
    public UserController(EmailSender emailSender)
```

**Instead of creating the
dependencies implicitly,
they're injected via the
constructor.**

```
    {
        _emailSender = emailSender;
    }

    public IActionResult RegisterUser(string username)
    {
        _emailSender.SendEmail(username);
        return View();
    }
}
```

> Instead of creating the dependencies implicitly, they're injected via the constructor.

> The action method is easy to read and understand again.

One of the advantages of a DI container is that it has a single responsibility: creating objects or services. You ask a container for an instance of a service and it takes care of figuring out how to create the dependency graph, based on how you configure it.

> **NOTE** It's common to refer to *services* when talking about DI containers, which is slightly unfortunate as it's one of the most overloaded terms in software engineering! In this context, a service refers to any class or interface that the DI container creates when required.

The beauty of this approach is that by using explicit dependencies, you never have to write the mess of code you saw in listing 10.3. The DI container can inspect your service's constructor and work out how to write the majority of the code itself. DI containers are always configurable, so if you *want* to describe how to manually create an instance of a service you can, but by default you shouldn't need to.

> **TIP** You can inject dependencies into a service in other ways; for example, by using property injection. But constructor injection is the most common and is the only one supported out of the box in ASP.NET Core, so I'll only be using that in this book.

Hopefully, the advantages of using DI in your code are apparent from this quick example, but DI provides additional benefits that you get for free. In particular, it helps keep your code loosely coupled by coding to interfaces.

10.1.2 *Creating loosely coupled code*

Coupling is an important concept in object-oriented programming. It refers to how a given class depends on other classes to perform its function. Loosely coupled code doesn't need to know a lot of details about a particular component to use it.

The initial example of `UserController` and `EmailSender` was an example of tight coupling; you were creating the `EmailSender` object directly and needed to know exactly how to wire it up. On top of that, the code was difficult to test. Any attempts to test `UserController` would result in an email being sent. If you were testing the controller with a suite of unit tests, that seems like a surefire way to get your email server blacklisted for spam!

Taking `EmailSender` as a constructor parameter and removing the responsibility of creating the object helps reduce the coupling in the system. If the `EmailSender` implementation changes so that it has another dependency, you no longer have to update UserController at the same time.

One issue that remains is that UserController is still tied to an *implementation* rather than an *interface*. Coding to interfaces is a common design pattern that helps further reduce the coupling of a system, as you're not tied to a single implementation. This is particularly useful in making classes testable, as you can create "stub" or "mock" implementations of your dependencies for testing purposes, as shown in figure 10.3.

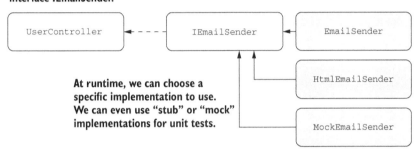

Instead of depending on a specific implementation, the UserController depends on the interface IEmailSender.

At runtime, we can choose a specific implementation to use. We can even use "stub" or "mock" implementations for unit tests.

Figure 10.3 By coding to interfaces instead of an explicit implementation, you can use different IEmailSender implementations in different scenarios, for example a MockEmailSender in unit tests.

TIP You can choose from many different mocking frameworks. My favorite is Moq, but NSubstitute and FakeItEasy are also popular options.

As an example, you might create an IEmailSender interface, which EmailSender would implement:

```
public interface IEmailSender
{
    public void SendEmail(string username);
}
```

UserController could then depend on this interface instead of the specific EmailSender implementation, as shown here. That would allow you to use a different implementation during unit tests, a DummyEmailSender for example.

Listing 10.5 Using interfaces with dependency injection

```
public class UserController : Controller
{
    private readonly IEmailSender _emailSender;
    public UserController(IEmailSender emailSender)
    {
        _emailSender = emailSender;
    }
```

You now depend on IEmailSender instead of the specific EmailSender implementation.

```
public IActionResult RegisterUser(string username)
{
    _emailSender.SendEmail(username);    ◁
    return View();
}
}
```

You don't care what the implementation is, as long as it implements IEmailSender.

The key point here is that the consuming code, UserController, doesn't care how the dependency is implemented, only that it implements the IEmailSender interface and exposes a SendEmail method. The application code is now independent of the implementation.

Hopefully, the principles behind DI seem sound—by having loosely coupled code, it's easy to change or swap out implementations completely. But this still leaves you with a question: how does the application know to use EmailSender in production instead of DummyEmailSender? The process of telling your DI container, "when you need IEmailSender, use EmailSender" is called *registration*.

> **DEFINITION**   You *register* services with a DI container so that it knows which implementation to use for each requested service. This typically takes the form of, "for interface X, use implementation Y."

Exactly how you register your interfaces and types with a DI container can vary depending on the specific DI container implementation, but the principles are generally all the same. ASP.NET Core includes a simple DI container out of the box, so let's look at how it's used during a typical request.

10.1.3 *Dependency injection in ASP.NET Core*

ASP.NET Core was designed from the outset to be modular and composable, with an almost plugin-style architecture, which is generally complemented by DI. Consequently, ASP.NET Core includes a simple DI container that all the framework libraries use to register themselves and their dependencies.

This container is used, for example, to register all of the MVC infrastructure—the formatters, the view engine, the validation system, and so on. It's only a basic container, so it only exposes a few methods for registering services, but you can also replace it with a third-party DI container. This can give you extra capabilities, such as auto-registration or setter injection. The DI container is built into the ASP.NET Core hosting model, as shown in figure 10.4.

The hosting model pulls dependencies from the DI container when they're needed. If the framework determines that UserController is required due to the incoming URL/route, the controller activator responsible for creating a Controller instance will ask the DI container for an IEmailSender implementation.

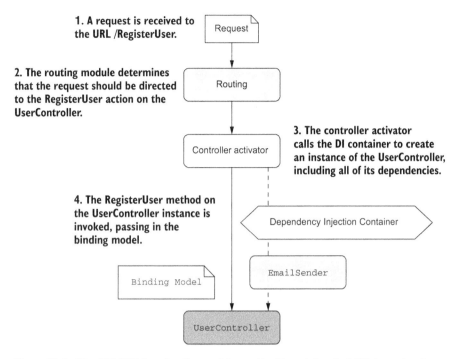

1. A request is received to the URL /RegisterUser.

2. The routing module determines that the request should be directed to the RegisterUser action on the UserController.

3. The controller activator calls the DI container to create an instance of the UserController, including all of its dependencies.

4. The RegisterUser method on the UserController instance is invoked, passing in the binding model.

Request

Routing

Controller activator

Dependency Injection Container

Binding Model

EmailSender

UserController

Figure 10.4   The ASP.NET Core hosting model uses the DI container to fulfill dependencies when creating controllers.

NOTE   This approach, where a class calls the DI container directly to ask for a class is called the *service locator* pattern. Generally speaking, you should try to avoid this pattern in your code; include your dependencies as constructor arguments directly and let the DI container provide them for you.[4]

The DI container needs to know what to create when asked for IEmailSender, so you must have registered an implementation, such as EmailSender, with the container. Once an implementation is registered, the DI container can inject it anywhere. That means you can inject framework-related services into your own custom services, as long as they are registered with the container. It also means you can register alternative versions of framework services and have the framework automatically use those in place of the defaults.

The flexibility to choose exactly how and which components you combine in your applications is one of the selling points of DI. In the next section, you'll learn how to configure DI in your own ASP.NET Core application, using the default, built-in container.

---

[4]   You can read about the Service Locator antipattern in *Dependency Injection in .NET* by Steven van Deursen and Mark Seemann (Manning, 2017), http://mng.bz/i995.

10.2   Using the dependency injection container

In previous versions of ASP.NET, using dependency injection was entirely optional. In contrast, to build all but the most trivial ASP.NET Core apps, some degree of DI is required. As I've mentioned, the underlying framework depends on it, so things like using MVC require you to configure the required services.

In this section, you'll see how to register these framework services with the built-in container, as well as how to register your own services. Once services are registered, you can use them as dependencies and inject them into any of the services in your application.

10.2.1   Adding ASP.NET Core framework services to the container

As I described earlier, ASP.NET Core uses DI to configure its internal components as well as your own custom services. In order to be able to use these components at runtime, the DI container needs to know about all the classes it will need. You register these in the `ConfigureServices` method of your `Startup` class.

> **NOTE**   The dependency injection container is set up in the `Configure-Services` method of your `Startup` class in Startup.cs.

Now, if you're thinking, "Wait, I have to configure the internal components myself?" then don't panic. Although true in one sense—you do need to explicitly register the components with the container in your app—all the libraries you'll use expose handy extension methods that you need to ensure you call.

For example, the MVC middleware exposes the `AddMvc()` extension method that you saw in chapters 2, 3, and 4. Invoke the extension method in `ConfigureServices` of `Startup`.

> **Listing 10.6   Registering the MVC services with the DI container**

```
public void ConfigureServices(IServiceCollection services)
{
    services.AddMvc();        ◁———————┐  The AddMvc extension method adds all
}                                     │  necessary services to the IServiceCollection.
```

It's as simple as that. Under the hood, this call is registering multiple components with the DI container, using the same APIs you'll see shortly for registering your own services.

Most nontrivial libraries that you add to your application will have services that you need to add to the DI container. By convention, each library that has necessary services should expose an `Add*()` extension method that you can call in `ConfigureServices`.

There's no way of knowing exactly which libraries will require you to add services to the container, it's generally a case of checking the documentation for any libraries you use. If you forget to add them, then you may find the functionality doesn't work, or you might get a handy exception like the one shown in figure 10.5. Keep an eye out for these and be sure to register any services that you need!

Figure 10.5 If you fail to call `AddMvc` in the `ConfigureServices` of `Startup`, you'll get a friendly exception message at runtime.

It's also worth noting that some of the `Add*()` extension methods allow you to specify additional options when you call them, often by way of a lambda expression. You can think of these as configuring the installation of a service into your application. The MVC middleware, for example, provides a wealth of options for fine-tuning its behavior if you want to get your fingers dirty, as shown by the IntelliSense snippet in figure 10.6.

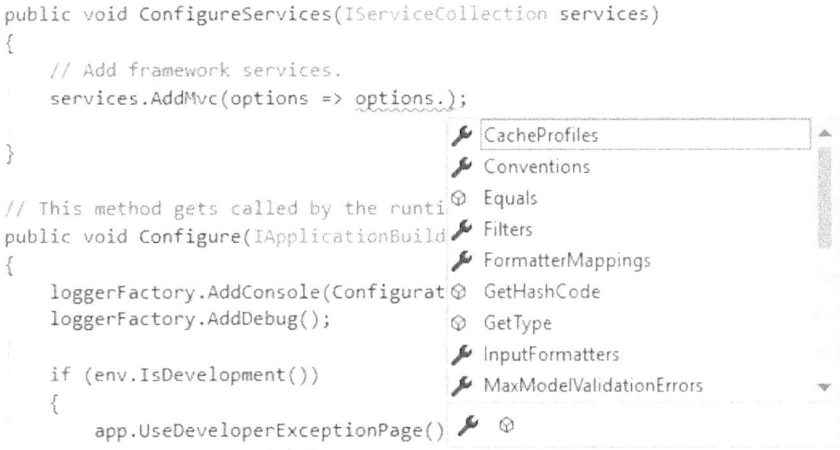

```
public void ConfigureServices(IServiceCollection services)
{
    // Add framework services.
    services.AddMvc(options => options.);

}                               CacheProfiles
                                Conventions
// This method gets called by the runti  Equals
public void Configure(IApplicationBuild  Filters
{                                        FormatterMappings
    loggerFactory.AddConsole(Configurat  GetHashCode
    loggerFactory.AddDebug();            GetType
                                         InputFormatters
    if (env.IsDevelopment())             MaxModelValidationErrors
    {
        app.UseDeveloperExceptionPage()
```

Figure 10.6 Configuring services when adding them to the service collection. The `AddMvc()` function allows you to configure a wealth of the internals of the MVC middleware.

Once you've added the required framework services, you can get down to business and register your own services, so you can use DI in your own code.

10.2.2 Registering your own services with the container

In the first section of this chapter, I described a system for sending emails when a new user registers on your application. Initially, `UserController` was manually creating an instance of `EmailSender`, but you subsequently refactored this, so you inject an instance of `IEmailSender` into the constructor instead.

The final step to make this refactoring work is to configure your services with the DI container. This will let it know what to use to fulfill the `IEmailSender` dependency. If you don't register your services, then you'll get an exception at runtime, like the one in figure 10.7. Luckily, this exception is useful, letting you know which service wasn't registered (`IEmailSender`) and which service needed it (`UserController`). That won't always be the case!

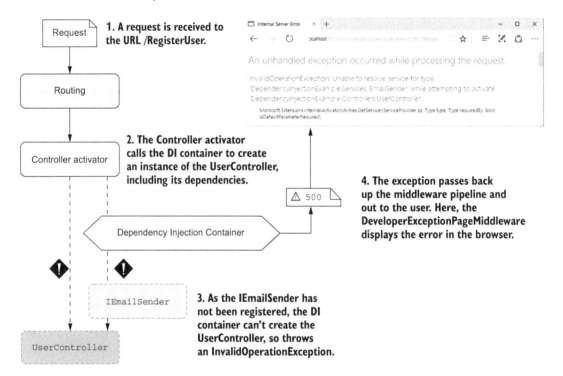

1. A request is received to the URL /RegisterUser.

2. The Controller activator calls the DI container to create an instance of the UserController, including its dependencies.

4. The exception passes back up the middleware pipeline and out to the user. Here, the DeveloperExceptionPageMiddleware displays the error in the browser.

3. As the IEmailSender has not been registered, the DI container can't create the UserController, so throws an InvalidOperationException.

Figure 10.7 If you don't register all of your required dependencies in `ConfigureServices`, you'll get an exception at runtime, telling you which service wasn't registered.

In order to completely configure the application, you need to register `EmailSender` and all of its dependencies with the DI container, as shown in figure 10.8.

Configuring DI consists of making a series of statements about the services in your app. For example:

- When a service requires `IEmailSender`, use an instance of `EmailSender`
- When a service requires `NetworkClient`, use an instance of `NetworkClient`
- When a service requires `MessageFactory`, use an instance of `MessageFactory`

NOTE You'll also need to register the `EmailServerSettings` object with the DI container—you'll do that slightly differently, in the next section.

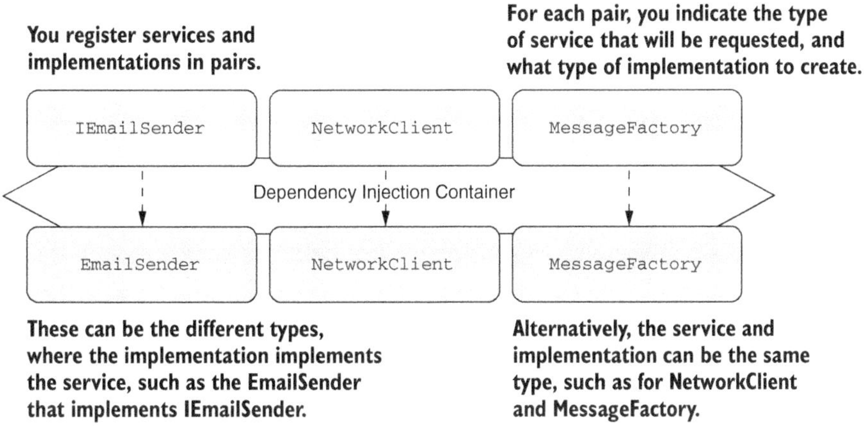

You register services and
implementations in pairs.

For each pair, you indicate the type
of service that will be requested, and
what type of implementation to create.

| IEmailSender | NetworkClient | MessageFactory |

Dependency Injection Container

| EmailSender | NetworkClient | MessageFactory |

These can be the different types,
where the implementation implements
the service, such as the EmailSender
that implements IEmailSender.

Alternatively, the service and
implementation can be the same
type, such as for NetworkClient
and MessageFactory.

Figure 10.8   Configuring the DI container in your application involves telling it what
type to use when a given service is requested; for example, "Use `EmailSender` when
`IEmailSender` is required."

These statements are made by calling various `Add*` methods on `IServiceCollection` in the `ConfigureServices` method. Each method provides three pieces of information to the DI container:

- *Service type*—TService. What class or interface will be requested as a dependency. Often an interface, such as `IEmailSender`, but sometimes a concrete type, such as `NetworkClient` or `MessageFactory`.
- *Implementation type*—TService or TImplementation. The class the container should create to fulfill the dependency. Must be a concrete type, such as `EmailSender`. May be the same as the service type, as for `NetworkClient` and `MessageFactory`.
- *Lifetime—Transient, Singleton, or Scoped.* How long an instance of the service should be used for. I'll discuss lifetimes in section 10.3.

The following listing shows how you can configure `EmailSender` and its dependencies in your application using three different methods: `AddScoped<TService>`, `AddSingleton<TService>`, and `AddScoped<TService, TImplementation>`. This tells the DI container how to create each of the `TService` instances when they're required.

Listing 10.7   Registering services with the DI container

You're using MVC, so
must call AddMvc.

```
public void ConfigureServices(IServiceCollection services)
{
    services.AddMvc();

    services.AddScoped<IEmailSender, EmailSender>();
```

Whenever you require
an IEmailSender, use
EmailSender.

```
        services.AddScoped<NetworkClient>();
        services.AddSingleton<MessageFactory>();
    }
```

Whenever you require a NetworkClient, use NetworkClient.

Whenever you require a MessageFactory, use MessageFactory.

And that's all there is to dependency injection! It may seem a little bit like magic,[5] but you're just giving the container instructions on how to make all of the constituent parts. You give it a recipe for how to cook the chili, shred the lettuce, and grate the cheese, so that when you ask for a burrito, it can put all the parts together and hand you your meal!

The service type and implementation type are the same for `NetworkClient` and `MessageFactory`, so there's no need to specify the same type twice in the `AddScoped` method, hence the slightly simpler signature. These generic methods aren't the only way to register services with the container, you can also provide objects directly, or by using lambdas, as you'll see in the next section.

10.2.3 *Registering services using objects and lambdas*

As I mentioned earlier, I didn't *quite* register all the services required by `UserController`. In all my previous examples, `NetworkClient` depends on `EmailServerSettings`, which you'll also need to register with the DI container for your project to run without exceptions.

I avoided registering this object in the preceding example because you have to use a slightly different approach. The preceding `Add*` methods use generics to specify the `Type` of the class to register, but they don't give any indication of *how* to construct an instance of that type. Instead, the container makes a number of assumptions that you have to adhere to:

- The class must be a concrete type.
- The class must have only a single "valid" constructor that the container can use.
- For a constructor to be "valid," all constructor arguments must be registered with the container, or must be an argument with a default value.

NOTE These limitations apply to the simple built-in DI container. If you choose to use a third-party container in your app, then they may have a different set of limitations.

The `EmailServerSettings` class doesn't meet these requirements, as it requires you to provide a `host` and `port` in the constructor, which are `strings` without default values:

---

[5] Under the hood, the built-in ASP.NET Core DI container uses reflection to create dependencies, but different DI containers may use other approaches.

```
public class EmailServerSettings
{
    public EmailServerSettings(string host, int port)
    {
        Host = host;
        Port = port;
    }
    public string Host { get; }
    public int Port { get; }
}
```

You can't register these primitive types in the container; it would be weird to say, "For every string constructor argument, in any type, use the "smtp.server.com" value!"

Instead, you can create an instance of the EmailServerSettings object yourself and provide *that* to the container, as shown next. The container will use the constructed object whenever an instance of the EmailServerSettings object is required.

Listing 10.8   Providing an object instance when registering services

```
public void ConfigureServices(IServiceCollection services)
{
    services.AddMvc();

    services.AddScoped<IEmailSender, EmailSender>();
    services.AddSingleton<NetworkClient>();
    services.AddScoped<MessageFactory>();
    services.AddSingleton(
        new EmailServerSettings
        (
            host: "smtp.server.com",      This instance of
            port: 25                       EmailServerSettings
        ));                                will be used whenever
}                                          an instance is required.
```

This works fine if you only want to have a single instance of EmailServerSettings in your application—*the same object* will be shared everywhere. But what if you want to create a *new* object each time one is requested?

> **NOTE**   When the same object is used whenever it's requested, it's known as a singleton. I'll discuss singletons along with other *lifetimes* in detail in the next section. The lifetime is how long the DI container should use a given object to fulfill a service's dependencies.

Instead of providing a single instance that the container will always use, you can also provide a *function* that the container will invoke when it needs an instance of the type, shown in figure 10.9.

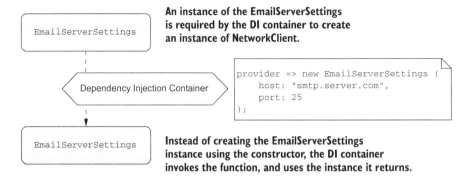

Figure 10.9   You can register a function with the DI container that will be invoked whenever a new instance of a service is required.

The easiest way to do this is to use a lambda function (an anonymous delegate), in which the container will create a new `EmailServerSettings` object when it's needed.

Listing 10.9   Using a lambda factory function to register a dependency

```
public void ConfigureServices(IServiceCollection services)
{
    services.AddMvc();

    services.AddScoped<IEmailSender, EmailSender>();
    services.AddSingleton<NetworkClient>();
    services.AddScoped<MessageFactory>();
    services.AddScoped(
        provider=>
            new EmailServerSettings
            (
                host: "smtp.server.com",
                port: 25
            ));
}
```

Because you're providing a function to create the object, you aren't restricted to singleton.

The lambda is provided an instance of IServiceProvider.

The constructor is now called every time an object is requested instead of only once.

In this example, I've changed the lifetime of the created `EmailServerSettings` object to be *scoped* instead of *singleton* and provided a factory lambda function that returns a new `EmailServerSettings` object. Every time the container requires a new `Email-ServerSettings`, it executes the function and uses the new object it returns.

> **NOTE**   I'll discuss lifetimes shortly, but it's important to notice that there are two concepts of a singleton here. If you create an object and pass it to the container, it's *always* registered as a singleton. You can also register any arbitrary class as a singleton and the container will only use one instance throughout your application.

When you use a lambda to register your services, you're provided with an `IService-Provider` instance at runtime, called `provider` in listing 10.9. This is the public API of the DI container itself, which you can access using `GetService()`. If you need to obtain dependencies to create an instance of your service, you can reach into the container at runtime in this way, but you should avoid doing so if possible.

TIP   Avoid calling `GetService()` in your factory functions if possible. Instead, favor constructor injection—it's more performant, as well as being simpler to reason about.

Open generics and dependency injection

As well as dependencies that have primitive dependencies in their constructor, you also can't use the generic registration methods to register *open generics*.

Open generics are types that contain a generic type parameter, such as `Repository<T>`. The normal use case for this sort of type is to define a base behavior that you can use with multiple generic types. In the `Repository<T>` example, you might inject `IRepository<Customer>` into your services, which should inject an instance of `DbRepository<Customer>`, for example.

To register these types, you must use a different overload of the `Add*` methods. For example,

```
services.AddScoped(typeof(IRespository<>), typeof(DbRepository<>));
```

This will ensure that whenever a service constructor requires `IRespository<T>`, the container will inject an instance of `DbRepository<T>`.

At this point, all your dependencies are registered. But `ConfigureServices` is starting to look a little messy, isn't it? It's entirely down to personal preference, but I like to group my services into logical collections and create extension methods for them, as in the following listing, to create an equivalent of the `AddMvc()` extension method. As you add more and more features to your app, I think you'll appreciate it too.

Listing 10.10   Creating an extension method to tidy up adding multiple services

```
public static class EmailSenderServiceCollectionExtensions
{
    public static IServiceCollection AddEmailSender(
        this IServiceCollection services)          ⟵——— Extend the IServiceCollection that's provided in the ConfigureServices method.
    {
        services.AddScoped<IEmailSender, EmailSender>();
        services.AddSingleton<NetworkClient>();
        services.AddScoped<MessageFactory>();
        services.AddSingleton(
            new EmailServerSettings               ⟵ Cut and paste your registration code from ConfigureServices.
            (
                host: "smtp.server.com",
                port: 25
            ));
        return services;      ⟵— By convention, return the IServiceCollection to allow method chaining.
    }
}
```

With the preceding extension method created, the `ConfigureServices` method is much easier to grok!

```
public void ConfigureServices(IServiceCollection services)
{
    services.AddMvc();
    services.AddEmailSender();
}
```

So far, you've seen how to register the simple DI cases where you have a single implementation. In some scenarios, you might find you have multiple implementations of an interface. In the next section, you'll see how to register these with the container to match your requirements.

10.2.4 Registering a service in the container multiple times

One of the advantages of coding to interfaces is that you can create multiple implementations of a service. For example, imagine you want to create a more generalized version of `IEmailSender` so that you can send messages via SMS or Facebook, as well as by email. You create an interface for it

```
public interface IMessageSender
{
    public void SendMessage(string message);
}
```

as well as several implementations: `EmailSender`, `SmsSender`, and `FacebookSender`. But how do you register these implementations in the container? And how can you inject these implementations into your `UserController`? The answer varies slightly depending on if you want to use all of the implementations or only one of them.

INJECTING MULTIPLE IMPLEMENTATIONS OF AN INTERFACE

Imagine you want to send a message using each of the `IMessageSender` implementations whenever a new user registers, so they get an email, an SMS, and a Facebook message, as shown in figure 10.10.

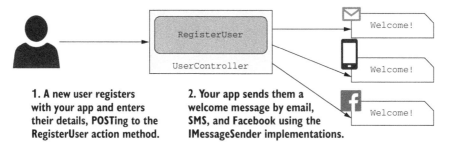

1. A new user registers with your app and enters their details, POSTing to the RegisterUser action method.

2. Your app sends them a welcome message by email, SMS, and Facebook using the IMessageSender implementations.

Figure 10.10   When a user registers with your application, they call the `RegisterUser` method. This sends them an email, an SMS, and a Facebook message using the `IMessageSender` classes.

The easiest way to achieve this is to register all of the implementations in your DI container and have it inject one of each type into `UserController`. `UserController` can then use a simple `foreach` loop to call `SendMessage()` on each implementation, as in figure 10.11.

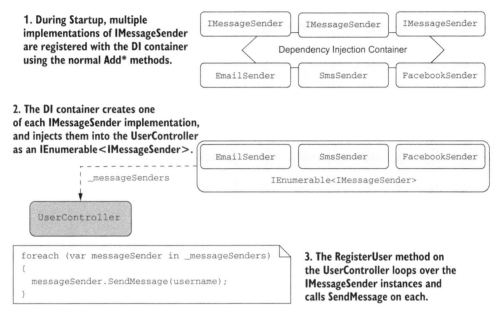

Figure 10.11 You can register multiple implementations of a service with the DI container, such as `IEmailSender` in this example. You can retrieve an instance of each of these implementations by requiring `IEnumerable<IMessageSender>` in the `UserController` constructor.

You register multiple implementations of the same service with a DI container in exactly the same way as for single implementations, using the `Add*` extension methods. For example:

```
public void ConfigureServices(IServiceCollection services)
{
    services.AddMvc();
    services.AddScoped<IMessageSender, EmailSender>();
    services.AddScoped<IMessageSender, SmsSender>();
    services.AddScoped<IMessageSender, FacebookSender>();
}
```

You can then inject `IEnumerable<IMessageSender>` into `UserController`, as shown in the following listing. The container will inject an array of `IMessageSender` containing one of each of the implementations you have registered, in the same order as you registered them. You can then use a standard `foreach` loop in the `RegisterUser` method to call `SendMessage` on each implementation.

Listing 10.11   Injecting multiple implementations of a service into a consumer

```
public class UserController : Controller
{
    private readonly IEnumerable<IMessageSender> _messageSenders;
    public UserController(
        IEnumerable<IMessageSender> messageSenders)
    {
        _messageSenders = messageSenders;
    }


    public IActionResult RegisterUser(string username)
    {
        foreach (var messageSender in _messageSenders)
        {
            messageSender.SendMessage(username);
        }

        return View();
    }
}
```

> Requesting an IEnumerable will inject an array of IMessageSender.

> Each IMessageSender in the IEnumerable is a different implementation.

> **WARNING**   You must use `IEnumerable<T>` as the constructor argument to inject all of the registered types of a service, `T`. Even though this will be injected as a `T[]` array, you can't use `T[]` or `ICollection<T>` as your constructor argument. Doing so will cause an `InvalidOperationException`, as you saw in figure 10.7.

It's simple enough to inject all of the registered implementations of a service, but what if you only need one? How does the container know which one to use?

INJECTING A SINGLE IMPLEMENTATION WHEN MULTIPLE SERVICES ARE REGISTERED

Imagine you've already registered all of the `IMessageSender` implementations, what happens if you have a service that requires only one of them? For example

```
public class SingleMessageSender
{
    private readonly IMessageSender _messageSender;
    public SingleMessageSender(IMessageSender messageSender)
    {
        _messageSender = messageSender;
    }
}
```

The container needs to pick a single `IMessageSender` to inject into this service, out of the three implementations available. It does this by using the last registered implementation—the `FacebookSender` from the previous example.

> **NOTE**   The DI container will use the last registered implementation of a service when resolving a single instance of the service.

This can be particularly useful for replacing built-in DI registrations with your own services. If you have a custom implementation of a service that you know is registered within a library's Add* extension method, you can override that registration by registering your own implementation afterwards. The DI container will use your implementation whenever a single instance of the service is requested.

The main disadvantage with this approach is that you end up with *multiple* implementations registered—you can inject an IEnumerable<T> as before. Sometimes you want to conditionally register a service, so you only ever have a single registered implementation.

CONDITIONALLY REGISTERING SERVICES USING TRYADD

Sometimes, you'll only want to add an implementation of a service if one hasn't already been added. This is particularly useful for library authors; they can create a default implementation of an interface and only register it if the user hasn't already registered their own implementation.

You can find a number of extension methods for conditional registration in the Microsoft.Extensions.DependencyInjection.Extensions namespace, such as Try-AddScoped. This checks to make sure a service hasn't been registered with the container before calling AddScoped on the implementation. The following listing shows you conditionally adding SmsSender, only if there are no existing IMessageSender implementations. As you just registered EmailSender, the container will ignore the SmsSender registration, so it won't be available in your app.

> **Listing 10.12   Conditionally adding a service using TryAddScoped**

```
public void ConfigureServices(IServiceCollection services)          EmailSender is
{                                                                   registered with
    services.AddScoped<IMessageSender, EmailSender>();       ◁─┘   the container.
    services.TryAddScoped<IMessageSender, SmsSender>();      ◁──┐
}
                               There's already an IMessageSender
                               implementation, so SmsSender isn't
                                                   registered.
```

Code like this often doesn't make a lot of sense at the application level, but it can be useful if you're building libraries for use in multiple apps. The ASP.NET Core framework, for example, uses TryAdd* in many places, which lets you easily register alternative implementations of internal components in your own application if you want.

That pretty much covers registering dependencies. Before we look in more depth at the "lifetime" aspect of dependencies, we'll take a quick detour and look at two ways other than a constructor to inject dependencies in your app.

10.2.5 Injecting services into action methods and view templates

I mentioned in section 10.1 that the ASP.NET Core DI container only supports constructor injection, but there are two additional locations where you can use dependency injection:

1 Action methods
2 View templates

In this section, I'll briefly discuss these two situations, how they work, and when you might want to use them.

INJECTING SERVICES DIRECTLY INTO ACTION METHODS USING [FROMSERVICES]

MVC controllers typically contain multiple action methods that logically belong together. You might group all the action methods related to managing user accounts into the same controller, for example. This allows you to apply filters and authorization to all of the action methods collectively, as you'll see in chapter 13.

As you add additional action methods to a controller, you may find the controller needs additional services to implement new action methods. With constructor injection, all of these dependencies are provided via the constructor. That means the DI container must create all of the services for every action method in a controller, even if none of them are required by the action method being called.

Consider listing 10.13 for example. This shows `UserController` with two stub methods: `RegisterUser` and `SignInUser`. Each action method requires a different dependency, so both dependencies will be created and injected, whichever action method is called by the request. If `ISignInManager` or `IMessageSender` have lots of dependencies themselves, the DI container may have to create lots of objects for a service that is often not used.

Listing 10.13 Injecting services into a controller via the constructor

```
public class UserController : Controller
{
    private readonly IMessageSender _messageSender;
    private readonly ISignInService _signInService;

    public UserController(
        IMessageSender messageSender, ISignInService signInService)
    {
        messageSenders = messageSender;
        _signInService = signInService;
    }

    public IActionResult RegisterUser(string username)
    {
        _messageSender.SendMessage(username);
        return View();
    }

    public IActionResult SignInUser(string username, string password)
    {
        _signInService.SignUserIn(username, password);
        return View();
    }
}
```

Both IMessageSender and ISignInService are injected into the constructor every time.

Only the RegisterUser method uses IMessageSender.

Only the SignInUser method uses ISignInService.

If you know a service is particularly expensive to create, you can choose to inject it as a dependency directly into the action method, instead of into the controller's constructor. This ensures the DI container only creates the dependency when the *specific* action method is invoked, as opposed to when *any* action method on the controller is invoked.

> **NOTE** Generally speaking, your controllers should be sufficiently cohesive that this approach isn't necessary. If you find you have a controller that's dependent on many services, each of which is used by a single action method, you might want to consider splitting up your controller.

You can directly inject a dependency into an action method by passing it as a parameter to the method and using the [FromServices] attribute. During model binding, MvcMiddleware will resolve the parameter from the DI container, instead of from the request values, like you saw in chapter 6. This listing shows how you could rewrite listing 10.13 to use [FromServices] instead of constructor injection.

Listing 10.14   Injecting services into a controller using the [FromServices] attribute

```
public class UserController : Controller
{
    public IActionResult RegisterUser(
        [FromServices] IMessageSender messageSender,
        string username)
    {
        messageSender.SendMessage(username);
        return View();
    }
    public IActionResult SignInUser(
        [FromServices] ISignInService signInService
        string username, string password)
    {
        signInService.SignUserIn(username, password);
        return View();
    }
}
```

The [FromServices] attribute ensures IMessageSender is resolved from the DI container.

IMessageSender is only available in RegisterUser.

ISignInService is resolved from the DI container and injected as a parameter.

Only the SignInUser method can use ISignInService.

You might be tempted to use the [FromServices] attribute in all of your action methods, but I'd encourage you to use standard constructor injection most of the time. Having the constructor as a single location that declares all the dependencies of a class can be useful, so I only use [FromServices] where creating an instance of a dependency is expensive and is only used in a single action method.

INJECTING SERVICES INTO VIEW TEMPLATES

Injecting dependencies into the constructor is recommended, but what if you don't have a constructor? In particular, how do you go about injecting services into a Razor view template when you don't have control over how the template is constructed?

Imagine you have a simple service, `HtmlGenerator`, to help you generate HTML in your view templates. The question is, how do you pass this service to your view templates, assuming you've already registered it with the DI container?

One option is to inject `HtmlGenerator` into your controller using constructor injection or the `[FromServices]` attribute. Then you can pass the service via `ViewData` or the view model, as you saw in chapter 7. In some cases, that approach may make sense, but other times, you might not want to have references to the `HtmlGenerator` service in your controller or view model at all. In those cases, you can directly inject `Html-Generator` into your view templates.

> **NOTE**   Some people take offense at injecting services into views in this way. You definitely shouldn't be injecting services related to business logic into your views, but I think it makes sense for services that are related to HTML generation.

You can inject a service into a Razor template with the `@inject` directive by providing the type to inject and a name for the injected service in the template.

Listing 10.15   Injecting a service into a Razor view template with `@inject`

```
@inject HtmlGenerator helper        ◁——┐    Injects an instance of HtmlGenerator
                                         │    into the view, named helper
<h1>The page title</h1>
<footer>
    @helper.Copyright()    ◁——    Uses the injected service by
</footer>                          calling the helper instance
```

Injecting services directly into views can be a useful way of exposing UI-related services to your view templates without having to closely couple your views to your controllers and actions. You shouldn't find you need to rely on it too much, but it's a useful tool to have.

That pretty much covers registering and using dependencies, but there's one important aspect I've only vaguely touched on: lifetimes, or, when does the container create a new instance of a service? Understanding lifetimes is crucial to working with DI containers, so it's important to pay close attention to them when registering your services with the container.

10.3   *Understanding lifetimes: when are services created?*

Whenever the DI container is asked for a particular registered service, for example an instance of `IMessageSender`, it can do one of two things:

- Create and return a new instance of the service
- Return an existing instance of the service

The *lifetime* of a service controls the behavior of the DI container with respect to these two options. You define the lifetime of a service during DI service registration. This dictates when a DI container will reuse an existing instance of the service to fulfill service dependencies, and when it will create a new one.

> **DEFINITION** The lifetime of a service is how long an instance of a service should *live* in a container before it creates a new instance.

It's important to get your head around the implications for the different lifetimes used in ASP.NET Core, so this section looks at each available lifetime option and when you should use it. In particular, you'll see how the lifetime affects how often the DI container creates new objects. In section 10.3.4, I'll show you a pattern of lifetimes to look out for, where a short-lifetime dependency is "captured" by a long-lifetime dependency. This can cause some hard-to-debug issues, so it's important to bear in mind when configuring your app!

In ASP.NET Core, you can specify three different lifetimes when registering a service with the built-in container:

- *Transient*—Every single time a service is requested, a new instance is created. This means you can potentially have different instances of the same class within the same dependency graph.
- *Scoped*—Within a *scope*, all requests for a service will give you the same object. For different scopes you'll get different objects. In ASP.NET Core, each web request gets its own scope.
- *Singleton*—You'll always get the same instance of the service, no matter which scope.

> **NOTE** These concepts align well with most other DI containers, but the terminology often differs. If you're familiar with a third-party DI container, be sure you understand how the lifetime concepts align with the built-in ASP.NET Core DI container.

To illustrate the behavior of the different lifetimes available to you, in this section, I'll use a simple representative example. Imagine you have `DataContext`, which has a connection to a database, as shown in listing 10.13. It has a single property, `RowCount`, which displays the number of rows in the `Users` table of a database. For the purposes of this example, fix the number of rows in the constructor, so it will display the same value every time you call `RowCount`, but different instances of the service will display a different number.

> **Listing 10.16 `DataContext` generating a random `RowCount` in its constructor**

```
public class DatabaseContext
{
    static readonly Random _rand = new Random();
    public DatabaseContext()
    {
        RowCount = _rand.Next(1, 1_000_000_000);    ⊲─── Generates a random
    }                                                      number between 1 and
                                                           1,000,000,000
```

> **Read-only properly set in the constructor,
> so always returns the same value.**

```
    public int RowCount { get; }    ⟵
}
```

You also have a `Repository` class that has a dependency on the `DataContext`, as shown in the next listing. This also exposes a `RowCount` property, but this property delegates the call to its instance of `DataContext`. Whatever value `DataContext` was created with, the `Repository` will display the same value.

Listing 10.17 Repository service that depends on an instance of `DataContext`

```
public class Repository
{
    private readonly DatabaseContext _dataContext;
    public Repository(DatabaseContext dataContext)
    {
        _dataContext = dataContext;
    }

    public int RowCount => _dataContext.RowCount;    ⟵
}
```

> **An instance of
> DataContext is
> provided using DI.**

> **RowCount returns the
> same value as the current
> instance of DataContext.**

Finally, you have `RowCountController`, which takes a dependency on both `Repository` and on `DataContext` directly. When the controller activator creates an instance of `RowCountController`, the DI container will inject an instance of `DataContext` and an instance of `Repository`. To create `Repository`, it will also inject an additional instance of `DataContext`. Over the course of two consecutive requests, a total of four instances of `DataContext` will be required, as shown in figure 10.12.

`RowCountController` records the value of `RowCount` from `Repository` and `DataContext` in a view model. This is then rendered using a Razor template (not shown).

Listing 10.18 `RowCountController` depends on `DataContext` and `Repository`

```
public class RowCountController : Controller
{
    private readonly Repository _repository;
    private readonly DataContext _dataContext;

    public RowCountController(
        Repository repository,
        DataContext dataContext)
    {
        _repository = repository;
        _dataContext = dataContext;
    }

    public IActionResult Index()
    {
        var viewModel = new RowCountViewModel
        {
            DataContextCount = _dataContext.RowCount,
            RepositoryCount = _repository.RowCount,
        };
```

> **DataContext and Repository
> are passed in using DI.**

> **When invoked, the
> action retrieves
> RowCount from both
> dependencies.**

```
        return View(viewModel);
    }
}
```

The view model is passed to the Razor
view and rendered to the screen.

The purpose of this example is to explore the relationship between the four Data-Context instances, depending on the lifetimes you use to register the services with the container. I'm generating a random number in DataContext as a way of uniquely identifying a DataContext instance, but you can think of this as being a point-in-time snapshot of the number of users logged in to your site, for example, or the amount of stock in a warehouse.

I'll start with the shortest-lived lifetime, move on to the common scoped lifetime, and then take a look at singletons. Finally, I'll show an important trap you should be on the lookout for when registering services in your own apps.

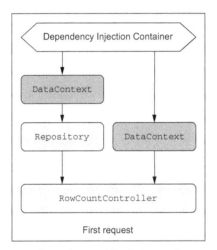 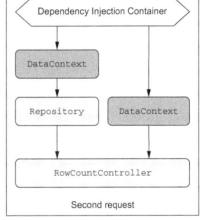

For each request, two instances of
DataContext are required to build the
RowCountController instance.

A total of four DataContext instances
is required for two requests.

Figure 10.12   The DI Container uses two instances of DataContext for each request. Depending on the lifetime with which the DataContext type is registered, the container might create one, two, or four different instances of DataContext.

10.3.1 *Transient: everyone is unique*

In the ASP.NET Core DI container, transient services are always created new, whenever they're needed to fulfill a dependency. You can register your services using the AddTransient extension methods:

```
services.AddTransient<DataContext>();
services.AddTransient<Repository>();
```

When registered in this way, every time a dependency is required, the container will create a new one. This applies both *between* requests but also *within* requests; the DataContext injected into the Repository will be a different instance to the one injected into the RowCountController.

> **NOTE**   Transient dependencies can result in different instances of the same type within a single dependency graph.

Figure 10.13 shows the results you get from two consecutive requests when you use the transient lifetime for both services. Note that, by default, Controller instances are also transient and are created new with every request.

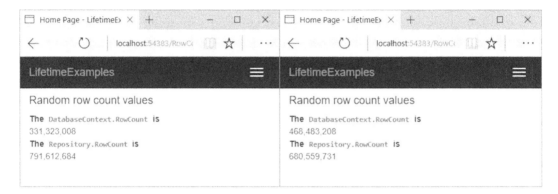

Figure 10.13   When registered using the transient lifetime, all four DataContext objects are different. That can be seen by the four different numbers displayed over two requests.

Transient lifetimes can result in a lot of objects being created, so they make the most sense for lightweight services with little or no state. It's equivalent to calling new every time you need a new object, so bear that in mind when using it. You probably won't use the transient lifetime too often; the majority of your services will probably be *scoped* instead.

10.3.2   *Scoped: let's stick together, guys*

The scoped lifetime states that a single instance of an object will be used within a given scope, but a different instance will be used between different scopes. In ASP.NET Core, a scope maps to a request, so within a single request the container will use the same object to fulfill all dependencies.

For the row count example, that means that, within a single request (a single scope), the same DataContext will be used throughout the dependency graph. The DataContext injected into the Repository will be the same instance as that injected into RowCountController.

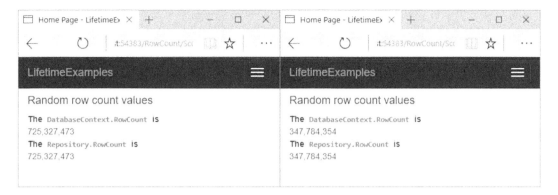

Figure 10.14 Scoped dependencies use the same instance of `DataContext` within a single request, but a new instance for a separate request. Consequently, the `RowCounts` are identical within a request.

In the next request, you'll be in a different scope, so the container will create a new instance of `DataContext`, as shown in figure 10.14. A different instance means a different `RowCount` for each request, as you can see.

You can register dependencies as scoped using the `AddScoped` extension methods. In this example, I registered `DataContext` as scoped and left `Repository` as transient, but you'd get the same results if they were both scoped:

```
services.AddScoped<DataContext>();
```

Due to the nature of web requests, you'll often find services registered as scoped dependencies in ASP.NET Core. Database contexts and authentication services are common examples of services that should be scoped to a request—anything that you want to share across your services *within* a single request, but that needs to change *between* requests.

Generally speaking, you'll find a lot of services registered using the scoped lifetime—especially anything that uses a database or is dependent on a specific request. But some services don't need to change between requests, such as a service that calculates the area of a circle, or that returns the current time in different time zones. For these, a singleton lifetime might be more appropriate.

10.3.3 Singleton: there can be only one

The singleton is a pattern that came before dependency injection; the DI container provides a robust and easy-to-use implementation of it. The singleton is conceptually simple: an instance of the service is created when it's first needed (or during registration, as in section 10.2.3) and that's it: you'll always get the same instance injected into your services.

The singleton pattern is particularly useful for objects that are either expensive to create or that don't hold state. The latter point is important—any service registered as a singleton should be thread safe.

WARNING Singleton services must be thread safe in a web application, as they'll typically be used by multiple threads during concurrent requests.

Let's consider what using singletons means for the row count example. I can update the registration of `DataContext` to be a singleton in `ConfigureServices`, using

```
services.AddSingleton<DataContext>();
```

I then call the `RowCountController.Index` action method twice and observe the results shown in figure 10.15. You can see that every instance has returned the same value, indicating that all four instances of `DataContext` are the same single instance.

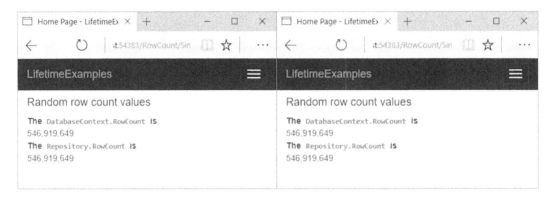

Figure 10.15 Any service registered as a singleton will always return the same instance. Consequently, all the calls to `RowCount` return the same value, both within a request and between requests.

Singletons are convenient for objects that need to be shared or that are immutable and expensive to create. A caching service should be a singleton, as all requests need to share it. It must be thread safe though. Similarly, you might register a settings object loaded from a remote server as a singleton, if you loaded the settings once at startup and reused them through the lifetime of your app.

On the face of it, choosing a lifetime for a service might not seem too tricky, but there's an important "gotcha" that can come back to bite you in subtle ways, as you'll see shortly.

10.3.4 Keeping an eye out for captured dependencies

Imagine you're configuring the lifetime for the `DataContext` and `Repository` examples. You think about the suggestions I've provided and decide on the following lifetimes:

- `DataContext`—*Scoped*, as it should be shared for a single request
- `Repository`—*Singleton*, as it has no state of its own and is thread safe, so why not?

> **WARNING** This lifetime configuration is to explore a bug—don't use it in your code or you'll experience a similar problem!

Unfortunately, you've created a *captured dependency* because you're injecting a *scoped* object, DataContext, into a *singleton*, Repository. As it's a singleton, the same Repository instance is used throughout the lifetime of the app, so the DataContext that was injected into it will also hang around, even though a new one should be used with every request. Figure 10.16 shows this scenario, where a new instance of Data-Context is created for each scope, but the instance inside Repository hangs around for the lifetime of the app.

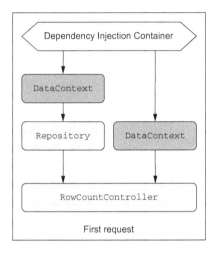 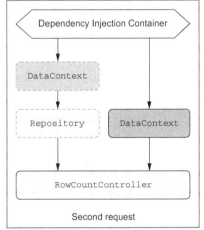

As the repository has been registered as a singleton, the DataContext it uses will act also as a singleton, even though it is registered as scoped.

The DataContext dependency has been captured by the repository, breaking the scoped lifetime.

Figure 10.16 DataContext **is registered as a scoped dependency, but** Repository **is a singleton. Even though you expect a new** DataContext **for every request,** Repository *captures* **the injected** DataContext **and causes it to be reused for the lifetime of the app.**

Captured dependencies can cause subtle bugs that are hard to root out, so you should always keep an eye out for them. These captured dependencies are relatively easy to introduce, so always think carefully when registering a singleton service.

> **WARNING** A service should only use dependencies with a lifetime longer than or equal to the lifetime of the service. A service registered as a singleton can only use singleton dependencies. A service registered as scoped can use scoped or singleton dependencies. A transient service can use dependencies with any lifetime.

At this point, I should mention that there's one glimmer of hope in this cautionary tale. ASP.NET Core 2.0 includes a new option that lets you check for these kinds of captured dependencies and will throw an exception on application startup if it detects them, as shown in figure 10.17.

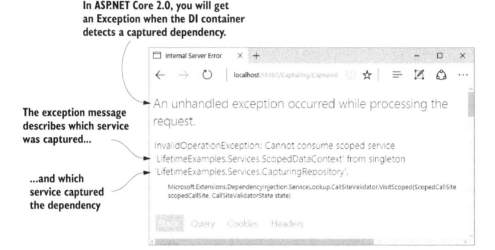

In ASP.NET Core 2.0, you will get an Exception when the DI container detects a captured dependency.

The exception message describes which service was captured...

...and which service captured the dependency

Figure 10.17   In ASP.NET Core 2.0, the DI container will throw an exception when it creates a service with a captured dependency. By default, this check is only enabled for development environments.

This scope validation check has a performance impact, so by default it's only enabled when your app is running in a development environment, but it should help you catch most issues of this kind. You can enable or disable this check regardless of environment by setting the `ValidateScopes` option when creating your `WebHostBuilder` in Program.cs, as shown in the following listing.

Listing 10.19   Setting the `ValidateScopes` property to always validate scopes

```
public class Program
{
    public static void Main(string[] args)
    {
        BuildWebHost(args).Run();
    }

    public static IWebHost BuildWebHost(string[] args) =>
        WebHost.CreateDefaultBuilder(args)
            .UseStartup<Startup>()
            .UseDefaultServiceProvider(options =>
            {
                options.ValidateScopes = true;
            })
            .Build();
}
```

The default builder sets ValidateScopes to validate only in development environments.

You can override the validation check with the UseDefaultService-Provider extension.

Setting to true will validate scopes in all environments. This has performance implications.

With that, you've reached the end of this introduction to DI in ASP.NET Core. You now know how to add framework services to your app using Add* extension methods like AddMvc(), as well as how to register your own service with the DI container. Hopefully, that will help you keep your code loosely coupled and easy to manage.

In the next chapter, we'll look at the ASP.NET Core configuration model. You'll see how to load settings from a file at runtime, how to store sensitive settings safely, and how to make your application behave differently depending on which machine it's running on. We'll even use a bit of DI; it gets everywhere in ASP.NET Core!

Summary

- Dependency injection is baked into the ASP.NET Core framework. You need to ensure your application adds all the framework's dependencies in Startup.
- The dependency graph is the set of objects that must be created in order to create a specific requested "root" object.
- You should aim to use explicit dependencies over implicit dependencies in most cases. ASP.NET Core uses constructor arguments to declare explicit dependencies.
- The DI or IoC container is responsible for creating instances of services. It knows how to construct an instance of a service by creating all of its dependencies and passing these to the constructor.
- When discussing DI, the term *service* is used to describe any class or interface registered with the container.
- You register services with a DI container so it knows which implementation to use for each requested service. This typically takes the form of, "for interface X, use implementation Y."
- The default built-in container only supports constructor injection. If you require other forms of DI, such as property injection, you can use a third-party container.
- You can register services with the container by calling Add* extension methods on IServiceCollection in ConfigureServices in Startup.
- If you forget to register a service that's used by the framework or in your own code, you'll get an InvalidOperationException at runtime.
- When registering your services, you describe three things: the service type, the implementation type, and the lifetime. The service type defines which class or interface will be requested as a dependency. The implementation type is the class the container should create to fulfill the dependency. The lifetime is how long an instance of the service should be used for.
- You can register a service using generic methods if the class is concrete and all its constructor arguments must be registered with the container or have default values.

- You can provide an instance of a service during registration, which will register that instance as a singleton.
- You can provide a lambda factory function that describes how to create an instance of a service with any lifetime you choose.
- Avoid calling `GetService()` in your factory functions if possible. Instead, favor constructor injection—it's more performant, as well as being simpler to reason about.
- You can register multiple implementations for a service. You can then inject `IEnumerable<T>` to get access to all of the implementations at runtime.
- If you inject a single instance of a multiple-registered service, the container injects the last implementation registered.
- You can use the `TryAdd*` extension methods to ensure that an implementation is only registered if no other implementation of the service has been registered.
- You define the lifetime of a service during DI service registration. This dictates when a DI container will reuse an existing instance of the service to fulfill service dependencies and when it will create a new one.
- The transient lifetime means that every single time a service is requested, a new instance is created.
- The scoped lifetime means that within a scope, all requests for a service will give you the same object. For different scopes, you'll get different objects. In ASP.NET Core, each web request gets its own scope.
- You'll always get the same instance of a singleton service, no matter which scope.
- A service should only use dependencies with a lifetime longer than or equal to the lifetime of the service.

Configuring an ASP.NET Core application

This chapter covers

- Loading settings from multiple configuration providers
- Storing sensitive settings safely
- Using strongly typed settings objects
- Using different settings in different hosting environments

In part 1 of this book, you learned the basics of getting an ASP.NET Core app up and running and how to use the MVC design pattern to create a traditional web app or a Web API. Once you start building real applications, you will quickly find that you want to tweak various settings at runtime, without having to recompile your application. This chapter looks at how you can achieve this in ASP.NET Core using configuration.

I know. Configuration sounds boring, right? But I have to confess, the configuration model is one of my favorite parts of ASP.NET Core. It's so easy to use, and so much more elegant than the previous version of ASP.NET. In section 11.2, you'll learn how to load values from a plethora of sources—JSON files, environment variables, and command-line arguments—and combine them into a unified configuration object.

On top of that, ASP.NET Core brings the ability to easily bind this configuration to strongly typed *options* objects. These are simple, POCO classes that are populated from the configuration object, which you can inject into your services, as you'll see in section 11.3. This lets you nicely encapsulate settings for different features in your app.

In the final section of this chapter, you'll learn about the ASP.NET Core *hosting environments*. You often want your app to run differently in different situations such as when running on your developer machine compared to when you deploy it to a production server. These different situations are known as *environments*. By letting the app know in which environment it's running, it can load a different configuration and vary its behavior accordingly.

Before we get to that, let's go back to basics: what is configuration, why do we need it, and how does ASP.NET Core handle these requirements?

11.1   *Introducing the ASP.NET Core configuration model*

Configuration is the set of external parameters provided to an application that controls the application's behavior in some way. It typically consists of a mixture of *settings* and *secrets* that the application will load at runtime.

> **DEFINITION**   A *setting* is any value that changes the behavior of your application. A *secret* is a special type of setting that contains sensitive data, such as a password, an API key for a third-party service, or a connection string.

The obvious question before we get started is to consider why you need app configuration, and what sort of things you need to configure. You should normally move anything that you can consider a setting or a secret out of your application code. That way, you can easily change these values at runtime, without having to recompile your application.

You might, for example, have an application that shows the locations of your brick-and-mortar stores. You could have a setting for the connection string to the database in which you store the details of the stores, but also settings such as the default location to display on a map, the default zoom level to use, maybe even the locations of the stores, as shown in figure 11.1. You wouldn't necessarily want to have to recompile your app to tweak these, so you can store them in external configuration sources instead.

There's also a security aspect to this; you don't want to hardcode secret values like API keys or passwords into your code, where they could be committed to source control and made publicly available. Even values embedded in your compiled application can be extracted, so it's best to externalize them whenever possible.

Virtually every web framework provides a mechanism for loading configuration and the previous version of ASP.NET was no different. It used the `<appsettings>`

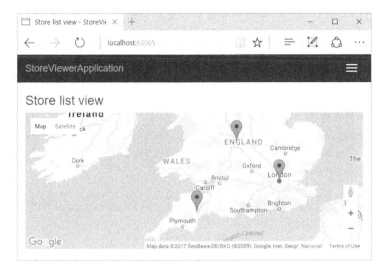

Figure 11.1   You can store the default map location, zoom level, and store locations in configuration and load them at runtime.

element in a web.config file to store key-value configuration pairs. At runtime, you'd use the static (*wince*) `ConfigurationManager` to load the value for a given key from the file. You could do more advanced things using custom configuration sections, but this was painful, and so was rarely used, in my experience.

ASP.NET Core gives you a totally revamped experience. At the most basic level, you're still specifying key-value pairs at strings, but instead of getting those values from a single file, you can now load them from multiple sources. You can load values from files, but they can now be any format you like: JSON, XML, YAML, and so on. On top of that, you can load values from environment variables, from command-line arguments, from a database or from a remote service. Or you could create your own custom *configuration provider*.

> **DEFINITION**   ASP.NET Core uses *configuration providers* to load key-value pairs from a variety of sources. Applications can use many different configuration providers.

The ASP.NET Core configuration model also has the concept of overriding settings. Each configuration provider can define its own settings, or it can overwrite settings from a previous provider. You'll see this super-useful feature in action in the next section.

ASP.NET Core makes it simple to bind these key-value pairs, which are defined as `strings`, to POCO-setting classes you define in your code. This model of strongly typed configuration makes it easy to logically group settings around a given feature and lends itself well to unit testing.

Before we get into the details of loading configuration from providers, we'll take a step back and look at *where* this process happens—inside `WebHostBuilder`. For ASP.NET Core 2.0 apps built using the default templates, that's invariably inside the `WebHost.CreateDefaultBuilder()` method.

11.2 Configuring your application with CreateDefaultBuilder

As you saw in chapter 2, the default templates in ASP.NET Core 2.0 use the `Create-DefaultBuilder` method. This is an opinionated helper method that sets up a number of defaults for your app.

Listing 11.1   Using `CreateDefaultBuilder` to set up configuration

```
public class Program
{
    public static void Main(string[] args)
    {
        BuildWebHost(args).Run();          ◁────── The entry point for your
    }                                              application creates
                                                   IWebHost and calls Run.
    public static IWebHost BuildWebHost(string[] args) =>
        WebHost.CreateDefaultBuilder(args)    ◁─┐
            .UseStartup<Startup>()              │ CreateDefaultBuilder sets up
            .Build();                           │ a number of defaults,
}                                               │ including configuration.
```

In chapter 2, I glossed over this method, as you will only rarely need to change it for simple apps. But as your application grows, and if you want to change how configuration is loaded for your application, you may find you need to break it apart.

This listing shows an overview of the `CreateDefaultBuilder` method, so you can see how `WebHostBuilder` is constructed.

Listing 11.2   The `WebHost.CreateDefaultBuilder` method

Creating an instance of   Kestrel is the default HTTP
WebHostBuilder   server in ASP.NET Core.

```
public static IWebHostBuilder CreateDefaultBuilder(string[] args)
{
    var builder = new WebHostBuilder()
        .UseKestrel()                                      ◁──
        .UseContentRoot(Directory.GetCurrentDirectory())
        .ConfigureAppConfiguration((hostingContext, config) =>
        {
            // Configuration provider setup
        })
```

The content root defines the   Configures application settings,
directory where configuration   the topic of this chapter
files can be found.

```
        .ConfigureLogging((hostingContext, logging) =>
        {
            logging.AddConfiguration(
              hostingContext.Configuration.GetSection("Logging"));
            logging.AddConsole();
            logging.AddDebug();                        Sets up the logging
        })                                             infrastructure
        .UseIISIntegration()
        .UseDefaultServiceProvider((context, options) =>    Configures the DI container.
        {                                                   The ValidateScopes option
            options.ValidateScopes =                        checks for captured
              context.HostingEnvironment.IsDevelopment();   dependencies.
        });

    return builder;    ◁─────────┐   Returns WebHostBuilder
}                                     for further configuration
                                      before calling Build()
When running on windows,
IIS integration is
automatically configured.
```

The first method called on `WebHostBuilder` is `UseKestrel`. This extension method configures the ASP.NET application to use the Kestrel HTTP server, the new high-performance, cross-platform HTTP server that was created specifically for ASP.NET Core.

The call to `UseContentRoot` tells the application in which directory it can find any configuration or view files it will need later. This is typically the folder in which the application is running, hence the call to `GetCurrentDirectory`.

TIP ContentRoot is *not* where you store static files that the browser can access directly—that's the *WebRoot*, typically wwwroot.

`ConfigureLogging` is where you can specify the logging settings for your application. We'll look at logging in detail in chapter 17; for now, it's enough to know that `CreateDefaultBuilder` sets this up for you.

When you're running ASP.NET Core applications in production, you need to run them behind a reverse proxy. The call to `UseIISIntegration` ensures that if you're running your application on Windows, IIS can talk to your application, monitor its health, and forward requests to it. When running the application on Linux or macOS, this method call has no effect.

The last method call in `CreateDefaultBuilder`, `UseDefaultServiceProvider`, configures your app to use the built-in DI container. It also sets the `ValidateScopes` option based on the current `HostingEnvironment`. When running the application in the development environment, the app will automatically check for captured dependencies, as you learned about in chapter 10. You'll learn more about hosting environments in section 11.5.

The `ConfigureAppConfiguration()` method is the focus of section 11.3. It's where you load the settings and secrets for your app, whether they're in JSON files, environment variables, or command-line arguments. In the next section, you'll see how to use this method to load configuration values from various configuration providers using the ASP.NET Core `ConfigurationBuilder`.

11.3 *Building a configuration object for your app*

The ASP.NET Core configuration model centers on two main constructs: `Configuration-Builder` and `IConfigurationRoot`.

> **NOTE** `ConfigurationBuilder` describes how to construct the final configuration representation for your app, and `IConfigurationRoot` holds the configuration values themselves.

You describe your configuration setup by adding a number of `IConfiguration-Providers` to `IConfigurationBuilder`. These describe how to load the key-value pairs from a particular source; for example, a JSON file or from environment variables, as shown in figure 11.2. Calling `Build()` on `ConfigurationBuilder` queries each of these providers for the values they contain to create the `IConfigurationRoot` instance.

ASP.NET Core ships with a number of configuration providers, each provided by a different NuGet package. In ASP.NET Core 2.0, all of these packages are included by

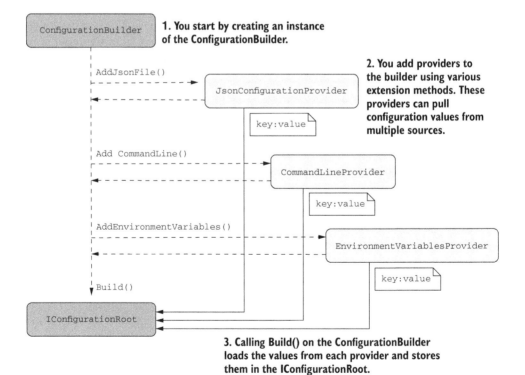

Figure 11.2 Using `ConfigurationBuilder` to create an instance of `IConfigurationRoot`.
Configuration providers are added to the builder with extension methods. Calling `Build()` queries
each provider to create `IConfigurationRoot`.

default, thanks to the Microsoft.AspNetCore.All metapackage. Some of the common providers are:

- *JSON files*—Microsoft.Extensions.Configuration.Json
- *XML files*—Microsoft.Extensions.Configuration.Xml
- *Environment variables*—Microsoft.Extensions.Configuration.EnvironmentVariables
- *Command-line arguments*—Microsoft.Extensions.Configuration.CommandLine
- *Azure Key Vault*—Microsoft.Extensions.Configuration.AzureKeyVault

If none of these fits your requirements, you can find a whole host of alternatives on GitHub and NuGet, and it's not difficult to create your own custom provider. For example, I wrote a simple configuration provider to read YAML files, available on NuGet or GitHub.[1]

In most cases, the default providers will be sufficient. In particular, most templates start with an appsettings.json file, which will contain a variety of settings, depending on the template you choose. This listing shows the default file generated by the ASP.NET Core 1.1 Web template without authentication.

Listing 11.3   Default appsettings.json file created by an ASP.NET Core Web template

```
{
  "Logging": {
    "IncludeScopes": false,
    "LogLevel": {
      "Default": "Warning"
    }
  }
}
```

As you can see, this file only contains settings to control logging to start with, but you can add additional configuration for your app here too.

> **WARNING** Don't store sensitive values, such as production passwords, API keys, or connection strings, in this file. You'll see how to store these securely in section 11.3.4.

Adding your own configuration values involves adding a key-value pair to the JSON. It's a good idea to "namespace" your settings by creating a base object for related settings, as in the MapDisplay object shown here.

Listing 11.4   Adding additional configuration values to an appsettings.json file

```
{
  "Logging": {
    "IncludeScopes": false,
    "LogLevel": {
      "Default": "Warning"
```

---

[1] You can find my YAML provider on GitHub at https://github.com/andrewlock/NetEscapades.Configuration.

```
    }
  },
  "MapDisplay": {
    "DefaultZoomLevel": 9,
    "DefaultLocation": {
      "latitude": 50.500,
      "longitude": -4.000
    }
  }
}
```

Nest all the configuration under the MapDisplay key.

Values can be numbers in the JSON file, but they'll be converted to strings when they're read.

You can create deeply nested structures to better organize your configuration values.

I've nested the map settings inside the `MapDisplay` parent key; this creates a section which will be useful later when it comes to binding your values to a POCO object. I also nested the `latitude` and `longitude` keys under the `DefaultLocation` key. You can create any structure of values that you like; the configuration provider will read them just fine. Also, you can store them as any data type—numbers, in this case—but be aware that the provider will read and store them internally as strings.

> **TIP** The configuration keys are *not* case-sensitive, so bear that in mind when loading from providers in which the keys *are* case-sensitive.

Now that you have a configuration file, it's time for your app to load it using `ConfigurationBuilder`! For this, return to the `ConfigureAppConfiguration()` method exposed by `WebHostBuilder` in Program.cs.

11.3.1 *Adding a configuration provider in Program.cs*

The default templates in ASP.NET Core use the `CreateDefaultBuilder` helper method to bootstrap `WebHostBuilder` for your app, as you saw in section 11.2. As part of this configuration, the `CreateDefaultBuilder` method calls `ConfigureApp-Configuration` and sets up a number of default configuration providers, which we'll look at in more detail throughout this chapter:

- *JSON file provider*—Loads settings from an optional JSON file called appsettings .json.
- *JSON file provider*—Loads settings from an optional environment-specific JSON file called appsettings.*ENVIRONMENT*.json. I'll show how to use environment-specific files in section 11.5.2.
- *User Secrets*—Loads secrets that are stored safely in development.
- *Environment variables*—Loads environment variables as configuration variables. Great for storing secrets in production.
- *Command-line arguments*—Uses values passed as arguments when you run your app.

Using the default builder ties you to this default set, but it's entirely optional. If you want to use different configuration providers, you can use your own `WebHostBuilder` instance instead. You can set up configuration using the `ConfigureAppConfiguration` method, as shown in the following listing, in which you configure a JSON provider to load the appsettings.json file. For brevity, I've omitted the logging and service provider configuration that you saw in listing 11.2, but you'd need to include this in practice.

Listing 11.5 Loading appsettings.json using a custom `WebHostBuilder`

```
public class Program
{
    public static void Main(string[] args)
    {
        BuildWebHost(args).Run();
    }

    public static IWebHost BuildWebHost(string[] args) =>
        new WebHostBuilder()
            .UseKestrel()
            .UseContentRoot(Directory.GetCurrentDirectory())
            .ConfigureAppConfiguration(AddAppConfiguration)
            .ConfigureLogging(
               (hostingContext, logging) => { /* Detail not shown */ })
            .UseIISIntegration()
            .UseDefaultServiceProvider(
               (context, options) =>{ /* Detail not shown */ })
            .UseStartup<Startup>()
            .Build();

    public static void AddAppConfiguration(
        WebHostBuilderContext hostingContext,
        IConfigurationBuilder config)
    {
        config.AddJsonFile("appsettings.json", optional: true);
    }
}
```

> Adds the configuration setup function to WebHostBuilder

> WebHostBuilder provides a hosting context and an instance of ConfigurationBuilder.

> Adds a JSON configuration provider, providing the filename of the configuration file

TIP In listing 11.5, I extracted the configuration to a static helper method, `AddAppConfiguration`, but you can also provide this inline as a lambda method.

In ASP.NET Core 2.0, `WebHostBuilder` creates an `IConfigurationBuilder` instance before invoking the `ConfigureAppConfiguration` method. All you need to do is add the configuration providers for your application.

In this example, you've added a single JSON configuration provider by calling the `AddJsonFile` extension method and providing a filename. You've also set the value of `optional` to `true`. This tells the configuration provider to skip over files it can't find at runtime, instead of throwing `FileNotFoundException`. Note that the extension method just registers the provider at this point, it doesn't try to load the file yet.

And that's it! The `WebHostBuilder` instance takes care of calling `Build()`, which generates `IConfigurationRoot`, which represents your configuration object. This is then registered as an `IConfiguration` instance with the DI container, so you can inject it into your classes. You'd commonly inject this into the constructor of your `Startup` class, so you can use it in the `Configure` and `ConfigureServices` methods:

```
public class Startup
{
    public Startup(IConfiguration config)
    {
        Configuration = config
    }
    public IConfiguration Configuration { get; }
}
```

> **NOTE** The ASP.NET Core 2.0 `WebHostBuilder` registers the configuration object as an `IConfiguration` in the DI container, not an `IConfiguration-Root`. In ASP.NET Core 1, you have to manually register the configuration with DI yourself.

At this point, at the end of the `Startup` constructor, you have a fully loaded configuration object! But what can you do with it? The `IConfigurationRoot` stores configuration as a set of key-value `string` pairs. You can access any value by its key, using standard dictionary syntax. For example, you could use

```
var zoomLevel = Configuration["MapDisplay:DefaultZoomLevel"];
```

to retrieve the configured zoom level for your application. Note that I used a : to designate a separate section. Similarly, to retrieve the `latitude` key, you could use

```
Configuration["MapDisplay:DefaultLocation:Latitude"];
```

You can also grab a whole section of the configuration using the `GetSection(section)` method. This grabs a chunk of the configuration and resets the namespace. Another way of getting the latitude key would be

```
Configuration.GetSection("MapDisplay")["DefaultLocation:Latitude"];
```

Accessing setting values like this is useful in the `ConfigureServices` and `Configure` methods of `Startup`, when you're defining your application. When setting up your application to connect to a database, for example, you'll often load a connection string from the `Configuration` object (you'll see a concrete example of this in the next chapter, when we look at Entity Framework Core).

If you need to access the configuration object like this from classes other than `Startup`, you can use DI to take it as a dependency in your service's constructor. But accessing configuration using `string` keys like this isn't particularly convenient; you should try to use strongly typed configuration instead, as you'll see in section 11.4.

> **WARNING** ASP.NET Core 1 doesn't register the configuration object with the DI container by default. If you need this functionality, you can register it yourself as a singleton by calling `services.AddSingleton(Configuration)` in `Startup.ConfigureServices`.

So far, this is probably all feeling a bit convoluted, and run-of-the-mill to load settings from a JSON file, and I'll grant you, it is. Where the ASP.NET Core configuration system shines is when you have multiple providers.

11.3.2 Using multiple providers to override configuration values

You've seen that ASP.NET Core uses the builder pattern to construct the configuration object, but so far, you've only configured a single provider. When you add providers, it's important to consider the order in which you add them, as that defines the order in which the configuration values are added to the underlying dictionary. Configuration values from later providers will overwrite values with the same key from earlier providers.

> **NOTE**   This bears repeating: the order you add configuration providers to `ConfigurationBuilder` is important. Later configuration providers can overwrite the values of earlier providers.

Think of the configuration providers as adding a layer of configuration values to a stack, where each layer may overlap with some or all of the layers below, as shown in figure 11.3. When you call `Build()`, `ConfigurationBuilder` collapses these layers down into one, to create the final set of configuration values stored in `IConfigurationRoot`.

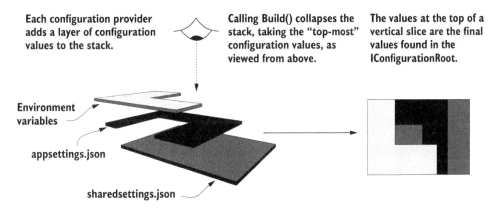

Each configuration provider adds a layer of configuration values to the stack.

Calling Build() collapses the stack, taking the "top-most" configuration values, as viewed from above.

The values at the top of a vertical slice are the final values found in the IConfigurationRoot.

Environment variables

appsettings.json

sharedsettings.json

Figure 11.3   Each configuration provider adds a "layer" of values to `ConfigurationBuilder`. Calling `Build()` collapses that configuration. Later providers will overwrite configuration values with the same key as earlier providers.

Update your code to load configuration from three different configuration providers—two JSON providers and an environment variable provider—by adding them to `ConfigurationBuilder`. I've only shown the `AddAppConfiguration` method in this listing for brevity.

Listing 11.6   Loading from multiple providers in Startup.cs using ASP.NET Core 2.0

```
public class Program
{
    /* Additional Program configuration*/
    public static void AddAppConfiguration(
        WebHostBuilderContext hostingContext,
        IConfigurationBuilder config)
    {
        config
            .AddJsonFile("sharedSettings.json", optional: true)
            .AddJsonFile("appsettings.json", optional: true)
            .AddEnvironmentVariables();
    }
}
```

> **Loads configuration from a different JSON configuration file before the appsettings.json file**

> **Adds the machine's environment variables as a configuration provider**

This design can be useful for a number of things. Fundamentally, it allows you to aggregate configuration values from a number of different sources into a single, cohesive object. To cement this in place, consider the configuration values in figure 11.4.

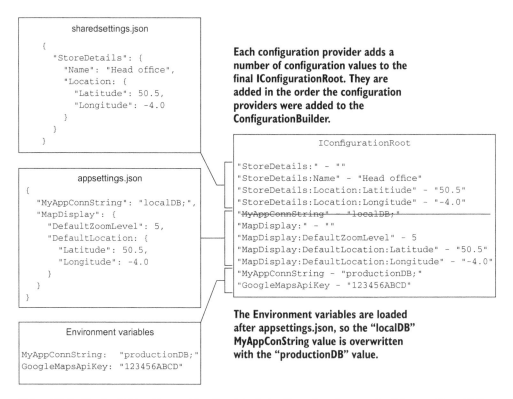

Figure 11.4   The final `IConfigurationRoot` **includes the values from each of the providers. Both appsettings.json and the environment variables include the** `MyAppConnString` **key. As the environment variables are added later, that configuration value is used.**

Most of the settings in each provider are unique and added to the final `IConfiguration-Root`. But the `"MyAppConnString"` key appears both in appsettings.json and as an environment variable. Because the environment variable provider is added after the JSON providers, the environment variable configuration value is used in `IConfiguration-Root`.

The ability to collate configuration from multiple providers is a handy trait on its own, but this design is also useful when it comes to handling sensitive configuration values, such as connection strings and passwords. The next section shows how to deal with this problem, both locally on your development machine and on production servers.

11.3.3 *Storing configuration secrets safely*

As soon as you build a nontrivial app, you'll find you have a need to store some sort of sensitive data as a setting somewhere. This could be a password, connection string, or an API key for a remote service, for example.

Storing these values in appsettings.json is generally a bad idea as you should never commit secrets to source control; the number of secret API keys people have committed to GitHub is scary! Instead, it's much better to store these values outside of your project folder, where they won't get accidentally committed.

You can do this in a number of ways, but the easiest and most commonly used approaches are to use environment variables for secrets on your production server and User Secrets locally.

Neither approach is truly secure, in that they don't store values in an encrypted format. If your machine is compromised, attackers will be able to read the stored values as they're stored in plaintext. They're intended to help you avoid committing secrets to source control.

> **TIP** Azure Key Vault[1] is a secure alternative, in that it stores the values encrypted in Azure. But you will still need to use the following approach for storing the Azure Key Value connection details!

Whichever approach you choose to store your application secrets, make sure you aren't storing them in source control, if possible. Even private repositories may not stay private forever, so it's best to err on the side of caution!

Storing secrets in environment variables in production

You can add the environment variable configuration provider using the `AddEnvironment-Variables` extension method, as you've already seen in listing 11.6. This will add all of the environment variables on your machine as key-value pairs in the configuration object.

---

[1] The Azure Key Vault configuration provider is available as a Microsoft.Extensions.Configuration.AzureKey-Vault NuGet package. For details on using it in your application, see the documentation at http://mng.bz/96aQ.

You can create the same hierarchical sections that you typically see in JSON files by using a colon, `:`, or a double underscore, `__`, to demarcate a section, for example: `MapSettings:MaxNumberOfPoints` or `MapSettings__MaxNumberOfPoints`.

> **TIP**   Some environments, such as Linux, don't allow ":" in environment variables, you must use the double underscore approach on these instead.

The environment variable approach is particularly useful when you're publishing your app to a self-contained environment, such as a dedicated server, Azure, or a Docker container. You can set environment variables on your production machine, or on your Docker container, and the provider will read them at runtime, overriding the defaults specified in your appsettings.json files.[1]

For a development machine, environment settings are less useful, as all your apps would be using the same variables. For example, if you set the `Connection-Strings__DefaultConnection` environment variable, then that would be added for every app you run locally. That sounds like more of a hassle than a benefit!

For development scenarios, you can use the User Secrets Manager. This effectively adds per-app environment variables, so you can have different settings for each app, but store them in a different location from the app itself.

STORING SECRETS WITH THE USER SECRETS MANAGER IN DEVELOPMENT

The idea behind User Secrets is to simplify storing per-app secrets outside of your app's project tree. This is similar to environment variables, but you use a unique key per-app to keep the secrets segregated.

> **WARNING**   The secrets aren't encrypted, so shouldn't be considered secure. They're an improvement on storing them in your project folder.

Setting up User Secrets takes a bit more effort than using environment variables, as you need to configure a tool to read and write them, add the User Secrets configuration provider, and define a unique key for your application:

1   ASP.NET Core 2.0 includes the User Secrets NuGet package by default as part of the Microsoft.AspNetCore.All metapackage. If you're not using the metapackage, you'll need to explicitly add the Microsoft.Extensions.Configuration .UserSecrets package to your project file:

```
<PackageReference
    Include="Microsoft.Extensions.Configuration.UserSecrets"
    Version="2.0.0" />
```

2   Add the SecretManager NuGet tools to your csproj file. Note, you need to do this manually by editing the csproj file—you can't use the NuGet UI in Visual Studio.[2]

---

[1]   For instructions on how to set environment variables for your operating system, see the documentation at http://mng.bz/R052.

[2]   ASP.NET Core 2.1 (in preview at the time of writing) introduces the concept of global tools so you can install the tools globally for all your applications. For preliminary details, see http://mng.bz/jGs6.

```
<ItemGroup>
  <DotNetCliToolReference
    Include="Microsoft.Extensions.SecretManager.Tools"
    Version="2.0.0" />
</ItemGroup>
```

3 Restore the NuGet package using `dotnet restore`. Visual Studio will do this automatically for you after you save your edits to the csproj file.

4 If you're using Visual Studio, right-click your project and choose Manage User Secrets. This opens an editor for a secrets.json file in which you can store your key-value pairs, as if it were an appsettings.json file, as shown in figure 11.5.

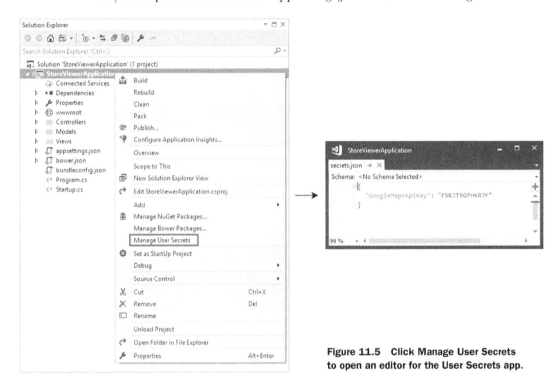

Figure 11.5   Click Manage User Secrets to open an editor for the User Secrets app.

5 Add a unique identifier to your csproj file. Visual Studio does this automatically when you click Manage User Secrets, but if you're using the command line, you'll need to add it yourself. Typically, you'd use a unique ID, like a GUID:

```
<PropertyGroup>
  <UserSecretsId>96eb2a39-1ef9-4d8e-8b20-8e8bd14038aa</UserSecretsId>
</PropertyGroup>
```

6 If you aren't using Visual Studio, you can add User Secrets using the command line:

```
dotnet user-secrets set GoogleMapsApiKey F5RJT9GFHKR7F
```

or you can edit the secret.json file directly using your favorite editor. The exact location of this file depends on your operating system and may vary. Check the documentation[1] for details.

Phew, that's a lot of setup, and you're not done yet! You still need to update your app to load the User Secrets at runtime. Thankfully, this is a lot simpler; you can use the extension method included as part of the UserSecrets NuGet package to add them to ConfigurationBuilder:

```
if(env.IsDevelopment())
{
    configBuilder.AddUserSecrets<Startup>();
}
```

> **NOTE** You should only use the User Secrets provider in development, *not* in production, so you're conditionally adding the provider to Configuration-Builder. In production, you should use environment variables or Azure Key Vault, as discussed earlier.

This method has a number of overloads, but the simplest is a generic method that you can call using your application's Startup class. The User Secrets provider needs to read the UserSecretsId property that you (or Visual Studio) added to the csproj. The Startup class acts as a simple marker to indicate which assembly contains this property.

> **NOTE** If you're interested, the User Secrets package uses the UserSecretsId property in your csproj file to generate an assembly-level UserSecretsId-Attribute. The provider then reads this attribute at runtime to determine the UserSecretsId of the app, and hence generates the path to the secrets.json file.

And there you have it, safe storage of your secrets outside your project folder during development. This might seem like overkill, but if you have anything that you consider remotely sensitive that you need to load into configuration, then I strongly urge you to use environment variables or User Secrets.

It's almost time to leave configuration providers behind, but before we do, I'd like to show you the ASP.NET Core configuration system's party trick: reloading files on the fly.

11.3.4 *Reloading configuration values when they change*

Besides security, not having to recompile your application every time you want to tweak a value is one of the advantages of using configuration and settings. In the previous version of ASP.NET, changing a setting by editing web.config would cause your

---

[1] The Secret Manager Tool 2.0.0 stores the secrets.json file in the user profile, but is subject to change in later versions. See http://mng.bz/1B2v for details.

app to have to restart. This beat having to recompile, but waiting for the app to start up before it could serve requests was a bit of a drag.

In ASP.NET Core, you finally get the ability to edit a file and have the configuration of your application automatically update, without having to recompile or restart.

A common scenario where you might find this useful is when you're trying to debug an app you have in production. You typically configure logging to one of a number of levels, for example:

- Error
- Warning
- Information
- Debug

Each of these settings is more verbose than the last, but also provides more context. By default, you might configure your app to only log warning- and error-level logs in production, so you don't generate too many superfluous log entries. Conversely, if you're trying to debug a problem, you want as much information as possible, so you might want to use the debug log level.

Being able to change configuration at runtime means you can easily switch on extra logs when you encounter an issue and switch them back afterwards by editing your appsettings.json file.

> **NOTE** Reloading is generally only available for file-based configuration providers, as opposed to the environment variable or User Secrets provider.

You can enable the reloading of configuration files when you add any of the file-based providers to your `ConfigurationBuilder`. The `Add*File` extension methods include an overload with a `reloadOnChange` parameter. If this is set to true, the app will monitor the filesystem for changes to the file and will trigger a rebuild of `IConfiguration-Root`, if needs be. This listing shows how to add configuration reloading to the appsettings.json file loaded inside the `AddAppConfiguration` method.

Listing 11.7   Reloading appsettings.json when the file changes

```
public class Program
{
    /* Additional Program configuration*/

    public static void AddAppConfiguration(
        WebHostBuilderContext hostingContext,
        IConfigurationBuilder config)
    {
        config.AddJsonFile(
            "appsettings.json",
            optional: true
            reloadOnChange: true);        ⟵——— IConfigurationRoot will be
    }                                            rebuilt if the appsettings.json
}                                                file changes.
```

With that in place, any changes you make to the file will be mirrored in `IConfiguration-Root`. But as I said at the start of this chapter, `IConfigurationRoot` isn't the preferred way to pass settings around in your application. Instead, as you'll see in the next section, you should favor strongly typed POCO objects.

11.4   *Using strongly typed settings with the options pattern*

Most of the examples I've shown so far have been how to get values *into* `IConfiguration-Root`, as opposed to how to *use* them. You've seen that you can access a key using the `Configuration["key"]` dictionary syntax, but using `string` keys like this feels messy and prone to typos.

Instead, ASP.NET Core promotes the use of strongly typed settings. These are POCO objects that you define and create and represent a small collection of settings, scoped to a single feature in your app.

The following listing shows both the settings for your store locator component and display settings to customize the homepage of the app. They're separated into two separate objects with `"MapDisplay"` and `"HomePageSettings"` keys corresponding to the different areas of the app they impact.

Listing 11.8   Separating settings into different objects in appsettings.json

```
{
  "MapDisplay": {
    "DefaultZoomLevel": 6,
    "DefaultLocation": {          Settings related to the store
      "latitude": 50.500,         locator section of the app
      "longitude": -4.000
    }
  },
  "HomePageSettings": {           General settings related to
    "Title":  "Acme Store Locator",   the app's homepage
    "ShowCopyright": true
  }
}
```

The simplest approach to making the homepage settings available to `HomeController` would be to inject `IConfiguration` and access the values using the dictionary syntax; for example:

```
public class HomeController : Controller
{
    public HomeController(IConfiguration config)
    {
        var title = config["HomePageSettings:Title"];
        var showCopyright = bool.Parse(
            config["HomePageSettings:ShowCopyright"]);
    }
}
```

But you don't want to do this; too many strings for my liking! And that `bool.Parse`? Yuk! Instead, you can use custom strongly typed objects, with all the type safety and IntelliSense goodness that brings.

You can inject a strongly typed
options class using the
IOptions<> wrapper interface.

The Value property
exposes the POCO
settings object.

```
public class HomeController : Controller
{
    public HomeController(IOptions<HomePageSettings> options)
    {
        HomePageSettings settings = options.Value;
        var title = settings.Title;
        var showCopyright = settings.ShowCopyright;
    }
}
```

The settings object
contains properties
that are bound to
configuration values
at runtime.

The binder can also
convert string values
directly to primitive types.

The ASP.NET Core configuration system includes a *binder*, which can take a collection of configuration values and *bind* them to a strongly typed object, called an *options class*. This is similar to the concept of binding from chapter 6, where request values were bound to the arguments of your application model.

This section shows how to set up the binding of configuration values to a POCO options class and how to make sure it reloads when the underlying configuration values change. We'll also have a look at the different sorts of objects you can bind.

11.4.1 Introducing the IOptions interface

ASP.NET Core introduced strongly typed settings as a way of letting configuration code adhere to the single responsibility principle and to allow injecting configuration classes as explicit dependencies. They also make testing easier; instead of having to create an instance of `IConfiguration` to test a service, you can create an instance of the POCO options class.

For example, the `HomePageSettings` class shown in the previous example could be simple, exposing just the values related to the homepage:

```
public class HomePageSettings
{
    public string Title { get; set; }
    public bool ShowCopyright { get; set; }
}
```

Your options classes need to be non-abstract and have a `public` parameterless constructor to be eligible for binding. The binder will set any public properties that match configuration values, as you'll see shortly.

To help facilitate the binding of configuration values to your custom POCO options classes, ASP.NET Core introduces the IOptions<T> interface. This is a simple interface with a single property, Value, which contains your configured POCO options class at runtime. Options classes are set up in the ConfigureServices section of Startup, as shown here.

> **Listing 11.10   Configuring the options classes using `Configure<T>` in Startup.cs**

```
public IConfiguration Configuration { get; }

public void ConfigureServices(IServiceCollection services)
{
    services.Configure<MapDisplaySettings>(
        Configuration.GetSection("MapDisplay"));

    services.Configure<HomePageSettings>(
        Configuration.GetSection("HomePageSettings"));
}
```

Binds the MapDisplay section to the POCO options class MapDisplaySettings

Binds the HomePageSettings section to the POCO options class HomePageSettings

TIP   If you get a compilation error with the preceding overload of Configure<>, add the Microsoft.Extensions.Options.ConfigurationExtensions NuGet package to your app. ASP.NET Core 2.0 includes this by default as part of the metapackage, so it's not often necessary.

Each call to Configure<T> sets up the following series of actions internally:

- Creates an instance of ConfigureOptions<T>, which indicates that IOptions<T> should be configured based on configuration.

  If Configure<T> is called multiple times, then multiple Configure-Options<T> objects will be used, all of which can be applied to create the final object, in much the same way as the IConfigurationRoot is built from multiple layers.

- Each ConfigureOptions<T> instance binds a section of IConfigurationRoot to an instance of the T POCO class. This sets any public properties on the options class based on the keys in the provided ConfigurationSection.

  Note that the section name ("MapDisplay" in listing 11.10) can have any value; it doesn't have to match the name of your options class.

- Registers the IOptions<T> interface in the DI container as a singleton, with the final bound POCO object in the Value property.

This last step lets you inject your options classes into controllers and services by injecting IOptions<T>, as you've seen. This gives you encapsulated, strongly typed access to your configuration values. No more magic strings, woo-hoo!

WARNING   If you forget to call Configure<T> and inject IOptions<T> into your services, you won't see any errors, but the T options class won't be bound to anything and will only have default values in its properties.

The binding of the `T` options class to `ConfigurationSection` happens when you first request `IOptions<T>`. The object is registered in the DI container as a singleton, so it's only bound once.

There's one catch with this setup: you can't use the `reloadOnChange` parameter I described in section 11.2.3 to reload your strongly typed options classes when using `IOptions<T>`. `IConfigurationRoot` will still be reloaded if you edit your appsettings.json files, but it won't propagate to your options class.

If that seems like a step backwards, or even a deal-breaker, then don't worry. `IOptions<T>` has a cousin, `IOptionsSnapshot<T>`, for such an occasion.

11.4.2 Reloading strongly typed options with IOptionsSnapshot

In the previous section, you used `IOptions<T>` to provide strongly typed access to configuration. This provided a nice encapsulation of the settings for a particular service, but with a specific drawback: the options class never changes, even if you modify the underlying configuration file from which it was loaded, for example appsettings.json.

This is often not a problem (you shouldn't be modifying files on live production servers anyway!), but if you need this functionality, you can use the `IOptions-Snapshot<T>` interface introduced with ASP.NET Core 1.1.

> **WARNING** `IOptionsSnapshot` is only available in ASP.NET Core 1.1 and above. If you're using ASP.NET Core 1.0, you won't be able to reload the `IOptions<T>` options classes when the underlying configuration changes.

Conceptually, `IOptionsSnaphot<T>` is identical to `IOptions<T>` in that it's a strongly typed representation of a section of configuration. The difference is when, and how often, the POCO options objects are created when each of these are used.

- `IOptions<T>`—The instance is created once, when first needed. It always contains the configuration when the object instance was first created.
- `IOptionsSnapshot<T>`—A new instance is created when needed, if the underlying configuration has changed since the last instance was created.

`IOptionsSnaphot<T>` is automatically set up for your options classes at the same time as `IOptions<T>`, so you can use it in your services in exactly the same way! This listing shows how you could update your `HomeController` so that you always get the latest configuration values in your strongly typed `HomePageSettings` options class.

Listing 11.11 Injecting reloadable options using `IOptionsSnapshot<T>`

```
public class HomeController : Controller
{
    public HomeController(
        IOptionsSnapshot<HomePageSettings> options)
    {
        HomePageSettings settings = options.Value;
        var title = settings.Title;
    }
}
```

IOptionsSnapshot<T> will update if the underlying configuration values change.

The Value property exposes the POCO settings object, the same as for IOptions<T>.

The settings object will match the configuration values at some point, instead of at first run.

Whenever you edit the settings file and cause `IConfigurationRoot` to be reloaded, `IOptionsSnapshot<HomePageSettings>` will be rebound. A new `HomePageSettings` object is created with the new configuration values and will be used for all future dependency injection. Until you edit the file again, of course! It's as simple as that; update your code to use `IOptionsSnapshot<T>` instead of `IOptions<T>` wherever you need it.

The final thing I want to touch on in this section is the design of your POCO options classes themselves. These are typically simple collections of properties, but there are a few things to bear in mind so that you don't get stuck debugging why the binding seemingly hasn't worked!

11.4.3 *Designing your options classes for automatic binding*

I've touched on some of the requirements for your POCO classes for the `IOptions<T>` binder to be able to populate them, but there are a few rules to bear in mind.

The first key point is that the binder will be creating instances of your options classes using reflection, so your POCO options classes need to:

- Be non-abstract
- Have a default (`public` parameterless) constructor

If your classes satisfy these two points, the binder will loop through all the properties on your class and bind any it can. In the broadest sense, the binder can bind any property which

- Is public
- Has a getter—the binder won't write set-only properties
- Has a setter or a non-null value
- Is not an indexer

This listing shows an extensive options class, with a whole host of different types of properties, some of which are valid to bind, and some of which aren't.

Listing 11.12   An options class containing binding and nonbinding properties

```
public class TestOptions
{
    public string String { get; set; }
    public int Integer { get; set; }
    public SubClass Object { get; set; }
    public SubClass ReadOnly { get; } = new SubClass();

    public Dictionary<string, SubClass> Dictionary { get; set; }
    public List<SubClass> List { get; set; }
    public IDictionary<string, SubClass> IDictionary { get; set; }
    public IEnumerable<SubClass> IEnumerable { get; set; }
    public ICollection<SubClass> IEnumerable { get; }
        = new List<SubClass>();
```

The binder can bind simple and complex object types, and read-only properties with a default.

The binder will also bind collections, including interfaces; dictionaries must have string keys.

```
            internal string NotPublic { get; set; }
            public SubClass SetOnly { set => _setOnly = value; }
            public SubClass NullReadOnly { get; } = null;
            public SubClass NullPrivateSetter { get; private set; } = null;
            public SubClass this[int i] {
                get => _indexerList[i];
                set => _indexerList[i] = value;
            }

            public List<SubClass> NullList { get; }
            public Dictionary<int, SubClass> IntegerKeys { get; set; }
            public IEnumerable<SubClass> ReadOnlyEnumerable { get; }
                = new List<SubClass>();

            public SubClass _setOnly = null;
            private readonly List<SubClass> _indexerList
                = new List<SubClass>();

            public class SubClass
            {
                public string Value { get; set; }
            }
        }
```

These collection properties can't be bound.

The binder can't bind nonpublic, set-only, null-read-only, or indexer properties.

The backing fields for SetOnly and Indexer properties

As shown in the listing, the binder generally supports collections too—both implementations and interfaces. If the collection property is already initialized, it will use that, but the binder can also create backing fields for them. If your property implements any of the following classes, the binder will create a List<> of the appropriate type as the backing object:

- IReadOnlyList<>
- IReadOnlyCollection<>
- ICollection<>
- IEnumerable<>

WARNING You can't bind to an IEnumerable<> property that has already been initialized, as the underlying type doesn't expose an Add function! You *can* bind to an IEnumerable<> if you leave its initial value as null.

Similarly, the binder will create a Dictionary<,> as the backing field for properties with dictionary interfaces, as long as they use string keys:

- IDictionary<,>
- IReadOnlyDictionary<,>

WARNING You can't bind dictionaries with nonstring values, such as int.

Clearly there are quite a few nuances here, but if you stick to the simple cases from the preceding example, you'll be fine. Be sure to check for typos in your JSON files!

That brings us to the end of this section on strongly typed settings. In the next section, we'll look at how you can dynamically change your settings at runtime, based on the environment in which your app is running.

11.5   *Configuring an application for multiple environments*

Any application that makes it to production will likely have to run in multiple environments. For example, if you're building an application with database access, you'll probably have a small database running on your machine that you use for development. In production, you'll have a completely different database running on a server somewhere else.

Another common requirement is to have different amounts of logging depending on where your app is running. In development, it's great to generate lots of logs as it helps debugging, but once you get to production, too much logging can be overwhelming. You'll want to log warnings and errors, maybe information-level logs, but definitely not debug-level logs!

To handle these requirements, you need to make sure your app loads different configuration values depending on the environment it's running in; load the production database connection string when in production and so on. You need to consider three aspects:

- How does your app identify which environment it's running in?
- How do you load different configuration values based on the current environment?
- How can you change the environment for a particular machine?

This section tackles each of these questions in turn, so you can easily tell your development machine apart from your production servers and act accordingly.

11.5.1   *Identifying the hosting environment*

ASP.NET Core identifies the current environment by using, perhaps unsurprisingly, an environment variable! The `WebHostBuilder` created in Program.cs looks for a magic environment variable called `ASPNETCORE_ENVIRONMENT` and uses it to create an `IHostingEnvironment` object.

The `IHostingEnvironment` interface exposes a number of useful properties about the running context of your app. Some of these you've already seen, such as `Content-RootPath`, which points to the folder containing your application's content files; for example, the appsettings.json files. The property you're interested in here is `EnvironmentName`.

The `IHostingEnvironment.EnvironmentName` property is set to the value of the `ASPNETCORE_ENVIRONMENT` environment variable, so it can be anything, but you should stick to three commonly used values in most cases:

- `"Development"`
- `"Staging"`
- `"Production"`

ASP.NET Core includes a number of helper methods for working with these three values, so you'll have an easier time if you stick to them. In particular, whenever you're testing whether your app is running in a particular environment, you should use one of the following extension methods:

- `IHostingEnvironment.IsDevelopment()`
- `IHostingEnvironment.IsStaging()`
- `IHostingEnvironment.IsProduction()`
- `IHostingEnvironment.IsEnvironment(string environmentName)`

These methods all make sure they do case-insensitive checks of the environment variable, so you don't get any wonky errors at runtime if you don't capitalize the environment variable value.

> **TIP** Where possible, use the `IHostingEnvironment` extension methods over direct string comparison with `EnvironmentValue`, as they provide case-insensitive matching.

`IHostingEnvironment` doesn't do anything other than expose the details of your current environment, but you can use it in a number of different ways. In chapter 8, you saw the Environment Tag Helper, which you used to show and hide HTML based on the current environment. Now you know where it was getting its information—`IHostingEnvironment`.

You can use a similar approach to customize which configuration values you load at runtime by loading different files when running in development versus production. This is common and is included out of the box in most ASP.NET Core templates, and in the ASP.NET Core 2.0 `CreateDefaultBuilder` helper method.

11.5.2 *Loading environment-specific configuration files*

The `EnvironmentName` value is determined early in the process of bootstrapping your application, before your `ConfigurationBuilder` is created. This means you can dynamically change which configuration providers are added to the builder, and hence which configuration values are loaded when the `IConfigurationRoot` is built.

A common pattern is to have an optional, environment-specific appsettings .ENVIRONMENT.json file that's loaded after the default appsettings.json file. This listing shows how you could achieve this in the `AddAppConfiguration` method of `Program`.

> **Listing 11.13 Adding environment-specific `appsettings.json` files**

```
public class Program
{
    /* Additional Program configuration*/

    public static void AddAppConfiguration(
        WebHostBuilderContext hostingContext,
        IConfigurationBuilder config)
    {
        var env = hostingContext.HostingEnvironment;    ⟵
        config
```

The current IHostingEnvironment is available on WebHostBuilderContext.

```
        .AddJsonFile(
            "appsettings.json",
            optional: false)     ◁
        .AddJsonFile
            $"appsettings.{env.EnvironmentName}.json",
            optional: true);
    }
}
```

It's common to make the base appsettings.json compulsory.

Adds an optional environment-specific JSON file where the filename varies with the environment

With this pattern, a global appsettings.json file contains settings applicable to most environments. Additional, optional, JSON files called appsettings.Development.json, appsettings.Staging.json, and appsettings.Production.json are subsequently added to ConfigurationBuilder, depending on the current EnvironmentName.

Any settings in these files will overwrite values from the global appsettings.json, if they have the same key, as you've seen previously. This lets you do things like set the logging to be verbose in the development environment only and switch to more selective logs in production.

Another common pattern is to completely add or remove configuration providers depending on the environment. For example, you might use the User Secrets provider when developing locally, but Azure Key Vault in production. This listing shows how you could use IHostingEnvironment to conditionally include the User Secrets provider.

Listing 11.14   Conditionally including the User Secrets configuration provider

```
public class Program
{
    /* Additional Program configuration*/

    public static void AddAppConfiguration(
        WebHostBuilderContext hostingContext,
        IConfigurationBuilder config)
    {
        var env = hostingContext.HostingEnvironment
        config
            .AddJsonFile(
                "appsettings.json",
                optional: false)
            .AddJsonFile
                $"appsettings.{env.EnvironmentName}.json",
                optional: true);
        if(env.IsDevelopment())      ◁
        {
            builder.AddUserSecrets<Startup>();      ◁
        }
    }
}
```

Extension methods make checking the environment simple and explicit.

In Staging and Production, the User Secrets provider wouldn't be used.

Another common place to customize your application based on the environment is when setting up your middleware pipeline. In chapter 3, you learned about

DeveloperExceptionPageMiddleware and how you should use it when developing locally. The following listing shows how you can use IHostingEnvironment to control your pipeline in this way, so that when you're in Staging or Production, your app uses ExceptionHandlerMiddleware instead.

Listing 11.15 Using `IHostingEnvironment` to customize your middleware pipeline

```
public void Configure(IApplicationBuilder app, IHostingEnvironment env)
{
    if (env.IsDevelopment())
    {                                            In Development,
        app.UseDeveloperExceptionPage();         DeveloperExceptionPageMiddleware
    }                                            is added to the pipeline.
    else
    {                                            In Production, the pipeline uses
        app.UseExceptionHandler("/Home/Error");  ExceptionHandlerMiddleware instead.
    }

    app.UseStaticFiles();

    app.UseMvc(routes =>
    {
        routes.MapRoute(
            name: "default",
            template: "{controller=Home}/{action=Index}/{id?}");
    });
}
```

You can inject IHostingEnvironment anywhere in your app, but I'd advise against using it in your own services, outside of Startup and Program. It's far better to use the configuration providers to customize strongly typed settings based on the current hosting environment.

As useful as it is, setting IHostingEnvironment can be a little cumbersome if you want to switch back and forth between different environments during testing. Personally, I'm always forgetting how to set environment variables on the various operating systems I use. The final skill I'd like to teach you is how to set the hosting environment when you're developing.

11.5.3 *Setting the hosting environment*

In this section, I'll show you a couple of ways to set the hosting environment when you're developing. These makes it easy to test a specific app's behavior in different environments, without having to change the environment for all the apps on your machine.

If your ASP.NET Core application can't find an ASPNETCORE_ENVIRONMENT environment variable when it starts up, it defaults to a production environment, as shown in figure 11.6. This means that when you deploy to your configuration providers, you'll be using the correct environment by default.

If the WebHostBuilder can't find the **ASPNETCORE_ENVIRONMENT** variable at runtime, it will default to Production.

```
dotnet run                                    —    □    ×
C:\Users\Sock\Repos\ch11>dotnet run
Hosting environment: Production
Content root path: C:\Users\Sock\Repos\ch11
Now listening on: http://localhost:5000
Application started. Press Ctrl+C to shut down.
```

Figure 11.6   By default, ASP.NET Core applications run in the Production hosting environment. You can override this by setting the ASPNETCORE_ENVIRONMENT variable.

TIP   By default, the current hosting environment is logged to the console at startup, which can be useful for quickly checking that the environment variable has been picked up correctly.

If you're working with the .NET CLI and a text editor, you're probably going to be comfortable setting environment variables from the command line for your OS, so you'll want to set your ASPNETCORE_ENVIRONMENT development machine environment to Development.

If you're using Visual Studio, you can set temporary environment variables for when you debug your application. Double-click the Properties node and choose the Debug tab; you can see in figure 11.7 that the ASPNETCORE_ENVIRONMENT is set to Development, so there's no need to dive back to the command line if you don't want to.

TIP   These values are all stored in the properties/launchSettings.json file, so you can edit them by hand if you prefer.[1]

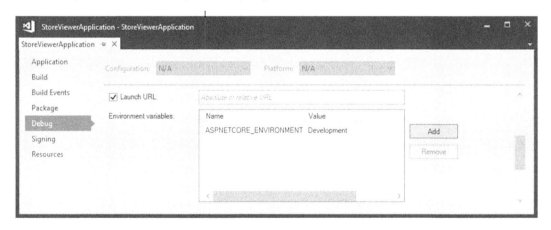

Figure 11.7   You can set temporary environment variables when you debug your application in Visual Studio.

---

[1]   In ASP.NET Core 2.1 you can use the launchSettings.json file with both the CLI tools and Visual Studio.

You can define temporary variables to
use when debugging your application
in the launch.json file.

Figure 11.8 Visual Studio code lets you define temporary environment variables to use when debugging. Your application will treat them the same as any other environment variable but they won't affect other applications, only the ASP.NET Core app you're debugging.

Visual Studio Code uses a similar approach with its own launch.json file. Add the ASPNETCORE_ENVIRONMENT variable, as shown in figure 11.8.

These temporary environment variables are a great way to test your application in different variables. In Visual Studio, you could even add a new debugging profile, IIS Express (Production) perhaps, so you can quickly switch between testing different environments.

There's one final trick I've seen used. If you want to completely hardcode the environment your app runs in to a single value, you can use the UseEnvironment extension method on WebHostBuilder, as shown next. This forces the app to use the value you provide. I still suggest using one of the standard values though, preferably EnvironmentName.Production.

Listing 11.16 Hardcoding EnvironmentName with UseEnvironment

```
public class Program
{
    public static void Main(string[] args)
    {
```

```
        BuildWebHost(args).Run();
    }

    public static IWebHost BuildWebHost(string[] args) =>
        new WebHostBuilder()
            .UseEnvironment(EnvironmentName.Production)
            .UseKestrel()
            .UseContentRoot(Directory.GetCurrentDirectory())
            .ConfigureAppConfiguration( /* Not shown*/)
            .UseIISIntegration()
            .UseStartup<Startup>()
            .Build();
}
```

This ignores **ASPNETCORE_ENVIRONMENT** and hardcodes the environment to Production.

TIP   This approach only makes sense if you always want to run your app in a single environment. That's overly restrictive, so I recommend setting the hosting environment using an environment variable or your IDE instead.

That brings us to the end of this chapter on configuration. Configuration isn't glamorous, but it's an essential part of all apps. The ASP.NET Core configuration provider model handles a wide range of scenarios, letting you store settings and secrets in a variety of locations.

Simple settings can be stored in appsettings.json, where they're easy to tweak and modify during development, and can be overwritten by using environment-specific JSON files. Meanwhile, your secrets and sensitive settings can be stored outside the project file, in the User Secrets manager, or as environment variables. This gives you both flexibility and safety—as long as you don't go writing your secrets to appsettings.json!

In the next chapter, we'll take a brief look at the new object relational mapper that fits well with ASP.NET Core: Entity Framework Core. We'll only be getting a taste of it in this book, but you'll learn how to load and save data, build a database from your code, and migrate the database as your code evolves.

Summary

- Anything that could be considered a setting or a secret is normally stored as a configuration value.
- ASP.NET Core uses configuration providers to load key-value pairs from a variety of sources. Applications can use many different configuration providers.
- `ConfigurationBuilder` describes how to construct the final configuration representation for your app and `IConfigurationRoot` holds the configuration values themselves.
- You create a configuration object by adding configuration providers to an instance of `ConfigurationBuilder` using extension methods such as `AddJsonFile()`. `WebHostBuilder` creates the `ConfigurationBuilder` instance for you and calls `Build()` to create an instance of `IConfigurationRoot`.
- ASP.NET Core includes built-in providers for JSON files, XML files, environment files, command-line arguments, and Azure Key Vault, among others.

- The order in which you add providers to `ConfigurationBuilder` is important; subsequent providers replace the values of settings defined in earlier providers.

- Configuration keys aren't case-sensitive.

- ASP.NET Core 1.x doesn't register the `IConfigurationRoot` object with the DI container by default. In ASP.NET Core 2.0, it's registered as an `IConfiguration` object.

- You can retrieve settings from `IConfiguration` directly using the indexer syntax, for example `Configuration["MySettings:Value"]`.

- In ASP.NET Core 2.0, the `CreateDefaultBuilder` method configures JSON, environment variable, command-line argument, and User Secret providers for you. You can customize the configuration providers used in your app by manually creating a `WebHostBuilder` and calling `ConfigureAppConfiguration`.

- In production, store secrets in environment variables. These can be loaded after your file-based settings in the configuration builder.

- On development machines, the User Secrets Manager is a more convenient tool than using environment variables. It stores secrets in your OS user's profile, outside the project folder.

- Be aware that neither environment variables nor the User Secrets Manager tool encrypt secrets, they merely store them in locations that are less likely to be made public, as they're outside your project folder.

- File-based providers, such as the JSON provider, can automatically reload configuration values when the file changes. This allows you to update configuration values in real time, without having to restart your app.

- Use strongly typed POCO options classes to access configuration in your app.

- Use the `Configure<T>()` extension method in `ConfigureServices` to bind your POCO options objects to `ConfigurationSection`.

- You can inject the `IOptions<T>` interface into your services using DI. You can access the strongly typed options object on the `Value` property.

- If you want to reload your POCO options objects when your configuration changes, use the `IOptionsSnapshot<T>` interface instead.

- Applications running in different environments, Development versus Production for example, often require different configuration values.

- ASP.NET Core determines the current hosting environment using the `ASPNETCORE_ENVIRONMENT` environment variable. If this variable isn't set, the environment is assumed to be Production.

- The current hosting environment is exposed as an `IHostingEnvironment` interface. You can check for specific environments using `IsDevelopment()`, `IsStaging()`, and `IsProduction()`.

- You can use the `IHostingEnvironment` object to load files specific to the current environment, such as appsettings.Production.json.

Saving data with Entity Framework Core

This chapter includes

- What Entity Framework Core is and why you should use it
- Adding Entity Framework Core to an ASP.NET Core application
- Building a data model and using it to create a database
- Querying, creating, and updating data using Entity Framework Core

Most applications that you'll build with ASP.NET Core will require storing and loading some kind of data. Even the examples so far in this book have assumed you have some sort of data store—storing exchange rates, user shopping carts, or the locations of physical main street stores. I've glossed over this for the most part but, typically, you'll store this data in a database.

Working with databases can often be a rather cumbersome process. You have to manage connections to the database, translate data from your application to a format the database can understand, as well as hande a plethora of other subtle issues.

You can manage this complexity in a variety of ways, but I'm going to focus on using a new library built for .NET Core: Entity Framework Core (EF Core). EF Core is a library that lets you quickly and easily build database access code for your ASP.NET Core applications. It's modeled on the popular Entity Framework 6.x library, but has significant changes that mean it stands alone in its own right and is more than an upgrade.

The aim of this chapter is to provide a quick overview of EF Core and how you can use it in your applications to quickly query and save to a database. You'll have enough knowledge to connect your app to a database, and to manage schema changes to the database, but I won't be going into great depth on any topics.

> **NOTE** For an in-depth look at EF Core I recommend, *Entity Framework Core in Action* by Jon P Smith (Manning, 2018). Alternatively, you can read about EF Core and its cousin, Entity Framework, on the Microsoft documentation website at https://docs.microsoft.com/en-us/ef/core/index.

Section 12.1 introduces EF Core and explains why you might want to use it in your applications. You'll learn how the design of EF Core helps you to quickly iterate on your database structure and reduce the friction of interacting with a database.

In section 12.2, you'll learn how to add EF Core to an ASP.NET Core app and configure it using the ASP.NET Core configuration system. You'll see how to build a model for your app that represents the data you'll store in the database and how to hook it into the ASP.NET Core DI container.

> **NOTE** For this chapter, and the rest of the book, I'm going to be using SQL Server Express' LocalDB feature. This is installed as part of Visual Studio 2017 (when you choose the .NET Desktop Development workload) and provides a lightweight SQL Server engine.[1] Very little of the code is specific to SQL Server, so you should be able to follow along with a different database if you prefer.

No matter how carefully you design your original data model, the time will come when you need to change it. In section 12.3, I show how you can easily update your model and apply these changes to the database itself, using EF Core for all the heavy lifting.

Once you have EF Core configured and a database created, section 12.4 shows how to use EF Core in your application code. You'll see how to create, read, update, and delete (CRUD) records, as well as some of the patterns to use when designing your data access.

---

[1] You can read more about LocalDB at http://mng.bz/24P8.

In section 12.5, I highlight a few of the issues you'll want to take into consideration when using EF Core in a production app. A single chapter on EF Core can only offer a brief introduction to all of the related concepts though, so if you choose to use EF Core in your own applications—especially if this is your first time using such a data access library—I strongly recommend reading more once you have the basics from this chapter.

Before we get into any code, let's look at what EF Core is, what problems it solves, and when you might want to use it.

12.1 Introducing Entity Framework Core

Database access code is ubiquitous across web applications. Whether you're building an e-commerce app, a blog, or the Next Big Thing™, chances are you'll need to interact with a database.

Unfortunately, interacting with databases from app code is often a messy affair and there are many different approaches you can take. For example, something as simple as reading data from a database requires handling network connections, writing SQL statements, and handling variable result data. The .NET ecosystem has a whole array of libraries you can use for this, ranging from the low-level ADO.NET libraries, to higher-level abstractions like EF Core.

In this section, I describe what EF Core is and the problem it's designed to solve. I cover the motivation behind using an abstraction such as EF Core, and how it helps to bridge the gap between your app code and your database. As part of that, I present some of the trade-offs you'll make by using it in your apps, which should help you decide if it's right for your purposes. Finally, we'll take a look at an example EF Core mapping, from app code to database, to get a feel for EF Core's main concepts.

12.1.1 What is EF Core?

EF Core is a library that provides an object-oriented way to access databases. It acts as an *object-relational mapper* (ORM), communicating with the database for you and mapping database responses to .NET classes and objects, as shown in figure 12.1.

> **DEFINITION** With an *object-relational mapper* (ORM), you can manipulate a database using object-oriented concepts such as classes and objects by mapping them to database concepts such as tables and columns.

EF Core is based on, but is distinct from, the existing Entity Framework libraries (currently, up to version 6.x). It was built as part of the .NET Core push to work cross-platform, but with additional goals in mind. In particular, the EF Core team wanted to make a highly performant library that could be used with a wide range of databases.

There are many different types of databases, but probably the most commonly used family is *relational* databases, accessed using Structured Query Language (SQL). This is the bread and butter of EF Core; it can map Microsoft SQL Server, MySQL,

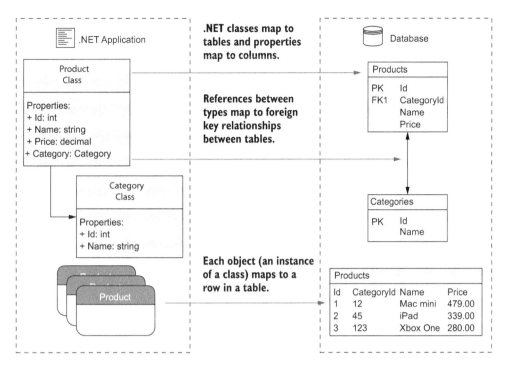

Figure 12.1   EF Core maps .NET classes and objects to database concepts such as tables and rows.

Postgres, and many other relational databases. It even has a cool in-memory feature you can use when testing to create a temporary database. EF Core uses a provider model, so that support for other relational databases can be plugged in later, as they become available.

NOTE   EF Core was designed to work with nonrelational, *NoSQL*, or *document* databases too but, at the time of writing, that feature hasn't yet been implemented.

That covers what EF Core is, but it doesn't dig into why you'd want to use it. Why not access the database directly using the traditional ADO.NET libraries? Most of the arguments for using EF Core can be applied to ORMs in general, so what are the advantages of an ORM?

12.1.2 *Why use an object-relational mapper?*

One of the biggest advantages an ORM brings is the speed with which you can develop an application. You can stay in the familiar territory of object-oriented .NET, in many cases without ever needing to directly manipulate a database or write custom SQL.

Imagine you have an e-commerce site and you want to load the details of a product from the database. Using low-level database access code, you'd have to open a connection to the database, write the necessary SQL using the correct table and column names, read the data over the connection, create a POCO to hold the data, and manually set the properties on the object, converting the data to the correct format as you go. Sounds painful, right?

An ORM, such as EF Core, takes care of most of this for you. It handles the connection to the database, generating the SQL, and mapping data back to your POCO objects. All you need to provide is a LINQ query describing the data you want to retrieve.

ORMs serve as high-level abstractions over databases, so they can significantly reduce the amount of plumbing code you need to write to interact with a database. At the most basic level, they take care of mapping SQL statements to objects and vice versa, but most ORMs take this a step further and provide a number of additional features.

ORMs like EF Core keep track of which properties have changed on any objects they rehydrate from the database. This lets you load an object from the database by mapping it from a database table, modify it in .NET code, and then ask the ORM to update the associated record in the database. The ORM will work out which properties have changed and issue update statements for the appropriate columns, saving you a bunch of work.

As is so often the case in software development, using an ORM has its drawbacks. One of the biggest advantages of ORMs is also their Achilles heel—they hide you from the database. Sometimes, this high level of abstraction can lead to problematic database query patterns in your apps. A classic example is the *N+1* problem, where what should be a single database request turns into separate requests for every single row in a database table.

Another commonly cited drawback is performance. ORMs are abstractions over a number of concepts, and so inherently do more work than if you were to hand craft every piece of data access in your app. Most ORMs, EF Core included, trade off some degree of performance for ease of development.

That said, if you're aware of the pitfalls of ORMs, you can often drastically simplify the code required to interact with a database. As with anything, if the abstraction works for you, use it, otherwise, don't. If you only have minimal database access requirements, or you need the best performance you can get, then an ORM such as EF Core may not be the right fit.

An alternative is to get the best of both worlds: use an ORM for the quick development of the bulk of your application, and then fall back to lower level APIs such as ADO.NET for those few areas that prove to be the bottlenecks in your application. That way, you can get good-enough performance with EF Core, trading off performance for development time, and only optimize those areas that need it.

Even if you do decide to use an ORM in your app, there are many different ORMs available for .NET, of which EF Core is one. Whether EF Core is right for you will depend on the features you need and the trade-offs you're willing to make to get them. The next section compares EF Core to Microsoft's other offering, Entity Framework, but there many other alternatives you could consider, such as Dapper and NHibernate, each with their own set of trade-offs.

12.1.3 *When should you choose EF Core?*

Microsoft designed EF Core as a reimagining of the mature Entity Framework 6.x (EF 6.x) ORM, which it released in 2008. With ten years of development behind it, EF 6.x is a stable and feature-rich ORM, though it runs on the full .NET Framework, not .NET Core.

In contrast, EF Core, like .NET Core and ASP.NET Core, is a relatively new project. The APIs of EF Core are designed to be close to that of EF 6.x—though they aren't identical—but the core components have been completely rewritten. You should consider EF Core as distinct from EF 6.x; upgrading directly from EF 6.x to EF Core is nontrivial.

Microsoft supports both EF Core and EF 6.x, and both will see ongoing improvements, so which should you choose? You need to consider a number of things:

- *Cross platform*—EF Core targets .NET Standard, so it can be used in cross-platform apps that target .NET Core. EF 6.x targets .NET Framework, so you're limited to Windows only.
- *Database providers*—Both EF 6.x and EF Core let you connect to various database types by using pluggable providers. EF Core has a growing number of providers, but there aren't as many for EF 6.x. If there isn't a provider for the database you're using, that's a bit of a deal breaker!
- *Performance*—The performance of EF 6.x has been a bit of a black mark on its record, so EF Core aims to rectify that. EF Core is designed to be fast and lightweight, significantly outperforming EF 6.x. But it's unlikely to ever reach the performance of a more lightweight ORM, such as Dapper, or handcrafted SQL statements.
- *Features*—Features are where you'll find the biggest disparity between EF 6.x and EF Core. EF Core has some features that EF 6.x doesn't have (batching statements, client-side key generation, in-memory database for testing), but EF 6.x is much more feature-rich than EF Core.

  At the time of writing, EF Core is missing some headline features, such as lazy-loading and full server-side Group By, but EF Core is under active development, so those features will no doubt appear soon.[1] For example, limited Group By

---

[1] For a detailed list of feature differences between EF 6.x and EF Core, see the documentation at https://docs.microsoft.com/en-us/ef/efcore-and-ef6/features.

support should be available in EF Core 2.1. In contrast, EF 6.x will likely only see incremental improvements and bug fixes, rather than major feature additions.

Whether these trade-offs and limitations are a problem for you will depend a lot on your specific app. It's a lot easier to start a new application bearing these limitations in mind than trying to work around them later.

> **WARNING**   EF Core isn't recommended for everyone. Be sure you understand the trade-offs involved, and keep an eye on the guidance from the EF team here: https://docs.microsoft.com/en-us/ef/efcore-and-ef6/choosing.

If you're working on a new ASP.NET Core application, you want to use an ORM for rapid development, and you don't require any of the unavailable features, then EF Core is a great contender. It's also supported out of the box by various other subsystems of ASP.NET Core. For instance, in chapter 14 you'll see how to use EF Core with the ASP.NET Core Identity authentication system for managing users in your apps.

Before we get into the nitty-gritty of using EF Core in your app, I'll describe the application we're going to be using as the case study for this chapter. We'll go over the application and database details and how to use EF Core to communicate between the two.

12.1.4 *Mapping a database to your application code*

EF Core focuses on the communication between an application and a database, so to show it off, we need an application! This chapter uses the example of a simple cooking app that lists recipes, and lets you view a recipe's ingredients, as shown in figure 12.2. Users can browse for recipes, add new ones, edit recipes, and delete old ones. This is obviously a simple application, but it contains all the database interactions you need with its two *entities*, Recipe and Ingredient.

> **DEFINITION**   An *entity* is a .NET class that's mapped by EF Core to the database. These are classes you define, typically as POCO classes that can be saved and loaded by mapping to database tables using EF Core.

When you interact with EF Core, you'll be primarily using POCO entities and a *database context* that inherits from the DbContext EF Core class. The entity classes are the object-oriented representations of the tables in your database; they represent the data you want to store in the database. You use the DbContext in your application to both configure EF Core and to access the database at runtime.

> **NOTE**   You can potentially have multiple DbContexts in your application and can even configure them to integrate with different databases.

When your application first uses EF Core, EF Core creates an internal representation of the database, based on the DbSet<T> properties on your application's DbContext and the entity classes themselves, as shown in figure 12.3.

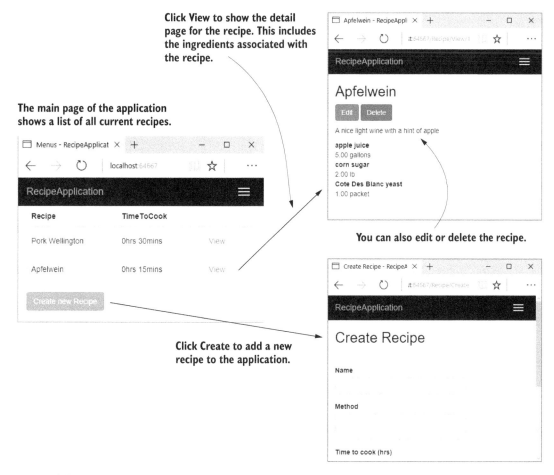

Click View to show the detail page for the recipe. This includes the ingredients associated with the recipe.

The main page of the application shows a list of all current recipes.

You can also edit or delete the recipe.

Click Create to add a new recipe to the application.

Figure 12.2   The cookery app lists recipes. You can view, update, and delete recipes, or create new ones.

For your recipe app, EF Core will build a model of the `Recipe` class because it's exposed on the `AppDbContext` as a `DbSet<Recipe>`. Furthermore, EF Core will loop through all the properties on `Recipe`, looking for types it doesn't know about, and add them to its internal model. In your app, the `Ingredients` collection on `Recipe` exposes the `Ingredient` entity as an `ICollection<Ingredient>`, so EF Core models the entity appropriately.

Each entity is mapped to a table in the database, but EF Core also maps the relationships between the entities. Each recipe can have *many* ingredients, but each ingredient (which has a name, quantity, and unit) belongs to *one* recipe, so this is a many-to-one relationship. EF Core uses that knowledge to correctly model the equivalent many-to-one database structure.

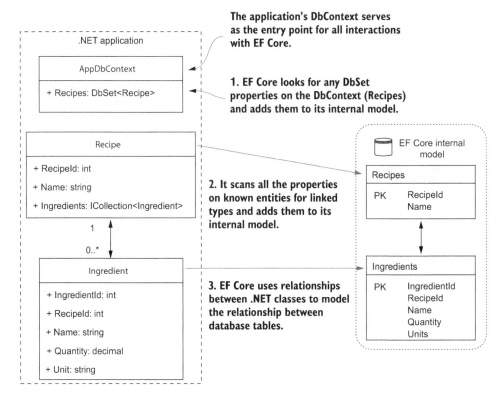

The application's DbContext serves as the entry point for all interactions with EF Core.

1. EF Core looks for any DbSet properties on the DbContext (Recipes) and adds them to its internal model.

2. It scans all the properties on known entities for linked types and adds them to its internal model.

3. EF Core uses relationships between .NET classes to model the relationship between database tables.

Figure 12.3   EF Core creates an internal model of your application's data model by exploring the types in your code. It adds all of the types referenced in the `DbSet<>` **properties on your app's** `DbContext`**, and any linked types.**

NOTE Two different recipes, say fish pie and lemon chicken, may use an ingredient that has both the same name and quantity, for example the juice of one lemon, but they're fundamentally two different instances. If you update the lemon chicken recipe to use two lemons, you wouldn't want this change to automatically update the fish pie to use two lemons too!

EF Core uses the internal model it builds when interacting with the database. This ensures it builds the correct SQL to create, read, update, and delete entities.

Right, it's about time for some code! In the next section, you'll start building the recipe app. You'll see how to add EF Core to an ASP.NET Core application, configure a database provider, and design your application's data model.

12.2   Adding EF Core to an application

In this section, we're going to focus on getting EF Core installed and configured in your ASP.NET Core recipe app. As we're talking about EF Core in this chapter, I'm

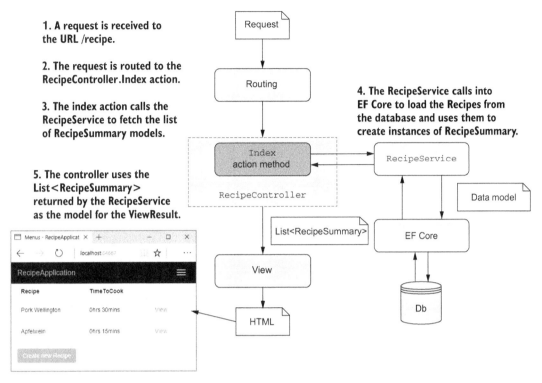

1. A request is received to the URL /recipe.

2. The request is routed to the RecipeController.Index action.

3. The index action calls the RecipeService to fetch the list of RecipeSummary models.

4. The RecipeService calls into EF Core to load the Recipes from the database and uses them to create instances of RecipeSummary.

5. The controller uses the List<RecipeSummary> returned by the RecipeService as the model for the ViewResult.

Figure 12.4 Handling a request by loading data from a database using EF Core. Interaction with EF Core is restricted to `RecipeService` only—the MVC controller doesn't access EF Core directly.

not going to go into how to create the application in general—I created a simple MVC app using Razor to render the HTML, nothing fancy.

Interaction with EF Core occurs in a service layer that encapsulates all of the data access outside of the MVC framework, as shown in figure 12.4. This keeps your concerns separated and makes both your services and MVC controllers testable.

Adding EF Core to an application is a multistep process:

1. Choose a database provider; for example, MySQL, Postgres, or MS SQL Server.
2. Install the EF Core NuGet packages.
3. Design your app's DbContext and entities that make up your data model.
4. Register your app's DbContext with the ASP.NET Core DI container.
5. Use EF Core to generate a *migration* describing your data model.
6. Apply the migration to the database to update the database's schema.

This might seem a little daunting already, but we'll walk through steps 1–4 in this section, and steps 5–6 in section 12.3, so it won't take long. Given the space constraints of this chapter, I'm going to be sticking to the default conventions of EF Core in the code I show. EF Core is far more customizable than it may initially appear, but I encourage you to stick to the defaults wherever possible. It will make your life easier in the long run!

The first step in setting up EF Core is to decide which database you'd like to interact with. It's likely that a client or your company's policy will dictate this to you, but it's still worth giving the choice some thought.

12.2.1 *Choosing a database provider and installing EF Core*

EF Core supports a range of databases by using a provider model. The modular nature of EF Core means you can use the same high-level API to program against different underlying databases, and EF Core knows how to generate the necessary implementation-specific code and SQL statements.

You probably already have a database in mind when you start your application, and you'll be pleased to know that EF Core has got most of the popular ones covered. Adding support for a particular database involves adding the correct NuGet package to your csproj file. For example

- *PostgreSQL*—Npgsql.EntityFrameworkCore.PostgreSQL
- *Microsoft SQL Server*—Microsoft.EntityFrameworkCore.SqlServer
- *MySQL*—MySql.Data.EntityFrameworkCore
- *SQLite*—Microsoft.EntityFrameworkCore.SQLite

Some of the database provider packages are maintained by Microsoft, some are maintained by the open source community, and some may require a paid license (for example, the Oracle provider, so be sure to check your requirements. You can find a list of providers here at https://docs.microsoft.com/en-us/ ef/core/providers/.

You install a database provider into your application in the same way as any other library: by adding a NuGet package to your project's csproj file and running `dotnet restore` from the command line (or letting Visual Studio automatically restore for you).

EF Core is inherently modular, so you'll want to install four different packages. I'm using the SQL Server database provider with LocalDB for the recipe app, so I'll be using the SQL Server packages.

- *Microsoft.EntityFrameworkCore.SqlServer*—This is the main database provider package for using EF Core at runtime. It also contains a reference to the main EF Core NuGet package.
- *Microsoft.EntityFrameworkCore.Design*—This contains shared design-time components for EF Core.
- *Microsoft.EntityFrameworkCore.SqlServer.Design*—More design-time components for EF Core, this time specific to Microsoft SQL Server.
- *Microsoft.EntityFrameworkCore.Tools.DotNet*—This package is optional, but you'll use it later on to create and update your database from the command line.

> **TIP**   ASP.NET Core 2.0 includes the EF Core libraries as part of the framework-provided Microsoft.AspNetCore.All package. If you reference this in your csproj

file, you won't need to explicitly include the default EF Core NuGet libraries. But there's no harm if you do! You'll still need to add the Microsoft.EntityFrameworkCore.Tools.DotNet tooling package to use the EF Core .NET CLI commands, unless you're using ASP.NET Core 2.1. ASP.NET Core 2.1 automatically installs the tooling packages globally, so you don't need to install them in your project.

Listing 12.1 shows the recipe app's csproj after adding the EF Core libraries. I'm going to be building a .NET Core 2.0 app, so the only package I need to add is the tooling package. Remember, you add NuGet packages as `PackageReference` elements, and tool packages as `DotNetCliToolReference` elements.

> **Listing 12.1 Installing EF Core into an ASP.NET Core 1.1 application**

```
<Project Sdk="Microsoft.NET.Sdk.Web">

  <PropertyGroup>
    <TargetFramework>netcoreapp2.0</TargetFramework>       ◁
  </PropertyGroup>

  <ItemGroup>
    <PackageReference
        Include="Microsoft.AspNetCore.All" Version="2.0.0 " />
  </ItemGroup>

  <ItemGroup>
    <DotNetCliToolReference
      Include="Microsoft.VisualStudio.Web.CodeGeneration.Tools"
      Version="2.0.0 " />
    <DotNetCliToolReference
      Include="Microsoft.EntityFrameworkCore.Tools.DotNet"
      Version="2.0.0" />
  </ItemGroup>

</Project>
```

The app targets .NET Core 2.0.

Default ASP.NET Core metapackage and tools for creating base MVC app

Tools for creating migrations and managing the database using the .NET CLI

With these packages installed and restored, you have everything you need to start building the data model for your application. In the next section, we'll create the entity classes and the `DbContext` for your recipe app.

12.2.2 Building a data model

In section 12.1.4, I showed an overview of how EF Core builds up its internal model of your database from the `DbContext` and entity models. Apart from this discovery mechanism, EF Core is pretty flexible in letting you define your entities the way *you* want to, as POCO classes.

Some ORMs require your entities to inherit from a specific base class or decorate your models with attributes to describe how to map them. EF Core heavily favors a convention over configuration approach, as you can see in this listing, which shows the `Recipe` and `Ingredient` entity classes for your app.

Listing 12.2   Defining the EF Core entity classes

```
public class Recipe
{
    public int RecipeId { get; set; }
    public string Name { get; set; }
    public TimeSpan TimeToCook { get; set; }
    public bool IsDeleted { get; set; }
    public string Method { get; set; }

    public ICollection<Ingredient> Ingredients { get; set; }    ⊲
}
public class Ingredient
{
    public int IngredientId { get; set; }
    public int RecipeId { get; set; }
    public string Name { get; set; }
    public decimal Quantity { get; set; }
    public string Unit { get; set; }
}
```

A Recipe can have many Ingredients, represented by ICollection.

These classes conform to certain default conventions that EF Core uses to build up a picture of the database it's mapping. For example, the `Recipe` class has a `RecipeId` property and the `Ingredient` class has an `IngredientId` property. EF Core identifies this pattern of `TId` as indicating the *primary key* of the table.

> **DEFINITION**   The *primary key* of a table is a value that uniquely identifies the row among all the others in the table. It's often an `int` or a `Guid`.

Another convention visible here is the `RecipeId` property on the `Ingredient` class. EF Core interprets this to be a *foreign key* pointing to the `Recipe` class. When considered with `ICollection<Ingredient>` on the `Recipe` class, this represents a many-to-one relationship, where each recipe has many ingredients, but each ingredient only belongs to a single recipe, as shown in figure 12.5.

> **DEFINITION**   A *foreign key* on a table points to the primary key of a different table, forming a link between the two rows.

Many other conventions are at play here, such as the names EF Core will assume for the database tables and columns, or the database column types it will use for each property, but I'm not going to discuss them here. The EF Core documentation contains details about all of the conventions, as well as how to customize them for your application: https://docs.microsoft.com/en-us/ef/core/modeling/relational/.

> **TIP**   You can also use `DataAnnotations` attributes to decorate your entity classes, controlling things like column naming or `string` length. EF Core will use these attributes to override the default conventions.

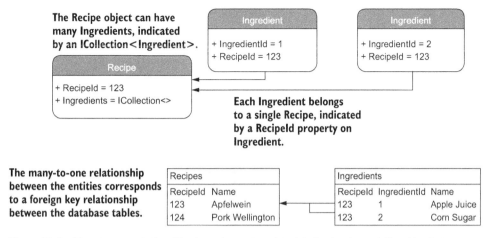

Figure 12.5 Many-to-one relationships in code are translated to foreign key relationships between tables.

As well as the entities, you also define the `DbContext` for your application. This is the heart of EF Core in your application, used for all your database calls. Create a custom `DbContext`, in this case called `AppDbContext`, and derive from the `DbContext` base class, as shown next. This exposes the `DbSet<Recipe>` so EF Core can discover and map the `Recipe` entity. You can expose multiple instances of `DbSet<>` in this way.

Listing 12.3 Defining the application `DbContext`

```
public class AppDbContext : DbContext
{
    public AppDbContext(DbContextOptions<AppDbContext> options)
        : base(options) { }

    public DbSet<Recipe> Recipes { get; set; }
}
```

The constructor options object, containing details such as the connection string

You'll use the Recipes property to query the database.

The `AppDbContext` for your app is simple, containing a list of your root entities, but you can do a lot more with it in a more complex application. If you wanted, you could completely customize how EF Core maps entities to the database, but for this app you're going to use the defaults.

> **NOTE** You didn't list `Ingredient` on `AppDbContext`, but it will be modeled by EF Core as it's exposed on the `Recipe`. You can still access the `Ingredient` objects in the database, but you have to go *via* the `Recipe` entity's `Ingredients` property to do so, as you'll see in section 12.4.

For this simple example, your data model consists of these three classes: `AppDb-Context`, `Recipe`, and `Ingredient`. The two entities will be mapped to tables and their columns to properties, and you'll use the `AppDbContext` to access them.

> **NOTE** This *code first* approach is typical, but if you have an existing database, you can automatically generate the EF entities and `DbContext` instead. (More information can be found at http://mng.bz/Ymtw.)

The data model is complete, but you're not quite ready to use it yet. Your ASP.NET Core app doesn't know how to create your `AppDbContext`, and your `AppDbContext` needs a connection string so that it can talk to the database. In the next section, we'll tackle both of these issues, and will finish setting up EF Core in your ASP.NET Core app.

12.2.3 Registering a data context

Like any other service in ASP.Net Core, you should register your `AppDbContext` with the DI container. When registering your context, you also configure a database provider and set the connection string, so EF Core knows how to talk with the database.

You register the `AppDbContext` in the `ConfigureServices` method of Startup.cs. EF Core provides a generic `AddDbContext<T>` extension method for this purpose, which takes a configuration function for a `DbContextOptionsBuilder` instance. This builder can be used to set a host of internal properties of EF Core and lets you completely replace the internal services of EF Core if you want.

The configuration for your app is, again, nice and simple, as you can see in the following listing. You set the database provider with the `UseSqlServer` extension method, made available by the Microsoft.EntityFrameworkCore.SqlServer package, and pass it a connection string.

> **Listing 12.4 Registering a `DbContext` with the DI container**

```
public void ConfigureServices(IServiceCollection services)
{
    var connString = Configuration
        .GetConnectionString("DefaultConnection");

    services.AddDbContext<AppDbContext>(
        options => options.UseSqlServer(connString));

    // Add other services.
}
```

The connection string is taken from configuration, from the ConnectionStrings section.

Specify the database provider in the customization options for the DbContext.

Register your app's DbContext by using it as the generic parameter.

> **NOTE** If you're using a different database provider, for example a provider for PostgreSQL, you will need to call the appropriate `Use*` method on the `options` object when registering your `AppDbContext`.

The connection string is a typical secret as I discussed in the previous chapter, so loading it from configuration makes sense. At runtime, the correct configuration string for your current environment will be used, so you can use different databases when developing locally and in production.

> **TIP** You can configure your `AppDbContext` in other ways and provide the connection string, such as with the `OnConfiguring` method, but I recommend the method shown here for ASP.NET Core websites.

You now have a `DbContext`, `AppDbContext`, registered with the DI container, and a data model corresponding to your database. Code-wise, you're ready to start using EF Core, but the one thing you *don't* have is a database! In the next section, you'll see how you can easily use the .NET CLI to ensure your database stays up to date with your EF Core data model.

12.3 *Managing changes with migrations*

Managing *schema* changes for databases, such as when you need to add a new table or a new column, is notoriously difficult. Your application code is explicitly tied to a particular *version* of a database, and you need to make sure the two are always in sync.

> **DEFINITION** *Schema* refers to how the data is organized in a database, including, among others, the tables, columns, and the relationships between them.

When you deploy an app, you can normally delete the old code/executable and replace it with the new code—job done. If you need to roll back a change, delete that new code and deploy an old version of the app.

The difficulty with databases is that they contain data! That means that blowing it away and creating a new database with every deployment isn't possible.

A common best practice is to explicitly version a database's schema in addition to your application's code. You can do this in a number of ways but, typically, you need to store a diff between the previous schema of the database and the new schema, often as a SQL script. You can then use libraries such as DbUp and FluentMigrator[1] to keep track of which scripts have been applied and ensure your database schema is up to date. Alternatively, you can use external tools that manage this for you.

EF Core provides its own version of schema management called *migrations*. Migrations provide a way to manage changes to a database schema when your EF Core data model changes. A migration is a C# code file in your application that defines how the data model changed—which columns were added, new entities, and so on. Migrations provide a record over time of how your database schema evolved as part of your application, so the schema is always in sync with your app's data model.

You can use command-line tools to create a new database from the migrations, or to update an existing database by *applying* new migrations to it. You can even rollback a migration, which will update a database to a previous schema.

---

[1] DbUp and FluentMigrator are open source projects, available at https://github.com/fluentmigrator/fluentmigrator and https://github.com/DbUp/DbUp, respectively.

WARNING   Applying migrations modifies the database, so you always have to be aware of data loss. If you remove a table from the database using a migration and then rollback the migration, the table will be recreated, but the data it previously contained will be gone forever!

In this section, you'll see how to create your first migration and use it to create a database. You'll then update your data model, create a second migration, and use it to update the database schema.

12.3.1 *Creating your first migration*

Before you can create migrations, you'll need to install the necessary tooling. There are two primary ways to do this:

- *Package manager console*—Provides a number of PowerShell cmdlets for use inside Visual Studio's Package Manager Console (PMC). You can install them directly from the PMC or by adding the Microsoft.EntityFrameworkCore.Tools package to your project. They're also included as part of the Microsoft.AspNet-Core.All metapackage.
- *.NET CLI*—Cross-platform tooling that you can run from the command line. You can install these by adding the Microsoft.EntityFrameworkCore.Tools.Dot-Net package to your project, as you did in listing 12.4.

In this book, I'll be using the cross-platform .NET CLI tools, but if you're familiar with EF 6.X or prefer to use the Visual Studio PMC, then there are equivalent commands for all of the steps you're going to take.[1] You've already installed the .NET CLI tools by adding the package to your csproj. You can check they installed correctly by running `dotnet ef --help`. This should produce a help screen like the one shown in figure 12.6.

TIP   If you get the *No executable found matching command "dotnet-ef"* message when running the preceding command, make sure you have restored packages and check the folder you're executing from. You need to run the `dotnet ef` tools from the *project* folder in which you have registered your `AppDbContext`, not at the solution-folder level.

With the tools installed, you can create your first migration by running the following command and providing a name for the migration—in this case, `"InitialSchema"`:

```
dotnet ef migrations add InitialSchema
```

This command creates three files in your solution:

- *Migration file*—A file with the Timestamp_MigrationName.cs format. This describes the actions to take on the database, such as Create table or Add column.
- *Migration designer.cs file*—This file describes EF Core's internal model of your data model at the point in time the migration was generated.

---

[1]   Documentation for PowerShell cmdlets can be found at http://mng.bz/lm6J.

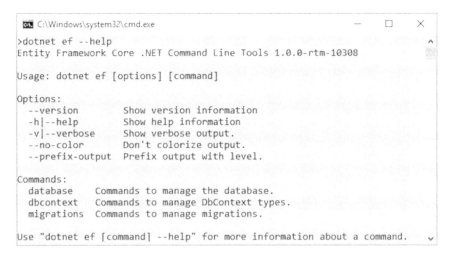

Figure 12.6 Running the `dotnet ef --help` command to check the .NET CLI EF Core tools are installed correctly.

- *AppDbContextModelSnapshot.cs*—This describes EF Core's *current* internal model. This will be updated when you add another migration, so it should always be the same as the current, latest migration.

  EF Core can use AppDbContextModelSnapshot.cs to determine a database's previous state when creating a new migration, without interacting with the database directly.

These three files encapsulate the migration process but adding a migration doesn't update anything in the database itself. For that, you must run a different command to apply the migration to the database.

> **TIP** You can, and should, look inside the migration file EF Core generates to check what it will do to your database before running the following commands. Better safe than sorry!

You can apply migrations in one of three ways:

- Using the .NET CLI
- Using the Visual Studio PowerShell cmdlets
- In code, by obtaining an instance of your `AppDbContext` and calling `context.Database.Migrate()`.

Which is best for you is a matter of how you've designed your application, how you'll update your production database, and your personal preference. I'll use the .NET CLI for now, but I'll discuss some of these considerations in section 12.5.

You can apply migrations to a database by running

```
dotnet ef database update
```

from the project folder of your application. I won't go into the details of how this works, but this command performs four steps:

1 Builds your application.
2 Loads the services configured in your app's Startup class, including AppDb-Context.
3 Checks whether the database in the AppDbContext connection string exists. If not, creates it.
4 Updates the database by applying any unapplied migrations.

If everything is configured correctly, as I showed in section 12.2, then running this command will set you up with a shiny new database, such as the one shown in figure 12.7!

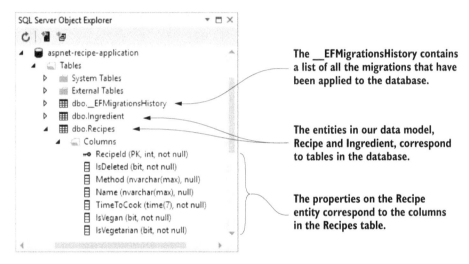

Figure 12.7 Applying migrations to a database will create the database if it doesn't exist and update the database to match EF Core's internal data model. The list of applied migrations is stored in the __EFMigrationsHistory table.

When you apply the migrations to the database, EF Core creates the necessary tables in the database and adds the appropriate columns and keys. You may have also noticed the __EFMigrationsHistory table. EF Core uses this to store the names of migrations that it's applied to the database. Next time you run dotnet ef database update, EF Core can compare this table to the list of migrations in your app and will apply only the new ones to your database.

In the next section, we'll look at how this makes it easy to change your data model, and update the database schema, without having to recreate the database from scratch.

12.3.2 Adding a second migration

Most applications inevitably evolve, whether due to increased scope or simple maintenance. Adding properties to your entities, adding new entities entirely, and removing obsolete classes—all are likely.

EF Core migrations make this simple. Change your entities to your desired state, generate a migration, and apply it to the database, as shown in figure 12.8. Imagine you decide that you'd like to highlight vegetarian and vegan dishes in your recipe app by exposing `IsVegetarian` and `IsVegan` properties on the `Recipe` entity.

Listing 12.5 Adding properties to the `Recipe` entity

```
public class Recipe
{
    public int RecipeId { get; set; }
    public string Name { get; set; }
    public TimeSpan TimeToCook { get; set; }
    public bool IsDeleted { get; set; }
    public string Method { get; set; }
    public bool IsVegetarian { get; set; }
    public bool IsVegan { get; set; }

    public ICollection<Ingredient> Ingredients { get; set; }
}
```

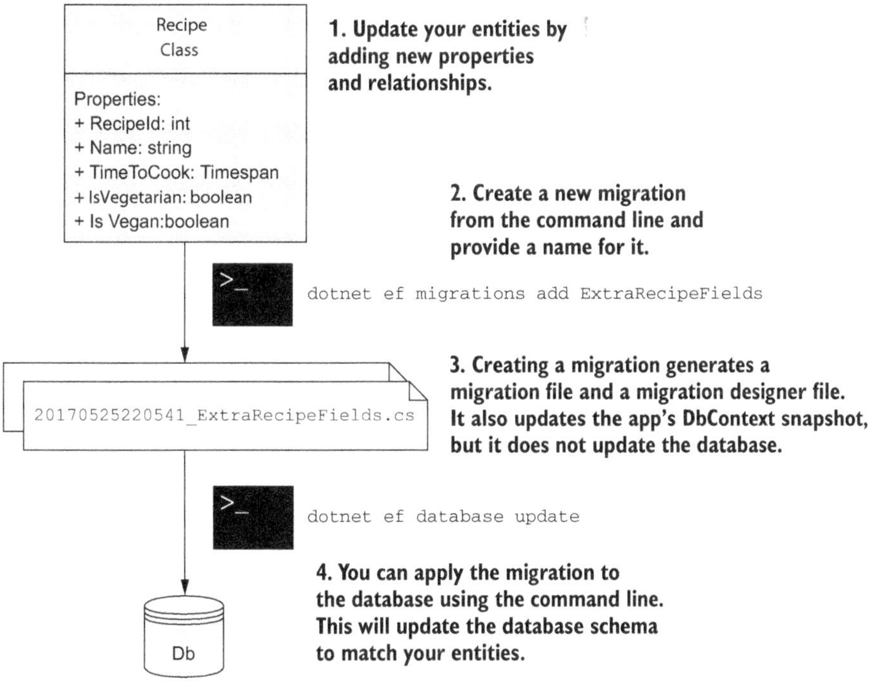

Recipe
Class

Properties:
+ RecipeId: int
+ Name: string
+ TimeToCook: Timespan
+ IsVegetarian: boolean
+ Is Vegan:boolean

1. Update your entities by adding new properties and relationships.

2. Create a new migration from the command line and provide a name for it.

```
dotnet ef migrations add ExtraRecipeFields
```

20170525220541_ExtraRecipeFields.cs

3. Creating a migration generates a migration file and a migration designer file. It also updates the app's DbContext snapshot, but it does not update the database.

```
dotnet ef database update
```

Db

4. You can apply the migration to the database using the command line. This will update the database schema to match your entities.

Figure 12.8 Creating a second migration and applying it to the database using the command-line tools.

After changing your entities, you need to update EF Core's internal representation of your data model. You do this in the exact same way as for the first migration, by calling `dotnet ef migrations add` and providing a name for the migration:

```
dotnet ef migrations add ExtraRecipeFields
```

This creates a second migration in your project by adding the migration file and its .designer.cs snapshot file and updating AppDbContextModelSnapshot.cs, as shown in figure 12.9.

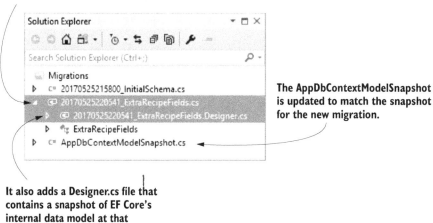

Creating a migration adds a cs file to your solution with a timestamp and the name you gave the migration.

The AppDbContextModelSnapshot is updated to match the snapshot for the new migration.

It also adds a Designer.cs file that contains a snapshot of EF Core's internal data model at that point in time.

Figure 12.9 Adding a second migration adds a new migration file and a migration Designer.cs file. It also updates AppDbContextModelSnapshot to match the new migration's Designer.cs file.

As before, this creates the migration's files, but it doesn't modify the database. You can apply the migration, and update the database, by running

```
dotnet ef database update
```

This compares the migrations in your application to the __EFMigrationsHistory table on your database to see which migrations are outstanding and then runs them. EF Core will run the 20170525220541_ExtraRecipeFields migration, adding the `IsVegetarian` and `IsVegan` fields to the database, as shown in figure 12.10.

Using migrations is a great way to ensure your database is versioned along with your app code in source control. You can easily check out your app's source code for a historical point in time and recreate the database schema that your application used at that point.

Migrations are easy to use when you're working alone, or when you're deploying to a single web server, but even in these cases, there are important things to consider

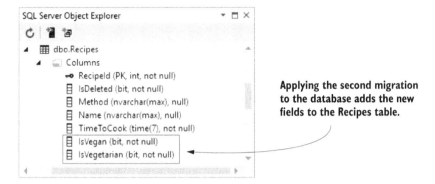

Figure 12.10　Applying the **ExtraRecipeFields** migration to the database adds the
IsVegetarian and **IsVegan** fields to the Recipes table.

when deciding how to manage your databases. For apps with multiple web servers
using a shared database, or for containerized applications, you have even more things
to think about.

This book is about ASP.NET Core, not EF Core, so I don't want to dwell on database management too much, but section 12.5 points out some of the things you need
to bear in mind when using migrations in production.

In the next section, we'll get back to the meaty stuff—defining our business logic
and performing CRUD operations on the database.

12.4　*Querying data from and saving data to the database*

Let's review where you are in creating the recipe application:

- You created a simple data model for the application, consisting of recipes and
  ingredients.
- You generated migrations for the data model, to update EF Core's internal
  model of your entities.
- You applied the migrations to the database, so its schema matches EF Core's
  model.

In this section, you'll build the business logic for your application by creating a
RecipeService. This will handle querying the database for recipes, creating new recipes, and modifying existing ones. As this app only has a simple domain, I'll be using
RecipeService to handle all of the requirements, but in your own apps you may have
multiple services that cooperate to provide the business logic.

> **NOTE**　For simple apps, you may be tempted to move this logic into your MVC
> Controllers. I'd encourage you to resist this urge; extracting your business
> logic to other services decouples the HTTP-centric nature of MVC from the
> underlying business logic. This will often make your business logic easier to
> test and more reusable.

Our database doesn't have any data in it yet, so we'd better start by letting you create a
recipe!

12.4.1 Creating a record

In this section, you're going to build the functionality to let users create a recipe in the app. This will primarily consist of a form that the user can use to enter all the details of the recipe using Razor Tag Helpers, which you learned about in chapters 7 and 8. This form is posted to the CreateRecipe action on RecipeController, which uses model binding and validation attributes to confirm the request is valid, as you saw in chapter 6.

If the request is valid, the action method calls RecipeService to create the new Recipe object in the database. As EF Core is the topic of this chapter, I'm going to focus on this service alone, but you can always check out the source code for this book if you want to see how the MVC controller and Razor templates fit together.

The business logic for creating a recipe in this application is simple—there *is* no logic! Map the *command* binding model provided by the controller to a Recipe entity and its Ingredients, add the Recipe object to AppDbContext, and save that in the database, as shown in figure 12.11.

> **WARNING**   Many simple, equivalent, sample applications using EF or EF Core allow you to bind directly to the Recipe entity as the view model for your MVC actions. Unfortunately, this exposes a security vulnerability known as overposting and is a bad practice. If you want to avoid the boilerplate mapping code in your applications, consider using a library such as AutoMapper (http://automapper.org/).

Creating an entity in EF Core involves adding a new row to the mapped table. For your application, whenever you create a new Recipe, you also add the linked Ingredient entities. EF Core takes care of linking these all correctly by creating the correct RecipeId for each Ingredient in the database.

The bulk of the code required for this example involves translating from Create-RecipeCommand to the Recipe entity—the interaction with the AppDbContext consists of only two methods: Add() and SaveChanges().

Listing 12.6   Creating a `Recipe` entity in the database

```
                                          An instance of the AppDbContext is
                                          injected in the class constructor using DI.
readonly AppDbContext _context;      ◁─┘

public int CreateRecipe(CreateRecipeCommand cmd)
{
    var recipe = new Recipe
    {
        Name = cmd.Name,
        TimeToCook = new TimeSpan(
            cmd.TimeToCookHrs, cmd.TimeToCookMins, 0),
        Method = cmd.Method,
        IsVegetarian = cmd.IsVegetarian,
        IsVegan = cmd.IsVegan,
        Ingredients = cmd.Ingredients?.Select(i =>
```

CreateRecipeCommand is passed in from the action method.

Create a Recipe by mapping from the command object to the Recipe entity.

```
new Ingredient
{
    Name = i.Name,
    Quantity = i.Quantity,
    Unit = i.Unit,
}).ToList()
};
_context.Add(recipe);
_context.SaveChanges();

return recipe.RecipeId;
}
```

Map each
CreateIngredientCommand
onto an **Ingredient** entity.

Tell **EF Core** to track the new entities.

Tell **EF Core** to write the
entities to the database.

EF Core populates the **RecipeId** field on
your new **Recipe** when it's saved.

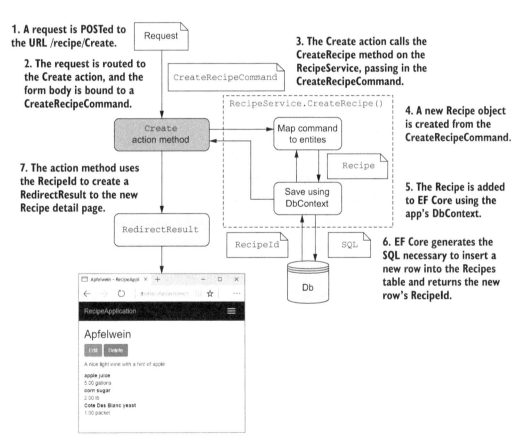

**1. A request is POSTed to
the URL /recipe/Create.**

**2. The request is routed to
the Create action, and the
form body is bound to a
CreateRecipeCommand.**

**3. The Create action calls the
CreateRecipe method on the
RecipeService, passing in the
CreateRecipeCommand.**

**4. A new Recipe object
is created from the
CreateRecipeCommand.**

**7. The action method uses
the RecipeId to create a
RedirectResult to the new
Recipe detail page.**

**5. The Recipe is added
to EF Core using the
app's DbContext.**

**6. EF Core generates the
SQL necessary to insert a
new row into the Recipes
table and returns the new
row's RecipeId.**

Figure 12.11 Calling the `Create` action method and creating a new entity. A `Recipe` is created from the
`CreateRecipeCommand` and is added to the `DbContext`. EF Core generates the SQL to add a new row
to the Recipes table in the database.

All interactions with EF Core and the database start with an instance of `AppDbContext`, which is typically DI injected via the constructor. Creating a new entity requires three steps:

1. Create the `Recipe` and `Ingredient` entities.
2. Add the entities to EF Core's list of tracked entities using `_context.Add` `(entity)`.
3. Execute the SQL `INSERT` statements against the database, adding the necessary rows to the `Recipe` and `Ingredient` tables, by calling `_context.SaveChanges()`.

If there's a problem when EF Core tries to interact with your database—you haven't run the migrations to update the database schema, for example—it will throw an exception. I haven't shown it here, but it's important to handle these in your application so you're not presenting users with an ugly error page when things go wrong.

Assuming all goes well, EF Core updates all the auto-generated IDs of your entities (`RecipeId` on `Recipe`, and both `RecipeId` and `IngredientId` on `Ingredient`). Return this ID to the MVC controller so it can use it, for example, to redirect to the View Recipe page.

And there you have it—you've created your first entity using EF Core. In the next section, we'll look at loading these entities from the database so you can view them in a list.

12.4.2 Loading a list of records

Now that you can create recipes, you need to write the code to view them. Luckily, loading data is simple in EF Core, relying heavily on LINQ methods to control which fields you need. For your app, you'll create a method on `RecipeService` that returns a summary view of a recipe, consisting of the `RecipeId`, `Name`, and `TimeToCook` as a `RecipeSummaryViewModel`, as shown in figure 12.12.

> **NOTE** Creating a view model is technically a UI concern rather than a business logic concern. I'm returning them directly from `RecipeService` here mostly to hammer home that you shouldn't be using EF Core entities directly in your action methods.

The `GetRecipes` method in `RecipeService` is conceptually simple and follows a common pattern for querying an EF Core database, as shown in figure 12.13.

EF Core uses a fluent chain of LINQ commands to define the query to return on the database. The `DbSet<Recipe>` property on `AppDataContext` is an `IQueryable`, so you can use all the usual `Select()` and `Where()` clauses that you would with other `IQueryable` providers. EF Core will convert these into a SQL statement to query the database with when you call an *execute* function such as `ToList()`, `ToArray()`, or `Single()`.

You can also use the `Select()` extension method to map to objects other than your entities as part of the SQL query. You can use this to efficiently query the database by only fetching the columns you need.

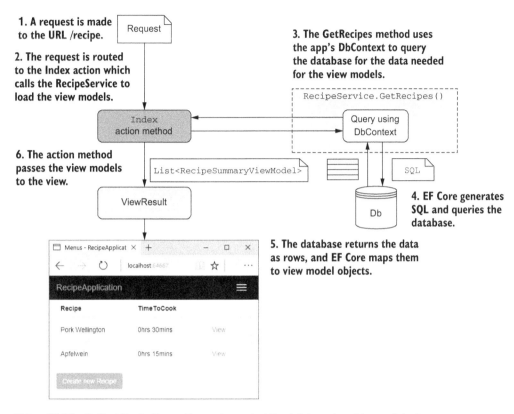

1. A request is made to the URL /recipe.

2. The request is routed to the Index action which calls the RecipeService to load the view models.

3. The GetRecipes method uses the app's DbContext to query the database for the data needed for the view models.

6. The action method passes the view models to the view.

4. EF Core generates SQL and queries the database.

5. The database returns the data as rows, and EF Core maps them to view model objects.

Figure 12.12 Calling the `Index` action and querying the database to retrieve a list of `RecipeSummaryViewModels`. EF Core generates the SQL to retrieve the necessary fields from the database and maps them to view model objects.

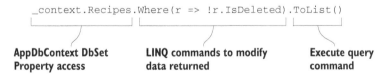

Figure 12.13 The three parts of an EF Core database query.

Listing 12.7 shows the code to fetch a list of `RecipeSummaryViewModels`, following the same basic pattern as in figure 12.12. It uses a `Where` LINQ expression to filter out recipes marked as deleted, and a `Select` clause to map to the view models. The `ToList()` command instructs EF Core to generate the SQL query, execute it on the database, and build `RecipeSummaryViewModel` from the data returned.

Listing 12.7   Loading a list of items using EF Core

```
public ICollection<RecipeSummaryViewModel> GetRecipes()
{
    return _context.Recipes     ◁─────────────────────────── A query starts from
        .Where(r => !r.IsDeleted)                              a DbSet property
        .Select(r => new RecipeSummaryViewModel                EF Core will only
        {                                                      query the Recipe
            Id = r.RecipeId,                                   columns it needs to
            Name = r.Name,                                     map the view model
            TimeToCook = "{r.TimeToCook.TotalMinutes}mins"     correctly
        })
        .ToList();   ◁──────────  This executes the SQL query and
}                                 creates the final view models.
```

Notice that in the `Select` method, you convert the `TimeToCook` property from a `Time-Span` to a `string` using string interpolation:

```
TimeToCook = $"{x.TimeToCook.TotalMinutes}mins"
```

I said before that EF Core converts the series of LINQ expressions into SQL, but that's only a half-truth; EF Core can't or doesn't know how to convert some expressions to SQL. For those cases, such as in this example, EF Core finds the fields from the DB that it needs in order to run the expression on the client side, selects those from the database, and then runs the expression in C# afterwards. This lets you combine the power and performance of database-side evaluation without compromising the functionality of C#.

> **WARNING**   Client-side evaluation is both powerful and useful but has the potential to cause issues. For certain queries, you could end up pulling back all the data from the database and processing it in memory, instead of in the database.

At this point, you have a list of records, displaying a summary of the recipe's data, so the obvious next step is to load the detail for a single record.

12.4.3   *Loading a single record*

For most intents and purposes, loading a single record is the same as loading a list of records. They share the same common structure you saw in figure 12.13, but when loading a single record, you'll typically use a `Where` clause and execute a command that restricts the data to a single entity.

Listing 12.8 shows the code to fetch a recipe by ID following the same basic pattern as before (figure 12.12). It uses a `Where()` LINQ expression to restrict the query to a single recipe, where `RecipeId == id`, and a `Select` clause to map to `RecipeDetail-ViewModel`. The `SingleOrDefault()` clause will cause EF Core to generate the SQL query, execute it on the database, and build the view model.

NOTE SingleOrDefault() will throw an exception if the previous Where clause returns more than one record. If you're loading a single record by ID, you can use the EF Core-specific Find method instead, which has some performance benefits when used.

Listing 12.8 Loading a single item using EF Core

**The id of the recipe to load
is passed as a parameter.**

**As before, a query starts
from a DbSet property.**

**Limit the query to
the recipe with the
provided id.**

```
public RecipeDetailViewModel GetRecipeDetail(int id)
{
    return _context.Recipes
        .Where(x => x.RecipeId == id)
        .Select(x => new RecipeDetailViewModel
        {
            Id = x.RecipeId,
            Name = x.Name,
            Method = x.Method,
            Ingredients = x.Ingredients
            .Select(item => new RecipeDetailViewModel.Item
            {
                Name = item.Name,
                Quantity = $"{item.Quantity} {item.Unit}"
            })
        })
        .SingleOrDefault();
}
```

**Map the Recipe to a
RecipeDetailViewModel.**

**Load and map linked
Ingredients as part of
the same query.**

**Execute the query and map
the data to the view model.**

Notice that, as well as mapping the Recipe to a RecipeDetailViewModel, you also map the related Ingredients for a Recipe, as though you're working with the objects directly in memory. This is one of the advantages of using an ORM—you can easily map child objects and let EF Core decide how best to build the underlying queries to fetch the data.

NOTE EF Core logs all the SQL statements it runs as LogLevel.Information events by default, so you can easily see what queries are being run against the database.

Our app is definitely shaping up; you can create new recipes, view them all in a list, and drill down to view individual recipes with their ingredients and method. Pretty soon though, someone's going to introduce a typo and want to change their model. To do this, you'll have to implement the *U* in CRUD: update.

12.4.4 *Updating a model with changes*

Updating entities when they have changed is generally the hardest part of CRUD operations, as there are so many variables. Figure 12.14 gives an overview of this process as it applies to your recipe app.

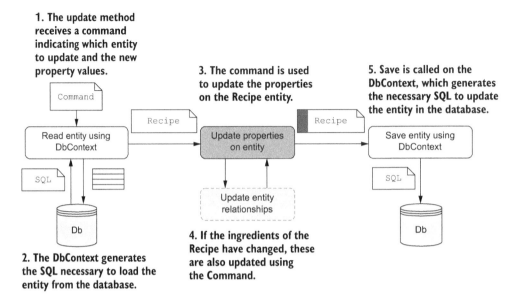

1. The update method receives a command indicating which entity to update and the new property values.

3. The command is used to update the properties on the Recipe entity.

5. Save is called on the DbContext, which generates the necessary SQL to update the entity in the database.

2. The DbContext generates the SQL necessary to load the entity from the database.

4. If the ingredients of the Recipe have changed, these are also updated using the Command.

Figure 12.14 **Updating an entity involves three steps: read the entity using EF Core, update the properties of the entity, and call** SaveChanges() **on the** DbContext **to generate the SQL to update the correct rows in the database.**

I'm not going to handle the relationship aspect in this book because that's generally a complex problem, and how you tackle it depends on the specifics of your data model. Instead, I'll focus on updating properties on the Recipe entity itself.[1]

For web applications, when you update an entity, you'll typically follow the steps outlined in Figure 12.14:

1   Read the entity from the database
2   Modify the entity's properties
3   Save the changes to the database

You'll encapsulate these three steps in a method on RecipeService, UpdateRecipe, which takes UpdateRecipeCommand, containing the changes to make to the Recipe entity.

> **NOTE** As with the Create command, you don't directly modify the entities in the MVC controllers, ensuring you keep the UI concern separate from the business logic.

The following listing shows the RecipeService.UpdateRecipe method, which updates the Recipe entity. It's the three steps you defined previously to read, modify,

---

[1]   For a detailed discussion on handling relationship updates in EF Core, see *EF Core in Action* by Jon P Smith (Manning, 2018) https://livebook.manning.com#!/book/smith3/Chapter-3/109.

and save the entity. I've extracted the code to update the recipe with the new values to a helper method.

Listing 12.9   Updating an existing entity with EF Core

```
public void UpdateRecipe(UpdateRecipeCommand cmd)
{
    var recipe = _context.Recipes.Find(cmd.Id);
    if(recipe == null) {
        throw new Exception("Unable to find the recipe");
    }

    UpdateRecipe(recipe, cmd);
    _context.SaveChanges();
}

static void UpdateRecipe(Recipe recipe, UpdateRecipeCommand cmd)
{
    recipe.Name = cmd.Name;
    recipe.TimeToCook =
        new TimeSpan(cmd.TimeToCookHrs, cmd.TimeToCookMins, 0);
    recipe.Method = cmd.Method;
    recipe.IsVegetarian = cmd.IsVegetarian;
    recipe.IsVegan = cmd.IsVegan;
}
```

> **Find is exposed directly by Recipes and simplifies reading an entity by id.**
>
> **If an invalid id is provided, recipe will be null.**
>
> **Set the new values on the Recipe entity.**
>
> **Execute the SQL to save the changes to the database.**
>
> **A helper method for setting the new properties on the Recipe entity**

In this example, I read the `Recipe` entity using the `Find(id)` method exposed by `DbSet`. This is a simple helper method for loading an entity by its ID, in this case `RecipeId`. I could've written an equivalent query directly using LINQ as

```
_context.Recipes.Where(r=>r.RecipeId == cmd.Id).FirstOrDefault();
```

Using `Find()` is a little more declarative and concise.

You may be wondering how EF Core knows which columns to update when you call `SaveChanges()`. The simplest approach would be to update every column—if the field hasn't changed, then it doesn't matter if you write the same value again. But EF Core is a bit more clever than that.

EF Core internally tracks the *state* of any entities it loads from the database. It creates a snapshot of all the entity's property values, so it can track which ones have changed. When you call `SaveChanges()`, EF Core compares the state of any tracked entities (in this case, the `Repair` entity) with the tracking snapshot. Any properties that have been changed are included in the `UPDATE` statement sent to the database, unchanged properties are ignored.

> **NOTE** EF Core provides other mechanisms to track changes, as well as options to disable change-tracking altogether. See the documentation or Jon P Smith's *EF Core in Action* (Manning, 2018) for details (https://livebook .manning.com#!/book/smith3/Chapter-3/59).

With the ability to update recipes, you're almost done with your recipe app. "But wait," I hear you cry, "we haven't handled the *D* in CRUD—delete!" And that's true, but in reality, I've found few occasions when you *want* to delete data.

Let's consider the requirements for deleting a recipe from the application, as shown in figure 12.15. You need to add a (scary-looking) Delete button next to a recipe. After the user clicks Delete, the recipe is no longer visible in the list and can't be viewed.

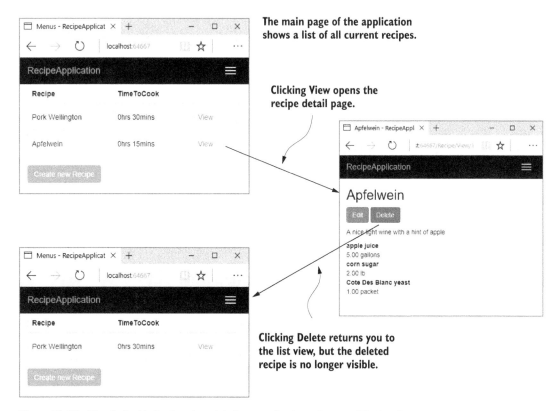

Figure 12.15   The desired behavior when deleting a recipe from the app. Clicking Delete should return you to the application's main list view, with the deleted recipe no longer visible.

Now, you could achieve this by deleting the recipe from the database, but the problem with data is once it's gone, it's gone! What if a user accidentally deletes a record? Also, deleting a row from a relational database typically has implications on other entities. For example, you can't delete a row from the Recipe table in your application without also deleting all of the Ingredient rows that reference it, thanks to the foreign key constraint on `Ingredient.RecipeId`.

EF Core can easily handle these *true deletion* scenarios for you with the `DbContext` `.Remove(entity)` command but, typically, what you *mean* when you find a need to delete data is to archive it or hide it from the UI. A common approach to handling this scenario is to include some sort of "Is this entity deleted" flag on your entity, such as the `IsDeleted` flag I included on the `Recipe` entity:

```
public bool IsDeleted {get;set;}
```

If you take this approach then, suddenly, deleting data becomes simpler, as it's nothing more than an update to the entity. No more issues of lost data and no more referential integrity problems.

> **NOTE** The main exception I've found to this pattern is when you're storing your users' personally identifying information. In these cases, you may be duty-bound (and, potentially, legally bound) to scrub their information from your database on request.

With this approach, you can create a *delete* method on `RecipeService`, which updates the `IsDeleted` flag, as shown in the following listing. In addition, you should ensure you have `Where()` clauses in all the other methods in your `RecipeService`, to ensure you can't display a deleted `Recipe`, as you saw in listing 12.9, for the `GetRecipes()` method.

Listing 12.10   Marking entities as deleted in EF Core

```
public void DeleteRecipe(int recipeId)                    Fetch the Recipe
{                                                         entity by id.
    var recipe = _context.Recipes.Find(recipeId);   ◁
    if(recipe == null) {                                  If an invalid id is
        throw new Exception("Unable to find the recipe"); provided, recipe
    }                                                     will be null.

    recipe.IsDeleted = true;   ◁────── Mark the Recipe as deleted.
    _context.SaveChanges();    ◁─┐ Execute the SQL to save the
}                                └ changes to the database.
```

This approach satisfies the requirements—it removes the recipe from the UI of the application—but it simplifies a number of things. This *soft delete* approach won't work for all scenarios, but I've found it to be a common pattern in projects I've worked on.

> **TIP** EF Core 2.0 gained a feature called *Model-level query filters*. These allow you to specify a `Where` clause at the model level, so you could, for example, ensure that EF Core never loads `Recipes` for which `IsDeleted` is true. See this announcement post for details: https://github.com/aspnet/EntityFrameworkCore/ issues/8923.

We're almost at the end of this chapter on EF Core. We've covered the basics of adding EF Core to your project and using it to simplify data access, but you'll likely need to read more into EF Core as your apps become more complex. In the final section of this chapter, I'd like to pinpoint a number of things you need to take into consideration before using EF Core in your own applications, so you're familiar with some of the issues you'll face as your apps grow.

12.5   *Using EF Core in production applications*

This book is about ASP.NET Core, not EF Core, so I didn't want to spend too much time exploring EF Core. This chapter should've given you enough to get up and running, but you'll definitely need to learn more before you even think about putting EF Core into production. As I've said a number of time, I recommend *EF Core in Action* by Jon P Smith (Manning, 2018) for details (https://livebook.manning.com/#!/book/smith3/Chapter-11/), or exploring the EF Core documentation site at https://docs.microsoft.com/en-us/ef/core/.

The following topics aren't essential to getting started with EF Core, but you'll quickly come up against them if you build a production-ready app. This section isn't a prescriptive guide to how to tackle each of these; it's more a set of things to consider before you dive into production!

- *Scaffolding of columns*—EF Core uses conservative values for things like `string` columns by allowing strings of unlimited length. In practice, you'll often want to restrict these and other data types to sensible values.
- *Validation*—You can decorate your entities with `DataAnnotations` validation attributes, but EF Core won't automatically validate the values before saving to the database. This differs from EF 6.x behavior, in which validation was automatic.
- *Handling concurrency*—EF Core provides a number of ways to handle concurrency, where multiple users attempt to update an entity at the same time. One partial solution is through the use of `Timestamp` columns on your entities.
- *Synchronous vs. asynchronous*—EF Core provides both synchronous and asynchronous commands for interacting with the database. Often, async is better for web apps, but there are nuances to this argument that make it impossible to recommend one approach over the other in all situations.

EF Core is a great tool for being productive when writing data-access code, but there are some aspects of working with a database that are unavoidably awkward. The issue of database management is one of the thorniest issues to tackle. This book is about ASP.NET Core, not EF Core, so I don't want to dwell on database management too much. Having said that, most web applications use some sort of database, so the following issues are likely to impact you at some point.

- *Automatic migrations*—If you automatically deploy your app to production as part of some sort of DevOps pipeline, you'll inevitably need some way of applying migrations to a database automatically. You can tackle this in a number of ways, such as scripting the .NET CLI, applying migrations in your app's startup code, or using a custom tool. Each approach has its pros and cons.
- *Multiple web hosts*—One specific consideration is whether you have multiple web servers hosting your app, all pointing to the same database. If so, then applying migrations in your app's startup code becomes harder, as you must ensure only one app can migrate the database at a time.

- *Making backward-compatible schema changes*—A corollary of the multiple-web host approach is that you'll often be in a situation where your app is accessing a database that has a *newer* schema than the app thinks. That means you should normally endeavor to make schema changes backward-compatible wherever possible.
- *Storing migrations in a different assembly*—In this chapter, I included all my logic in a single project, but in larger apps, data access is often in a different project to the web app. For apps with this structure, you must use slightly different commands when using the .NET CLI or PowerShell cmdlets.
- *Seeding data*—When you first create a database, you often want it to have some initial *seed* data, such as a default user. EF 6.X had a mechanism for seeding data built in, whereas EF Core requires you to explicitly seed your database yourself.

How you choose to handle each of these issues will depend on the infrastructure and deployment approach you take with your application. None of them are particularly fun to tackle but they're an unfortunate necessity. Take heart though, they can all be solved one way or another!

That brings us to the end of this chapter on EF Core. In the next chapter, we'll look at one of the slightly more advanced topics of MVC, the filter pipeline, and how you can use it to reduce duplication in your code.

Summary

- EF Core is an object-relational mapper (ORM) that lets you interact with a database by manipulating standard POCO classes, called entities, in your application.
- EF Core maps entity classes to tables, properties on the entity to columns in the tables, and instances of entity objects to rows in these tables.
- EF Core uses a database-provider model that lets you change the underlying database without changing any of your object manipulation code. EF Core has database providers for Microsoft SQL Server, SQLite, PostgreSQL, MySQL, and many others.
- EF Core is cross-platform and has good performance for an ORM, but has fewer features than some other ORMs, such as EF 6.x.
- EF Core stores an internal representation of the entities in your application and how they map to the database, based on the `DbSet<T>` properties on your application's `DbContext`. EF Core builds a model based on the entity classes themselves and any other entities they reference.
- You add EF Core to your app by adding a NuGet database provider package. You should also install the Design packages for both EF Core and your database provider (if available). These are used to generate and apply migrations to a database.

- EF Core includes a number of conventions for how entities are defined, such as primary keys and foreign keys. You can customize how entities are defined either declaratively, using `DataAnotations`, or using a fluent API.

- Your application uses a `DbContext` to interact with EF Core and the database. You register it with a DI container using `AddDbContext<T>`, defining the database provider and providing a connection string.

- EF Core uses migrations to track changes to your entity definitions. They're used to ensure your entity definitions, EF Core's internal model, and the database schema all match.

- After changing an entity, you can create a migration either using the .NET CLI tool or using Visual Studio PowerShell cmdlets.

- To create a new migration with the .NET CLI, run `dotnet ef migrations add NAME` in your project folder, where `NAME` is the name you want to give the migration.

- You can apply the migration to the database using `dotnet ef database update`. This will create the database if it doesn't already exist and apply any outstanding migrations.

- EF Core doesn't interact with the database when it creates migrations, only when you explicitly update the database.

- You can add entities to an EF Core database by creating a new entity, e, calling `_context.Add(e)` on an instance of your application's data context, `_context`, and calling `_context.SaveChanges()`. This generates the necessary SQL `INSERT` statements to add the new rows to the database.

- You can load records from a database using the `DbSet<T>` properties on your app's `DbContext`. These expose the `IQueryable` interface, so you can use LINQ statements to filter and transform the data in the database before it's returned. If you use a C# expression that EF Core can't translate to SQL, it will load the data necessary to perform the operation in your app, instead of in the database.

- Updating an entity consists of three steps: read the entity from the database, modify the entity, and save the changes to the database. EF Core will keep track of which properties have changed so that it can optimize the SQL it generates.

- You can delete entities in EF Core using the `Remove` method, but you should consider carefully whether you need this functionality. Often a *soft delete* technique using an `IsDeleted` flag on entities is safer and easier to implement.

- This chapter only covers a subset of the issues you must consider when using EF Core in your application. Before using it in a production app, you should consider, among other things: the data types generated for fields, validation, how to handle concurrency, the seeding of initial data, handling migrations on a running application, and handling migrations in a web-farm scenario.

The MVC filter pipeline

This chapter covers

- The MVC filter pipeline and how it differs from middleware
- Creating custom filters to refactor complex action methods
- Using authorization filters to protect your action methods
- Short-circuiting the filter pipeline to bypass action execution
- Injecting dependencies into filters

In part 1, I covered the MVC framework of ASP.NET Core in some detail. You learned about MvcMiddleware and how routing is used to select an action method to execute. You also saw model binding, validation, and how to generate a response by returning an IActionResult from your actions. In this chapter, I'm going to head deeper into MvcMiddleware and look at the *MVC filter pipeline*, sometimes called the *MVC action invocation pipeline*.

369

MVC uses a number of built-in filters to handle crosscutting concerns, such as authorization (controlling which users can access which action methods in your application). Any application that has the concept of users will use authorization filters as a minimum, but filters are much more powerful than this single use case.

This chapter describes the MVC filter pipeline in the context of an MVC request. You'll learn how to create custom filters that you can use in your own apps, and how you can use them to reduce duplicate code in your action methods. You'll learn how to customize your application's behavior for specific actions, as well as how to apply filters globally to modify all of the actions in your app.

Think of the filter pipeline as a mini middleware pipeline running inside `Mvc-Middleware`. Like the middleware pipeline in ASP.NET Core, the filter pipeline consists of a series of components connected as a pipe, so the output of one filter feeds into the input of the next.

This chapter starts by looking at the similarities and differences between MVC filters and middleware, and when you should choose one over the other. You'll learn about all the different types of filters and how they combine to create the filter pipeline for a request that reaches `MvcMiddleware`.

In section 13.2, I'll take you through each filter type in detail, how they fit into the MVC pipeline, and what to use them for. For each one, I'll provide example implementations that you might use in your own application.

A key feature of filters is the ability to short-circuit a request by generating a response and halting progression through the MVC filter pipeline. This is similar to the way short-circuiting works in middleware, but there are subtle differences. On top of that, the exact behavior is slightly different for each filter, which I cover in section 13.3.

You typically add MVC filters to the pipeline by implementing them as attributes added to your controller classes and action methods. Unfortunately, you can't easily use DI with attributes due to the limitations of C#. In section 13.4, I'll show you how to use the `ServiceFilterAttribute` and `TypeFilterAttribute` base classes to enable dependency injection in your filters.

Before we can start writing code, we should get to grips with the basics of the MVC filter pipeline. The first section of this chapter explains what the pipeline is, why you might want to use it, and how it differs from the middleware pipeline.

13.1   *Understanding filters and when to use them*

The MVC filter pipeline is a relatively simple concept, in that it provides *hooks* into the normal MVC request, as shown in figure 13.1. Say you wanted to ensure that users can create or edit products on an e-commerce app only if they're logged in. The app would redirect anonymous users to a login page instead of executing the action.

Without filters, you'd need to include the same code to check for a logged-in user at the start of each specific action method. With this approach, `MvcMiddleware` would still execute the model binding and validation, even if the user were not logged in.

With filters, you can use the *hooks* in the MVC request to run common code across all, or a subset of, requests. This way, you can do a wide range of things, such as

- Ensuring a user is logged in before an action method, model binding, or validation runs
- Customizing the output format of particular action methods
- Handling model validation failures before an action method is invoked
- Catching exceptions from an action method and handling them in a special way

In many ways, the MVC filter pipeline is like a middleware pipeline, but restricted to Mvc-Middleware only. Like middleware, filters are good for handling crosscutting concerns for your application and are a useful tool for reducing code duplication in many cases.

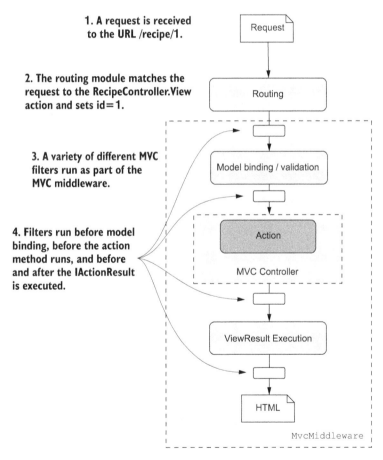

Figure 13.1 Filters run at multiple points in `MvcMiddleware` in the normal handling of a request.

In this section, I'll describe the MVC filter pipeline and how it fits into the overall MVC request. You'll learn about the types of MVC filters, how you can add them to your own apps, and how to control the order in which they execute when handling a request.

13.1.1 The MVC filter pipeline

As you saw in figure 13.1, MVC filters run at a number of different points in the MVC request. This linear view of an MVC request and the filter pipeline that you've used so far doesn't *quite* match up with how these filters execute. There are five types of filter, each of which runs at a different *stage* in MvcMiddleware, as shown in figure 13.2.

Each stage lends itself to a particular use case, thanks to its specific location in Mvc-Middleware, with respect to model binding, action execution, and result execution.

- *Authorization filters*—These run first in the pipeline, so are useful for protecting your APIs and action methods. If an authorization filter deems the request unauthorized, it will short-circuit the request, preventing the rest of the filter pipeline from running.
- *Resource filters*—After authorization, resource filters are the next filters to run in the pipeline. They can also execute at the *end* of the pipeline, in much the same way that middleware components can handle both the incoming request and the outgoing response. Alternatively, they can completely short-circuit the request pipeline and return a response directly.

  Thanks to their early position in the pipeline, resource filters can have a variety of uses. You could add metrics to an action method, prevent an action method from executing if an unsupported content type is requested, or, as they run before model binding, control the way model binding works for that request.
- *Action filters*—Action filters run just before and after an action is executed. As model binding has already happened, action filters let you manipulate the arguments to the method—before it executes—or they can short-circuit the action completely and return a different IActionResult. Because they also run after the action executes, they can optionally customize IActionResult before it's executed.
- *Exception filters*—Exception filters can catch exceptions that occur in the filter pipeline and handle them appropriately. They let you write custom MVC-specific error-handling code, which can be useful in some situations. For example, you could catch exceptions in Web API actions and format them differently to exceptions in your MVC actions.
- *Result filters*—Result filters run before and after an action method's IAction-Result is executed. This lets you control the execution of the result, or even short-circuit the execution of the result.

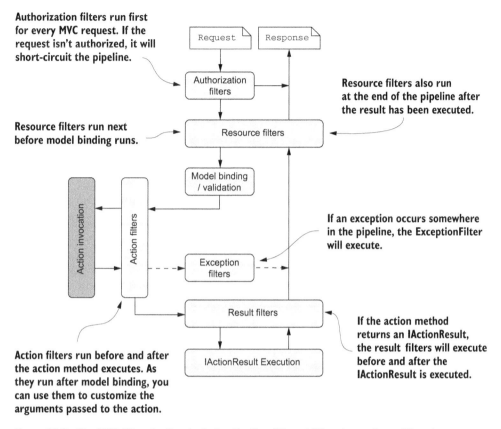

Authorization filters run first for every MVC request. If the request isn't authorized, it will short-circuit the pipeline.

Resource filters run next before model binding runs.

Action filters run before and after the action method executes. As they run after model binding, you can use them to customize the arguments passed to the action.

Resource filters also run at the end of the pipeline after the result has been executed.

If an exception occurs somewhere in the pipeline, the ExceptionFilter will execute.

If the action method returns an IActionResult, the result filters will execute before and after the IActionResult is executed.

Figure 13.2 The MVC filter pipeline, including the five different filter stages. Some filter stages (resource, action, and result) run twice, before and after the remainder of the pipeline.

Exactly which filter you pick to implement will depend on the functionality you're trying to introduce. Want to short-circuit a request as early as possible? Resource filters are a good fit. Need access to the action method parameters? Use an action filter.

Think of the filter pipeline as a small middleware pipeline that lives by itself in MvcMiddleware. Alternatively, you could think of filters as *hooks* into the MVC action invocation process, which let you run code at a particular point in a request's lifecycle.

One of the main questions I hear when people learn about filters in ASP.NET Core is "Why do we need them?" If the filter pipeline is like a mini middleware pipeline, why not use a middleware component directly, instead of introducing the filter concept? That's an excellent point, which I'll tackle in the next section.

13.1.2 *Filters or middleware: which should you choose?*

The filter pipeline is similar to the middleware pipeline in many ways, but there are a number of subtle differences that you should consider when deciding which approach to use. When considering the similarities, they have three main parallels:

- *Requests pass through a middleware component on the way "in" and responses pass through again on the way "out."* Resource, action, and result filters are also two-way, though authorization and exception filters run only once for a request.
- *Middleware can short-circuit a request by returning a response, instead of passing it on to later middleware.* Filters can also short-circuit the MVC filter pipeline by returning a response.
- *Middleware is often used for crosscutting application concerns, such as logging, performance profiling, and exception handling.* Filters also lend themselves to crosscutting concerns.

In contrast, there are three main differences between middleware and filters:

- Middleware can run for all requests; filters will only run for requests that reach `MvcMiddleware`.
- Filters have access to MVC constructs such as `ModelState` and `IActionResults`. Middleware, in general, is independent from MVC, so can't use these concepts.
- Filters can be easily applied to a subset of requests; for example, all actions on a single controller. Middleware doesn't have this concept as a first-class idea (though you could achieve something similar with custom middleware components).

That's all well and good, but how should we interpret these differences? When should we choose one over the other?

I like to think of middleware versus filters as a question of specificity. Middleware is the more general concept, so has the wider reach. If the functionality you need has no MVC-specific requirements, then you should use a middleware component. Exception handling is a great example of this; exceptions could happen anywhere in your application, and you need to handle them, so using exception-handling middleware makes sense.

On the other hand, if you *do* need access to MVC constructs, or you want to behave differently for some MVC actions, then you should consider using a filter. Ironically, this can also be applied to exception handling. You don't want exceptions in your Web API controllers to automatically generate HTML error pages when the client is expecting JSON. Instead, you could use an exception filter on your Web API actions to render the exception to JSON, while letting the exception-handling middleware catch errors from elsewhere in your app.

> **TIP**   Where possible, consider using middleware for crosscutting concerns. Use filters when you need different behavior for different action methods, or where the functionality relies on MVC concepts like `ModelState` validation.

The middleware versus filters argument is a subtle one, and it doesn't matter which you choose as long as it works for you. You can even use middleware components *inside* the filter pipeline as filters, but that's outside the scope of this book.[1]

---

[1]   The "middleware as filters" feature was introduced in ASP.NET Core 1.1. If you're interested, I wrote an introduction to the feature here: http://mng.bz/Mg97.

TIP   The middleware as filters feature was introduced in ASP.NET Core 1.1 and is also available in 2.0. The canonical use case is for localizing requests to multiple languages. I have a blog series on how to use the feature here: http://mng.bz/a6Rb.

Filters can be a little abstract in isolation, so in the next section, we'll look at some code and learn how to write a custom filter in ASP.NET Core.

13.1.3 Creating a simple filter

In this section, I show how to create your first filters; in section 13.1.4, you'll see how to apply them to your MVC actions. We'll start small, creating filters that just write to the console, but in section 13.2, we'll look at some more practical examples and discuss some of their nuances.

You implement an MVC filter for a given stage by implementing one of a pair of interfaces—one synchronous (sync), one asynchronous (async):

- *Authorization filters*—IAuthorizationFilter or IAsyncAuthorizationFilter
- *Resource filters*—IResourceFilter or IAsyncResourceFilter
- *Action filters*—IActionFilter or IAsyncActionFilter
- *Exception filters*—IExceptionFilter or IAsyncExceptionFilter
- *Result filters*—IResultFilter or IAsyncResultFilter

You can use any POCO class to implement a filter, but you'll typically implement them as C# attributes, which you can use to decorate your MVC controllers and actions, as you'll see in section 13.1.4. You can achieve the same results with either the sync or async interface, so which you choose should depend on whether any services you call in the filter require async support.

NOTE   You should implement *either* the sync interface *or* the async interface, *not both*. If you implement both, then only the async interface will be used.

Listing 13.1 shows a resource filter that implements IResourceFilter and writes to the console when it executes. The OnResourceExecuting method is called when a request first reaches the resource filter stage of the filter pipeline. In contrast, the OnResourceExecuted method is called after the rest of the pipeline has executed; after model binding, action execution, result execution, and all intermediate filters have run.

Listing 13.1   Example resource filter implementing IResourceFilter

```
public class LogResourceFilter : Attribute, IResourceFilter       Executed at the start
{                                                                  of the pipeline, after
    public void OnResourceExecuting(    ◁─────────────────────     authorization filters.
        ResourceExecutingContext context)    ◁──────────
    {                                                         The context contains the
        Console.WriteLine("Executing!");                      HttpContext, routing details,
    }                                                         and information about the
}                                                             current action.
```

```
public void OnResourceExecuted(
    ResourceExecutedContext context)
{
    Console.WriteLine("Executed"");
}
```

Executed after model binding, action execution, and result execution.

Contains additional context information, such as the IActionResult returned by the action

The interface methods are simple and are similar for each stage in the filter pipeline, passing a context object as a method parameter. Each of the two-method sync filters has an *Executing and an *Executed method. The type of the argument is different for each filter, but it contains all of the details for the filter pipeline.

For example, the ResourceExecutingContext passed to the resource filter contains the HttpContext object itself, details about the route that selected this action, details about the action itself, and so on. Contexts for later filters will contain additional details, such as the action method arguments for an action filter and the Model-State.

The context object for the ResourceExecutedContext method is similar, but it also contains details about how the rest of the pipeline executed. You can check whether an unhandled exception occurred, you can see if another filter from the same stage short-circuited the pipeline, or you can see the IActionResult used to generate the response.

These context objects are powerful and are the key to advanced filter behaviors like short-circuiting the pipeline and handling exceptions. We'll make use of them in section 13.2 when creating more complex filter examples.

The async version of the resource filter requires implementing a single method, as shown in listing 13.2. As for the sync version, you're passed a ResourceExecuting-Context object as an argument, and you're passed a delegate representing the remainder of the filter pipeline. You must call this delegate (asynchronously) to execute the remainder of the pipeline, which will return an instance of ResourceExecutedContext.

Listing 13.2   Example resource filter implementing IAsyncResourceFilter

Executed at the start of the pipeline, after authorization filters.

You're provided a delegate, which encapsulates the remainder of the MVC filter pipeline.

```
public class LogAsyncResourceFilter : Attribute, IAsyncResourceFilter
{
    public async Task OnResourceExecutionAsync(
        ResourceExecutingContext context,
        ResourceExecutionDelegate next)
    {
        Console.WriteLine("Executing async!");
        ResourceExecutedContext executedContext = await next();
        Console.WriteLine("Executed async!");
    }
}
```

Called before the rest of the pipeline executes.

Called after the rest of the pipeline executes.

Executes the rest of the pipeline and obtains a ResourceExecutedContext instance

The sync and async filter implementations have subtle differences, but for most purposes they're identical. I recommend implementing the sync version if possible, and only falling back to the async version if you need to.

You've created a couple of filters now, so we should look at how to use them in the application. In the next section, we'll tackle two specific issues: how to control which requests execute your new filters and how to control the order in which they execute.

13.1.4 Adding filters to your actions, your controllers, and globally

In section 13.1.2, I discussed the similarities and differences between middleware and filters. One of those differences is that filters can be scoped to specific actions or controllers, so that they only run for certain requests. Alternatively, you can apply a filter globally, so that it runs for every MVC action.

By adding filters in different ways, you can achieve a number of different results. Imagine you have a filter that forces you to log in to view an action. How you add the filter to your app will significantly change your app's behavior:

- *Apply the filter to a single action*—Anonymous users could browse the app as normal, but if they tried to access the protected action, they would be forced to log in.
- *Apply the filter to a controller*—Anonymous users could access actions from other controllers, but accessing any action on the protected controller would force them to log in.
- *Apply the filter globally*—Users couldn't use the app without logging in. Any attempt to access an action would redirect the user to the login page.

NOTE ASP.NET Core comes with just such a filter out of the box, `Authorize-Filter`. I'll discuss this filter in section 13.2.1, and you'll be seeing a lot more of it in chapter 15.

As I described in the previous section, you normally create filters as attributes, and for good reason—it makes applying them to MVC controllers and actions easy. In this section, you'll see how to apply `LogResourceFilter` from listing 13.1 to an action, a controller, and globally. The level at which the filter applies is called its *scope*.

DEFINITION The *scope* of a filter refers to how many different actions it applies to. A filter can be scoped to the action method, to the controller, or globally.

You'll start at the most specific scope—applying filters to a single action. The following listing shows an example of an MVC controller that has two action methods: one with `LogResourceFilter` and one without.

> **Listing 13.3 Applying filters to an action method**

```
public class HomeController : Controller
{
    [LogResourceFilter]
    public IActionResult Index()
    {
        return View();
    }
```
LogResourceFilter will run as part of the pipeline when executing this action.

```
public IActionResult About()
{
    return View();
}
```

This action method has no
filters at the action level.

```
}
```

Alternatively, if you want to apply the same filter to every action method, you could add the attribute at the controller scope, as in the next listing. Every action method in the controller will use `LogResourceFilter`, without having to specifically decorate each method:

Listing 13.4   Applying filters to a controller

```
[LogResourceFilter]         ◁──────────────
public class HomeController : Controller
{
    public IActionResult Index ()
    {
        return View();
    }

    public IActionResult SendInvoice()
    {
        return View();
    }
}
```

The LogResourceFilter Is
added to every action on
the controller.

Every action in the
controller is decorated
with the filter.

Filters you apply as attributes to controllers and actions are automatically discovered by `MvcMiddleware` when your application starts up. For common attributes, you can go one step further and apply filters globally, without having to decorate individual controllers.

You add global filters in a different way to controller- or action-scoped filters—by adding a filter directly to the MVC services, when configuring MVC in `Startup`. This listing shows three equivalent ways to add a globally scoped filter.

Listing 13.5   Applying filters globally to an application

```
public class Startup
{
    public void ConfigureServices(IServiceCollection services)
    {
        services.AddMvc(options =>          ◁───────────────
        {
            options.Filters.Add(new LogResourceFilter());
            options.Filters.Add(typeof(LogAsyncResourceFilter));
            options.Filters.Add<LogAsyncResourceFilter>();  ◁──
        });
    }
}
```

Adds filters using
the MvcOptions
object

You can pass
an instance
of the filter
directly. . .

Alternatively, the
framework can
create a global
filter using a
generic type
parameter.

. . . or pass in the Type of the filter
and let the framework create it.

With three different scopes in play, you'll often find action methods that have multiple filters applied to them, some applied directly to the action method, and others inherited from the controller or globally. The question then becomes: Which filters run first?

13.1.5 Understanding the order of filter execution

You've seen that the filter pipeline contains five different *stages*, one for each type of filter. These stages always run in the fixed order I described in section 13.1.1. But within each stage, you can also have multiple filters of the same type (for example, multiple resource filters) that are part of a single action method's pipeline. These could all have multiple *scopes*, depending on how you added them, as you saw in the last section.

In this section, we're thinking about the *order of filters within a given stage* and how scope affects this. We'll start by looking at the default order, then move on to ways to customize the order to your own requirements.

THE DEFAULT SCOPE EXECUTION ORDER

When thinking about filter ordering, it's important to remember that resource, action, and result filters implement two methods: an *Executing before method and an *Executed after method. The order in which each method executes depends on the scope of the filter, as shown in figure 13.3 for the resource filter stage.

By default, filters execute from the broadest scope (global) to the narrowest (action) when running the *Executing method for each stage. The *Executed methods run in reverse order, from the narrowest scope (action) to the broadest (global).

You'll often find you need a bit more control over this order, especially if you have, for example, multiple action filters applied at the same scope. The MVC framework caters to this requirement by way of the IOrderedFilter interface.

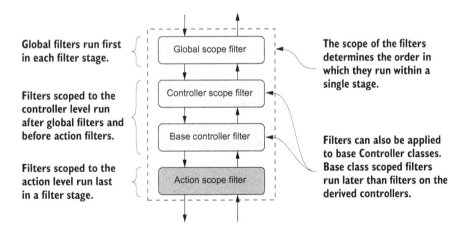

Global filters run first in each filter stage.

Filters scoped to the controller level run after global filters and before action filters.

Filters scoped to the action level run last in a filter stage.

Global scope filter

Controller scope filter

Base controller filter

Action scope filter

The scope of the filters determines the order in which they run within a single stage.

Filters can also be applied to base Controller classes. Base class scoped filters run later than filters on the derived controllers.

Figure 13.3   The default filter ordering within a given stage, based on the scope of the filters. For the *Executing method, globally scoped filters run first, followed by controller-scoped, and finally, action-scoped filters. For the *Executed method, the filters run in reverse order.

OVERRIDING THE DEFAULT ORDER OF FILTER EXECUTION WITH IORDEREDFILTER

Filters are great for extracting crosscutting concerns from your controller actions, but if you have multiple filters applied to an action, then you'll often need to control the precise order in which they execute.

Scope can get you some of the way, but for those other cases, you can implement IOrderFilter. This interface consists of a single property, Order:

```
public interface IOrderedFilter
{
    int Order { get; }
}
```

You can implement this property in your filters to set the order in which they execute. MvcMiddleware will order the filters for a stage based on this value first, from lowest to highest, and use the default scope order to handle ties, as shown in figure 13.4.

The filters for Order = -1 execute first, as they have the lowest Order value. The controller filter executes first because it has a broader scope than the action filter. The filters with Order=0 execute next, in the default scope order, as shown in figure 13.4. Finally, the filter with Order=1 executes.

By default, if a filter doesn't implement IOrderedFilter, it's assumed to have Order = 0. All of the filters that ship as part of ASP.NET Core have Order = 0, so you can implement your own filters relative to these.

This section has covered most of the technical details you need to use filters and create custom implementations for your own application. In the next section, you'll

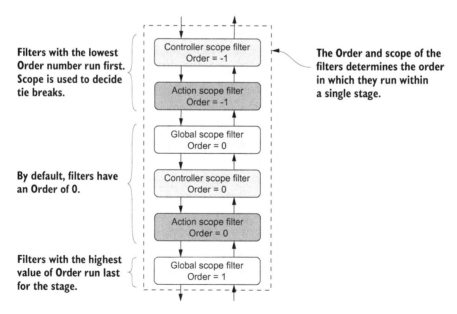

Figure 13.4   Controlling the filter order for a stage using the IOrderedFilter interface. Filters are ordered by the Order property first, and then by scope.

see some of the built-in filters provided by ASP.NET Core, as well as some practical examples of filters you might want to use in your own applications.

13.2 Creating custom filters for your application

ASP.NET Core includes a number of filters that you can use, but often, the most useful filters are the custom ones that are specific to your own apps. In this section, you'll work through each of the five types of filters. I'll explain in more detail what they're for and when you should use them. I'll point out examples of these filters that are part of ASP.NET Core itself and you'll see how to create custom filters for an example application.

To give you something realistic to work with, you'll start with a Web API controller for accessing the recipe application from chapter 12. This controller contains two actions: one for fetching a `RecipeDetailViewModel` and another for updating a `Recipe` with new values. This listing shows your starting point for this chapter, including both of the action methods.

Listing 13.6 Recipe Web API controller before refactoring to use filters

```
[Route("api/recipe")]
public class RecipeApiController : Controller
{
    private const bool IsEnabled = true;
    public RecipeService _service;
    public RecipeApiController(RecipeService service)
    {
        _service = service;
    }

    [HttpGet("{id}")]
    public IActionResult Get(int id)
    {
        if (!IsEnabled) { return BadRequest(); }

        try
        {
            if (!_service.DoesRecipeExist(id))
            {
                return NotFound();
            }

            var detail = _service.GetRecipeDetail(id);

            Response.GetTypedHeaders().LastModified =
                detail.LastModified;

            return Ok(detail);
        }
        catch (Exception ex)
        {
            return GetErrorResponse(ex);
        }
    }
}
```

These fields would be passed in as configuration values and are used to control access to actions.

If the API isn't enabled, block further execution.

If the requested Recipe doesn't exist, return a 404 response.

Fetch RecipeDetailViewModel.

Sets the Last-Modified response header to the value in the model

Returns the view model with a 200 response

If an exception occurs, catch it, and return the error in an expected format, as a 500 error.

```
[HttpPost("{id}")]
public IActionResult Edit(
    int id, [FromBody] UpdateRecipeCommand command)
{
    if (!IsEnabled) { return BadRequest(); }          ⟵    If the API isn't enabled,
                                                            block further execution.
    try
    {
        if (!ModelState.IsValid)                            Validates the binding model
        {                                                   and returns a 400 response
            return BadRequest(ModelState);                  if there are errors
        }

        if (!_service.DoesRecipeExist(id))                  If the requested Recipe
        {                                                   doesn't exist, return a
            return NotFound();                              404 response.
        }

        _service.UpdateRecipe(command);                     Updates the Recipe from the command
        return Ok();                                        and returns a 200 response
    }
    catch (Exception ex)
    {                                                       If an exception occurs, catch it,
        return GetErrorResponse(ex);                        and return the error in an
    }                                                       expected format, as a 500 error.
}

private static IActionResult GetErrorResponse(Exception ex)
{
    var error = new
    {
        Success = false,
        Errors = new[]
        {
            ex.Message
        }
    };

    return new ObjectResult(error)
    {
        StatusCode = 500
    };
}
}
```

These action methods currently have a lot of code to them, which hides the intent of each action. There's also quite a lot of duplication between the methods, such as checking that the Recipe entity exists, and formatting exceptions.

In this section, you're going to refactor this controller to use filters for all the code in the methods that's unrelated to the intent of each action. By the end of the chapter, you'll have a much simpler controller that's far easier to understand, as shown here.

Listing 13.7 Recipe Web API controller after refactoring to use filters

```
[Route("api/recipe")]
[ValidateModel, HandleException, FeatureEnabled(IsEnabled = true)]    ◁────────┐
public class RecipeApiController : Controller                      The filters encapsulate
{                                                                   the majority of logic
    public RecipeService _service;                                 common to multiple
    public RecipeApiController(RecipeService service)              action methods.
    {
        _service = service;                            Placing filters at the action level
    }                                                  limits them to a single action.

    [HttpGet("{id}"), EnsureRecipeExists, AddLastModifedHeader]    ◁──────────┐
    public IActionResult Get(int id)
    {
        var detail = _service.GetRecipeDetail(id);     The intent of the action,
        return Ok(detail);                             return a Recipe view model,
                                                       is much clearer.

    }

    [HttpPost("{id}"), EnsureRecipeExists]    ◁──────  Placing filters at the action level
    public IActionResult Edit(                         can be used to control the order
        int id, [FromBody] UpdateRecipeCommand command)  in which they execute.
    {
        _service.UpdateRecipe(command);     The intent of the action, update
        return Ok();                        a Recipe, is much clearer.
    }
}
```

I think you'll have to agree, the controller in listing 13.7 is much easier to read! In this section, you'll refactor the controller bit by bit, removing crosscutting code to get to something more manageable. All the filters I'll create in this section will use the sync filter interfaces—I'll leave it as an exercise for the reader to create their async counterparts. You'll start by looking at authorization filters and how they relate to security in ASP.NET Core.

13.2.1 Authorization filters: protecting your APIs

Authentication and *authorization* are related, fundamental concepts in security that we'll be looking at in detail in chapters 14 and 15.

> **DEFINITION** *Authentication* is concerned with determining *who* made a request. *Authorization* is concerned with *what* a user is allowed to access.

Authorization filters run first in the MVC filter pipeline, before any other filters. They control access to the action method by immediately short-circuiting the pipeline when a request doesn't meet the necessary requirements.

ASP.NET Core has a built-in authorization framework that you should use when you need to protect your MVC application or your Web APIs. You can configure this framework with custom policies that let you finely control access to your actions.

TIP It's possible to write your own authorization filters by implementing
`IAuthorizationFilter` or `IAsyncAuthorizationFilter`, but I strongly advise
against it. The ASP.NET Core authorization framework is highly configurable
and should meet all your needs.

At the heart of the ASP.NET Core authorization framework is an Authorization filter,
`AuthorizeFilter`, which you can add to the filter pipeline by decorating your actions
or controllers with the `[Authorize]` attribute. In its simplest form, adding the
`[Authorize]` attribute to an action, as in the following listing, means the request must
be made by an authenticated user to be allowed to continue. If you're not logged in, it
will short-circuit the pipeline, returning a 401 Unauthorized response to the browser.

Listing 13.8 Adding `[Authorize]` to an action method

```
public class RecipeApiController : Controller       The Get method has no
{                                                   [Authorize] attribute, so can
    public IActionResult Get(int id)        ◁──     be executed by anyone.
    {
        // method body                              Adds the AuthorizeFilter to the MVC
    }                                               filter pipeline using [Authorize]

    [Authorize]                     ◁──────────
    public IActionResult Edit(
        int id, [FromBody] UpdateRecipeCommand command)    The Edit method can
    {                                                      only be executed if
        // method body                                    you're logged in.
    }
}
```

As with all filters, you can apply the `[Authorize]` attribute at the controller level to
protect all the actions on a controller, or even globally, to protect every method in
your app.

NOTE We'll explore authorization in detail in chapter 15, including how to
add more detailed requirements, so that only specific sets of users can execute an action.

The next filters in the pipeline are resource filters. In the next section, you'll extract
some of the common code from `RecipeApiController` and see how easy it is to create
a short-circuiting filter.

13.2.2 Resource filters: short-circuiting your action methods

Resource filters are the first general-purpose filters in the MVC filter pipeline. In section 13.1.3, you saw minimal examples of both sync and async resource filters, which
logged to the console. In your own apps, you can use resource filters for a wide range
of purposes, thanks to the fact they execute so early (and late) in the filter pipeline.

The ASP.NET Core framework includes a few different implementations of resource filters you can use in your apps, for example:

- `ConsumesAttribute`—Can be used to restrict the allowed formats an action method can accept. If your action is decorated with `[Consumes("application/json")]` but the client sends the request as XML, then the resource filter will short-circuit the pipeline and return a 415 Unsupported Media Type response.
- `DisableFormValueModelBindingAttribute`—This filter prevents model binding from binding to form data in the request body. This can be useful if you know an action method will be handling large file uploads that you need to manage manually yourself. The resource filters run before model binding, so you can disable the model binding for a single action in this way.[2]

resource filters are useful when you want to ensure the filter runs early in the pipeline, before model binding. They provide an early hook into the pipeline for your logic, so you can quickly short-circuit the request if you need to.

Look back at listing 13.6 and see if you can refactor any of the code into a Resource filter. One candidate line appears at the start of both the `Get` and `Edit` methods:

```
if (!IsEnabled) { return BadRequest(); }
```

This line of code is a *feature toggle* that you can use to disable the availability of the whole API, based on the `IsEnabled` field. In practice, you'd probably load the `IsEnabled` field from a database or configuration file so you could control the availability dynamically at runtime but, for this example, I'm using a hardcoded value.

This piece of code is self-contained, crosscutting logic, which is somewhat tangential to the main action method intent—a perfect candidate for a filter. You want to execute the feature toggle early in the pipeline, before any other logic, so a resource filter makes sense.

> **TIP** Technically, you could also use an Authorization filter for this example, but I'm following my own advice of "Don't write your own Authorization filters!"

The next listing shows an implementation of `FeatureEnabledAttribute`, which extracts the logic from the action methods and moves it into the filter. I've also exposed the `IsEnabled` field as a property on the filter.

Listing 13.9 The FeatureEnabledAttribute resource filter

```
public class FeatureEnabledAttribute : Attribute, IResourceFilter
{
    public bool IsEnabled { get; set; }    ⟵—— Defines whether the feature is enabled
```

---

[2] For details on handling file uploads, see http://mng.bz/2rrk.

```
public void OnResourceExecuting(          Executes before model binding,
    ResourceExecutingContext context)      early in the filter pipeline

{
    if (!IsEnabled)                         If the feature isn't enabled,
    {                                       short-circuits the pipeline
        context.Result = new BadRequestResult();   by setting the
    }                                       context.Result property
}
public void OnResourceExecuted(            Must be implemented to satisfy
    ResourceExecutedContext context) { }   IResourceFilter, but not needed
}                                           in this case.
```

This simple resource filter demonstrates a number of important concepts, which are applicable to most filter types:

- The filter is an attribute as well as a filter. This lets you decorate your controller and action methods with it using [FeatureEnabled(IsEnabled = true)].
- The filter interface consists of two methods—*Executing that runs before model binding and *Executed that runs after the result has been executed. You must implement both, even if you only need one for your use case.
- The filter execution methods provide a context object. This provides access to, among other things, the HttpContext for the request and metadata about the action method the middleware will execute.
- To short-circuit the pipeline, set the context.Result property to IAction-Result. The MVC pipeline will execute this result to generate the response, bypassing any remaining filters in the pipeline and the action method itself. In this example, if the feature isn't enabled, you bypass the pipeline by returning BadRequestResult, which will return a 400 error to the client.

By moving this logic into the resource filter, you can remove it from your action methods, and instead decorate the whole API controller with a simple attribute:

```
[Route("api/recipe"), FeatureEnabled(IsEnabled = true)]
public class RecipeApiController : Controller
```

You've only extracted two lines of code from your action methods so far, but you're on the right track. In the next section, we'll move on to Action filters and extract two more filters from the action method code.

13.2.3 *Action filters: customizing model binding and action results*

Action filters run just after model binding, before the action method executes. Thanks to this positioning, action filters can access all the arguments that will be used to execute the action method, which makes them a powerful way of extracting common logic out of your actions.

On top of this, they also run just after the action method has executed and can completely change or replace the IActionResult returned by the action if you want. They can even handle exceptions thrown in the action.

The ASP.NET Core framework includes a number of action filters out of the box. One of these commonly used filters is `ResponseCacheFilter`, which sets HTTP caching headers on your action-method responses.

> **TIP** Caching is a broad topic that aims to improve the performance of an application over the naive approach. But caching can also make debugging issues difficult and may even be undesirable in some situations. Consequently, I often apply `ResponseCacheFilter` to my action methods to set HTTP caching headers that *disable* caching! You can read about this and other approaches to caching in the docs at http://mng.bz/AMSQ.

The real power of action filters comes when you build filters tailored to your own apps by extracting common code from your action methods. To demonstrate, I'm going to create two custom filters for `RecipeApiController`:

- `ValidateModelAttribute`—This will return `BadRequestResult` if the model state indicates that the binding model is invalid and will short-circuit the action execution.
- `EnsureRecipeExistsAttribute`—This will use each action method's `id` argument to validate that the requested `Recipe` entity exists before the action method runs. If the `Recipe` doesn't exist, the filter will return `NotFoundResult` and will short-circuit the pipeline.

As you saw in chapter 6, `MvcMiddleware` automatically validates your binding models for you before your actions execute, but it's up to you to decide what to do about it. For Razor pages, this can be somewhat complicated by the need to build a view model, so you'll often need some custom code in each action method to handle this. But for Web API controllers, it's common to return a 400 Bad Request response containing a list of the errors, as shown in figure 13.5.

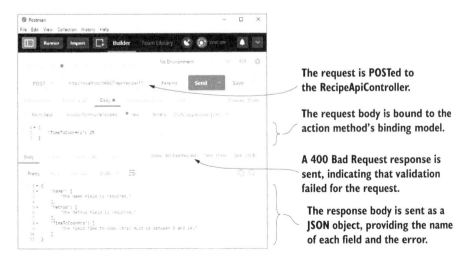

Figure 13.5 Posting data to a Web API using Postman. The data is bound to the action method's binding model and validated. If validation fails, it's common to return a 400 BadRequest response with a list of the validation errors.

It's likely that all of your Web API controllers will use this approach, so an action filter that automatically validates your binding models is a perfect fit. It's normally the first filter I create for any new project. Listing 13.10 shows a simple implementation that you can use in your own apps.[3]

Listing 13.10   The action filter for validating `ModelState`

For convenience, you derive from
the ActionFilterAttribute base class.

```
public class ValidateModelAttribute : ActionFilterAttribute
{
    public override void OnActionExecuting(            Overrides the Executing
        ActionExecutingContext context)               method to run the filter
    {                                                  before the Action executes
        if (!context.ModelState.IsValid)
        {
            context.Result =
                new BadRequestObjectResult(context.ModelState);
        }
    }
}
```

Overrides the Executing
method to run the filter
before the Action executes

Model binding and validation have already
run at this point, so you can check the state.

If the model isn't valid, set the
Result property; this short-
circuits the action execution.

This attribute is self-explanatory and follows a similar pattern to the resource filter in section 13.2.2, but with a few interesting points:

- I have derived from the abstract `ActionFilterAttribute`. This class implements `IActionFilter` and `IResultFilter`, as well as their async counterparts, so you can override the methods you need as appropriate. This avoids needing to add an unused `OnActionExecuted()` method, but is entirely optional and a matter of preference.

- Action filters run after model binding has taken place, so `context.ModelState` contains the validation errors if validation failed.

- Setting the `Result` property on `context` short-circuits the pipeline. But, due to the position of the action filter stage, only the action method execution and later action filters are bypassed; all the other stages of the pipeline run as though the action had executed as normal.

If you apply this action filter to your `RecipeApiController`, you can remove

```
if (!ModelState.IsValid)
{
    return BadRequest(ModelState);
}
```

---

[3] ASP.NET Core 2.1 added this behavior by default for controllers decorated with the `[ApiController]` attribute. For details, see https://blogs.msdn.microsoft.com/webdev/2018/02/27/asp-net-core-2-1-web-apis/.

from the start of both the action methods, as it will run automatically in the filter pipeline. You'll use a similar approach to remove the duplicate code checking whether the id provided as an argument to the action methods corresponds to an existing Recipe entity.

This listing shows the EnsureRecipeExistsAttribute action filter. This uses an instance of RecipeService to check whether the Recipe exists and returns a 404 Not Found if it doesn't.

Listing 13.11 An action filter to check whether a Recipe exists

```
public class EnsureRecipeExistsAtribute : ActionFilterAttribute
{
    public override void OnActionExecuting(
        ActionExecutingContext context)
    {
        var service = (RecipeService) context.HttpContext
            .RequestServices.GetService(typeof(RecipeService));

        var recipeId = (int) context.ActionArguments["id"];
        if (!service.DoesRecipeExist(recipeId))
        {
            context.Result = new NotFoundResult();
        }
    }
}
```

Fetches an instance of RecipeService from the DI container

Retrieves the id parameter that will be passed to action method when it executes

If it doesn't exist, returns a 404 Not Found result and short-circuits the pipeline.

Checks whether a Recipe entity with the given RecipeId exists

As before, you've derived from ActionFilterAttribute for simplicity and overridden the OnActionExecuting method. The main functionality of the filter relies on the DoesRecipeExist() method of RecipeService, so the first step is to obtain an instance of RecipeService. The context parameter provides access to the Http-Context for the request, which in turn lets you access the DI container and use RequestServices.GetService() to return an instance of RecipeService.

> **WARNING** This technique for obtaining dependencies is known as *service location* and is generally considered an antipattern.[4] In section 13.4, I'll show a much better way to use the DI container to inject dependencies into your filters.

As well as RecipeService, the other piece of information you need is the id argument of the Get and Edit action methods. In action filters, model binding has already occurred, so the arguments that the MVC middleware will use to execute the action method are already known and are exposed on context.ActionArguments.

The action arguments are exposed as Dictionary<string, object>, so you can obtain the id parameter using the "id" string key. Remember to cast the object to the correct type.

---

[4] For a detailed discussion on DI patterns and antipatterns, see *Dependency Injection in .NET* by Mark Seemann (Manning, 2012) https://livebook.manning.com/#!/book/dependency-injection-in-dot-net/chapter-5/.

TIP   Whenever I see magic strings like this, I always like to try to replace them by using the `nameof` operator. Unfortunately, `nameof` won't work for method arguments like this, so be careful when refactoring your code. I suggest explicitly applying the action filter to the action method (instead of globally, or to a controller) to remind you about that implicit coupling.

With `RecipeService` and `id` in place, it's a case of checking whether the identifier corresponds to a `Recipe` entity and, if not, setting `context.Result` to `NotFoundResult`. This will short-circuit the pipeline and bypass the action method altogether.

NOTE   Remember, you can have multiple action filters running in a single stage. Short-circuiting the pipeline by setting `context.Result` will prevent later filters in the stage from running, as well as bypassing the action method execution.

Before we move on, it's worth mentioning a special case for action filters. The `Controller` base class implements `IActionFilter` and `IAsyncActionFilter` itself. If you find yourself creating an action filter for a single controller and you want to apply it to every action in that controller, then you can override the appropriate methods on your controller.

> ### Listing 13.12   Overriding action filter methods directly on a `Controller`

```
public class HomeController : Controller    ◁── Derives from the Controller base class
{
    public override void OnActionExecuting(
        ActionExecutingContext context)
    { }
    public override void OnActionExecuted(
        ActionExecutedContext context)
    { }
}
```

Runs before any other action filters for every action in the controller

Runs after all other action filters for every action in the controller

If you override these methods on your controller, they'll run in the action filter stage of the filter pipeline for every action on the controller. The `OnActionExecuting` `Controller` method runs before any other action filters, regardless of ordering or scope, and the `OnActionExecuted` method runs after all other filters.

TIP   The controller implementation can be useful in some cases, but you can't control the ordering related to other filters. Personally, I generally prefer to break logic into explicit, declarative filter attributes but, as always, the choice is yours.

With the resource and action filters complete, your controller is looking much tidier, but there's one aspect in particular that would be nice to remove: the exception handling. In the next section, we'll look at how to create a custom exception filter for your controller, and why you might want to do this instead of using exception-handling middleware.

13.2.4 Exception filters: custom exception handling for your action methods

In chapter 3, I went into some depth about types of error-handling middleware you can add to your apps. These let you catch exceptions thrown from any later middleware and handle them appropriately. If you're using exception-handling middleware, you may be wondering why we need exception filters at all!

The answer to this is pretty much the same as I outlined in section 13.1.2: filters are great for crosscutting concerns, when you need behavior that's either specific to MVC or should only apply to certain routes.

Both of these can apply in exception handling. Exception filters run within `Mvc-Middleware`, so they have access to the context in which the error occurred, such as the action that was executing. This can be useful for logging additional details when errors occur, such as the action parameters that caused the error.

> **WARNING** If you use exception filters to record action method arguments, make sure you're not storing sensitive data, such as passwords or credit card details, in your logs.

You can also use exception filters to handle errors from different routes in different ways. Imagine you have both MVC and Web API controllers in your app, as we do in the recipe app. What happens when an exception is thrown by an MVC controller?

As you saw in chapter 3, the exception travels back up the middleware pipeline, and is caught by exception-handler middleware. The exception-handler middleware will re-execute the pipeline and generate an MVC error page.

That's great for your MVC controllers, but what about exceptions in your Web API controllers? If your API throws an exception, and consequently returns HTML generated by the exception-handler middleware, that's going to break a client who has called the API expecting a JSON response!

Instead, exception filters let you handle the exception inside `MvcMiddleware` and generate an appropriate response body. The exception handler middleware only intercepts errors without a body, so it will let the modified Web API response pass untouched.

Exception filters can catch exceptions from more than your action methods. They'll run if an exception occurs in `MvcMiddleware`

- During model binding or validation
- When the action method is executing
- When an action filter is executing

You should note that exception filters won't catch exceptions thrown in any filters other than action filters, so it's important your resource and result filters don't throw exceptions. Similarly, they won't catch exceptions thrown when executing `IAction-Result` itself.

Now that you know why you might want an exception filter, go ahead and implement one for RecipeApiController, as shown next. This lets you safely remove the try-catch block from your action methods, knowing that your filter will catch any errors.

Listing 13.13   The HandleExceptionAttribute exception filter

ExceptionFilterAttribute is an abstract base class that implements IExceptionFilter.

There's only a single method to override for IExceptionFilter.

```
public class HandleExceptionAttribute : ExceptionFilterAttribute
{
    public override void OnException(ExceptionContext context)
    {
        var error = new
        {
            Success = false,
            Errors = new [] { context.Exception.Message }
        };

        context.Result = new ObjectResult(error)
        {
            StatusCode = 500
        };
        context.ExceptionHandled = true;
    }
}
```

Building a custom object to return in the response

Creates an ObjectResult to serialize the error object and to set the response status code

Marks the exception as handled to prevent it propagating out of MvcMiddleware

It's quite common to have one or two different exception filters in your application, one for your MVC controllers and one for your Web API controllers, but they're not always necessary. If you can handle all the exceptions in your application with a single piece of middleware, then ditch the exception filters and go with that instead.

You're coming to the last type of filter now, result filters, and with it, you're almost done refactoring your RecipeApiController. Custom result filters tend to be relatively rare in the apps I've written, but they have their uses, as you'll see.

13.2.5   Result filters: customizing action results before they execute

If everything runs successfully in the pipeline, and there's no short-circuiting, then the next stage of the pipeline after action filters are result filters. These run just before and after the IActionResult returned by the Action method (or action filters) is executed.

> **WARNING** If the pipeline is short-circuited by setting context.Result, the result filter stage won't be run, but IActionResult will still be executed to generate the response. The one exception to this rule is action filters—these only short-circuit the action execution, as you saw in figure 13.2, and so result filters run as normal, as though the action itself generated the response.

Result filters run immediately after action filters, so many of their use cases are similar, but you typically use result filters to customize the way the `IActionResult` executes. For example, ASP.NET Core has several result filters built into its framework:

- `ProducesAttribute`—This forces the Web API result to be serialized to a specific output format. For example, decorating your action method with `[Produces("application/xml")]` forces the formatters to try to format the response as XML, even if the client doesn't list XML in its `Accept` header.
- `FormatFilterAttribute`—Decorating an action method with this filter tells the formatter to look for a route value or query string parameter called `format`, and to use that to determine the output format. For example, you could call `/api/recipe/11?format=json` and `FormatFilter` will format the response as JSON, or call `api/recipe/11?format=xml` and get the response as XML.[5]

As well as controlling the output formatters, you can use result filters to make any last-minute adjustments before `IActionResult` is executed and the response is generated.

As an example of the kind of flexibility available to you, in the following listing I demonstrate setting the `Last-Modified` header, based on the object returned from the action. This is a somewhat contrived example—it's specific enough to a single action that it doesn't warrant being moved to a result filter—but, hopefully, you get the idea!

Listing 13.14   Setting a response header in a result filter

ResultFilterAttribute provides a useful base class you can override

You could also override the Executed method, but the response would already be sent by then.

```
public class AddLastModifedHeaderAttribute : ResultFilterAttribute
{
    public override void OnResultExecuting(
        ResultExecutingContext context)
    {
        if (context.Result is OkObjectResult result
            && result.Value is RecipeDetailViewModel detail)
        {
            var viewModelDate = detail.LastModified;
            context.HttpContext.Response
                .GetTypedHeaders().LastModified = viewModelDate;
        }
    }
}
```

Checks whether the action result returned a 200 Ok result with a view model

Checks whether the view model type is RecipeDetailViewModel . . .

. . . if it is, fetches the LastModified field and sets the Last-Modified header in the response

I've used another helper base class here, `ResultFilterAttribute`, so you only need to override a single method to implement the filter. Fetch the current `IActionResult`,

---

[5] Remember, you need to explicitly configure the XML formatters if you want to serialize to XML. For details, see http://mng.bz/0J2z.

exposed on `context.Result`, and check that it's `OkObjectResult` with `RecipeDetail-ViewModel`. If it is, then fetch the `LastModified` field from the view model and add a `Last-Modified` header to the response.

> **TIP** `GetTypedHeaders()` is an extension method that provides strongly typed access to request and response headers. It takes care of parsing and formatting the values for you. You can find it in the `Microsoft.AspNetCore.Http` namespace.

As with resource and action filters, result filters can implement a method that runs *after* the result has been executed, `OnResultExecuted`. You can use this method, for example, to inspect exceptions that happened during the execution of `IAction-Result`.

> **WARNING** Generally, you can't modify the response in the `OnResult-Executed` method, as `MvcMiddleware` may have already started streaming the response to the client.

That brings us to the end of this detailed look at each of the filters in the MVC pipeline. Looking back and comparing listings 13.6 and 13.7, you can see filters allowed us to refactor the controllers and make the intent of each action method much clearer. Writing your code in this way makes it easier to reason about, as each filter and action has a single responsibility.

In the next section, I'll take a slight detour into exactly what happens when you short-circuit a filter. I've described *how* to do this, by setting the `context.Result` property on a filter, but I haven't yet described exactly what happens. For example, what if there are multiple filters in the stage when it's short-circuited? Do those still run?

13.3 *Understanding pipeline short-circuiting*

A brief warning: the topic of filter short-circuiting can be a little confusing. Unlike middleware short-circuiting, which is cut-and-dried, the MVC filter pipeline is a bit more nuanced. Luckily, you won't often find you need to dig into it, but when you do, you'll be glad of the detail.

You short-circuit the authorization, resource, action, and result filters by setting `context.Result` to `IActionResult`. Setting an action result in this way causes some, or all, of the remaining pipeline to by bypassed. But the filter pipeline isn't entirely linear, as you saw in figure 13.2, so short-circuiting doesn't always do an about-face back down the pipeline. For example, short-circuited action filters only bypass action method execution—the result filters and result execution stages still run.

The other difficulty is what happens if you have more than one type of filter. Let's say you have three resource filters executing in a pipeline. What happens if the second filter causes a short circuit? Any remaining filters are bypassed, but the first resource filter has already run its *Executing command, as shown in figure 13.6. This earlier filter gets to run its *Executed command too, with `context.Cancelled = true`, indicating that a filter in that stage (the resource filter stage) short-circuited the pipeline.

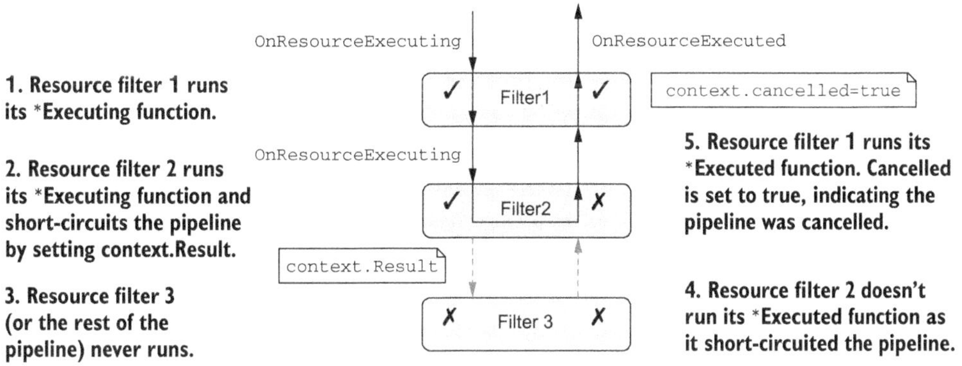

1. Resource filter 1 runs its *Executing function.

2. Resource filter 2 runs its *Executing function and short-circuits the pipeline by setting context.Result.

3. Resource filter 3 (or the rest of the pipeline) never runs.

5. Resource filter 1 runs its *Executed function. Cancelled is set to true, indicating the pipeline was cancelled.

4. Resource filter 2 doesn't run its *Executed function as it short-circuited the pipeline.

Figure 13.6 The effect of short-circuiting a resource filter on other resource filters in that stage. Later filters in the stage won't run at all, but earlier filters run their `OnResourceExecuted` function.

Understanding which other filters will run when you short-circuit a filter can be somewhat of a chore, but I've summarized each filter in table 13.1. You'll also find it useful to refer to figure 13.2 to visualize the shape of the pipeline when thinking about short-circuits.

Table 13.1   The effect of short-circuiting filters on filter-pipeline execution

Filter type	How to short-circuit?	What else runs?
Authorization filters	Set `context.Result`	Nothing, the pipeline is immediately halted.
Resource filters	Set `context.Result`	Resource-filter `*Executed` functions from earlier filters run with `context.Cancelled = true`.
Action filters	Set `context.Result`	Only bypasses action method execution. Action filters earlier in the pipeline run their `*Executed` methods with `context.Cancelled = true`, then result filters, result execution, and resource filters' `*Executed` methods all run as normal.
Exception filters	Set `context.Result` and `Exception.Handled = true`	All resource-filter `*Executed` functions run.
Result filters	Set `context.Cancelled = true`	Result filters earlier in the pipeline run their `*Executed` functions with `context.Cancelled = true`. All resource-filter `*Executed` functions run as normal.

The most interesting point here is that short-circuiting an action filter doesn't short-circuit much of the pipeline at all. In fact, it only bypasses later action filters and the action method execution itself. By primarily building action filters, you can ensure that other filters, such as result filters that define the output format, run as usual, even when your action filters short-circuit.

The last thing I'd like to talk about in this chapter is how to use DI with your filters. You saw in chapter 10 that DI is integral to ASP.NET Core, and in the next section, you'll see how to design your filters so that the framework can inject service dependencies into them for you.

13.4 *Using dependency injection with filter attributes*

The previous version of ASP.NET used filters, but they suffered from one problem in particular: it was hard to use services from them. This was a fundamental issue with implementing them as attributes that you decorate your actions with. C# attributes don't let you pass dependencies into their constructors (other than constant values), and they're created as singletons, so there's only a single instance for the lifetime of your app.

In ASP.NET Core, this limitation is still there in general, in that filters are typically created as attributes that you add to your controller classes and action methods. What happens if you need to access a transient or scoped service from inside the singleton attribute?

Listing 13.11 showed one way of doing this, using a pseudo service locator pattern to reach into the DI container and pluck out `RecipeService` at runtime. This works but is generally frowned upon as a pattern, in favor of proper DI. How can you add DI to your filters?

The key is to split the filter into two. Instead of creating a class that's both an attribute and a filter, create a filter class that contains the functionality and an attribute that tells `MvcMiddleware` when and where to use the filter.

Let's apply this to the action filter from listing 13.11. Previously, I derived from `ActionFilterAttribute` and obtained an instance of `RecipeService` from the context passed to the method. In the following listing, I show two classes, `EnsureRecipeExistsFilter` and `EnsureRecipeExistsAttribute`. The filter class is responsible for the functionality and takes in `RecipeService` as a constructor dependency.

Listing 13.15   Using DI in a filter by not deriving from `Attribute`

```
public class EnsureRecipeExistsFilter : IActionFilter    ◁────    Doesn't derive from
{                                                                  an Attribute class
    private readonly RecipeService _service;
    public EnsureRecipeExistsFilter(RecipeService service)
    {
        _service = service;
    }

    public void OnActionExecuting(ActionExecutingContext context)
    {
        var recipeId = (int) context.ActionArguments["id"];
        if (!_service.DoesRecipeExist(recipeId))
        {
            context.Result = new NotFoundResult();
        }
    }
}
```

RecipeService is injected into the constructor.

The rest of the method remains the same.

```
        public void OnActionExecuted(ActionExecutedContext context) { }
    }
    public class EnsureRecipeExistsAttribute : TypeFilterAttribute
    {
        public EnsureRecipeExistsAttribute()
            : base(typeof(EnsureRecipeExistsFilter)) {}
    }
```

You must implement the Executed action to satisfy the interface.

Passes the type EnsureRecipeExistsFilter as an argument to the base TypeFilter constructor

Derives from TypeFilter, which is used to fill dependencies using the DI container.

EnsureRecipeExistsFilter is a valid filter; you could use it on its own by adding it as a global filter (as global filters don't need to be attributes). But you can't use it directly by decorating controller classes and action methods, as it's not an attribute. That's where EnsureRecipeExistsAttribute comes in.

You can decorate your methods with EnsureRecipeExistsAttribute instead. This attribute inherits from TypeFilterAttribute and passes the Type of filter to create as an argument to the base constructor. This attribute acts as a *factory* for EnsureRecipe-ExistsFilter by implementing IFilterFactory.

When MvcMiddleware initially loads your app, it scans your actions and controllers, looking for filters and filter factories. It uses these to form a filter pipeline for every action in your app, as shown in figure 13.7.

When an action decorated with EnsureRecipeExistsAttribute is called, Mvc-Middleware calls CreateInstance() on the attribute. This creates a new instance of EnsureRecipeExistsFilter and uses the DI container to populate its dependencies (RecipeService).

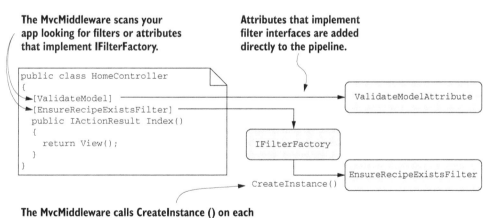

The MvcMiddleware scans your app looking for filters or attributes that implement IFilterFactory.

Attributes that implement filter interfaces are added directly to the pipeline.

```
public class HomeController
{
    [ValidateModel]
    [EnsureRecipeExistsFilter]
    public IActionResult Index()
    {
        return View();
    }
}
```

ValidateModelAttribute

IFilterFactory

EnsureRecipeExistsFilter

CreateInstance()

The MvcMiddleware calls CreateInstance () on each IFilterFactory when a request is received to create a filter instance, which is added to the pipeline.

Figure 13.7 The MvcMiddleware scans your app on startup to find both filters and attributes that implement IFilterFactory. At runtime, the middleware calls CreateInstance() to get an instance of the filter.

By using this `IFilterFactory` approach, you get the best of both worlds; you can decorate your controllers and actions with attributes, and you can use DI in your filters. Out of the box, two similar classes provide this functionality, which have slightly different behaviors:

- `TypeFilterAttribute`—Loads all of the filter's dependencies from the DI container and uses them to create a new instance of the filter.
- `ServiceFilterAttribute`—Loads the filter *itself* from the DI container. The DI container takes care of the service lifetime and building the dependency graph. Unfortunately, you also have to explicitly register your filter with the DI container in `ConfigureServices` in `Startup`:

```
services.AddTransient<EnsureRecipeExistsFilter>();
```

Whether you choose to use `TypeFilterAttribute` or `ServiceFilterAttribute` is somewhat a matter of preference, and you can always implement a custom `IFilterFactory` if you need to. The key takeaway is that you can now use DI in your filters. If you don't need to use DI for a filter, then implement it as an attribute directly for simplicity.

> **TIP** I like to create my filters as a nested class of the attribute class when using this pattern. This keeps all the code nicely contained in a single file and indicates the relationship between the classes.

That brings us to the end of this chapter on the filter pipeline. Filters are a somewhat advanced topic, in that they aren't strictly necessary for building basic apps, but I find them extremely useful for ensuring my controller and action methods are simple and easy to understand.

In the next chapter, we'll take our first look at securing your app. We'll discuss the difference between authentication and authorization, the concept of identity in ASP.NET Core, and how you can use the ASP.NET Core Identity system to let users register and log in to your app.

Summary

- The filter pipeline executes as part of `MvcMiddleware` after routing has selected an action method.
- The filter pipeline consists of authorization filters, resource filters, action filters, exception filters, and Result filters. Each filter type is grouped into a *stage*.
- Resource, action, and result filters run twice in the pipeline: an `*Executing` method on the way in and an `*Executed` method on the way out.
- Authorization and exception filters only run once as part of the pipeline; they don't run after a response has been generated.
- Each type of filter has both a sync and an async version. For example, resource filters can implement either the `IResourceFilter` interface or the `IAsync-ResourceFilter` interface. You should use the synchronous interface unless your filter needs to use asynchronous method calls.

- You can add filters globally, at the controller level, or at the action level. This is called the *scope* of the filter.
- Within a given stage, global-scoped filters run first, then controller-scoped, and finally, action-scoped.
- You can override the default order by implementing the `IOrderedFilter` interface. Filters will run from lowest to highest `Order` and use scope to break ties.
- Authorization filters run first in the pipeline and control access to APIs. ASP.NET Core includes an `[Authorization]` attribute that you can apply to action methods so that only logged-in users can execute the action.
- Resource filters run after authorization filters, and again after a result has been executed. They can be used to short-circuit the pipeline, so that an action method is never executed. They can also be used to customize the model binding process for an action method.
- Action filters run after model binding has occurred, just before an action method executes. They also run after the action method has executed. They can be used to extract common code out of an action method to prevent duplication.
- The `Controller` base class also implements `IActionFilter` and `IAsyncAction-Filter`. They run at the start and end of the action filter pipeline, regardless of the ordering or scope of other action filters.
- Exception filters execute after action filters, when an action method has thrown an exception. They can be used to provide custom error handling specific to the action executed.
- Generally, you should handle exceptions at the middleware level, but exception filters let you customize how you handle exceptions for specific actions or controllers.
- Result filters run just before and after an `IActionResult` is executed. You can use them to control how the action result is executed, or to completely change the action result that will be executed.
- You can use `ServiceFilterAttribute` and `TypeFilterAttribute` to allow dependency injection in your custom filters. `ServiceFilterAttribute` requires that you register your filter and all its dependencies with the DI container, whereas `TypeFilterAttribute` only requires that the filter's dependencies have been registered.

Authentication: adding users to your application with Identity

14

This chapter covers

- How authentication works in web apps in ASP.NET Core
- Creating a project using the ASP.NET Core Identity system
- Adding user functionality to an existing web app

One of the selling points of a web framework like ASP.NET Core is the ability to provide a dynamic app, customized to individual users. Many apps have the concept of an "account" with the service, which you can "sign in" to and get a different experience.

Depending on the service, an account gives you varying things: on some apps you may have to sign in to get access to additional features, on others you might see suggested articles. On an e-commerce app, you'd be able to make and view your past orders, on Stack Overflow you can post questions and answers, whereas on a news site you might get a customized experience based on previous articles you've viewed.

When you think about adding users to your application, you typically have two aspects to consider:

- *Authentication*—The process of creating users and letting them log in to your app
- *Authorization*—Customizing the experience and controlling what users can do, based on the current logged-in user

In this chapter, I'm going to be discussing the first of these points, authentication and membership, and in the next chapter, I'll tackle the second point, authorization. In section 14.1, I discuss the difference between authentication and authorization, how authentication works in a traditional ASP.NET Core web app, and ways you can architect your system to provide sign-in functionality.

I also touch on the typical differences in authentication between a traditional web app and Web APIs used with client-side or mobile web apps. This book focuses on traditional web apps for authentication, but many of the principles are applicable to both.

In section 14.2, I introduce a user management system called ASP.NET Core Identity (or Identity for short). Identity integrates with EF Core and provides a number of services for creating and managing users, storing and validating passwords, and signing users in and out of your app.

In section 14.3, you'll create an app using a default template that includes ASP.NET Core Identity out of the box. This will give you an app to explore, to see the features Identity provides, as well as everything it doesn't.

Creating an app is great for seeing an example of how the pieces fit together, but you'll often need to add users to an existing app. In section 14.4, you'll see how you can extract the Identity elements from the default template and apply it to an existing app: the recipe application from chapters 12 and 13.

In section 14.5, you'll customize the login process. It's common to need to store additional information about a user (such as their name or date of birth) and to provide permissions to them that you can later use to customize the app's behavior (if the user is a VIP, for example).

NOTE The authentication and authorization subsystem of ASP.NET Core underwent some breaking changes between ASP.NET Core 1.1 and 2.0 to solve some general design deficiencies. I only talk about the ASP.NET Core 2.0 system in this book. You can read about the changes at https://github .com/aspnet/Announcements/issues/232. Additionally, ASP.NET Core 2.1, in preview at the time of writing, hides much of the UI code from you by default. You can generate the UI code again, if required, using the scaffolder described in the following post http://mng.bz/tZZz.

Before we break out the braces, let's take a look at authentication and authorization in ASP.NET Core, what's happening when you sign in to a website, and some of the ways to design your apps to provide this functionality.

14.1   *Introducing authentication and authorization*

When you add sign-in functionality to your app and control access to certain functions based on the currently-signed-in user, you're using two distinct aspects of security:

- *Authentication*—The process of determining *who you are*
- *Authorization*—The process of determining *what you're allowed to do*

Generally, you need to know *who* the user is before you can determine *what* they're allowed to do, so authentication typically comes first, followed by authorization. In this chapter, we're only looking at authentication; we'll cover authorization in chapter 15.

I'll start by discussing how ASP.NET Core thinks about users, and cover some of the terminology and concepts that are central to authentication. I always found this to be the hardest part to grasp when first learning about authentication, so I'll take it slow!

Next, we'll look at what it *means* to sign in to a traditional web app. After all, you only provide your password and sign in to an app on a single page—how does the app know the request came from *you* for subsequent requests?

Finally, we'll look at how authentication works when you need to support client-side apps and mobile apps that call Web APIs, in addition to traditional web apps. Many of the concepts are similar, but the requirement to support multiple types of users, traditional apps, client-side apps, and mobile apps has led to alternative solutions.

In the next section, we'll look at a practical implementation of a user management system called ASP.NET Core Identity, and how you can use this in your own projects.

14.1.1   *Understanding users and claims in ASP.NET Core*

The concept of a user is baked-in to ASP.NET Core. In this section, we'll look at the fundamental model used to describe a user, including its properties, such as an associated email address, as well as any permission-related properties, such as whether the user is an admin user.

In chapter 3, you learned that the HTTP server, Kestrel, creates an `HttpContext` object for every request it receives. This object is responsible for storing all of the details related to that request, such as the request URL, any headers sent, the body of the request, and so on.

The `HttpContext` object also exposes the current *principal* for a request as the `User` property. This is ASP.NET Core's view of which user made the request. Any time your app needs to know who the current user is, or what they're allowed to do, it can look at the `HttpContext.User` principal.

> **DEFINITION** You can think of the *principal* as the user of your app.

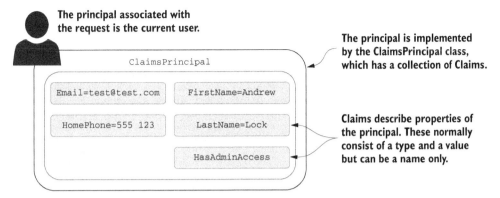

Figure 14.1   The principal is the current user, implemented as `ClaimsPrincipal`. It contains a collection of `Claims` that describe the user.

In ASP.NET Core, principals are implemented as `ClaimsPrincipals`, which has a collection of *claims* associated with it, as shown in figure 14.1.

You can think about claims as properties of the current user. For example, you could have claims for things like email, name, or date of birth.

> **DEFINITION**   A claim is a single piece of information about a principal, which consists of a *claim type* and an optional *value*.

Claims can also be indirectly related to permissions and authorization, so you could have a claim called `HasAdminAccess` or `IsVipCustomer`. These would be stored in exactly the same way—as claims associated with the user principal.

> **NOTE**   Earlier versions of ASP.NET used a role-based approach to security, rather than claims-based. The `ClaimsPrincipal` used in ASP.NET Core is compatible with this approach for legacy reasons, but you should use the claims-based approach for new apps.

Kestrel assigns a user principal to every request that arrives at your app. Initially, that principal is a generic, anonymous, unauthenticated principal with no claims. How do you log in, and how does ASP.NET Core know that you've logged in on subsequent requests?

In the next section, we'll look at how authentication works in a traditional web app using ASP.NET Core, and the process of signing in to a user account.

14.1.2   *Authentication in ASP.NET Core: services and middleware*

Adding authentication to any web app involves a number of moving parts. The same general process applies whether you're building a traditional web app or a client-side app, though there are often differences in implementation, as I'll discuss in section 14.1.3:

- The client sends an identifier and a secret to the app, which identify the current user. For example, you could send an email (identifier) and a password (secret).
- The app verifies that the identifier corresponds to a user known by the app and that the corresponding secret is correct.
- If the identifier and secret are valid, the app can set the principal for the current request, but it also needs a way of storing these details for subsequent requests. For traditional web apps, this is typically achieved by storing an encrypted version of the user principal in a cookie.

This is the typical flow for most web apps, but in this section, I'm going to look at how it works in ASP.NET Core. The overall process is the same, but it's good to see how this pattern fits into the services, middleware, and MVC aspects of an ASP.NET Core application. We'll step through the various pieces at play in a typical app when you sign in as a user, what that means, and how you can make subsequent requests as that user.

SIGNING IN TO AN ASP.NET CORE APPLICATION

When you first arrive on a site and sign in to a traditional web app, the app will send you to a sign-in page and ask you to enter your username and password. After you submit the form to the server, the app redirects you to a new page, and you're magically logged in! Figure 14.2 shows what's happening behind the scenes in an ASP.NET Core app when you submit the form.

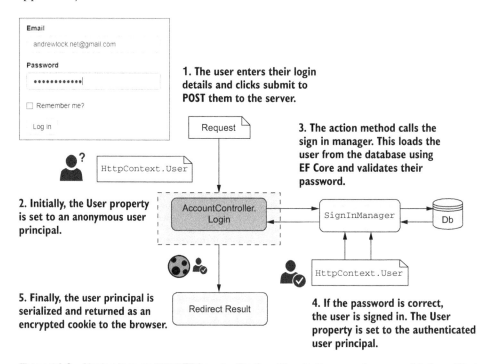

Figure 14.2   Signing in to an ASP.NET Core application. `SignInManager` is responsible for setting `HttpContext.User` to the new principal and serializing the principal to the encrypted cookie.

This shows the series of steps from the moment you submit the login form, to the point the redirect is returned to the browser. When the request first arrives, Kestrel creates an anonymous user principal and assigns it to the `HttpContext.User` property. The request is then routed to a normal MVC controller, `AccountController`, which reads the email and password from the request.

The meaty work happens inside the `SignInManager` service. This is responsible for loading a user entity from the database with the provided username and validating that the password they provided is correct.

> **WARNING** Never store passwords in the database directly. They should be *hashed* using a strong one-way algorithm. The ASP.NET Core Identity system does this for you, but it's always wise to reiterate this point!

If the password is correct, `SignInManager` creates a new `ClaimsPrincipal` from the user entity it loaded from the database and adds the appropriate claims, such as the email. It then replaces the old, anonymous, `HttpContext.User` principal with the new, authenticated principal.

Finally, `SignInManager` serializes the principal, encrypts it, and stores it as a *cookie*. A cookie is a small piece of text that's sent back and forth between the browser and your app along with each request, consisting of a name and a value.

This authentication process explains how you can set the user for a request when they first log in to your app, but what about subsequent requests? You only send your password when you first log in to the app, so how does the app know that it's the same user making the request?

AUTHENTICATING USERS FOR SUBSEQUENT REQUESTS

The key to persisting your identity across multiple requests lies in the final step of figure 14.2, where you serialized the principal in a cookie. Browsers will automatically send this cookie with all requests made to your app, so you don't need to provide your password with every request.

ASP.NET Core uses the authentication cookie sent with the requests to rehydrate `ClaimsPrincipal` and set the `HttpContext.User` principal for the request, as shown in figure 14.3. The important thing to note is *when* this process happens—in `AuthenticationMiddleware`.

When a request containing the authentication cookie is received, Kestrel creates the default, unauthenticated, anonymous principal and assigns it to the `HttpContext .User` principal. Any middleware that runs at this point, before `Authentication-Middleware`, will see the request as unauthenticated, even if there's a valid cookie.

> **TIP** If it looks like your authentication system isn't working, double-check your middleware pipeline. Only middleware that runs after `Authentication-Middleware` will see the request as authenticated.

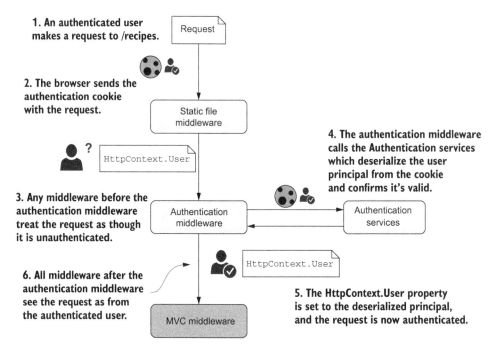

1. An authenticated user makes a request to /recipes.

Request

2. The browser sends the authentication cookie with the request.

Static file middleware

4. The authentication middleware calls the Authentication services which deserialize the user principal from the cookie and confirms it's valid.

`HttpContext.User`

3. Any middleware before the authentication middleware treat the request as though it is unauthenticated.

Authentication middleware

Authentication services

6. All middleware after the authentication middleware see the request as from the authenticated user.

`HttpContext.User`

5. The HttpContext.User property is set to the deserialized principal, and the request is now authenticated.

MVC middleware

Figure 14.3   A subsequent request after signing in to an application. The cookie sent with the request contains the user principal, which is validated and used to authenticate the request.

`AuthenticationMiddleware` is responsible for setting the current user for a request. The middleware calls authentication services, which will read the cookie from the request and deserialize it to obtain the `ClaimsPrincipal` created when the user logged in.

`AuthenticationMiddleware` sets the `HttpContext.User` principal to the new, authenticated principal. All subsequent middleware will now know the user principal for the request and can adjust behavior accordingly (for example, displaying the user's name on the homepage, or restricting access to some areas of the app).

The process described so far, in which a single app authenticates the user when they log in and sets a cookie that's read on subsequent requests, is common with traditional web apps, but it isn't the only possibility. In the next section, we'll take a look at authentication for client-side and mobile apps, and how the authentication system changes for those scenarios.

14.1.3   *Authentication for APIs and distributed applications*

The process I've outlined so far applies to traditional web apps, where you have a single endpoint that's doing all the work. It's responsible for authenticating and managing users, as well as serving your app data, as shown in figure 14.4.

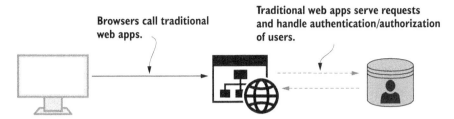

Figure 14.4 Traditional apps typically handle all the functionality of an app: the business logic, generating the UI, authentication, and user management.

In addition to this traditional web app, it's common to use ASP.NET Core as a Web API to serve data for mobile and client-side SPAs. Similarly, the trend towards microservices on the backend means that even traditional web apps using Razor often need to call Web APIs behind the scenes, as shown in figure 14.5.

In this situation, you have multiple apps and APIs, all of which need to understand that the same user is making a request across all of the apps and APIs. If you keep the same approach as before, where each app manages its own users, things can quickly become complicated!

You'll need to duplicate all of the sign-in logic between the apps and APIs, as well as needing to have some central database holding the user details. Users may need to sign in multiple times to access different parts of the service. On top of that, using cookies becomes problematic for some mobile clients in particular, or where you're making requests to multiple domains (as cookies only belong to a single domain).

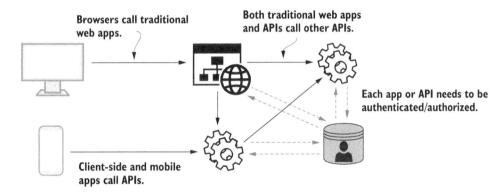

Figure 14.5 Modern applications typically need to expose Web APIs for mobile and client-side apps, as well as potentially calling APIs on the backend. When all of these services need to authenticate and manage users, this becomes complicated logistically.

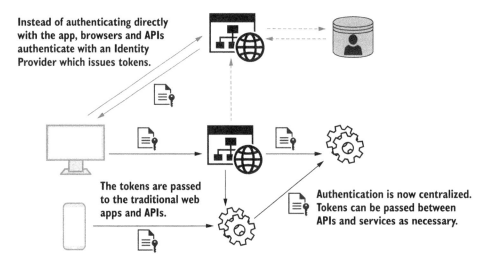

Instead of authenticating directly with the app, browsers and APIs authenticate with an Identity Provider which issues tokens.

The tokens are passed to the traditional web apps and APIs.

Authentication is now centralized. Tokens can be passed between APIs and services as necessary.

Figure 14.6   An alternative architecture involves using a central identity provider to handle all the authentication and user management for the system. Tokens are passed back and forth between the identity provider, apps, and APIs.

How can you improve this? The typical approach is to extract the code that's common to all of the apps and APIs, and move it to an *identity provider*, as shown in figure 14.6.

Instead of signing in to an app directly, the app redirects to an identity provider app. The user signs in to this identity provider, which passes *bearer tokens* back to the client that indicate who the user is and what they're allowed to access. The clients and apps can pass these tokens to the APIs, to provide information about the logged-in user, without needing to re-authenticate or manage users directly.

This architecture is clearly more complicated on the face of it, as you've thrown a whole new service—the identity provider—into the mix, but in the long run this has a number of advantages:

- *Users can share their identity between multiple services.* As you're logged in to the central identity provider, you're essentially logged in to *all* apps that use that service. This gives you the "single-sign-on" experience, where you don't have to keep logging in to multiple services.
- *Reduced duplication.* All of the sign-in logic is encapsulated in the identity provider, so you don't need to add sign-in screens to all your apps.
- *Can easily add new providers.* Whether you use the identity provider approach or the traditional approach, it's possible to use external services to handle the authentication of users. You'll have seen this on apps that allow you to "log in using Facebook" or "log in using Google," for example. If you use a centralized identity provider, adding support for additional providers can be handled in one place, instead of having to configure every app and API explicitly.

Out of the box, ASP.NET Core supports architectures like this, and for *consuming* issued bearer tokens, but it doesn't include support for *issuing* those tokens. That means you'll need to use another library or service for the identity provider.

One option for an identity provider is to delegate all the authentication responsibilities to a third-party identity provider, such as Okta, Auth0, or Azure Active Directory B2C. These will manage users for you, so user information and passwords are stored in their database, rather than your own. The biggest advantage of this approach is that you don't have to worry about making sure your customer data is safe; you can be pretty sure that a third party will protect it, as it's their whole business!

> **TIP** Wherever possible, I recommend this approach, as it delegates security responsibilities to someone else. You can't lose your user's details if you never had them!

Another common option is to build your own identity provider. This may sound like a lot of work, but thanks to excellent libraries like OpenIddict (https://github.com/openiddict) and IdentityServer4 (http://docs.identityserver.io), it's perfectly possible to write your own identity provider to serve bearer tokens that will be consumed by an application.

An aspect often overlooked by people getting started with OpenIddict and IdentityServer is that they aren't prefabricated solutions. You, as a developer, need to write the code that knows how to create a new user (normally in a database), how to load a user's details, and how to validate their password. In that respect, the development process of creating an identity provider is similar to the traditional web app with cookie authentication that I discussed in section 14.1.2.

In fact, you can almost think of an identity provider as a traditional web app that only has account management pages. It also has the ability to generate tokens for other services, but it contains no other app-specific logic. The need to manage users in a database, as well as providing an interface for users to log in, is common to both approaches and is the focus of this chapter.

> **NOTE** Hooking up your apps and APIs to use an identity provider requires a fair amount of tedious configuration, both of the app and the identity provider. For simplicity, this book will focus on traditional web apps using the process outlined in section 14.1.2. For details on how to configure your apps and client-side SPAs to use IdentityServer, see the excellent documentation at http://docs.identityserver.io.

ASP.NET Core Identity (hereafter shortened to Identity) is a system that makes building the user management aspect of your app (or identity provider app) simpler. It handles all of the boilerplate for saving and loading users to a database, as well as a number of best practices for security, such as user lock out, password hashing, and *two-factor authentication*.

> **DEFINITION**   *Two-factor authentication* (2FA) is where you require an extra piece of information to sign in, in addition to a password. This could involve sending a code to a user's phone by SMS, or using a mobile app to generate a code, for example.

In the next section, I'm going to talk about the ASP.NET Core Identity system, the problems it solves, when you'd want to use it, and when you might not want to use it. In section 14.3, we'll take a look at some code and see ASP.NET Core Identity in action.

14.2   *What is ASP.NET Core Identity?*

Whether you're writing a traditional web app using Razor templates or are setting up a new identity provider using a library like IdentityServer, you'll need a way of persisting details about your users, such as their usernames and passwords.

This might seem like a relatively simple requirement but, given this is related to security and people's personal details, it's important you get it right. As well as storing the claims for each user, it's important to store passwords using a strong hashing algorithm, to allow users to use 2FA where possible, and to protect against brute force attacks, to name a few of the many requirements!

Although it's perfectly possible to write all the code to do this manually and to build your own authentication and membership system, I highly recommend you don't.

I've already mentioned third-party identity providers such as Auth0 or Azure Active Directory B2C. These are Software-as-a-Service (SaaS) solutions that take care of the user management and authentication aspects of your app for you. If you're in the process of moving apps to the cloud generally, then solutions like these can make a lot of sense.

If you can't or don't want to use these solutions, then I recommend you consider using the ASP.NET Core Identity system to store and manage user details in your database. ASP.NET Core Identity takes care of some of the boilerplate associated with authentication, but remains flexible and lets you control the login process for users.

> **NOTE**   ASP.NET *Core* Identity is an evolution of ASP.NET Identity, with some design improvements and converted to work with ASP.NET Core.

By default, ASP.NET Core Identity uses EF Core to store user details in the database. If you're already using EF Core in your project, then this is a perfect fit. Alternatively, it's possible to write your own stores for loading and saving user details in another way.

Identity takes care of the low-level parts of user management, as shown in table 14.1. As you can see from this list, Identity gives you a lot, but not everything—by a long shot!

The biggest missing piece is the fact that you need to provide all the UI for the application, as well as tying all the individual Identity services together to create a functioning sign-in process. That's a pretty big missing piece, but it makes the Identity system extremely flexible.

Table 14.1 Which services are and aren't handled by ASP.NET Core Identity

Managed by ASP.NET Core Identity	Implemented by the developer
Database schema for storing users and claims.	UI for logging in, creating, and managing users (controller, actions, view models). This is included in the default templates.
Creating a user in the database.	Sending emails and SMS messages.
Password validation and rules.	Customizing claims for users (adding new claims).
Handling user account lockout (to prevent brute-force attacks).	Configuring third-party identity providers.
Managing and generating 2FA codes.	
Generating password-reset tokens.	
Saving additional claims to the database.	
Managing third-party identity providers (for example Facebook, Google, Twitter).	

Luckily, the .NET CLI and Visual Studio come with templates that give you a huge amount of the UI boilerplate for free. And I do mean a huge amount—if you're using all of the features of Identity, such as 2FA and external login providers, then there's a lot of Razor to write!

> **NOTE** ASP.NET Core 2.1 (in preview at the time of writing) uses new features to deliver this UI code as a library package, drastically reducing the amount of code you need to write. For details, see http://mng.bz/tZZz.

For that reason, I strongly recommend using one of the templates as a starting point, whether you're creating an app or adding user management to an existing app. But the question still remains: when should you use Identity, and when should you consider rolling your own?

I'm a big fan of Identity, so I tend to suggest it in most situations, as it handles a lot of security-related things for you that are easy to mess up. I've heard a number of arguments against it, some of which are valid, and others less so:

- *I already have user authentication in my app.* Great! In that case, you're probably right, Identity may not be necessary. But does your custom implementation use 2FA? Do you have account lockout? If not, and you need to add them, then considering Identity may be worthwhile.
- *I don't want to use EF Core.* That's a reasonable stance. You could be using Dapper, some other ORM, or even a document database for your database access. Luckily, the database integration in Identity is pluggable, so you could swap out the EF Core integration and use your own database integration libraries instead.

- *My use case is too complex for Identity.* Identity provides lower-level services for authentication, so you can compose the pieces however you like. It's also extensible, so if you need to, for example, transform claims before creating a principal, you can.

- *I don't want to build my own identity system.* I'm glad to hear it. Using an external identity provider like Azure Active Directory B2C or Auth0 is a great way of shifting the responsibility and risk associated with storing users' personal information onto a third party.

Any time you're considering adding user management to your ASP.NET Core application, I'd recommend looking at Identity as a great option for doing so. In the next section, I'll demonstrate what Identity provides by creating a new MVC application using the default Identity templates. In section 14.4, we'll take that template and apply it to an existing app instead.

14.3 Creating a project that uses ASP.NET Core Identity

I've covered authentication and Identity in general terms a fair amount now, but the best way to get a feel for it is to see some working code. In this section, we're going to look at the default code generated by the ASP.NET Core templates with Identity, how it works, and how Identity fits in.

14.3.1 Creating the project from a template

You'll start by using the Visual Studio templates to generate a simple MVC application that uses Identity for storing individual user accounts in a database.

> **TIP** You can create an equivalent project using the .NET CLI by running
> ```
> dotnet new mvc -au Individual -uld
> ```

To create the template using Visual Studio, you must be using VS 2017 Update 3 or later and have the ASP.NET Core 2.0 SDK installed:[1]

1 Choose File > New > Project.
2 From the New Project dialog, choose .NET Core, and then select ASP.NET Core Web Application.
3 Enter a Name, Location, and optionally a solution name, and click OK.
4 Choose the Web Application (Model-View-Controller) template and click Choose Authentication to bring up the Authentication dialog, shown in figure 14.7.

5 Choose Individual User Accounts to create an application configured with EF Core and ASP.NET Core Identity. Click OK.

---

[1] ASP.NET Core 2.1 (in preview at the time of writing) uses new features to deliver this UI code as a library package. If you have the 2.1 SDK installed, the templates won't generate all the UI code as described, though the behavior will be similar. For details, see http://mng.bz/tZZz.

Choose Individual User Accounts to store local user accounts using **ASP.NET Core Identity and EF Core.**

Choose No Authentication to create a template without authentication.

Choose Store user accounts in-app.

Work or School Accounts will configure the application to use an external **Identity Provider,** using **Active Directory** (or **Office365** for example) to handle user management and authentication.

Choose Windows Authentication for intranet sites where the **Windows** login of the user provides the authentication mechanism.

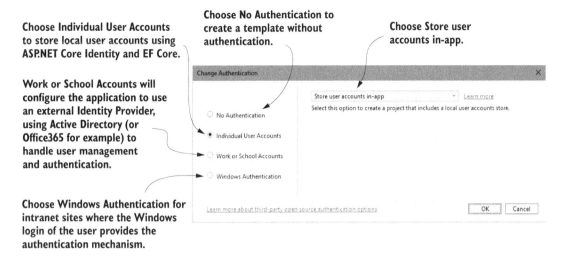

Figure 14.7 Choosing the authentication mode of the new ASP.NET Core application template in VS 2017

6 Click OK to create the application. Visual Studio will automatically run `dotnet restore` to restore all the necessary NuGet packages for the project.

7 Run the application to see the default app, as shown in figure 14.8.

You can create new users and sign in using the log in widget.

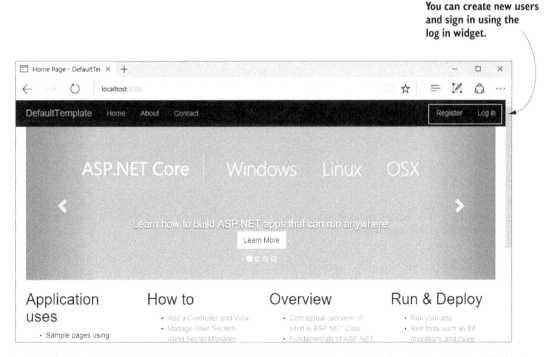

Figure 14.8 The default template with individual account authentication looks similar to the no authentication template, with the addition of a login widget in the top right of the page.

This template should look familiar, with one particular twist: you now have Register and Log-in buttons! Feel free to play with the template—creating a user, logging in and out—to get a feel for the app. Once you're happy, look at the code generated by the template and the boilerplate it saved you from writing!

14.3.2   *Exploring the template in Solution Explorer*

At first glance, the number of files in the solution for a new template can be a bit overwhelming, so I'll talk through each aspect first. The template uses the standard folder layout for the templates, where files are split by role (controller, service, data, and so on), as shown in figure 14.9.

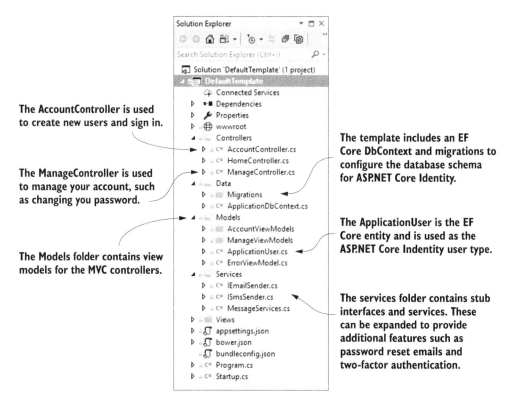

Figure 14.9   The project layout of the default template. Depending on your version of Visual Studio, the exact files may vary slightly.

Starting from the top, the first folder contains your MVC controllers. Of particular interest are `AccountController` and `ManageController`:

- `AccountController`—Used for registering as a new user, logging in, and sending password reset emails.
- `ManageController`—Used for managing your user account when logged in. Changing user details, password, and enabling two-factor authentication.

Most of the direct interaction between your app and the Identity system happens in here, in the default templates, so we'll look at these files in more detail in section 14.3.4.

The next folder, the Data folder, contains your application's EF Core `DbContext`, called `ApplicationDbContext`, and the migrations for configuring the database schema to use Identity. I'll discuss this schema in more detail in section 14.3.3.

The Models folder contains two types of models:

- The binding/view models for use with action methods and Razor view results.
- `ApplicationUser`, an EF Core entity model. This is the entity that the Identity system stores in the database.

Next up is the Services folder. This contains stub services for sending an email and an SMS, which are required in order to allow password resets and two-factor authentication.

> **NOTE**   These services are stubs and don't do anything. You'll need to hook them up, often to a third-party service, to make them functional.[2] In some versions of Visual Studio, the stub SMS service may be missing.

The last folder, Views, contains all the Razor view templates for the app. Of particular note are the Account and Manage folders, which contain the view templates for `AccountController` and `ManageController`.

In addition to all the new files included thanks to ASP.NET Core Identity, it's worth opening up Startup.cs and looking at the changes there. The most obvious change is the additional configuration in `ConfigureServices`, which adds all the services Identity requires.

Listing 14.1   Adding ASP.NET Core Identity services to `ConfigureServices`

ASP.NET Core Identity uses EF Core, so it includes the standard EF Core configuration.

Adds the Identity system, and configures the user and role types

```
public void ConfigureServices(IServiceCollection services)
{
    services.AddDbContext<ApplicationDbContext>(options =>
        options.UseSqlServer(
            Configuration.GetConnectionString("DefaultConnection")));

    services.AddIdentity<ApplicationUser, IdentityRole>()
        .AddEntityFrameworkStores<ApplicationDbContext>()
        .AddDefaultTokenProviders();

    services.AddTransient<IEmailSender, AuthMessageSender>();
    services.AddTransient<ISmsSender, AuthMessageSender>();

    services.AddMvc();
}
```

Configures Identity to store its data in EF Core

Uses the default Identity providers for generating 2FA codes

Registers the stub service for sending SMS; may be missing in some versions of Visual Studio

Registers the stub service for sending email

---

[2]   The documentation shows how to create a provider to send an email using SendGrid (https://docs.microsoft .com/en-us/aspnet/core/security/authentication/accconfirm) and SMS using Twilio or ASPSMS (2FA).

There's one other change in `Startup`, in the `Configure` method:

```
app.UseAuthentication();
```

This adds `AuthenticationMiddleware` to the pipeline, so that you can authenticate incoming requests, as you saw in figure 14.3. It's placed early in the pipeline, before `MvcMiddleware`, so that the `HttpContext.User` principal will be set correctly when the MVC controllers execute.

Now you've got an overview of the additions made by Identity, we'll look in a bit more detail at the database schema and how Identity stores users in the database.

14.3.3   *The ASP.NET Core Identity data model*

Out of the box, and in the default templates, Identity uses EF Core to store user accounts. It provides a base `DbContext` that you can inherit from, called `Identity-Context<TUser>`, where `TUser` is the user entity in your app. It also provides a base user entity, `IdentityUser`, to inherit from.

In the template, the app's `DbContext` is called `ApplicationDbContext`, and the user entity is called `ApplicationUser`. If you open up these files, you'll see they're sparse; they only inherit from the Identity classes I described earlier. What do those base classes give you? The easiest way to see is to update a database with the migrations and take a look!

Applying the migrations is the same process as in chapter 12. Ensure the connection string points to where you want to create the database, and run

```
dotnet ef database update
```

to update the database with the migrations. If the database doesn't yet exist, the CLI will create it. Figure 14.10 shows what the database looks like for the default template.

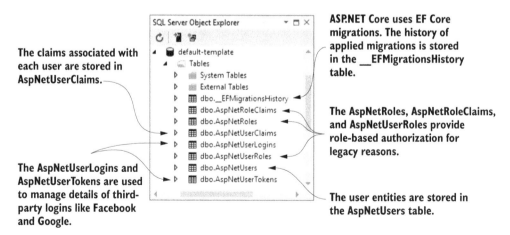

Figure 14.10   The database schema used by ASP.NET Core Identity

That's a lot of tables! You shouldn't need to interact with these tables directly—Identity handles that for you—but it doesn't hurt to have a basic grasp of what they're for:

- *__EFMigrationsHistory*—The EF Core migrations table that records which migrations have been applied.
- *AspNetUsers*—The user profile table itself. This is where `ApplicationUser` is serialized to. We'll take a closer look at this table shortly.
- *AspNetUserClaims*—The claims associated with a given user. A user can have many claims, so it's modeled as a many-to-one relationship.
- *AspNetUserLogins and AspNetUserTokens*—These are related to third-party logins. When configured, these let users sign in with a Google or Facebook account (for example), instead of creating a password on your app.
- *AspNetUserRoles, AspNetRoles, and AspNetRoleClaims*—These tables are somewhat of a legacy left over from the old role-based permission model of the pre-.NET 4.5 days, instead of the claims-based permission model. These tables let you define roles that multiple users can belong to. Each role can be assigned a number of claims. These claims are effectively inherited by a user principal when they are assigned that role.

You can explore these tables yourself, but the most interesting of them is the AspNet-Users table, shown in figure 14.11.

All of the columns in the AspNetUsers table are security related—their email and password hash, whether they have confirmed their email, whether they have 2FA enabled, and so on. There's no room for additional information, like the user's name, for example.

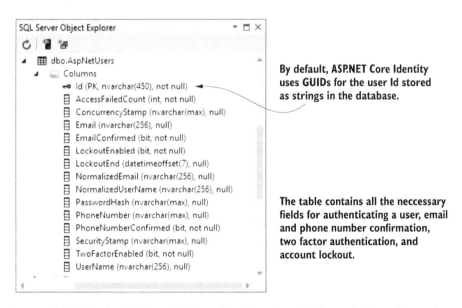

Figure 14.11   The AspNetUsers table is used to store all the details required to authenticate a user.

> **NOTE** You can see from figure 14.11 that the primary key Id is stored as a string column. By default, Identity uses Guid for the identifier. To customize the data type, see http://mng.bz/Z7Y2.

Any extra properties of the user are stored as claims in the AspNetUserClaims table associated with that user. This lets you add arbitrary additional information, without having to change the database schema to accommodate it. Want to store the user's date of birth? Add a claim to that user—no need to change the database. You can see this in action in section 14.5, when you add a Name claim to every new user.

It's useful to have a mental model of the underlying database schema Identity uses, but in day-to-day work, you won't have to interact with it directly—that's what Identity is for! In the next section, we'll look at the other end of the scale—the UI of the app—and how the action methods and controllers interact with the Identity system.

14.3.4 *Interacting with ASP.NET Core Identity: the MVC controllers*

You saw in table 14.1 that Identity provides low-level constructs and services for adding users to your application, but that you still need to put all the pieces together to create your app. In the templates, this all happens in the MVC Controllers.

In this section, we'll look at the main action methods they expose for creating users and logging in, to get a feel for the authentication process and how you need to interact with Identity.

> **NOTE** I'm only going to cover the main action methods in this chapter. It's worth exploring the code in the templates to see how to include additional functionality like two-factor authentication, external authentication, and password reset emails.

CREATING NEW USERS WITH THE ACCOUNTCONTROLLER.REGISTER ACTION

AccountController is responsible for registering new users and logging them in. The first action method a user will hit is the Register action, which will display the login form, asking the user to provide an email and password, as shown in figure 14.12.

When they click submit, this will POST the form to the Register method of AccountController, as shown in listing 14.2. This action is responsible for creating a new user entity and signing the user in. This involves several steps:

- Create the user entity in the database
- Create and store claims associated with the user (the email and username claims)
- Set the principal for the current request
- Serialize the principal to a cookie for subsequent requests

These steps would be relatively involved if you had to do them manually but, luckily, Identity takes care of most of that for us.

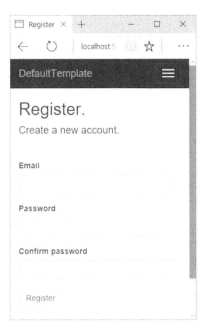

Figure 14.12 The user registration form in the default template

```
public async Task<IActionResult> Register(
    RegisterViewModel model, string returnUrl = null)
{
    ViewData["ReturnUrl"] = returnUrl;
    if (ModelState.IsValid)
    {
        var user = new ApplicationUser {
            UserName = model.Email, Email = model.Email };
        var result = await _userManager.CreateAsync(
            user, model.Password);

        if (result.Succeeded)
        {
            await _signInManager.SignInAsync(user);
            return RedirectToLocal(returnUrl);
        }
        AddErrors(result);
    }

    return View(model);
}
```

The form is bound to RegisterViewModel.

If the binding mode is valid, creates an instance of the user entity

Checks that the provided password is valid and creates the new user in the database

If the user was created successfully, sign them in.

Updates the HttpContext.User principal and sets a cookie containing the serialized principal

Redirects to the previous page using a helper method to protect against open redirect attacks

If something went wrong, adds the errors to the model state and redisplays the form

As with all action methods for modifying data, the action first validates the binding model. If that's successful, the action creates a new instance of `ApplicationUser` and attempts to create it in the database using the `UserManager` provided by the Identity system. This validates that the password passes some password-strength validation (it is of sufficient length for example) and creates the user in the database.

> **TIP** You can customize the password rules used by Identity when you configure your services. I'll show how to do this in section 14.4.1.

If `UserManager` created the user successfully, then you use `SignInManager` to sign the new user in. `SignInManager` is responsible for setting the `HttpContext.User` property to your user principal and serializing the principal to a cookie for use in subsequent requests, as you saw in figure 14.2.

Once the user is signed in, you can redirect them to what they were doing before they signed in. Identity takes care of all the heavy lifting; you're left to coordinate individual services and to generate the appropriate user interaction using `IAction-Results`.

SIGNING OUT WITH THE ACCOUNTCONTROLLER.LOGOUT ACTION

Great—so you can create a new user and sign in, but what if a user is finished with the app and wants to sign out? Funnily enough, there's a `Logout` action!

The `Logout` action method, shown in listing 14.3, is simple and asks `SignInManager` to sign the user out. This will clear the `HttpContext.User` property and removes the authentication cookie from the response so that, in subsequent requests, you'll be anonymous again. Finally, it redirects you to the `HomeController` index page.

Listing 14.3   The `AccountController.Logout` POST action for signing out

```
public async Task<IActionResult> Logout()          Replaces the HttpContext.User with
{                                                  an anonymous principal and deletes
    await _signInManager.SignOutAsync();    ◁      the authentication cookie
    return RedirectToAction(nameof(HomeController.Index), "Home");  ◁
}
                                                   Redirects to the app's homepage
```

On subsequent requests, there won't be an authentication cookie, so the request will be unauthenticated.

SIGNING IN WITH THE ACCOUNTCONTROLLER.LOGIN ACTION

The final method I want to look at is the `Login` action method. As with the `Register` action, this displays a form to the user to enter their email and password, as shown in figure 14.13, and POSTs it to the `Login` action on `AccountController`.

The login screen is a standard setup, with fields for email and password, and a link to reset your password if you've forgotten it. On the right-hand side of the screen, you can see a section for logging in using an external identity provider, such as Facebook or Google.

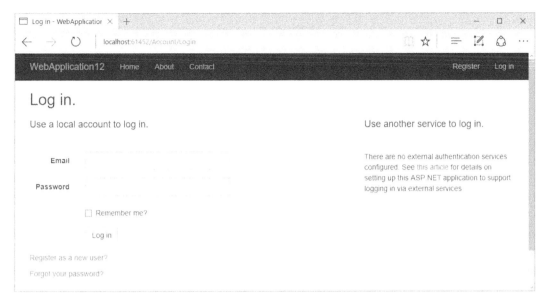

Figure 14.13 The login form in the default templates. The right-hand side of the screen can be used to configure external identity providers, so users can log in to your app using their Google or Facebook accounts.

NOTE Adding external providers is a fully supported feature of Identity, which requires relatively minimal configuration to your app. Unfortunately, you also have to register your app with the external provider, Google or Facebook, for example, which can be a convoluted process![3]

As with the `Register` method, the Identity system does all the hard work associated with loading a user from the database, validating the password, checking that the account isn't locked, and whether they have enabled 2FA on the account. The following listing shows that the `SignInManager` handles all this; you only need to display a view or redirect to an action, as appropriate.

Listing 14.4 The `AccountController.Login` POST action for logging in

```
public async Task<IActionResult> Login(                    Attempts to sign
    LoginViewModel model, string returnUrl = null)         in with the email
{                                                           and password
    ViewData["ReturnUrl"] = returnUrl;
    if (ModelState.IsValid)
    {
        var result = await _signInManager.PasswordSignInAsync(
            model.Email, model.Password, model.RememberMe);
        if (result.Succeeded)
        {                                        The sign-in succeeded, so the
            return RedirectToLocal(returnUrl);   HttpContext.User and authentication
        }                                        cookie have been set.
```

---

[3] For documentation on adding external providers see http://mng.bz/MR2m.

```
        if (result.RequiresTwoFactor)
        {
            return RedirectToAction(nameof(SendCode),
                new { ReturnUrl = returnUrl, model.RememberMe });
        }
        if (result.IsLockedOut)
        {
            return View("Lockout");
        }
        else
        {
            ModelState.AddModelError(
                string.Empty, "Invalid login attempt.");
            return View(model);
        }
    }
    return View(model);
}
```

> **If 2FA is enabled for the user, they'll be redirected to an action to generate and validate a code.**

> **Too many failed login attempts have been made for the email and lockout is enabled.**

> **An error occurred, or the view model wasn't valid. Redisplays the form.**

This method also showcases some of the additional features included in the templates, such as 2FA and account lockout. These are disabled by default in the templates, but the templates include comments that describe how to enable them.

You've covered the most important methods of `AccountController` now. If you browse the templates, you'll see others that handle 2FA and external login providers. I strongly recommend turning on these features by following the comments in the code and the tutorials in the documentation.

`AccountController` contains the most important Identity-related actions for logging in and out. `ManageController` allows users to manage their account by configuring 2FA or managing their third-party logins. As I said earlier, these features are optional for the most part, but you'll probably need the `ChangePassword` action in your apps!

CHANGING YOUR PASSWORD WITH THE MANAGECONTROLLER.CHANGEPASSWORD ACTION

As you might expect by now, the Identity system exposes methods to handle the change password functionality for you—your job is to wire it all up! This shows the `ChangePassword` method from the default templates.

Listing 14.5 The `ManageController.ChangePassword` action method

```
public async Task<IActionResult> ChangePassword(
    ChangePasswordViewModel model)
{
    if (!ModelState.IsValid)
    {
        return View(model);
    }
    var user = await _userManager.GetUserAsync(HttpContext.User);
    if (user != null)
    {
```

> **Loads the user entity for the currently-signed-in principal**

```
                        var result = await _userManager.ChangePasswordAsync(
                            user, model.OldPassword, model.NewPassword);
                        if (result.Succeeded)
                        {
                            await _signInManager.SignInAsync(user);
                            return RedirectToAction(nameof(Index)));
                        }
                        AddErrors(result);
                        return View(model);
                    }
                    return RedirectToAction(nameof(Index)));
                }
```

If the password was changed successfully, sign in again to update the principal. — (left annotation for `if (result.Succeeded)` block)

Validates the old password is correct and the new password is valid, and updates the password — (right annotation for `ChangePasswordAsync`)

If something went wrong, add the errors to ModelState and redisplay the form. — (annotation for `AddErrors` / `return View(model)`)

The action goes through several steps to change a user's password:

1 If the binding model isn't valid, redisplay the form (never forget to do this!).

2 Load the current user using `UserManager`.

3 Attempt to change the user's password by providing both the old and new password. `UserManager` will validate that the old password matches the existing hash and that the new password meets the configured password-strength requirements.

4 If `UserManager` changed the password successfully, use `SignInManager` to sign in the user principal again. This ensures the principal on `HttpContext.User`, and stored in the cookie, matches the values on the database user entity.

Even with the Identity system handling all of the low-level security aspects for you, there's still quite a lot of code to configure correctly here. In fact, there's so much code associated with the Identity templates in general, that I rarely add Identity to an existing app manually. Instead, I take a shortcut.

In the next section, you'll see how easy it is to take the code generated by the templates and add it to an existing app, without having to figure it all out for yourself from scratch.

14.4 Adding ASP.NET Core Identity to an existing project

In this section, we're going to add users to the recipe application from chapters 12 and 13. This is a working app that you want to add user functionality to. In chapter 15, we'll extend this work to restrict control regarding who's allowed to edit recipes on the app.

By the end of this section, you'll have an application with a registration page, a login screen, and a manage account screen, like the default templates. You'll also have a persistent widget in the top right of the screen, showing the login status of the current user, as shown in figure 14.14.

As with the default templates, I'm not going to set up external login providers or 2FA; I'm only concerned with adding ASP.NET Core Identity to an existing app that's already using EF Core.

The Login widget shows the
current signed in user's email
and a link for them to log out.

Figure 14.14   The recipe app after adding authentication

TIP   It's worth making sure you're comfortable with the new project templates before you go about adding Identity to an existing project. Create a test app, set up an external login provider, configure the email and SMS, and enable 2FA. This will take a bit of time, but it'll be invaluable for deciphering errors when you come to adding Identity to your own apps.

To add Identity to your app, you'll need to:

1   Add the ASP.NET Core Identity NuGet packages.
2   Configure `Startup` to use `AuthenticationMiddleware` and add Identity services to the DI container.
3   Update the EF Core data model with the Identity entities.
4   Add `AccountController` and `ManageController`, as well as the associated views and view models.

This section will tackle each of these steps in turn. At the end of the section, you'll have successfully added user accounts to your recipe app.

14.4.1   Configuring the ASP.NET Core Identity services and middleware

You can add ASP.NET Core Identity to an existing app by referencing a single NuGet package in your csproj, Microsoft.AspNetCore.Identity.EntityFrameworkCore:

```
<PackageReference
  Include="Microsoft.AspNetCore.Identity.EntityFrameworkCore"
  Version="2.0.0" />
```

This one package will bring in all the additional required dependencies you need to add Identity. Be sure to run `dotnet restore` after adding it to your project.

> **NOTE** If your app uses the Microsoft.AspNetCore.All or Microsoft.AspNet-Core.App package (used by the default templates), then the Identity package is already included and you don't need an explicit reference.

Once you've added the Identity package, you can update your Startup.cs file to include the Identity services, as shown next. This is similar to the default template setup you saw in listing 14.1, but make sure to reference your existing AppDbContext.

Listing 14.6 Adding ASP.NET Core Identity services to the recipe app

```
public void ConfigureServices(IServiceCollection services)                    The existing
{                                                                              service
    services.AddDbContext<AppDbContext>(options =>                             configuration
        options.UseSqlServer(                                                  is unchanged.
            Configuration.GetConnectionString("DefaultConnection")));

    services.AddIdentity<ApplicationUser, IdentityRole>(options =>
        options.Password.RequiredLength = 10)          ◁
        .AddEntityFrameworkStores<AppDbContext>()      ◁
        .AddDefaultTokenProviders();

    services.AddTransient<IEmailSender, AuthMessageSender>();
    services.AddTransient<ISmsSender, AuthMessageSender>();

    services.AddMvc();
    services.AddScoped<RecipeService>();
}
```

Adds the Identity services to the DI container

Updates the password rules to set the minimum password length to 10

Makes sure you use the name of your existing DbContext app

Adds the stub services to the DI container

This adds all the necessary services and configures Identity to use EF Core. You can also see that I've customized the password strength requirements in the AddIdentity call, increasing the minimum password length to 10 characters.

You've also configured the IEmailSender and ISmsSender interfaces used by the default templates. If your app already has email- or SMS-sending capabilities, you can configure them to use your existing classes. For now, I copied across the stub implementations from the default templates.

> **NOTE** You'll need to implement IEmailSender at a minimum if you want users to be able to reset their password when they forget it! See the documentation for details: http://mng.bz/pJp3.

Configuring AuthenticationMiddleware is somewhat easier: add it to the pipeline in the Configure method. As you can see in listing 14.7, I've added the middleware after StaticFileMiddleware, but before MvcMiddleware. In this position, serving static files won't come with the overhead of authentication, but your MVC controllers will be able to correctly read the user principal from HttpContext.User.

Listing 14.7   Adding `AuthenticationMiddleware` to the recipe app

**StaticFileMiddleware will never see requests
as authenticated, even after you sign in.**

```
public void Configure(IApplicationBuilder app, IHostingEnvironment env)
{
    app.UseStaticFiles();
    app.UseAuthentication();

    app.UseMvc(routes =>
    {
        routes.MapRoute(
            name: "default",
            template: "{controller=Recipe}/{action=Index}/{id?}");
    });
}
```

**Adds AuthenticationMiddleware
to the pipeline**

**Middleware after
AuthenticationMiddleware can read the
user principal from HttpContext.User.**

You've configured your app to use Identity, so the next step is to update EF Core's
data model. You're already using EF Core in this app, so you need to update your database schema to include the tables Identity requires.

14.4.2   *Updating the EF Core data model to support Identity*

You saw in section 14.3.3 that Identity provides a `DbContext` called `IdentityDb-
Context`, which you can inherit from. The `IdentityDbContext` base class includes the
necessary `DbSet<T>` to store your user entities using EF Core.

Updating an existing `DbContext` for Identity is simple—update your app's `DbContext`
to inherit from `IdentityDbContext`, as shown in the following listing. You'll also need to
copy the `ApplicationUser` entity class to your app.

Listing 14.8   Updating `AppDbContext` to use `IdentityDbContext`

**The remainder
of the class
remains
the same**

```
public class AppDbContext : IdentityDbContext<ApplicationUser>
{
    public AppDbContext(DbContextOptions<AppDbContext> options)
        : base(options)
    { }

    public DbSet<Recipe> Recipes { get; set; }
}
```

**Updates to inherit from the
Identity context, instead of
directly from DbContext**

Effectively, by updating the base class of your context in this way, you've added a whole
load of new entities to EF Core's data model. As you saw in chapter 12, whenever EF
Core's data model changes, you need to create a new migration and apply those
changes to the database.

At this point, your app should compile, so you can add a new migration called
`AddIdentitySchema` using

```
dotnet ef migrations add AddIdentitySchema.
```

The final—biggest—step is adding the controllers, view models, and view templates for the app. Normally, this would be a lot of work, but by using the default templates as a base, you can add the code much faster.

14.4.3 Adding the controllers, view models, and views

One of the most tedious parts of adding Identity to an existing app is adding all the UI code to interact with it. You need the login page and the register page, obviously, but if you're also implementing features like 2FA and external login providers, there's a whole host of other pages you need.

To get around this, I like to copy and paste the default code from the templates and tweak it later! I copied `AccountController` and `ManageController`, their view models, and the associated view templates into their corresponding parts of the existing recipe app, and it pretty much works.

> **TIP** To avoid namespace issues, I create a fresh, temporary project with the same name as the project I'm moving to. This generates the code with all the correct namespaces.

You need to make a couple more changes before you're done. First off, you'll need to make sure your view templates are importing the correct namespaces for view models and Identity. The best place for these is the _ViewImports.cshtml file, as you saw in chapter 7.

Listing 14.9 Updating _ViewImports.cshtml to use additional namespaces

```
@using Microsoft.AspNetCore.Identity       ◁——— The Identity namespace
@using RecipeApplication
@using RecipeApplication.Models
@using RecipeApplication.Models.AccountViewModels        The namespace of the Identity
@using RecipeApplication.Models.ManageViewModels         view models for the recipe app
@addTagHelper *, Microsoft.AspNetCore.Mvc.TagHelpers
```

The last tweak is to add the login widget from figure 14.8. This shows the current login status of the user and lets you register or sign in. This widget is implemented as a shared partial template, _LoginPartial.cshtml, which you can copy directly across to the views/shared folder. All that remains is to invoke the partial by calling

```
@await Html.PartialAsync("_LoginPartial")
```

in the layout file of your app, _Layout.cshtml.

And there you have it, you've added Identity to an existing application. Admittedly, copying the templates like this is a bit of a cheat, but as long as you can read through and understand what they're doing, there's no harm in saving yourself some work. On top of that, it reduces the chance of introducing accidental security bugs at the same time![4]

---

[4] In ASP.NET Core 2.1 (currently in preview), using the default UI will be easier, as described in https://blogs.msdn.microsoft.com/webdev/2018/03/02/aspnetcore-2-1-identity-ui/.

Getting started with Identity like this is pretty easy, and the documentation for enabling additional features like 2FA and external providers is easily accessible and highlighted in the code comments. One area where people quickly get confused is when they want to extend the default templates. In the next section, I show how you can tackle a common follow requirement: how to add additional claims to users when they register.

14.5   Managing users: adding new claims to users

Very often, the next step after adding Identity to an application is to customize it. The default templates only require an email and password to register. What if you need more details, like a friendly name for the user? Also, I've mentioned that we use claims for security, so what if you want to add a claim called `IsAdmin` to certain users?

You know that every user principal has a collection of claims so, conceptually, adding any claim just requires adding it to the user's collection. There are two main times that you would want to grant a claim to a user:

- *For every user, when they first register on the app.* For example, you might want to add a "Name" field to the Register form and add that as a claim to the user when they register.
- *Manually, after the user has already registered.* This is common for claims used as "permissions," where an existing user might want to add an `IsAdmin` claim to a specific user after they have registered on the app.

In this section, I show you the first approach, automatically adding new claims to a user when they're created. The latter approach is the more flexible and, ultimately, is the approach many apps will need, especially line-of-business apps. Luckily, there's nothing conceptually difficult to it; it requires a simple UI that lets you view users and add a claim through the same mechanism I'll show here.

Let's say you want to add a new Claim to a user called `FullName`. A typical approach would be:

1   Add a "Name" field to the `RegisterViewModel` model of the `Register` action.
2   Add a "Name" input field to the Register.cshtml Razor template.
3   Create the new `ApplicationUser` entity as before, by calling `CreateAsync` on `UserManager<ApplicationUser>`.
4   Add a new Claim to the user by calling `_userManager.AddClaimAsync()`.
5   Sign the user in as before, using `_signInManager.SignInAsync()`.

Steps 1 and 2 are fairly self-explanatory and just require updating the existing templates with the new field. Steps 3-5 all take place in the `AccountController.Register` method, which you can compare to listing 14.2, where you didn't add the extra claim.

Listing 14.10 Adding a custom claim to a new user in the Register action

```
public async Task<IActionResult> Register(
        RegisterViewModel model, string returnUrl = null)
{
    ViewData["ReturnUrl"] = returnUrl;
    if (ModelState.IsValid)
    {
        var user = new ApplicationUser {
            UserName = model.Email, Email = model.Email };
        var result = await _userManager.CreateAsync(
            user, model.Password);

        if (result.Succeeded)
        {
            var claim = new Claim("FullName", model.Name);
            await _userManager.AddClaimAsync(user, nameClaim);

            await _signInManager.SignInAsync(user);
            return RedirectToLocal(returnUrl);
        }
        AddErrors(result);
    }

    return View(model);
}
```

Creates an instance of the ApplicationUser entity, as usual

Validates that the provided password is valid and creates the user in the database

Adds the new claim to the ApplicationUser's collection

Creates a claim, with a string name of "FullName" and the provided value

Signs the user in by setting the HttpContext.User, the principal will include the custom claim

This is all that's required to add the new claim, but you're not using it anywhere currently. What if you want to display it? Well, you've added a claim to the user principal, which was assigned to the `HttpContext.User` property when you called `SignInAsync`. That means you can access the claims anywhere you have access to `HttpContext`—in your controllers or in view templates. For example, you could display the user's `FullName` claim anywhere in a Razor template with the following statement:

```
@User.Claims.FirstOrDefault(x=>x.Type == "FullName").Value
```

This finds the first claim on the current users with a `Type` of `"FullName"` and prints the assigned value. The Identity system even includes a handy extension method that tidies up this LINQ expression (found in the `System.Security.Claims` namespace):

```
@User.FindFirstValue("FullName")
```

And with that last titbit, we've reached the end of this chapter on ASP.NET Core Identity. I hope you've come to appreciate the amount of effort using Identity can save you, especially when you make use of the templates that come with Visual Studio and the .NET CLI.

ASP.NET Core Identity provides so many additional features, such as 2FA and external login providers, that there isn't space to cover them here. Although not essential for adding user functionality to your app, I strongly recommend looking into them. In particular, consider adding 2FA to give your users additional protection.

Adding user accounts and authentication to an app is typically the first step to customizing your app further. Once you have authentication, you can have authorization, which lets you lock down certain actions in your app, based on the current user. In the next chapter, you'll learn about the ASP.NET Core authorization system and how you can use it to customize your apps, in particular, the recipe application, which is coming along nicely!

Summary

- Authentication is the process of determining who you are.
- Authorization is the process of determining what you're allowed to do.
- Every request in ASP.NET Core is associated with a user, also known as a principal. By default, without authentication, this is an anonymous user.
- The current principal for a request is exposed on `HttpContext.User`.
- Every user has a collection of claims. These claims are single pieces of information about the user. Claims could be properties of the physical user, such as `Name` and `Email`, or they could be related to things the user has, such as `HasAdminAccess` or `IsVipCustomer`.
- Earlier versions of ASP.NET used roles instead of claims. You can still use roles if you need to, but you should use claims where possible.
- Authentication in ASP.NET Core is provided by `AuthenticationMiddleware` and a number of authentication services. These services are responsible for setting the current principal when a user logs in, saving it to a cookie, and loading the principal from the cookie on subsequent requests.
- ASP.NET Core 2.0 includes support for consuming bearer tokens for authenticating API calls, but it doesn't include a way to create them. You can use a third-party provider such as Azure AD B2C, or a library such as IdentityServer if you need this ability.
- ASP.NET Core Identity handles low-level services needed for storing users in a database, ensuring their passwords are stored safely, and for logging users in and out. You must provide the UI for the functionality yourself and wire it up to the Identity sub-system.
- The default template for an MVC Application with Individual Account Authentication uses ASP.NET Core Identity to store users in the database with EF Core. It includes all the boilerplate code required to wire the UI up to the Identity system.
- You can use the `UserManager<T>` class to create new user accounts, load them from the database, and change their passwords.
- `SignInManager<T>` is used to sign a user in and out, by assigning the principal for the request and by setting an authentication cookie.
- You can update an EF Core `DbContext` to support Identity by deriving from `IdentityDbContext<TUser>` where `TUser` is a class that derives from `IdentityUser`, called `ApplicationUser` in the default templates.

- You can add additional claims to a user using the `UserManager<TUser>` `.AddClaimAsync(TUser user, Claim claim)` method.
- Claims consist of a type and a value. Both values are strings. You can use standard values for types exposed on the `ClaimTypes` class, such as `ClaimTypes` `.GivenName` and `ClaimTypes.FirstName`, or you can use a custom string, such as `"FullName"`.

Authorization: securing your application

This chapter covers

- Using authorization to control who can use your app
- Using claims-based authorization with policies
- Creating custom policies to handle complex requirements
- Authorizing a request depending upon the resource being accessed
- Hiding elements from a Razor template that the user is unauthorized to access

In chapter 14, I showed how to add users to an ASP.NET Core application by adding authentication. With authentication, users can register and log in to your app using an email and password. Whenever you add authentication to an app, you inevitably find you want to be able to restrict what some users can do. The process of determining whether a user can perform a given action on your app is called *authorization*.

432

On an e-commerce site, for example, you may have admin users who are allowed to add new products and change prices, sales users who are allowed to view completed orders, and customer users who are only allowed to place orders and buy products.

In this chapter, I show how to use authorization in an app to control what your users can do. In section 15.1, I introduce authorization and put it in the context of a real-life scenario you've probably experienced: an airport. I describe the sequence of events, from checking in, passing through security, to entering an airport lounge, and how these relate to the authorization concepts you'll see in this chapter.

In section 15.2, I show how authorization fits into an ASP.NET Core web application and how it relates to the `ClaimsPrincipal` class that you saw in the previous chapter. You'll see how to enforce the simplest level of authorization in an ASP.NET Core app, ensuring that only authenticated users can execute an MVC action.

We'll extend that approach in section 15.3 by adding in the concept of policies. These let you make specific requirements about a given authenticated user, requiring that they have a specific claim in order to execute an action.

You'll use policies extensively in the ASP.NET Core authorization system, so in section 15.4, we explore how to handle more complex scenarios. You'll learn about authorization requirements and handlers, and how you can combine them to create specific policies that you can apply to your MVC actions.

Sometimes, whether a user is authorized for an action depends on which resource or document they're attempting to access. A resource is anything that you're trying to protect, so it could be a document or a post in a social media app.

For example, you may allow users to create documents and read documents from other users, but only to edit documents that they created themselves. This type of authorization, where you need the details of the document to determine authorization, is called resource-based authorization, and is the focus of section 15.5.

In the final section of this chapter, I show how you can extend the resource-based authorization approach to your MVC view models and Razor templates. This lets you modify the UI to hide elements that users aren't authorized to interact with. In particular, you'll see how to hide the Edit button when a user isn't authorized to edit the entity.

We'll start by looking more closely at the concept of authorization, how it differs from authentication, and how it relates to real-life concepts you might see in an airport.

15.1 Introduction to authorization

For people who are new to web apps and security, authentication and authorization can sometimes be a little daunting. It certainly doesn't help that the words look so similar! The two concepts are often used together, but they're definitely distinct:

- *Authentication*—The process of determining who made a request
- *Authorization*—The process of determining whether the requested action is allowed

Typically, authentication occurs first, so that you know who is making a request to your app. For traditional web apps, your app authenticates a request by checking the encrypted cookie that was set when the user logged in (as you saw in the previous chapter). Web APIs typically use a header instead of a cookie for authentication, but the process is the same.

Once a request is authenticated and you know who is making the request, you can determine whether they're allowed to execute an action on your server. This process is called authorization and is the focus of this chapter.

Before we dive into code and start looking at authorization in ASP.NET Core, I'll put these concepts into a real-life scenario you're hopefully familiar with: checking in at an airport. To enter an airport and board a plane, you must pass through several steps. In simplified form, these might look like:

1 Show passport at check-in desk. Receive a boarding pass.
2 Show boarding pass to enter security. Pass through security.
3 Show frequent flyer card to enter the airline lounge. Enter lounge.
4 Show boarding pass to board flight. Enter airplane.

Obviously, these steps, also shown in figure 15.1, will vary somewhat (I don't have a frequent flyer card!), but we'll go with them for now. Let's explore each step a little further.

When you arrive at the airport, the first thing you do is go to the check-in counter. Here, you can purchase a plane ticket, but in order to do so, you need to prove who you are by providing a passport; you *authenticate* yourself. If you've forgotten your passport, you can't authenticate, and you can't go any further.

Once you've purchased your ticket, you're issued a boarding pass, which says which flight you're on. We'll assume it also includes a `BoardingPassNumber`. You can think of this number as an additional *claim* associated with your identity.

> **DEFINITION** A *claim* is a piece of information about a user that consists of a *type* and an optional *value*.

The next step is security. The security guards will ask you to present your boarding pass for inspection, which they'll use to check that you have a flight and so are allowed deeper into the airport. This is an authorization process: you must have the required claim (a `BoardingPassNumber`) to proceed.

If you don't have a valid `BoardingPassNumber`, there are two possibilities for what happens next:

- *If you haven't yet purchased a ticket*—You'll be directed back to the check-in desk, where you can authenticate and purchase a ticket. At that point, you can try to enter security again.
- *If you have an invalid ticket*—You won't be allowed through security and there's nothing else you can do. If, for example, you show up with a boarding pass a week late for your flight, they probably won't let you through. (Ask me how I know!)

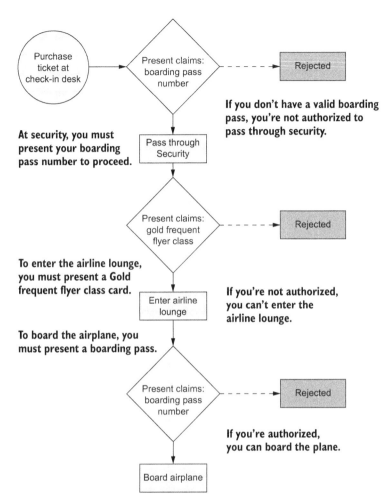

Figure 15.1   When boarding a plane at an airport, you pass through a number of authorization steps. At each authorization step, you must present a claim in the form of a boarding pass or a frequent flyer card. If you're not authorized, then access will be denied.

Once you're through security, you need to wait for your flight to start boarding, but unfortunately there aren't any seats free. Typical! Luckily, you're a regular flier, and you've notched up enough miles to achieve a "Gold" frequent flyer status, so you can use the airline lounge.

You head to the lounge, where you're asked to present your Gold Frequent Flyer card to the attendant and they let you in. This is another example of authorization. You must have a `FrequentFlyerClass` claim with a value of `Gold` in order to proceed.

NOTE   You've used authorization twice so far in this scenario. Each time, you presented a claim in order to proceed. In the first case, the presence of any BoardingPassNumber was sufficient, whereas for the FrequentFlyerClass claim, you needed the specific value of Gold.

When you're boarding the airplane, you have one final authorization step, in which you must present the BoardingPassNumber claim again. You presented this claim earlier, but boarding the aircraft is a distinct action from entering security, so you have to present it again.

This whole scenario has lots of parallels with requests to a web app:

- Both processes start with authentication.
- You have to prove *who* you are in order to retrieve the *claims* you need for authorization.
- You use authorization to protect sensitive actions like entering security and the airline lounge.

I'll reuse this airport scenario throughout the chapter to build a simple web application that simulates the steps you take in an airport. We've covered the concept of authorization in general, so in the next section, we'll look at how authorization works in ASP.NET Core. You'll start with the most basic level of authorization, ensuring only authenticated users can execute an action, and look at what happens when you try to execute such an action.

15.2 *Authorization in ASP.NET Core*

The ASP.NET Core framework has authorization built in,[1] so you can use it anywhere in your app, but it's most common to apply authorization as part of MVC. For both traditional web apps and web APIs, users execute actions on your controllers. Authorization occurs before these actions execute, as shown in figure 15.2. This lets you use different authorization requirements for different action methods.

As you can see in figure 15.2, authorization occurs as part of MvcMiddleware, after AuthenticationMiddeware has authenticated the request. You saw in chapter 13 that authorization occurs as part of the MVC filter pipeline, in the (cunningly named) authorization filters.

15.2.1 *Preventing anonymous users from accessing your application*

When you think about authorization, you typically think about checking whether a particular user has permission to execute an action. In ASP.NET Core, you'd achieve this by checking whether a user has a particular claim.

---

[1] You can find the authentication and authorization packages for ASP.NET Core on GitHub at https://github .com/aspnet/security.

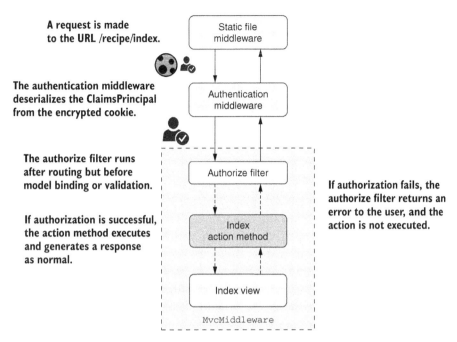

A request is made to the URL /recipe/index.

The authentication middleware deserializes the ClaimsPrincipal from the encrypted cookie.

The authorize filter runs after routing but before model binding or validation.

If authorization is successful, the action method executes and generates a response as normal.

Static file middleware

Authentication middleware

Authorize filter

Index action method

Index view

MvcMiddleware

If authorization fails, the authorize filter returns an error to the user, and the action is not executed.

Figure 15.2   Authorization occurs before an action method executes as part of the MVC filter pipeline in `MvcMiddleware`.

There's an even more basic level of authorization that you haven't considered yet—only allowing authenticated users to execute an action. This is even simpler than the claims scenario (which we'll come to later) as there are only two possibilities:

- *The user is authenticated*—The action executes as normal.
- *The user is unauthenticated*—The user can't execute the action.

You can achieve this basic level of authorization by using the [Authorize] attribute, as you saw in chapter 13, when we discussed authorization filters. You can apply this attribute to your actions, as shown in the following listing, to restrict them to authenticated (logged-in) users only. If an unauthenticated user tries to execute an action protected with the [Authorize] attribute in this way, they'll be redirected to the login page.

Listing 15.1   Applying [Authorize] to an action

```
public class HomeController : Controller        This action can be
{                                               executed by anyone, even
    public IActionResult Index()        ◁───────when not logged in.
    {
        return View();          Applies [Authorize] to
    }                           individual actions or
                                whole controllers
    [Authorize]        ◁───────
```

```
public IActionResult AuthedUsersOnly()          ◁─────    This action can only be executed
{                                                          by authenticated users.
    return View();
}
}
```

You can apply the [Authorize] attribute at the action scope, controller scope, or globally, as you saw in chapter 13. Any action that has the [Authorize] attribute applied in this way can be executed only by an authenticated user. Unauthenticated users will be redirected to the login page.

Sometimes, especially when you apply the [Authorize] attribute globally, you might need to "poke holes" in this authorization requirement. If you apply the [Authorize] attribute globally, then any unauthenticated request will be redirected to the login page for your app. But the [Authorize] attribute is global, so when the login page tries to load, you'll be unauthenticated and redirected to the login page again. And now you're stuck in an infinite redirect loop.

To get around this, you can designate specific actions to ignore the [Authorize] attribute by applying the [AllowAnonymous] attribute to an action, as shown next. This allows unauthenticated users to execute the action, so you can avoid the redirect loop that would otherwise result.

Listing 15.2 Applying [AllowAnonymous] to allow unauthenticated access

```
[Authorize]                                      ◁────    Applied at the controller scope,
public class AccountController : Controller               so user must be authenticated
{                                                         for all actions on the controller.
    public IActionResult ManageAccount()         ◁──┐
    {                                                │      Only authenticated users may
        return View();                               │      execute ManageAccount.
    }

    [AllowAnonymous]                             ◁──┐      [AllowAnonymous] overrides
    public IActionResult Login()                 ◁──┤      [Authorize] to allow
    {                                                │      unauthenticated users.
        return View();
    }                                                       Login can be executed
}                                                           by anonymous users.
```

> **WARNING** If you apply the [Authorize] attribute globally, be sure to add the [AllowAnonymous] attribute to your login actions, error actions, password reset actions, and any other actions that you need unauthenticated users to execute.

If an unauthenticated user attempts to execute an action protected by the [Authorize] attribute, traditional web apps will redirect them to the login page. But what about web APIs? And what about more complex scenarios, where a user is logged in but doesn't have the necessary claims to execute an action? In the next section, we'll look at how the ASP.NET Core authentication services handle all of this for you.

15.2.2 *Handling unauthorized requests*

In the previous section, you saw how to apply the [Authorize] attribute to an action to ensure only authenticated users can execute it. In section 15.3, we'll look at more complex examples that require you to also have a specific claim. In both cases, you must meet one or more authorization requirements (for example, you must be authenticated) to execute the action.

If the user meets the authorization requirements, then they can execute the action as normal and the request continues down the MVC filter pipeline. If they don't meet the requirements, the authorization filter will short-circuit the request. Depending on why they failed authorization, the authorization filter will return one of two different types of IActionResult:

- ChallengeResult—This indicates that the user was not authorized to execute the action because they weren't yet logged in.
- ForbidResult—This indicates that the user was logged in but didn't meet the requirements to execute the action. They didn't have a required claim, for example.

NOTE If you apply the [Authorize] attribute in basic form, as you did in section 15.2.1, then the filter will only create ChallengeResults. The filter will return ChallengeResult for unauthenticated users, but authenticated users will always be authorized.

When authorization fails, the authorization filter short-circuits the MVC filter pipeline, and the ChallengeResult or ForbidResult executes to generate a response. This response passes back through the middleware pipeline as usual. The exact response generated depends on the type of application you're building, and so the type of authentication your application uses.

For traditional web apps using cookie authentication, such as when you use ASP.NET Core Identity, as in chapter 14, ChallengeResult and ForbidResult redirect users to a different page in your application. ChallengeResult indicates the user isn't yet authenticated, so they're redirected to the login page for the app. After logging in, they can attempt to execute the protected resource again.

ForbidResult means the request was from a user that already logged in, but they're still not allowed to execute the action. Consequently, the user is redirected to a Forbidden or Access Denied web page, as shown in figure 15.3, which informs them they can't execute the action.

The preceding behavior is typical for traditional web apps, but web APIs typically use a different approach to authentication, as you saw in chapter 14. Instead of logging in using the web API directly, you'd typically log in to a third-party application that provides a token to the client-side SPA or mobile app. The client-side app sends this token when it makes a request to your web API.

Authenticating a request for a web API using tokens is essentially identical to a traditional web app that uses cookies; AuthenticationMiddleware deserializes the

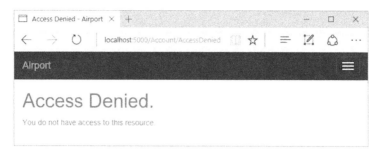

Figure 15.3   In traditional web apps using cookie authentication, if you don't have permission to execute an action and you're already logged in, you'll be redirected to an Access Denied page.

cookie or token to create the `ClaimsPrincipal`. The difference is in how a web API handles `ChallengeResult` and `ForbidResult`.

When a web API app executes a `ChallengeResult`, it returns a 401 Unauthorized error response to the caller. Similarly, when the app executes a `ForbidResult`, it returns a 403 Forbidden response. The traditional web app essentially handled these errors by automatically redirecting unauthorized users to the login or Access Denied page, but the web API doesn't do this. It's up to the client-side SPA or mobile app to detect these errors and handle them as appropriate.

The important takeaway from all this is that the framework largely handles these intricacies for you. Whether you're building a web API or a traditional MVC web app, the authorization code looks the same in both cases. Apply your [`Authorize`] attributes as normal and let the framework take care of the differences for you.

> **NOTE**   In chapter 14, you saw how to configure ASP.NET Core Identity as a traditional web app. This chapter assumes you're building a traditional web app, but it's equally applicable if you're building a web API. Remember that a web API will return 401 and 403 status codes directly, instead of redirecting unauthorized users.

You've seen how to apply the most basic authorization requirement—restricting an action to authenticated users only—but most apps need something more subtle than this all-or-nothing approach.

Consider the airport scenario from section 15.1. Being authenticated (having a passport) isn't enough to get you through security. Instead, you also need a specific claim: `BoardingPassNumber`. In the next section, we'll look at how you can implement a similar requirement in ASP.NET Core.

15.3   *Using policies for claims-based authorization*

In the previous chapter, you saw that authentication in ASP.NET Core centers around a `ClaimsPrincipal` object, which represents the user. This object has a collection of claims that contain pieces of information about the user, such as their name, email, and date of birth.

You can use these to customize the app for each user, by displaying a welcome message addressing the user by name, but you can also use claims for authorization. For example, you might only authorize a user if they have a specific claim (such as Boarding-PassNumber) or if a claim has a specific value (FrequentFlyerClass claim with the value Gold).

In ASP.NET Core, the rules that define whether a user is authorized are encapsulated in a *policy*.

> **DEFINITION** A *policy* defines the requirements you must meet in order for a request to be authorized.

Policies can be applied to an action using the [Authorize] attribute, similar to the way you saw in section 15.2.1. This listing shows a controller and action that represent the first step in the airport scenario. The AirportSecurity action method is protected by an [Authorize] attribute, but you've also provided a policy name: "CanEnterSecurity".

> **Listing 15.3 Applying an authorization policy to an action**

```
public class AirportController : Controller        The Index method can be
{                                                  executed by
    public IActionResult Index()        ◁────────  unauthenticated users.
    {
        return View();
    }                                              Applying the
                                                   "CanEnterSecurity" policy
    [Authorize("CanEnterSecurity")]     ◁────────  using [Authorize]
    public IActionResult AirportSecurity()   ◁───
    {                                              Only users that satisfy the
        return View();                             "CanEnterSecurity" policy can
    }                                              execute the AirportSecurity action.
}
```

If a user attempts to execute the AirportSecurity action, the authorize filter will verify whether the user satisfies the policy's requirements (we'll look at the policy itself shortly). This gives one of three possible outcomes:

- *The user satisfies the policy.*—The action will execute as normal.
- *The user is unauthenticated.*—The user will be redirected to the login page.
- *The user is authenticated but doesn't satisfy the policy.*—The user will be redirected to a "Forbidden" or "Access Denied" page.

These three outcomes correlate with the real-life outcomes you might expect when trying to pass through security at the airport:

- *You have a boarding pass.*—You can enter security as normal.
- *You're unauthenticated.*—You're redirected to purchase a ticket.
- *Your boarding pass is invalid (you turned up a day late, for example).*—You're blocked from entering.

Listing 15.3 shows how you can apply a policy to an action using the [Authorize] attribute, but you still need to define the CanEnterSecurity policy.

You add policies to an ASP.NET Core application in the ConfigureServices method of Startup.cs, as shown in listing 15.4. First, you add the authorization services using AddAuthorization(), and then you can add policies by calling AddPolicy() on the AuthorizationOptions object. You define the policy itself by calling methods on a provided AuthorizationPolicyBuilder (called policyBuilder here).

Listing 15.4   Adding an authorization policy using `AuthorizationPolicyBuilder`

```
public void ConfigureServices(IServiceCollection services)        Calls AddAuthorization
{                                                                  to configure
    services.AddAuthorization(options =>          <————           AuthorizationOptions
    {
        options.AddPolicy(      <————— Adds a new policy
            "CanEnterSecurity",       <————— Provides a name for the policy
            policyBuilder => policyBuilder
                .RequireClaim("BoardingPassNumber"));       ┐ Defines the policy
    });                                                     │ requirements using
    // Additional service configuration                     ┘ AuthorizationPolicyBuilder
}
```

When you call AddPolicy you provide a name for the policy, which should match the value you use in your [Authorize] attributes, and you define the requirements of the policy. In this example, you have a single simple requirement: the user must have a claim of type BoardingPassNumber. If a user has this claim, whatever its value, then the policy will be satisfied and they'll be authorized.

AuthorizationPolicyBuilder contains several methods for creating simple policies like this, as shown in table 15.1. For example, an overload of the RequireClaim() method lets you specify a specific value that a claim must have. The following would let you create a policy that the "BoardingPassNumber" claim must have a value of "A1234":

```
policyBuilder => policyBuilder.RequireClaim("BoardingPassNumber", "A1234");
```

Table 15.1   Simple policy builder methods on `AuthorizationPolicyBuilder`

Method	Policy behavior
RequireAuthenticatedUser()	The required user must be authenticated. Creates a policy similar to the default [Authorize] attribute, where you don't set a policy.
RequireClaim(claim, values)	The user must have the specified claim. Optionally, with one of the specified values.
RequireUsername(username)	The user must have the specified username.
RequireAssertion(function)	Executes the provided lambda function, which returns a bool, indicating whether the policy was satisfied.

Role-based authorization vs. claims-based authorization

If you look at all of the methods available on the `AuthorizationPolicyBuilder` type, you might notice that there's a method I didn't mention in table 15.1, `Require-Role()`. This is a remnant of the role-based approach to authorization used in previous versions of ASP.NET, and I don't recommend using it.

Before Microsoft adopted the claims-based authorization used by ASP.NET Core and recent versions of ASP.NET, role-based authorization was the norm. Users were assigned to one or more roles, such as `Administrator` or `Manager`, and authorization involved checking whether the current user was in the required role.

This role-based approach to authorization is possible in ASP.NET Core, but it's primarily for legacy compatibility reasons. Claims-based authorization is the suggested approach. Unless you're porting a legacy app that uses roles, I suggest you embrace claims-based authorization and leave those roles behind!

You can use these methods to build simple policies that can handle basic situations, but often you'll need something more complicated. What if you wanted to create a policy that enforces only users over the age of 18 can execute the action method?

The `DateOfBirth` claim provides the information you need, but there's not a single correct value, so you couldn't use the `RequireClaim()` method. You *could* use the `RequireAssertion()` method and provide a function that calculates the age from the `DateOfBirth` claim, but that could get messy pretty quickly.

For more complex policies that can't be easily defined using the `RequireClaim()` method, I recommend you take a different approach and create a custom policy, as you'll see in the following section.

15.4 *Creating custom policies for authorization*

You've already seen how to create a policy by requiring a specific claim, or requiring a specific claim with a specific value, but often the requirements will be more complex than that. Also, you'll sometimes need to account for there being multiple ways to satisfy a policy, any of which are valid.

Let's return to the airport example. You've already configured the policy for passing through security, and now you're going to configure the policy that controls whether you're authorized to enter the airline lounge.

As you saw in figure 15.1, you're allowed to enter the lounge if you have a `Frequent-FlyerClass` claim with a value of `Gold`. If this was the only requirement, you could use `AuthorizationPolicyBuilder` to create a policy using:

```
options.AddPolicy("CanAccessLounge", policyBuilder =>
    policyBuilder.RequireClaim("FrequentFlyerClass", "Gold");
```

But what if the requirements are more complicated than this? For example, you can enter the lounge if

- You're a gold-class frequent flyer (have a `FrequentFlyerClass` claim with value `"Gold"`)
- You're an employee of the airline (have an `EmployeeNumber` claim)
- You're at least 18 years old (as calculated from the `DateOfBirth` claim)

If you've ever been banned from the lounge (you have an `IsBannedFromLounge` claim), then you won't be allowed in, even if you satisfy the other requirements.

There's no way of achieving this complex set of requirements with the basic usage of `AuthorizationPolicyBuilder` you've seen so far. Luckily, these methods are a wrapper around a set of building blocks that you can combine to achieve the desired policy.

15.4.1 *Requirements and handlers: the building blocks of a policy*

Every policy in ASP.NET Core consists of one or more *requirements*, and every requirement can have one or more *handlers*. For the airport lounge example, you have a single policy (`"CanAccessLounge"`), two requirements (`MinimumAgeRequirement` and `AllowedInLoungeRequirement`), and several handlers, as shown in figure 15.4.

For a policy to be satisfied, a user must fulfill *all* the requirements. If the user fails *any* of the requirements, the authorize filter won't allow the protected action to be executed. A user must be allowed to access the lounge *and* must be over 18 years old.

Each requirement can have one or more handlers, which will confirm that the requirement has been satisfied. For example, as shown in figure 15.4, `AllowedIn-LoungeRequirement` has two handlers that can satisfy the requirement:

- `FrequentFlyerHandler`
- `IsAirlineEmployeeHandler`

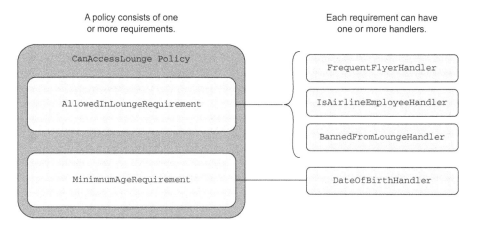

Figure 15.4   A policy can have many requirements, and every requirement can have many handlers.

If the user satisfies either of these handlers, then `AllowedInLoungeRequirement` is satisfied. You don't need all handlers for a requirement to be satisfied, you just need one.

> **NOTE** Figure 15.4 showed a third handler, `BannedFromLoungeHandler`, which I'll cover in the next section. It's slightly different, in that it can only *fail* a requirement, not *satisfy* it.

You can use requirements and handlers to achieve most any combination of behavior you need for a policy. By combining handlers for a requirement, you can validate conditions using a logical OR: if any of the handlers are satisfied, the requirement is satisfied. By combining requirements, you create a logical AND: all of the requirements must be satisfied for the policy to be satisfied, as shown in figure 15.5.

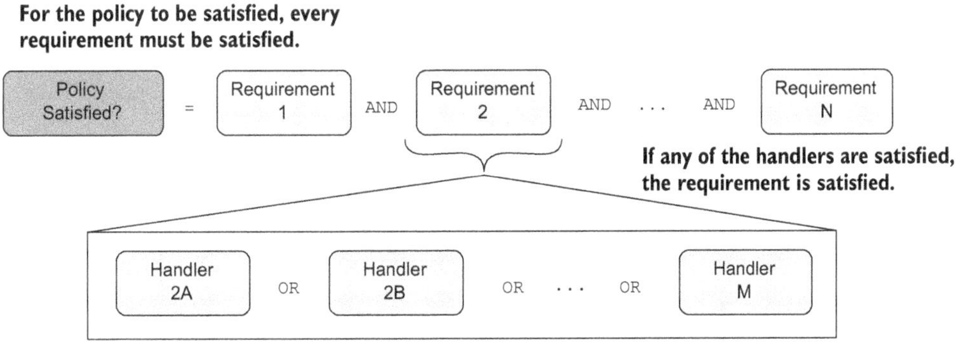

Figure 15.5 **For a policy to be satisfied, every requirement must be satisfied. A requirement is satisfied if any of the handlers are satisfied.**

> **TIP** You can also add multiple policies to an action method by applying the `[Authorize]` attribute multiple times, for example `[Authorize("Policy1"), Authorize("Policy2")]`. All policies must be satisfied for the request to be authorized.

I've highlighted requirements and handlers that will make up your `"CanAccessLounge"` policy, so in the next section, you'll build each of the components and apply them to the airport sample app.

15.4.2 *Creating a policy with a custom requirement and handler*

You've seen all the pieces that make up a custom authorization policy, so in this section, we'll explore the implementation of the `"CanAccessLounge"` policy.

CREATING AN IAUTHORIZATIONREQUIREMENT TO REPRESENT A REQUIREMENT

As you've seen, a custom policy can have multiple requirements, but what *is* a requirement in code terms? Authorization requirements in ASP.NET Core are any class that implements the `IAuthorizationRequirement` interface. This is a blank, marker interface, which you can apply to any class to indicate that it represents a requirement.

If the interface doesn't have any members, you might be wondering what the requirement class needs to look like. Typically, they're simple, POCO classes. The following listing shows `AllowedInLoungeRequirement`, which is about as simple as a requirement can get! It has no properties or methods; it implements the required `IAuthorizationRequirement` interface.

Listing 15.5   `AllowedInLoungeRequirement`

```
public class AllowedInLoungeRequirement          The interface identifies the class
    : IAuthorizationRequirement { }              as an authorization requirement.
```

This is the simplest form of requirement, but it's also common for them to have one or two properties that make the requirement more generalized. For example, instead of creating the highly specific `MustBe18YearsOldRequirement`, you instead create a parametrized `MinimumAgeRequirement`, as shown in the following listing. By providing the minimum age as a parameter to the requirement, you can reuse the requirement for other policies with different minimum age requirements.

Listing 15.6   The parameterized `MinimumAgeRequirement`

```
public class MinimumAgeRequirement : IAuthorizationRequirement    The interface
{                                                                 identifies the
    public MinimumAgeRequirement(int minimumAge)    The minimum   class as an
    {                                               age is        authorization
        MinimumAge = minimumAge;                    provided      requirement.
    }                                               when the
                                                    requirement
    public int MinimumAge { get; }                  is created.
}
            Handlers can use the exposed
         minimum age to determine whether
           the requirement is satisfied.
```

The requirements are the easy part. They represent each of the components of the policy that must be satisfied for the policy to be satisfied overall.

CREATING A POLICY WITH MULTIPLE REQUIREMENTS

You've created the two requirements, so now you can configure the "CanAccess-Lounge" policy to use them. You configure your policies as you did before, in the `ConfigureServices` method of Startup.cs. Listing 15.7 shows how you could do this by creating an instance of each requirement and passing them to `Authorization-PolicyBuilder`. The authorization handlers will use these requirement objects when attempting to authorize the policy.

Listing 15.7   Creating an authorization policy with multiple requirements

```
public void ConfigureServices(IServiceCollection services)
{
    services.AddAuthorization(options =>
```

```
{
    options.AddPolicy(
        "CanEnterSecurity",
        policyBuilder => policyBuilder
            .RequireClaim(Claims.BoardingPassNumber));
```

Adds the previous simple policy for passing through security

```
    options.AddPolicy(
        "CanAccessLounge",
        policyBuilder => policyBuilder.AddRequirements(
            new MinimumAgeRequirement(18),
            new AllowedInLoungeRequirement()
        ));
});
```

Adds a new policy for the airport lounge, called CanAccessLounge

```
    // Additional service configuration
}
```

Adds an instance of each IAuthorizationRequirement object

You now have a policy called "CanAccessLounge" with two requirements, so you can apply it to an action method using the [Authorize] attribute, in exactly the same way you did for the "CanEnterSecurity" policy:

```
[Authorize("CanAccessLounge")]
public IActionResult AirportLounge()
{
    return View();
}
```

When a user attempts to execute the AirportLounge action, the authorize filter policy will be executed and each of the requirements will be inspected. But you saw earlier that the requirements are purely data; they indicate what needs to be fulfilled, they don't describe how that has to happen. For that, you need to write some handlers.

CREATING AUTHORIZATION HANDLERS TO SATISFY YOUR REQUIREMENTS
Authorization handlers contain the logic of how a specific IAuthorizationRequirement can be satisfied. When executed, a handler can do one of three things:

- Mark the requirement handling as a success
- Not do anything
- Explicitly fail the requirement

Handlers should implement AuthorizationHandler<T>, where T is the type of requirement they handle. For example, the following listing shows a handler for AllowedInLounge-Requirement that checks whether the user has a claim called FrequentFlyerClass with a value of Gold.

Listing 15.8 FrequentFlyerHandler for AllowedInLoungeRequirement

```
public class FrequentFlyerHandler :
    AuthorizationHandler<AllowedInLoungeRequirement>
{
    protected override Task HandleRequirementAsync(
```

The handler implements AuthorizationHandler<T>.

You must override the abstract HandleRequirementAsync method.

```
                                                              The context contains details
                                                              such as the ClaimsPrincipal
            AuthorizationHandlerContext context,    ◁─────────  user object.
            AllowedInLoungeRequirement requirement)
The     ┌─▷                                                       
requirement │  {                                                 
to handle   │      if(context.User.HasClaim("FrequentFlyerClass", "Gold"))  ◁───────┐
            │      {                                                                
            │          context.Succeed(requirement);   ◁──────┐   Checks whether the user
            │      }                                            has the FrequentFlyerClass
            │                                                   claim with the Gold value
            │      return Task.CompletedTask;   ◁──────┐
            }                                          
        }            If the requirement wasn't      If the user had the necessary claim,
                     satisfied, do nothing.         then mark the requirement as
                                                    satisfied by calling Succeed.
```

This handler is functionally equivalent to the simple `RequireClaim()` handler you saw at the start of section 15.4, but using the requirement and handler approach instead.

When a user attempts to execute the `AirportLounge` action method, the authorization filter added by the `[Authorize]` attribute validates the `"CanAccessLounge"` policy. It loops through all of the requirements in the policy, and all of the handlers for each requirement, calling the `HandleRequirementAsync` method for each.

The filter passes in the current `AuthorizationHandlerContext` and the requirement to be checked. The current `ClaimsPrincipal` being authorized is exposed on the context as the `User` property. In listing 15.8, `FrequentFlyerHandler` uses the context to check for a claim called `FrequentFlyerClass` with the `Gold` value, and if it exists, concludes that the user is allowed to enter the airline lounge, by calling `Succeed()`.

> **NOTE** Handlers mark a requirement as being successfully satisfied by calling `context.Succeed()` and passing in the requirement.

It's important to note the behavior when the user *doesn't* have the claim. `FrequentFlyerHandler` doesn't do anything if this is the case (it returns a completed `Task` to satisfy the method signature).

> **NOTE** Remember, if any of the handlers associated with a requirement pass, then the requirement is a success. Only one of the handlers has to succeed for the requirement to be satisfied.

This behavior, whereby you either call `context.Succeed()` or do nothing, is typical for authorization handlers. This listing shows the implementation of `IsAirline-EmployeeHandler`, which uses a similar claim check to determine whether the requirement is satisfied.

Listing 15.9   IsAirlineEmployeeHandler handler

```
public class IsAirlineEmployeeHandler :                The handler implements
    AuthorizationHandler<AllowedInLoungeRequirement>   ◁─┤ AuthorizationHandler<T>.
{
```

```
protected override Task HandleRequirementAsync(
    AuthorizationHandlerContext context,
    AllowedInLoungeRequirement requirement)
{
    if(context.User.HasClaim(c => c.Type == "EmployeeNumber"))
    {
        context.Succeed(requirement);
    }
    return Task.CompletedTask;
}
}
```

You must override the abstract HandleRequirementAsync method.

Checks whether the user has the EmployeeNumber claim

If the user has the necessary claim, then mark the requirement as satisfied by calling Succeed.

If the requirement wasn't satisfied, do nothing.

This pattern of authorization handler is common,[2] but in some cases, instead of checking for a success condition, you might want to check for a failure condition. In the airport example, you don't want to authorize someone who was previously banned from the lounge, even if they would otherwise be allowed to enter.

You can handle this scenario by using the `context.Fail()` method exposed on the context, as shown in the following listing. Calling `Fail()` in a handler will always cause the requirement, and hence the whole policy, to fail. You should only use it when you want to guarantee failure, even if other handlers indicate success.

Listing 15.10 Calling `context.Fail()` in a handler to fail the requirement

```
public class BannedFromLoungeHandler :
    AuthorizationHandler<AllowedInLoungeRequirement>
{
    protected override Task HandleRequirementAsync(
        AuthorizationHandlerContext context,
        AllowedInLoungeRequirement requirement)
    {
        if(context.User.HasClaim(c => c.Type == "IsBanned"))
        {
            context.Fail();
        }
        return Task.CompletedTask;
    }
}
```

The handler implements AuthorizationHandler<T>.

You must override the abstract HandleRequirementAsync method.

Checks whether the user has the IsBanned claim

If the user has the claim, then fail the requirement by calling Fail. The whole policy will fail.

If the claim wasn't found, do nothing.

In most cases, your handlers will either call `Succeed()` or will do nothing, but the `Fail()` method is useful when you need this kill-switch to guarantee that a requirement won't be satisfied.

NOTE Whether a handler calls `Succeed()`, `Fail()`, or neither, the authorization system will always execute all of the handlers for a requirement, so you can be sure your handlers will always be called.

---

[2] I'll leave the implementation of `MinimumAgeHandler` for `MinimumAgeRequirement` as an exercise for the reader. You can find an example in the code samples for the chapter.

The final step to complete your authorization implementation for the app is to register the authorization handlers with the DI container, as shown in listing 15.11.

Listing 15.11   Registering the authorization handlers with the DI container

```
public void ConfigureServices(IServiceCollection services)
{
    services.AddAuthorization(options =>
    {
        options.AddPolicy(
            "CanEnterSecurity",
            policyBuilder => policyBuilder
                .RequireClaim(Claims.BoardingPassNumber));

        options.AddPolicy(
            "CanAccessLounge",
            policyBuilder => policyBuilder.AddRequirements(
                new MinimumAgeRequirement(18),
                new AllowedInLoungeRequirement()
            ));
    });

    services.AddSingleton<IAuthorizationHandler, MinimumAgeHandler>();
    services.AddSingleton<IAuthorizationHandler, FrequentFlyerHandler>();
    services
        .AddSingleton<IAuthorizationHandler, BannedFromLoungeHandler>();
    Services
        .AddSingleton<IAuthorizationHandler, IsAirlineEmployeeHandler>();

    // Additional service configuration
}
```

For this app, the handlers don't have any constructor dependencies, so I've registered them as singletons with the container. If your handlers have scoped or transient dependencies (the EF Core DbContext, for example), then you might want to register them as scoped instead, as appropriate.

You can combine the concepts of policies, requirements, and handlers in many different ways to achieve your goals for authorization in your application. The example in this section, although contrived, demonstrates each of the components you need to apply authorization at the action method level, by creating policies and applying the [Authorize] attribute as appropriate.

There's one area, however, where the [Authorize] attribute falls short: resource-based authorization. The [Authorize] attribute uses an authorization filter to authorize the user before the action method is executed, but what if you need to authorize the action *during* the action method?

This is common when you're applying authorization at the document or resource level. If users are only allowed to edit documents they created, then you need to load the document before you can tell whether you're allowed to edit it! This isn't possible with the declarative [Authorize] attribute approach, so you must use an alternative, imperative approach. In the next section, you'll see how to apply this resource-based authorization to an action method.

15.5   *Controlling access with resource-based authorization*

Resource-based authorization is a common problem for applications, especially when you have users that can create or edit some sort of document. Consider the recipe application you built in the previous 3 chapters. This app lets users create, view, and edit recipes.

Up to this point, everyone is able to create new recipes, and anyone can edit a recipe, even if they haven't logged in. Now you want to add some additional behavior:

- Only authenticated users should be able to create new recipes
- You can only edit recipes you created

You've already seen how to achieve the first of these requirements; decorate the `Create` action method with an `[Authorize]` attribute and don't specify a policy, as shown in this listing. This will force the user to authenticate before they can create a new recipe.

Listing 15.12   Adding `AuthorizeAttribute` to `RecipeController.Create`

```
public class RecipeController : Controller
{
    [Authorize]                    ◁            Users must be authenticated
    public IActionResult Create()               to execute the Create action.
    {
        return View(new CreateRecipeCommand());
    }
                                                It's important to protect
    [HttpPost, Authorize]          ◁            the HttpPost actions, too.
    public async Task<IActionResult> Create(CreateRecipeCommand command)
    {
        // Method body not shown for brevity
    }
}
```

> **TIP**   When applying the `[Authorize]` attribute to single actions, it's important to protect both the GET method and the POST action method.

Adding the `[Authorize]` attribute fulfills your first requirement, but unfortunately, with the techniques you've seen so far, you have no way to fulfill the second. You could apply a policy that either permits or denies a user the ability to edit *all* recipes, but there's currently no way to restrict this so that a user can only edit *their own* recipes.

In order to find out who created the `Recipe`, you must first load it from the database. Only then can you attempt to authorize the user, taking the specific recipe (resource) into account. The following listing shows a partially implemented method for how this might look, where authorization occurs part way through the method, after the `Recipe` object has been loaded.

The id of the recipe to edit is
provided by model binding.

```
public IActionResult Edit(int id)     ⟵
{
    var recipe = _service.GetRecipe(id);
    var createdById = recipe.CreatedById;

        // Authorize user based on createdById    ⟵

    if(isAuthorized)
    {
        return View(recipe);
    }
}
```

You must load the Recipe from the
database before you know who created it.

You must authorize the
current user, to verify
they're allowed to edit this
specific Recipe.

The action method
can only continue if
the user was
authorized.

The [Authorize] attribute can't help you here; authorization filters run before model binding and before the action method executes. In the next section, you'll see the approach you need to take to handle these situations and to apply authorization inside the action.

> **WARNING**   Be careful when exposing the integer ID of your entities in the URL, as in listing 15.13. Users will be able to edit every entity by modifying the ID in the URL to access a different entity. Be sure to apply authorization checks, otherwise you could expose a security vulnerability called Insecure Direct Object Reference.[3]

15.5.1 *Manually authorizing requests with IAuthorizationService*

All of the approaches to authorization so far have been *declarative*. You apply the [Authorize] attribute, with or without a policy name, and you let the framework take care of performing the authorization itself.

For this recipe-editing example, you need to use *imperative* authorization, so you can authorize the user after you've loaded the Recipe from the database. Instead of applying a marker saying "Authorize this method," you need to write some of the authorization code yourself.

> **DEFINITION**   *Declarative* and *imperative* are two different styles of programming. Declarative programming describes *what* you're trying to achieve, and lets the framework figure out how to achieve it. Imperative programming describes *how* to achieve something by providing each of the steps needed.

ASP.NET Core exposes IAuthorizationService, which you can inject into your controllers for imperative authorization. This listing shows how you can update the Edit action shown in listing 15.13 to use the IAuthorizationService and verify whether the action is allowed to continue execution.

---

[3]   You can read about this vulnerability and ways to counteract it on the Open Web Application Security Project (OWASP): www.owasp.org/index.php/Top_10_2007-Insecure_Direct_Object_Reference.

Listing 15.14 Using `IAuthorizationService` for resource-based authorization

```
public class RecipeController : Controller
{
    private IAuthorizationService _authService
    public RecipeController(IAuthorizationService authService)
    {
        _authService = authService;
    }

    [Authorize]
    public async Task<IActionResult> Edit(int id)
    {
        var recipe = _service.GetRecipe(id);
        var authResult = await _authService
            .AuthorizeAsync(User, recipe, "CanManageRecipe");

        if (!authResult.Succeeded)
        {
            return new ForbidResult();
        }

        return View(recipe);
    }
}
```

IAuthorizationService is injected into the class constructor using DI.

Only authenticated users should be allowed to edit recipes.

Load the recipe from the database.

Calls **IAuthorizationService**, providing ClaimsPrinicipal, resource, and the policy name

If authorization failed, returns a 403 Forbidden result

If authorization was successful, continues the action method

IAuthorizationService exposes an `AuthorizeAsync` method, which requires three things to authorize the request:

- The `ClaimsPrincipal` user object, exposed on the `Controller` as `User`
- The resource being authorized: `recipe`
- The policy to evaluate: `"CanManageRecipe"`

The authorization attempt returns an `AuthorizationResult` object, which indicates whether the attempt was successful via the `Succeeded` property. If the attempt wasn't successful, then you should return a new `ForbidResult`, which will return a 403 Forbidden response to the user.

> **WARNING** In ASP.NET Core 1.x resource-based authorization, you'd return a `ChallengeResult` instead of a `ForbidResult` and the framework would generate the appropriate 401 or 403 response, depending on whether you were logged in or not. In the changes that came with ASP.NET Core 2.0, this behavior was lost, so you have to work out whether to return a 401 or 403 yourself. The easiest approach is: mark your action methods with the `[Authorize]` attribute and always return a `ForbidResult`.

You've configured the imperative authorization in the `Edit` method itself, but you still need to define the `"CanManageRecipe"` policy that you use to authorize the user. This is the same process as for declarative authorization, so you have to:

- Create a *policy* in `ConfigureServices` by calling `AddAuthorization()`
- Define one or more *requirements* for the policy

- Define one or more *handlers* for each requirement
- Register the handlers in the DI container

With the exception of the handler, these steps are all identical to the declarative authorization approach with the [Authorize] attribute, so I'll only run through them briefly here.

First, you can create a simple IAuthorizationRequirement. As with all requirements, this contains no functionality and simply implements the marker interface.

```
public class IsRecipeOwnerRequirement : IAuthorizationRequirement { }
```

Defining the policy in ConfigureServices is similarly simple, as you have only this single requirement. Note that there's nothing resource-specific in any of this code so far:

```
public void ConfigureServices(IServiceCollection services)
{
    services.AddAuthorization(options => {
        options.AddPolicy("CanManageRecipe", policyBuilder =>
            policyBuilder.AddRequirements(new IsRecipeOwnerRequirement()));
    });
}
```

You're halfway there; all you need to do now is create an authorization handler for IsRecipeOwnerRequirement and register it with the DI container.

15.5.2 *Creating a resource-based AuthorizationHandler*

Resource-based authorization handlers are essentially the same as the authorization handler implementations you saw in section 15.4.2. The only difference is that the handler also has access to the resource being authorized.

To create a resource-based handler, you should derive from the Authorization-Handler<TRequirement, TResource> base class, where TRequirement is the type of requirement to handle, and TResource is the type of resource that you provide when calling IAuthorizationService. Compare this to the AuthorizationHandler<T> class you implemented previously, where you only specified the requirement.

This listing shows the handler implementation for your recipe application. You can see that you've specified the requirement as IsRecipeOwnerRequirement, the resource as Recipe, and have implemented the HandleRequirementAsync method.

Listing 15.15 IsRecipeOwnerHandler for resource-based authorization

```
public class IsRecipeOwnerHandler :
        AuthorizationHandler<IsRecipeOwnerRequirement, Recipe>    ⊲─────────┐
    {                                                                       │
        private readonly UserManager<ApplicationUser> _userManager;         │
                                                                            │
        public IsRecipeOwnerHandler(              Implements the            │
            UserManager<ApplicationUser> userManager)   necessary base class,│
        {                                             specifying the        │
            _userManager = userManager;               requirement and       │
        }                                             resource type         │
```

Injects an instance of the UserManager<T> class using DI

```
protected override async Task HandleRequirementAsync(
    AuthorizationHandlerContext context,
    IsRecipeOwnerRequirement requirement,
    Recipe resource)
{
    var appUser = await _userManager.GetUserAsync(context.User);
    if(appUser == null)
    {
        return;
    }

    if(resource.CreatedById == appUser.Id)
    {
        context.Succeed(requirement);
    }
}
}
```

As well as the context and requirement, you're also provided the resource instance.

If you aren't authenticated, then appUser will be null.

Checks whether the current user created the Recipe by checking the CreatedById property

If the user created the document, Succeed the requirement; otherwise, do nothing.

This handler is slightly more complicated than the examples you've seen previously, primarily because you're using an additional service, UserManager<>, to load the ApplicationUser entity based on ClaimsPrincipal from the request.

The other significant difference is that the HandleRequirementAsync method is called with a Recipe resource. This is the same object that you provided when calling AuthorizeAsync on IAuthorizationService. You can use this resource to verify whether the current user created it. If so, you Succeed() the requirement, otherwise you do nothing.

Our final task is to add IsRecipeOwnerHandler to the DI container. Your handler uses an additional dependency, UserManager<>, which you know uses EF Core, so you should register the handler as a scoped service:

```
services.AddScoped<IAuthorizationHandler, IsRecipeOwnerHandler>();
```

> **TIP** If you're wondering how to know whether you register a handler as scoped or a singleton, think back to chapter 10. Essentially, if you have scoped dependencies, then you must register the handler as scoped; otherwise, singleton is fine.

With everything hooked up, you can take the application for a spin. If you try to edit a recipe you didn't create by clicking the Edit button on the recipe, you'll either be redirected to the login page (if you hadn't yet authenticated) or you'll be presented with an Access Denied page, as shown in figure 15.6.

By using resource-based authorization, you're able to enact more fine-grained authorization requirements that you can apply at the level of an individual document or resource. Instead of only being able to authorize that a user can edit *any* recipe, you can authorize whether a user can edit *this* recipe.

All of the authorization techniques you've seen so far have focused on server-side checks. Both the [Authorize] attribute and resource-based authorization approaches focus on stopping users from executing a protected action on the server. This is

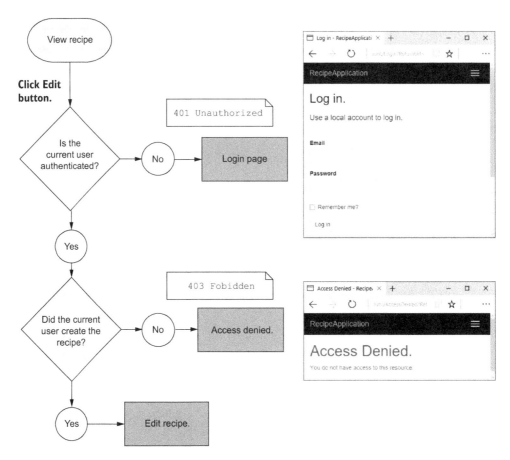

Figure 15.6   If you're not authorized to edit a recipe, you'll be redirected to an Access Denied page. If you're not logged in, you'll be redirected to the login page.

important from a security point of view, but there's another aspect you should consider too: the user experience when they don't have permission.

Now you've protected the code executing on the server, but arguably, the Edit button should never have been visible to the user if they weren't going to be allowed to edit the recipe! In the next section, we'll look at how you can conditionally hide the Edit button by using resource-based authorization in your view models.

15.6 *Hiding elements in Razor templates from unauthorized users*

All of the authorization code you've seen so far has revolved around protecting action methods on the server side, rather than modifying the UI for users. This is important and should be the starting point whenever you add authorization to an app.

WARNING   Malicious users can easily circumvent your UI, so it's important to always authorize your actions on the server, never on the client alone.

From a user-experience point of view, however, it's not friendly to have buttons or links that look like they're available but present you with an Access Denied page when they're clicked. A better experience would be for the links to be disabled, or not visible at all.

You can achieve this in several ways in your own Razor templates. In this section, I'm going to show you how to add an additional property to the page view model, `CanEditRecipe`, which the view template will use to change the rendered HTML.

TIP   An alternative approach would be to inject `IAuthorizationService` directly into the view template using the `@inject` directive, as you saw in chapter 10.

When you're finished, the rendered HTML will look unchanged for recipes you created, but the Edit button will be hidden when viewing a recipe someone else created, as shown in figure 15.7.

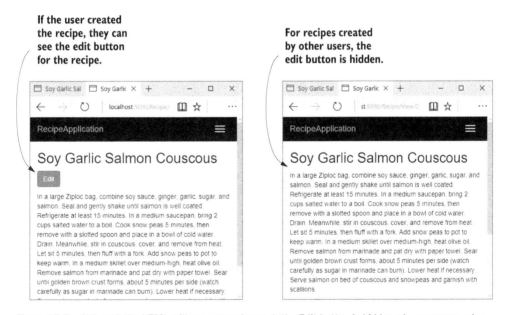

Figure 15.7   Although the HTML will appear unchanged, the Edit button is hidden when someone else has created the recipe.

The following listing shows `RecipeDetailViewModel`, which is used to render the recipe page shown in figure 15.7. I've added an additional property, called `CanEdit-Recipe`, which you'll set in the `RecipeDetail` action method, based on whether the current user can edit the recipe.

Listing 15.16 `RecipeDetailViewModel` used by the View.cshtml template

```
public class RecipeDetailViewModel
{
    public int Id { get; set; }
    public string Name { get; set; }
    public string Method { get; set; }
    public DateTimeOffset LastModified { get; set; }
    public IEnumerable<Item> Ingredients { get; set; }
    public bool CanEditRecipe {get; set;}          ◁⎯⎯⎯   The CanEditRecipe property will
                                                           be used to control whether the
    public class Item                                      Edit button is rendered.
    {
        public string Name { get; set; }
        public string Quantity { get; set; }
    }
}
```

The View.cshtml Razor template only requires a simple change: adding an `if` clause around the rendering of the edit link:

```
@if(Model.CanEditRecipe)
{
    <a asp-action="Edit" asp-route-id="@Model.Id"
        class="btn btn-primary">Edit</a>
}
```

The final step is to set the `CanEditRecipe` value as appropriate in the `View` action method. But how do you set that value?

Hopefully, the previous section has given you a clue—you can use `IAuthorization-Service` to determine whether the current user has permission to edit the `Recipe`, by calling `AuthorizeAsync`, as shown here.

Listing 15.17 Setting a view model property using `IAuthorizationService`

```
public async Task<IActionResult> View(int id)          Loads the Recipe resource for
{                                                      use with IAuthorizationService
    var recipe = _service.GetRecipe(id);       ◁⎯⎯
    var authResult = await _authService.AuthorizeAsync(       Verifies whether
        User, recipe, "CanManageRecipe");                     the user is
                                                              authorized to edit
    model.CanEditRecipe = authResult.Succeeded;    ◁⎯⎯        the Recipe

    return View(model);          Sets the CanEditRecipe property on
}                                the view model as appropriate
```

Instead of blocking execution of the method (as you did in the `Edit` action), use the result of the call to `AuthorizeAsync` to set the `CanEditRecipe` value on the view model. This ensures that only users who will be able to execute the `Edit` action see the link to that page.

WARNING Note that you didn't remove the server-side authorization check from the `Edit` action. This is important for preventing malicious users from circumventing your UI.

With that final change, you've finished adding authorization to the recipe application. Anonymous users can browse the recipes created by others, but they must log in to create new recipes. Additionally, users can only edit the recipes that they created, and won't see an edit link for other people's recipes.

Authorization is a key aspect of most apps, so it's important to bear it in mind from an early point. Although it's possible to add authorization later, as you did with the recipe app, it's normally preferable to consider authorization sooner rather than later in the app's development.

In the next chapter, we're going to be looking at your ASP.NET Core application from a different point of view. Instead of focusing on the code and logic behind your app, we're going to look at how you prepare an app for production. You'll see how to specify the URLs your application uses, and how to publish an app so that it can be hosted in IIS. Finally, you'll learn about the bundling and minification of client-side assets, why you should care, and how to use `BundlerMinifier` in ASP.NET Core.

Summary

- Authorization is the process of determining what a user can do. It's distinct from authentication, the process of determining who a user is. Authentication typically occurs before authorization.

- You can use authorization in any part of your application, but it's typically applied to MVC controllers and actions, using the `[Authorize]` attribute to control which actions a user can execute.

- The simplest form of authorization requires that a user is authenticated before executing an action. You can achieve this by applying the `[Authorize]` attribute to an action, to a controller, or globally.

- Claims-based authorization uses the current user's claims to determine whether they're authorized to execute an action. You define the claims needed to execute an action in a *policy*.

- Policies have a name and are configured in Startup.cs as part of the call to `AddAuthorization()` in `ConfigureServices`. You define the policy using `AddPolicy()`, passing in a name and a lambda that defines the claims needed.

- You can apply a policy to an action or controller by specifying the policy in the authorize attribute, for example `[Authorize("CanAccessLounge")]`.

- If an unauthenticated user attempts to execute a protected action, they'll typically be redirected to the login page for your app. If they're already authenticated, but don't have the required claims, they'll be shown an Access Denied page instead.

- For complex authorization policies, you can build a custom policy. A custom policy consists of one or more requirements, and a requirement can have one or more handlers.

- For a policy to be authorized, every requirement must be satisfied. For a requirement to be satisfied, one or more of the associated handlers must indicate success, and none must indicate explicit failure.

- `AuthorizationHandler<T>` contains the logic that determines whether a requirement is satisfied. If a requirement requires that users are over 18, the handler could look for a `DateOfBirth` claim and calculate the user's age.

- Handlers can mark a requirement as satisfied by calling `context.Succeed (requirement)`. If a handler can't satisfy the requirement, then it shouldn't call anything on the context, as a different handler could call `Succeed()` and satisfy the requirement.

- If a handler calls `context.Fail()`, then the requirement will fail, even if a different handler marked it as a success using `Succeed()`.

- Resource-based authorization uses details of the resource being protected to determine whether the current user is authorized. For example, if a user is only allowed to edit their own documents, then you need to know the author of the document before you can determine whether they're authorized.

- Resource-based authorization uses the same policy, requirements, and handlers system as before. Instead of applying authorization with the `[Authorize]` attribute, you must manually call `IAuthorizationService` and provide the resource you're protecting.

- You can modify the user interface to account for user authorization by adding additional properties to your view models. If a user isn't authorized to execute an action, you can remove or disable the link to that action method in the UI. You should always authorize on the server, even if you've removed links from the UI.

Publishing and deploying your application

This chapter covers

- Publishing an ASP.NET Core application
- Hosting an ASP.NET Core application in IIS
- Customizing the URLs for an ASP.NET Core app
- Optimizing client-side assets with bundling and minification

We've covered a vast amount of ground so far in this book. We've gone over the basic mechanics of building an ASP.NET Core application, such as configuring dependency injection, loading app settings, and building a middleware pipeline. We've looked at the UI side, using Razor templates and layouts to build an HTML response. And we've looked at higher-level abstractions, such as EF Core and ASP.NET Core Identity, that let you interact with a database and add users to your application.

In this chapter, we're taking a slightly different route. Instead of looking at ways to build bigger and better applications, we focus on what it means to deploy your application so that users can access it. You'll learn about

- The process of publishing an ASP.NET Core application so that it can be deployed to a server.
- How to prepare a reverse proxy (IIS) to host your application.
- How to optimize your app so that it's performant once deployed.

We start by looking again at the ASP.NET Core hosting model in section 16.1 and examining why it's a good idea to host your application behind a reverse proxy instead of exposing your app directly to the internet. I show you the difference between running an ASP.NET Core app in development using `dotnet run` and publishing the app for use on a remote server. Finally, I describe some of the options available to you when deciding how and where to deploy your app.

In section 16.2, I show you how to deploy your app to one such option, a Windows server running IIS (Internet Information Services). This will be a typical deployment scenario for many developers already familiar with ASP.NET, so it acts as a useful case study, but it's certainly not the only possibility. I won't go into all the technical details of configuring the venerable IIS system, but I'll show the bare minimum required to get it up and running. If your focus is cross-platform development, then don't worry, I don't dwell on IIS for too long!

In section 16.3, I provide an introduction to hosting on Linux. You'll see how it differs from hosting applications on Windows, learn the changes you need to make to your apps, and find out about some gotchas to look out for. I describe how reverse proxies on Linux differ from IIS and point you to some resources you can use to configure your environments, rather than giving exhaustive instructions in this book.

If you're *not* hosting your application using IIS, then you'll likely need to set the URL that your ASP.NET Core app is using when you deploy your application. In section 16.4, I show two approaches to this: using the special `ASPNETCORE_URLS` environment variable and loading the URLs using `ConfigurationBuilder`. Although generally not an issue during development, setting the correct URLs for your app is critical when you need to deploy it.

In the final section of this chapter, we look at a common optimization step used when deploying your application. Bundling and minification are used to reduce the number and size of requests that browsers must make to your app to fully load a page. I show you how to use a simple tool to create bundles when you build your application, and how to conditionally load these when in production to optimize your app's page size.

This chapter covers a relatively wide array of topics, all related to deploying your app. But before we get into the nitty-gritty, I'll go over the hosting model for ASP.NET Core so that we're all on the same page. This is significantly different from the hosting model of the previous version of ASP.NET, so if you're coming from that background, it's best to try to forget what you know!

16.1 Understanding the ASP.NET Core hosting model

If you think back to chapter 1, you may remember that we discussed the hosting model of ASP.NET Core. ASP.NET Core applications are, essentially, console applications. They have a `static void Main` function that serves as the entry point for the application, like a standard .NET console app would.

What makes an app an ASP.NET Core app is that it runs a web server, Kestrel, inside the console app process. Kestrel provides the HTTP functionality to receive requests and return responses to clients. Kestrel passes any requests it receives to the body of your application to generate a response, as shown in figure 16.1. This hosting model decouples the server and reverse proxy from the application itself, so that the same application can run unchanged in multiple environments.

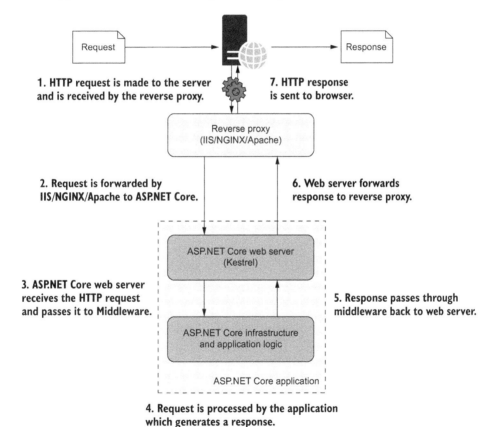

Figure 16.1   The hosting model for ASP.NET Core. Requests are received by the reverse proxy and are forwarded to the Kestrel web server. The same application can run behind various reverse proxies without modification.

In this book, we've focused on the lower half of figure 16.1—the ASP.NET Core application itself—but the reality is that you'll generally want to place your ASP.NET Core apps behind a reverse proxy, such as IIS on Windows, or NGINX or Apache on Linux. The *reverse proxy* is the program that listens for HTTP requests from the internet and then makes requests to your app as though the request had come from the internet directly.

> **DEFINITION**   A *reverse proxy* is software that's responsible for receiving requests and forwarding them to the appropriate web server. The reverse proxy is exposed directly to the internet, whereas the underlying web server is exposed only to the proxy.

Using a reverse proxy has a number of benefits:

- *Security*—Reverse proxies are specifically designed to be exposed to malicious internet traffic, so they're typically well-tested and battle-hardened.
- *Performance*—You can configure reverse proxies to provide performance improvements by aggressively caching responses to requests.
- *Process management*—An unfortunate reality is that apps sometimes crash. Some reverse proxies can act as a monitor/scheduler to ensure that if an app crashes, the proxy can automatically restart it.
- *Support for multiple apps*—It's common to have multiple apps running on a single server. Using a reverse proxy makes it easier to support this scenario by using the host name of a request to decide which app should receive the request.

Using a reverse proxy isn't all sunshine and roses. One of the biggest complaints is how complex they are. Another common concern is that communication between two processes (a reverse proxy and your web app) is slower than if you directly exposed your web app to requests from the internet.

In ASP.NET Core 1.x, exposing your app directly to the internet is *explicitly unsupported*, but in ASP.NET Core 2.0, Kestrel has undergone some security hardening that means directly exposing your app to the internet is possible, though generally discouraged.

> **WARNING**   I strongly suggest you use a reverse proxy when exposing your ASP.NET Core app to the internet. If you don't, you'll need to configure some sort of scheduler to restart your app if it crashes, and you generally won't be able to host more than one app on a server. A reverse proxy makes sense in most cases.

Whichever approach you take, when the time comes to host your app, you can't copy your code files directly on to the server. First, you need to *publish* your ASP.NET Core app, to optimize it for production. In the next section, we'll look at building an ASP.NET Core app so it can be run on your development machine, compared to publishing it so that it can be run on a server.

16.1.1 Running vs. publishing an ASP.NET Core app

One of the key changes in ASP.NET Core from previous versions of ASP.NET is making it easy to build apps using your favorite code editors and IDEs. Previously, Visual Studio was required for ASP.NET development, but with the .NET CLI and the OmniSharp plugin, you can now build apps with the tools you're comfortable with, on any platform.

As a result, whether you build using Visual Studio or the .NET CLI, the same tools are being used under the hood. Visual Studio provides an additional GUI, functionality, and wrappers for building your app, but it executes the same commands as the .NET CLI behind the scenes.

As a refresher, you've used four main .NET CLI commands so far to build your apps:

- `dotnet new`—Creates an ASP.NET Core application from a template
- `dotnet restore`—Downloads and installs any referenced NuGet packages for your project
- `dotnet build`—Compiles and builds your project
- `dotnet run`—Executes your app, so you can send requests to it

If you've ever built a .NET application, whether it's an ASP.NET app or a .NET Framework Console app, then you'll know that the output of the build process is written to the bin folder. The same is true for ASP.NET Core applications.

If your project compiles successfully when you call `dotnet build`, then the .NET CLI will write its output to a bin folder in your project's directory. Inside this bin folder are several files required to run your app, including a dll file that contains the code for your application. Figure 16.2 shows the output of the bin folder for the recipe application from previous chapters:

The bin folder contains the compiled output of your app.

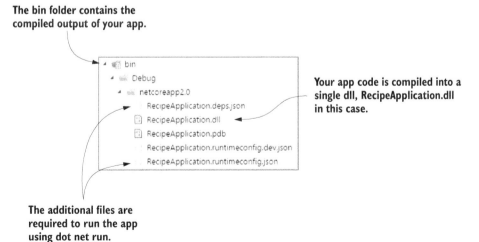

Your app code is compiled into a single dll, RecipeApplication.dll in this case.

The additional files are required to run the app using dot net run.

Figure 16.2   The bin folder for the RecipeApplication app after running `dotnet build`. The application is compiled into a single dll, RecipeApplication.dll.

> **NOTE**   If your ASP.NET Core app targets .NET Framework instead of .NET Core, then you won't have a file called RecipeApplication.dll. Instead, you'll have a file called RecipeApplication.exe. Apart from this difference, the output is similar.

When you call `dotnet run` in your project folder (or run your application using Visual Studio), the .NET CLI uses the DLL to run your application. But this doesn't contain everything you need to deploy your app.

In order to host and deploy your app on a server, you first need to *publish* it. You can publish your ASP.NET Core app from the command line using the `dotnet publish` command. This will build and package everything your app needs to run. The following command will package the app from the current directory and build it to a subfolder called publish. I've used the `Release` configuration, instead of the default `Debug` configuration, so that the output will be fully optimized for running in production:

```
dotnet publish --output publish --configuration release
```

> **TIP**   Always use the release configuration when publishing your app for deployment. This ensures the compiler generates optimized code for your app.

Once the command completes, you'll find your published application in the publish folder, as shown in figure 16.3.

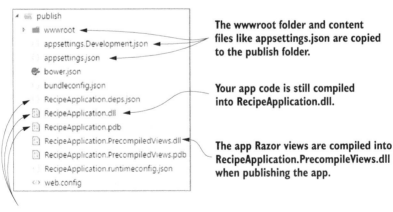

The published output includes many additional files compared to the bin folder.

The wwwroot folder and content files like appsettings.json are copied to the publish folder.

Your app code is still compiled into RecipeApplication.dll.

The app Razor views are compiled into RecipeApplication.PrecompileViews.dll when publishing the app.

The same files from the bin folder are also copied to the publish folder.

Figure 16.3   The publish folder for the RecipeApplication after running `dotnet publish`. The app is still compiled into a single dll, but all the additional files, such as wwwroot and appsettings.json are also copied to the output.

As you can see, the RecipeApplication.dll file is still there, along with a lot of additional files. Most notably, the publish process has copied across the wwwroot folder and your appsettings.json files. When running your application locally with `dotnet run`, the .NET CLI uses these files from your application directly. Running `dotnet publish` copies the files to the output directory, so they're included when you deploy your app to a server.

You may be surprised to note that the Views folder, containing your Razor templates, was *not* copied across to the publish folder. In development, your app uses the Razor cshtml files directly by compiling them as necessary. This means you can edit templates and refresh to see your changes immediately, without having to restart your app. By default, ASP.NET Core 2.0 precompiles your Razor templates into a dll when you publish. This means your app doesn't need to compile the templates at runtime, which has significant performance benefits, especially in terms of the time taken for your app to start.

> **NOTE** If you want, you can disable view precompilation by adding the `<MvcRazorCompileOnPublish>false</MvcRazorCompileOnPublish>` property to your csproj project file.

If your first instinct is to try running the application in the publish folder using the `dotnet run` command you already know and love, then you'll be disappointed. Instead of the application starting up, you're presented with a somewhat confusing message: "Couldn't find a project to run."

To run a published application, you need to use a slightly different command. Instead of calling `dotnet run`, you must pass the path to your application's dll file to the `dotnet` command. If you're running the command from the publish folder, then for the Recipe application, that would look something like

```
dotnet RecipeApplication.dll
```

This is the command that your server will run when running your application in production. When you're developing, the `dotnet run` command does a whole load of work to make things easier on you: it makes sure your application is built, looks for a project file in the current folder, works out where the corresponding dlls will be (in the bin folder), and finally, runs your app.

In production, you don't need any of this extra work. Your app is already built, it only needs to be run. The `dotnet <dll>` syntax does this alone, so your app starts much faster.

> **NOTE** The `dotnet` command used to run your published application is part of the .NET Core Runtime, whereas the `dotnet` command used to build and run your application during development is part of the .NET Core SDK.

Framework-dependent deployments vs. self-contained deployments

If you're creating an ASP.NET Core app built on the .NET Core framework (instead of the full .NET Framework), then you have two different ways to deploy your app: framework-dependent deployments (FDD) and self-contained deployments (SCD).

Most of the time, you'll use an FDD. This relies on the .NET Core runtime being installed on the target machine that runs your published app, but you can run your app on any platform—Windows, Linux, or macOS—without having to recompile.

In contrast, an SCD contains *all* of the code required to run your app, so the target machine doesn't need to have .NET Core installed. Instead, publishing your app will package up the .NET Core runtime with your app's code and libraries.

Each approach has its pros and cons, but in most cases, you'll create FDDs for ASP.NET Core. The final size of FDDs is much smaller, as they only contain your app code, instead of the whole .NET Core framework, as for SCDs. Also, you can deploy your FDD apps to any platform, whereas SCDs must be compiled specifically for the target machine's operating system, such as Windows 10 64-bit or Ubuntu 16.04 64-bit.

In this book, I'll only discuss FDDs, but if you want to create an SCD, add a `<Runtime-Identifiers>` element to your csproj file

```
<PropertyGroup>
  <RuntimeIdentifiers>win10-x64;ubuntu.16.04-x64</RuntimeIdentifiers>
</PropertyGroup>
```

and provide a runtime identifier when you publish your app.

```
dotnet publish -c Release -r win10-x64 -o publish_folder
```

The output will contain an exe file, which is your application, and a *ton* of dlls (100 MB of dlls for a sample app), which are the .NET Core framework. You need to deploy this whole folder to the target machine to run your app. For more details, see the documentation at https://docs.microsoft.com/en-us/dotnet/core/deploying/.

We've established that publishing your app is important for preparing it to run in production, but how do you go about deploying it? How do you get the files from your computer on to a server so that people can access your app? You have many, many options for this, so in the next section, I'll give you a brief list of approaches to consider.

16.1.2 *Choosing a deployment method for your application*

To deploy any application to production, you generally have two fundamental requirements:

- A server that can run your app
- A means of loading your app on to the server

Historically, putting an app into production was a laborious, and error-prone, process. For many people, this is still the case. If you're working at a company that hasn't changed practices in recent years, then you may need to request a server or virtual machine for your app and provide your application to an operations team who will install it for you. If that's the case, you may have your hands tied regarding how you deploy.

For those who have embraced continuous integration (CI) or continuous deployment (CD), there are many more possibilities. CI/CD is the process of detecting changes in your version control system (for example Git, SVN, Mercurial, Team Foundation Version Control) and automatically building, and potentially deploying, your application to a server, with little to no human intervention.

You can find many different CI/CD systems out there: Jenkins, TeamCity, Visual Studio Team Services (VSTS), AppVeyor, Travis, and Octopus Deploy, to name a few. Each can manage some or all of the CI/CD process and can integrate with many different systems.

Rather than pushing any particular system, I suggest trying out some of the services available and seeing which works best for you. Some are better suited to open source projects, some are better when you're deploying to cloud services—it all depends on your particular situation.

If you're getting started with ASP.NET Core and don't want to have to go through the setup process of getting CI working, then you still have lots of options. The easiest way to get started with Visual Studio is to use the built-in deployment options. These are available from Visual Studio via the Build > Publish *AppName* menu option, which presents you with the screen shown in figure 16.4.

From here, you can publish your application directly from Visual Studio to many different locations.[1] This is great when you're getting started, though I recommend looking at a more automated and controlled approach for larger applications, or when you have a whole team working on a single app.

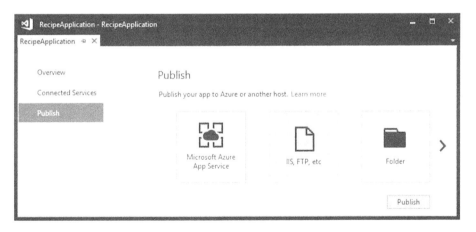

Figure 16.4 The Publish application screen in Visual Studio 2017. This provides easy options for publishing your application directly to Azure App Service, to IIS, to an FTP site, or to a folder on the local machine.

---

[1] For guidance on choosing your Visual Studio publishing options, see http://mng.bz/a2pE.

Given the number of possibilities available in this space, and the speed with which these options change, I'm going to focus on one specific scenario in this chapter: you've built an ASP.NET Core application and you need to deploy it; you have access to a Windows server that's already serving (previous version) ASP.NET applications using IIS and you want to add your ASP.NET Core app to it.

In the next section, you'll see an overview of the steps required to run an ASP.NET Core application in production, using IIS as a reverse proxy. It won't be a master class in configuring IIS (there's so much depth to the 20-year-old product that I wouldn't know where to start!), but I'll cover the basics needed to get your application serving requests.

16.2   Publishing your app to IIS

In the previous section, you learned about the need to publish an app before you deploy it, and the benefits of using a reverse proxy when you run an ASP.NET Core app in production. If you're deploying your application to Windows, then IIS will be your reverse proxy, and will be responsible for managing your application.

IIS is an old and complex beast, and I can't possibly cover everything related to configuring it in this book. Nor would you want me to—it would be very boring! Instead, in this section, I provide an overview of the basic requirements for running ASP.NET Core behind IIS, along with the changes you need to make to your application to support IIS.

If you're on Windows and want to try out these steps locally, then you'll need to manually enable IIS on your development machine. If you've done this with older versions of Windows, nothing much has changed. You can find a step-by-step guide to configuring IIS and troubleshooting tips in the ASP.NET Core documentation at https://docs.microsoft.com/en-us/aspnet/core/publishing/iis.

In this section, I briefly show how to publish your first app to IIS. You'll add an application pool and website to IIS, and ensure your app has the necessary configuration to work with IIS as a reverse proxy. The deployment itself will be as simple as copying your published app to IIS's hosting folder.

16.2.1   Configuring IIS for ASP.NET Core

The first step in preparing IIS to host ASP.NET Core applications is to install the .NET Core Windows Server Hosting Bundle.[2] This includes several components needed to run .NET Core apps:

- *The .NET Core Runtime*—Runs your .NET Core application
- *The .NET Core libraries*—Used by your .NET Core apps
- *The IIS AspNetCore Module*—Provides the link between IIS and your app, so that IIS can act as a reverse proxy

---

[2] You can download the bundle from https://go.microsoft.com/fwlink/?linkid=848766.

If you're going to be running IIS on your development machine, then Visual Studio will install all of these components for you automatically, but you can always install the bundle again if you have any issues.

> **TIP** Wherever you're hosting your app, whether in IIS on Windows, or NGINX on Linux, the server will need to have the .NET Core Runtime to run .NET Core apps.

Once you've installed the bundle, you need to configure an *application pool* in IIS for your ASP.NET Core apps. Previous versions of ASP.NET would run in a managed app pool, but for ASP.NET Core you must create a *No Managed Code* pool. Only the native ASP.NET Core Module runs inside the pool itself; your ASP.NET Core application runs in a separate process, and IIS uses the ASP NET Core Module to send requests to your app.

> **DEFINITION** An *application pool* in IIS represents an application process. You can run each app in IIS in a separate application pool to keep them isolated from one another.

To create an unmanaged application pool, right-click Application Pools in IIS and choose Add Application Pool. Provide a name for the app pool in the resulting dialog, for example NetCore, and set the .NET CLR version to No Managed Code, as shown in figure 16.5.

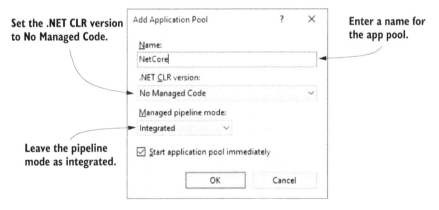

Figure 16.5 Creating an app pool in IIS for your ASP.NET Core app. The .NET CLR version must be set to No Managed Code.

Now you have an app pool, you can add a new website to IIS. Right-click the Sites node and choose Add Website. In the Add Website dialog, shown in figure 16.6, you provide a name for the website and the path to the folder where you'll publish your website. I've created a folder that I'll use to deploy the RecipeApplication app. It's important to change the Application pool for the app to the new NetCore app pool you created. In production, you'd also provide a hostname for the application, but

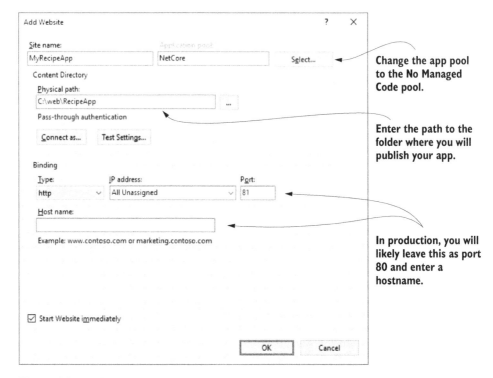

Figure 16.6   **Adding a new website to IIS for your app. Be sure to change the Application pool to the No Managed Code pool created in the previous step. You also provide a name, the path where you'll publish your app files, and the URL IIS will use for your app.**

I've left it blank for now and changed the port to 81, so the application will bind to the URL http://localhost:81.

Once you click OK, IIS will create the application and attempt to start it. But you haven't published your app to the folder, so you won't be able view it in a browser yet.

You need to carry out one more critical setup step before you can publish and run your app: you must grant permissions for the NetCore app pool to access the path where you'll publish your app. To do this, right-click the publish folder in Windows Explorer and choose Properties. In the Properties dialog, choose Security > Edit > Add... Enter IIS AppPool\NetCore in the textbox, as shown in figure 16.7, where NetCore is the name of your app pool, and click OK. Close all the dialog boxes by clicking OK and you're all set.

Out of the box, the ASP.NET Core templates are configured to work seamlessly with IIS, but if you've created an app from scratch, then you may need to make a couple of changes. In the next section, I briefly show the changes you need to make and explain why they're necessary.

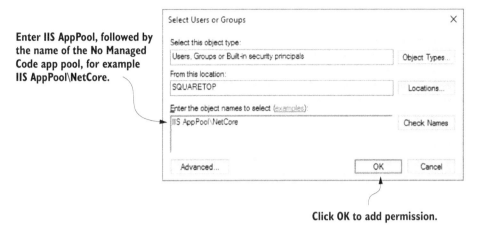

Enter IIS AppPool, followed by the name of the No Managed Code app pool, for example IIS AppPool\NetCore.

Click OK to add permission.

Figure 16.7 Adding permission for the NetCore app pool to the website publish folder.

16.2.2 *Preparing and publishing your application to IIS*

As I discussed in section 16.1, IIS acts as a reverse proxy for your ASP.NET Core app. That means IIS needs to be able to communicate directly with your app in order to forward incoming requests and outgoing responses to and from your app.

IIS handles this with the ASP.NET Core Module, but there's a certain degree of negotiation required between IIS and your app. In order for this to work correctly, you need to configure your app to use IIS integration.

IIS integration is added by default when you use the `WebHost.CreateDefault-Builder()` helper method used in the ASP.NET Core 2.0 templates. If you're creating your own `WebHostBuilder`, or you're using ASP.NET Core 1.x, then you need to ensure you add IIS integration with the `UseIISIntegration()` extension method.

Listing 16.1 Adding IIS integration to a web host builder in ASP.NET Core 2.x

```
public class Program
{
    public static void Main(string[] args)
    {
        BuildWebHost(args).Run();
    }

    public static IWebHost BuildWebHost(string[] args) =>
        new WebHostBuilder()
        .UseKestrel()
        .UseContentRoot(Directory.GetCurrentDirectory())
        .UseIISIntegration()          ⊲──   Configures your application
        .UseStartup<Startup>()               for use with IIS
        .Build();
}
```

> **NOTE**   If you're not using your application with IIS, the `UseIISIntegration()` method will have no effect on your app, so it's safe to include it anyway.

When running behind IIS, this extension method configures your app to pair with the IIS reverse proxy so that it can seamlessly accept requests. Among other things, the extension

- Defines the URL that IIS will use to forward requests to your app and configure your app to listen on this URL
- Configures your app to interpret requests coming from IIS as coming from the client by setting up header forwarding
- Enables Windows authentication if required

Adding the `UseIISIntegration()` extension is the only change you need to make to your application to be able to host in IIS, but there's one additional aspect to be aware of when you publish your app.

As with previous versions of ASP.NET, IIS relies on a web.config file to configure the applications it runs. It's important your application includes a web.config file when it's published to IIS, otherwise you could get broken behavior, or even expose files that shouldn't be exposed.[3]

If your ASP.NET Core project already includes a web.config file, the .NET CLI or Visual Studio will copy it to the publish directory when you publish your app. If your app doesn't include a web.config file, the publish command will create the correct one for you. If you don't need to customize the web.config file, it's generally best not to include one in your project, and let the CLI create the correct file for you.

With these changes, you're finally in a position to publish your application to IIS. Publish your ASP.NET Core to a folder, either from Visual Studio, or with the .NET CLI by running

```
dotnet publish --output publish_folder --configuration release
```

This will publish your application to the publish_folder folder. You can then copy your application to the path specified in IIS in figure 16.6. At this point, if all has gone smoothly, you should be able to navigate to the URL you specified for your app (http://localhost:81, in my case) and see it running, as in figure 16.8.

And there you have it, your first application running behind a reverse proxy. Even though ASP.NET Core uses a different hosting model to previous versions of ASP.NET, the process of configuring IIS is similar.

As is often the case when it comes to deployment, the success you have is highly dependent on your precise environment and your app itself. If, after following these steps, you find you can't get your application to start, I highly recommend checking out the documentation at https://docs.microsoft.com/en-us/aspnet/core/publishing/iis. This contains many troubleshooting steps to get you back on track if IIS decides to throw a hissy fit.

---

[3]   For details on using web.config to customize the IIS AspNetCore Module, see http://mng.bz/VpK3.

The app is served using IIS
as a reverse proxy and using
the URL sepecified in the Add
Website dialog.

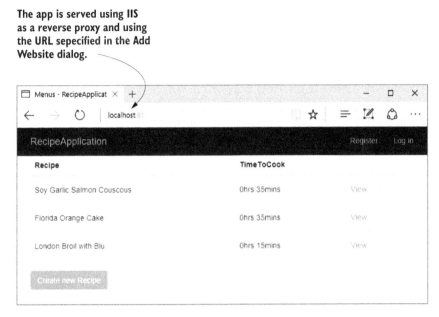

Figure 16.8   Figure 16.8 The published application, using IIS as a reverse proxy listening at the URL http://localhost:81

This section was deliberately tailored to deploying to IIS, as it provides a great segue for developers who are already used to deploying ASP.NET apps and want to deploy their first ASP.NET Core app. But that's not to say that IIS is the only, or best, place to host your application.

In the next section, I'll provide a brief introduction to hosting your app on Linux, behind a reverse proxy like NGINX or Apache. I won't go into configuration of the reverse proxy itself, but will provide an overview of things to consider, and resources you can use to run your applications on Linux.

16.3   *Hosting an application on Linux*

One of the great new features in ASP.NET is the ability to develop and deploy applications cross-platform, whether that be on Windows, Linux, or macOS. The ability to run on Linux, in particular, opens up the possibility of cheaper deployments to cloud hosting, deploying to small devices like a Raspberry Pi or to Docker containers.

One of the characteristics of Linux is that it's almost infinitely configurable. Although that's definitely a feature, it can also be extremely daunting, especially if coming from the Windows world of wizards and GUIs. This section provides an overview of what it takes to run an application on Linux. It focuses on the broad steps you need to take, rather than the somewhat tedious details of the configuration itself. Instead, I point to resources you can refer to as necessary.

16.3.1 *Running an ASP.NET Core app behind a reverse proxy on Linux*

You'll be glad to hear that running your application on Linux is broadly the same as running your application on Windows with IIS:

1 *Publish your app using* dotnet publish. If you're creating an FDD, the output is the same as you'd use with IIS. For an SCD, you must provide the target platform moniker, as described in section 16.1.1.

2 *Install the necessary prerequisites on the server.* For an FDD deployment, you must install the .NET Core Runtime and the necessary prerequisites. You can find details on this in the docs at http://mng.bz/0I4A.

3 *Copy your app to the server.* You can use any mechanism you like, FTP, USB stick, whatever you need to get your files onto the server!

4 *Configure a reverse proxy and point it to your app.* As you know by now, you shouldn't expose your app directly to the internet, instead you should run it behind a reverse proxy. On Windows, you'd use IIS, but on Linux you have more options. NGINX, Apache, and HAProxy are all commonly used options.

5 *Configure a process-management tool for your app.* On Windows, IIS acts both as a reverse proxy and a process manager, restarting your app if it crashes or stops responding. On Linux, you typically need to configure a separate process manager to handle these duties; the reverse proxies won't do it for you.

The first three points are generally the same whether you're running on Windows with IIS or on Linux, but the last two points are more interesting. In contrast to the monolithic IIS, Linux has a philosophy of small applications with a single responsibility.

IIS runs on the same server as your app and takes on multiple duties—proxying traffic from the internet to your app, but also monitoring the app process itself. If your app crashes or stops responding, IIS will restart the process to ensure you can keep handling requests.

In Linux, the reverse proxy might be running on the same server as your app, but it's also common for it to be running on a different server entirely, as shown in figure 16.9. This is similarly true if you choose to deploy your app to Docker; your app would typically be deployed in a container without a reverse proxy, and a reverse proxy on a server would point to your Docker container.

As the reverse proxies aren't necessarily on the same server as your app, they can't be used to restart your app if it crashes. Instead, you need to use a process manager such as systemd to monitor your app. If you're using Docker, you'd typically use a container orchestrator such as Kubernetes (https://kubernetes.io) or Apache Mesos (http://mesos.apache.org) to monitor the health of your containers.

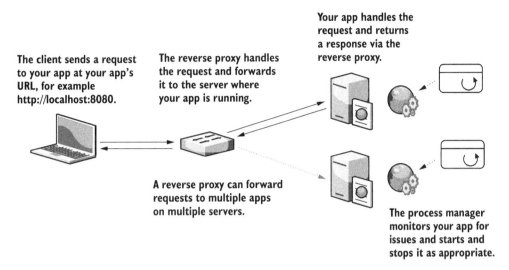

The client sends a request to your app at your app's URL, for example http://localhost:8080.

The reverse proxy handles the request and forwards it to the server where your app is running.

Your app handles the request and returns a response via the reverse proxy.

A reverse proxy can forward requests to multiple apps on multiple servers.

The process manager monitors your app for issues and starts and stops it as appropriate.

Figure 16.9   On Linux, it's common for a reverse proxy to be on a different server to your app. The reverse proxy forwards incoming requests to your app, while the process manager, for example systemd, monitors your apps for crashes and restarts it as appropriate.

Running ASP.NET Core applications in Docker

Docker is the most commonly used engine for *containerizing* your applications. A container is like a small, lightweight virtual machine, specific to your app. It contains an operating system, your app, and any dependencies for your app. This container can then be run on any machine that runs Docker, and your app will run exactly the same, regardless of the host operating system and what's installed on it. This makes deployments highly repeatable: you can be confident that if the container runs on your machine, it will run on the server too.

ASP.NET Core is well-suited to container deployments, but moving to Docker involves a big shift in your deployment methodology, and may or may not be right for you and your apps. If you're interested in the possibilities afforded by Docker and want to learn more, I suggest checking out the following resources:

- *Docker in Practice, Second Edition* by Ian Miell and Aidan Hobson Sayers (Manning, 2017) provides a vast array of practical techniques to help you get the most out of Docker (http://mng.bz/wuz9).
- Even if you're not deploying to Linux, you can use Docker with Docker for Windows. Check out the free e-book, *Introduction to Windows Containers* by John McCabe and Michael Friis (Microsoft Press, 2017) from https://aka.ms/containersebook.
- You can find a lot of details on building and running your ASP.NET Core applications on Docker in the .NET documentation at http://mng.bz/NODY.
- Steve Gordon has an excellent blog post series on Docker for ASP.NET Core developers at www.stevejgordon.co.uk/docker-dotnet-developers-part-1.

Configuring these systems is a laborious task that makes for dry reading, so I won't detail them here. Instead, I recommend checking out the ASP.NET Core docs. They have a guide for NGINX and systemd (http://mng.bz/bvCF), and a guide for configuring Apache with systemd (http://mng.bz/20g0).

Both guides cover the basic configuration of the respective reverse proxy and systemd supervisor, but more importantly, they also show how to configure them *securely*. The reverse proxy sits between your app and the unfettered internet, so it's important to get it right!

Configuring the reverse proxy and the process manager is typically the most complex part of deploying to Linux, and isn't specific to .NET development: the same would be true if you were deploying a Node.js web app. But you need to consider a few things *inside* your application when you're going to be deploying to Linux, as you'll see in the next section.

16.3.2 *Preparing your app for deployment to Linux*

Generally speaking, your app doesn't care which reverse proxy it sits behind, whether it's NGINX, Apache, or IIS—your app receives requests and responds to them without the reverse proxy affecting things. Just as when you're hosting behind IIS, you need to add `UseIISIntegration()`; when you're hosting on Linux, you need to add a similar extension method to your app setup.

When a request arrives at the reverse proxy, it contains some information that is lost after the request is forwarded to your app. For example, the IP address of the client/browser connecting to your app: once the request is forwarded from the reverse proxy, the IP address is that of the *reverse proxy*, not the *browser*. Also, if the reverse proxy is used for SSL offloading (see chapter 18) then a request that was originally made using HTTPS may arrive at your app as an HTTP request.

The standard solution to these issues is for the reverse proxy to add additional headers before forwarding requests to your app. For example, the `X-Forwarded-For` header identifies the original client's IP address, while the `X-Forwarded-Proto` header indicates the original scheme of the request (`http` or `https`).

For your app to behave correctly, it needs to look for these headers in incoming requests and modify the incoming request as appropriate. A request to http://localhost with the `X-Forwarded-Proto` header set to `https` should be treated the same as if the request was to https://localhost.

You can use `ForwardedHeadersMiddleware` in your middleware pipeline to achieve this. This middleware overrides `Request.Scheme` and other properties on `Http-Context` to correspond to the forwarded headers. Add the middleware to the start of your middleware pipeline, as shown in listing 16.2, and configure it with the headers to look for.

> **WARNING** It's important that `ForwardedHeadersMiddleware` is placed early in the middleware pipeline to correct `Request.Scheme` before any middleware that depends on the scheme runs.

> **Listing 16.2   Configuring an app to use forwarded headers in Startup.cs**

```
public class Startup                                              Adds
{                                                     ForwardedHeadersMiddle
    public class Configure(IApplicationBuilder app)   ware early in your pipeline
    {
        app.UseForwardedHeaders(new ForwardedHeadersOptions     <─────────
        {
            ForwardedHeaders = ForwardedHeaders.XForwardedFor |
                               ForwardedHeaders.XForwardedProto
        });                                    Configures the headers
                                               the middleware should
        app.UseAuthentication();                  look for and use
        app.UseMvc();
    }                              The forwarded headers middleware
}                                  must be placed before the
                                   authentication or MVC middleware.
```

NOTE   This behavior isn't specific to reverse proxies on Linux; the UseIis-Integration extension adds ForwardedHeadersMiddleware under the hood as part of its configuration when your app is running behind IIS.

Aside from considering the forwarded headers, you need to consider a few minor things when deploying your app to Linux that may trip you up if you're used to deploying to Windows alone:

- *Line endings (LF on Linux versus CRLF on Windows).* Windows and Linux use different character codes in text to indicate the end of a line. This isn't often an issue for ASP.NET Core apps, but if you're writing text files on one platform and reading them on a different platform, then it's something to bear in mind.
- *Path directory separator ("\" on Windows, "/" on Linux).* This is one of the most common bugs I see when Windows developers move to Linux. Each platform uses a different separator in file paths, so while loading a file using the "subdir\myfile.json" path will work fine on Windows, it won't on Linux. Instead, you should use Path.Combine to create the appropriate string for the current platform, for example Path.Combine("subdir", "myfile.json").
- Environment variables can't contain ":". On some Linux distributions, the colon character, ":", isn't allowed in environment variables. As you saw in chapter 11, this character is typically used to denote different sections in ASP.NET Core configuration, so you often need to use it in environment variables. Instead, you can use a double underscore in your environment variables ("__") and ASP.NET Core will treat it the same as if you'd used a colon.

As long as you set up ForwardedHeadersMiddleware and take care to use cross-platform constructs like Path.Combine, you shouldn't have any problems running your applications on Linux. But configuring a reverse proxy isn't the simplest of activities, so wherever you're planning on hosting your app, I suggest checking the documentation for guidance at https://docs.microsoft.com/en-us/aspnet/core/publishing.

16.4   *Configuring the URLs for your application*

At this point, you've deployed an application, but there's one aspect you haven't configured: the URLs for your application. When you're using IIS as a reverse proxy, you don't have to worry about this inside your app. IIS integration with the ASP.NET Core Module works by dynamically creating a URL that's used to forward requests between IIS and your app. The hostname you configure in IIS (in figure 16.6) is the URL that external users see for your app; the internal URL that IIS uses when forwarding requests is never exposed.

If you're not using IIS as a reverse proxy, maybe you're using NGINX or exposing your app directly to the internet (shudder); in this case, you may find you need to configure the URLs your application listens to directly.

By default, ASP.NET Core will listen for requests to the URL http://localhost: 5000. You have two main ways to customize this URL: using environment variables or using configuration. In this section, I'll show both techniques and describe when you might want to use one over the other.

16.4.1   *Using an environment variable*

In chapter 10, you learned about configuration in ASP.NET Core, and in particular about the concept of hosting environments so that you can use different settings when running in development compared to production. You choose the hosting environment by setting an environment variable on your machine called `ASPNETCORE_ENVIRONMENT`. The ASP.NET Core framework magically picks up this variable when your app starts and uses it to set the hosting environment.

You can use a similar special environment variable to specify the URL that your app uses; this variable is called `ASPNETCORE_URLS`. When your app starts up, it looks for this value and uses it as the application's URL. By changing this value, you can change the default URL used by all ASP.NET Core apps on the machine.

For example, you could set a temporary environment variable in Windows from the command window using

```
set ASPNETCORE_URLS=http://localhost:5001
```

Running `dotnet run` within the same command window, as shown in figure 16.10, shows that the app is now listening on the URL provided in the `ASPNETCORE_URLS` variable.

You can instruct an app to listen on multiple URLs by separating them with a semi-colon, or you can listen to a specific port, without specifying a hostname. If you set the `ASPNETCORE_URLS` environment variable to

```
http://localhost:5001;http://tastyrecipes.com;http://*:5002
```

then your ASP.NET Core apps would listen for requests to:

- http://localhost:5001
- http://tastyrecipes.com
- Any URL on port 5002

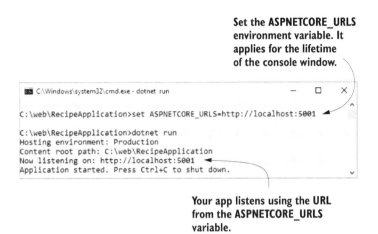

Set the ASPNETCORE_URLS environment variable. It applies for the lifetime of the console window.

Your app listens using the URL from the ASPNETCORE_URLS variable.

Figure 16.10 Change the `ASPNETCORE_URLS` environment variable to change the URL used by ASP.NET Core apps.

NOTE If you run your app from within Visual Studio or VS Code, rather than directly using the .NET CLI, you may notice that the app uses a different port number from the default 5000. That's because the launch.json and launchSettings.json files these apps use specify a custom, semi-random URL for the `ASPNETCORE_URLS` value. In ASP.NET Core 2.1, the CLI adopts this behavior such that it too can use the launchSettings.json file.

Setting the URL of an app using a single environment variable works great for some scenarios, most notably when you're running a single application in a virtual machine, or within a Docker container.[4]

If you're not using Docker containers, the chances are you're hosting multiple apps side-by-side on the same machine. A single environment variable is no good for setting URLs in this case, as it would change the URL of every app. In these scenarios, it's common to set the URL from a configuration file in much the same way you load configuration for your app from an appsettings.json.

16.4.2 Using configuration values

In chapter 10, we looked at the configuration system of ASP.NET Core. You saw that it was possible to load configuration values from multiple sources—such as JSON files, environment variables, and the command-line argument—and combine them into a single dictionary of key-value pairs. This used a `ConfigurationBuilder` object to configure the sources and to generate an `IConfiguration` object.

---

[4] ASP.NET Core is well-suited to running in containers, but working with containers is a separate book in its own right. For details on hosting and publishing apps using Docker, see http://mng.bz/tGuf.

It's common to store app configuration in an appsettings.json file for your application. This stores any settings related to the behavior of your application, making them easy to change without needing to recompile your application.

The default `IWebHost` created in Program.cs creates and configures `Configuration-Builder` for your app settings, but there's no reason you can't use the `Configuration-Builder` class in other areas of your app too. If you need a way of reading values from multiple sources, then using `ConfigurationBuilder` provides an easy interface to work with.

In fact, the `WebHostBuilder` object internally uses a separate instance of the `IConfiguration` object when bootstrapping itself during startup, to set the URLs it listens on and the `IHostingEnvironment` for the app, as shown in figure 16.11.

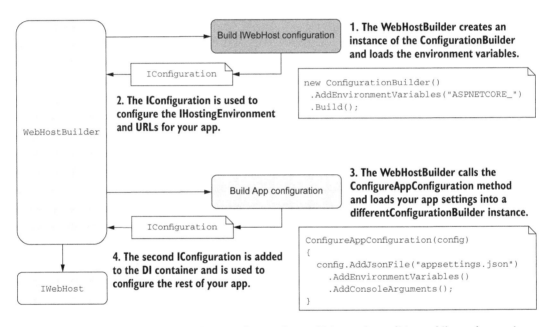

Figure 16.11 `WebHostBuilder` creates `ConfigurationBuilder` and uses it to read the environment variables for the app. These are used to set `IHostingEnvironment` and URLs. A second `ConfigurationBuilder` is created and passed to `ConfigureAppConfiguration` to build `IConfiguration` for the rest of your app.

It uses this to set the hosting environment and the URLs for the app. Internally, the `WebHostBuilder` creates a `ConfigurationBuilder` object to load the special environment variables using:

```
new ConfigurationBuilder()
    .AddEnvironmentVariables(prefix: "ASPNETCORE_")
    .Build();
```

TIP The prefix argument passed to the AddEnvironmentVariables method acts as a filter for the environment variables. Only variables starting with the prefix are added and the variable name is trimmed before it's added to IConfiguration. The ASPNETCORE_URLS and ASPNETCORE_ENVIRONMENT variables are added with the URLS and ENVIRONMENT key values.

This configuration occurs internally in the WebHostBuilder object, but you can override this behavior and provide a completely different IConfiguration object with the UseConfiguration method.

You could create a simple JSON file for setting the environment and URLs for the app, instead of using environment variables. You can then create Configuration-Builder, load the JSON file using a configuration provider, and inject the resulting IConfiguration into WebHostBuilder. WebHostBuilder will use this replacement configuration for its initial bootstrapping to set IHostingEnvironment and URLs, as shown in figure 16.12.

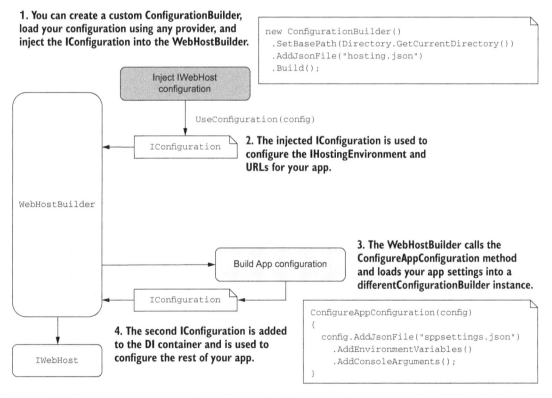

Figure 16.12   You can customize the IWebHost configuration by creating your own ConfigurationBuilder and injecting IConfiguration into WebHostBuilder. This lets you set IHostingEnvironment and URLs for your app from any configuration source, for example a JSON file.

This listing shows how you could customize the default WebHostBuilder in this way to use configuration values loaded from a JSON file called hosting.json.

> **Listing 16.3   Loading configuration values for WebHost from hosting.json**

```
public class Program                                          Uses a custom
{                                                             configuration for
    public static void Main(string[] args)                   the WebHost only,
    {                                                         separate from the
        BuildWebHost(args).Run();                            app configuration
    }

    public static IWebHost BuildWebHost(string[] args) =>
        WebHost.CreateDefaultBuilder(args)                    Creates an
            .UseConfiguration(GetLaunchConfiguration())  <──  IConfiguration
            .UseStartup<Startup>()                            object using
            .Build();                                         Configuration
                                                              Builder
    public static IConfiguration GetLaunchConfiguration() =>  <──
        new ConfigurationBuilder()
            .SetBasePath(Directory.GetCurrentDirectory())
            .AddJsonFile("hosting.json")         <──  Loads configuration values
            .Build();                                 from the hosting.json file
}
```

Remember, the configuration values in hosting.json are for WebHost, not for your app itself. The CreateDefaultBuilder method defines your *app* configuration, and loads configuration values from environment variables and appsettings.json as normal. The hosting.json file would look something like the following:

```
{
  "Environment": "Testing",
  "Urls": "http://localhost:5080"
}
```

This would set the hosting environment to "Testing" and the app URL to http://localhost:5080, in the same way as if you'd used the environment variables instead, as you can see in figure 16.13.

The approach of using ConfigurationBuilder with the UseConfiguration method is flexible. You could load the values from a JSON file as in figure 16.13, but you could also use command-line arguments, XML files, or any other supported

The WebHost configuration values are loaded from hosting.json and are used to set both the hosting environment and the URLs.

Figure 16.13   Setting the hosting environment and URLs for an application by loading them from a custom IConfiguration. You can load the values using any configuration provider.

configuration provider. You could even use multiple sources, so that, for example, your app loads the environment and URLs from a JSON configuration file if it exists, but falls back to environment variables if it doesn't.

Remember, you don't need to set your URLs in this way if you're using IIS as a reverse proxy; IIS integration handles this for you. Setting the URLs is only necessary when you're manually configuring the URL your app is listening on, for example if you're using NGINX or are exposing Kestrel directly to clients.

Continuing the theme of deployment-related tasks, in the next section, we take a look at optimizing some of your client-side assets for production. If you're building a Web API, then this isn't something you'll have to worry about in your ASP.NET Core app, but for traditional web apps it's worth considering.

16.5 Optimizing your client-side assets using BundlerMinifier

Have you ever used a web app or opened a web page that seemed to take forever to load? Once you stray off the beaten track of Amazon, Google, or Microsoft, it's only a matter of time before you're stuck twiddling your thumbs while the web page slowly pops into place.

Next time this happens to you, open the browser developer tools (for example, press F12 in Edge or Chrome) and take a look at the number, and size, of the requests the web app is making. In the majority of cases, a high number of requests generating large responses will be responsible for the slow loading of a web page.

In this section, we'll explore the performance of your ASP.NET Core application in terms of the number and size of requests. You'll see how to improve the performance of your app using bundling and minification, but ensuring your app is still easy to debug while you're building it. Finally, we'll look at a common technique for improving app performance in production: using a content delivery network (CDN).

We'll start by exploring the problem of performance by looking at a single page from your recipe application: the login page. This is a simple page, and it isn't inherently slow, but even this is sufficient to investigate the impact of request size.

As a user, when you click the login button, the browser sends a request to `/Account/Login`. Your ASP.NET Core app executes the `Login` action on `Account-Controller`, which executes a Razor template and returns the generated HTML in the response, as shown in figure 16.14. That's a single request-response; a single round-trip.

But that's not it for the web page. The HTML returned by the page includes links to CSS files (for styling the page), JavaScript files (for client-side functionality—client-side form validation, in this case), and, potentially, images and other resources (though you don't have any others in this recipe app).

The browser must request each of these additional files and wait for the server to return them before the whole page is loaded. When you're developing locally, this all happens quickly, as the request doesn't have far to go at all, but once you deploy your app to production, it's a different matter.

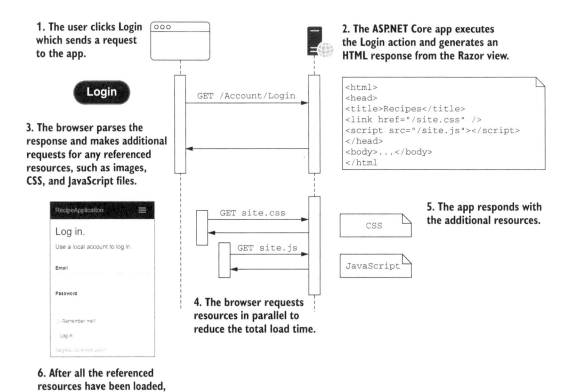

Figure 16.14   Loading a complete page for your app. The initial request returns the HTML for the page, but this may include links to other resources, such as CSS and JavaScript files. The browser must make additional requests to your app for all of the outstanding resources before the page can be fully loaded.

Users will be requesting pages from your app from a wide variety of distances from the server, and over a wide variety of network speeds. Suddenly, the number and size of the requests and responses for your app will have a massive impact on the overall perceived speed of your app. This, in turn, can have a significant impact on how users perceive your site and, for e-commerce sites, even how much money they spend.[5]

A great way to explore how your app will behave for non-optimal networks is to use the network-throttling feature in Chrome's developer tools. This simulates the delays and network speeds associated with different types of networks, so you can get an idea of how your app behaves in the wild. In figure 16.15, I've loaded the login page for the recipe app, but this time with the network set to a modest Regular 3G speed.

> **NOTE**   I've added additional files to the template, navigation.css and global.js, to make the page more representative of a real app.

---

[5]   There has been a lot of research done on this, including stats such as "a 1-second delay in page load time equals 7% loss in conversions" from http://mng.bz/Mi70.

Right click the reload button and choose Empty Cache and Hard Reload.

Throttling adds latency to each request and reduces the maximum data rate.

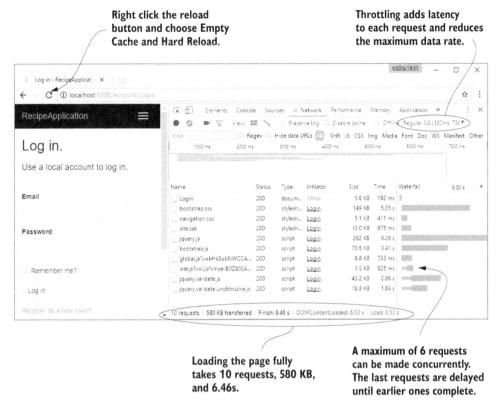

Loading the page fully takes 10 requests, 580 KB, and 6.46s.

A maximum of 6 requests can be made concurrently. The last requests are delayed until earlier ones complete.

Figure 16.15   Exploring the effect of network speed on application load times. Chrome lets you simulate a slower network, so you can get an impression of the experience users will get when loading your application once it's in production.

Throttling the network doesn't change anything about the page or the data requested—there are 8 separate requests and 580 KB loaded for this single page—but it dramatically impacts the time for the page to load. Without throttling, the login page loads locally in 90ms; with Regular 3G throttling, the login page takes 6.45 seconds to load!

> **NOTE**   Don't be too alarmed by these numbers. I'm making a point of reloading all of the files with every request to emphasize the point, whereas in practice, browsers go to great lengths to cache files to avoid having to send this amount of data.

The time it takes to fully load a page of your app is based primarily on two things:

- *The total size of the responses*—This is straight-up math; you can only return data at a certain speed, so the more data you need to return, the longer it takes.
- *The number of requests*—In general, the more requests the browser must make, the longer it takes to fully load the page. In HTTP/1.0 and HTTP/1.1, you can

only make six concurrent requests to a server, so any requests after the sixth must wait for an earlier request to *finish* before they can even *start*.

How can you improve your app speed, assuming all the files you're serving are needed? In general, this is a big topic, with lots of possibilities, such as using a CDN to serve your static files. Two of the simplest ways to improve your site's performance are to use *bundling* and *minification* to reduce the number and size of requests the browser must make to load your app.

16.5.1 Speeding up an app using bundling and minification

In figure 16.15, for the recipe app, you made a total of 10 requests to the server:

- One initial request for the HTML
- Three requests for CSS files
- Six requests for JavaScript files

Some of the CSS and JavaScript files are standard vendor libraries, like Bootstrap and jQuery, that are included as part of the default Razor templates, and some (navigation .css, site.css, global.js, and site.js) are files specific to your app. In this section, we're going to look at optimizing your custom CSS and JavaScript files.

If you're trying to reduce the number of requests for your app, then an obvious first thought is to avoid creating multiple files in the first place! For example, instead of creating a navigation.css file and a site.css file, you could use a single file that contains all of the CSS, instead of separating it out.

That's a valid solution but putting all your code into one file will make it harder to manage and debug. As developers, we generally try to avoid this sort of monster file. A better solution is to let you split your code into as many files as you want, and then *bundle* the files when you come to deploy your code.

> **DEFINITION** *Bundling* is the process of concatenating multiple files into a single file, to reduce the number of requests.

Similarly, when you write JavaScript, you should use descriptive variables names, comments where necessary, and whitespace to create easily readable and debuggable code. When you come to deploy your scripts, you can process and optimize them for size, instead of readability. This process is called *minification*.

> **DEFINITION** *Minification* involves processing code to reduce its size, without changing the behavior of the code. Processing has many different levels, which typically includes removing comments and whitespace, and can extend to renaming variables to give them shorter names or removing whole sections of code entirely if they're unused.

As an example, look at the JavaScript in the following listing. This (very contrived) function adds up some numbers and returns them. It includes (excessively) descriptive variable names, comments, and plenty of use of whitespace, but is representative of the JavaScript you might find in your own app.

Listing 16.4   Example JavaScript function before minification

```
function myFunc() {
    // this function doesn't really do anything,
    // it's just here so that we can show off minifying!
    function innerFunctionToAddTwoNumbers(
        thefirstnumber, theSecondNumber) {

        // i'm nested inside myFunc
        return thefirstnumber + theSecondNumber;
    }

    var shouldAddNumbers = true;
    var totalOfAllTheNumbers = 0;

    if (shouldAddNumbers == true) {
        for (var index = 0; i < 10; i++) {
            totalOfAllTheNumbers =
                innerFunctionToAddTwoNumbers(totalOfAllTheNumbers, index);
        }
    }

    return totalOfAllTheNumbers;
}
```

This function takes a total of 588 bytes as it's currently written, but after minification, that's reduced to 95 bytes—16% of its original size. The behavior of the code is identical, but the output, shown in the following listing, is optimized to reduce its size. It's clearly not something you'd want to debug, but you'd only use minified versions of your file in production; you'd use the original source files when developing.

Listing 16.5   Example JavaScript function after minification

```
function myFunc(){function r(n,t){return n+t}var
n=0,t;if(1)for(t=0;i<10;i++)n=r(n,t);return n}
```

Optimizing your static files using bundling and minification can provide a free boost to your app's performance when you deploy your app to production, while letting you develop using easy-to-read and separated files.

Figure 16.16 shows the impact of bundling and minifying the files for the login page of your recipe app. Each of the vendor files has been minified to reduce its size, and your custom assets have been bundled and minified to reduce both their size and the number of requests. This reduced the number of requests from 10 to 8, the total amount of data from 580 KB to 270 KB, and the load time from 6.45 s to 3.15 s.

> **NOTE** The vendor assets, such as jQuery and Bootstrap, aren't bundled with your custom scripts in figure 16.16. This lets you load those files from a CDN, as I'll touch on in section 16.5.4.

This performance improvement can be achieved with little effort on your part, and no impact on your development process. In the next section, I'll show how you can

The vendor assets like
Bootstrap and JQuery
are individually minified.

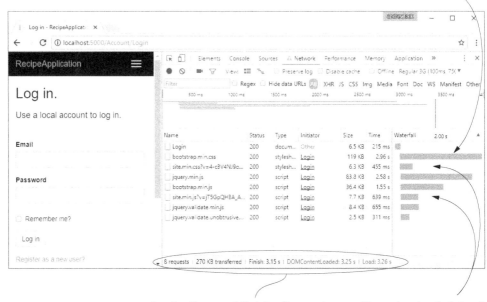

Loading the page fully takes 8 requests,
270 KB, and 3.15s—50% faster and
50% less data than before.

The custom JavaScript and
CSS assets for the app are
bundled into a single file.

Figure 16.16   By bundling and minifying your client-side resources, you can reduce both the number of requests required and the total data to transfer, which can significantly improve performance. In this example, bundling and minification cut the time to fully loaded in half.

include bundling and minification as part of your ASP.NET Core build process, and how to customize the bundling and minification processes for your app.

16.5.2 *Adding BundlerMinifier to your application*

Bundling and minification isn't a new idea, so you have many ways to achieve the same result. The previous version of ASP.NET performed bundling and minification in managed code, whereas JavaScript task runners such as gulp, grunt, and webpack are commonly used for these sorts of tasks. In fact, if you're writing an SPA, then you're almost certainly already performing bundling and minification as a matter of course.

The ASP.NET Core templates include support for bundling and minification via a NuGet package called BuildBundlerMinifier or a Visual Studio extension version called Bundler & Minifier. You don't have to use either of these, and if you're already using other tools such as gulp or webpack, then I suggest you continue to use them instead. But if you're getting started with a new project, then I suggest considering BundlerMinifier; you can always switch to a different tool later.

You have two options for adding BundlerMinifier to your project:

- You can install the Bundler & Minifier Visual Studio extension from Tools > Extensions and Updates.
- You can add the BuildBundlerMinifier NuGet package to your project.

Whichever approach you use, they both use the same underlying BundlerMinifier library.[6] I prefer to use the NuGet package approach as it's cross-platform and will automatically bundle your resources for you, but the extension is useful for performing ad hoc bundling. If you do use the Visual Studio extension, make sure to enable Bundle on build, as you'll see shortly.

The BundlerMinifier library is controlled using a bundleconfig.json file in the root folder of your project. ASP.NET Core templates in Visual Studio and the .NET CLI include this file automatically. You can install the BuildBundlerMinifier NuGet package in your project with this command:

```
dotnet add package BuildBundlerMinifier
```

Alternatively, if you're using Visual Studio and have installed the Bundler & Minifier extension, you can right-click the bundleconfig.json file and choose Enable bundle on build, as shown in figure 16.17. Doing so will install the BuildBundlerMinifier package into your project.

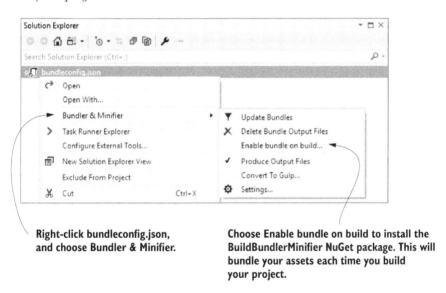

Right-click bundleconfig.json, and choose Bundler & Minifier.

Choose Enable bundle on build to install the BuildBundlerMinifier NuGet package. This will bundle your assets each time you build your project.

Figure 16.17 Enabling bundle on build in Visual Studio using the Bundler & Minifier extension. This installs the BuildBundlerMinifier tooling package in your project file.

---

[6] The library and extension are open source on GitHub: https://github.com/madskristensen/Bundler-Minifier/.

With the BuildBundlerMinifier package installed, whenever you build your project the BundlerMinifier will check your CSS and JavaScript files for changes. If something has changed, new bundled and minified files are created, as shown in figure 16.18, where I modified a JavaScript file.

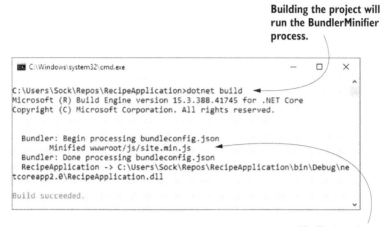

Building the project will run the BundlerMinifier process.

If a file has changed, the BundlerMinifier will rebuild and minify the bundle.

Figure 16.18   Whenever the project is built, the BuildBundlerMinifier tool looks for changes in the input files and builds new bundles as necessary.

As you can see in figure 16.18, the bundler minified your JavaScript code and created a new file at wwwroot/js/site.min.js. But why did it pick this name? Well, because you told it to in bundleconfig.json.

Listing 16.6 shows the default bundleconfig.json that's included in the ASP.NET Core templates. This defines which files to include in each bundle, where to write each bundle, and what minification options to use. Two bundles are configured by default: one for CSS and one for JavaScript. You can add bundles to the JSON array, or you can customize the existing provided bundles.

Listing 16.6   The default bundleconfig.json file

```
[
  {
    "outputFileName": "wwwroot/css/site.min.css",
    "inputFiles": [
      "wwwroot/css/site.css"
    ]
  },
  {
    "outputFileName": "wwwroot/js/site.min.js",
    "inputFiles": [
      "wwwroot/js/site.js"
    ],
```

The bundler will create a file with this name.

The files listed in inputFiles are minified and concatenated into outputFileName.

You should create separate bundles for CSS and JavaScript.

You can specify multiple bundles, each with an output filename.

```
    "minify": {                    The JavaScript bundler has
      "enabled": true,             some additional options.
      "renameLocals": true
    },
    "sourceMap": false   ◁─┐  You can optionally create a source
  }                          │  map for the bundled JavaScript file.
]
```

By default, each bundle only includes a specific list of files, as specified in the `input-Files` property. That means if you add a new CSS or JavaScript file to your project, you have to remember to come back to bundleconfig.json and add it to the list. Instead, I like to use *globbing* patterns to automatically include new files by default. This isn't always possible, for example when you need to ensure that files are concatenated in a particular order, but I find it preferable in most cases.

> **DEFINITION**   *Globbing* patterns use wildcards to represent many different characters. For example, *.css would match all files with a .css extension, whatever the filename.

You can update the bundleconfig.json file to automatically include all of your custom CSS and JavaScript files, as shown in the following listing. I've added the navigation .css file to the CSS bundle explicitly and have updated the JavaScript bundle to use a globbing pattern. This pattern includes all .js files in the wwwroot/js folder but excludes the minified output file itself.

> **Listing 16.7   Customizing the bundleconfig.json file to include additional files**

```
[
  {
    "outputFileName": "wwwroot/css/site.min.css",
    "inputFiles": [
      "wwwroot/css/site.css",            You can list all of the files to
      "wwwroot/css/navigation.css"  ◁────  include in a bundle explicitly.
    ]
  },
  {
    "outputFileName": "wwwroot/js/site.min.js",
    "inputFiles": [                        You can use globbing patterns
      "wwwroot/js/*.js",  ◁──────────────  to specify files to include.
      "!wwwroot/js/site.min.js"  ◁───  The ! symbol excludes
    ],                                 the matching file from
    "minify": {                        the bundle.
      "enabled": true,
      "renameLocals": true
    },
    "sourceMap": false
  }
]
```

Now when you build your project, the BundlerMinifier optimizes your css files into a single wwwroot/css/site.min.css file, and your JavaScript into a single wwwroot/js/

site.min.js file. In the next section, we'll look at how to include these files when you run in production, continuing to use the original files when developing locally.

> **NOTE**   The BundlerMinifier package is great for optimizing your CSS and JavaScript resources. But images are another important resource to consider for optimization and can easily constitute the bulk of your page's size. Unfortunately, there aren't any built-in tools for this, so you'll need to look at other options; https://tinypng.com is one.

16.5.3   Using minified files in production with the environment tag helper

Optimizing files using bundling and minification is great for performance, but you want to use the original files during development. The easiest way to achieve this split in ASP.NET Core is to use the Environment Tag Helper to conditionally include the original files when running in the Development hosting environment, and to use the optimized files in other environments.

You learned about the Environment Tag Helper in chapter 8, in which we used it to show a banner on the homepage when the app was running in the Testing environment. Listing 16.7 shows how you can achieve a similar approach in the _Layout .cshtml for the CSS files of your Recipe app by using two Environment Tag Helpers: one for when you're in Development, and one for when you aren't in Development (you're in Production or Staging, for example). You can use similar Tag Helpers for the JavaScript files in the app.

Listing 16.8   Using Environment Tag Helpers to conditionally render optimized files

```
<environment include="Development">
    <link rel="stylesheet"
        href="~/lib/bootstrap/dist/css/bootstrap.css" />
    <link rel="stylesheet" href="~/css/navigation.css" />
    <link rel="stylesheet" href="~/css/site.css" />
</environment>

<environment exclude="Development">
    <link rel="stylesheet"
        href="~/lib/bootstrap/dist/css/bootstrap.min.css" />
    <link rel="stylesheet" href="~/css/site.min.css" />
</environment>
```

The development version of Bootstrap

Only render these links when running in Development environment.

The development version of your styles

The minified version of Bootstrap

Only render these links when not in Development, such as in Staging or Production.

The bundled and minified version of your styles

When the app detects it isn't running in the Development hosting environment (as you learned in chapter 11), it will switch to rendering links for the optimized files. This gives you the best of both worlds: performance in production and ease of development.

The example in listing 16.8 also included a minified version of Bootstrap, even though you didn't configure this as part of the BundlerMinifier. It's common for CSS and JavaScript libraries like Bootstrap to include a pre-minified version of the file for you to use in Production. For those that do, it's often better to exclude them from your bundling process, as this allows you to potentially serve the file from a public CDN.

16.5.4 *Serving common files from a CDN*

A public CDN is a website that hosts commonly used files, such as Bootstrap or jQuery, which you can reference from your own apps. They have a number of advantages:

- They're normally fast.
- They save your server having to serve the file, saving bandwidth.
- Because the file is served from a different server, it doesn't count toward the six concurrent requests allowed to your server in HTTP/1.0 and HTTP/1.1.
- Many different apps can reference the same file, so a user visiting your app may have already cached the file by visiting a different website, so may not need to download it at all.

It's easy to use a CDN in principle: reference the CDN file instead of the file on your own server. Unfortunately, you need to cater for the fact that, like any server, CDNs can sometimes fail. If you don't have a fallback mechanism to load the file from a different location, such as your server, then this can result in your app looking broken.

Luckily, ASP.NET Core includes several tag helpers to make working with CDNs and fallbacks easier. In fact, the default MVC templates come configured to serve Bootstrap and jQuery from a CDN in production, and to fall back to the version included with your app if the CDN fails.

Listing 16.9 shows how you could update your CSS Environment Tag Helper to serve Bootstrap from a CDN when running in production, and to include a fallback. The fallback test creates a temporary HTML element and applies a Bootstrap style to it. If the element has the expected CSS properties, then the fallback test passes, because Bootstrap must be loaded. If it doesn't have the required properties, Bootstrap will be loaded from the alternative, local link instead.

> **Listing 16.9   Serving Bootstrap CSS styles from a CDN with a local fallback**

By default, Bootstrap is loaded from a CDN.

If the fallback check fails, the CDN must have failed, so Bootstrap is loaded from the local link.

```
<environment include="Development">
    <link rel="stylesheet" href="~/lib/bootstrap/dist/css/bootstrap.css" />
    <link rel="stylesheet" href="~/css/navigation.css" />
    <link rel="stylesheet" href="~/css/site.css" />
</environment>
<environment exclude="Development">
    <link rel="stylesheet"  href="https://ajax.aspnetcdn.com/ajax/
    bootstrap/3.3.7/css/bootstrap.min.css"
    asp-fallback-href="~/lib/bootstrap/dist/css/bootstrap.min.css"
```

```
        asp-fallback-test-class="sr-only"
        asp-fallback-test-property="position"
        asp-fallback-test-value="absolute" />
      <link rel="stylesheet" href="~/css/site.min.css" />
    </environment>
```

The fallback test applies the
sr-only class to an element ...

... and checks the element has a CSS
position of absolute. This indicates
Bootstrap was loaded.

Optimizing your static files is an important step to consider before you put your app into production, as it can have a significant impact on performance. Luckily, the BuildBundlerMinifier package makes it easy to optimize your CSS and JavaScript files. If you couple that with serving common files from a CDN, your app will be as speedy as possible for users in production.

That brings us to the end of this chapter on publishing your app. This last mile of app development, deploying an application to a server where users can access it, is a notoriously thorny issue. Publishing an ASP.NET Core application is easy enough, but the multitude of hosting options available makes providing concise steps for every situation difficult.

Whichever hosting option you choose, there's one critical topic which is often overlooked, but is crucial for resolving issues quickly: logging. In the next chapter, you'll learn about the logging abstractions in ASP.NET Core, and how you can use them to keep tabs on your app once it's in production.

Summary

- ASP.NET Core apps are console applications that self-host a web server.
- .NET Core has two parts: the .NET Core SDK (also known as the .NET CLI) and the .NET Core Runtime.
- When you're developing an application, you use the .NET CLI to restore, build, and run your application. Visual Studio uses the same .NET CLI commands from the IDE.
- When you want to deploy your app to production, you need to publish your application. This creates a folder containing your application as a dll, along with all its dependencies.
- By default, Razor templates are precompiled into a dll. This gives performance benefits, as your app doesn't need to compile the templates at runtime. You can disable precompilation by setting the MvcRazorCompileOnPublish property to false in your csproj file.
- To run a published application, you don't need the .NET CLI as you won't be building the app. You only need the .NET Core Runtime to run a published app. You can run a published application using the dotnet app.dll command, where app.dll is the application dll created by the dotnet publish command.

- In order to host ASP.NET Core applications in IIS, you must install the ASP.NET Core Module. This allows IIS to act as a reverse proxy for your ASP.NET Core app.
- To prepare your application for publishing with ASP.NET Core, ensure you call `UseIISIntegration()` on `WebHostBuilder`. The `WebHost.CreateDefault-Builder` static helper method does this automatically.
- When you publish your application using the .NET CLI, a web.config file will be added to the output folder. It's important that this file is deployed with your application when publishing to IIS, as it defines how your application should be run.
- The URL that your app will listen on is specified by default using the environment variable `ASPNETCORE_URLS`. Setting this value will change the URL for all the apps on your machine.
- To customize the URL for a single app, use an additional `Configuration-Builder` to load configuration from a JSON file, or from command-line arguments. Build it using `Build()`, and pass `IConfiguration` to `WebHostBuilder` with the `UseConfiguration` method. This approach is highly flexible and lets you specify the URLs for your app in many different ways.
- It's important to optimize your client-side assets to reduce the size and number of files that must be downloaded by a client's web browser when a page loads. You can achieve this by bundling and minifying your assets.
- You can use the BuildBundlerMinifier package to combine multiple JavaScript or CSS files together in a process called bundling. You can reduce the size of the files in a process called minification, in which unnecessary whitespace is removed and variables are renamed while preserving the function of the file.
- You can install a Visual Studio extension to control bundling and minification, or you can install the BuildBundlerMinifier package to automatically perform bundling and minification on each build of the project.
- The settings for bundling and minification are stored in the bundleconfig.json file, where you can define the different output bundle files and choose which files to include in the bundle. You can explicitly specify files, or you can use globbing patterns to include multiple files using wildcard characters.
- Use the Environment Tag Helper to conditionally render your bundles in production only. This lets you optimize for performance in production and readability in development.
- For common files shared by multiple apps, such as jQuery or Bootstrap, you can serve files from a CDN. These are websites that host the common files, so your app doesn't need to serve them itself.
- Use Link and Script Tag Helpers to check that the file has loaded correctly from the CDN. These can test that a file has been downloaded by a client and ensures that your server is used as a fallback should the CDN fail.

Part 3

Extending your applications

We covered a huge amount of content in parts 1 and 2: we looked at all the main functional components you'll use to build both traditional MVC web apps and web APIs. In part 3, we look at four different topics that build on what you've learned so far: logging, security, custom components, and testing.

Adding logging to your application is one of those activities that's often left until after you discover a problem in production. Adding sensible logging from the get-go will help you quickly diagnose and fix errors as they arise. Chapter 17 introduces the logging framework built in to ASP.NET Core. You'll see how you can use it to write log messages to a wide variety of locations, whether it's the console, a file, or a third-party remote-logging service.

Correctly securing your app is an important part of web development these days. Even if you don't feel you have any sensitive data in your application, you have to make sure you protect your users from attacks by adhering to security best practices. In chapter 18, I describe some common vulnerabilities, how attackers can exploit them, and what you can do to protect your applications.

As you saw in parts 1 and 2, the MVC middleware is the workhorse for most ASP.NET Core applications, allowing you to easily customize your application's UI and exposed URLs, but sometimes you need to customize more than that. In chapter 19, I show you how to build various custom components, from custom middleware to custom Tag Helpers and validation attributes. You'll also see how to handle complex configuration requirements and how to replace the built-in dependency injection container with a third-party alternative.

Chapter 20, the final chapter, covers testing your application. The exact role of testing in application development can sometimes lead to philosophical arguments, but in chapter 20, I stick to the practicalities of testing your app using the xUnit test framework. You'll see how to create unit tests for your controllers and middleware, how to test code that's dependent on EF Core using an in-memory database provider, and how to write integration tests that can test multiple aspects of your application at once.

Monitoring
and troubleshooting
errors with logging

This chapter covers

- Understanding the components of a log message
- Writing logs to multiple output locations
- Controlling log verbosity in different environments using filtering
- Using structured logging to make logs searchable

Logging is one of those topics that seems unnecessary, right up until the point when you desperately need it! There's nothing more frustrating than finding an issue that you can only reproduce in production, and then discovering there are no logs to help you debug it.

Logging is the process of recording events or activities in an app and often involves writing a record to a console, a file, the Windows Event Log, or some other system. You can record anything in a log message, though there are generally two different types of message:

- *Informational messages*—A standard event occurred: a user logged in, a product was placed in a shopping cart, or a new post was created on a blogging app.
- *Warning and errors*—An error or unexpected condition occurred: a user had a negative total in the shopping cart, or an exception occurred.

Historically, a common problem with logging in larger applications was that each library and framework would generate logs in a slightly different format, if at all. When an error occurred in your app and you were trying to diagnose it, this inconsistency made it harder to connect the dots in your app to get the full picture and understand the problem.

Luckily, ASP.NET Core includes a new, generic logging interface that you can plug into. It's used throughout the ASP.NET Core framework code itself, as well as by third-party libraries, and you can easily use it to create logs in your own code. With the ASP.NET Core logging framework, you can control the verbosity of logs coming from each part of your code, including the framework and libraries, and you can write the log output to any destination that plugs into the framework.

In this chapter, I cover the ASP.NET Core logging framework in detail and explain how you can use it to record events and diagnose errors in your own apps. In section 17.1, I describe the architecture of the logging framework. You'll learn how DI makes it easy for both libraries and apps to create log messages, as well as to write those logs to multiple destinations.

In section 17.2, you'll learn how to write your own log messages in your apps with the `ILogger` interface. We'll break down the anatomy of a typical log record and look at its properties, such as the log level, category, and message.

Writing logs is only useful if you can read them, so in section 17.3, you'll learn how to add *logging providers* to your application. Logging providers control where your app writes your log messages. This could be to the console, to a file, or even an external service. I'll show you how to add a logging provider that writes logs to a file, and how to configure a popular third-party logging provider called Serilog in your app.

Logging is an important part of any application, but determining *how much* logging is enough can be a tricky question. On the one hand, you want to provide sufficient information to be able to diagnose any problems. On the other, you don't want to fill your logs with data that makes it hard to find the important information when you need it. Even worse, what is sufficient in development might be far too much once you're running in production.

In section 17.4, I explain how you can filter log messages from various sections of your app, such as the ASP.NET Core infrastructure libraries, so that your logging providers only write the important messages. This lets you keep that balance between extensive logging in development and only writing important logs in production.

In the final section of this chapter, I touch on some of the benefits of *structured logging*, an approach to logging that you can use with some providers for the ASP.NET Core logging framework. Structured logging involves attaching data to log messages as key-value pairs to make logs more easily searched and queried. You might attach a unique customer ID to every log message generated by your app, for example. Finding all the log messages associated with a user is much simpler with this approach, compared to recording the customer ID in an inconsistent manner as part of the log message.

We'll start this chapter by digging into what logging involves, and why your future self will thank you for using logging effectively in your application. Then we'll look at the pieces of the ASP.NET Core logging framework you'll use directly in your apps, and how they fit together.

17.1 Using logging effectively in a production app

Imagine you've just deployed a new app to production, when a customer calls saying that they're getting an error message using your app.

How would you identify what caused the problem? You could ask the customer what steps they were taking, and potentially try to recreate the error yourself, but if that doesn't work then you're left trawling through the code, trying to spot errors with nothing else to go on.

Logging can provide the extra context you need to quickly diagnose a problem. Arguably, the most important logs capture the details about the error itself, but the events that led to the error can be just as useful in diagnosing the cause of an error.

There are many reasons for adding logging to an application, but typically, the reasons fall into one of two categories:

- Logging for auditing or analytics reasons, to trace when events have occurred
- Logging errors, or to provide a breadcrumb trail of events when an error does occur

The first of these reasons is simple. You may be required to keep a record of every time a user logs in, for example, or you may want to keep track of how many times a particular API method is called. Logging is an easy way to record the behavior of your app, by writing a message to the log every time an interesting event occurs.

I find the second reason for logging to be the most common. When an app is working perfectly, logs often go completely untouched. It's when there's an issue and a customer comes calling that logs become invaluable. A good set of logs can help you understand the conditions in your app that caused an error, including the context of the error itself, but also the context in previous requests.

> **TIP** Even with extensive logging in place, you may not realize you have an issue in your app unless you look through your logs regularly! For any medium to large app this becomes impractical, so monitoring services such as https://raygun.io can be invaluable for notifying you of issues quickly.

If this sounds like a lot of work, then you're in luck. ASP.NET Core does a ton of the "breadcrumb" logging for you so that you can focus on creating high-quality log messages that provide the most value when diagnosing problems.

17.1.1 Highlighting problems using custom log messages

ASP.NET Core uses logging throughout its libraries. Depending on how you configure your app, you'll have access to the details of each request and EF Core query, even without adding additional logging messages to your own code. In figure 17.1 you can see the log messages created when you view a single recipe in the recipe application.

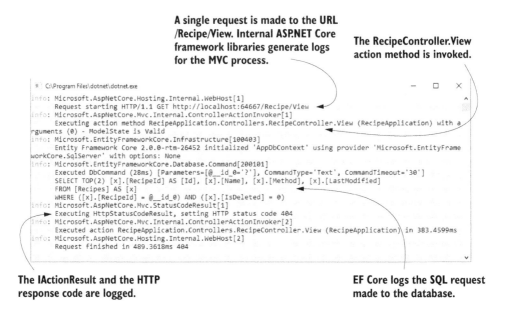

A single request is made to the URL /Recipe/View. Internal ASP.NET Core framework libraries generate logs for the MVC process.

The RecipeController.View action method is invoked.

The IActionResult and the HTTP response code are logged.

EF Core logs the SQL request made to the database.

Figure 17.1   The ASP.NET Core Framework libraries use logging throughout. A single request generates multiple log messages that describe the flow of the request through your application.

This gives you a lot of useful information. You can see which URL was requested, the action method that was invoked (and its arguments), the EF Core database command, the action result invoked, and the response. This information can be invaluable when trying to isolate a problem, whether a bug in a production app or a feature in development when you're working locally.

This infrastructure logging can be useful, but log messages that you create yourself can have even greater value. For example, you may be able to spot the cause of the error from the log messages in figure 17.1—we're attempting to view a recipe with an unknown RecipeId of 0, but it's far from obvious. If you explicitly add a log message to your app when this happens, as in figure 17.2, then the problem is much more apparent.

This custom log message easily stands out, and clearly states both the problem (the recipe with the requested ID doesn't exist) and the parameters/variables that led to the issue (the ID value of 0). Adding similar log messages to your own applications will make it easier for you to diagnose problems, track important events, and generally give you an idea of what your app is doing.

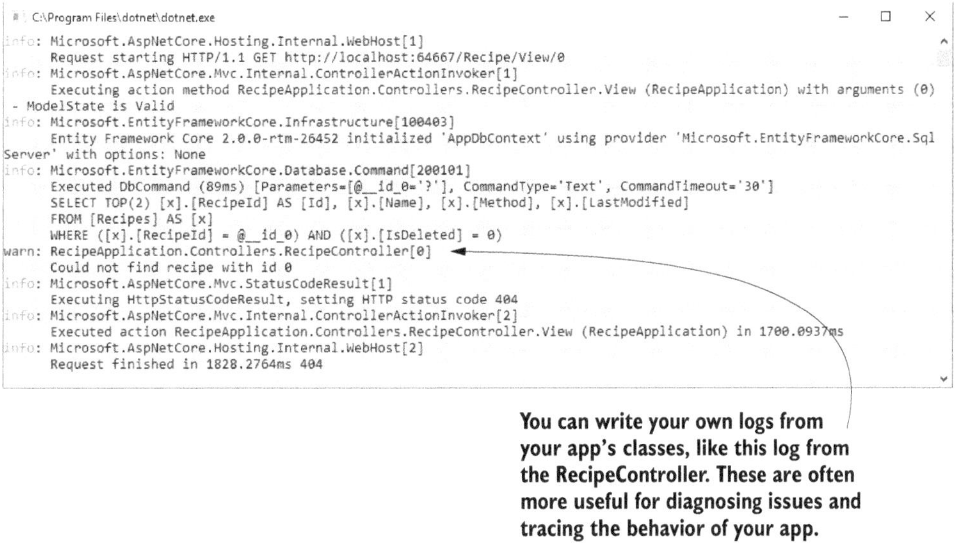

```
C:\Program Files\dotnet\dotnet.exe                                           —   □   ×
info: Microsoft.AspNetCore.Hosting.Internal.WebHost[1]
      Request starting HTTP/1.1 GET http://localhost:64667/Recipe/View/0
info: Microsoft.AspNetCore.Mvc.Internal.ControllerActionInvoker[1]
      Executing action method RecipeApplication.Controllers.RecipeController.View (RecipeApplication) with arguments (0)
- ModelState is Valid
info: Microsoft.EntityFrameworkCore.Infrastructure[100403]
      Entity Framework Core 2.0.0-rtm-26452 initialized 'AppDbContext' using provider 'Microsoft.EntityFrameworkCore.Sql
Server' with options: None
info: Microsoft.EntityFrameworkCore.Database.Command[200101]
      Executed DbCommand (89ms) [Parameters=[@__id_0='?'], CommandType='Text', CommandTimeout='30']
      SELECT TOP(2) [x].[RecipeId] AS [Id], [x].[Name], [x].[Method], [x].[LastModified]
      FROM [Recipes] AS [x]
      WHERE ([x].[RecipeId] = @__id_0) AND ([x].[IsDeleted] = 0)
warn: RecipeApplication.Controllers.RecipeController[0]   ◄
      Could not find recipe with id 0
info: Microsoft.AspNetCore.Mvc.StatusCodeResult[1]
      Executing HttpStatusCodeResult, setting HTTP status code 404
info: Microsoft.AspNetCore.Mvc.Internal.ControllerActionInvoker[2]
      Executed action RecipeApplication.Controllers.RecipeController.View (RecipeApplication) in 1700.0937ms
info: Microsoft.AspNetCore.Hosting.Internal.WebHost[2]
      Request finished in 1828.2764ms 404
```

You can write your own logs from your app's classes, like this log from the RecipeController. These are often more useful for diagnosing issues and tracing the behavior of your app.

Figure 17.2   You can write your own logs. These are often more useful for identifying issues and interesting events in your apps.

Hopefully, you're now motivated to add logging to your apps, so we'll dig in to the details of what that involves. In section 17.1.2, you'll see how to create a log message, and how to define where the log messages are written. We'll look in detail at these two aspects in section 17.2 and 17.3; for now, we'll only look at where they fit in terms of the ASP.NET Core logging framework as a whole.

17.1.2   *The ASP.NET Core logging abstractions*

The ASP.NET Core logging framework consists of a number of logging abstractions (interfaces, implementations, and helper classes), the most important of which are shown in figure 17.3:

- ILogger—This is the interface you'll interact with in your code. It has a Log() method, which is used to write a log message.
- ILoggerProvider—This is used to create a custom instance of an ILogger, depending on the provider. A console ILoggerProvider would create an ILogger that writes to the console, whereas a file ILoggerProvider would create an ILogger that writes to a file.
- ILoggerFactory—The glue between the ILoggerProvider instances and the ILogger you use in your code. You register ILoggerProvider instances with an ILoggerFactory and call CreateLogger() on the ILoggerFactory when you need an ILogger. The factory creates an ILogger that wraps each of the providers, so when you call the Log() method, the log is written to every provider.

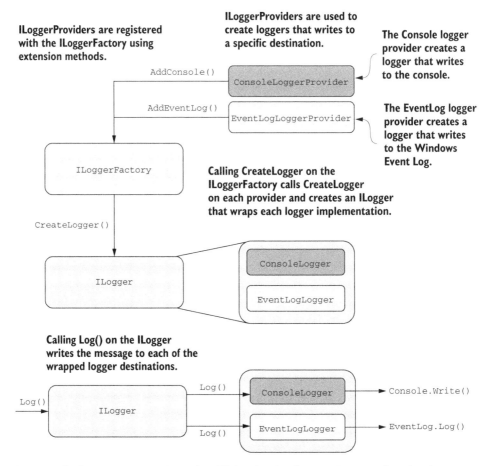

Figure 17.3   The components of the ASP.NET Core logging framework. You register logging providers with an `ILoggerFactory`, which are used to create implementations of `ILogger`. You write logs to the `ILogger`, which uses the `ILogger` implementations to output logs to the console or a file.

This design in figure 17.3 makes it easy to add or change where your application writes the log messages, without having to change your application code. This listing shows all the code required to add an `ILoggerProvider` that writes logs to the console.

Listing 17.1   Adding a console log provider to `IWebHost` in Program.cs

```
public class Program
{
    public static void Main(string[] args)
    {
        BuildWebHost(args).Run();
    }
```

```
public static IWebHost BuildWebHost(string[] args) =>
    new WebHostBuilder()
        .UseStartup<Startup>()
        .ConfigureLogging(builder =>builder.AddConsole())   ◁───┐
        .Build();
}                                           Add new providers with the
                                            ConfigureLogging extension
                                            method on WebHostBuilder.
```

NOTE The console logger is added by default in the `CreateDefaultBuilder` method, as you'll see in section 17.3.

Other than this configuration on `WebHostBuilder`, you don't interact with `ILogger-Provider` instances directly. Instead, you write logs using an instance of `ILogger`, as you'll see in the next section.

17.2 *Adding log messages to your application*

In this section, we'll look in detail at how to create log messages in your own application. You'll learn how to create an instance of `ILogger`, and how to use it to add logging to an existing application. Finally, we'll look at the properties that make up a logging record, what they mean, and what you can use them for.

Logging, like almost everything in ASP.NET Core, is available through DI. To add logging to your own services, you only need to inject an instance of `ILogger<T>`, where `T` is the type of your service.

NOTE When you inject `ILogger<T>`, the DI container indirectly calls `ILogger-Factory.CreateLogger<T>()` to create the wrapped `ILogger` of figure 17.3. In section 17.2.2, you'll see how to work directly with `ILoggerFactory` if you prefer. The `ILogger<T>` interface also implements the nongeneric `ILogger` interface.

You can use the injected `ILogger` instance to create log messages, which writes the log to each configured `ILoggerProvider`. The following listing shows how to inject an `ILogger<>` instance into the `RecipeController` of the recipe application from previous chapters and write a log message indicating how many recipes were found.

Listing 17.2 Injecting `ILogger` into a class and writing a log message

```
public class RecipeController : Controller
{
    private readonly RecipeService _service;
    private readonly ILogger _log;   ◁───────────────────┐

    public RecipeController(RecipeService service,
            ILogger<RecipeController> log)   ◁───────────┐  Injects the generic
    {                                                     │  ILogger<T> using
        _service = service;                               │  DI, which
        _log = log;   ◁───────────────────────────────────┘  implements ILogger
    }

    public IActionResult Index()
```

```
    {
        var models = _service.GetRecipes();
        _log.LogInformation(
            "Loaded {RecipeCount} recipes", models.Count);
        return View(models);
    }
}
```

> This writes an Information-level log. The RecipeCount variable is substituted in the message.

In this example, you're using one of the many extension methods on `ILogger` to create the log message, `LogInformation()`. There are many extension methods on `ILogger` that let you easily specify a `LogLevel` for the message.

> **DEFINITION**   The *log level* of a log is how important it is and is defined by the `LogLevel` enum. Every log message has a log level.

You can also see that the message you pass to the `LogInformation` method has a placeholder indicated by braces, `{RecipeCount}`, and you pass an additional parameter, `models.Count`, to the logger. The logger will replace the placeholder with the parameter at runtime.

> **TIP**   You could've used normal string interpolation to create the log message, for example, `$"Loaded {models.Count} recipes"`. But I recommend always using placeholders, as they provide additional information for the logger that can be used for structured logging, as you'll see in section 17.5.

When the `RecipeController.Index` action executes (due to a request to /recipes/index), `ILogger` writes a message to any configured logging providers. The exact format of the log message will vary from provider to provider, but figure 17.4 shows how the console provider would display the log message from listing 17.2.

Figure 17.4   An example log message, as it's written to the default console provider

The exact presentation of the message will vary depending on where the log is written, but each log record includes up to six common elements:

- *Log level*—The log level of the log is how important it is and is defined by the `LogLevel` enum.
- *Event category*—The category may be any string value, but it's typically set to the name of the class creating the log. For `ILogger<T>`, the full name of the type `T` is the category.

- *Message*—This is the content of the log message. It can be a static string, or it can contain placeholders for variables, as shown in listing 17.2. Placeholders are indicated by braces, {}, and are substituted with the provided parameter values.
- *Parameters*—If the message contains placeholders, then they're associated with the provided parameters. For the example in listing 17.2, the value of `models`.`Count` is assigned to the placeholder called `RecipeCount`. Some loggers can extract these values and expose them in your logs, as you'll see in section 17.5.
- *Exception*—If an exception occurs, you can pass the exception object to the logging function along with the message and other parameters. The logger will log the exception, in addition to the message itself.
- *EventId*—This is an optional integer identifier for the error, which can be used to quickly find all similar logs in a series of log messages. You might use an `EventId` of `1000` when a user attempts to load a non-existent recipe, and an `EventId` of `1001` when a user attempts to access a recipe they don't have permission to access. If you don't provide an `EventId`, the value `0` will be used.

Not every log message will have all these elements—you won't always have an `Exception` or parameters—but each message will have, at the very least, a level, category, and message. These are the key features of the log, so we'll look at each in turn.

17.2.1 Log level: how important is the log message?

Whenever you create a log using `ILogger`, you must specify the *log level*. This indicates how serious or important the log message is and is an important factor when it comes to filtering which logs get written by a provider, as well as finding the important log messages after the fact.

You might create an `Information` level log when a user starts to edit a recipe. This is useful for tracing the application's flow and behavior, but it's not important, because everything is normal. But if an exception is thrown when the user attempts to save the recipe, you might create a `Warning` or `Error` level log.

The log level is typically set by using one of several extension methods on the `ILogger` interface, as shown in listing 17.3. This example creates an `Information` level log when the `View` method executes, and a `Warning` level error if the requested recipe isn't found.

> **Listing 17.3 Specifying the log level using extension methods on `ILogger`**

```
private readonly ILogger _log;          ⊲──────────   An ILogger instance is injected into the
public async Task<IActionResult> View(int id)          controller using constructor injection.
{
    _log.LogInformation(                               Writes an Information
        "Loading recipe with id {RecipeId}", id);      level log message

    var model = _service.GetRecipeDetail(id);
    if (model == null)
    {
```

```
        _log.LogWarning(
            "Could not find recipe with id {RecipeId}", id);
        return NotFound();
    }
    return View(model)
}
```

Writes a warning
level log message

The `LogInformation` and `LogWarning` extension methods create log messages with a log level of `Information` and `Warning`, respectively. There are six log levels to choose from, ordered here from most to least serious:

- `Critical`—For disastrous failures that may leave the app unable to function correctly, such as out of memory exceptions, if the hard drive is out of disk space, or the server is on fire.

- `Error`—For errors and exceptions that you can't handle gracefully, for example, exceptions thrown when saving an edited entity in EF Core. The operation failed, but the app can continue to function for other requests and users.

- `Warning`—For when an unexpected or error condition arises that you can work around. You might log a `Warning` for handled exceptions, or when an entity isn't found, as in listing 17.3.

- `Information`—For tracking normal application flow, for example, logging when a user logs in, or when they view a specific page in your app. Typically, these log messages provide context when you need to understand the steps leading up to an error message.

- `Debug`—For tracking detailed information that's particularly useful during development. Generally, this only has short-term usefulness.

- `Trace`—For tracking very detailed information, which may contain sensitive information like passwords or keys. It's rarely used, and not used at all by the framework libraries.

Think of these log levels in terms of a pyramid, as shown in figure 17.5. As you progress down the log levels, the importance of the messages goes down, but the frequency goes up. Generally, you'll find many `Debug` level log messages in your application, but (hopefully) few `Critical` or `Error` level messages.

This pyramid shape will become more meaningful when we look at filtering in section 17.4. When an app is in production, you typically don't want to record all the `Debug` level messages generated by your application. The sheer volume of messages would be overwhelming to sort through and could end up filling your disk with messages that say "Everything's OK!" Additionally, `Trace` messages shouldn't be enabled in production, as they may leak sensitive data. By filtering out the lower log levels, you can ensure that you generate a sane number of logs in production, while still having access to all of the log levels in development.

In general, logs of a higher level are more important than lower-level logs, so a `Warning` log is more important than an `Information` log, but there's another aspect to

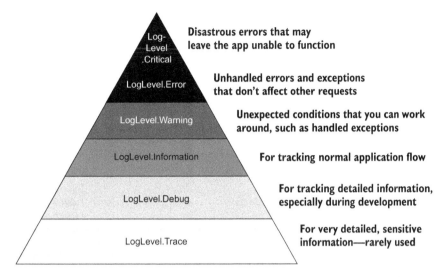

Figure 17.5 The pyramid of log levels. Logs with a level near the base of the pyramid are used more frequently but are less important. Logs with a level near the top should be rare but are important.

consider. Where the log came from, or who created the log, is a key piece of information that's recorded with each log message and is called the *category*.

17.2.2 Log category: which component created the log

As well as a log level, every log message also has a *category*. You set the log level independently for every log message, but the category is set when you create the ILogger instance. Like log levels, the category is particularly useful for filtering, as you'll see in section 17.4, but it's also written to every log message, as shown in figure 17.6

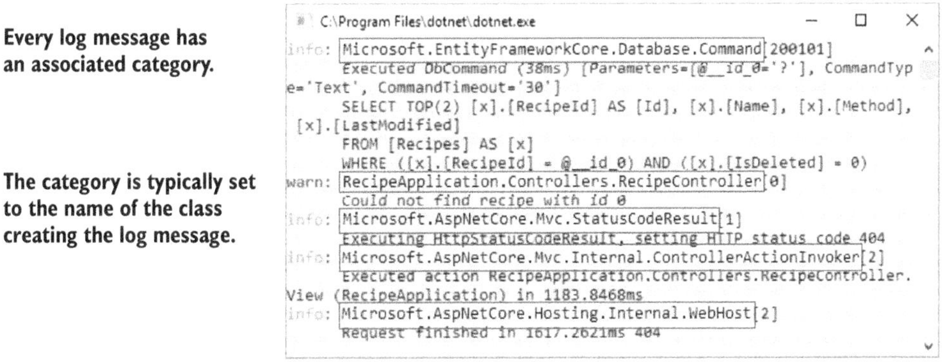

Every log message has an associated category.

The category is typically set to the name of the class creating the log message.

```
C:\Program Files\dotnet\dotnet.exe                        —    □    ×
info: Microsoft.EntityFrameworkCore.Database.Command[200101]
      Executed DbCommand (38ms) [Parameters=[@__id_0='?'], CommandTyp
e='Text', CommandTimeout='30']
      SELECT TOP(2) [x].[RecipeId] AS [Id], [x].[Name], [x].[Method],
[x].[LastModified]
      FROM [Recipes] AS [x]
      WHERE ([x].[RecipeId] = @__id_0) AND ([x].[IsDeleted] = 0)
warn: RecipeApplication.Controllers.RecipeController[0]
      Could not find recipe with id 0
info: Microsoft.AspNetCore.Mvc.StatusCodeResult[1]
      Executing HttpStatusCodeResult, setting HTTP status code 404
info: Microsoft.AspNetCore.Mvc.Internal.ControllerActionInvoker[2]
      Executed action RecipeApplication.Controllers.RecipeController.
View (RecipeApplication) in 1183.8468ms
info: Microsoft.AspNetCore.Hosting.Internal.WebHost[2]
      Request finished in 1617.2621ms 404
```

Figure 17.6 Every log message has an associated category, which is typically the class name of the component creating the log. The default console logging provider outputs the log category for every log.

The category is a `string`, so you can set it to anything, but the convention is to set it to the fully qualified name of the type that's using `ILogger`. In section 17.2, I achieved this by injecting `ILogger<T>` into `RecipeController`; the generic parameter `T` is used to set it to the category of the `ILogger`.

Alternatively, you can inject `ILoggerFactory` into your methods and pass an explicit category when creating an `ILogger` instance. This lets you change the category to an arbitrary string.

Listing 17.4 Injecting `ILoggerFactory` to use a custom category

```
public class RecipeService
{
    private readonly ILogger _log;
    public RecipeService(ILoggerFactory factory)      ◁──────  Injects an
    {                                                           ILoggerFactory instead
        _log = factory.CreateLogger("RecipeApp.RecipeService");   ◁──  of an ILogger directly
    }
}                                                     Passes a category as a string
                                                      when calling CreateLogger
```

There is also an overload of `CreateLogger()` with a generic parameter that uses the provided class to set the category. If the `RecipeService` in listing 17.4 was in the Recipe-App namespace, then the `CreateLogger` call could be written equivalently as

```
_log = factory.CreateLogger<RecipeService>();.
```

Similarly, the final `ILogger` instance created by this call would be the same as if you'd directly injected `ILogger<RecipeService>` instead of `ILoggerFactory`.

> **TIP** Unless you're using heavily customized categories for some reason, favor injecting `ILogger<T>` into your methods over `ILoggerFactory`.

The final compulsory part of every log entry is fairly obvious: the *log message*. At the simplest level, this can be any string, but it's worth thinking carefully about what information it would be useful to record—anything that will help you self-diagnose issues later on!

17.2.3 *Formatting messages and capturing parameter values*

Whenever you create a log entry, you must provide a *message*. This can be any string you like, but as you saw in listing 17.2, you can also include placeholders indicated by braces, `{}`, in the message string:

```
_log.LogInformation("Loaded {RecipeCount} recipes", models.Count);
```

Including a placeholder and a parameter value in your log message effectively creates a key-value pair, which some logging providers can store as additional information associated with the log. The previous log message would assign the value of `models` `.Count` to a key, `RecipeCount`, and the log message itself is generated by replacing the placeholder with the parameter value, to give (if `models.Count=3`):

```
"Loaded 3 recipes"
```

You can include multiple placeholders in a log message, and they'll be associated with the additional parameters passed to the log method. The order of the placeholders in the format string must match the order of the parameters you provide.

> **WARNING** You must pass at least as many parameters to the log method as there are placeholders in the message. If you don't pass enough parameters, you'll get an exception at runtime.

For example, the log message

```
_log.LogInformation("User {UserId} loaded recipe {RecipeId}", 123, 456)
```

would create the parameters UserId=123 and RecipeId=456. *Structured logging* providers could store these values, in addition to the formatted log message "User 123 loaded recipe 456". This makes it easier to search the logs for a particular UserId or RecipeId.

> **DEFINITION** *Structured or semantic logging* attaches additional structure to log messages to make them more easily searchable and filterable. Rather than storing only text, it stores additional contextual information, typically as key-value pairs.

Not all logging providers use semantic logging. The default console logging provider doesn't, for example—the message is formatted to replace the placeholders, but there's no way of searching the console by key-value.

But even if you're not using structured logging initially, I recommend writing your log messages as though you are, with explicit placeholders and parameters. That way, if you decide to add a structured logging provider later, then you'll immediately see the benefits. Additionally, I find that thinking about the parameters that you can log in this way prompts you to record more parameter values, instead of only a log message. There's nothing more frustrating than seeing a message like "Cannot insert record due to duplicate key" but not having the key value logged!

> **TIP** Generally speaking, I'm a fan of C# 6's interpolated strings, but don't use them for your log messages when a placeholder and parameter would also make sense. Using placeholders instead of interpolated strings will give you the same output message, but will also create key-value pairs that can be searched later.

We've looked a lot at how you can create log messages in your app, but we haven't focused on where those logs are written. In the next section, we'll look at the built-in ASP.NET Core logging providers, how they're configured, and how you can replace the defaults with a third-party provider.

17.3   Controlling where logs are written using logging providers

Up to this point, we've been writing all our log messages to the console. If you've run any ASP.NET Core sample apps locally, you'll have probably already seen the log messages written to the console window.

> **NOTE**   If you're using Visual Studio and debugging using the IIS Express option (the default), then you won't see the console window (though the log messages are written to the Debug Output window instead). For that reason, I normally ensure I select the app name from the dropdown in the debug toolbar, instead of IIS Express.

Writing log messages to the console is great when you're debugging, but it's not much use for production. No one's going to be monitoring a console window on a server, and the logs wouldn't be saved anywhere or searchable. Clearly, you'll need to write your production logs somewhere else when in production.

As you saw in section 17.1, *logging providers* control the destination of your log messages in ASP.NET Core. They take the messages you create using the `ILogger` interface and write them to an output location, which varies depending on the provider.

> **NOTE**   This name always gets to me—the log *provider* effectively *consumes* the log messages you create and outputs them to a destination. You can probably see the origin of the name from figure 17.3, but I still find it somewhat counterintuitive!

Microsoft have written a number of first-party log providers for ASP.NET Core, which are available out-of-the-box in ASP.NET Core 2.0. These include

- *Console provider*—Writes messages to the console, as you've already seen.
- *Debug provider*—Writes messages to the debug window when you're debugging an app in Visual Studio or Visual Studio Code, for example.
- *EventLog provider*—Writes messages to the Windows Event Log. Only available when targeting .NET Framework, not .NET Core, as it requires Windows-specific APIs.
- *EventSource provider*—Writes messages using Event Tracing for Windows (ETW). Available in .NET Core, but only creates logs when running on Windows.
- *Azure App Service provider*—Writes messages to text files or blob storage if you're running your app in Microsoft's Azure cloud service. The provider is automatically added when you run an ASP.NET Core 2.0 app in Azure.[1]

There are also many third-party logging provider implementations, such as NLog, Loggr, and Serilog. It's always worth looking to see whether your favorite .NET logging library or service has a provider for ASP.NET Core, as many do.

---

[1]   The Azure App Service provider uses a feature in ASP.NET Core 2.0 called `IHostingStartup` to automatically configure itself. You can read more about the provider at http://mng.bz/gaZP.

You configure the logging providers for your app in Program.cs using `WebHost-Builder`. In ASP.NET Core 2.0, the `CreateDefaultBuilder` method configures the console and debug providers for your application, but it's likely you'll want to change or add to these.

You have two options when you need to customize logging for your app:

- Use `WebHostBuilder` instead of `CreateDefaultBuilder` and configure it explicitly.
- Add an additional `ConfigureLogging` call after `CreateDefaultBuilder`.

If you only need to customize logging, then the latter approach is simpler. But if you find you also want to customize the other aspects of the `WebHostBuilder` created by `CreateDefaultBuilder` (such as your app configuration settings), then it may be worth ditching the `CreateDefaultBuilder` method and creating your own instance instead.

In section 17.3.1, I'll show how to add a simple third-party logging provider to your application that writes log messages to a file, so that your logs are persisted. In section 17.3.2, I'll show how to go one step further and replace the default `ILoggerFactory` in ASP.NET Core with an alternative implementation using the popular open source Serilog library.

17.3.1 *Adding a new logging provider to your application*

In this section, we're going to add a logging provider that writes to a rolling file, so our application writes logs to a new file each day. We'll continue to log using the console and debug providers as well, because they will be more useful than the file provider when developing locally.

To add a third-party logging provider in ASP.NET Core, you must

1 Add the logging provider NuGet package to the solution. I'm going to be using a provider called NetEscapades.Extensions.Logging.RollingFile, which is available on NuGet and GitHub. You can add it to your solution using the NuGet Package Manager in Visual Studio, or using the .NET CLI by running

```
dotnet add package NetEscapades.Extensions.Logging.RollingFile
```

from your application's project folder.

NOTE This package is a simple file logging provider, available at https://github.com/andrewlock/NetEscapades.Extensions.Logging, which is based on the Azure App Service logging provider. If you would like more control over your logs, such as the file format, consider using Serilog instead, as described in section 17.3.2.

2 Add the logging provider using the `WebHostBuilder.ConfigureLogging()` extension method. You can add the file provider by calling `AddFile()`, as shown in the next listing. This is an extension method, provided by the logging provider package, to simplify adding the provider to your app.

Listing 17.5   Adding a third-party logging provider to `WebHostBuilder`

```
public class Program
{
    public static void Main(string[] args)
    {
        BuildWebHost(args).Run();
    }

    public static IWebHost BuildWebHost(string[] args) =>
        WebHost.CreateDefaultBuilder(args)
            .ConfigureLogging(builder => builder.AddFile())
            .UseStartup<Startup>()
            .Build();
}
```

> The CreateDefaultBuilder method configures the console and debug providers as normal.

> Adds the new file logging provider to the logger factory

NOTE   Adding a new provider doesn't replace existing providers. Listing 17.5 uses the `CreateDefaultBuilder` helper method, so the console and debug logging providers have already been added. To remove them, call `builder.ClearProviders()` at the start of the `ConfigureLogging` method, or use a custom `WebHostBuilder`.

With the file logging provider configured, you can run the application and generate logs. Every time your application writes a log using an `ILogger` instance, `ILogger` writes the message to all configured providers, as shown in figure 17.7. The console messages are conveniently available, but you also have a persistent record of the logs stored in a file.

> **TIP**   By default, the rolling file provider will write logs to a subdirectory of your application. You can specify additional options such as filenames and file size limits using overloads of `AddFile()`. For production, I recommend using a more established logging provider, such as Serilog.

The key takeaway from this listing is that the provider system makes it easy to integrate existing logging frameworks and providers with the ASP.NET Core logging abstractions. Whichever logging provider you choose to use in your application, the principles are the same: call `ConfigureLogging` on `WebHostBuilder` and add a new logging provider using extension methods like `AddConsole()`, or `AddFile()` in this case.

Logging your application messages to a file can be useful in some scenarios, and it's certainly better than logging to a non-existent console window in production, but it may still not be the best option.

If you discovered a bug in production and you needed to quickly look at the logs to see what happened, for example, you'd need to log on to the remote server, find the log files on disk, and trawl through them to find the problem. If you have multiple web servers, then suddenly you'd have a mammoth job to fetch all the logs before you could even start to tackle the bug. Not fun. Add to that the possibility of file permission or drive space issues and file logging seems less attractive.

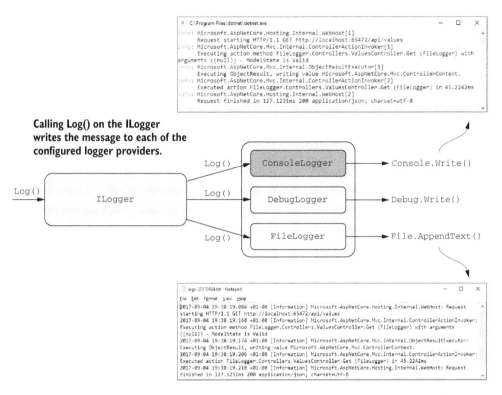

Figure 17.7   Logging a message with `ILogger` writes the log using all of the configured providers.

Instead, it's often better to send your logs to a centralized location, separate from your application itself. Exactly where this location may be is up to you; the key is that each instance of your app sends its logs to the same location, separate from the app itself.

If you're running your app on Azure, then you get centralized logging for free because you can collect logs using the Azure App Service provider. Alternatively, you could send your logs to a third-party log aggregator service such as Loggr (http://loggr.net/), elmah.io (https://elmah.io/), or Seq (https://getseq.net/). You can find ASP.NET Core logging providers for each of these services on NuGet, so adding them is the same process as adding the file provider you've seen already.

Another popular option is to use the open source Serilog library to simultaneously write to a variety of different locations. In the next section, I'll show how you can replace the default `ILoggerFactory` implementation with Serilog in your application, opening up a wide range of possible options for where your logs are written.

17.3.2   *Replacing the default ILoggerFactory with Serilog*

In this section, we'll replace the default `ILoggerFactory` in the Recipe app with an implementation that uses Serilog. Serilog (https://serilog.net) is an open source project that can write logs to many different locations, such as files, the console, an Elasticsearch cluster,[2] or a database.

Serilog predates ASP.NET Core, but thanks to the logging abstractions around `ILoggerFactory` and `ILoggerProvider`, you can easily integrate with Serilog while still using the `ILogger` abstractions in your application code.

Serilog uses a similar design philosophy to the ASP.NET Core logging abstractions—you write logs to a central logging object and the log messages are written to multiple locations, such as the console or a file. Serilog calls each of these locations a *sink*.[3]

When you use Serilog with ASP.NET Core, you'll typically replace the default `ILoggerFactory` with a custom factory that contains a single logging provider, `SerilogLoggerProvider`. This provider can write to multiple locations, as shown in figure 17.8. This configuration is a bit of a departure from the standard ASP.NET Core logging setup, but it prevents Serilog's features from conflicting with equivalent features of the default `LoggerFactory`, such as filtering (see section 17.4).

> **TIP**   If you're familiar with Serilog, you can use the examples in this section to easily integrate a working Serilog configuration with the ASP.NET Core logging infrastructure.

In this section, we'll add a single sink to write the log messages to the console, but using the Serilog logging provider instead of the built-in console provider. Once you've set this up, adding additional sinks to write to other locations is trivial. Adding the Serilog logging provider to an application involves three steps:

1   Add the required Serilog NuGet packages to the solution.
2   Create a Serilog logger and configure it with the required sinks.
3   Call `UseSerilog()` on `WebHostBuilder` to replace the default `ILoggerFactory` implementation with `SerilogLoggerFactory`. This configures the Serilog provider automatically and hooks up the already-configured Serilog logger.

To install Serilog into your ASP.NET Core app, you need to add the base NuGet package and the NuGet packages for any sinks you need. You can do this through the Visual Studio NuGet GUI, using the PMC, or using the .NET CLI. To add the Serilog ASP.NET Core package and a sink for writing to the console, run

```
dotnet add package Serilog.AspNetCore
dotnet add package Serilog.Sinks.Console
```

This adds the necessary NuGet packages to your project file and restores them. Next, create a Serilog logger and configure it to write to the console by adding the console sink, as shown in listing 17.6. This is the most basic of Serilog configurations, but you

---

[2]   Elasticsearch is a REST-based search engine that's often used for aggregating logs. You can find out more at www.elastic.co/products/elasticsearch.

[3]   For a full list of available sinks, see https://github.com/serilog/serilog/wiki/Provided-Sinks. There are 67 different sinks at the time of writing!

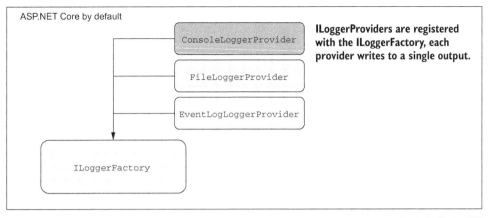

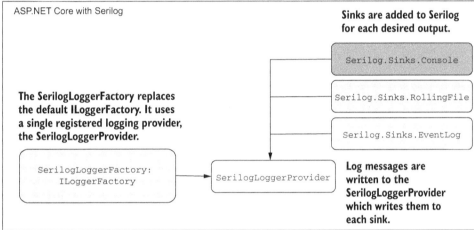

Figure 17.8 Configuration differences when using Serilog with ASP.NET Core 2.0 compared to the default logging configuration.

can add extra sinks and configuration here too.[4] I've also added a try-catch-finally block around our call to BuildWebHost, to ensure that logs are still written if there's an error starting up the web host or there's a fatal exception. Finally, the Serilog logger factory is configured by calling UseSerilog() on the WebHostBuilder.

Listing 17.6 Configuring a Serilog logging provider to use a console sink

```
public class Program
{
    public static void Main(string[] args)
    {
        Log.Logger = new LoggerConfiguration()
```

Creates a LoggerConfiguration
for configuring the Serilog logger

---

[4] You can customize Serilog until the cows come home, so it's worth consulting the documentation to see what's possible. The wiki is particularly useful: https://github.com/serilog/serilog/wiki/Configuration-Basics.

```
        .WriteTo.Console()              ◄──────  Serilog will write logs to the console.
        .CreateLogger();        ◄─┐
                                   │  This creates a Serilog logger
    try                           │  instance on the static
    {                             │  Log.Logger property.
        BuildWebHost(args).Run();
    }
    catch (Exception ex)
    {
        Log.Fatal(ex, "Host terminated unexpectedly");
    }
    finally
    {
        Log.CloseAndFlush();
    }
}

public static IWebHost BuildWebHost(string[] args) =>
    WebHost.CreateDefaultBuilder(args)
        .UseSerilog()           ◄─┐
        .UseStartup<Startup>()    │  Registers the SerilogLoggerFactory
        .Build();                 │  and connects the Log.Logger as
}                                 │  the sole logging provider
```

With the Serilog logging provider configured, you can run the application and generate some logs. Every time the app generates a log, `ILogger` writes the message to the Serilog provider, which writes it to every sink. In the example, you've only configured the console sink, so the output will look something like figure 17.9. The Serilog console sink colorizes the logs more than the built-in console provider, so I find it's somewhat easier to parse the logs visually.

**Serilog colorizes the various
parameters passed to the logger.**

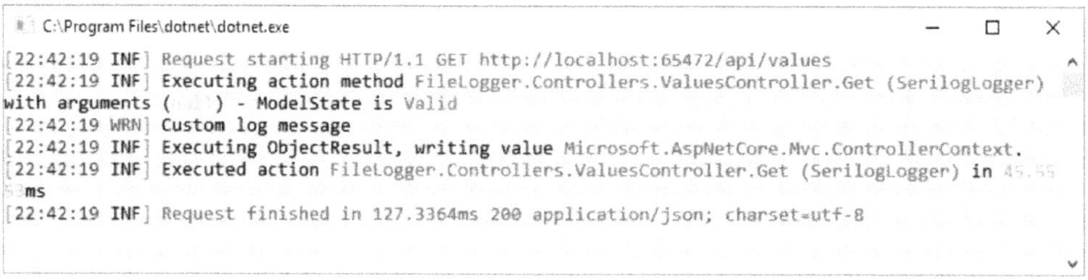

```
C:\Program Files\dotnet\dotnet.exe                                    —   □   ×
[22:42:19 INF] Request starting HTTP/1.1 GET http://localhost:65472/api/values
[22:42:19 INF] Executing action method FileLogger.Controllers.ValuesController.Get (SerilogLogger)
with arguments (    ) - ModelState is Valid
[22:42:19 WRN] Custom log message
[22:42:19 INF] Executing ObjectResult, writing value Microsoft.AspNetCore.Mvc.ControllerContext.
[22:42:19 INF] Executed action FileLogger.Controllers.ValuesController.Get (SerilogLogger) in 45.55
 ms
[22:42:19 INF] Request finished in 127.3364ms 200 application/json; charset=utf-8
```

**In contrast to the default console provider,
it doesn't display the log category.**

Figure 17.9   Example output using the Serilog provider and a console sink. The output has more colorization than the built-in console provider, though by default it doesn't display the log category for each log.[5]

---

[5] If you wish to display the log category in the console sink, you can customize the `outputTemplate` and add `{SourceContext}`. For details, see https://github.com/serilog/serilog-sinks-console#output-templates.

> **TIP** Serilog has many great features in addition to this. One of my favorites is the ability to add *enrichers*. These automatically add additional information to all your log messages, such as the process ID or environment variables, which can be useful when diagnosing problems.

Serilog lets you easily plug in additional sinks to your application, in much the same way as you do with the default ASP.NET Core abstractions. Whether you choose to use Serilog or stick to other providers is up to you; the feature sets are quite similar, though Serilog is more mature. Whichever you choose, once you start running your apps in production, you'll quickly discover a different issue: the sheer number of log messages your app generates!

17.4 Changing log verbosity with filtering

If you've been playing around with the logging samples, then you'll probably have noticed that you get a lot of log messages, even for a single request like the one in figure 17.2: messages from the Kestrel server, messages from EF Core, not to mention your own custom messages. When you're debugging locally, having access to all that detailed information is extremely useful, but in production you'll be so swamped by noise that it'll make picking out the important messages difficult.

ASP.NET Core includes the ability to filter out log messages *before* they're written based on a combination of three things:

- The log level of the message
- The category of the logger (who created the log)
- The logger provider (where the log will be written)

You can create multiple rules using these properties, and for each log that's created, the most specific rule will be applied to determine whether the log should be written to the output. You could create the following three rules:

- *The default minimum log level is* `Information`. If no other rules apply, only logs with a log level of `Information` or above will be written to providers.
- *For categories that start with* `Microsoft`, *the minimum log level is* `Warning`. Any logger created in a namespace that starts with `Microsoft` will only write logs that have a log level of `Warning` or above. This would filter out the "noisy" framework messages you saw in figure 17.6.
- *For the console provider, the minimum log level is* `Error`. Logs written to the console provider must have a minimum log level of `Error`. Logs with a lower level won't be written to the console, though they might be written using other providers.

Typically, the goal with log filtering is to reduce the number of logs written to certain providers, or from certain namespaces (based on the log category). Figure 17.10 shows a possible set of filtering rules that apply filtering rules to the console and file logging providers.

In this example, the console logger explicitly restricts logs written in the `Microsoft` namespace to `Warning` or above, so the console logger ignores the log message shown. Conversely, the file logger doesn't have a rule that explicitly restricts the `Microsoft` namespace, so it uses the configured minimum level of `Information` and writes the log to the output.

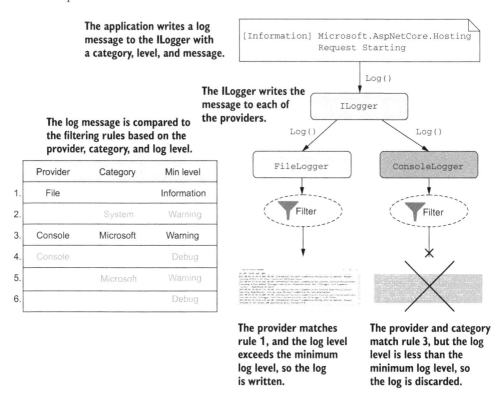

Figure 17.10   Applying filtering rules to a log message to determine whether a log should be written. For each provider, the most specific rule is selected. If the log exceeds the rule's required minimum level, the provider writes the log, otherwise it discards it.

TIP   Only a single rule is chosen when deciding whether a log message should be written; they aren't combined. In figure 17.10, rule 1 is considered more specific than rule 5, so the log is written to the file provider, even though both could technically apply.

You typically define your app's set of logging rules using the layered configuration approach discussed in chapter 11, because this lets you easily have different rules when running in development and production. You do this by calling `AddConfiguration` when configuring logging in Program.cs, but `CreateDefaultBuilder()` also does this for you automatically.

This listing shows how you'd add configuration rules to your application when configuring your own `WebHostBuilder`, instead of using the `CreateDefaultBuilder` helper method.

Listing 17.7 Loading logging configuration in `ConfigureLogging`

```
public class Program
{
    public static void Main(string[] args)
    {
        BuildWebHost(args).Run();
    }

    public static IWebHost BuildWebHost(string[] args) =>
        new WebHostBuilder()
            .UseKestrel()
            .UseContentRoot(Directory.GetCurrentDirectory())
            .ConfigureAppConfiguration(config =>
                config.AddJsonFile("appsettings.json"))
            .ConfigureLogging((ctx, builder) =>
            {
                builder.AddConfiguration(
                    ctx.Configuration.GetSection("Logging"));
                builder.AddConsole();
            })
            .UseStartup<Startup>()
            .Build();
}
```

Loads the log filtering configuration from the Logging section and adds to ILoggingBuilder

Loads configuration values from appsettings.json

Adds a console provider to the app

In this example, I've loaded the configuration from a single file, appsettings.json, which contains all of our app configuration. The logging configuration is specifically contained in the `"Logging"` section of the `IConfiguration` object, which is available when you call `Configurelogging()`.

> **TIP** As you saw in chapter 11, you can load configuration settings from multiple sources, like JSON files and environment variables, and can load them conditionally based on the `IHostingEnvironment`. A common practice is to include logging settings for your production environment in appsettings.json, and overrides for your local development environment in appsettings .Development.json.

The logging section of your configuration should look similar to the following listing, which shows how you could define the rules shown in figure 17.10.

Listing 17.8 The log filtering configuration section of appsettings.json

```
{
  "Logging": {
    "LogLevel": {
      "Default": "Debug",
      "System": "Warning",
      "Microsoft": "Warning"
    },
```

Rules to apply if there are no applicable rules for a provider

```
      "File": {
        "LogLevel": {
          "Default": "Information"
        }
      },
      "Console": {
        "LogLevel": {
          "Default": "Debug",
          "Microsoft": "Warning"
        }
      }
    }
  }
}
```

Rules to apply to the File provider

Rules to apply to the Console provider

When creating your logging rules, the important thing to bear in mind is that if you have *any* provider-specific rules, these will take precedence over the category-based rules defined in the `"LogLevel"` section. Therefore, for the configuration defined in listing 17.8, if your app *only* uses the file or console logging providers, then the `"System"` and `"Microsoft"` category-specific rules will effectively never apply.

If you find this confusing, don't worry, so do I. Whenever I'm setting up logging, I check the algorithm used to determine which rule will apply for a given provider and category, which is as follows:

- Select all rules for the given provider. If no rules apply, select all rules that don't define a provider (the top `"LogLevel"` section from listing 17.8).
- From the selected rules, select rules with the longest matching category prefix. If no selected rules match the category prefix, select any that don't specify a category.
- If multiple rules are selected, use the last one.
- If no rules are selected, use the global minimum level, `"LogLevel:Default"` (Debug in listing 17.8).

Each of these steps (except the last) narrows down the applicable rules for a log message, until you're left with a single rule. You saw this in effect for a `"Microsoft"` category log in figure 17.10. Figure 17.11 shows the process in more detail.

> **WARNING** Log filtering rules aren't merged together; a single rule is selected. Including provider-specific rules will override global category-specific rules, so I tend to stick to category-specific rules in my apps in order to make the overall set of rules easier to understand.

With some effective filtering in place, your production logs should be much more manageable, as shown in figure 17.12. Generally, I find it's best to limit the logs from the ASP.NET Core infrastructure and referenced libraries to Warning or above, while keeping logs that my app writes to Debug in development and Information in production.

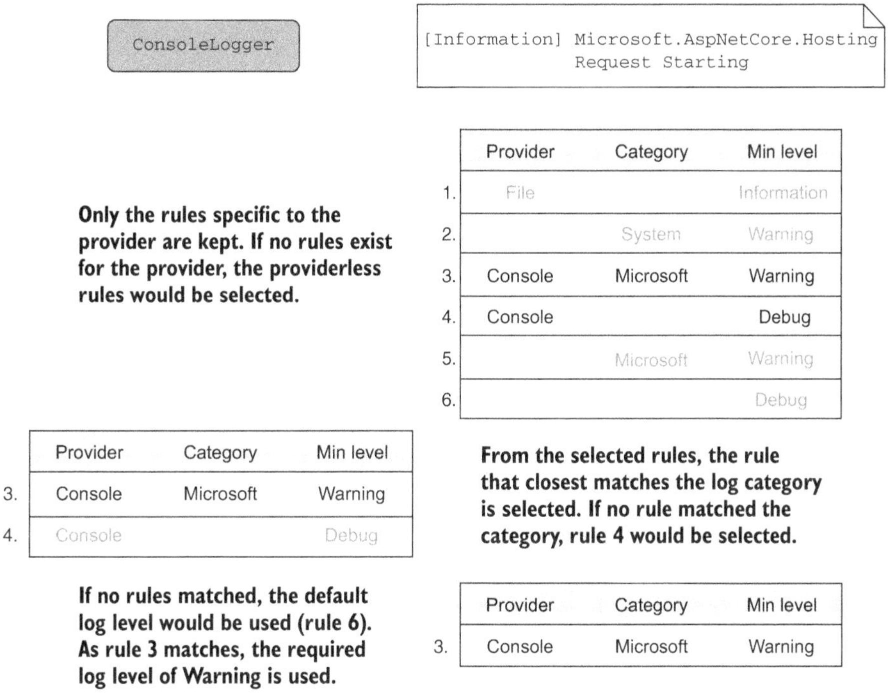

	Provider	Category	Min level
1.	File		Information
2.		System	Warning
3.	Console	Microsoft	Warning
4.	Console		Debug
5.		Microsoft	Warning
6.			Debug

Only the rules specific to the provider are kept. If no rules exist for the provider, the providerless rules would be selected.

	Provider	Category	Min level
3.	Console	Microsoft	Warning
4.	Console		Debug

From the selected rules, the rule that closest matches the log category is selected. If no rule matched the category, rule 4 would be selected.

If no rules matched, the default log level would be used (rule 6). As rule 3 matches, the required log level of Warning is used.

	Provider	Category	Min level
3.	Console	Microsoft	Warning

Figure 17.11 Selecting a rule to apply from the available set for the console provider and an `Information` level log.

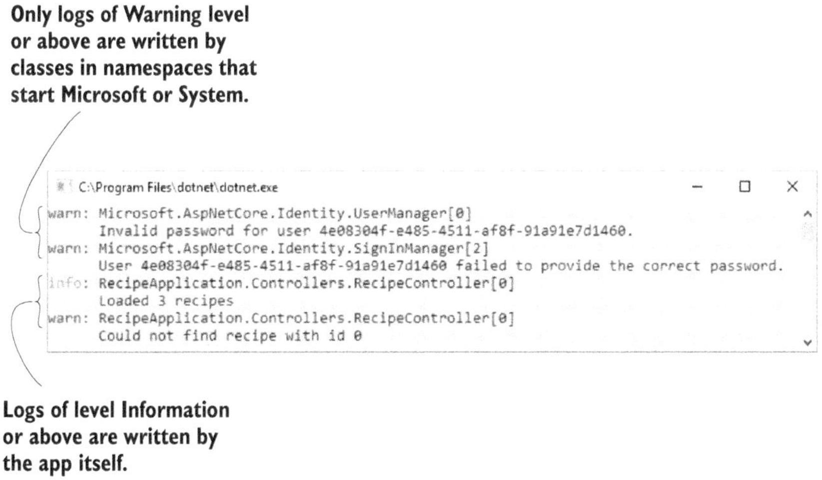

Only logs of Warning level or above are written by classes in namespaces that start Microsoft or System.

Logs of level Information or above are written by the app itself.

Figure 17.12 Using filtering to reduce the number of logs written. In this example, category filters have been added to the Microsoft and System namespaces, so only logs of Warning and above are recorded.

This is close to the default configuration used in the ASP.NET Core templates. You may find you need to add additional category-specific filters, depending on which NuGet libraries you use and the categories they write to. The best way to find out is generally to run your app and see if you get flooded with uninteresting log messages!

Even with your log verbosity under your control, if you stick to the default logging providers like the file or console loggers, then you'll probably regret it in the long run. These log providers work perfectly well, but when it comes to finding specific error messages, or analyzing your logs, you'll have your work cut out for you. In the next section, you'll see how structured logging can help tackle this problem.

17.5   *Structured logging: creating searchable, useful logs*

Let's imagine you've rolled out the recipe application we've been working on into production. You've added logging to the app so that you can keep track of any errors in your application, and you're storing the logs in a file.

One day, a customer calls and says they can't view their recipe. Sure enough, when you look through the log messages you a see a warning:

```
warn: RecipeApplication.Controllers.RecipeController[12]
        Could not find recipe with id 3245
```

This piques your interest—why did this happen? Has it happened before for this *customer*? Has it happened before for this *recipe*? Has it happened for *other* recipes? Does it happen regularly?

How would you go about answering these questions? Given that the logs are stored in a text file, you might start doing basic text searches in your editor of choice, looking for the phrase `"Could not find recipe with id"`. Depending on your notepad-fu skills, you could probably get a fair way in answering your questions, but it would likely be a laborious, error-prone, and painful process.

The limiting factor is that the logs are stored as *unstructured* text, so text processing is the only option available to you. A better approach is to store the logs in a *structured* format, so that you can easily query the logs, filter them, and create analytics. Structured logs could be stored in any format, but these days they're typically represented as JSON. For example, a structured version of the same recipe warning log might look something like

```
{
  "eventLevel": "Warning",
  "cateogry": "RecipeApplication.Controllers.RecipeController",
  "eventId": "12",
  "messageTemplate": "Could not find recipe with {recipeId}",
  "message": "Could not find recipe with id 3245",
  "recipeId": "3245"
}
```

This structured log message contains all the same details as the unstructured version, but in a format that would easily let you search for specific log entries. It makes it simple to filter logs by their EventLevel, or to only show those logs relating to a specific recipe ID.

> **NOTE** This is only an example of what a structured log could look like. The format used for the logs will vary depending on the logging provider used and could be anything. The key point is that properties of the log are available as key-value pairs.

Adding structured logging to your app requires a logging provider that can create and store structured logs. Elasticsearch is a popular general search and analytics engine that can be used to store and query your logs. Serilog includes a sink for writing logs to Elasticsearch that you can add to your app in the same way as you added the console sink in section 17.3.2.

> **TIP** If you want to learn more about Elasticsearch, *Relevant Search* by Doug Turnbull and John Berryman (Manning, 2016) is a great choice, and will show how you can make the most of your structured logs.

Elasticsearch is a powerful production-scale engine for storing your logs, but setting it up isn't for the faint of heart. Even after you've got it up and running, there's a somewhat steep learning curve associated with the query syntax. If you're interested in something more user-friendly for your structured logging needs, then Seq (https://getseq.net) is a great option. In the next section, I'll show how adding Seq as a structured logging provider makes analyzing your logs that much easier.

17.5.1 Adding a structured logging provider to your app

To demonstrate the advantages of structured logging, in this section, you'll configure an app to write logs to Seq. You'll see that configuration is essentially identical to unstructured providers, but that the possibilities afforded by structured logging make considering it a no-brainer.

Seq is installed on a server or your local machine and collects structured log messages over HTTP, providing a web interface for you to view and analyze your logs. It is currently a Windows-only app, but thanks to .NET Core, work is underway to add Linux support. You can install a free version for development,[6] which will allow you to experiment with structured logging in general.

From the point of view of your app, the process for adding the Seq provider should be familiar:

1. Install the Seq logging provider using Visual Studio or the .NET CLI with

   ```
   dotnet add package Seq.Extensions.Logging
   ```

2. Add the Seq logging provider in Program.cs inside the ConfigureLogging method. To add the Seq provider in addition to the console and debug providers included as part of CreateDefaultBuilder, use

---

[6] You can download the Windows installer for Seq from https://getseq.net/Download.

```
WebHost.CreateDefaultBuilder(args)
    .ConfigureLogging(builder => builder.AddSeq())
    .UseStartup<Startup>()
    .Build();
```

That's all you need to add Seq to your app. This will send logs to the default local URL when you have Seq installed in your local environment. The `AddSeq()` extension method includes additional overloads to customize Seq when you move to production, but this is all you need to start experimenting locally.

If you haven't already, install Seq on your development machine and navigate to the Seq app at http://localhost:5341. In a different tab, open up your app and start browsing around and generating logs. Heading back to Seq, if you refresh the page, you'll see a list of logs, something like in figure 17.13. Clicking on a log expands it and shows you the structured data recorded for the log.

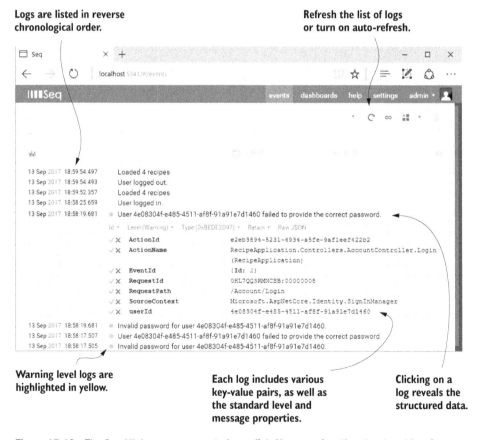

Logs are listed in reverse chronological order.

Refresh the list of logs or turn on auto-refresh.

Warning level logs are highlighted in yellow.

Each log includes various key-value pairs, as well as the standard level and message properties.

Clicking on a log reveals the structured data.

Figure 17.13 The Seq UI. Logs are presented as a list. You can view the structured logging details of individual logs, view analytics for logs in aggregates, and search by log properties.

ASP.NET Core supports structured logging by treating each captured parameter from your message format string as a key-value-pair. If you create a log message using the format string

```
_log.LogInformation("Loaded {RecipeCount} recipes", models.Count);
```

then the logging provider will create a `RecipeCount` parameter with a value of `models.Count`. These parameters are added as properties to each structured log, as you can see in figure 17.13.

Structured logs are generally easier to read than your standard-issue console output, but their real power comes when you need to answer a specific question. Consider the problem from before, where you see the error

```
Could not find recipe with id 3245
```

and you want to get a feel for how widespread the problem is. The first step would be to identify how many times this error has occurred, and to see whether it's happened to any other recipes. Seq lets you filter your logs, but it also lets you craft SQL queries to analyze your data, so finding the answer to the question takes a matter of seconds, as shown in figure 17.14.

> **NOTE** You don't need query languages like SQL for simple queries, but it makes digging into the data easier. Other structured logging providers may provide query languages other than SQL, but the principal is the same as this Seq example.

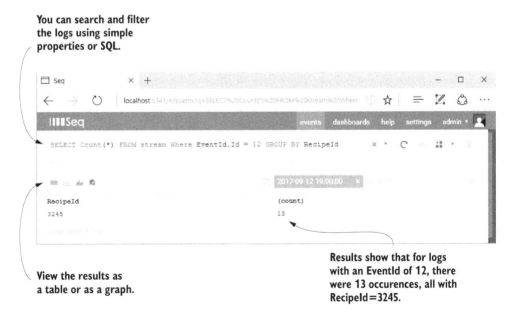

You can search and filter the logs using simple properties or SQL.

View the results as a table or as a graph.

Results show that for logs with an EventId of 12, there were 13 occurences, all with RecipeId=3245.

Figure 17.14 Querying logs in Seq. Structured logging makes log analysis like this example easy.

A quick search shows that you've recorded the log message with `EventId.Id=12` (the `EventId` of the warning we're interested in) 13 times, and every time the offending `RecipeId` was 3245. This suggests that there may be something wrong with that recipe in particular, which points you in the right direction to find the problem.

More often than not, figuring out errors in production involves logging detective work like this to isolate where the problem occurred. Structured logging makes this process significantly easier, so it's well worth considering, whether you choose Seq, Elasticsearch, or a different provider.

I've already described how you can add structured properties to your log messages using variables and parameters from the message, but as you can see in figure 17.13, there are far more properties visible than exist in the message alone.

Scopes provide a way to add arbitrary data to your log messages. They're available in some unstructured logging providers, but they shine when used with structured logging providers. In the final section of this chapter, I'll demonstrate how you can use them to add additional data to your log messages.

17.5.2 *Using scopes to add additional properties to your logs*

You'll often find in your apps that you have a group of operations that all use the same data, which would be useful to attach to logs. For example, you might have a series of database operations that all use the same transaction ID, or you might be performing multiple operations with the same user ID or recipe ID. *Logging scopes* provide a way of associating the same data to every log message in such a group.

> **DEFINITION** *Logging scopes* are used to group a number of operations by adding the same data to each log message.

Logging scopes in ASP.NET Core are created by calling `ILogger.BeginScope<T>` `(T state)` and providing the `state` data to be logged. You create scopes inside a `using` block; any log messages written inside the scope block will have the associated data, whereas those outside won't.

Listing 17.9 Adding scope properties to log messages with `BeginScope`

Log messages written outside the scope block don't include the scope state.

Calling BeginScope starts a scope block, with a scope state of "Scope value".

You can pass anything as the state for a scope.

Log messages written inside the scope block include the scope state.

```
_logger.LogInformation("No, I don't have scope");

using(_logger.BeginScope("Scope value"))
using(_logger.BeginScope(new Dictionary<string, object>
    {{ "CustomValue1", 12345 } }))
{
    _logger.LogInformation("Yes, I have the scope!");
}

_logger.LogInformation("No, I lost it again");
```

The scope state can be any object at all: an `int`, a `string`, or a `Dictionary`, for example. It's up to each logging provider implementation to decide how to handle the state you provide in the `BeginScope` call, but typically it will be serialized using `ToString()`.

> **TIP** The most common use for scopes I've found is to attach additional key-value pairs to logs. To achieve this behavior in Seq and Serilog, you need to pass `Dictionary<string, object>` as the state object.[7]

When the log messages inside the scope block are written, the scope state is captured and written as part of the log, as shown in figure 17.15. The `Dictionary<>` of key-value

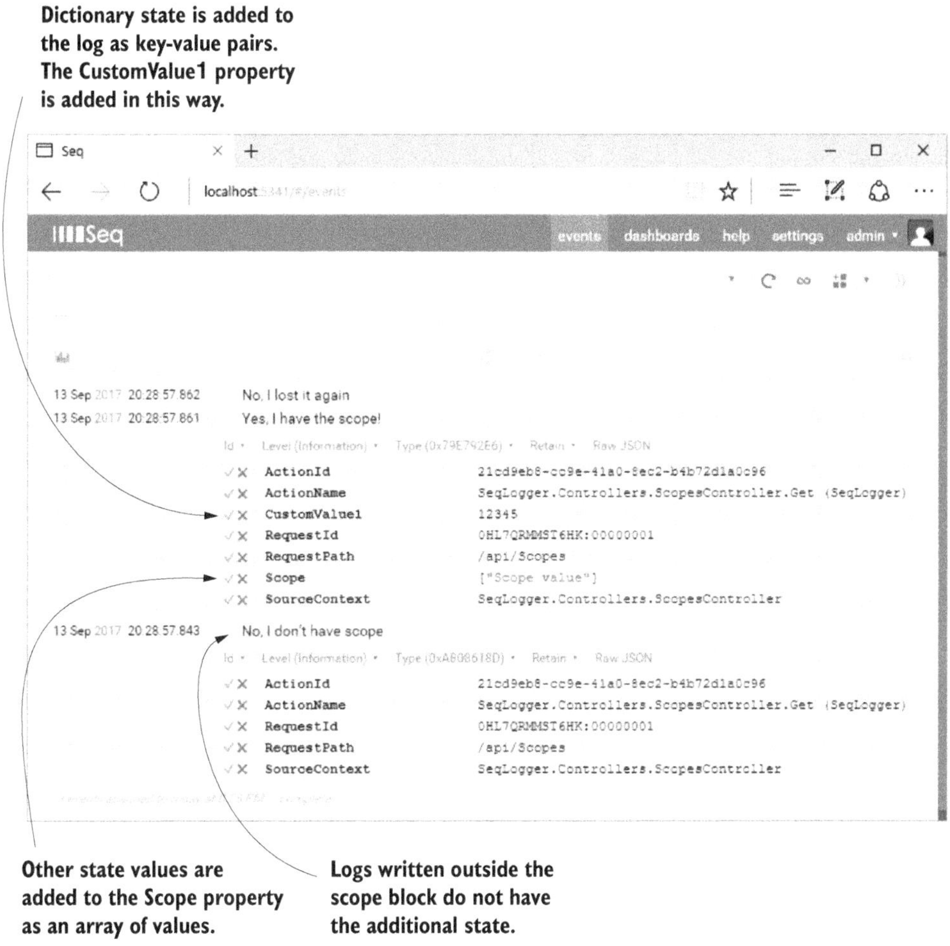

Dictionary state is added to the log as key-value pairs. The CustomValue1 property is added in this way.

Other state values are added to the Scope property as an array of values.

Logs written outside the scope block do not have the additional state.

Figure 17.15 Adding properties to logs using scopes. Scope state added using the dictionary approach is added as structured logging properties, but other state is added to the `Scope` property.

---

[7] Nicholas Blumhardt, the creator of Serilog and Seq, has examples and the reasoning for this on his blog: https://nblumhardt.com/2016/11/ilogger-beginscope/.

pairs is added directly to the log message (`CustomValue1`), and the remaining state values are added to the `Scope` property. You will likely find the dictionary approach the more useful of the two, as the added properties are more easily filtered on, as you saw in figure 17.14.

That brings us to the end of this chapter on logging. Whether you use the built-in logging providers or opt to use a third-party provider like Serilog or NLog, ASP.NET Core makes it easy to get detailed logs not only for your app code, but of the libraries that make up your app's infrastructure, like Kestrel and EF Core. Whichever you choose, I encourage you to add more logs than you *think* you'll need—future-you will thank me when it comes to tracking down a problem!

In the next chapter, we'll look in detail at a variety of web security problems that you should consider when building your apps. ASP.NET Core takes care of some of these issues for you automatically, but it's important to understand where your app's vulnerabilities lie, so you can mitigate them as best you can.

Summary

- Logging is critical to quickly diagnosing errors in production apps. You should always configure logging for your application so that logs are written to a durable location.

- You can add logging to your own services by injecting `ILogger<T>`, where `T` is the name of the service. Alternatively, inject `ILoggerFactory` and call `Create-Logger()`.

- The log level of a message is how important it is and ranges from `Trace` to `Critical`. Typically, you'll create many low-importance log messages, and a few high-importance log messages.

- You specify the log level of a log by using the appropriate extension method of `ILogger` to create your log. To write an `Information` level log, use `ILogger`
  `.LogInformation(message)`.

- The log category indicates which component created the log. It is typically set to the fully qualified name of the class creating the log, but you can set it to any string if you wish. `ILogger<T>` will have a log category of `T`.

- You can format messages with placeholder values, similar to the `string.Format` method, but with meaningful names for the parameters. Calling `logger.LogInfo`
  `("Loading Recipe with id {RecipeId}", 1234 )` would create a log reading
  `"Loading Recipe with id 1234"`, but would also capture the value `RecipeId=`
  `1234`. This *structured logging* makes analyzing log messages much easier.

- ASP.NET Core includes many logging providers out of the box. These include the console, debug, EventLog, EventSource, and Azure App service providers. Alternatively, you can add third-party logging providers.

- You can configure multiple `ILoggerProvider` instances in ASP.NET Core, which define where logs are output. The `CreateDefaultBuilder` method adds the console and debug providers, and you can add additional providers by calling `ConfigureLogging()`.

- Serilog is a mature logging framework that includes support for a large number of output locations. You can add Serilog to your app with the Serilog.AspNet-Core package. This replaces the default `ILoggerFactory` with a Serilog-specific version.

- You can control logging output verbosity using configuration. The `Create-DefaultBuilder` helper uses the `"Logging"` configuration section to control output verbosity.

- Only a single log filtering rule is selected for each logging provider when determining whether to output a log message. The most specific rule is selected based on the logging provider and the category of the log message.

- Structured logging involves recording logs so that they can be easily queried and filtered, instead of the default unstructured format that's output to the console. This makes analyzing logs, searching for issues, and identifying patterns easier.

- You can add additional properties to a structured log by using scope blocks. A scope block is created by calling `ILogger.BeginScope<T>(state)` in a `using` block. The state can be any object and is added to all log messages inside the scope block.

18

Improving your application's security

This chapter covers

- Encrypting traffic using HTTPS and configuring local SSL certificates
- Defending against cross-site scripting attacks
- Protecting from cross-site request forgery attacks
- Allowing calls to your API from other apps using CORS

Web application security is a hot topic at the moment. Practically every week another breach is reported, or confidential details are leaked. It may seem like the situation is hopeless, but the reality is that the vast majority of breaches could've been avoided with the smallest amount of effort.

In this chapter, we look at a few different ways to protect your application and your application's users from attackers. Because security is an extremely broad topic that covers lots of different avenues, this chapter is by no means an exhaustive guide. It's intended to make you aware of some of the most common threats to your app and how to counteract them, and to highlight areas where you can inadvertently introduce vulnerabilities if you're not careful.

> **TIP** I strongly advise exploring additional resources around security after you've read this chapter. The Open Web Application Security Project (OWASP) (www.owasp.org) is an excellent resource, though it can be a little dry. Alternatively, Troy Hunt (www.troyhunt.com/) has some excellent courses and workshops on security, geared towards .NET developers.

We'll start by looking at how to add HTTPS encryption to your website so that users can access your app without the risk of third parties spying on or modifying the content as it travels over the internet. This is effectively a requirement for any app these days, and it is heavily encouraged by the makers of modern browsers such as Chrome, Firefox, and Edge. You'll see how to create a self-signed SSL certificate to add HTTPS to your development machine, how to configure an app for HTTPS in production, and how to enforce HTTPS for your whole app.

In sections 18.2 and 18.3, you'll learn about two potential attacks that should be on your radar: cross-site scripting (XSS) and cross-site request forgery (CSRF). We'll explore how the attacks work and how you can prevent them in your apps. ASP.NET Core has built-in protection against both types of attack, but you have to remember to use the protection correctly and resist the temptation to circumvent it, unless you're certain it's safe to do so.

Section 18.4 deals with a common scenario—you have an application that wants to use JavaScript AJAX (Asynchronous JavaScript and XML) requests to retrieve data from a second app. By default, web browsers block requests to other apps, so you need to enable cross-origin resource sharing (CORS) in your API to achieve this. We'll look at how CORS works, how to create a CORS policy for your app, and how to apply it to specific action methods.

The final section of this chapter, section 18.5, is a collection of common threats to your application. Each one represents a potentially critical flaw that an attacker could use to compromise your application. The solutions to each threat are generally relatively simple; the important thing is to recognize where the flaws could exist in your own apps so that you can ensure you don't leave yourself vulnerable.

We'll start by looking at HTTPS and why you should use it to encrypt the traffic between your users' browsers and your app. Without HTTPS, attackers could subvert many of the safeguards you add to your app, so it's an important first step to take.

18.1 Adding HTTPS to an application

So far in this book, I've shown how the user's browser sends a request across the internet to your app using the HTTP protocol. We haven't looked too much into the details of that protocol, other than to establish that it uses *verbs* to describe the type of request (such as GET and POST), that it contains *headers* with metadata about the request, and optionally a *body* payload of data.

By default, HTTP requests are unencrypted; they're plain text files being sent over the internet. Anyone on the same network as a user (such as using the same public Wi-Fi in a coffee shop) can read the requests and responses sent back and forth. Attackers can even *modify* the requests or responses as they're in transit.

Using unencrypted web apps in this way presents both a privacy and a security risk to your users. Attackers could read the data sent in forms and returned by your app, inject malicious code into your responses to attack users, or steal authentication cookies and impersonate the user on your app.

To protect your users, your app should encrypt the traffic between the user's browser and your app as it travels over the network by using the HTTPS protocol. This is the same as HTTP, but it uses an SSL[1] certificate to encrypt requests and responses, so attackers cannot read or modify the contents. In browsers, you can tell a site is using HTTPS by the https:// prefix to URLs (notice the "s"), or by a padlock, as shown in figure 18.1.

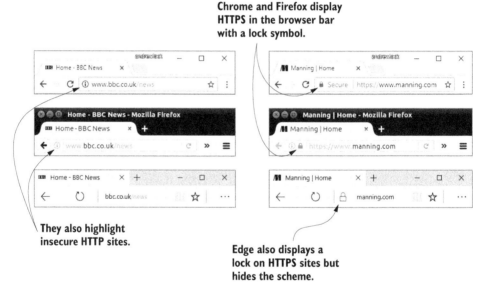

Chrome and Firefox display HTTPS in the browser bar with a lock symbol.

They also highlight insecure HTTP sites.

Edge also displays a lock on HTTPS sites but hides the scheme.

Figure 18.1   Encrypted apps using HTTPS and unencrypted apps using HTTP in Chrome (top), Firefox (middle), and Edge (bottom)

The reality is that, these days, you should always serve your production websites over HTTPS. The industry is pushing toward HTTPS by default, with browsers like Chrome and Firefox moving to mark HTTP sites as explicitly "not secure." Skipping HTTPS will hurt the perception of your app in the long run, so even if you're not interested in the security benefits, it's in your best interest to set up HTTPS.

---

[1]   Technically, the SSL protocol has been superseded by TLS. But SSL is commonly used to refer to the protocol that facilitates HTTPS, so I'll be using SSL throughout. Just think SSL/TLS whenever you see SSL.

In order to configure HTTPS, you need to obtain and configure an SSL certificate for your server. Unfortunately, although that process is a lot easier than it used to be, and is now essentially free thanks to Let's Encrypt (https://letsencrypt.org/), it's still far from simple. If you're setting up a production server, I recommend carefully following the tutorials on the Let's Encrpyt site. It's easy to get it wrong, so take your time!

> **TIP** If you're hosting your app in the cloud, then most providers will provide "one-click" SSL certificates so that you don't have to manage certificates yourself. This is *extremely* useful, and I highly recommended it for everyone.[2]

Luckily, as an ASP.NET Core application developer, you can often get away without directly supporting HTTPS in your app by taking advantage of the reverse proxy architecture, as shown in figure 18.2, in a process called SSL offloading/termination. Instead of your application handling requests using HTTPS directly, it continues to use HTTP. The reverse proxy is responsible for encrypting and decrypting HTTPS traffic to the browser. This often gives you the best of both worlds—data is encrypted between the user's browser and the server, but you don't have to worry about SSL in your application.[3]

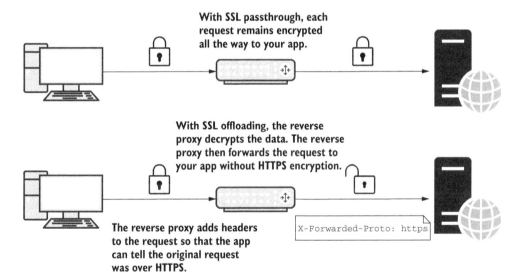

With SSL passthrough, each request remains encrypted all the way to your app.

With SSL offloading, the reverse proxy decrypts the data. The reverse proxy then forwards the request to your app without HTTPS encryption.

The reverse proxy adds headers to the request so that the app can tell the original request was over HTTPS.

`X-Forwarded-Proto: https`

Figure 18.2 You have two options when adding HTTPS to an ASP.NET Core app: SSL passthrough and SSL offloading. In SSL passthrough, the data is encrypted all the way to your ASP.NET Core app. For SSL termination, the reverse proxy handles decrypting the data, so your app doesn't have to.

---

[2] You don't even have to be hosting your application in the cloud to take advantage of this. Cloudflare (www.cloudflare.com/) provides a CDN service that you can add SSL to. You can even use it for free.

[3] If you're concerned that the traffic is unencrypted between the reverse proxy and your app, then I recommend reading this post by Troy Hunt: http://mng.bz/eHCi. It discusses the pros and cons of the issue as it relates to using Cloudflare to provide HTTPS encryption.

Depending on the specific infrastructure where you're hosting your app, SSL could be offloaded to a dedicated device on your network, a third-party service like Cloudflare, or a reverse proxy (such as IIS, NGINX, or HAProxy), running on the same or a different server.

Nevertheless, in some situations, you may need to handle SSL directly in your app so that requests are encrypted all the way to the Kestrel server. When developing locally, you may find this is necessary when you're testing without a reverse proxy. For example, some identity providers such as Azure Active Directory require that requests come from an app running over HTTPS. If you're not using IIS or IIS Express locally, then in this situation you'll have to configure Kestrel to handle HTTPS directly.

> **TIP** HTTPS support has been greatly improved in ASP.NET Core 2.1 (in preview at the time of writing). The 2.1 .NET CLI will automatically install a self-signed development certificate for you, and the 2.1 default templates configure Kestrel to use HTTPS by default. See http://mng.bz/3t6W for details. If you're using ASP.NET Core 2.0 or below, then you'll still need to follow the steps in this section.

In order to test HTTPS locally, you'll need to set up an SSL certificate on your development machine and configure Kestrel to use it. For the rest of this section, we'll look at ways to achieve that.

18.1.1 Setting up IIS and IIS Express to use encryption

If you're on Windows and are using Visual Studio and IIS Express for development, I have some good news—you can still avoid handling SSL certificates directly. IIS Express acts as a reverse proxy when you're developing locally, so it can handle the SSL setup and the configuration of Kestrel. You get this for free when you add the `UseIntegration()` extension to your `WebHostBuilder` in Program.cs and enable SSL in the Debug screen of your project's Properties page, as shown in figure 18.3.

This sets up IIS Express to handle HTTPS for you, so that IIS Express terminates the SSL and your app runs over HTTPS without having to change your app code at all. You can achieve a similar setup when using full IIS by adding a secure binding to your website.

Open Properties > Debug >
IIS profile for your app.

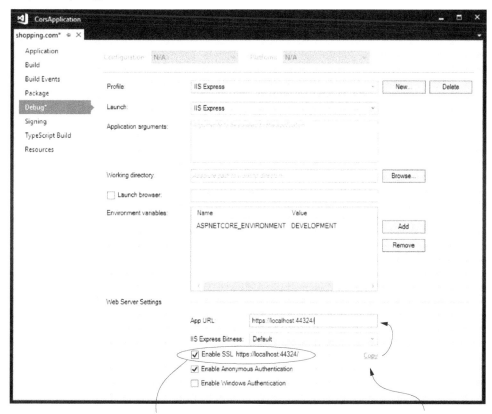

**Check the Enable SSL box
to enable SSL offloading
to IIS Express.**

**Copy the generated HTTPS
URL into the App URL, so the
browser opens the right URL.**

Figure 18.3 You can enable SSL for an IIS Express profile by checking the Enable SSL box in the Debug
screen. IIS Express acts as a reverse proxy, so Kestrel doesn't have to handle the SLL directly.

Select https.

The default port
for https is 443.

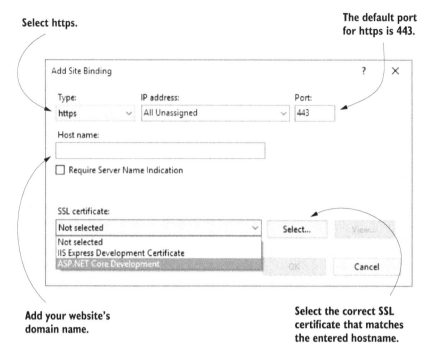

Add your website's
domain name.

Select the correct SSL
certificate that matches
the entered hostname.

**Figure 18.4   The Add Site Binding screen in IIS. When you select an HTTPS binding,
IIS terminates the SSL for your app, serving your app over HTTPS without having to
change any app code.**

To add a new binding to an existing IIS website, right-click your website in the Sites
node of IIS and choose Edit Bindings > Add. This opens the Add Site Binding dialog,
where you can add an HTTPS binding for your application, as shown in figure 18.4.

Where possible, I recommend this model of letting a reverse proxy like IIS or IIS
Express handle the SSL termination, as it moves the concern out of your application
code.

> **TIP** Visual Studio installs a development SSL certificate (the IIS Express
> Development Certificate shown in figure 18.4) you can use when testing
> locally. Visual Studio sets it up for you, so it's the easiest route to enabling
> HTTPS for local development.

If you're not using Visual Studio for development, aren't on Windows, or want to have
Kestrel handle the SSL directly, you'll need to install a development SSL certificate on
your machine. In the next section, we'll look at how to install a self-signed certificate
for development purposes, and how to trust it so your browsers will use it.

18.1.2 *Creating a self-signed certificate for local development*

Creating an SSL certificate for production is often a laborious process, as it requires proving to a third-party certificate authority (CA) that you own the domain you're creating the certificate for. This an important step in the "trust" process and ensures that attackers can't impersonate your servers.

When you're only creating an SSL certificate to use for local testing, that step isn't something you want to (or even can) go through. Instead, you can create a *self-signed certificate*, and use that to add HTTPS to your application.

> ### A brief primer on certificates and signing
>
> HTTPS uses *public key cryptography* as part of the data-encryption process. This uses two keys: a *public* key that *anyone* can see, and a *private* key that only *your* server can see. Anything encrypted with the public key can only be decrypted with the private key. That way, a browser can encrypt something with your server's public key, and only your server can decrypt it. A complete SSL certificate consists of both the public and private parts.
>
> When a browser connects to your app, the server sends the public key part of the SSL certificate. But how does the browser know that it was definitely *your* server that sent the certificate? To achieve this, your SSL certificate contains additional certificates, including a certificate from a trusted CA, called a root certificate.
>
> CAs are special trusted entities. Browsers are hardcoded to trust certain root certificates. So, in order for the SSL certificate for your app to be trusted, it must contain (or be signed by) a trusted root certificate.
>
> When you create a self-signed certificate for local development, you don't have that trusted root certificate. That means browsers won't trust your certificate and won't connect to your server, so you can't use it in production. In development, a self-signed certificate is OK because you can tell your development computer to explicitly trust it.

You can create self-signed certificates in many different ways. In this section, I'll show you how to create one using PowerShell on Windows, and an equivalent using OpenSSL on Linux or macOS.

CREATING A SELF-SIGNED CERTIFICATE USING POWERSHELL ON WINDOWS

You can create a self-signed certificate in multiple ways in Windows, but one of the easiest ways is using PowerShell, because you can easily script it.

> **NOTE** As a reminder, if you're using Visual Studio, then you may not need to create a new certificate, because IIS Express creates a self-signed certificate called IIS Express Development Certificate.

To create a certificate using PowerShell, make sure you use an administrative Power-Shell prompt. Listing 18.1 shows how you to create the certificate and export it to a file using the provided password.

Listing 18.1   Creating a self-signed certificate using PowerShell

```
$cert = New-SelfSignedCertificate -Subject localhost `
    -DnsName localhost -KeyUsage DigitalSignature `
    -FriendlyName "ASP.NET Core Development" `
    -TextExtension @("2.5.29.37={text}1.3.6.1.5.5.7.3.1")
$mypwd = ConvertTo-SecureString -Force -AsPlainText `
    -String "testpassword"
Export-PfxCertificate -Cert $cert -Password $mypwd `
    -FilePath .\test-certificate.pfx
```

Creates a self-signed certificate for the localhost domain

Sets the friendly name of the certificate to make it easier to identify

Creates a password for the certificate (testpassword)

Exports the certificate to a .pfx file in the current directory, using the provided password

> **WARNING**   You must provide a password to use the certificate in ASP.NET Core 2.0. If you use a blank password, then Kestrel will throw an exception when it attempts to read the certificate.

After you run this script, you should have a self-signed certificate in the current directory called test-certificate.pfx. This contains both the public part and the private part of the certificate, so Kestrel can use it to handle HTTPS connections. Because the certificate is self-signed, if you try to use it to add HTTPS to Kestrel, you'll be greeted with a warning that the certificate isn't secure, as shown in figure 18.5.

To fix this, you need to *trust* the certificate. You can do this by running the following PowerShell snippet, which adds the certificate file to the trusted store for the current user, using the password you provided earlier:

```
Import-PfxCertificate -FilePath .\test-certificate.pfx -Password $mypwd -
    CertStoreLocation cert:/CurrentUser/Root
```

You may see a warning when you run this snippet, but if you click OK and trust the certificate, then your browser warnings should go away. Note that you may need to restart your browser for it to detect the change in trust.

> **TIP**   This aspect of convincing browsers to trust your certificate can sometimes be a bit finicky. When in doubt, consult the online help for your browser for trusting a self-signed certificate.

After running these scripts, you should have a trusted self-signed certificate that you can use to add HTTPS to Kestrel. In the next section, I'll show you how to create the certificate if you're using Linux or macOS.

The request is made over HTTPS, but the SSL certificate isn't trusted, so the request is marked not secure.

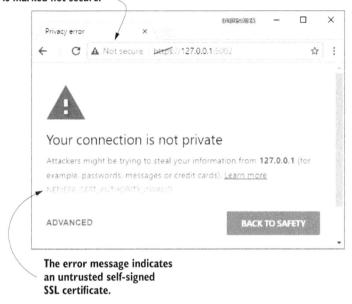

The error message indicates an untrusted self-signed SSL certificate.

Figure 18.5 A certificate error warning in Chrome caused by an untrusted self-signed certificate

CREATING A SELF-SIGNED CERTIFICATE USING OpenSSL ON LINUX OR macOS

On Linux or macOS, you can use the OpenSSL program to create a self-signed certificate and to export it to a file. The following script creates a similar test-certificate.pfx certificate in the current directory:

```
openssl req -new -x509 -newkey rsa:2048 -keyout test-certificate.key -out
    test-certificate.cer -days 365 -subj /CN=localhost
openssl pkcs12 -export -out test-certificate.pfx -inkey test-certificate.key
    -in test-certificate.cer
```

TIP OpenSSL contains many different configuration options. The code samples for chapter 18 include a script that adds more properties to the certificate, which some newer browsers (Chrome) may require.

This creates the certificate, but you still need to trust it to avoid browser warnings. On macOS, you can import the certificate into your keychain, and trust it using

```
security import test-certificate.pfx -k ~/Library/Keychains/login.keychain-db
security add-trusted-cert test-certificate.cer
```

Unfortunately, trusting the certificate in Linux is a little trickier, and depends on the particular flavor you're using. On top of that, software on Linux often uses its own certificate store, so you'll probably need to add the certificate directly to your favorite browser. I suggest looking at the documentation for your favorite browser to figure out the best approach.

18.1.3   Using HTTPS directly in Kestrel

Once you have a certificate, you can configure Kestrel to serve requests over HTTPS by specifying the URL and port to listen on. In chapter 16, you saw how to set the URLs for your application with the `ASPNETCORE_URLS` environment variable and the `UseConfiguration()` extension method, but unfortunately you can only use those to configure HTTP endpoints, not HTTPS. If you want to use Kestrel with HTTPS directly, you need to configure your URLs in a slightly different way.

The `UseKestrel()` extension method is used to add the Kestrel web server to the `WebHostBuilder` in Program.cs. The `CreateDefaultBuilder` extension method calls `UseKestrel()` automatically, but you can call the method a second time and provide additional configuration options.

The `UseKestrel` method takes an optional action to configure `KestrelServerOptions`. You can specify the URL and port to listen on by calling the `Listen` method, which has a `UseHttps()` extension that will enable HTTPS for the endpoint.

> **TIP** You can provide the SSL certificate to the `UseHttps()` method in many different ways. For example, you could load it from a .pfx file, or you could load it from the machine certificate store. Working with SSL X509 certificates is a bit tricky, and there are differences in the availability of the certificate store between Windows and Linux. It's not ideal, but I've had the most success loading from files instead.

The following listing shows a basic example of configuring Kestrel to listen to insecure HTTP requests on http://localhost:5001, and secure HTTPS requests on https://localhost:5002. In this example, I've hardcoded the addresses and certificate information, but you should load these from configuration in practice.[4]

Listing 18.2   Configuring Kestrel to use HTTPS directly

CreateDefaultBuilder calls UseKestrel(), but you can add options by calling it a second time.

```
public static IWebHost BuildWebHost(string[] args) =>
    WebHost.CreateDefaultBuilder()
        .UseKestrel(options =>
        {
            options.Listen(IPAddress.Loopback, 5001);
```

Sets Kestrel to listen to the loopback address (localhost) on port 5001 using HTTP

---

[4]   Kestrel was supposed to have a configuration-based API for defining these values in ASP.NET Core 2.0, but that API was delayed. You can see an example of manually loading the values from configuration in the source code for the book.

```
                          options.Listen(IPAddress.Loopback, 5002, listenOptions =>
                          {
                              listenOptions.UseHttps(
                                  "test-certificate.pfx", "testpassword");
                          });
                      })
                      .UseStartup<Startup>()
                      .Build();
```

Sets Kestrel to also listen to port 5002, and customize the listener for this address

Connections to port 5002 must use HTTPS.

HTTPS should use the provided SSL certificate file and password.

> **WARNING** Listing 18.2 has hardcoded the certificate filename and password for simplicity, but you should either load these from a configuration store like user-secrets, or you should load the certificate from the local store.

If you run the app and access the website over HTTPS, you should see that the connection is secure, as shown in figure 18.6. If you receive any browser warnings, then the certificate hasn't been trusted correctly.

Now the certificate is trusted, so it's marked secure as indicated by a green lock symbol.

Figure 18.6 A trusted SSL certificate will show a green lock. Chrome or Firefox will explicitly mark the connection as secure.

You now have an application that can serve both HTTP and HTTPS traffic, but currently which endpoint you end up using will depend on the URL users use when they first browse to your app. For listing 18.2, if a user navigates to http://localhost:5001, then their traffic will be unencrypted. Seeing as you've gone to all the trouble to set up HTTPS, it's probably best that you force users to use it!

18.1.4 *Enforcing HTTPS for your whole app*

Enforcing SSL across your whole website is practically required these days. Browsers are beginning to explicitly label HTTP pages as insecure, for security reasons you *must* use SSL any time you're transmitting sensitive data across the internet, and thanks to HTTP/2,[5] adding SSL can *improve* your app's performance.

---

[5] HTTP/2 offers many performance improvements over HTTP/1.x, and all modern browsers require HTTPS to enable it. For a great introduction to HTTP/2, see http://mng.bz/K6M2.

Unfortunately, browsers default to loading apps over HTTP unless otherwise specified, so you typically don't want to remove that option entirely. A best practice is to add an HTTP Strict Transport Security (HSTS) header to your responses. In the next chapter, you'll create custom middleware to add this header to your own app.

Another common approach is to redirect any insecure requests to your application to their HTTPS equivalent instead.[6] You can do this in two main ways:

- *In middleware*—When you want to enforce HTTPS across your whole app, not only for specific MVC actions
- *In MVC*—When you only want specific actions to use HTTPS

TIP   I strongly recommend going whole hog and using SSL throughout your site. It might seem like overkill, but in the long run it's easier to reason about and avoids hard-to-debug errors caused by cross-origin requests (see section 18.4).

ASP.NET Core comes with `RewriteMiddleware`, which you can use to enforce HTTPS across your whole app. You add it to the middleware pipeline in the `Configure` section of `Startup`, and it ensures that any requests that pass through it are secure. If an HTTP request reaches `RewriteMiddleware`, the middleware immediately short-circuits the pipeline with a redirect to the HTTPS version of the request. The following listing shows how you could configure the app from listing 18.2 to automatically redirect all requests to the secure endpoint using an HTTP 302 Temporary Redirect response code.

> **Listing 18.3   Using `RewriteMiddleware` to enforce HTTPS for an application**

```
public void Configure(IApplicationBuilder app, IHostingEnvironment env)
{
    app.UseRewriter(new RewriteOptions()
        .AddRedirectToHttps(statusCode: 302, sslPort: 5002));

    if (env.IsDevelopment())
    {
        app.UseDeveloperExceptionPage();
    }

    app.UseMvc();
}
```

Adds the rewriter middleware to the pipeline

Configures the rewriter to redirect insecure requests to the secure endpoint (port 5002)

If you're sure you don't want to enforce HTTPS for the whole application, then you can apply a similar redirect behavior to specific controllers or actions by using the `[RequireHttps]` attribute. This authorization filter behaves like `RewriteMiddleware`—it redirects insecure HTTP requests to HTTPs. You can add this filter to any controller, action, or globally, as you saw in chapter 13.

---

[6] Scott Helme has some great guidance on, this and other security headers you can add to your site: http://mng.bz/K8it.

TIP If you're using HTTPS over a nonstandard port (anything other than 443), then you need to let MVC know which port to use for the redirects when you add MVC to your app in `ConfigureServices`. For example, you could set the SSL port to 5002 by using `services.AddMvc(options => options.SslPort = 5002);`.

SSL offloading, header forwarding, and detecting secure requests

At the start of this section, I encouraged you to consider terminating SSL requests at a reverse proxy. That way, the user uses HTTPS to talk to the reverse proxy, and the reverse proxy talks to your app using HTTP. With this setup, your users are protected but your app doesn't have to deal with SSL certificates itself.

In order for `RewriteMiddleware` and the `[RequireHttps]` attribute to work correctly, Kestrel needs some way of knowing whether the original request that the reverse proxy received was over HTTP or HTTPS. The reverse proxy communicates to your app over HTTP, so Kestrel can't figure that out without extra help.

The standard approach used by most reverse proxies (such as IIS, NGINX, and HAProxy) is to add additional headers to the request before forwarding it to your app. Specifically, a header called `X-Forwarded-Proto` is added, indicating whether the original request protocol was HTTP or HTTPS.

ASP.NET Core includes middleware to look for this forwarded header (and others) and update the request accordingly, so your app treats a request that was originally secured by HTTPS as secure for all intents and purposes.

If you're using IIS with the `UseIisIntegration()` extension, the header forwarding is handled for you automatically. If you're using a different reverse proxy, such as NGINX or HAProxy, then you'll need to add `ForwardedHeadersMiddleware` to your pipeline in `Startup.Configure`.

```
public void Configure(IApplicationBuilder app)
{
    app.UseForwardedHeaders(new ForwardedHeadersOptions {
        ForwardedHeaders = ForwardedHeaders.XForwardedProto
    });

    app.UseRewriter(new RewriteOptions().AddRedirectToHttps())
    // Other app configuration
    app.UseMvc()
}
```

When the reverse proxy forwards a request, `ForwardedHeadersMiddleware` will look for the `X-Forwarded-Proto` header and will update the request details as appropriate. For all subsequent middleware, the request is considered secure. It's important you place `ForwardedHeadersMiddleware` before the call to `UseMvc` or `UseRewriter`, so that the forwarded headers are read and the request is marked secure, as appropriate.

HTTPS is one of the most basic requirements for adding security to your application these days. It can be tricky to set up initially, but once you're up and running, you can largely forget about it, especially if you're using SSL termination at a reverse proxy.

Unfortunately, most other security practices require rather more vigilance to ensure you don't accidentally introduce vulnerabilities into your app as it grows and develops. Many attacks are conceptually simple and have been known about for years, yet they're still commonly found in new applications. In the next section, we'll take a look at one such attack and see how to defend against it when building apps using Razor templates.

18.2 *Defending against cross-site scripting (XSS) attacks*

Attackers can exploit a vulnerability in your app to create cross-site scripting (XSS) attacks[7] that execute code in another user's browser. Commonly, attackers submit content using a legitimate approach, such as an input form, which is later rendered somewhere to the page. By carefully crafting malicious input, the attacker can execute arbitrary JavaScript on user's browsers, and so can steal cookies, impersonate the user, and generally do bad things.

Figure 18.7 shows a basic example of an XSS attack. Legitimate users of your app can send their name to your app by submitting a form. The app then adds the name to an internal list and renders the whole list to the page. If the names are not rendered safely, then a malicious user can execute JavaScript in the browser of every other user that views the list.

In figure 18.7, the user entered a snippet of HTML as their name. When users viewed the list of names, the Razor template rendered the names using `@Html.Raw()`, which writes the `<script>` tag directly to the document. The user's input has become part of the page's HTML structure. As soon as the page is loaded in the user's browser, the `<script>` tag executes and the user is compromised. Once an attacker can execute arbitrary JavaScript on a user's browser, they can do pretty much anything.

The vulnerability here is due to rendering the user input in an unsafe way. If the data isn't encoded to make it safe before it's rendered, then you could open your users to attack. By default, Razor protects against XSS attacks by HTML-encoding any data written using Tag Helpers, HTML Helpers, or the @ syntax. So, generally, you should be safe, as you saw in chapter 7.

Using `@Html.Raw()` is where the danger lies—if the HTML you're rendering contains user input (even indirectly), then you could have an XSS vulnerability. By rendering the user input with @ instead, the content is encoded before it's written to the output, as shown in figure 18.8.

This example demonstrates using HTML encoding to prevent elements being directly added to the HTML DOM, but it's not the only case you have to think about.

---

[7] For a detailed discussion, see OWASP at www.owasp.org/index.php/Cross-site_Scripting_(XSS).

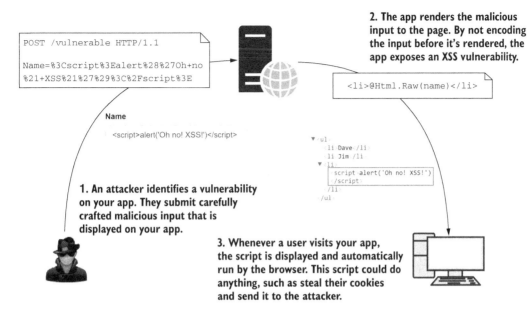

Figure 18.7 How an XSS vulnerability is exploited. An attacker submits malicious content to your app, which is displayed in the browser of other users. If the app doesn't encode the content when writing to the page, the input becomes part of the HTML of the page and can run arbitrary JavaScript.

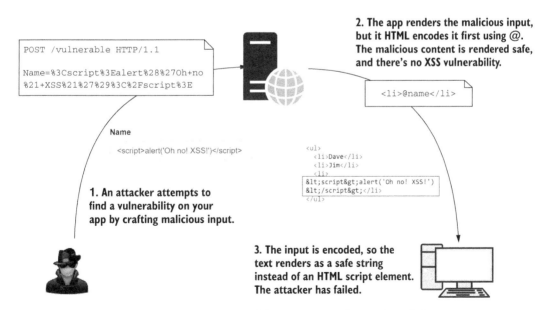

Figure 18.8 Protecting against XSS attacks by HTML encoding user input using @ in Razor templates

If you're passing untrusted data to JavaScript, or using untrusted data in URL query values, you must make sure you encode the data correctly.

A common scenario is when you're using jQuery or JavaScript with Razor pages, and you want to pass a value from the server to the client. If you use the standard @ symbol to render the data to the page, then the output will be HTML-encoded. Unfortunately, if you HTML encode a string and inject it directly into JavaScript, you probably won't get what you expect. If you have a variable in your Razor file called name, and you want to make it available in JavaScript, you might be tempted to use something like

```
<script>var name = '@name'</script>
```

If the name contains special characters, Razor will encode them using HTML encoding, which probably isn't what you want in this JavaScript context. For example, if name was Arnold "Arnie" Schwarzenegger, then rendering it as you did previously would give

```
<script>var name = 'Arnold &quot;Arnie&quot; Schwarzenegger';</script>
```

Note how the quotation marks " have been HTML-encoded to ". If you use this value in JavaScript directly, expecting it to be a "safe" encoded value, then it's going to look wrong, as shown in figure 18.9.

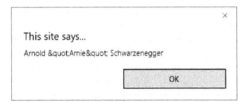

With HTML encoding, the quote marks are displayed incorrectly in JavaScript.

JavaScript encoding gives a safe way to render the user input in the expected format.

Figure 18.9   Comparison of alerts when using JavaScript encoding compared to HTML encoding

Instead, you should encode the variable using JavaScript encoding so that the " is rendered as a safe Unicode character, \u0022. You can achieve this by injecting a Java-ScriptEncoder into the view as you saw in chapter 10 and calling Encode() on the name:

```
@inject System.Text.Encodings.Web.JavaScriptEncoder encoder;
<script>var name = '@encoder.Encode(name)'</script>
```

To avoid having to remember to use JavaScript encoding, I recommend you don't write values into JavaScript like this. Instead, write the value to an HTML element's attributes, and then read that into the JavaScript variable later. That avoids the need for the JavaScript encoder entirely.

Listing 18.4   Passing values to JavaScript by writing them to HTML attributes

```
<div id="data" data-name="@name"></div>
<script>
var ele = document.getElementById('data');
var name = ele.getAttribute('data-name');
</script>
```

Gets a reference to
the HTML element

Reads the data-* attribute into
JavaScript, which will convert it
to JavaScript encoding

Write the value you want in
JavaScript to a data-* attribute.
This will HTML encode the data.

XSS attacks are still common, and it's easy to expose yourself to them whenever you allow users to input data. Validation of the incoming data can sometimes help, but it's often a tricky problem. For example, a naive name validator might require that you only use letters, which would prevent most attacks. Unfortunately, that doesn't account for users with hyphens or apostrophes in their name, let alone users with non-western names. People get (understandably) upset when you tell them their name is invalid, so be wary of this approach!

Whether or not you use strict validation, you should always encode the data when you render it to the page. Think carefully whenever you find yourself writing @Html.Raw(). Is there any way for a user to get malicious data into that field? If so, you'll need to find another way to display the data.

XSS vulnerabilities allow attackers to execute JavaScript on a user's browser. The next vulnerability we're going to consider lets them make requests to your API as though they're a different logged-in user, even when the user isn't using your app. Scared? I hope so!

18.3   *Protecting from cross-site request forgery (CSRF) attacks*

Cross-site (request forgery (CSRF) attacks can be a problem for websites or APIs that use cookies for authentication. A CSRF attack involves a malicious website making an authenticated request to your API on behalf of the user, without the user initiating the request. In this section, we'll explore how these attacks work and how you can mitigate them with anti-forgery tokens.

The canonical example of this attack is a bank transfer/withdrawal. Imagine you have a banking application that stores authentication tokens in a cookie, as is common (especially in traditional server-side rendered applications). Browsers automatically send the cookies associated with a domain with every request, so the app knows whether a user is authenticated.

Now imagine your application has a page that lets a user transfer funds from their account to another account, the WithdrawFunds action method. You have to be logged in to access the form (you've protected the action with the [Authorize] attribute), but otherwise you post a form that says how much you want to transfer, and where you want to transfer it.

Imagine a user visits your site, logs in, and performs a transaction. They then visit a second website that the attacker has control of. The attacker has embedded a form on their website that performs a POST to your bank's website, identical to the transfer funds form on your banking website. This form does something malicious, such as transfer all the user's funds to the attacker, as shown in figure 18.10. Browsers automatically send the cookies for the application when the page does a full form post, and the banking app has no way of knowing that this is a malicious request. The unsuspecting user has given all their money to the attacker!

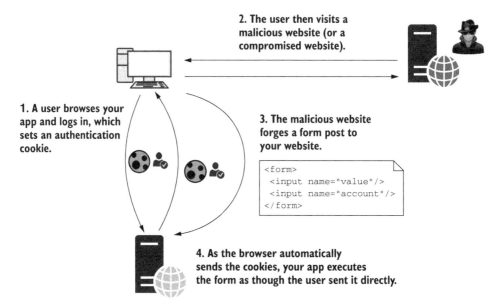

Figure 18.10   A CSRF attack occurs when a logged-in user visits a malicious site. The malicious site crafts a form that matches one on your app and POSTs it to your app. The browser sends the authentication cookie automatically, so your app sees the request as a valid request from the user.

The vulnerability here revolves around the fact that browsers automatically send cookies when a page is requested (using a GET request) or a form is POSTed. There's no difference between a legitimate POST of the form in your banking app and the attacker's malicious POST. Unfortunately, this behavior is baked into the web; it's what allows you to navigate websites seamlessly after initially logging in.

A common solution to the attack is the *synchronizer token* pattern,[8] which uses user-specific, unique, anti-forgery tokens to enforce a difference between a legitimate

---

[8]   The OWASP site gives a thorough discussion of the CSRF vulnerability, including the synchronizer token pattern: http://mng.bz/Qt49.

POST and a forged POST from an attacker. One token is stored in a cookie and another is added to the form you wish to protect. Your app generates the tokens at runtime based on the current logged-in user, so there's no way for an attacker to create one for their forged form.

When the `WithdrawFunds` action receives a form POST, it compares the value in the form with the value in the cookie. If either value is missing, or they don't match, then the request is rejected. If an attacker creates a POST, then the browser will post the cookie token as usual, but there won't be a token in the form itself, or the token won't be valid. The action method will reject the request, protecting from the CSRF attack, as in figure 18.11.

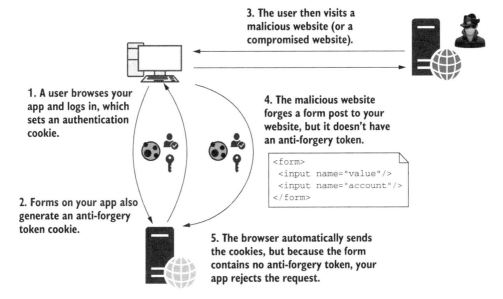

Figure 18.11   Protecting against a CSRF attack using anti-forgery tokens. The browser automatically forwards the cookie token, but the malicious site can't read it, and so can't include a token in the form. The app rejects the malicious request as the tokens don't match.

The Form Tag Helper automatically sets an anti-forgery token cookie and renders the token to a hidden field called `__RequestVerificationToken` for every `<form>` element in your app (unless you specifically disable them). For example, take this simple Razor template that posts to the `WithdrawFunds` action:

```
<form asp-action="WithdrawFunds">
    <label>Amount</label>
    <input type="number" name="amount" />
    <button type="submit">Withdraw funds</button>
</form>
```

When rendered to HTML, the anti-forgery token is stored in the hidden field and posted back with a legitimate request:

```
<form action="/Balance/Withdraw" method="post">
    <label>Amount</label>
    <input type="number" name="amount" />
    <button type="submit" class="btn btn-default">Withdraw funds</button>
    <input name="__RequestVerificationToken" type="hidden"
        value="CfDJ8Daz26qb0hBGsw7QCK">
</form>
```

ASP.NET Core automatically adds the anti-forgery tokens to every form, but unfortunately the framework *doesn't* automatically validate them. Instead, you have to decorate your controllers and actions with [ValidateAntiForgeryToken] attributes. These ensure the anti-forgery tokens exist in both the cookie and the form data, ensures they match, and will reject any requests where they don't.

> **WARNING**   ASP.NET Core automatically generates anti-forgery tokens, but it doesn't automatically validate them. You must make sure you mark all vulnerable methods with [ValidateAntiForgeryToken]. Alternatively, configure automatic validation, as discussed in the next section.

You can apply the [ValidateAntiForgeryToken] attribute to a controller or an action method, as you do with other filters. Technically, you can apply it globally, but there's a better alternative in this case: the [AutoValidateAntiForgeryToken] attribute.

Generally, you only need to use anti-forgery tokens for POST, DELETE, and other dangerous request types that are used for modifying state. GET requests shouldn't be used for this purpose, so you typically don't want to use anti-forgery tokens with them. The [AutoValidateAntiForgeryToken] attribute uses this behavior; it validates anti-forgery tokens for dangerous verbs like POST and ignores safe verbs like GET. As long as you create your MVC app following this pattern (and you should!), then the attribute will do the right thing to keep you safe.

You can add the [AutoValidateAntiForgeryToken] attribute to your app's global filters collection in Startup.ConfigureServices when you add MVC to your app using

```
services.AddMvc(options =>
    options.Filters.Add(new AutoValidateAntiforgeryTokenAttribute()));
```

If you need to explicitly ignore anti-forgery tokens on a method for some reason, you can disable the validation for an action by applying the [IgnoreAntiforgeryToken] attribute to a method. This will bypass both the [ValidateAntiForgeryToken] and [AutoValidateAntiForgeryToken] attributes if you're doing something that you know is safe and doesn't need protecting, but in most cases it's better to play it safe and validate, just in case.

CSRF attacks can be a tricky thing to get your head around from a technical point of view, but if you're using the built-in Razor views and forms, then everything *should* work without much effort on your part. Razor will add anti-forgery tokens to your forms, and the attributes will take care of validation for you. Similarly, if you're using the Razor Pages functionality introduced in ASP.NET Core 2.0, then anti-forgery token generation and validation is completely handled for you.

Where things get trickier is if you're making a lot of requests to an API using JavaScript and you're posting JSON objects rather than form data. In these cases, you won't be able to send the verification token as part of a form (as you're sending JSON), so you'll need to add it as a header in the request instead.[9]

> **TIP** If you're not using cookie authentication, and instead have an SPA that sends authentication tokens in a header, then good news—you don't have to worry about CSRF at all! Malicious sites can only send cookies, not headers, to your API, so they can't make authenticated requests.

Generating unique tokens with the Data Protection APIs

The anti-forgery tokens used to prevent CSRF attacks rely on the ability of the framework to use strong symmetric encryption to encrypt and decrypt data. Encryption algorithms typically rely on one or more keys, which are used to initialize the encryption and to make the process reproducible. If you have the key, you can encrypt and decrypt data; without it, the data is secure.

In ASP.NET Core, encryption is handled by the Data Protection APIs. They're used to create the anti-forgery tokens, to encrypt authentication cookies, and to generate secure tokens in general. Crucially, they also control the management of the *key files* that are used for encryption.

A key file is a small XML file that contains the random key value used for encryption in ASP.NET Core apps. It's critical that it's stored securely—if an attacker got hold of it, they could impersonate any user of your app, and generally do bad things!

The Data Protection system stores the keys in a safe location, depending on how and where you host your app. For example:

- *Azure Web App*—In a special synced folder, shared between regions.
- *IIS without user profile*—Encrypted in the registry.
- *Account with user profile*—In %LOCALAPPDATA%\ASP.NET\DataProtection-Keys on Windows, or ~/.aspnet/DataProtection-Keys on Linux or macOS.
- *All other cases*—In memory. When the app restarts, the keys will be lost.

So why do you care? In order for your app to be able to read your users' authentication cookies, it must decrypt them using the same key that was used to encrypt them. If you're running in a web-farm scenario, then, by default, each server will have its own key and won't be able to read cookies encrypted by other servers.

To get around this, you must configure your app to store its data protection keys in a central location. This could be a shared folder on a hard drive, a Redis instance, or an Azure blob storage instance, for example.

---

[9] Exactly how you do this varies depending on the JavaScript framework you're using. The documentation contains examples using JQuery and AngularJS, but you should be able to extend this to your JavaScript framework of choice: http://mng.bz/54Sl.

(continued)

The documentation on the data protection APIs is extremely detailed, but it can be overwhelming. I recommend reading the section on configuring data protection, (http://mng.bz/d40i) and configuring a key storage provider for use in a web-farm scenario (http://mng.bz/5pW6).

It's worth clarifying that the CSRF vulnerability discussed in this section requires that a malicious site does a full form POST to your app. The malicious site can't make the request to your API using *client-side only* JavaScript, as browsers will block JavaScript requests to your API that are from a different origin.

This is a safety feature, but it can often cause you problems. If you're building a client-side SPA, or only have a little JavaScript on an otherwise server-side rendered app, you may find you need to make such *cross-origin* requests. In the next section, I'll describe a common scenario you're likely to run into and show how you can modify your apps to work arounds it.

18.4   *Calling your web APIs from other domains using CORS*

As you've already seen, CSRF attacks can be powerful, but they would be even more dangerous if it weren't for browsers implementing the *same-origin* policy. This policy blocks apps from using JavaScript to call a web API at a different location, unless the web API explicitly allows it.

> **DEFINITION**   *Origins* are deemed the same if they match the scheme (HTTP or HTTPS), domain (example.com), and port (80 by default for HTTP, and 443 for HTTPS). If an app attempts to access a resource using JavaScript and the origins aren't identical, the browser blocks the request.

The same-origin policy is strict—the origins of the two URLs must be identical for the request to be allowed. For example, the following origins are the same:

- http://example.com/home
- http://example.com/site.css

The paths are different for these two URLs (`/home` and `/sites.css`), but the scheme, domain, and port (80) are identical. So, if you were on the homepage of your app, you could request the `/sites.css` file using JavaScript without any issues.

In contrast, the origins of the following sites are all different, so you couldn't request any of these URLs using JavaScript from the http://example.com origin:

- *https://example.com*—Different scheme (https)
- *http://www.example.com*—Different domain (includes a subdomain)
- *http://example.com:5000*—Different port (default HTTP port is 80)

For simple apps, where you have a single web app handling all of your functionality, this limitation might not be a problem, but it's extremely common for an app to make requests to another domain.

You might have an e-commerce site hosted at http://shopping.com, and you're attempting to load data from http://api.shopping.com to display details about the products available for sale. With this configuration, you'll fall foul of the same-origin policy. Any attempt to make a request using JavaScript to the API domain will fail, with an error similar to figure 18.12.

The browser won't allow cross-origin requests by default and will block your app from accessing the response.

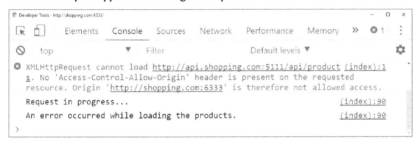

Figure 18.12   The console log for a failed cross-origin request. Chrome has blocked a cross-origin request from the app http://shopping.com:6333 to the API at http://api .shopping.com:5111.

Obviously, the need to make cross-origin requests from JavaScript is increasingly common with the rise of client-side SPAs and the move away from monolithic apps. Luckily, there's a web standard that lets you work around this in a safe way; this standard is called cross-origin resource sharing (CORS). You can use CORS to control which apps are allowed to call your API, so you can enable scenarios like the one described earlier.

18.4.1 *Understanding CORS and how it works*

CORS is a web standard that allows your Web API to make statements about who can make cross-origin requests to it. For example, you could make statements such as

- Allow cross-origin requests from http://shopping.com and https://app.shopping .com
- Only allow GET cross-origin requests
- Allow returning the `Server` header in responses to cross-origin requests
- Allow credentials (such as authentication cookies or authorization headers) to be sent with cross-origin requests

You can combine these rules into a *policy* and apply different policies to different endpoints of your API. You could apply a policy to your entire application, or a different policy to every action.

CORS works using HTTP headers. When your application receives a request, it sets special headers on the response to indicate whether cross-origin requests are allowed, which origins they're allowed from, and which HTTP verbs and headers the request can use—pretty much everything about the request.

In some cases, before sending a real request to your API, the browser sends a *pre-flight* request. This is a request sent using the OPTIONS verb, which the browser uses to check whether it's allowed to make the real request. If the API sends back the correct headers, the browser will send the true cross-origin request, as shown in figure 18.13.

> **TIP** For a more detailed discussion of CORS, see *CORS in Action* by Monsur Hossain (Manning, 2014), available at http://mng.bz/aD41.

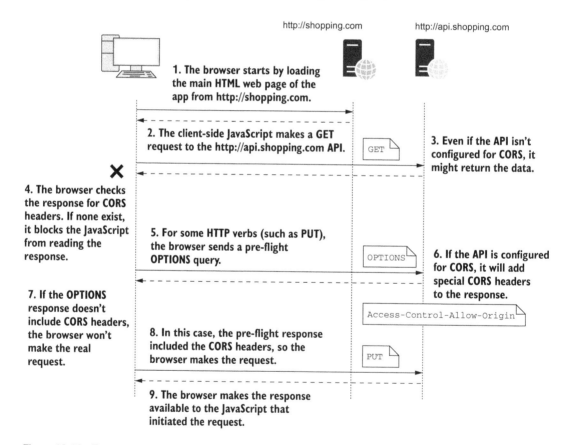

Figure 18.13 Two cross-origin-requests. The response to the first request doesn't contain any CORS headers, so the browser blocks the app from reading it. The second request requires a preflight OPTIONS request, to check if CORS is enabled. As the response contains CORS headers, the real request can be made, and the response provided to the JavaScript app.

The CORS specification, as with many technical documents, is pretty complicated,[10] with a variety of headers and processes to contend with. Thankfully, ASP.NET Core handles the details of the specification for you, so your main concern is working out exactly *who* needs to access your API, and under what circumstances.

18.4.2 *Adding CORS to your whole app with middleware*

Typically, you shouldn't set up CORS for your APIs until you need it. Browsers block cross-origin communication for a reason—it closes an avenue of attack—they're not being awkward! Wait until you have an API on a different domain to an app that needs to access it.

Adding CORS support to your application requires three things:

- Add the CORS services to your app
- Configure at least one CORS policy
- Add the CORS middleware to enable CORS for your entire app or decorate your MVC action with the `[EnableCors]` attribute to selectively enable CORS

Adding the CORS services to your application involves calling `AddCors` in your `Startup.ConfigureServices` method:

```
services.AddCors();
```

The bulk of your effort in configuring CORS will go into policy configuration. A CORS policy controls how your application will respond to cross-origin requests. It defines which origins are allowed, which headers to return, which HTTP methods to allow, and so on. You normally define your policies inline when you add the CORS services to your application.

For example, consider the previous e-commerce site example. You want your API that is hosted at http://api.shopping.com to be available from the main app, hosted at http://shopping.com. You therefore need to configure the *API* to allow cross-origin requests.

> **NOTE** Remember, it's the main app that will get errors when attempting to make cross-origin requests, but it's the API you're accessing you need to add CORS to, not the app making the requests.

The following listing shows how to configure a policy called `"AllowShoppingApp"` to enable cross-origin requests from http://shopping.com to the API. Additionally, you explicitly allow any HTTP verb type; without this call, only simple methods (GET, HEAD, and POST) are allowed. The policies are built up using the familiar "fluent builder" style you've seen throughout this book.

---

[10] If that's the sort of thing that floats your boat, you can read the spec here: https://www.w3.org/TR/cors/.

Listing 18.5   Configuring a CORS policy to allow requests from a specific origin

```
public void ConfigureServices(IServiceCollection services)
{
    services.AddCors(options => {
        options.AddPolicy("AllowShoppingApp", policy =>
            policy.WithOrigins("http://shopping.com")
                .AllowAnyMethod());
    });
    // other service configuration
}
```

Every policy has a unique name.

The AddCors method exposes an Action<CorsOptions> overload.

The WithOrigins method specifies which origins are allowed. Note the URL has no trailing /.

Allows all HTTP verbs to call the API

WARNING   When listing origins in WithOrigins(), ensure that they don't have a trailing "/", otherwise the origin will never match and your cross-origin requests will fail.

Once you've defined a CORS policy, you can apply it to your application. In the following listing, apply the "AllowShoppingApp" policy to the whole application using CorsMiddleware by calling UseCors(). This method also includes an overload that lets you define a policy inline. If you opt for this approach, you don't need to create a policy in ConfigureServices.

Listing 18.6   Adding the CORS middleware and configuring a default CORS policy

```
public void Configure(IApplicationBuilder app)
{
    app.UseCors("AllowShoppingApp");

    app.UseMvc()
}
```

Adds the CORS middleware and uses AllowShoppingApp as the default policy

The CORS middleware must come before the MVC middleware.

NOTE   It's important that you add the CORS middleware before the MVC middleware. The CORS middleware needs to intercept cross-origin requests to your MVC actions, so it can generate the correct responses to preflight requests and add the necessary headers.

With the CORS middleware in place for the API, the shopping app can now make cross-origin requests. You can call the API from the http://shopping.com site and the browser lets the CORS request through, as shown in figure 18.14. If you make the same request from a domain other than http://shopping.com, the request continues to be blocked.

Applying CORS globally to your application in this way may be overkill. If there's only a subset of actions in your API that need to be accessed from other origins, then it's prudent to only enable CORS for those specific actions. This can be achieved with the [EnableCors] attribute.

Without CORS

The browser won't allow cross-origin requests by default and will block your app from accessing the response.

With CORS

With CORS enabled, the API sends CORS headers with the response. The browser sees these headers and passes the response to the JavaScript.

Figure 18.14 With CORS enabled, cross-origin requests can be made and the browser will make the response available to the JavaScript. Compare this to figure 18.12, in which the request was blocked.

18.4.3 Adding CORS to specific MVC actions with EnableCorsAttribute

Browsers block cross-origin requests by default for good reason—they have the potential to be abused by malicious or compromised sites. Enabling CORS for your entire app may not be worth the risk if you know that only a subset of actions will ever need to be accessed cross-origin.

If that's the case, it's best to only enable CORS for those specific actions. ASP.NET Core provides the [EnableCors] attribute, which lets you select a specific policy to apply to a given controller or action method.

This approach lets you apply different CORS policies to different action methods. For example, you could allow GET requests access to your entire API from the http://shopping.com domain, but only allow other HTTP verbs for a specific controller, while allowing anyone to access your product list action method.

You define these policies in ConfigureServices using AddPolicy() and giving the policy a name, as you saw in listing 18.5. To apply a policy to a controller or an action method, apply the [EnableCors] attribute, as shown in the following listing. An [Enable-Cors] attribute on an action takes precedence over an attribute on a controller, or you can use the [DisableCors] attribute to disable cross-origin access to the method entirely.

Applies the AllowShoppingApp
CORS policy to every action method

```
[EnableCors("AllowShoppingApp")]
public class ProductController: Controller
{
    [EnableCors("AllowAnyOrigin")]
    public IActionResult GetProducts() { /* Method */ }

    public IActionResult GetProductPrice(int id) { /* Method */ }

    [DisableCors]
    public IActionResult DeleteProduct(int id) { /* Method */ }
}
```

The AllowAnyOrigin policy is "closer"
to the action, so it takes precedence.

The AllowShoppingApp
policy will be applied.

The DisableCors attribute
disables CORS for the action
method completely.

> **WARNING**   The [DisableCors] attribute will only disable CORS for an action method that has CORS enabled using the [EnableCors] attribute. It won't disable CORS for an action method when CORS has been enabled using Cors-Middleware.

If you want to apply CORS to all your actions, but you also want to disable CORS for some actions, you can't use CorsMiddleware. Instead, you can add the [EnableCors] attribute globally to MvcMiddleware, so that it applies to all action methods, but can still be disabled. To add the AllowShoppingApp CORS policy globally, update the call to AddMvc() in ConfigureServices with the global filter (as you saw in chapter 13):

```
services.AddMvc(options => {
    options.Filters.Add(
        new CorsAuthorizationFilterFactory("AllowShoppingApp"));
}
```

> **NOTE**   The [EnableCors] attribute is a *marker* attribute—it contains no functionality; it's used by MvcMiddleware to decide which filter to apply. Consequently, instead of adding an [EnableCors] attribute to the global filters, you must add CorsAuthorizationFilterFactory.

Whether you choose to use CorsMiddleware or the [EnableCors] attribute, you need to configure the CORS policy for your application. Many different options are available when configuring CORS; in the next section, I'll provide an overview of the possibilities.

18.4.4 Configuring CORS policies

Browsers implement the cross-origin policy for security reasons, so you should carefully consider the implications of relaxing any of the restrictions they impose. Even if you enable cross-origin requests, you can still control what data cross-origin requests are allowed to send, and what your API will return. For example, you can configure

- The origins that may make a cross-origin request to your API
- The HTTP verbs (such as GET, POST, and DELETE) that can be used
- The headers the browser is allowed to send
- The headers that the browser is allowed to read from your app's response
- Whether the browser will send authentication credentials with the request

You define all of these options when creating a CORS policy in your call to `AddCors()` using the `CorsPolicyBuilder`, as you saw in listing 18.7. A policy can set all, or none of these options, so you can customize the results to your heart's content. Table 18.1 shows some of the options available, and their effects.

Table 18.1   The methods available for configuring a CORS policy, and their effect on the policy

`CorsPolicyBuilder` method example	Result
`WithOrigins("http://shopping.com")`	Allows cross-origin requests from http://shopping.com.
`AllowAnyOrigin()`	Allows cross-origin requests from any origin. This means *any* website can make JavaScript requests to your API.
`WithMethods()/AllowAnyMethod()`	Sets the allowed methods (such as GET, POST, and DELETE) that can be made to your API.
`WithHeaders()/AllowAnyHeader()`	Sets the headers that the browser may send to your API. If you restrict the headers, you must include at least `"Accept"`, `"Content-Type"`, and `"Origin"` to allow valid requests.
`WithExposedHeaders()`	Allows your API to send extra headers to the browser. By default, only the `Cache-Control`, `Content-Language`, `Content-Type`, `Expires`, `Last-Modified`, and `Pragma` headers are sent in the response.
`AllowCredentials()`	By default, the browser won't send authentication details with cross-origin requests unless you explicitly allow it. You must also enable sending credentials client-side in JavaScript when making the request.

One of the first issues in setting up CORS is realizing you have a cross-origin problem at all. Several times I've been stumped trying to figure out why a request won't work, until I realize the request is going cross-domain, or from HTTP to HTTPS, for example.

Whenever possible, I recommend avoiding cross-origin requests completely. You can end up with subtle differences in the way browsers handle them, which can cause more headaches. In particular, avoid HTTP to HTTPS cross-domain issues by running all of your applications behind HTTPS. As discussed in section 18.1, that's a best practice anyway, and it'll help avoid a whole class of CORS headaches.

Once I've established I definitely need a CORS policy, I typically start with the `WithOrigins()` method. I then expand or restrict the policy further, as need be, to provide cross-origin lock-down of my API, while still allowing the required functionality. CORS can be tricky to work around, but remember, the restrictions are there for your safety.

Cross-origin requests are only one of many potential avenues attackers could use to compromise your app. Many of these are trivial to defend against, but you need to be aware of them, and know how to mitigate them.[11] In the next section, we'll look at common threats and how to avoid them.

18.5   *Exploring other attack vectors*

So far in this chapter, I've described two potential ways attackers can compromise your apps—XSS and CSRF attacks—and how to prevent them. Both of these vulnerabilities regularly appear on the OWASP top ten list of most critical web app risks,[12] so it's important to be aware of them, and to avoid introducing them into your apps. In this section, I'll provide an overview of some of the other most common vulnerabilities and how to avoid them in your apps.

18.5.1 *Detecting and avoiding open redirect attacks*

The number ten OWASP vulnerability is due to *open redirect* attacks. An open redirect attack is where a user clicks a link to an otherwise safe app and ends up being redirected to a malicious website; for example, one that serves malware. The safe app contains no direct links to the malicious website, so how does this happen?

Open redirect attacks occur where the next page is passed as a parameter to an action method. The most common example is when logging in to an app. Typically, apps remember the page a user is on before redirecting them to a login page by passing the current page as a `returnUrl` query string parameter. After the user logs in, the app redirects the user to the `returnUrl` to carry on where they left off.

Imagine a user is browsing an e-commerce site. They click Buy on a product and are redirected to the login page. The product page they were on is passed as the `returnUrl`, so after they log in, they're redirected to the product page, instead of being dumped back to the home screen.

An open redirect attack takes advantage of this common pattern, as shown in figure 18.15. A malicious attacker creates a login URL where the `returnUrl` is set to the website they want to send the user and convinces the user to click the link to your web app. After the user logs in, a vulnerable app will then redirect the user to the malicious site.

---

[11] For an example of how incorrectly configured CORS policies could expose vulnerabilities in your app, see http://mng.bz/211b.

[12] OWASP publishes the list online, with descriptions of each attack and how to prevent those attacks. You can view the lists dating back to 2003 at http://mng.bz/yXd3.

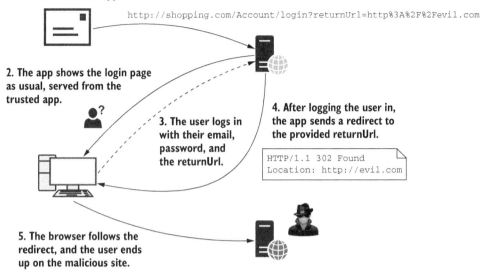

1. The user clicks a link to the login page of a trusted app, which looks safe.

`http://shopping.com/Account/login?returnUrl=http%3A%2F%2Fevil.com`

2. The app shows the login page as usual, served from the trusted app.

3. The user logs in with their email, password, and the returnUrl.

4. After logging the user in, the app sends a redirect to the provided returnUrl.

```
HTTP/1.1 302 Found
Location: http://evil.com
```

5. The browser follows the redirect, and the user ends up on the malicious site.

Figure 18.15 An open redirect makes use of the common return URL pattern. This is typically used for login pages but may be used in other areas of your app too. If your app doesn't verify the URL is safe before redirecting the user, it could redirect users to malicious sites.

The simple solution to this attack is to always validate that the `returnUrl` is a local URL that belongs to your app before redirecting users to it. ASP.NET Core provide a couple of helper methods for this, the most useful of which, I find, is `Url.IsLocal-Url()`. The following listing shows how you could verify a provided return URL is safe, and if it isn't, redirect to the app's homepage. You can also use the `LocalRedirect()` helper method on the `Controller` base class, which throws an exception if the provided URL isn't local.

Listing 18.8 Detecting open redirect attacks by checking for local return URLs

```
[HttpPost]
public async Task<IActionResult> Login(          ⟵ The return URL is
    LoginViewModel model, string returnUrl = null)     provided as an argument
{                                                       to the action method.
    // Verify password, and sign user in

    if (Url.IsLocalUrl(returnUrl))          ⟵ Returns true if the return
    {                                          URL starts with / or ~/
        return Redirect(returnUrl);      ⟵ The URL is local, so it's
    }                                       safe to redirect to it.
    else
    {                                                ⟵ The URL was not local,
        return RedirectToAction("Index", "Home");      could be an open redirect
    }                                                   attack, so redirect to the
}                                                       homepage for safety.
```

This simple pattern protects against open redirect attacks that could otherwise expose your users to malicious content. Whenever you're redirecting to a URL that comes from a query string or other user input, you should use this pattern.

> **NOTE** The default templates use exactly this pattern for redirecting to return URLs in `AccountController` by wrapping the `if-else` clause into a simple helper called `RedirectToLocal()`.

Open redirect attacks present a risk to your users rather than to your app directly. The next vulnerability represents a critical vulnerability in your app itself.

18.5.2 Avoiding SQL injection attacks with EF Core and parameterization

SQL injection attacks represent one of the most dangerous threats to your application. Attackers craft simple malicious input, which they send to your application as traditional form-based input or by customizing URLs and query strings to execute arbitrary code on your database. An SQL injection vulnerability could expose your entire database to attackers, so it's critical that you spot and remove any such vulnerabilities in your apps.

Hopefully, I've scared you a little with that introduction, so now for the good news—if you're using EF Core (or pretty much any other ORM) in a standard way, then you should be safe. EF Core has built-in protections against SQL injection, so as long as you're not doing anything funky, you should be fine.

SQL injection vulnerabilities occur when you build SQL statements yourself and include dynamic input that an attacker provides, even indirectly. EF Core provides the ability to create raw SQL queries using the `FromSql()` method, so you must be careful when using this method.

Imagine your recipe app has a search form that lets you search for a recipe by name. If you write the query using LINQ extension methods (as discussed in chapter 12), then you would have no risk of SQL injection attacks. However, if you decide to write your SQL query by hand, you open yourself up to such a vulnerability.

Listing 18.9   An SQL injection vulnerability in EF Core due to string concatenation

```
public IList<User> FindRecipe(string search)       ◁——— The search parameter comes
{                                                        from user input, so it's unsafe.
    return _context.Recipes
        .FromSql("SELECT * FROM Recipes" +         ◁———
                "WHERE Name = '" + search + "'")    ◁———
        .ToList();
}
```

The current EF Core DbContext is held in the `_context` field.

This introduces the vulnerability—including unsafe content directly in an SQL string.

You can write queries by hand using the FromSql extension method.

In this listing, the user input held in `search` is included *directly* in the SQL query. By crafting malicious input, users can potentially perform any operation on your database. Imagine an attacker searches your website using the text

```
'; DROP TABLE Recipes; --
```

Your app assigns this to the `search` parameter, and the SQL query executed against your database becomes

```
SELECT * FROM Recipes WHERE Name = ''; DROP TABLE Recipes; --'
```

By simply entering text into the search form of your app, the attacker has deleted the entire Recipes table from your app! That's catastrophic, but an SQL injection vulnerability provides more or less unfettered access to your database. Even if you've set up database permissions correctly to prevent this sort of destructive action, attackers will likely be able to read all the data from your database, including your users' details.

The simple way to avoid this happening is to avoid creating SQL queries by hand like this. If you do need to write your own SQL queries, then don't use string concatenation, as you did in listing 18.9. Instead, use parameterized queries, in which the (potentially unsafe) input data is separate from the query itself, as shown here.

> **Listing 18.10 Avoiding SQL injection by using parameterization**

```
public IList<User> FindRecipe(string search)          The SQL query uses a
{                                                      placeholder {0} for
    return _context.Recipes                            the parameter.
        .FromSql("SELECT * FROM Recipes WHERE Name = '{0}'",   ⟵
                        search)     ⟵
        .ToList();                        The dangerous input is passed as a
}                                         parameter, separate from the query.
```

Parameterized queries are not vulnerable to SQL injection attacks, so the same attack presented earlier won't work. If you use EF Core (or other ORMs) to access data using standard LINQ queries, you won't be vulnerable to injection attacks. EF Core will automatically create all SQL queries using parameterized queries to protect you.

> **NOTE** I've only talked about SQL injection attacks in terms of a relational database, but this vulnerability can appear in NoSQL and document databases too. Always use parameterized queries (or equivalent) and don't craft queries by concatenating strings with user input.

Injection attacks have been the number one vulnerability on the web for over a decade, so it's crucial that you're aware of them and how they arise. Whenever you need to write raw SQL queries, make sure you always use parameterized queries.

The next vulnerability is also related to attackers accessing data they shouldn't be able to. It's a little subtler than a direct injection attack but is trivial to perform—the only skill the attacker needs is the ability to add one to a number.

18.5.3 Preventing insecure direct object references

Insecure direct object reference is a bit of a mouthful, but it means users accessing things they shouldn't by noticing patterns in URLs. Let's revisit our old friend the recipe app. As a reminder, the app shows you a list of recipes. You can view any of them, but you can only edit recipes you created yourself. When you view someone else's recipe, there's no Edit button visible.

For example, a user clicks the edit button on one of their recipes and notices the URL is `/Recipes/Edit/120`. That "120" is a dead giveaway as the underlying database ID of the entity you're editing. A simple attack would be to change that ID to gain access to a *different* entity, one that you wouldn't normally have access to. The user could try entering `/Recipes/Edit/121`. If that lets them edit or view a recipe they shouldn't be able to, you have an insecure direct object reference vulnerability.

The solution to this problem is simple—you should have resource-based authentication and authorization in your action methods. If a user attempts to access an entity they're not allowed to access, they should get a permission denied error. They shouldn't be able to bypass your authorization by typing a URL directly into the search bar of their browser.

In ASP.NET Core apps, this vulnerability typically arises when you attempt to restrict users by hiding elements from your UI, for example, by hiding the Edit button. Instead, you should use resource-based authorization, as discussed in chapter 15.

> **WARNING** You must always use resource-based authorization to restrict which entities a user can access. Hiding UI elements provides an improved user experience, but it isn't a security measure.

You can sidestep this vulnerability somewhat by avoiding integer IDs for your entities in the URLs; for example, using a pseudorandom GUID (for instance, `C2E296BA-7EA8-4195-9CA7-C323304CCD12`) instead. This makes the process of guessing other entities harder as you can't just add one to an existing number, but it's only masking the problem rather than fixing it. Nevertheless, using GUIDs can be useful when you want to have publicly accessible pages (that don't require authentication), but you don't want their IDs to be easily discoverable.

The final section in this chapter doesn't deal with a single vulnerability. Instead, I discuss a separate, but related, issue: protecting your users' data.

18.5.4 Protecting your users' passwords and data

For many apps, the most sensitive data you'll be storing is the personal data of your users. This could include emails, passwords, address details, or payment information. You should be careful when storing any of this data. As well as presenting an inviting target for attackers, you may have legal obligations for how you handle it, such as data protection laws and PCI compliance requirements.

The easiest way to protect yourself is to not store data that you don't need. If you don't *need* your user's address, don't ask for it. That way, you can't lose it! Similarly, if you use a third-party identity service to store user details, as described in chapter 14, then you won't have to work as hard to protect your users' personal information.

If you store user details in your own app, or build your own identity provider, then you need to make sure to follow best practices when handling user information. The new project templates that use ASP.NET Core Identity follow most of these practices by default, so I highly recommend you start from one of these. You need to consider many different aspects—too many to go into detail here[13]—but they include:

- Never store user passwords anywhere directly. You should only store cryptographic hashes, computed using an expensive hashing algorithm, such as BCrypt or PBKDF2.
- Don't store more data than you need. You should never store credit card details.
- Allow users to use two-factor authentication (2FA) to sign in to your site.
- Prevent users from using passwords that are known to be weak or compromised.
- Mark authentication cookies as "http" (so they can't be read using JavaScript) and "secure" so they'll only be sent over an HTTPS connection, never over HTTP.
- Don't expose whether a user is already registered with your app or not. Leaking this information can expose you to enumeration attacks.[14]

These are all guidelines, but they represent the minimum you should be doing to protect your users. The most important thing is to be aware of potential security issues as you're building your app. Trying to bolt on security at the end is always harder than thinking about it from the start, so it's best to think about it earlier rather than later.

This chapter has been a whistle-stop tour of things to look out for. We've touched on most of the big names in security vulnerabilities, but I strongly encourage you to check out the other resources mentioned in this chapter. They provide a more exhaustive list of things to consider to complement the defenses mentioned in this chapter. On top of that, don't forget about input validation and mass assignment/over-posting, as discussed in chapter 6. ASP.NET Core includes basic protections against some of the most common attacks, but you can still shoot yourself in the foot. Make sure it's not your app making headlines for being breached!

Summary

- HTTPS is used to encrypt your app's data as it travels from the server to the browser and back. This prevents third parties from seeing or modifying it.
- HTTPS is effectively becoming required, with modern browsers like Chrome and Firefox marking non-HTTPS apps as explicitly "not secure."

---

[13] The NIST (National Institute of Standards and Technology) recently released their Digital Identity Guidelines on how to handle user details: https://pages.nist.gov/800-63-3/sp800-63-3.html.

[14] You can learn more about website enumeration in this video tutorial from Troy Hunt: http://mng.bz/PAAA.

- In production, you can avoid handling the SSL in your app by using SSL off-loading. This is where a reverse proxy uses HTTPS to talk to the browser, but the traffic is unencrypted between your app and the reverse proxy. The reverse proxy could be on the same or a different server, such as IIS or NGINX, or it could be a third-party service, such as Cloudflare.

- You can use a self-signed certificate to test SSL during development. This can't be used for production, but it's sufficient for testing locally. You can use Power-Shell on Windows, or OpenSSL on Linux and macOS to create a self-signed certificate.

- You can't use the `UseUrls()` extension method to configure HTTPS in Kestrel. Instead, you must use the `Listen` endpoint configuration methods and provide the certificate to use.

- You can enforce HTTPS for your whole app using `RewriteMiddleware`. This will redirect HTTP requests to HTTPS endpoints. Alternatively, you can apply the `[RequireHttps]` authorization filter to specific controllers, actions, or globally, to enforce SSL only in the MVC middleware.

- Cross-site scripting (XSS) attacks involve malicious users injecting content into your app, typically to run malicious JavaScript when users browse your app. You can avoid XSS injection attacks by always encoding unsafe input before writing it to a page. Razor does this automatically unless you use the `@Html.Raw()` method, so use it sparingly and carefully.

- Cross-site request forgery (CSRF) attacks are a problem for apps that use cookie-based authentication, such as ASP.NET Core Identity. It relies on the fact browsers automatically send cookies to a website. A malicious website could create a form that POSTs to your API, and the browser will send the authentication cookie with the request. This allows malicious websites to send requests as though they're the logged-in user.

- You can mitigate CSRF attacks using anti-forgery tokens. These involve writing a hidden field in every form that contains a random string based on the current user. A similar token is stored in a cookie. A legitimate request will have both parts, but a forged request from a malicious website will only have the cookie half; they cannot create the hidden field in the form. By validating these tokens, your API can reject forged requests.

- ASP.NET Core automatically adds anti-forgery tokens to any forms you create using Razor. You can validate the tokens by adding the `[ValidateAntiForgery-Token]` attribute to your controllers and actions. Alternatively, you can apply the `[AutoValidateAntiForgeryToken]` attribute globally to protect your whole app, and only disable the check as necessary using the `[IgnoreAntiForgery-Token]` attribute.

- Browsers won't allow a website to make a JavaScript AJAX request from one app to another at a different origin. To match the origin, the app must have the same scheme, domain, and port. If you wish to make cross-origin requests like this, you must enable cross-origin resource sharing (CORS) in your API.

- CORS uses HTTP headers to communicate with browsers and defines which origins are allowed to call your API. In ASP.NET Core, you can define multiple policies, which can be applied either globally to your whole app, or to specific controllers and actions.

- You can add the CORS middleware by calling `UseCors()` in `Startup.Configure` and passing the name of the CORS policy to apply. You can apply CORS to an MVC action or controller by adding the `[EnableCors]` attribute and providing the name of the policy to apply.

- Open redirect attacks use the common `returnURL` mechanism after logging in to redirect users to malicious websites. You can prevent this attack by ensuring you only redirect to local URLs, URLs that belong to your app.

- Insecure direct object references are a common problem where you expose the ID of database entities in the URL. You should always verify that users have permission to access or change the requested resource by using resource-based authorization in your action methods.

- SQL injection attacks are a common attack vector when you build SQL requests manually. Always use parameterized queries when building requests, or instead use a framework like EF Core, which isn't vulnerable to SQL injection.

- The most sensitive data in your app is often the data of your users. Mitigate this risk by only storing data that you need. Ensure you only store passwords as a hash, protect against weak or compromised passwords, and provide the option for 2FA. ASP.NET Core Identity provides all of this out of the box, so it's a great choice if you need to create an identity provider.

Building custom components

This chapter covers

- Building custom middleware and branching middleware pipelines
- Using configuration values to set up other configuration providers
- Replacing the built-in DI container with a third-party container
- Creating custom Razor Tag Helpers and view components
- Creating a custom `DataAnnotations` validation attribute

When you're building apps with ASP.NET Core, most of your creativity and specialization goes into the services and models that make up your business logic, and the MVC controllers that expose them through views or APIs. Eventually, however, you're likely to find that you can't quite achieve a desired feature using the components that come out of the box. At that point, you may need to build a custom component.

This chapter shows how to create ASP.NET Core components that you're likely to need as your app grows. You probably won't need to use all of them, but each solves a specific problem you may run into.

We'll start by looking at the middleware pipeline. You saw how to build pipelines by piecing together existing middleware in chapter 3, but in this chapter, you'll create your own custom middleware. You'll explore the basic middleware constructs of the Map, Use, and Run methods, and how to create standalone middleware classes. You'll use these to build middleware components that can add headers to all your responses, that act as simple health-check endpoints to confirm your app is running correctly, and to create branching middleware pipelines. These will give you everything you need to build more complex middleware, should the need arise.

Chapter 11 described the configuration provider system used by ASP.NET Core, but in section 19.2, we look at more complex scenarios. In particular, I'll show you how to handle the situation where a configuration provider itself needs some configuration values. For example, a configuration provider that reads values from a database might need a connection string. You'll also see how to use DI when configuring strongly typed IOptions objects, something not possible using the methods you've seen so far.

We'll stick with DI in section 19.3 and see how to replace the built-in DI container with a third-party alternative. The built-in container is fine for most small apps, but your ConfigureServices function can quickly get bloated as your app grows and you register more services. I'll show you how to integrate StructureMap into an existing app, so you can make use of extra features such as automatic service registration by convention.

In the second half of the chapter, we look at custom MVC components, in particular Tag Helpers, view components, and custom validation attributes. In section 19.4, I'll show you how to create two different Tag Helpers: one that generates HTML to describe the current machine, and one that lets you write if statements in Razor templates without having to use C#. These will give you the details you need to create your own custom Tag Helpers in your own apps, if the need arises.

View components are a new concept in ASP.NET Core Razor templates. They're a bit like partial views, but they can contain business logic and database access. For example, on an e-commerce site, you might have a shopping cart, a dynamically populated menu, and a login widget, all on one page. Each of those sections is independent of the main page content and has its own logic and data-access needs. In an ASP.NET Core app using Razor, you'd implement each of those as a View Component.

In section 19.6, I'll show you how to create a custom validation attribute. As you saw in chapter 6, validation is a key responsibility of action methods in MVC, and the Data-Annotations attributes provide a clean, declarative way for doing so. We previously only looked at the built-in attributes, but you'll often find you need to add attributes tailored to your app's domain. In section 19.6, you'll see how to create a simple validation attribute, and how to extend it to use services registered with the DI container.

ASP.NET Core is highly customizable, so you can replace the vast majority of the framework with custom implementations, but the components in this chapter will likely cover the majority of your use cases. In particular, I use the subject of the first topic—custom middleware—in almost every project I build.

19.1 *Customizing your middleware pipeline*

The middleware pipeline is one of the fundamental building blocks of ASP.NET Core apps, so we covered it in depth in chapter 3. Every request passes through the middleware pipeline, and each middleware component in turn gets an opportunity to modify the request, or to handle it and return a response.

ASP.NET Core includes middleware out of the box for handling common scenarios. You'll find middleware for serving static files, for handling errors, for authentication, and many more. The largest of these components is the MVC middleware.

The MVC middleware is a particularly large component and is commonly where you'll spend most of your time during development. It serves as the entry point for most of your app's business logic, as it routes incoming requests to action methods, which call methods on your app's various business services and models.

Sometimes, however, you don't need all of the power (and associated complexity) that comes with the MVC middleware. You might want to create a simple service that, when called, returns the current time. Or you might want to add a health-check URL to an existing app, where calling the URL doesn't do any significant processing, but checks the app is running. Although you *could* use the MVC middleware for these, you could also create small, dedicated middleware components that handle these requirements.

Other times, you might have requirements that lie outside the remit of the MVC middleware. You might want to ensure all responses generated by your app include a specific header. This sort of cross-cutting concern is a perfect fit for custom middleware. You could add the custom middleware early in your middleware pipeline to ensure every response from your app includes the required header, whether it comes from the static file middleware, the error-handling middleware, or the MVC middleware.

In this section, I show three ways to create custom middleware components, as well as how to create branches in your middleware pipeline where a request can flow down either one branch or another. By combining the methods demonstrated in this section, you'll be able to create custom solutions to handle your specific requirements.

We'll start by creating a middleware component that returns the current time as plain text, whenever the app receives a request. From there, we'll look at branching the pipeline, creating general-purpose middleware components, and finally, how to encapsulate your middleware into standalone classes.

19.1.1 Creating simple endpoints with the Run extension

As you've seen in previous chapters, you define the middleware pipeline for your app in the `Configure` method of your `Startup` class. You add middleware to a provided `IApplicationBuilder` object, typically using extension methods. For example

```
public void Configure(IApplicationBuilder)
{
    app.UseStaticFiles();
    app.UseMvc();
}
```

When your app receives a request, the request passes through each middleware, which gets a chance to modify the request, or to handle it by generating a response. If a middleware component generates a response, it effectively short-circuits the pipeline; no subsequent middleware in the pipeline will see the request. The response passes back through the earlier middleware components on its way back to the browser.

You can use the `Run` extension method to build a simple middleware component that always generates a response. This extension takes a single lambda function that runs whenever a request reaches the component. The `Run` extension always generates a response, so no middleware placed after it will ever execute. For that reason, you should always place the `Run` middleware last in a middleware pipeline.

> **TIP** Remember, middleware runs in the order you add them to the pipeline. If a middleware handles a request and generates a response, later middleware will never see the request.

The `Run` extension method provides access to the request in the form of the `Http-Context` object you saw in chapter 3. This contains all the details of the request via the `Request` property, such as the URL path, the headers, and the body of the request. It also contains a `Response` property you can use to return a response.

The following listing shows how you could build a simple middleware that returns the current time. It uses the provided `HttpContext` context object and the `Response` property to set the `content-type` of the response and writes the body of the response using `WriteAsync(text)`.

Listing 19.1 Creating simple middleware using the `Run` extension

```
public void Configure(IApplicationBuilder app)       Uses the Run extension to create
{                                                    a simple middleware that always
    app.Run(async (context) =>        ◁───────────   returns a response
    {
        context.Response.ContentType = "text/plain";   ◁──   You should set the content-
        await context.Response.WriteAsync(                   type of the response you're
            DateTime.UtcNow.ToString());                     generating.
    });

    app.UseMvc();   ◁─────   Any middleware added after the     Returns the time as a string in
}                            Run extension will never execute.  the response. The 200 OK status
                                                                code is used if not explicitly set.
```

The Run extension is useful for building simple middleware. You can use it to create basic endpoints that always generate a response. But as the component always generates some sort of response, you must always place it at the end of the pipeline, as no middleware placed after it will execute.

A more common scenario is where you want your middleware component to only respond to a specific URL path. In the next section, you'll see how you can combine Run with the Map extension method to create branching middleware pipelines.

19.1.2 *Branching middleware pipelines with the Map extension*

So far, when discussing the middleware pipeline, we've always considered it as a single pipeline of sequential components. Each request passes through every middleware, until a component generates a response, which passes back through the previous middleware.

The Map extension method lets you change that simple pipeline into a branching structure. Each branch of the pipeline is independent; a request passes through one branch or the other, but not both, as shown in figure 19.1.

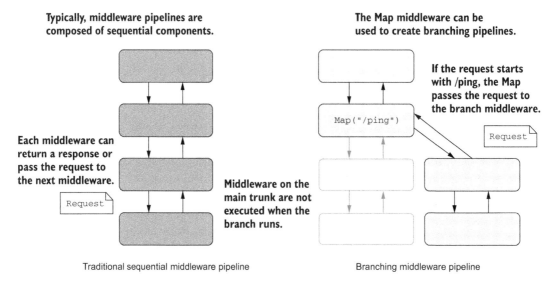

Typically, middleware pipelines are composed of sequential components.

Each middleware can return a response or pass the request to the next middleware.

Request

Traditional sequential middleware pipeline

The Map middleware can be used to create branching pipelines.

Map("/ping")

If the request starts with /ping, the Map passes the request to the branch middleware.

Request

Middleware on the main trunk are not executed when the branch runs.

Branching middleware pipeline

Figure 19.1 A sequential middleware pipeline compared to a branching pipeline created with the Map extension. In branching middleware, requests only pass through one of the branches at most. Middleware on the other branch never see the request and aren't executed.

The Map extension method looks at the path of the request's URL; if the path matches the required pattern, the request travels down the branch of the pipeline, otherwise it remains on the main trunk. This lets you have completely different behavior in different branches of your middleware pipeline.

For example, imagine you want to add a health-check endpoint to your existing app. This endpoint is a simple URL that you can call that indicates whether your app is running correctly. You could easily create a health-check middleware using the Run extension, as you saw in listing 19.1, but then that's *all* your app can do. You only want the health-check to respond to a specific URL, /ping; the MVC middleware should handle all other requests as normal.

One solution to this would be to create a branch using the Map extension method and to place the health-check middleware on that branch, as shown next. Only those requests that match the Map pattern /ping will execute the branch, all other requests will be handled by the MVC middleware on the main trunk instead.

Listing 19.2 Using the Map extension to create branching middleware pipelines

```
public void Configure(IApplicationBuilder app)
{
    app.UseDeveloperExceptionPage();          ◁──────

    app.Map("/ping", branch =>                ◁──────
    {
        branch.UseExceptionHandler();         ◁──────

        branch.Run(async (context) =>
        {
            context.Response.ContentType = "text/plain";
            await context.Response.WriteAsync("pong");
        });
    });

    app.UseMvc();          ◁──────
}
```

Every request will pass though this middleware.

The Map extension method will branch if a request starts with /ping.

This middleware will only run for requests matching the /ping branch.

The MvcMiddleware will run for requests that don't match the /ping branch.

The Run extension always returns a response, but only on the /ping branch.

The Map middleware creates a completely new IApplicationBuilder (called branch in the listing), which you can customize as you would your main app pipeline. Middleware added to the branch builder are only added to the branch pipeline, not the main trunk pipeline.

In this example, you added the Run middleware to the branch, so it will only execute for requests that start with /ping, such as /ping, /ping/go, or /ping?id=123. Any requests that don't start with /ping are ignored by the Map extension. Those requests stay on the main trunk pipeline and execute the next middleware in the pipeline after Map (in this case, MvcMiddleware).

If you need to, you can create elaborate branching pipelines in this way, where each branch is independent of every other. You could also nest calls to Map, so you have branches coming off branches.

The Map extension can be useful, but if you try to get too elaborate, it can quickly get confusing. Remember, you should use middleware for implementing cross-cutting concerns or simple endpoints. MvcMiddleware is better suited to more complex routing requirements, so don't be afraid to use it.

> **NOTE**   Under the hood, MvcMiddleware uses RouterMiddleware, which you can use independently of MVC if you want. I won't go into it in detail here, but can think of it as the Map extension on steroids (http://mng.bz/QDes).

The final point you should be aware of when using the Map extension is that it modifies the effective Path seen by middleware on the branch. When it matches a URL prefix, it cuts off the matched segment from the path, as shown in figure 19.2. The removed segments are stored on a property of HttpContext called PathBase, so they're still accessible if you need them. This lets you, for example, move MvcMiddleware to a branch without having to change all your routes, ensuring that URLs are still generated correctly.

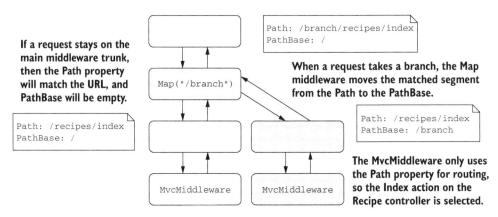

Figure 19.2   When the Map extension diverts a request to a branch, it removes the matched segment from the Path property and adds it to the PathBase property.

You've seen the Run extension, which always returns a response, and the Map extension which creates a branch in the pipeline. The next extension we'll look at is the general-purpose Use extension.

19.1.3   *Adding to the pipeline with the Use extension*

You can use the Use extension method to add a general-purpose piece of middleware. You can use it to view and modify requests as they arrive, to generate a response, or to pass the request on to subsequent middleware in the pipeline.

Similar to the Run extension, when you add the Use extension to your pipeline, you specify a lambda function that runs when a request reaches the middleware. The app passes two parameters to this function:

- The HttpContext representing the current request and response. You can use this to inspect the request or generate a response, as you saw with the Run extension.

- A pointer to the rest of the pipeline as a `Func<Task>`. By executing this task, you can execute the rest of the middleware pipeline.

By providing a pointer to the rest of the pipeline, you can use the `Use` extension to control exactly how and when the rest of the pipeline executes, as shown in figure 19.3. If you don't call the provided `Func<Task>` at all, then the rest of the pipeline doesn't execute for the request, so you have complete control.

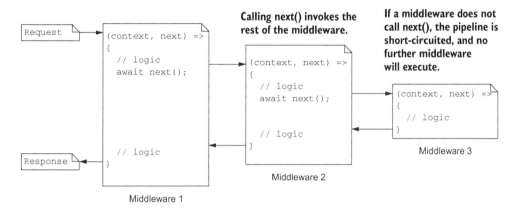

Figure 19.3   Three pieces of middleware, created with the `Use` extension. Invoking the provided `Func<Task>` using `next()` invokes the rest of the pipeline. Each middleware can run code before and after calling the rest of the pipeline, or it can choose to not call `next()` at all to short-circuit the pipeline.

Exposing the rest of the pipeline as a `Func<Task>` makes it easy to conditionally short-circuit the pipeline, which opens up many different scenarios. Instead of branching the pipeline to implement the health-check middleware with `Map` and `Run`, as you did in listing 19.2, you could use a single instance of the `Use` extension. This provides the same required functionality as before but does so without branching the pipeline.

Listing 19.3   Using the `Use` extension method to create a health-check middleware

The Use extension takes a lambda with HttpContext (context) and Func<Task> (next) parameters.

The StartsWithSegments method looks for the provided segment in the current path.

```
public void Configure(IApplicationBuilder app)
{
    app.Use(async (context, next) =>
    {
        if (context.Request.Path.StartsWithSegments("/ping"))
        {
            context.Response.ContentType = "text/plain";
            await context.Response.WriteAsync("pong");
        }
        else
```

If the path matches, generate a response, and short-circuit the pipeline

```
        {
                await next();          ◁
        }
    });

    app.UseMvc();
}
```

> If the path doesn't match,
> call the next middleware in
> the pipeline, in this case
> the MvcMiddleware.

If the incoming request starts with the required path segment (/ping), then the middleware responds and doesn't call the rest of the pipeline. If the incoming request doesn't start with /ping, then the extension calls the next middleware in the pipeline, no branching necessary.

With the Use extension, you have control over when, and if, you call the rest of the middleware pipeline. But it's important to note that you generally shouldn't modify the Response object after calling next(). Calling next() runs the rest of the middleware pipeline, so a subsequent middleware may have already started sending the response to the browser. If you try to modify the response after executing the pipeline, you may end up corrupting the response or sending invalid data.

> **WARNING**   Don't modify the Response object after calling next(). Also, don't call next() if you've written to the response body with WriteAsync(), as the response may have already started sending and you could cause invalid data to be sent.

Another common use for the Use extension method is to modify every request or response that passes through it. For example, HTTP Strict-Transport-Security (HSTS) is a header you can send with every response that tells the browser to always load your app over HTTPS rather than HTTP.[1]

Imagine you've been tasked with adding the HSTS header to every response generated by your app. This sort of cross-cutting concern is perfect for middleware. You can use the Use extension method to intercept every request, set the response header, and then execute the rest of the middleware pipeline. No matter what response the pipeline generates, whether it's a static file, an error, or a Razor-rendered view, the response will always have the HSTS header.

Listing 19.4 shows a robust way to achieve this. When the middleware receives a request, it registers a callback that runs before Kestrel starts sending the response back to the browser. It then calls next() to run the rest of the middleware pipeline. When the pipeline generates a response, the callback runs and adds the HSTS header. This approach ensures the header isn't accidentally removed by other middleware in the pipeline.

---

[1] You can use this header in combination with the techniques described in chapter 18 to enforce HTTPS. For a summary of how the Strict-Transport-Header works and its benefits, check out this post by Scott Helme: https://scotthelme.co.uk/hsts-the-missing-link-in-tls/.

Listing 19.4 Adding headers to a response with the Use extension

```
public void Configure(IApplicationBuilder app)          Adds the middleware at
{                                                        the start of the pipeline
    app.Use(async (context, next) =>          ◄─┐
    {                                             ├── Sets a function that should be
        context.Response.OnStarting(() =>       ◄─┘    called before the response is
        {                                             sent to the browser
            context.Response.Headers["Strict-Transport-Security"] = ┐
                "max-age=60";                                       │
            return Task.CompletedTask;                              ├── Adds an HSTS header. For
        });                                                         │   60 seconds the browser
        await next();          ◄──┐                                 │   will only send HTTPS
    }                             │ Invokes the rest of the         ┘   requests to your app.
                                  │ middleware pipeline
    app.UseMvc();      ◄──┐
}                         │ No matter what response the
                          │ MvcMiddleware generates, it'll
                          │ have the HSTS header.
```

The function passed to OnStarting must return a Task.

Simple cross-cutting middleware like the health-check and HSTS examples in this section are common, but they can quickly clutter your Configure method, and make it difficult to understand the pipeline at a glance. Instead, it's common to encapsulate your middleware into a class that's functionally equivalent to the Use extension, but which can be easily tested and reused.

19.1.4 Building a custom middleware component

Creating middleware with the Use extension, as you did in listings 19.3 and 19.4, is convenient but it's not easy to test, and you're somewhat limited in what you can do. You can't easily use DI to inject scoped services inside of these basic middleware components. Normally, rather than calling the Use extension directly, you'll encapsulate your middleware into a class that's functionally equivalent.

Custom middleware components don't derive from a particular base class, but they have a certain shape, as shown in listing 19.5. In particular, middleware classes should have a constructor that takes a RequestDelegate object, which represents the rest of the middleware pipeline, and they should have an Invoke function with a signature similar to

```
public Task Invoke(HttpContext context);
```

The Invoke() function is equivalent to the lambda function from the Use extension, and is called when a request is received. Here's how you could convert the headers middleware from listing 19.4 into a standalone middleware class.[2]

---

[2] Using this shape approach makes the middleware more flexible. In particular, it means you can easily use DI to inject services into the Invoke method. This wouldn't be possible if the Invoke method were an overridden base class method or an interface.

Listing 19.5   Adding headers to a `Response` using a custom middleware component

```
public class HeadersMiddleware
{
    private readonly RequestDelegate _next;
    public HeadersMiddleware(RequestDelegate next)      The RequestDelegate
    {                                                    represents the rest of
        _next = next;                                    the middleware pipeline
    }

    public async Task Invoke(HttpContext context)       The Invoke method is
    {                                                    called with HttpContext
        context.Response.OnStarting(() =>                when a request is received.
        {
            context.Response.Headers["Strict-Transport-Security"] =
                "max-age=60";
            return Task.CompletedTask;
        });                                              Invokes the rest of the middleware
                                                         pipeline. Note that you must pass
        await _next(context);                            in the provided HttpContext.
    }
}
```

Adds the HSTS header response as before

Adds the HSTS header response as before

This middleware is effectively identical to the example in listing 19.4 but encapsulated in a class called `HeadersMiddleware`. You can add this middleware to your app in `Startup.Configure` by calling

```
app.UseMiddleware<HeadersMiddleware>();
```

A common pattern is to create helper extension methods to make it easy to consume your extension method from `Startup.Configure` (IntelliSense reveals it as an option on the `IApplicationBuilder` instance). Here's how you could create a simple extension method for `HeadersMiddleware`.

Listing 19.6   Creating an extension method to expose `HeadersMiddleware`

```
public static class MiddlewareExtensions                By convention, the
{                                                        extension method should
    public static IApplicationBuilder UseSecurityHeaders(  return an
        this IApplicationBuilder app)                    IApplicationBuilder to
    {                                                    allow chaining
        return app.UseMiddleware<HeadersMiddleware>();
    }                                                    Adds the middleware
}                                                        to the pipeline
```

With this extension method, you can now add the headers middleware to your app using

```
app.UseSecurityHeaders();
```

This is a simple example, but you can create middleware for many different purposes. In some cases, you may need to use DI to inject services and use them to handle a request. You can inject singleton services into the constructor of your middleware component, or you can inject services with any lifetime into the `Invoke` method of your middleware, as demonstrated in the following listing.

Listing 19.7   Using DI in middleware components

```
public class ExampleMiddleware                      You can inject additional
{                                                   services in the constructor.
    private readonly RequestDelegate _next;         These must be singletons.
    private readonly ServiceA _a;
    public HeadersMiddleware(RequestDelegate next, ServiceA a)
    {
        _next = next;
        _a = a;       ◁─────────────────────────
    }
                                                    You can inject services into
                                                    the Invoke method. These
    public async Task Invoke(                        may have any lifetime
        HttpContext context, Service b, service c)  ◁──┘
    {
        // use services a, b, and c
        // and/or call _next.Invoke(context);
    }
}
```

WARNING   ASP.NET Core creates the middleware only once for the lifetime of your app, so any dependencies injected in the constructor must be singletons. If you need to use scoped or transient dependencies, inject them into the `Invoke` method.

That covers pretty much everything you need to start building your own middleware components. By encapsulating your middleware into custom classes, you can easily test their behavior, or distribute them in NuGet packages, so I strongly recommend taking this approach. Apart from anything else, it will make your `Startup.Configure()` method less cluttered and easier to understand.

In the next section, we'll look at how to handle complex configuration requirements. In particular, you'll see how to set up complex configuration providers that require their own configuration values, and how to use DI services to build your strongly typed `IOptions` objects.

19.2   *Handling complex configuration requirements*

In chapter 11, we discussed the ASP.NET Core configuration system in depth. You saw how an `IConfiguration` object is built from multiple layers, where subsequent layers can add to or replace configuration values from previous layers. Each layer is added by a configuration provider, which can read values from a file, from environment variables, from User Secrets, or from any number of possible locations.

You also saw how to *bind* configuration values to strongly typed POCO objects, using the `IOptions` interface. You can inject these strongly typed objects into your classes to provide easy access to your settings, instead of having to read configuration using string keys.

In this section, we'll look at two scenarios that are slightly more complex. In the first scenario, you're trying to use a configuration provider that requires some configuration itself.

As an example, imagine you want to store some configuration in a database table. In order to load these values, you'd need some sort of connection string, which would most likely also come from your IConfiguration. You're stuck with a chicken-and-egg situation: you need to build the IConfiguration object to add the provider, but you can't add the provider without building the IConfiguration object!

In the second scenario, you want to configure a strongly typed IOptions object with values returned from a service. But the service won't be available until after you've configured all of the IOptions objects. In section 19.2.2, you'll see how to handle this by implementing the IConfigureOptions interface.

19.2.1 *Partially building configuration to configure additional providers*

ASP.NET Core includes many configuration providers, such as file and environment variable providers, that don't require anything more than basic details to set up. All you need to read a JSON file, for example, is the path to the file.

But the configuration system is extensible, so this might not be the case for more complex configuration providers. You may have a configuration provider that loads configuration values from a database, a provider that loads values from a remote API, or a provider that loads secrets from Azure Key Vault.[3]

These more complex configuration providers typically require some sort of configuration themselves, such as a connection string for a database, a URL for a remote service, or a secret to decrypt the data. Unfortunately, this leaves you with a circular problem: you need to add the provider to build your configuration object, but you need a configuration object in order to add the provider!

The solution is to use a two-stage process to build your final IConfiguration configuration object, as shown in figure 19.4. In the first stage, you load the configuration values that are available locally, such as JSON files and environment variables, and build a temporary IConfiguration. You can use this object to configure the complex providers, add them to your configuration builder, and build the final IConfiguration for your app.

You can use this two-phase process whenever you have configuration providers that need configuration themselves. In listing 19.8, you'll create a temporary IConfiguration

---

[3] Azure Key Vault is a service that lets you securely store secrets in the cloud. Your app retrieves the secrets from Azure Key Vault at runtime by calling an API and providing a client ID and a secret. The client ID and secret must come from local configuration values, so that you can retrieve the rest from Azure Key Vault. Read more, including how to get started, at http://mng.bz/96aQ.

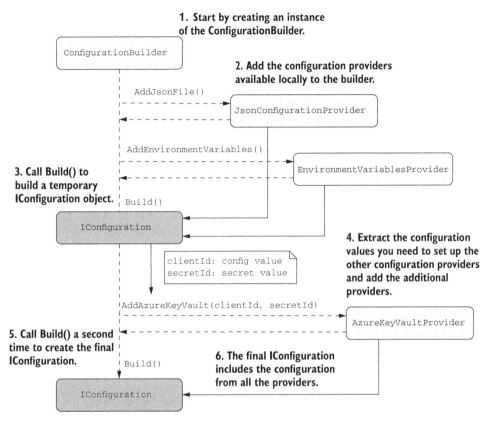

1. Start by creating an instance of the ConfigurationBuilder.

ConfigurationBuilder

2. Add the configuration providers available locally to the builder.

AddJsonFile()

JsonConfigurationProvider

AddEnvironmentVariables()

EnvironmentVariablesProvider

3. Call Build() to build a temporary IConfiguration object.

Build()

IConfiguration

clientId: config value
secretId: secret value

4. Extract the configuration values you need to set up the other configuration providers and add the additional providers.

AddAzureKeyVault(clientId, secretId)

AzureKeyVaultProvider

5. Call Build() a second time to create the final IConfiguration.

Build()

6. The final IConfiguration includes the configuration from all the providers.

IConfiguration

Figure 19.4 Adding a configuration provider that requires configuration. Start by adding configuration providers that you have the details for and build a temporary IConfiguration object. You can use this configuration object to load the settings required by the complex provider, add the provider to your builder, and build the final IConfiguration object using all three providers.

object built using the contents of an XML file. This contains a configuration property called "SettingsFile" with the filename of a JSON file.

In the second phase of configuration, add the JSON file provider (using the filename from the partial IConfiguration) and the environment variable provider. When you finally call Build() on the WebHostBuilder, a new IConfiguration object will be built, containing the configuration values from the XML file, the JSON file, and the environment variables.

Listing 19.8 Using multiple IConfiguration objects to configure providers

```
public static IWebHost BuildWebHost(string[] args) =>
    new WebHostBuilder()
        .UseKestrel()
        .UseContentRoot(Directory.GetCurrentDirectory())
        .ConfigureAppConfiguration((context, config) =>
```

**Builds the
IConfiguration
to read the
XML file**

**Adds an XML file to the
configuration, which contains
configuration for other providers**

```
{
    config.AddXmlFile("baseconfig.xml");
    IConfiguration partialConfig = config.Build();
    string filename = partialConfig["SettingsFile"];

    config.AddJsonFile(filename)
        .AddEnvironmentVariables();
})
.UseStartup<Startup>()
.Build();
```

**Extracts the
configuration
required by
other
providers**

**Calling Build() rebuilds the IConfiguration
with the XML file, JSON file, and
environment variables**

**Remember, values from
subsequent providers
will overwrite values
from previous providers.**

**Uses the extracted
configuration to
configure other
providers**

This is a somewhat contrived example—it's unlikely that you'd need to load configuration values to read a JSON file—but the principle is the same no matter which provider you use. A good example of this is the Azure Key Value provider. In order to load configuration from Azure Key Vault, you need a URL, a client ID, and a secret. These must be loaded from other configuration providers, so you have to use the same two-phase process.

Once you've loaded the configuration for your app, it's common to *bind* this configuration to strongly typed objects using the IOptions pattern. In the next section, we look at other ways to configure your IOptions objects and how to use DI services.

19.2.2 *Using services to configure IOptions with IConfigureOptions*

A common and encouraged practice is to bind your configuration object to strongly typed IOptions<T> objects, as you saw in chapter 11. Typically, you configure this binding in ConfigureServices by calling services.Configure<T>() and providing an IConfiguration object or section to bind.

To bind a strongly typed object, called CurrencyOptions, to the "Currencies" section of an IConfiguration object, you'd use

```
public void ConfigureServices(IServiceCollection services)
{
    services.Configure<CurrencyOptions>(
        Configuration.GetSection("Currencies"));
}
```

This sets the properties of the CurrencyOptions object, based on the values in the "Currencies" section of your IConfiguration object. Sometimes, you might want to customize the configuration of your IOptions<T> objects, or you might not want to bind them to configuration at all. The IOptions pattern only requires you to configure a strongly typed object before it's injected into a dependent service, it doesn't mandate that you *have* to bind it to an IConfiguration section.

The services.Configure<T>() method has an overload that lets you provide a lambda function that will also be used to configure the CurrencyOptions object. For example, in the following snippet, use a lambda function to set the `Currencies` property on the configured `CurrencyOptions` object to an array of strings:

```
public void ConfigureServices(IServiceCollection services)
{
    services.Configure<CurrencyOptions>(
        Configuration.GetSection("Currencies"));
    services.Configure<CurrencyOptions>(options =>
        options.Currencies = new string[] { "GBP", "USD"});
    services.AddMvc();
}
```

Each call to `Configure<T>()`, both the binding to `IConfiguration` and the lambda function, adds another configuration step to the `CurrencyOptions` object. When the DI container first requires an instance of `IOptions<CurrencyOptions>`, each of the steps run in turn, as shown in figure 19.5.

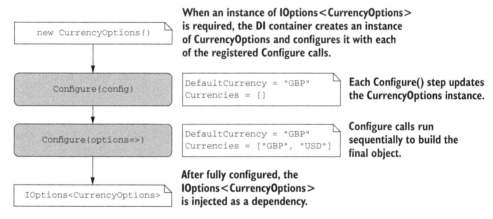

Figure 19.5 Configuring a `CurrencyOptions` object. When the DI container needs an `IOptions<>` instance of a strongly typed object, the container creates the object, and then uses each of the registered `Configure()` methods to set the object's properties.

In the example, you set the `Currencies` property to a static array of strings in a lambda function. But what if you don't know the correct values ahead of time? You might need to load the available currencies from a database, or from some other service.

Unfortunately, this situation, where you need a configured service to configure your `IOptions<T>` is hard to resolve. Remember, you declare your `IOptions<T>` configuration inside `ConfigureServices`, as part of the DI configuration. How can you get a fully configured instance of a currency service if you haven't registered it with the container yet?

The solution is to defer the configuration of your `IOptions<T>` object until the last moment, just before the DI container needs to create it to handle an incoming request. At that point, the DI container will be completely configured and will know how to create the currency service.

ASP.NET Core provides this mechanism with the `IConfigureOptions<T>` interface. You implement this interface in a configuration class and use it to configure the `IOptions<T>` object in any way you need. This class can use DI, so you can easily use any other required services.

> **Listing 19.9   Implementing `IConfigureOptions<T>` to configure an options object**

```
public class ConfigureCurrencyOptions : IConfigureOptions<CurrencyOptions>
{
    private readonly ICurrencyProvider _currencyProvider;
    public ConfigureCurrencyOptions(ICurrencyProvider currencyProvider)
    {
        _currencyProvider = currencyProvider;
    }

    public void Configure(CurrencyOptions options)
    {
        options.Currencies = _currencyProvider.GetCurrencies();
    }
}
```

Configure is called when an instance of IOptions `<CurrencyOptions>` is required.

You can inject services that are only available after the DI is completely configured.

You can use the injected service to load the values from a remote API, for example.

All that remains is to register this implementation in the DI container. As always, order is important, so if you want `ConfigureCurrencyOptions` to run *after* binding to configuration, you must add it after the first call to `services.Configure<T>()`:

```
public void ConfigureServices(IServiceCollection services)
{
    services.Configure<CurrencyOptions>(
        Configuration.GetSection("Currencies"));
    services.AddSingleton
        <IConfigureOptions<CurrencyOptions>, ConfigureCurrencyOptions>();
}
```

> **WARNING**   The `CurrencyConfigureOptions` object is registered as a singleton, so it will capture any injected services of scoped or transient lifetimes.[4]

With this configuration, when `IOptions<CurrencyOptions>` is injected into a controller or service, the `CurrencyOptions` object will first be bound to the `"Currencies"` section of your `IConfiguration` and will then be configured by the `ConfigureCurrencyOptions` class.

One piece of configuration not yet shown is `ICurrencyProvider` used by `ConfigureCurrencyOptions`. In the sample code for this chapter, I created a simple `CurrencyProvider` service and registered it with the DI container using

```
services.AddSingleton<ICurrencyProvider, CurrencyProvider>();
```

---

[4]   If you inject a scoped service into your configuration class (for example, a DbContext), you need to do a bit more work to ensure it's disposed of correctly. I describe how to achieve that here: http://mng.bz/6m17.

As your app grows and you add extra features and services, you'll probably find yourself writing more and more of these simple DI registrations, where you register a `Service` that implements `IService`. The built-in ASP.NET Core DI container requires you to explicitly register each of these services manually. If you find yourself getting frustrated, it may be time to look at third-party DI containers that can take care of this boilerplate for you.

19.3 *Using a third-party dependency injection container*

The .NET community had been using DI containers for years before ASP.NET Core decided to include one that is built-in. The ASP.NET Core team wanted a way to use DI in their own framework libraries, and to create a common abstraction[5] that allows you to replace the built-in container with your favorite third-party alternative, such as

- Autofac
- StructureMap
- Ninject
- Simple Injector

The built-in container is intentionally limited in the features it provides, and it won't be getting many more realistically. In contrast, third-party containers can provide a host of extra features. These are some of the features available in StructureMap (http://structuremap.github.io/):

- Assembly scanning for interface/implementation pairs based on conventions
- Automatic concrete class registration
- Property injection and constructor selection
- Automatic `Lazy<T>`/`Func<T>` resolution
- Debugging/testing tools for viewing inside your container

None of these features is a requirement for getting an application up and running, so using the built-in container makes a lot of sense if you're building a small app or you're new to DI containers in general. But if, at some undefined tipping point, the simplicity of the built-in container becomes too much of a burden, it may be worth replacing it.

In this section, I show how you can configure an ASP.NET Core app to use Structure-Map for dependency resolution. It won't be a complex example, or an in-depth discussion of StructureMap itself. Instead, I'll cover the bare minimum to get up and running.

Whichever third-party container you choose to install into an existing app, the overall process is pretty much the same:

---

[5] Although the promotion of DI as a core practice has been applauded, this abstraction has seen some controversy. This post from one of the maintainers of the SimpleInjector DI library describes many of the arguments and concerns: http://mng.bz/KLuU. You can also read more about the decisions here: https://github.com/aspnet/DependencyInjection/issues/433.

1   Install the container NuGet package.
2   Return an `IServiceProvider` from `Startup.ConfigureServices`.
3   Configure the third-party container to register your services and populate with services already registered in the built-in container.

Most of the major .NET DI containers have been ported to work on .NET Core and include an adapter that lets you add them to ASP.NET Core apps. For details, it's worth consulting the specific guidance for the container you're using. For Structure-Map, that process looks like this:

1   Install the StructureMap.Microsoft.DependencyInjection NuGet package using the NuGet package manager, by running dotnet add package

```
dotnet add package StructureMap.Microsoft.DependencyInjection
```

or by adding a `<PackageReference>` to your csproj file

```
<PackageReference
    Include="StructureMap.Microsoft.DependencyInjection" Version="1.4.0" />
```

2   Update the signature of your `Startup.ConfigureServices()` method to return an `IServiceProvider` instead of `void`. For example, change

```
public void ConfigureServices(IServiceCollection services)
```

to

```
public IServiceProvider ConfigureServices(IServiceCollection services)
```

3   Configure the StructureMap container and call `Populate(services)` to add the built-in container's registered services to the StructureMap container, as shown here. This is a basic configuration, but you can see a more complex example in the source code for this chapter.

> **Listing 19.10   Configuring StructureMap as a third-party DI container**

```
public IServiceProvider ConfigureServices(          Updates ConfigureServices to return
    IServiceCollection services)                    IServiceProvider instead of void
{
    services.AddAuthorization();                You can add ASP.NET Core services to the
    services.AddMvc()                           IServiceCollection as usual.
        .AddControllersAsServices();        ◁
                                                Required so that StructureMap is
    var container = new Container();            used to build your MVC controllers.

    container.Configure(config => {
        config.Scan(_ => {
            _.AssemblyContainingType(typeof(Startup));      StructureMap can
            _.WithDefaultConventions();                     automatically scan for
        })                                                  services to register.
```

Creates a StructureMap container

Configures the StructureMap container
with your service registrations

```
        config.Populate(services);          ◁─────────────────────
    });

    return container.GetInstance<IServiceProvider>();  ◁───
}
```

Calls Populate() to add the services registered in the built-in container to StructureMap

Returns an IServiceProvider. ASP.NET Core will use this instead of the built-in container.

In this example, I've used the default conventions to register services. This will automatically register concrete classes and services that are named following expected conventions (for example, `Service` implements `IService`). You can change these conventions or add other registrations in the `container.Configure` method.

The call to `Populate()` adds all services previously registered with the built-in container with StructureMap. That means you can use the built-in extension methods, such as `AddMvc()` and `AddAuthorization()`, and the associated services will automatically be added to StructureMap.

> **WARNING** If you're using DI in your MVC controllers (almost certainly!) and you register those dependencies with StructureMap, rather than the built-in container, you may need to call `AddControllersAsServices()`, as shown in listing 19.10. This is due to an implementation detail in the way the MVC middleware creates your MVC controllers.

Finally, by calling `GetInstance<IServiceProvider>` on your StructureMap container, and returning the instance from `ConfigureServices()`, ASP.NET Core knows to use StructureMap instead of the built-in container. Whenever the framework needs to create a service, it will request it from the StructureMap container, which will create the dependency tree for the class and create an instance.

That marks the end of the first half of this chapter. You've seen how to create custom middleware, how to add complex configuration providers, how to use DI when configuring `IOptions`, and how to add a third-party DI container. In the second half of the chapter, we focus on building custom MVC components.

19.4 Creating a custom Razor Tag Helper

In my opinion, Tag Helpers are one of the best new additions to Razor in ASP.NET Core. They allow you to write Razor templates that are easier to read, as they require less switching between C# and HTML, and they *augment* your HTML tags, rather than replacing them (as opposed to the HTML Helpers used extensively in the previous version of ASP.NET).

ASP.NET Core comes with a wide variety of Tag Helpers (see chapter 8), which will cover many of your day-to-day requirements, especially when it comes to building forms. But you can also create your own custom Tag Helpers to help reduce the duplication in your code, or to simplify common patterns.

In this section, I show how to create two simple Tag Helpers. In section 19.4.1, you create a system information Tag Helper, which prints details about the name and

operating system of the server your app is running on. In section 19.4.2, you create a
Tag Helper that you can use to conditionally show or hide an element based on a C#
Boolean property.

19.4.1 Printing environment information with a custom Tag Helper

A common problem you may run into when you start running your web applications
using a server-farm setup is working out which machine rendered the page you're currently looking at. When I'm developing and testing, I sometimes like to add a little
"info dump" at the bottom of my layouts, so I can easily work out which server generated the current page, which environment it's running in, and so on.

In this section, I'm going to show you how to build a custom Tag Helper to output
system information to your layout. You'll be able to toggle the information it displays,
but by default, it will display the machine name and operating system on which the
app is running, as shown in figure 19.6.

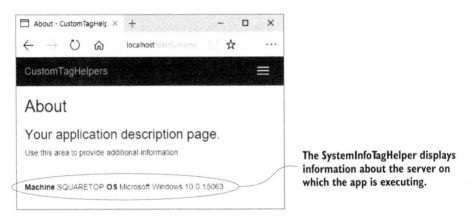

The SystemInfoTagHelper displays
information about the server on
which the app is executing.

**Figure 19.6   The `SystemInfoTagHelper` displays the machine name and operating system
on which the application is running. It can be useful for identifying which instance of your app
handled the request when running in a web farm scenario.**

You can call this Tag Helper from Razor by creating a `<system-info>` element in your
template, for example:

```
<footer>
  <system-info></system-info>
</footer>
```

> **TIP**   You probably don't want to expose this sort of information in produc-
> tion, so you could also wrap it in an `<environment>` Tag Helper, as you saw in
> chapter 8.

The easiest way to create a custom Tag Helper is to derive from the `TagHelper` base
class and override the `Process()` or `ProcessAsync()` function that describes how the
class should render itself. The following listing shows your complete custom Tag

Helper, the `SystemInfoTagHelper`, which renders the system information to a `<div>`. You could easily extend this class if you wanted to display additional fields or add additional options.

Listing 19.11 `SystemInfoTagHelper` to render system information to a view

Derives from the TagHelper base class

```
public class SystemInfoTagHelper : TagHelper
{
    private readonly HtmlEncoder _htmlEncoder;
    public SystemInfoTagHelper(HtmlEncoder htmlEncoder)
    {
        _htmlEncoder = htmlEncoder;
    }

    [HtmlAttributeName("add-machine")]
    public bool IncludeMachine { get; set; } = true;

    [HtmlAttributeName("add-os")]
    public bool IncludeOS { get; set; } = true;

    public override void Process(
        TagHelperContext context, TagHelperOutput output)
    {
        output.TagName = "div";
        output.TagMode = TagMode.StartTagAndEndTag;

        var sb = new StringBuilder();
        if (IncludeMachine)
        {
            sb.Append(" <strong>Machine</strong> ");
            sb.Append(_htmlEncoder.Encode(Environment.MachineName));
        }
        if (IncludeOS)
        {
            sb.Append(" <strong>OS</strong> ");
            sb.Append(
                _htmlEncoder.Encode(RuntimeInformation.OSDescription));
        }

        output.Content.SetHtmlContent(sb.ToString());
    }
}
```

An HtmlEncoder is necessary when writing HTML content to the page.

Decorating properties with HtmlAttributeName allows you to set their value from Razor markup

The main function called when an element is rendered.

Renders both the `<div>` `</div>` start and end tag

Replaces the `<system-info>` element with a `<div>` element

If required, adds a `<strong>` element and the HTML-encoded machine name

Sets the inner content of the `<div>` tag with the HTML-encoded value stored in the string builder

If required, adds a `<strong>` element and the HTML-encoded OS name

There's a lot of new code in this sample, so we'll work through it line by line. First, the class name of the Tag Helper defines the name of the element you must create in the Razor template, with the suffix removed and converted to kebab-case. As this Tag Helper is called `SystemInfoTagHelper`, you must create a `<system-info>` element.

> **TIP**   If you want to customize the name of the element, for example to `<env-info>`, and keep the same class name, you can apply the `[HtmlTarget-Element]` with the desired name, such as `[HtmlTargetElement("EnvInfo")]`.

Inject an `HtmlEncoder` into your Tag Helper so you can HTML-encode any data you write to the page. As you saw in chapter 18, you should always HTML-encode data you write to the page to avoid XSS vulnerabilities (and to ensure the data is displayed correctly).

You've defined two properties on your Tag Helper, `IncludeMachine` and `IncludeOS`, which you'll use to control which data is written to the page. These are decorated with a corresponding `[HtmlAttributeName]`, which enables setting the properties from the Razor template. In Visual Studio, you'll even get IntelliSense and type checking for these values, as shown in figure 19.7.

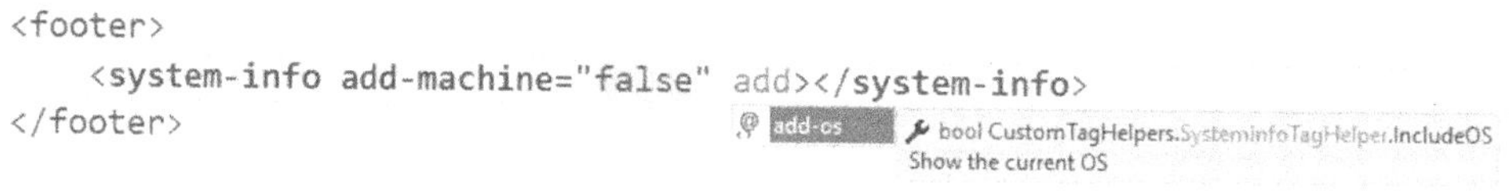

```
<footer>
    <system-info add-machine="false" add></system-info>
</footer>
```

Figure 19.7   In Visual Studio, Tag Helpers are shown in a purple font and you get IntelliSense for properties decorated with [HtmlAttributeName].

Finally, we come to the `Process()` method. The Razor engine calls this method to execute the Tag Helper when it identifies it in a view template. This method defines the type of tag to render (`<div>`), whether it should render a start and end tag (or a self-closing tag, it depends on the type of tag you're rendering), and the HTML content of the `<div>`. You set the HTML content to be rendered inside the tag by calling `Content.SetHtmlContent()` on the provided instance of `TagHelperOutput`.

> **WARNING**   Always HTML-encode your output before writing to your tag with `SetHtmlContent()`. Alternatively, pass unencoded input to `SetContent()` and the output will be automatically HTML-encoded for you.

Before you can use your new Tag Helper in a Razor template, you need to register it. You can do this in the _ViewImports.cshtml file, using the `@addTagHelper` directive and specifying the fully qualified name of the Tag Helper and the assembly. For example,

```
@addTagHelper CustomTagHelpers.SystemInfoTagHelper, CustomTagHelpers
```

Alternatively, you can add all the Tag Helpers from a given assembly by using the wildcard syntax, `*`, and specifying the assembly name:

```
@addTagHelper *, CustomTagHelpers
```

With your custom Tag Helper created and registered, you're now free to use it in any of your Razor views, partial views, or layouts.

The `SystemInfoTagHelper` is an example of a Tag Helper that generates content, but you can also use Tag Helpers to control how existing elements are rendered. In the next section, you'll create a simple Tag Helper that can control whether or not an element is rendered, based on an attribute.

19.4.2 Creating a custom Tag Helper to conditionally hide elements

If you want to control whether an element is displayed in a Razor template based on some C# variable, then you'd typically wrap the element in a C# `if` statement:

```
@{
    var showContent = true;
}
@if(showContent)
{
    <p>The content to show</p>
}
```

Falling back to C# constructs like this can be useful, as it allows you to generate any markup you like. Unfortunately, it can be mentally disruptive having to switch back and forth between C# and HTML, and it makes it harder to use HTML editors that don't understand Razor syntax.

In this section, you'll create a simple Tag Helper to avoid the dissonance problem. You can apply this Tag Helper to existing elements to achieve the same result as shown previously, but without having to fall back to C#:

```
@{
    var showContent = true;
}
<p if="showContent">
    The content to show
</p>
```

Instead of creating a new *element*, as you did for `SystemInfoTagHelper` (`<system-info>`), you'll create a Tag Helper that you apply as an *attribute* to existing HTML elements. This Tag Helper does one thing: it controls the visibility of the element it's attached to. If the value passed in the `if` attribute is `true`, the element and its content is rendered as normal. If the value passed is `false`, the Tag Helper removes the element and its content from the template. Here's how you could achieve this.

Listing 19.12 Creating an `IfTagHelper` to conditionally render elements

```
[HtmlTargetElement(Attributes = "if")]     ⤝  Setting the Attributes property ensures the
public class IfTagHelper : TagHelper            Tag Helper is triggered by an if attribute.
{
    [HtmlAttributeName("if")]              ⤝  Binds the value of the if attribute
    public bool RenderContent { get; set; } = true;   to the RenderContent property

    public override void Process(          ⤝  The Razor engine calls
        TagHelperContext context, TagHelperOutput output)   Process() to execute
                                                            the Tag Helper.
```

```
    {
        if(RenderContent == false)
        {
            output.TagName = null;
            output.SuppressOutput();
        }
        output.Attributes.RemoveAll("if");
    }
    public override int Order => int.MinValue;
}
```

If the RenderContent property evaluates to false, removes the element

Sets the element the Tag Helper resides on to null, removing it from the page

Doesn't render or evaluate the inner content of the element

Ensures this Tag Helper runs before any others attached to the element

If you render the element, remove the if attribute. It's only there to attach the Tag Helper.

Instead of a standalone `<if>` element, the Razor engine executes the `IfTagHelper` whenever it finds an element with an `if` attribute. Define a Boolean property for whether you should render the content, which is bound to the value in the `if` attribute.

The `Process()` function is much simpler here. If `RenderContent` is `false`, then set the `TagHelperOutput.TagName` to `null`, which removes the element from the page. You also call `SuppressOutput()`, which prevents any content inside the element from being rendered. If `RenderContent` is `true`, then you skip these steps and the content is rendered as normal.

Finally, remove the `if` attribute itself from the output. You don't want the `if` attribute to be rendered in the final HTML (it's only there to enable your Tag Helper to run) so remove it from the `Attributes` collection.

One other point of note is the overridden `Order` property. This controls the order in which Tag Helpers run when multiple Tag Helpers are applied to an element. By setting `Order` to `int.MinValue`, you ensure `IfTagHelper` will run first, removing the element if required, before other Tag Helpers execute. There's no point running other Tag Helpers if the element is going to be removed from the page anyway!

> **NOTE** Remember to register your custom Tag Helpers in _ViewImports .cshtml with the `@addTagHelper` directive.

With a simple HTML attribute, you can now conditionally render elements in Razor templates, without having to fall back to C#. The Tag Helpers in this section represent a small sample of possible avenues you could explore,[6] but they cover the two broad categories: Tag Helpers for rendering new content, and Tag Helpers for controlling the rendering of other elements.

---

[6] For further details and examples, see the documentation at http://mng.bz/ldb0. Damian Edwards, project manager for ASP.NET Core, also has source code for additional Tag Helpers available on GitHub: https://github.com/DamianEdwards/TagHelperPack/.

Tag Helpers can be useful for providing small pieces of isolated, reusable functionality like this, but they're not designed to provide larger, application-specific sections of an app or to make calls to business-logic services. Instead, you should use view components, as you'll see in the next section.

19.5 View components: adding logic to partial views

If you think about a typical website, you'll notice that they often have multiple independent dynamic sections, in addition to the main content. Consider Stack Overflow, shown in figure 19.8, for example. As well as the main body of the page showing questions and answers, there's a section showing the current logged-in user, a panel for blog posts and related items, and a section for job suggestions.

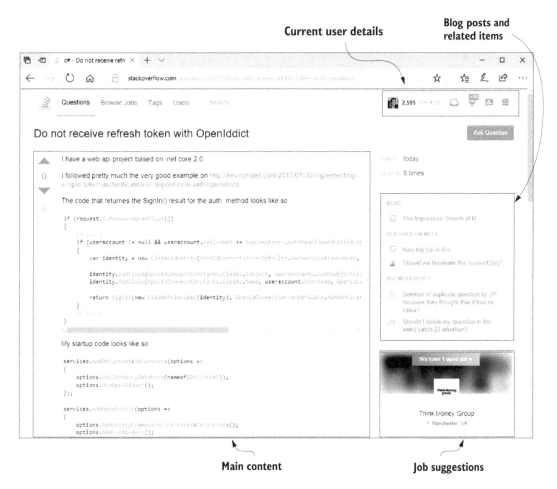

Figure 19.8 The Stack Overflow website has multiple sections that are independent of the main content but which contain business logic and complex rendering logic. Each of these sections could be rendered as a view Component in ASP.NET Core.

Each of these sections is effectively independent of the main content, and contains business logic (deciding which posts to show), database access (loading the details of the posts), and rendering logic for how to display the data. In chapter 7, you saw that you can use layouts and partial views to split up the rendering of a view template into similar sections, but partial views aren't a good fit for this example. Partial views let you encapsulate *view rendering* logic, but not *business* logic that's independent of the main page content.

Instead, view components provide this functionality. View components can contain business logic. You can use DI to provide access to a database context, and you can test them independently of the view they generate, much like MVC controllers. Think of them a bit like mini-MVC controllers, but you invoke them directly from a view template or layout, instead of in response to an HTTP request.

> **TIP** View components are comparable to *child actions* from the previous version of ASP.NET, in that they provide similar functionality. Child actions don't exist in ASP.NET Core.

In this section, you'll see how to create a custom view component for the recipe app you built in previous chapters, as shown in figure 19.9. If the current user is logged in, the view component displays a panel with a list of links to the user's recently created recipes. For unauthenticated users, the view component displays links to the login and register actions.

This component is a good candidate for a view component as it contains database access and business logic (choosing which recipes to display), as well as rendering logic (how the panel should be displayed).

> **TIP** Use partial views when you want to encapsulate the rendering of a specific view model, or part of a view model. When you have rendering logic that requires business logic or database access, or where the section is logically distinct from the main page content, consider using a view component.

You invoke view components directly from views and layouts. You can invoke them in two different ways, but from ASP.NET Core 1.1 onward, the preferred way is to use a declarative Tag Helper-style syntax, using a `vc:` prefix:

```
<vc:my-recipes number-of-recipes="3">
</vc:my-recipes>
```

Custom view components typically derive from the `ViewComponent` base class, and implement an `InvokeAsync()` method, as shown in listing 19.13. Deriving from this base class allows access to useful helper methods, in much the same way that deriving from the `Controller` base class does for MVC controllers. But the parameters to `InvokeAsync` don't come from model binding like they do for MVC controllers. Instead, you pass the parameters to the view component using properties on the Tag Helper element, as you saw previously.

When the user is logged in, the View
Component displays a list of recipes
created by the current user, loaded
from the database.

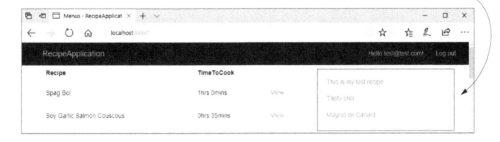

When the user is not logged
in, the View Component displays
links to the Register and Log in pages.

**Figure 19.9   The view component displays different content based on the currently logged-in user.
It includes both business logic (which recipes to load from the database) and rendering logic (how
to display the data).**

Listing 19.13   A custom view component to display the current user's recipes

```
public class MyRecipesViewComponent : ViewComponent
{
    private readonly RecipeService _recipeService;
    private readonly UserManager<ApplicationUser> _userManager;
    public MyRecipesViewComponent(RecipeService recipeService,
        UserManager<ApplicationUser> userManager)
    {
        _recipeService = recipeService;
        _userManager = userManager;
    }

    public async Task<IViewComponentResult> InvokeAsync(
        int numberOfRecipes)
```

You can use
DI in a view
Component.

Deriving from the
ViewComponent base
class provides useful
methods like View().

InvokeAsync renders the view
component. It should return a
Task<IViewComponentResult>

You can pass parameters to
the component from the view.

```
    {
        if(!User.Identity.IsAuthenticated)
        {
            return View("Unauthenticated");
        }

        var userId = _userManager.GetUserId(HttpContext.User);
        var recipes = await _recipeService.GetRecipesForUser(
            userId, numberOfRecipes);

        return View(recipes);
    }
}
```

Calling View() will render a partial view with the provided name.

You can pass a view model to the partial view. If you don't specify a name, Default.cshtml is used.

This custom view component handles all the logic you need to render a list of recipes when the user is logged in, or a different view if the user isn't authenticated. The name of the component is derived from the class name, like Tag Helpers. Alternatively, you can apply the [ViewComponent] attribute to the class and set a different name.

The InvokeAsync method must return a Task<IViewComponentResult>. This is similar to the way you return an IActionResult from an action method, but more restrictive; view components must render some sort of content, they can't send status codes or redirects. You'll typically use the View() helper method to render a partial view template, though you can also return a string directly using the Content() helper method, which will HTML-encode the content and render it to the page directly.

You can pass any number of parameters to the InvokeAsync method. The name of the parameters (in this case, numberOfRecipes) is converted to kebab-case and exposed as a property in the Tag Helper (number-of-recipes). You can provide these parameters when you invoke the view component from a view.

View components have access to the current request and HttpContext. In listing 19.13, you can see that we're checking whether the current request was from an authenticated user. You can also see that we've used some conditional logic: if the user isn't authenticated, render the "Unauthenticated" view template, if they're authenticated, render the default view template and pass in the view models loaded from the database.

In *action methods*, if you don't specify a view template name, the template name matches the name of the action method. For *view components*, if you don't specify a different name, the template name is "Default.cshtml."

The partial views for view components work similarly to other Razor partial views but they're stored separately from them. You must create partial views for view components at Views/Shared/Components/ComponentName/TemplateName. For the view component in listing 19.13, for example, you'd create your view templates at

- Views/Shared/Components/MyRecipes/Default.cshtml
- Views/Shared/Components/MyRecipes/Unauthenticated.cshtml

This was only a quick introduction to view components, but it should get you a long way. View components are a simple method to embed pockets of isolated, complex logic in your Razor layouts. Having said that, be mindful of these caveats:

- View component classes must be public, non-nested, and non-abstract classes.
- Although similar to MVC controllers, you can't use filters with view components.
- You can't use Razor @sections in partial views returned by a view component.
- When using the <vc:my-recipes> Tag Helper syntax to invoke your view component, you must import it as a custom Tag Helper, as you saw in section 19.4.
- Instead of using the Tag Helper syntax, you can invoke the view component from a view directly by using IViewComponentHelper Component. For example

```
@await Component.InvokeAsync("MyRecipes", new { numberOfRecipes = 3 })
```

We've covered Tag Helpers and view components, which are both new features of ASP.NET Core. In the final section of this chapter, you'll see how to create a custom DataAnnotations attribute. If you've used previous versions of ASP.NET, then this will be familiar, but ASP.NET Core has a couple of tricks up its sleeve to help you out.

19.6 Building a custom validation attribute

We looked at model binding in chapter 6, where you saw how to use the built-in DataAnnotations in your binding models to validate user input. These provide a number of built-in validations, such as

- [Required]—The property isn't optional and must be provided.
- [StringLength(min, max)]—The length of the string value must be between min and max characters.
- [EmailAddress]—The value must be a valid email address format.

But what if these attributes don't meet your requirements? Consider the following listing, which shows a binding model from a currency converter application. The model contains three properties: the currency to convert from, the currency to convert to, and the quantity.

> **Listing 19.14 Currency converter initial binding model**

```
public class CurrencyConverterModel
{
    [Required]
    [StringLength(3, MinimumLength = 3)]
    public string CurrencyFrom { get; set; }

    [Required]
    [StringLength(3, MinimumLength = 3)]
    public string CurrencyTo { get; set; }

    [Required]
    [Range(1, 1000)]
    public decimal Quantity { get; set; }
}
```

All the properties are required.

The strings must be exactly 3 characters.

The quantity can be between 1 and 1000.

There's some basic validation on this model, but during testing you identify a problem: users are able to enter any three-letter string for the `CurrencyFrom` and `CurrencyTo` properties. Users should only be able to choose a valid currency code, like `"USD"` or `"GBP"`, but someone attacking your application could easily send `"XXX"` or `"£$%"`!

Assuming we support a limited set of currencies, say GBP, USD, EUR, and CAD, you could handle the validation in a few different ways. One way would be to validate this within the action method, after model binding and attribute validation has already occurred.

Another way would be to use a `[RegularExpresssion]` attribute to look for the allowed strings. The approach I'm going to take here is to create a custom `Validation-Attribute`. The goal is to have a custom validation attribute you can apply to the `CurrencyFrom` and `CurrencyTo` attributes, to restrict the range of valid values. This will look something like this example.

Listing 19.15   Applying custom validation attributes to the binding model

```
public class CurrencyConverterModel
{
    [Required]
    [StringLength(3, MinimumLength = 3)]
    [CurrencyCode("GBP", "USD", "CAD", "EUR")]        ◁      CurrencyCodeAttribute
    public string CurrencyFrom { get; set; }                 validates that the
                                                             property has one of the
    [Required]                                               provided values
    [StringLength(3, MinimumLength = 3)]
    [CurrencyCode("GBP", "USD", "CAD", "EUR")].       ◁

    [Required]
    [Range(1, 1000)]
    public decimal Quantity { get; set; }
}
```

Creating a custom validation attribute is simple, as you can start with the `Validation-Attribute` base class and you only have to override a single method. The next listing shows how you could implement `CurrencyCodeAttribute` to ensure that the currency codes provided match the expected values.

Listing 19.16   Custom validation attribute for currency codes

Derives from ValidationAttribute to ensure
your attribute is used during validation

```
public class CurrencyCodeAttribute : ValidationAttribute      ◁
{
    private readonly string[] _allowedCodes;
    public CurrencyCodeAttribute(params string[] allowedCodes)
    {                                            The attribute takes in
        _allowedCodes = allowedCodes;              an array of allowed
    }                                              currency codes.
```

```
      protected override ValidationResult IsValid(
         object value, ValidationContext context)
      {
         var code = value as string;
         if(code == null || !_allowedCodes.Contains(code))
         {
            return new ValidationResult("Not a valid currency code");
         }

         return ValidationResult.Success;
      }
   }
```

The IsValid method is passed the value to validate plus a context object.

If the value provided isn't a string, is null, or isn't an allowed code, then return an error . . .

. . . otherwise, return a success result

Validation occurs in the MVC action pipeline after model binding, but before the action or action filters have executed. The MvcMiddleware calls IsValid() for each instance of the attribute and passes in value (the value of the property being validated) and the ValidationContext. This context object contains details that you can use to validate the property.

Of particular note is the ObjectInstance property. You can use this to access the top-level model being validated, for example the CurrencyConvertModel in the example, using

```
var model = validationContext.ObjectInstance as CurrencyConverterModel;
```

This can be useful if the validity of a property depends on the value of another property of the model. For example, you might want a validation rule that says that GBP is a valid value for CurrencyTo, *except* when CurrencyFrom is EUR. The ObjectInstance makes these sorts of comparison validations easy.

Within the IsValid method, you can safely cast the value provided to the required data type (in this case, string) and check against the list of allowed codes. If the code isn't allowed, then the attribute returns a ValidationResult with an error message indicating there was a problem. If the code is allowed, then ValidationResult.Success is returned and the validation succeeds.

Putting your attribute to the test in figure 19.10 shows that when CurrencyTo is an invalid value (£$%), the validation for the property fails and an error is added to the ModelState. You could do some tidying up of this attribute to let you set a custom message, to allow nulls, or to display the name of the property that's invalid, but the important features are all there.

The main feature missing from this custom attribute is client-side validation. You've seen that the attribute works well on the server side, but if the user entered an invalid value they wouldn't be informed until after the invalid value had been sent to the server.

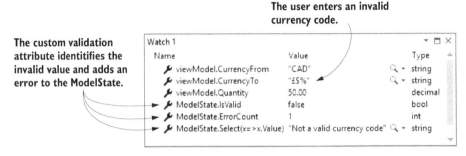

The user enters an invalid currency code.

The custom validation attribute identitifies the invalid value and adds an error to the ModelState.

Figure 19.10   The Watch window of Visual Studio showing the result of validation using the custom `ValidationAttribute`. The user has provided an invalid `currencyTo` value, £$%. Consequently, `ModelState` isn't valid and contains a single error with the message "Not a valid currency code."

You can implement client-side validation in several ways, but it's heavily dependent on the client-side framework and libraries you're using. By default, ASP.NET Core Razor templates use jQuery for client-side validation. For a complete jQuery example, see http://mng.bz/0Pul.

Another improvement to your custom validation attribute is to load the list of currencies from a DI service, such as `ICurrencyProvider`. Unfortunately, you can't use constructor DI in your `CurrencyCodeAttribute`, as you can only pass constant values to the constructor of an `Attribute` in .NET. In chapter 13, we worked around this limitation for filters by using `[TypeFilter]` or `[ServiceFilter]`, but there's no such solution for `ValidationAttribute`.

Instead, for validation attributes, you have to use the service locator pattern. As I discussed in chapter 10, this antipattern is best avoided, but unfortunately, it's necessary in this case. Instead of declaring an explicit dependency via a constructor, you must ask the DI container directly for an instance of the required service.

Listing 19.17 shows how you could rewrite listing 19.16 to load the allowed currencies from an instance of `ICurrencyProvider`, instead of hardcoding the allowed values in the attribute's constructor. The attribute calls the `GetService<T>()` method on `ValidationContext` to resolve an instance of `ICurrencyProvider` from the DI container.

Listing 19.17   Using the service-locator pattern to access services

```
public class CurrencyCodeAttribute : ValidationAttribute
{
    protected override ValidationResult IsValid(
        object value, ValidationContext context)
    {
        var provider = context.GetService<ICurrencyProvider>();
        var allowedCodes = provider.GetCurrencies();
        var code = value as string;
        if(code == null || !_allowedCodes.Contains(code))
```

Retrieves an instance of ICurrencyProvider directly from the DI container

Fetches the currency codes using the provider

Validates the property as before

```
      {
          return new ValidationResult("Not a valid currency code");
      }

      return ValidationResult.Success;
   }
}
```

TIP The generic `GetService<T>` method is an extension method available in the `Microsoft.Extensions.DependencyInjection` namespace. As an alternative, you can use the native `GetService(Type type)` method.

That brings us to the end of this chapter on custom components. In this chapter, I focused on some of the most common components you'll need to build. The ASP.NET Core framework is eminently pluggable, so it's theoretically possible to replace almost any part with your own custom implementation should you so desire, but you should find the components I've shown in this chapter get you a long way.

In the final chapter of this book, I'll describe an important aspect of web development which, sometimes despite the best of intentions, is often left until last: testing. You'll learn how to write simple unit tests for your classes, how to design for testability, and how to build integration tests that test your whole app.

Summary

- Use the `Run` extension method to create middleware components that always return a response. You should always place the `Run` extension at the end of a middleware pipeline or branch, as middleware placed after it will never execute.

- You can create branches in the middleware pipeline with the `Map` extension. If an incoming request matches the specified path prefix, the request will execute the pipeline branch, otherwise it will execute the trunk.

- When the `Map` extension matches a request path segment, it removes the segment from the request's `HttpContext.Path` and moves it to the `PathBase` property.

- You can use the `Use` extension method to create generalized middleware components that can generate a response, modify the request, and pass the request on to subsequent middleware in the pipeline.

- You can encapsulate middleware in a reusable class. The class should take a `RequestDelegate` object in the constructor, and should have a public `Invoke()` method that takes an `HttpContext` and returns a `Task`. To call the next middleware in the pipeline, invoke the `RequestDelegate` with the provided `HttpContext`.

- Some configuration providers require configuration values themselves. For example, a configuration provider that loads settings from a database might need a connection string. You can load these configuration providers by partially building an `IConfiguration` object using the other providers and reading the required configuration from it. You can then configure the database provider and add it to the `ConfigurationBuilder` before rebuilding to get the final `IConfiguration`.

- If you need services from the DI container to configure an `IOptions<T>` object, then you should create a separate class that implements `IConfigure-Options<T>`. This class can use DI in the constructor.

- You can add a third-party container to an existing application, which can provide additional features, such as convention-based dependency registration.

- To use a third-party container such as StructureMap, configure the built-in container with framework services as usual and then transfer those registrations to StructureMap by calling `Populate()`. Configure the third-party container with your own services, and finally, return an instance of `IServiceProvider` from `Startup.ConfigureServices`.

- The name of a Tag Helper class dictates the name of the element in the Razor templates, so the `SystemInfoTagHelper` corresponds to the `<system-info>` element.

- You can set properties on your Tag Helper object from Razor syntax by decorating the property with an `[HtmlAttributeName("name")]` attribute and providing a name. This can be set from Razor using `<system-info name="value">`, for example.

- The `TagHelperOutput` parameter passed to the `Process` or `ProcessAsync` methods control the HTML that's rendered to the page. Set the element type with the `TagName` property, and set the inner content using `Content.SetContent()` or `Content.SetHtmlContent()`.

- You can prevent inner Tag Helper content being processed by calling `Supress-Output()` and you can remove the element entirely by setting `TagName=null`.

- View components are like partial views, but they allow you to use complex business and rendering logic. You can use them for sections of a page, such as the shopping cart, a dynamic navigation menu, or suggested articles.

- Create a view component by deriving from the `ViewComponent` base class, and implement `InvokeAsync()`. You can pass parameters to this function from the Razor view template.

- View components can use DI, have access to the `HttpContext`, and can render partial views. The partial views should be stored in the Views/Shared/Components/<Name>/ folder, where Name is the name of the view component. If not specified, view templates use the name Default.cshtml.

- You can create a custom `DataAnnotations` attribute by deriving from `ValidationAttribute` and overriding the `IsValid` method. You can use this to decorate your binding model properties.

- You can't use constructor DI with custom validation attributes. If the validation attribute needs access to services from the DI container, you must use the service locator pattern to load them from the validation context, using the `Get-Service<T>` method.

Testing your application

This chapter covers

- Creating unit test projects with xUnit
- Writing unit tests for custom middleware and MVC controllers
- Using the Test Host package to write integration tests
- Testing code dependent on EF Core with the in-memory database provider

When I first started programming, I didn't understand the benefits of automated testing. It involved writing so much more code—wouldn't it be more productive to be working on new features instead? It was only when my projects started getting bigger that I appreciated the advantages. Instead of having to manually run my app and test each scenario, I could press Play on a suite of tests and have my code tested for me automatically.

Testing is universally accepted as good practice, but how it fits into your development process can often turn into a religious debate. How many tests do you need? Is anything less than 100% coverage of your code base adequate? Should you write tests before, during, or after the main code?

This chapter won't address any of those questions. Instead, I focus on the *mechanics* of testing an ASP.NET Core application. I show you how to use isolated *unit tests* to verify the behavior of your services in isolation, how to test your MVC controllers and custom middleware, and how to create *integration tests* that exercise multiple components of your application at once. Finally, I touch on the EF Core in-memory provider, a feature that lets you test components that depend on a `DbContext` without having to connect to a database.

> **TIP**   For a broader discussion around testing, or if you're brand new to unit testing, see *The Art of Unit Testing* by Roy Osherove (Manning, 2013). Alternatively, for an in-depth look at testing with xUnit in .NET Core, see *.NET Core in Action* by Dustin Metzgar (Manning, 2018).

In section 20.1, I introduce the .NET SDK testing framework, and how you can use it to create unit testing apps. I describe the components involved, including the testing SDK and the testing frameworks themselves, like xUnit and MSTest. Finally, I cover some of the terminology I use throughout the chapter.

In section 20.2, you'll create your first test project. You'll be testing a simple class at this stage, but it'll allow you to come to grips with the various testing concepts involved. You'll create several tests using the xUnit test framework, make assertions about the behavior of your services, and execute the test project both from Visual Studio and the command line.

In sections 20.3 and 20.4, we'll look at how to test common features of your ASP.NET Core apps: MVC controllers and custom middleware. I show you how to write isolated unit tests for both, much like you would any other service, as well as the tripping points to look out for.

To ensure components work correctly, it's important to test them in isolation. But you also need to test they work correctly when you combine them in your app. ASP.NET Core provides a handy Test Host package that lets you easily write these *integration tests* for your application. In section 20.5, you'll see how to use the Test Host to simulate requests to your application, and to verify it generates the correct response.

In the final section of this chapter, I demonstrate how to use the SQLite database provider for EF Core with an in-memory database. You can use this provider to test services that depend on an EF Core `DbContext`, without having to use a real database. That avoids the pain of having a known database infrastructure, of resetting the database between tests, and of different people having slightly different database configurations.

Let's start by looking at the overall testing landscape for ASP.NET Core, the options available to you, and the components involved.

20.1   *An introduction to testing in ASP.NET Core*

If you have experience building apps with the full .NET Framework or mobile apps with Xamarin, then you might have some experience with unit testing frameworks. If you were building apps in Visual Studio, exactly how to create a test project would vary between testing frameworks (xUnit, NUnit, MSTest), and running the tests in Visual Studio often required installing a plugin. Similarly, running tests from the command line varied between frameworks.

With the .NET Core SDK, testing in ASP.NET Core and .NET Core is now a first-class citizen, on a par with building, restoring packages, and running your application. Just as you can run `dotnet build` to build a project, or `dotnet run` to execute it, you can use `dotnet test` to execute the tests in a test project, regardless of the testing framework used.

The `dotnet test` command uses the underlying .NET Core SDK to execute the tests for a given project. This is exactly the same as when you run your tests using the Visual Studio test runner, so whichever approach you prefer, the results are the same.

> **NOTE** As I have throughout the book, I'm referring to testing .NET Core apps, but you can also use the same tools to execute tests against the full .NET framework if your app targets .NET Framework instead of .NET Core.

Test projects are console apps that contain a number of *tests*. A test is typically a method that evaluates whether a given class in your app behaves as expected. The test project will typically have dependencies on at least three components:

- The .NET Test SDK
- A unit testing framework, for example xUnit, NUnit, Fixie, or MSTest
- A test-runner adapter for your chosen testing framework, so that you can execute your tests by calling `dotnet test`

These dependencies are normal NuGet packages that you can add to a project, but they allow you to hook in to the `dotnet test` command and the Visual Studio test runner. You'll see an example csproj from a test app in the next section.

Typically, a test consists of a method that runs a small piece of your app in isolation and checks that it has the desired behavior. If you were testing a `Calculator` class, you might have a test that checks that passing the values 1 and 2 to the `Add()` method returns the expected result, 3.

You can write lots of small, isolated tests like this for your app's classes to verify that each component is working correctly, independent of any other components. Small isolated tests like these are called *unit tests*.

Using the ASP.NET Core framework, you can build apps that you can easily unit test; you can test your controllers in isolation from your action filters and model binding. This is because the framework

- Avoids static types.
- Uses interfaces instead of concrete implementations.
- Has a highly modular architecture; you can test your controllers in isolation from your action filters and model binding, for example.

But just because all your components work correctly independently, doesn't mean they'll work when you put them together. For that, you need *integration tests*, which test the interaction between multiple components.

The definition of an integration test is another somewhat contentious issue, but I think of integration tests as any time you're testing multiple components together, or you're testing large vertical slices of your app. Testing a user manager class can save values to a database, or testing that a request made to a health-check endpoint returns the expected response, for example. Integration tests don't necessarily include the *entire* app, but they definitely use more components than unit tests.

> **NOTE**   I don't cover UI tests which, for example, interact with a browser to provide true end-to-end automated testing. Selenium (www.seleniumhq.org) is one of the best known tools for UI testing, but you can find other services, such as Ghost Inspector (https://ghostinspector.com), which are worth investigating.

ASP.NET Core has a couple of tricks up its sleeve when it comes to integration testing. You can use the Test Host package to run an in-process ASP.NET Core server, which you can send requests to and inspect the responses. This saves you from the orchestration headache of trying to spin up a web server on a different process, making sure ports are available and so on, but still allowing you to exercise your whole app.

At the other end of the scale, the EF Core SQLite in-memory database provider lets you isolate your tests from the database. Interacting and configuring a database is often one of the hardest aspects of automating tests, so this provider lets you sidestep the issue entirely. You'll see how to use it in section 20.6.

The easiest way to get to grips with testing is to give it a try, so in the next section, you'll create your first test project and use it to write unit tests for a simple custom service.

20.2   *Unit testing with xUnit*

As I described in section 20.1, to create a test project you need to use a testing framework. You have many options, such as NUnit or MSTest, but the most commonly used test framework with .NET Core is xUnit (https://xunit.github.io/). The ASP.NET Core framework project itself uses xUnit as its testing framework, so it's become somewhat of a convention. If you're familiar with a different testing framework, then feel free to use that instead.

In this section, you'll see how to create unit test projects, how to reference classes in other projects, and how to run tests with Visual Studio or the .NET CLI. You'll create an xUnit test project and use it to test the behavior of a basic currency converter service, using xUnit Fact and Theory tests. You'll write some simple unit tests that check that the service returns the expected results, and that it throws exceptions when you expect it to.

20.2.1 *Creating your first test project*

Visual Studio includes a template to create a .NET Core xUnit test project, as shown in figure 20.1. Choose File > New Project and choose xUnit Test Project from the New Project dialog. If you choose Unit Test Project, Visual Studio will create an MSTest unit project instead.

Choose .NET Core.

Choose xUnit Test Project (.NET Core).

Enter a name for the project.

Figure 20.1   The New Project Dialog in Visual Studio. Choose xUnit Test Project to create an xUnit project or choose Unit Test Project to create an MSTest project.

Alternatively, if you're not using Visual Studio, you can create a similar template using the .NET CLI with

```
dotnet new xunit
```

Whether you use Visual Studio or the .NET CLI, the template creates a console project and adds the required testing NuGet packages to your csproj file, as shown in the following listing. If you chose to create an MSTest (or other framework) test project, then the xUnit and xUnit runner packages would be replaced with packages appropriate to your testing framework of choice.

Listing 20.1   The csproj file for an xUnit test project

```
<Project Sdk="Microsoft.NET.Sdk">
  <PropertyGroup>
    <TargetFramework>netcoreapp2.0</TargetFramework>
```

The test project is a standard .NET Core project targeting .NET Core 2.0.

```
        <IsPackable>false</IsPackable>
      </PropertyGroup>

      <ItemGroup>
        <PackageReference
          Include="Microsoft.NET.Test.Sdk" Version="15.3.0" />
        <PackageReference Include="xunit" Version="2.3.0" />
        <PackageReference
          Include="xunit.runner.visualstudio" Version="2.3.0" />
      </ItemGroup>
    </Project>
```

The .NET Test SDK, required
by all test projects

The xUnit
test
framework

The xUnit test adapter
for the .NET Test SDK

In addition to the NuGet packages, the template includes a single example unit test. This doesn't *do* anything, but it's a valid xUnit test all the same, as shown in the following listing. In xUnit, a test is a method on a public class, decorated with a [Fact] attribute.

Listing 20.2   An example xUnit unit test, created by the default template

```
public class UnitTest1            xUnit tests must be in public classes.
{
    [Fact]                        The [Fact] attribute indicates the method is a test method.
    public void Test1()
    {                             The Fact must be public
    }                             and have no parameters.
}
```

Even though this test doesn't test anything, it highlights some characteristics of xUnit [Fact] tests:

- Tests are denoted by the [Fact] attribute.
- The method should be public, with no method arguments.
- The method returns void. It could also be an async method and return Task.
- The method resides inside a public, nonstatic class.

NOTE   The [Fact] attribute, and these restrictions, are specific to the xUnit testing framework. Other frameworks will use other ways to denote test classes and have different restrictions on the classes and methods themselves.

It's also worth noting that, although I said that test projects are console apps, there's no Program class or static void main method. Instead, the app looks more like a class library. This is because the test SDK automatically injects a Program class at build time. It's not something you have to worry about in general, but you may have issues if you try to add your own Program.cs file to your test project.[1]

Before we go any further and create some useful tests, we'll run the test project as it is, using both Visual Studio and the .NET SDK tooling, to see the expected output.

---

[1]   This isn't a common thing to do, but I've seen it used occasionally. I describe this issue in detail, and how to fix it, at http://mng.bz/1NyQ.

20.2.2 *Running tests with dotnet test*

When you create a test app that uses the .NET Test SDK, you can run your tests either with Visual Studio or using the .NET CLI. In Visual Studio, you run tests by choosing Tests > Run > All Tests from the main menu, or by clicking Run All in the Test Explorer window, as shown in figure 20.2.

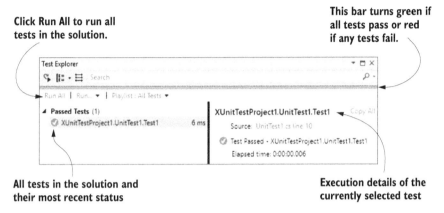

Click Run All to run all tests in the solution.

This bar turns green if all tests pass or red if any tests fail.

All tests in the solution and their most recent status

Execution details of the currently selected test

Figure 20.2   The Test Explorer window in Visual Studio lists all tests found in the solution, and their most recent pass/fail status. Click a test in the left-hand pane to see details about the most recent test run in the right-hand pane.

The Test Explorer window lists all the tests found in your solution, the results of each test, and overall, whether all the tests in your solution passed successfully. In xUnit, a test will pass if it doesn't throw an exception, so Test1 passed successfully.

Alternatively, you can run your tests from the command line using the .NET CLI by running

```
dotnet test
```

from the unit test project's folder, as shown in in figure 20.3.

> **WARNING**   Make sure you run dotnet test from the *project* folder, which contains the test project's csproj file. If you try to run it from the *solution* folder, you'll get an error that the project can't be found.

Calling dotnet test runs a restore and build of your test project and then runs the tests, as you can see from the console output in figure 20.3. Under the hood, the .NET CLI calls into the same underlying infrastructure as Visual Studio does (the .NET Core SDK), so you can use whichever approach better suits your development style.

> **TIP**   You can also use the dotnet xunit command to run tests with xUnit. This provides additional options specific to xUnit test projects. You can read more about the xunit command here https://xunit.github.io/docs/getting-started-dotnet-core.html.

**dotnet test builds and
restores the project.**

**Run dotnet
test from the test
project folder.**

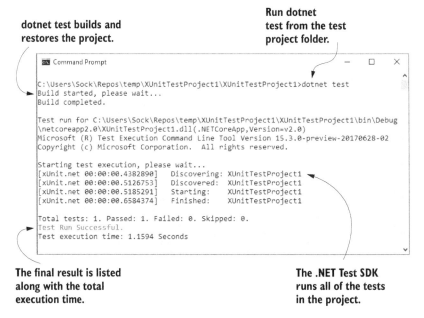

**The final result is listed
along with the total
execution time.**

**The .NET Test SDK
runs all of the tests
in the project.**

Figure 20.3   You can run tests from the command line using `dotnet test`**. This
restores and builds the test project before executing all the tests in the project.**

You've seen a successful test run, so it's time to replace that placeholder test with something useful. First things first, you need something to test.

20.2.3   *Referencing your app from your test project*

In test-driven development (TDD), you typically write your unit tests before you write the actual class you're testing, but I'm going to take a more traditional route here and create the class to test first. You'll write the tests for it afterwards.

Let's assume you've created an app called ExchangeRates.Web, which is used to convert between different currencies, and you want to add tests for it. You've added a test project to your solution as described in section 20.2.1, so your solution looks like figure 20.4.

In order for the ExchangeRates.Web.Test project to be able to test the classes in the ExchangeRates.Web project, you need to add a reference from the web project to

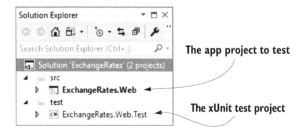

The app project to test

The xUnit test project

**Figure 20.4   A basic solution,
containing an ASP.NET Core app called
ExchangeRates.Web and a test project
called ExchangeRates.Web.Test**

your test project. In Visual Studio, you can do this by right-clicking the Dependencies node of your Unit test project and choosing Add Reference, as shown in figure 20.5. You can then select the web project from the Add Reference Dialog. After adding it to your project, it shows up inside the Dependencies node, under Projects.

Alternatively, you can edit the csproj file directly and add a `<ProjectReference>` element inside an `<ItemGroup>` element with the relative path to the referenced project's csproj file.

```
<ItemGroup>
  <ProjectReference
    Include="..\..\src\ExchangeRates.Web\ExchangeRates.Web.csproj" />
</ItemGroup>
```

Note that the path is the *relative* path. A `".."` in the path means the parent folder, so the relative path shown correctly traverses the directory structure for the solution, including both the src and test folders shown in Solution Explorer in figure 20.5.

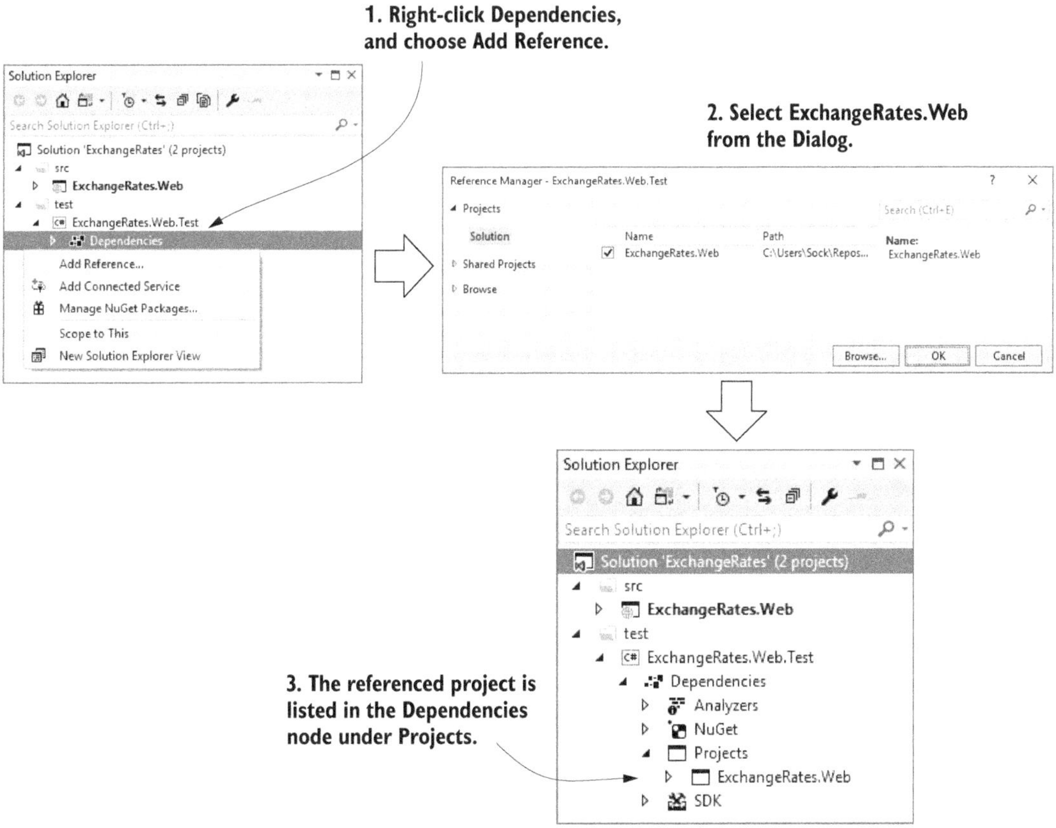

1. Right-click Dependencies, and choose Add Reference.

2. Select ExchangeRates.Web from the Dialog.

3. The referenced project is listed in the Dependencies node under Projects.

Figure 20.5 To test your app project, you need to add a reference to it from the test project. Right-click the Dependencies node and choose Add Reference. The app project is shown referenced inside the Dependencies Node, under Projects.

TIP   Remember, you can edit the csproj file directly in Visual Studio by right-clicking the project and choosing Edit projectname.csproj.

Common conventions for project layout

The layout and naming of projects within a solution is completely up to you, but ASP.NET Core projects have generally settled on a couple of conventions that differ slightly from the Visual Studio File New defaults. These conventions are used by the ASP.NET team on GitHub, as well as many other open source C# projects.

The following figure shows an example of these layout conventions. In summary, these are:

- The .sln solution file is in the root directory.
- The main projects are placed in an src sub-directory.
- The test projects are placed in a test sub-directory.
- Each main project has a test project equivalent, named the same as the associated main project with a ".Test" or ".Tests" suffix.
- Other folders, such as samples, tools, or docs contain sample projects, tools for building the project, or documentation.

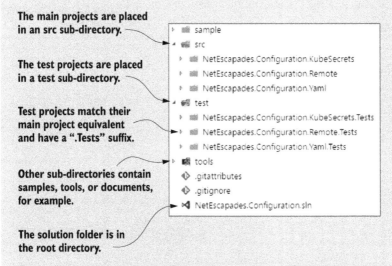

The main projects are placed in an src sub-directory.

The test projects are placed in a test sub-directory.

Test projects match their main project equivalent and have a ".Tests" suffix.

Other sub-directories contain samples, tools, or documents, for example.

The solution folder is in the root directory.

- sample
- src
  - NetEscapades.Configuration.KubeSecrets
  - NetEscapades.Configuration.Remote
  - NetEscapades.Configuration.Yaml
- test
  - NetEscapades.Configuration.KubeSecrets.Tests
  - NetEscapades.Configuration.Remote.Tests
  - NetEscapades.Configuration.Yaml.Tests
- tools
- .gitattributes
- .gitignore
- NetEscapades.Configuration.sln

Conventions around project structures have emerged in the ASP.NET Core framework libraries and open source projects on GitHub. You don't have to follow them for your own project, but it's worth being aware of them.

Whether or not you choose to follow these conventions is entirely up to you, but it's good to be aware of them at least, so you can easily navigate other projects on GitHub.

Your test project is now referencing your web project, so you can write tests for classes in the web project. You're going to be testing a simple class used for converting between currencies, as shown in the following listing.

Listing 20.3   Example `CurrencyConverter` class to convert currencies to GBP

```
public class CurrencyConverter
{
    public decimal ConvertToGbp(
        decimal value, decimal exchangeRate, int decimalPlaces)
    {
        if (exchangeRate <= 0)
        {
            throw new ArgumentException(
                "Exchange rate must be greater than zero",
                nameof(exchangeRate));
        }

        var valueInGbp = value / exchangeRate;

        return decimal.Round(valueInGbp, decimalPlaces);
    }
}
```

The ConvertToGbp method converts a value using the provided exchange rate and rounds it.

Guard clause, as only positive exchange rates are valid.

Converts the value

Rounds the result and return it

This class only has a single method, `ConvertToGbp()`, which converts a `value` from one currency into GBP, given the provided `exchangeRate`. It then rounds the value to the required number of decimal places and returns it.

> **WARNING**   This class is only a basic implementation. In practice, you'd need to handle arithmetic overflow/underflow for large or negative values, as well as considering other edge cases. This is only for demonstration purposes!

Imagine you want to convert 5.27 USD to GBP, and the exchange rate from GBP to USD is 1.31. If you want to round to 4 decimal places, you'd call

```
converter.ConvertToGbp(value: 5.27, exchangeRate: 1.31, decimalPlaces:4);
```

You have your sample application, a class to test, and a test project, so it's about time you wrote some tests.

20.2.4   Adding Fact and Theory unit tests

When I write unit tests, I usually target one of three different paths through the method under test:

- *The happy path*—Where typical arguments with expected values are provided
- *The error path*—Where the arguments passed are invalid and tested for
- *Edge cases*—Where the provided arguments are right on the edge of expected values

I realize this is a broad classification, but it helps me think about the various scenarios I need to consider. Let's start with the happy path, by writing a unit test that verifies that the `ConvertToGbp()` method is working as expected with typical input values.

Listing 20.4   Unit test for `ConvertToGbp` using expected arguments

```
                     The [Fact] attribute marks the
                     method as a test method.
                                                        You can call the test
[Fact]      ◁──┘                                        anything you like.
public void ConvertToGbp_ConvertsCorrectly()    ◁──┘
{
    var converter = new CurrencyConverter();    ◁────── The class to test
    decimal value = 3;          The parameters of the
    decimal rate = 1.5m;        test that will be passed
    int dp = 4;                 to ConvertToGbp
                                                         Executes the
    decimal expected = 2;    ◁────── The result you expect.    method and
                                                         captures the result
    var actual = converter.ConvertToGbp(value, rate, dp);  ◁──┘

    Assert.Equal(expected, actual);   ◁──┐
}                                          Verifies the expected and actual
                                           values match. If they don't, this
                                           will throw an exception.
```

This is your first proper unit test, which has been configured using the Arrange, Act, Assert (AAA) style:

- *Arrange*—Define all the parameters and create the class under test
- *Act*—Execute the method being tested and capture the result
- *Assert*—Verify that the result of the Act stage had the expected value

Most of the code in this test is standard C#, but if you're new to testing, the `Assert` call will be unfamiliar. This is a helper class provided by xUnit for making assertions about your code. If the parameters provided to `Assert.Equal()` aren't equal, the `Equal()` call will throw an exception and fail the test. If you change the `expected` variable in listing 20.4 to be `2.5` instead of `2`, for example, and run the test, you can see that Test Explorer shows the failure in figure 20.6.

> **NOTE**   The names of your test class and method are used throughout the test framework to describe your test. If you'd rather not display the class name, you can configure an xunit.runner.json file as described here: https://xunit .github.io/docs/configuring-with-json.html.

In listing 20.4, you chose specific values for `value`, `exchangeRate`, and `decimalPlaces` to test the happy path. But this is only one set of values in an infinite number of possibilities, so you should probably at least test *a few* different combinations.

One way to achieve this would be to copy and paste the test multiple times, tweak the parameters, and change the test method name to make it unique. xUnit provides an alternative way to achieve the same thing without requiring so much duplication.

The top bar turns red to indicate one or more failing tests.

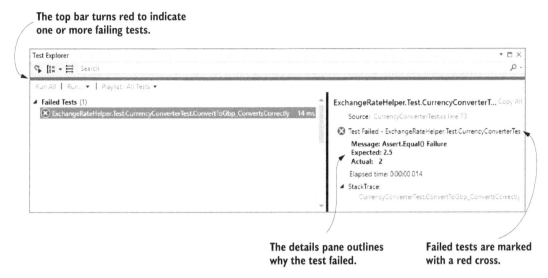

The details pane outlines why the test failed.

Failed tests are marked with a red cross.

Figure 20.6   When a test fails, it's marked with a red cross in Test Explorer. Clicking the test in the left pane shows the reason for the failure in the right pane. In this case, the expected value was 2.5, but the actual value was 2.

Instead of creating a [Fact] test method, you can create a [Theory] test method. A Theory provides a way of parameterizing your test methods, effectively taking your test method and running it multiple times with different arguments. Each set of arguments is considered a different test.

You could rewrite the [Fact] test in listing 20.4 to be a [Theory] test, as shown next. Instead of specifying the variables in the method body, pass them as parameters to the method, then decorate the method with three [InlineData] attributes that provide the parameter for a single run of the test.

Listing 20.5   Theory test for `ConvertToGbp` testing multiple sets of values

```
[Theory]          ◁──┐  Marks the method as a
[InlineData(0, 3, 0)]     parameterized test
[InlineData(3, 1.5, 2)]
[InlineData(3.75, 2.5, 1.5)]
public void ConvertToGbp_ConvertsCorrectly (
    decimal value, decimal rate, decimal expected)
{
    var converter = new CurrencyConverter();
    int dps = 4;

    var actual = converter.ConvertToGbp(value, rate, dps);   ◁──

    Assert.Equal(expected, actual);   ◁────── Verifies the result
}
```

Marks the method as a parameterized test

Each [InlineData] attribute provides all the parameters for a single run of the test method.

The method takes parameters, which are provided by the [InlineData] attributes.

Executes the method under test

Figure 20.7   Each set of parameters in an `[InlineData]` attribute for a `[Theory]` test creates a separate test run. In this example, a single `[Theory]` has three `[InlineData]` attributes, so it creates three tests, named according to the method name and the provided parameters.

If you run this `[Theory]` test using `dotnet test` or Visual Studio, then it will show up as three separate tests, one for each set of `[InlineData]`, as shown in figure 20.7.

`[InlineData]` isn't the only way to provide the parameters for your theory tests, though it's one of the most commonly used. You can also use a static property on your test class with the `[MemberData]` attribute, or a class itself using the `[ClassData]` attribute.[2]

You have some tests for the happy path of the `ConvertToGbp()` method, and I even sneaked an edge case into listing 20.5 by testing the case where `value = 0`. The final concept I'll cover is testing error cases, where invalid values are passed to the method under test.

20.2.5   *Testing failure conditions*

A key part of unit testing is checking that your class under test handles edge cases and errors correctly. For the `CurrencyConverter`, that would mean checking how the class handles negative values, small or zero exchange rates, large values and rates, and so on.

Some of these edge cases might be rare but valid cases, whereas other cases might be technically invalid. Calling `ConvertToGbp` with a negative `value` is probably valid; the converted result should be negative too. A negative exchange rate doesn't make sense conceptually, so should be considered an invalid value.

Depending on the design of the method, it's common to throw exceptions when invalid values are passed to a method. In listing 20.3 you saw that we throw an `ArgumentException` if the `exchangeRate` parameter is less than or equal to zero.

xUnit includes a variety of helpers on the `Assert` class for testing whether a method throws an exception of an expected type. You can then make further assertions on the exception, for example to test whether the exception had an expected message.

> **WARNING**   Take care not to tie your test methods too closely to the internal implementation of a method. Doing so can make your tests brittle, where trivial changes to a class break the unit tests.

---

[2]   I describe how you to use the `[ClassData]` and `[MemberData]` attributes in a blog post at http://mng.bz/8ayP.

The following listing shows a [Fact] test to check the behavior of the ConvertToGbp() method when you pass it a zero exchangeRate. The Assert.Throws method takes a lambda function that describes the action to execute, which should throw an exception when run.

```
[Fact]
public void ThrowsExceptionIfRateIsZero()
{
    var converter = new CurrencyConverter();
    const decimal value = 1;
    const decimal rate = 0;    <──── An invalid value
    const int dp = 2;

    var ex = Assert.Throws<ArgumentException>(     <────────  You expect an
        () => converter.ConvertToGbp(value, rate, dp));  <─┐  ArgumentException
                                                          │  to be thrown.
    // Further assertions on the exception thrown, ex      └─ The method to
}                                                             execute, which should
                                                              throw an exception
```

The Assert.Throws method executes the lambda and catches the exception. If the exception thrown matches the expected type, the test will pass. If no exception is thrown or the exception thrown isn't of the expected type, then the Assert.Throws method will throw an exception and fail the test.

That brings us to the end of this introduction on unit testing with xUnit. The examples in this section describe how to use the new .NET Test SDK, but we didn't cover anything specific to ASP.NET Core. In the rest of this chapter, we'll focus on testing ASP.NET Core projects specifically. We'll start by unit testing middleware and MVC controllers.

20.3 Unit testing custom middleware

In chapter 19, you saw how to create custom middleware and how you could encapsulate middleware as a class with an Invoke function. In this section, you'll create unit tests for a simple health-check middleware, similar to the one in chapter 19. This is a basic class, but it demonstrates the approach you can take for more complex middleware components.

The middleware you'll be testing is shown in listing 20.7. When invoked, this middleware checks that the path starts with /ping and, if it does, returns a plain text "pong" response. If the request doesn't match, it calls the next middleware in the pipeline (the provided RequestDelegate).

```
public class StatusMiddleware
{
    private readonly RequestDelegate _next;      The RequestDelegate
    public StatusMiddleware(RequestDelegate next)  representing the rest of
                                                   the middleware pipeline
```

```
    {
        _next = next;
    }

    public async Task Invoke(HttpContext context)
    {
        if(context.Request.Path.StartsWithSegments("/ping"))
        {
            context.Response.ContentType = "text/plain";
            await context.Response.WriteAsync("pong");
            return;
        }
        await _next(context);
    }
}
```

Called when the
middleware is executed

If the path starts
with "/ping", a
"pong" response is
returned . . .

. . . otherwise, the next middleware
in the pipeline is invoked.

In this section, you're only going to test two simple cases with two unit tests:

- When a request is made with a path of `"/ping"`
- When a request is made with a different path

Testing middleware is made slightly complicated by the fact that the HttpContext object is conceptually a *big* class. It contains all the details for the request and the response, which can mean there's a lot of surface area for your middleware to interact with. For that reason, I find unit tests tend to be tightly coupled to the middleware implementation, which is generally undesirable.

For the first test, you'll look at the case where the incoming request Path *doesn't* start with /ping. In this case, StatusMiddleware should leave the HttpContext unchanged, and should call the RequestDelegate provided in the constructor, representing the next middleware in the pipeline.

You could test this behavior in several ways, but in listing 20.8 you test that the RequestDelegate is executed by setting a variable when it's invoked. In the Assert at the end of the method, you verify the variable was set and therefore that the delegate was invoked. To invoke StatusMiddleware, create and pass in a DefaultHttp-Context,[3] which is an implementation of HttpContext.

> **Listing 20.8   Unit testing `StatusMiddleware` when a nonmatching path is provided**

```
[Fact]
public async Task ForNonMatchingRequest_CallsNextDelegate()
{
    var context = new DefaultHttpContext();
    context.Request.Path = "/somethingelse";

    var wasExecuted = false;
    RequestDelegate next = (ctx) =>
    {
        wasExecuted = true;
        return Task.CompletedTask;
    };
```

Creates a DefaultHttpContext and
sets the path for the request

Tracks whether the
RequestDelegate was executed

The RequestDelegate representing the next
middleware, should be invoked in this example.

---

[3]   The DefaultHttpContext derives from HttpContext and is part of the base ASP.NET Core framework abstractions. If you're so inclined, you can explore the source code for it at http://mng.bz/7b43.

```
    var middleware = new StatusMiddleware(next: next);    ◁──────
    await middleware.Invoke(context);    ◁─┐
    Assert.True(wasExecuted);    ◁─┐
}
```

Creates an instance of the middleware, passing in the next RequestDelegate

Invokes the middleware with the HttpContext, should invoke the RequestDelegate

Verifies RequestDelegate was invoked

When the middleware is invoked, it checks the provided `Path` and finds that it doesn't match the required value of `/ping`. The middleware therefore calls the next `Request-Delegate` and returns.

The other obvious case to test is when the request `Path` is `"/ping"`, and so the middleware should generate an appropriate response. You could test several different characteristics of the response:

- The response should have a `200 OK` status code
- The response should have a `Content-Type` of `text/plain`
- The response body should contain the `"pong"` string

Each of these characteristics represents a different requirement, so you'd typically codify each as a separate unit test. This makes it easier to tell exactly which requirement hasn't been met when a test fails. For simplicity, in listing 20.9 I show all of these assertions in the same test.

The positive case unit test is made more complex by the need to read the response body to confirm it contains `"pong"`. `DefaultHttpContext` uses `Stream.Null` for the `Response.Body` object, which means anything written to `Body` is lost. In order to capture the response and read it out to verify the contents, you must replace the `Body` with a `MemoryStream`. After the middleware executes, you can use a `StreamReader` to read the contents of the `MemoryStream` into a `string` and verify it.

Listing 20.9 Unit testing `StatusMiddleware` when a matching `Path` is provided

```
[Fact]
public async Task ReturnsPongBodyContent()
{
    var bodyStream = new MemoryStream();
    var context = new DefaultHttpContext();
    context.Response.Body = bodyStream;
    context.Request.Path = "/ping";

    RequestDelegate next = (ctx) => Task.CompletedTask;
    var middleware = new StatusMiddleware(next: next);

    await middleware.Invoke(context);    ◁─┐

    string response;
    bodyStream.Seek(0, SeekOrigin.Begin);
    using (var stringReader = new StreamReader(bodyStream))
    {
        response = await stringReader.ReadToEndAsync();
    }
```

Creates a DefaultHttpContext and initializes the body with a MemoryStream to capture the response

Creates an instance of the middleware and passes in a simple RequestDelegate

Invokes the middleware

Rewinds the MemoryStream and reads the response body into a string

The path is set to the required value for the StatusMiddleware.

```
Assert.Equal("pong", response);
    Assert.Equal("text/plain", context.Response.ContentType);
    Assert.Equal(200, context.Response.StatusCode);
}
```

**Verifies the response
has the correct value**

**Verifies the Status Code
response is correct**

**Verifies the
Content-Type
response is correct**

As you can see, unit testing middleware requires a fair amount of setup to get it working. On the positive side, it allows you to test your middleware in isolation, but in some cases, especially for simple middleware without any dependencies on databases or other services, integration testing can (somewhat surprisingly) be easier. In section 20.5, you'll create integration tests for this middleware in order to see the difference.

Custom middleware is common in ASP.NET Core projects, but whether you're building a traditional server-side rendered app or a Web API, you'll also probably use MVC controllers. In the next section, you'll see how you can unit test them in isolation from other components.

20.4   *Unit testing MVC controllers*

Unit tests are all about isolating behavior; you want to test only the logic contained in the component itself, separate from the behavior of any dependencies. MvcMiddleware as a whole contains complex behavior in the form of a filter pipeline, routing, and model binding, but these are all external to the MVC controller. MVC controllers themselves are responsible for only a limited number of things. Typically,

- For invalid requests (that have failed validation, for example), return an appropriate IActionResult.
- For valid requests, call the required business logic services and return an appropriate IActionResult (or alternatively an object to serialize, in the case of Web API Controllers).
- Optionally, apply resource-based authorization as required.

MVC Controllers generally shouldn't contain business logic themselves; instead, they should call out to other services. Think of an MVC controller as more of an orchestrator, serving as the intermediary between the HTTP interfaces your app exposes and your business logic services.

If you follow this separation, you'll find it easier to write unit tests for your business logic, as well as providing more flexibility to change your controllers to meet your needs. With that in mind, there's often a drive to make your controllers as thin as possible,[4] to the point where there's not much left to test!

---

[4] One of my first introductions to this idea was a series of posts by Jimmy Bogard. The following is a link to the last post in the series, but it contains links to all the earlier posts too. Jimmy Bogard is also behind the MediatR library (https://github.com/jbogard/MediatR), which makes creating thin controllers even easier. See http://mng.bz/q0QV.

All that said, MVC controllers and actions are simple classes and methods, so you can easily write unit tests for them. The following listing shows that you can create an instance of a controller, call an action method, and verify that the response is an `IActionResult` of the expected type, a `ViewResult`. You even test that the `ViewModel` passed to the `ViewResult` is the correct type, an `IndexViewModel`.

> **Listing 20.10   A simple MVC Controller unit test**

```
public class HomeControllerTest
{
    [Fact]
    public void Index_ReturnsIndexViewModelInViewResult()
    {
        var controller = new HomeController();

        IActionResult result = controller.Index(model);
        Assert.IsType<ViewResult>(result);

        var viewModel = (result as ViewResult).Model;
        Assert.IsType<IndexViewModel>(viewModel);
    }
}
```

Creates an instance of the HomeController to test

Invokes the Index method and captures the IActionResult returned

Asserts that the IActionResult is a ViewResult

Extracts the ViewModel from the ViewResult and asserts it's of the IndexViewModel type

An important point to note here is that you're testing the return type of the controller, the `IActionResult`, not the response that's sent back to the user. The `IActionResult` isn't executed, so no HTML is generated; you're purely testing the action method in isolation.

> **TIP** You can write unit tests around the name of the view template in `ViewResult`, but it can be tricky to do this in a way that isn't brittle. As you saw in chapter 7, the MVC framework has conventions for locating a view template when you don't specify the view or controller name. Consider all these conventions if you want to verify which view template will be rendered.

When you unit test MVC Controllers in this way, you're testing them separately from the MVC infrastructure, such as model binding, routing, and authentication. This is obviously by design, but as with testing middleware in section 20.3, it can make testing some aspects of your controller somewhat complex.

Consider model validation. As you saw in chapter 6, one of the key responsibilities of an action method is to check the `ModelState.IsValid` property and act accordingly if a binding model is invalid. Testing that your controller correctly handles validation failures is a good candidate for a unit test.

Unfortunately, `MvcMiddleware` automatically sets the `ModelState` property as part of the model binding process. In practice, when your action method is invoked, you know that the `ModelState` will match the binding model parameter passed to your method. But in a unit test, there's no model binding, so you have to handle the validation yourself.

Imagine you have an MVC Controller that should return a 400 Bad Request response when validation fails, as in the following listing.

```
[Route("api/[controller]")]
public class CurrencyController : Controller          The ConvertInputModel is
{                                                     automatically validated
    [HttpPost]                                        during model binding.
    public IActionResult Convert(ConvertInputModel model)  ◁─────
    {
        if (!ModelState.IsValid)  ◁────── If the input model is invalid . . .
        {
            return BadRequest(ModelState);  ◁───── . . .return a 400 Bad Request
        }                                           including the ModelState.
        // Other processing + business logic
        return Json(new { Success = true });  ◁──── The model was valid so
    }                                               process it and return a result.
}
```

In this example, you're interested in testing the sad path, where the model is invalid, and the controller should return `BadRequestObjectResult`. Unfortunately, in a unit test you can't rely on the `ModelState` property being correct for the binding model. Instead, you have to manually add a model-binding error to the controller's `Model-State` before calling the action, as shown here.

```
[Fact]                                                   Creates an instance of
public void Convert_ReturnsBadRequestWhenInvalid()       the Controller to test
{
    var controller = new CurrencyController();  ◁──────
    var model = new ConvertInputModel
    {
        Value = 1,                             Creates an invalid binding
        ExchangeRate = -2,                     model. ExchangeRate should
        DecimalPlaces = 2,                     be a positive value.
    };

    controller.ModelState.AddModelError(            Manually adds a model error
        nameof(model.ExchangeRate),                 to the Controller's
        "Exchange rate must be greater than zero"   ModelState. This sets
    );                                              ModelState.IsValid to false.

    var result = controller.Convert(model);  ◁──────   Invokes the action
                                                        method, passing in
    Assert.IsType<BadRequestObjectResult>(result);  ◁──  the binding models
}
                    Verifies the action method returned
                    a BadRequestObjectResult
```

> **NOTE** In listing 20.12, I passed in an invalid model, but I could just as easily have passed in a *valid* model, or even `null`; the controller doesn't use the binding model if the `ModelState` isn't valid, so the test would still pass. But if you're writing unit tests like this one, I recommend trying to keep your model consistent with your `ModelState`, otherwise your unit tests aren't testing a situation that occurs in practice!

Personally, I tend to shy away from unit testing MVC controllers directly in this way. As you've seen with model binding, the controllers are somewhat dependent on earlier stages of the `MvcMiddleware`, which you often need to emulate. Similarly, if your controllers access the `HttpContext` (available on the `Controller` and `ControllerBase` base classes), you may need to perform additional setup.

Instead, I try to keep controllers as thin as possible, pushing as much of the behavior into business logic services that can be easily unit tested, or into middleware and filters, which can similarly be tested independently.

> **NOTE** This is a personal preference. Some people like to get as close to 100% test coverage for their code base as possible, but I find testing orchestration classes is often more hassle than it's worth.

Although I often forgo *unit* testing MVC controllers, I write *integration* tests that test the controllers in the context of a complete application. In the next section, we'll look at ways to write integration tests for your app, so you can test its various components in the context of the ASP.NET Core framework as a whole.

20.5 Integration testing: testing your whole app with a Test Host

If you search the internet for the different types of testing,[5] you'll find a host of different types to choose from. The differences between them are sometimes subtle and people don't universally agree upon the definitions. I chose not to dwell on it in this book—I consider unit tests to be isolated tests of a component and integration tests to be tests that exercise multiple components at once.

In this section, I'm going to show how you can write integration tests for the `StatusMiddleware` from section 20.3 and an MVC controller similar to that tested in section 20.4. Instead of isolating the components from the surrounding framework and invoking them directly, you'll specifically test them in a similar context to when you use them in practice.

Integration tests are an important part of confirming that your components function correctly, but they don't remove the need for unit tests. Unit tests are excellent for testing small pieces of logic contained in your components and are typically quick to execute. Integration tests are normally significantly slower, as they require much more configuration and may rely on external infrastructure, such as a database.

---

[5] Or let me do it for you: https://lmgtfy.com/?q=different+types+of+software+testing.

Consequently, it's normal to have far more unit tests for an app than integration tests. As you saw in section 20.2, unit tests typically verify the behavior of a component, using valid inputs, edge cases, and invalid inputs, to ensure that the component behaves correctly in all cases. Once you have an extensive suite of unit tests, you'll likely only need a few integration tests to be confident your application is working correctly.

You could write many different types of integration tests for an application. You could test that a service can write to a database correctly, that it can integrate with a third-party service (for sending emails, for example), or that it can handle HTTP requests made to it.

In this section, you're going to focus on the last point, verifying that your app can handle requests made to it, just as you would if you were accessing the app from a browser. For this, you're going to use a useful library provided by the ASP.NET Core team called Microsoft.AspNetCore.TestHost.

20.5.1 *Creating a TestServer using the Test Host package*

Imagine you want to write some integration tests for the `StatusMiddleware` from section 20.3. You've already written unit tests for it, but you want to have at least one integration test that tests the middleware in the context of the ASP.NET Core infrastructure.

You could go about this in many ways. Perhaps the most complete approach would be to create a separate project and configure `StatusMiddleware` as the only middleware in the pipeline. You'd then need to run this project, wait for it to start up, send requests to it, and inspect the responses.

This would possibly make for a good test, but it would also require a lot of configuration, and be fragile and error-prone. What if the test app can't start because it tries to use an already-taken port? What if the test app doesn't shut down correctly? How long should the integration test wait for the app to start?

The ASP.NET Core Test Host package lets you get close to this setup, without having the added complexity of spinning up a separate app. You add the Test Host to your test project by adding the Microsoft.AspNetCore.TestHost NuGet package, either using the Visual Studio NuGet GUI, Package Manager Console, or the .NET CLI. Alternatively, add the `<PackageReference>` element directly to your csproj file:

```
<PackageReference Include="Microsoft.AspNetCore.TestHost" Version="2.0.0"/>
```

In a typical ASP.NET Core app, you create a `WebHostBuilder` in your `Program` class, configure a web server (Kestrel) and define your application's configuration, services, and middleware pipeline (using a Startup file). Finally, you call `Build()` on the `WebHostBuilder` to create an instance of a `WebHost` that can be run and will listen for requests on a given URL and port.

The Test Host package uses the same `WebHostBuilder` to define your test application, but it takes care of building and running the web host for you, as shown in figure

20.8. Instead of listening for requests at the network level, it creates an `IWebHost` that uses in-memory request objects. It even exposes an `HttpClient` that you can use to send requests to the test app. You can interact with the `HttpClient` as though it were sending requests over the network, but in reality, the requests are kept entirely in memory.

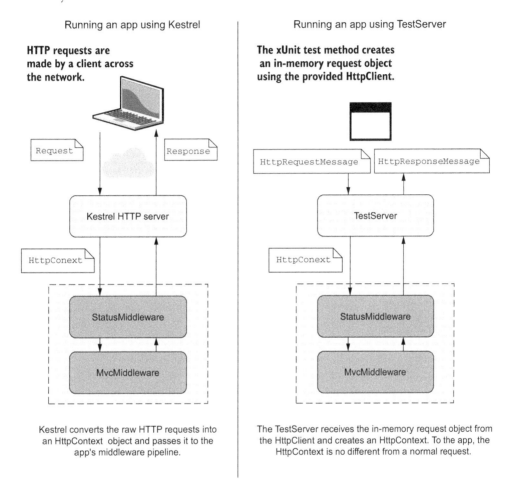

Figure 20.8 When your app runs normally, it uses the Kestrel server. This listens for HTTP requests and converts requests into an `HttpContext`, which is passed to the middleware pipeline. The `TestServer` doesn't listen for requests on the network. Instead, you use an `HttpClient` to make in-memory requests. From the point of view of the middleware, there's no difference.

Listing 20.13 shows how to use the Test Host package to create an integration test for the `StatusMiddleware`. First, create a `WebHostBuilder` and configure the middleware as the only component in the pipeline, then pass the builder to a `TestServer`. The `TestServer` is the main component in the Test Host package, which makes all the magic possible. You can then create an `HttpClient`, use it to make requests to the server, and verify the response.

Listing 20.13   Creating an integration test with `TestServer`

```
public class StatusMiddlewareTests
{
    [Fact]
    public async Task StatusMiddlewareReturnsPong()
    {
        var hostBuilder = new WebHostBuilder()
            .Configure(app =>
            {
                app.UseMiddleware<StatusMiddleware>();
            });

        using (var server = new TestServer(hostBuilder))
        {
            HttpClient client = server.CreateClient();

            var response = await client.GetAsync("/ping");

            response.EnsureSuccessStatusCode();
            var content = await response.Content.ReadAsStringAsync();
            Assert.Equal("pong", content);
        }
    }
}
```

- Configures a WebHostBuilder that defines your app
- Creates an instance of the TestServer, passing in the WebHostBuilder app
- Creates an HttpClient, or you can interact directly with the server object
- Makes an in-memory request, which is handled by the app as normal.
- Reads the body content and verifies that it contained "pong"
- Verifies the response was a success (2xx) status code

This test ensures that the test application defined by `WebHostBuilder` returns the expected value when it receives a request to the `/ping` path. The request is entirely in-memory, but from the point of view of `StatusMiddleware`, it's the same as if the request came from the network.

The `WebHostBuilder` in this example is simple. Even though it's an integration test, you're specifically testing the `StatusMiddleware` on its own, rather than in the context of a whole application. You may want to test the middleware in the context of your *real* application, including all of your configured middleware, and maybe even database access.

If you want to run integration tests based on an existing app, then you don't want to have to configure your test `WebHostBuilder` manually like you did in listing 20.13. Instead, you can use the app's Startup.cs file directly.

20.5.2   *Using your application's Startup file for integration tests*

In listing 20.13, you configured the `WebHostBuilder` by calling `Configure()` and defining the middleware pipeline in a lambda function. This method is the same as the `Configure` method of your `Startup` class in a normal app: it defines the middleware pipeline. You can configure your real apps in this way too, but generally you should call `UseStartup<T>()` instead, and define your middleware pipeline in a `Startup` class.

> **TIP** The `Startup` class approach has a couple of advantages. You can explicitly inject services into the `Configure` method when you use a `Startup` class and it separates the aspects of configuration that are likely to change (your services and middleware pipeline) from the static configuration that typically resides in `Program`.

You can use the same approach of a `Startup` class to configure your `WebHostBuilder` in integration tests, too. You could rewrite the test from listing 20.13 to use a `Startup` class from a referenced project, as shown next. In this example, you've added a reference from the test project to the main app, and reference the `Startup` class directly using `UseStartup<Startup>()`.

Listing 20.14 Creating an integration test with `TestServer` and a Startup class

```
public class StatusMiddlewareTests
{
    [Fact]
    public async Task StatusMiddlewareReturnsPong()          Instead of configuring
    {                                                        WebHostBuilder manually,
        var hostBuilder = new WebHostBuilder()               you can use the Startup
            .UseStartup<Startup>();      ◁──────             from your real app.

        using (var server = new TestServer(hostBuilder))
        {
            HttpClient client = server.CreateClient();

            var response = await client.GetAsync("/ping");

            response.EnsureSuccessStatusCode();
            var content = await response.Content.ReadAsStringAsync();
            Assert.Equal("pong", content);
        }
    }
}
```

Instead of creating a minimal pipeline with only `StatusMiddleware`, listing 20.14 uses the full middleware pipeline for your app. If the pipeline contains `StatusMiddleware`, then the test would pass, as the middleware should return a `"pong"`.

These two tests are both integration tests, but they're fundamentally rather different. The first test, listing 20.13, represents an integration test specifically for `Status-Middleware`; it tests the behavior of the middleware in the larger context of the ASP.NET Core framework. The second test, listing 20.14, is more like an integration test for your *app*. The second test doesn't care *how* the pong is generated—maybe it was generated by an MVC controller, for example—it ensures your *app* behaves as expected. You may want to have both sorts of tests for your app, depending on your requirements.

Listing 20.14 works as expected when you make a request to `StatusMiddleware` using the `/ping` URL, but if you try to call an MVC controller you'll run into some strange exceptions. In the next section, you'll explore these issues and how to resolve them.

20.5.3 *Rendering Razor views in TestServer integration tests*

In the previous section, I described how you could write integration tests using a real app's Startup class, so that the `TestServer` has the same middleware pipeline as your app. But as you've seen throughout this book, the Startup.cs file doesn't describe *all* of your application's setup.

> **NOTE** ASP.NET Core 2.1 introduces the Microsoft.AspNetCore.Mvc.Testing package, which solves the issues described in this section. For details, see http://mng.bz/2QP2.

In your app's `Program` class, you create an instance of `WebHostBuilder`, either using the default `WebHost.CreateBuilder()`, or by creating `WebHostBuilder` manually and customizing it by calling `UseConfiguration()`, `UseEnvironment()`, `UseKestrel()`, and so on.

If you're running integration tests using the `Startup` approach shown in listing 20.14, you have to be aware of the differences between the `WebHostBuilder` created in your app and the `WebHostBuilder` in your test.

If you change the request path in listing 20.14 to `"/"`, this request will be routed to the `Index` action on `HomeController` for a default MVC application. But if that action returns a `ViewResult`, the `TestServer` will generate an error like the following:

```
System.InvalidOperationException: The view 'Index' was not found. The
    following locations were searched:
/Views/Home/Index.cshtml
/Views/Shared/Index.cshtml
```

The problem stems from the fact that you've only *partially* configured the application. You defined the middleware pipeline and the DI container by specifying a Startup class, but you didn't add any other configuration to the `WebHostBuilder`. You didn't configure the app configuration (such as appsettings.json and environment variables) or the hosting environment, but most importantly, you didn't configure the *content root* directory.

> **DEFINITION** The *content root* is the base directory for the application. It defines where the app should look for configuration files and the Views folder, for example.

If you don't specify a content root path by calling `UseContentRoot()` on the `WebHost-Builder()`, then the app uses the directory where the app is running. In the context of a unit test, that will be the bin folder of the test project, something like

```
test\ExchangeRates.Web.Test\bin\debug\netcreapp2.0
```

whereas you need the content root to be the root of your actual app, as shown in figure 20.9, something like

```
src\ExchangeRates.Web
```

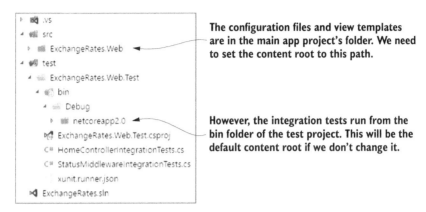

The configuration files and view templates are in the main app project's folder. We need to set the content root to this path.

However, the integration tests run from the bin folder of the test project. This will be the default content root if we don't change it.

Figure 20.9 The default content root for an application is the directory it's running in. For integration tests using Razor files, you need to set the content root to the main app's project folder instead.

The simple solution to this issue is to explicitly set the content root path of the `Web-HostBuilder` in your integration test to point to your real app's project folder. The biggest pain-point is calculating the *relative* path from the test project's bin folder to your real app's project folder.

From figure 20.9, you can see that, in this example, you have to navigate to the fifth parent folder, and then into the src and ExhangeRates.Web folders. The following listing is similar to listing 20.14, but instead of creating a `WebHostBuilder` directly, you're using the `WebHost.CreateDefaultBuilder()` method and passing in a calculated content root for the application.

Listing 20.15 Creating an integration test with the TestServer and a Startup file

```
[Fact]
public async Task IndexReturnsHtml()
{
    var projectRootPath = Path.Combine(
        Directory.GetCurrentDirectory(),
        "..", "..", "..", "..", "..", "src", "ExchangeRates.Web");

    var builder = WebHost.CreateDefaultBuilder()
        .UseStartup<Startup>()
        .UseContentRoot(projectRootPath);

    using (var server = new TestServer(hostBuilder))
```

Calculates the project root path and uses Path.Combine to ensure cross-platform path separators

Creates a default WebHostBuilder which loads configuration like the real app

Sets the content root for the test to the real app's project folder

```
    {
        HttpClient client = server.CreateClient();

        var response = await client.GetAsync("/");

        response.EnsureSuccessStatusCode();
        var content = await response.Content.ReadAsStringAsync();
        Assert.Contains("<h1>Home page</h1>", content);
}
```

> **TIP**   In this example, you created a `WebHostBuilder` using the static helper. If
> your app doesn't use the `CreateDefaultBuilder` helper, then with a little bit
> of refactoring of your app's `Program` class, you can expose the same `WebHost-`
> `Builder` configuration to your integration tests. See the code samples for this
> chapter for an example.

There's one more thing you need to do before running this test to ensure the Test-
Server can compile your Razor pages at runtime. The details are rather technical, so I
won't go into them here.[6] Copy and paste the code in listing 20.16 into your *test* project's csproj file. Remember you can right-click a project in Visual Studio and choose
Edit projectname.csproj. Add the code before the final `</Project>` element in the file.

Listing 20.16   MSBuild target to allow compilation of Razor pages in integration tests

```
<Target Name="CopyDepsFiles" AfterTargets="Build"
        Condition="'$(TargetFramework)'!=''">
  <ItemGroup>
    <DepsFilePaths Include="$([System.IO.Path]::ChangeExtension(
'%(_ResolvedProjectReferencePaths.FullPath)','.deps.json'))" />
  </ItemGroup>
  <Copy SourceFiles="%(DepsFilePaths.FullPath)"
        DestinationFolder="$(OutputPath)"
        Condition="Exists('%(DepsFilePaths.FullPath)')" />
</Target>
```

With this in place, you'll be able to test an app that uses Razor templates. Remember
that if you're genuinely using the same configuration as your real app, you'll also be
calling the same services and writing to the same database! If you're doing full end-to-
end integration tests of your app, then this may be desirable; make sure you understand the implications.

> **WARNING**   If you load a real app's configuration in an integration test, then any
> requests you make will have the same effect as if you made them to the running
> app. This includes calling third-party services and writing to a database.

---

[6] If you're interested in the details, you can read about the issue at https://github.com/aspnet/Razor/
issues/1212.

If you want to use a slightly different configuration when running integration tests for your app, I suggest you define a `"Testing"` hosting environment and use it to configure the app differently, as I described in chapter 11.

If you have more than one integration test for your application, then you may find yourself creating a new `TestServer` inside every test. This is effectively starting up a new test server, which can be an expensive process performance-wise, especially if the server has to load configuration files from disk. To get around this, in xUnit you can share a single configured `TestServer` instance between multiple tests by using a *test fixture*.

20.5.4 *Extracting common setup into an xUnit test fixture*

A *test fixture* is a class that's shared among all the test methods in a class. Normally, xUnit creates an instance of a test class and runs a single [Fact] or [Theory] test method. Every test method is run in its own separate instance, so you can't easily share objects between test methods.

Sometimes, as is the case for integration tests, the setup for a test (its context) is expensive, which makes running your tests slower. Instead, you can use a fixture to ensure the expensive setup happens *once per test class*, instead of *every test method*. To create a fixture, you must

1 Create the fixture class, `T`. This is the class that will be passed to the test method.
2 Implement `IClassFixture<T>` on your test class. This interface has no methods, but signals to xUnit that it should create an instance of `T` before calling the first test method.
3 Inject an instance of `T` into the test class constructor.

In listing 20.17, you'll create a test fixture for your integration tests. In this example, I'm using the `CreateDefaultBuilder` method to create the `WebHostBuilder` and setting the content root path as you saw in listing 20.15. This is used to create a `TestServer` and `HttpClient`, which the `TestFixture` exposes for use in test methods. If a test fixture implements `IDisposable`, xUnit will automatically call `Dispose()` after your tests have run, to clean up any resources.

> **Listing 20.17 Creating a test fixture for use in integration tests**

```
public class TestFixture : IDisposable                          Defines the content
{                                                               root path for the app
    public TestFixture()
    {
        var projectRootPath = Path.Combine(
            Directory.GetCurrentDirectory(),
            "..", "..", "..", "..", "..", "src", "ExchangeRates.Web");

        var builder = WebHost.CreateDefaultBuilder()            Defines the WebHostBuilder
            .UseStartup<Startup>()                              for the app
            .UseContentRoot(projectRootPath);
```

```
        Server = new TestServer(builder);    ◁——— Creates the TestServer

        Client = Server.CreateClient();    ◁
  ┌———▷ Client.BaseAddress = new Uri("http://localhost:5000");
  │   }
  │
  │   public HttpClient Client { get; }
  │   public TestServer Server { get; }
  │
  │   public void Dispose()
  │   {
  │       Client?.Dispose();
  │       Server?.Dispose();
  │   }
  │ }
```

**Creates a test
HttpClient for use
in the test methods**

**xUnit will call Dispose
after all the test methods
in a class have run.**

**Exposes the TestServer
and HttpClient for use
in integration tests**

**Optionally, sets the base path to
use for requests. Note that
requests are still sent in-memory.**

Now that you've defined your fixture, you can update your integration test class to use
it in its test methods. The following listing shows two integration tests, one for the
StatusMiddleware and one for the HomeController Index page. Both tests use the
same TestFixture instance, hence, the same TestServer instance. Once both tests
have run, the TestFixture is disposed.

Listing 20.18   Integration tests using `TestFixture`

```
public class IntegrationTests : IClassFixture<TestFixture>    ◁
{
    private readonly HttpClient _client;
    public IntegrationTests(TestFixture fixture)
    {
        _client = fixture.Client;
    }

    [Fact]
    public async Task PingReturnsPong()
    {
        var response = await _client.GetAsync("/ping");    ◁

        var content = await response.Content.ReadAsStringAsync();
        Assert.Contains("pong", content);
    }

    [Fact]
    public async Task IndexReturnsHtml()
    {
        var response = await _client.GetAsync("/");    ◁

        var content = await response.Content.ReadAsStringAsync();
        Assert.Contains("<h1>Home page</h1>", content);
    }
}
```

**The test class
must implement
IClassFixture< >.**

**An instance of TestFixture
is created before the first
test run and is injected
into the test class.**

**You can use the HttpClient
from the fixture to test the
"/ping" route.**

**The test fixture encapsulates the
complex WebHostBuilder setup so
you can easily test MVC.**

Running integration using your real app's configuration requires a fair amount of configuration, but it has the definite advantage that your app's behavior in the integration tests will be about as close to your real app's behavior as possible.

We've almost reached the end of this section on integration testing, but I'll leave you with one small ray of hope. In ASP.NET Core 2.1 (in preview at the time of writing), the process of creating integration tests should be simplified by the introduction of the Microsoft.AspNetCore.Mvc.Testing package. This will simplify creating test fixtures and remove the need to add custom MSBuild targets to your test files. For details, see the post at http://mng.bz/2QP2.

In the final section of this chapter, we'll look at how to use the SQLite provider for EF Core with an in-memory database. You can use this approach to write tests for services that use an EF Core database context, without needing access to a database.

20.6 Isolating the database with an in-memory EF Core provider

As you saw in chapter 12, EF Core is an ORM that is used primarily with relational databases. In this section, I'm going to discuss one way to test services that depend on an EF Core DbContext, without having to configure or interact with a real database.

> **NOTE** To learn more about testing your EF Core code, see *Entity Framework Core in Action* by Jon P Smith (Manning, 2018), http://mng.bz/k0dz.

The following listing shows a highly stripped-down version of the RecipeService you created in chapter 12 for the recipe app. It shows a single method to fetch the details of a recipe using an injected EF Core DbContext.

Listing 20.19 RecipeService to test, which uses EF Core to store and load entities

```
public class RecipeService
{
    readonly AppDbContext _context;
    public RecipeService(AppDbContext context)       An EF Core DbContext is
    {                                                 injected in the constructor.
        _context = context;
    }

    public RecipeViewModel GetRecipe(int id)
    {
        return _context.Recipes        ◁────         Uses the DbSet<Recipes>
            .Where(x => x.RecipeId == id)             property to load recipes and
            .Select(x => new RecipeViewModel          creates a RecipeViewModel
            {
                Id = x.RecipeId,
                Name = x.Name
            })
            .SingleOrDefault();
    }
}
```

Writing unit tests for this class is a bit of a problem. Unit tests should be fast, repeatable, and isolated from other dependencies, but you have a dependency on your app's DbContext. You don't want to be writing to a real database in unit tests, as it would make the tests slow, potentially unrepeatable, and highly dependent on the configuration of the database: a fail on all three requirements!

Luckily, Microsoft ships two *in-memory* database providers for this scenario. Recall from chapter 12 that when you configure your app's DbContext in Startup.Configure-Services, you configure a specific database provider, such as SQL Server, for example:

```
services.AddDbContext<AppDbContext>(options =>
    options.UseSqlServer(connectionSttring);
```

The in-memory database providers are alternative providers designed *only for testing*. Microsoft includes two in-memory providers in ASP.NET Core:

- *Microsoft.EntityFrameworkCore.InMemory*—This provider doesn't simulate a database, instead, it stores objects directly in memory. It isn't a relational database as such, so it doesn't have all the features of a normal database. You can't execute SQL against it directly, and it won't enforce constraints, but it's fast.
- *Microsoft.EntityFrameworkCore.Sqlite*—SQLite is a relational database. It's limited in features compared to a database like SQL Server, but it's a true relational database, unlike the in-memory database provider. Normally, a SQLite database is written to a file, but the provider includes an in-memory mode, in which the database stays in memory. This makes it much faster and easier to create and use for testing.

Instead of storing data in a database on disk, both of these providers store data in memory, as shown in figure 20.10. This makes them fast, easy to create and tear down, and allows you to create a new database for every test, to ensure your tests stay isolated from one another.

> **TIP**   In this post, I describe how to use the SQLite provider as an in-memory database, as it's more fully featured than the in-memory provider. For details on using the in-memory provider see http://mng.bz/hdIq.

To use the SQLite provider in memory, add the Microsoft.EntityFramework-Core.Sqlite package to your test project's csproj file. This adds the UseSqlite() extension method, which you'll use to configure the database provider for your unit tests.

> **TIP**   If you're using ASP.NET Core 2.0, this package is already included via the Microsoft.AspNetCore.All metapackage.

Listing 20.20 shows how you could use the in-memory SQLite provider to test the Get-Recipe() method of RecipeService. Start by creating a SqliteConnection object and using the "DataSource=:memory:" connection string. This tells the provider to store the database in memory and then open the connection.

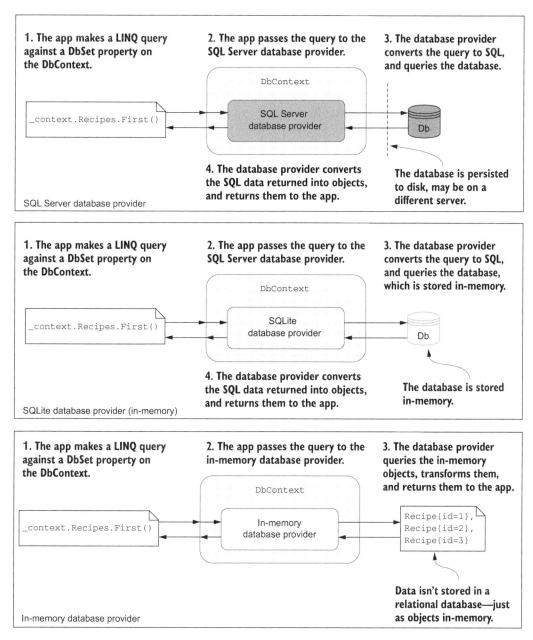

Figure 20.10 The in-memory database provider and SQLite provider (in-memory mode) compared to the SQL Server database provider. The in-memory database provider doesn't simulate a database as such. Instead, it stores objects in memory and executes LINQ queries against them directly.

> **WARNING**   The in-memory database is destroyed when the connection is closed. If you don't open the connection yourself, EF Core will close the connection to the in-memory database when you dispose the DbContext. If you want to share an in-memory database between DbContexts, you must explicitly open the connection yourself.

Next, pass the SqlLiteConnection instance into the DbContextOptionsBuilder<> and call UseSqlite(). This configures the resulting DbContextOptions<> object with the necessary services for the SQLite provider and provides the connection to the in-memory database. By passing this options object into an instance of AppDbContext, all calls to the DbContext result in calls to the in-memory database provider.

Listing 20.20   Using the in-memory database provider to test an EF Core DbContext

Configures an in-memory SQLite connection using the special "in-memory" connection string

Opens the connection so EF Core won't close it automatically

```
[Fact]
public void GetRecipeDetails_CanLoadFromContext()
{
    var connection = new SqliteConnection("DataSource=:memory:");
    connection.Open();

    var options = new DbContextOptionsBuilder<AppDbContext>()
        .UseSqlite(connection)
        .Options;

    using (var context = new AppDbContext(options))
    {
        context.Database.EnsureCreated();

        context.Recipes.AddRange(
            new Recipe { RecipeId = 1, Name = "Recipe1" },
            new Recipe { RecipeId = 2, Name = "Recipe2" },
            new Recipe { RecipeId = 3, Name = "Recipe3" });
        context.SaveChanges();
    }

    using (var context = new AppDbContext(options))
    {
        var service = new RecipeService(context);

        var recipe = service.GetRecipe (id: 2);

        Assert.NotNull(recipe);
        Assert.Equal(2, recipe.Id);
        Assert.Equal("Recipe2", recipe.Name);
    }
}
```

Creates a DbContext and passes in the options

Creates an instance of DbContextOptions<> and configures it to use the SQLite connection

Adds some recipes to the DbContext

Ensures the in-memory database matches EF Core's model (similar to running migrations)

Saves the changes to the in-memory database

Creates a fresh DbContext to test that you can retrieve data from the DbContext

Executes the GetRecipe function. This executes the query against the in-memory database.

Creates the RecipeService to test and pass in the fresh DbContext

Verifies that you correctly retrieved the recipe from the in-memory database

This is a simple example, but it follows the standard format for any time you need to test a class that depends on an EF Core `DbContext`:

1 Create a `SqliteConnection` with the `"DataSource=:memory:"` connection string and open the connection.

2 Create a `DbContextOptionsBuilder<>` and call `UseSqlite()`, passing in the open connection.

3 Retrieve the `DbContextOptions` object from the `Options` property.

4 Pass the options to an instance of your `DbContext` and ensure the database matches EF Core's model by calling `context.Database.EnsureCreated()`. This is similar to running migrations on your database. Create and add any required test data to the in-memory database and call `SaveChanges()` to persist the data.

5 Create a new instance of your `DbContext` and inject it into your test class. All queries will be executed against the in-memory database.

By using two separate `DbContexts`, you can avoid bugs in your tests due to EF Core caching data without writing it to the database. With this approach, you can be sure that any data read in the second `DbContext` was definitely persisted to the underlying in-memory database provider.

This was a relatively brief introduction to using the SQLite provider as an in-memory database provider, and EF Core testing in general, but if you follow the setup shown in listing 20.20, it should take you a long way. For more details on testing EF Core, including additional options and strategies, see *Entity Framework Core in Action* by Jon P Smith (Manning, 2018).

Summary

- Unit test apps are console apps that have a dependency on the .NET Test SDK, a test framework such as xUnit, MSTest, or NUnit, and a test runner adapter.

- You can run the tests in a test project by calling `dotnet test` from the command line in your test project or using the Test Explorer in Visual Studio.

- Many testing frameworks are compatible with the .NET Test SDK, but xUnit has emerged as an almost *de facto* standard for ASP.NET Core projects. The ASP.NET Core team themselves use it to test the framework.

- To create an xUnit test project, choose .NET Core xUnit Test Project in Visual Studio or use the `dotnet new xunit` CLI command. This creates a test project containing the Microsoft.NET.Test.Sdk, xunit, and xunit.runner.visualstudio NuGet packages.

- xUnit includes two different attributes to identify test methods. `[Fact]` methods should be public and parameterless. `[Theory]` methods can contain parameters, so they can be used to run a similar test repeatedly with different parameters. You can provide the data for each `[Theory]` run using the `[InlineData]` attribute.

- Use assertions in your test methods to verify that the service under test returned an expected value. Assertions exist for most common scenarios, including verifying that a method call raised an exception of a specific type.

- Use the `DefaultHttpContext` class to unit test your custom middleware components. If you need access to the response body, you must replace the default `Stream.Null` with a `MemoryStream` instance and manually read the stream after invoking the middleware.

- MVC controllers can be unit tested just like other classes. But they should generally contain little business logic, so it may not be worth the effort. In particular, the MVC controller is tested independently of routing, model validation, and filters, so you can't easily test logic that depends on any of these aspects.

- Integration tests allow you to test multiple components of your app at once, typically within the context of the ASP.NET Core framework itself. The Microsoft .AspNetCore.TestHost package provides a `TestServer` object that you can use to create a simple web host for testing. This creates an in-memory version of your app that you can make requests to and receive responses from.

- Create a `TestServer` by passing in a configured `WebHostBuilder`. The `TestServer` exposes an `HttpClient` property, `Client`. You can make requests with this client as you would a normal `HttpClient`, and they'll be served by `TestServer`.

- You can configure the `WebHostBuilder` using your application's Startup file to closely match your real application. If you need to load configuration files or Razor views from your ASP.NET Core app, you'll need to configure the correct relative `ContentRootPath` for your app.

- To correctly render Razor views, you must currently add an additional `MSBuild` target to your test csproj file. In ASP.NET Core 2.1, you can avoid this by installing the Microsoft.AspNetCore.Mvc.Testing package in your test project.

- If you're using the same `TestHost` configuration for all your integration tests, you can configure the host in a custom `T` class, implement `IClassFixture<T>` in your test class, and inject an instance of `T` into your test class' constructor. All tests in that class will use the same instance of `T`, reducing the number of times the `TestHost` is created.

- You can use the EF Core SQLite provider as an in-memory database to test code that depends on an EF Core database context. You configure the in-memory provider by creating a `SqliteConnection` with a `"DataSource=:memory:"` connection string. Create a `DbContextOptionsBuilder<>` object and call `UseSqlite()`, passing in the connection. Finally, pass `DbContextOptions<>` into an instance of your app's `DbContext` and call `context.Database.EnsureCreated()` to prepare the in-memory database for use with EF Core.

- The SQLite in-memory database is maintained as long as there's an open `SqliteConnection`. By opening the connection manually, the database can be used with multiple `DbContexts`. If you don't call `Open()` on the connection, EF Core will close the connection (and delete the in-memory database) when the `DbContext` is disposed.

appendix A
Getting to grips with
.NET Core and .NET Standard

This appendix covers

- Understanding the position of .NET Core in the .NET ecosystem
- Sharing code between projects using .NET Standard libraries
- Using the .NET Framework compatibility shim

The .NET ecosystem has changed a lot since .NET was first introduced, but the development of .NET Core has resulted in a particularly large degree of churn and the introduction of many new concepts.

This churn isn't surprising given Microsoft's newfound transparency regarding the development process, building in the open on GitHub. Unfortunately, it can be confusing for developers new to the .NET Framework, and even to seasoned veterans! In this appendix, I'll try to straighten out some of the terms that developers new to .NET Core often find confusing, as well as provide some context for the changes.

I begin by discussing the .NET ecosystem prior to .NET Core, to highlight the issues Microsoft is attempting to solve by developing .NET Core. I describe the structure of a typical .NET platform and how that relates to .NET Core, as well as the similarities and differences between .NET Core and other platforms like the .NET Framework.

.NET Core wasn't developed in isolation, and one of its primary design goals was to improve the ability to share code between multiple frameworks. In section A.2, I describe how this was achieved in pre-.NET Core days, using Portable Class Libraries (PCLs), and the new approach using .NET Standard.

Finally, I provide some guidance on how to choose a target framework for your applications and libraries. With so many different target frameworks to choose from—.NET Core, the .NET Framework, .NET Standard—it can be hard to understand what the pros and cons are. In section A.3, I provide some best practices that I stick to that ensure the greatest code reuse for my libraries and avoid incompatibilities between libraries.

A.1 *Exploring the motivations for .NET Core*

If you're a .NET developer, chances are you're already familiar with the .NET Framework. The .NET Framework, version 4.7.1 at the time of writing, is a Windows-only development platform that you can use for both desktop and web development. It's installed by default on Windows and contains a variety of functionality for building applications.

If you're a Xamarin developer, you might also be familiar with the Xamarin framework, which uses the cross-platform Mono implementation of the .NET Framework. This is an alternative *platform* to the .NET Framework that you can use to build mobile applications on Windows, Android, and iOS.

These two platforms are separate, but they consist of many similar components and implement similar APIs. Each platform contains libraries and app-models specific to their platform, but they use similar fundamental libraries and types, as shown in figure A.1.

At the bottom of each stack is the tooling that allows you to compile and run .NET applications such as the compiler and the common language runtime (CLR). At the top of each stack, you have the app-specific libraries that you use to build applications for your platform. For example, you could build a Windows Forms app on the .NET Framework, but not using the Xamarin platform, and vice-versa for an iOS app.

In the middle of each stack you have the Base Class Libraries (BCL). These are the fundamental .NET types you use in your apps on a daily basis: the `int` and `string` types, the file-reading APIs, the `Task` APIs, and so on. Although both .NET platforms have many similar types, they're fundamentally different, so you can't guarantee a type will exist on both platforms, or that it will expose the same methods and properties.

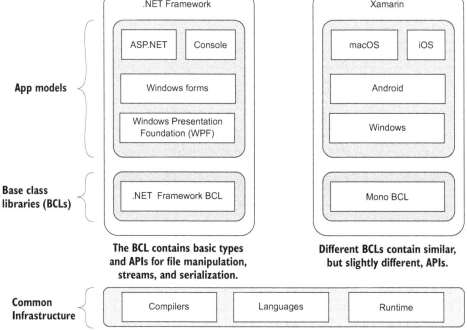

Figure A.1   The layers that make up the .NET Framework. Each builds on the capabilities of the layer below, with the highest layer providing the app models that you'll use to build your applications.

I've only discussed two platforms so far, the .NET Framework and Xamarin, but .NET has *many* different implementations, of which these are only two. Windows also has the Windows 8/8.1 platform and the Universal Windows Platform (UWP). On phones, in addition to Xamarin, there's the Windows Phone 8.1 and Silverlight Phone platforms. The list goes on and on (Unity, .NET Compact Framework (CF), .NET Micro …)!

Each of these platforms uses a slightly different set of APIs (classes and methods) in their BCL. Platforms have a certain number of similar APIs between them in their BCLs, but the intersection is patchy. On top of that, the libraries that make up the BCL of a platform are fundamentally not interoperable. Any source code written for a given set of APIs must be specifically recompiled for each target platform.

Several years ago, Microsoft realized this sharding of .NET was a problem. Developers had to know a *slightly* different set of APIs for each platform, and sharing code so that it could be used on more than one platform was a pain.

On top of that, the primary web development platform of the .NET Framework was showing its age. The software industry was moving toward small, lightweight, cloud-native frameworks that you could deploy in cross-platform environments. The centrally installed Windows-only .NET Framework was not designed for these scenarios.

The .NET Core platform was Microsoft's solution. .NET Core is highly modular, can be deployed side-by-side with other .NET Core installations (or alternatively, distributed with the app), and is cross-platform. The term .NET Core is somewhat overloaded, in that it was used through development as a general umbrella term to describe a variety of changes. The .NET Core platform consists of

- *A cross-platform BCL*—The BCL libraries of the .NET Core platform, sometimes called CoreFX, were developed in the open on GitHub at https://github.com/dotnet/corefx.
- *A new cross-platform runtime*—The runtime for .NET Core, called CoreCLR. It was also developed on GitHub at https://github.com/dotnet/coreclr.
- *The .NET CLI tooling*—The dotnet tool used for building and running apps as you've seen, again on GitHub https://github.com/dotnet/cli.
- *The ASP.NET Core libraries*—Used to build ASP.NET Core applications. These were later moved to run on the .NET Framework as well as .NET Core.

These components make up the .NET Core platform and find their analogs to the various components that make up the .NET Framework and Xamarin platforms you saw in figure A.1. By creating a new platform, Microsoft was able to maintain backward compatibility for apps that used the .NET Framework, which allowed new apps to be developed using .NET Core and take advantage of its cross-platform and isolated deployment story.

> **NOTE** You might be thinking, "Wait, they had too many .NET platforms, so they created *another* one?" If so, you're on the ball. But luckily, with .NET Core, came .NET Standard.

On its own, .NET Core would've meant *yet another* BCL of APIs for .NET developers to learn. But as part of the development of .NET Core, Microsoft introduced .NET Standard. .NET Standard, as the name suggests, ensures a *standard set* of APIs is available on every .NET platform. You no longer have to learn the specific set of APIs available for the flavor of .NET you're using; if you can use the .NET Standard APIs, you know you'll be fine.

Before I dig into the details of .NET Standard, I'll briefly discuss its predecessor, Portable Class Libraries, and why they're now obsolete thanks to .NET Standard.

A.2 *Sharing code between projects*

With so many different .NET implementations, the .NET ecosystem needed a way to share code between libraries long before .NET Core was envisaged. What if you wanted to use the same classes in both your ASP.NET .NET Framework project and your Silverlight project? You'd have to create a separate project for each platform, copy and paste files between them, and recompile your code for each platform. The result was two different libraries from the same code. PCLs were the initial solution to this problem.

A.2.1 *Finding a common intersection with Portable Class Libraries*

PCLs were introduced to make the process of compiling and sharing code between multiple platforms simpler. When creating a library, developers could specify the platforms they wanted to support, and the project would only have access to the set of APIs common among all of them. Each additional platform supported would reduce the API surface to only those APIs available in *all* the selected platforms, as shown in figure A.2.

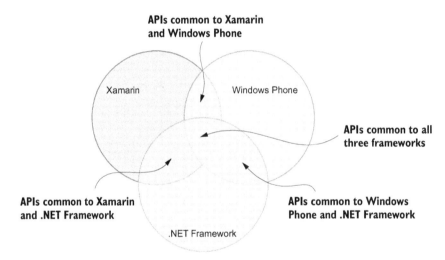

Figure A.2   Each additional framework that must be supported by a PCL reduces the APIs available to your application.

To create a PCL library, you'd create a library that targeted a specific PCL profile. This profile contained a precomputed list of APIs known to be available on the associated platforms. That way, you could create one library that you could share across your selected platforms. You could have a single project and a single resulting package—no copy and paste or duplicate projects required.

This approach was a definite improvement over the previous option, but creating PCLs was often tricky. There were inherent tooling complexities to contend with, and understanding the APIs available for each different combination of platforms that made up a PCL profile was difficult.[1]

---

[1]   See here for the full horrifying list: https://portablelibraryprofiles.stephencleary.com/.

On top of these issues, every additional platform you targeted would reduce the BCL API surface available for you to use in your library. For example, the .NET Framework might contain APIs A, B, and C. But if Xamarin only has API A and Windows Phone only has API C, then your library can't use any of them, as shown in figure A.3.

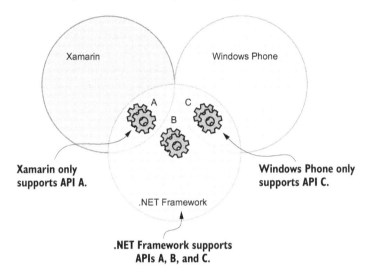

Figure A.3 Each platform exposes slightly different APIs. When creating PCLs, only those APIs that are available in all of the targeted platforms are available. In this case, none of the APIs, A, B, or C, is available in all targeted platforms, so none of them can be used in the PCL.

One additional issue with PCL libraries was that they were inherently tied to the underlying platforms they targeted. In order to work with a new target platform, you'd have to recompile the PCL, even if no source code changes were required.

Say you're using a PCL library that supports Windows Phone 8.1 and .NET 4.5. If Microsoft were to release a new platform, let's say, .NET Fridge, which exposes the same API as Windows Phone 8.1, you wouldn't be able to use the existing library with your new .NET Fridge application. Instead, you'd have to wait for the library author to recompile their PCL to support the new platform, and who knows when that would be!

PCLs had their day, and they solved a definite problem, but for modern development you should focus your attention on .NET Standard instead.

A.2.2   *.NET Standard: a common interface for .NET*

As part of the development of .NET Core, Microsoft announced .NET Standard as the successor to PCL libraries. .NET Standard takes the PCL relationship between platform support and APIs available, and flips it on its head:

- *PCLs*—A PCL profile targets a specific set of *platforms*. The APIs available to a PCL library are the common APIs shared by all the platforms in the profile.

- *.NET Standard*—A .NET Standard version defines a specific set of *APIs*. These APIs are always available in a .NET Standard library. Any platform that implements all these APIs supports that version of .NET Standard.

.NET Standard isn't something you download. Instead, it's a list of APIs that a .NET Standard-compatible platform must implement. You can create libraries that target .NET Standard, and you can use that library in any app that targets a .NET Standard-compatible platform.

.NET Standard has multiple *versions*, each of which is a superset of the previous. .NET Standard 1.2 includes all the APIs from .NET Standard 1.1, which in turn includes all the APIs from .NET Standard 1.0, as shown in figure A.4.

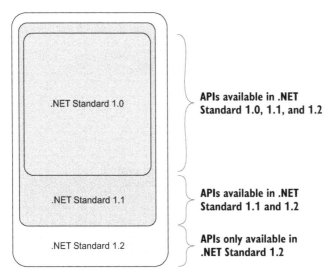

Figure A.4   Each version of .NET Standard includes all the APIs from previous versions. The smaller the version of .NET Standard, the smaller the number of APIs.

When you create a .NET Standard library, you target a specific version of .NET Standard and can reference any library that targets that version or earlier. If you're writing a library that targets .NET Standard 1.2, you can reference packages that target .NET Standard 1.2, 1.1, or 1.0. Your package can in turn be referenced by any library that targets .NET Standard 1.2 or later or any library that targets a *platform that implements* .NET Standard 1.2 or later.

A platform implements a specific version of .NET Standard if it contains all the APIs required by that version of .NET Standard. By extension, a platform that supports a specific version of .NET Standard also supports all previous versions of .NET Standard. For example, UWP version 10 supports .NET Standard 1.4, which means it also supports .NET Standard versions 1.0-1.3, as shown in figure A.5.

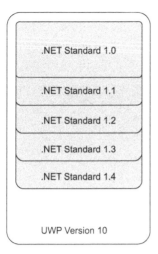

UWP Version 10 includes all the APIs for .NET Standard 1.4 and below.

It also includes platform-specific APIs that are not part of any .NET Standard.

Figure A.5   The UWP Platform version 10 supports .NET Standard 1.4. That means it contains all the APIs required by the .NET Standard specification version 1.4. By definition, that means it also contains all the APIs in earlier versions of .NET Standard. It also contains additional platform-specific APIs that aren't part of any version of .NET Standard.

Each version of a platform supports a different version of .NET Standard. .NET Framework 4.5 supports .NET Standard 1.1, but .NET Framework 4.7.1 supports .NET Standard 2.0. Table A.1 shows some of the versions supported by various .NET platforms. For a more complete list, see https://docs.microsoft.com/en-us/dotnet/standard/net-standard.

Table A.1   Highest supported .NET Standard version for various .NET platform versions. A blank cell means that version of .NET Standard isn't supported on the platform.

.NET Standard Version	1.0	1.1	1.2	1.3	1.4	1.5	1.6	2.0
.NET Core	1.0	1.0	1.0	1.0	1.0	1.0	1.0	2.0
.NET Framework	4.5	4.5	4.5.1	4.6	4.6.1	4.6.2		4.7.1
Mono	4.6	4.6	4.6	4.6	4.6	4.6	4.6	5.4
Windows	8.0	8.0	8.1					
Windows Phone	8.1	8.1	8.1					

A version of this table is often used to explain .NET Standard, but for me, the relationship between .NET Standard and a .NET Platform all made sense when I saw an example that explained .NET Standard in terms of C# constructs.[2]

---

[2] The example was by David Fowler from the ASP.NET team. You can view the original on GitHub at http://mng.bz/F9q3.

You can think of each version of .NET Standard as a series of inherited interfaces, and the .NET platforms as implementations of one of these interfaces. In the following listing, I use the last two rows of table A.1 to illustrate this, considering .NET Standard 1.0-1.2 and looking at the Windows 8.0 platform and Windows Phone 8.1.

Listing A.1   An interpretation of .NET Standard in C#

```
interface NETStandard1_0        ◁——   Defines the APIs
{                                       available in .NET
    void SomeMethod();                  Standard 1.0
}


interface NETStandard1_1 : NETStandard1_0        ◁——   .NET Standard 1.1
{                                                         inherits all the APIs from
    void OtherMethod();        ◁——                        .NET Standard 1.0.
}
                               APIs available in .NET
                               Standard 1.1 but not in 1.0

                                                    .NET Standard 1.2
                                                    inherits all the APIs from
interface NETStandard1_2 : NETStandard1_1    ◁——   .NET Standard 1.1.
{
    void YetAnotherMethod(){ /* Method implementation */ }  ◁
}                                                    APIs available in
                                                     .NET Standard
                                                     1.2 but not in
                                                     1.1 or 1.0

class Windows8 : NETStandard1_1
{                                                   Implementations of the
    void SomeMethod () { /* Method implementation */ }   APIs required by .NET
    void OtherMethod();                             Standard 1.1 and 1.0

    void ADifferentMethod() { /* Method implementation */ }  ◁————
}
                                                    Additional APIs that aren't part of
                                                    .NET Standard, but exist on the
                                                    Windows 8.0 platform

class WindowsPhone81 : NETStandard1_2
{                                                   Implementations of
    void SomeMethod () { /* Method implementation */ }    the APIs required by
    void OtherMethod() { /* Method implementation */ }    .NET Standard 1.2,
    void YetAnotherMethod () { /* Method implementation */ }   1.1, and 1.0

    void ExtraMethod1() { /* Method implementation */ }
    void ExtraMethod2() { /* Method implementation */ }
}
         Additional APIs that aren't part of
         .NET Standard, but exist on the
         Windows Phone 8.1 platform
```

Windows 8.0 implements .NET Standard 1.1.

Windows Phone 8.1 implements .NET Standard 1.2.

In the same way that you write programs to use interfaces rather than specific implementations, you can target your *libraries* against a .NET Standard interface without worrying about the individual implementation details of the platform. You can then use your library with any platform that implements the required interface version.

One of the advantages you gain by targeting .NET Standard is the ability to target new platforms without having to recompile any of your libraries or wait for dependent library authors to recompile theirs. It also makes reasoning about the exact APIs available far simpler—the higher the .NET Standard version you target, the more APIs will be available to you.

> **WARNING** Even if a platform implements a given version of .NET Standard, the method implementation might throw a `PlatformNotSupportedException`. For example, some reflection APIs might not be available on all platforms. I discuss how to counteract this issue in section A.3.

Unfortunately, things are never as simple as you want them to be. Although .NET Standard 2.0 is a strict superset of .NET Standard 1.6, apps targeting .NET Framework 4.6.1 can reference .NET Standard 2.0 libraries, even though it technically only implements .NET Standard 1.4, as shown in Table A.1.[3]

> **WARNING** Even though .NET Framework 4.6.1 technically only implements .NET Standard 1.4, it can reference .NET Standard 2.0 libraries. This is a special case and applies only to versions 4.6.1-4.7.0. .NET Framework 4.7.1 implements .NET Standard 2.0, so it can reference .NET Standard 2.0 libraries natively.

The reasoning behind this move was to counteract a chicken-and-egg problem. One of the early complaints about .NET Core 1.x was how few APIs were available, which made porting projects to .NET Core tricky. Consequently, in .NET Core 2.0, Microsoft added thousands of APIs that were available in .NET Framework 4.6.1, the most widely installed .NET Framework version, and added these APIs to .NET Standard 2.0. The intention was for .NET Standard 2.0 to provide the same APIs as .NET Framework 4.6.1.

Unfortunately, .NET Framework 4.6.1 *doesn't* contain the APIs in .NET Standard 1.5 or 1.6. Given .NET Standard 2.0 is a strict superset of .NET Standard 1.6, .NET Framework 4.6.1 can't support .NET Standard 2.0 directly.

This left Microsoft with a problem. If the most popular version of the .NET Framework didn't support .NET Standard 2.0, no one would write .NET Standard 2.0 libraries, which would hamstring .NET Core 2.0 as well. Consequently, Microsoft took the decision to *allow* .NET Framework 4.6.1 *to reference* .NET Standard 2.0 libraries, as shown in figure A.6.

All this leads to some fundamental technical difficulties. .NET Framework 4.6.1 can reference .NET Standard 2.0 libraries, even though it *technically* doesn't support them, but you must have the .NET Core 2.0 SDK installed to ensure everything works correctly.

---

[3] The reasoning behind this move was laid out in a post on the .NET blog which I highly recommend reading: http://mng.bz/tU6u.

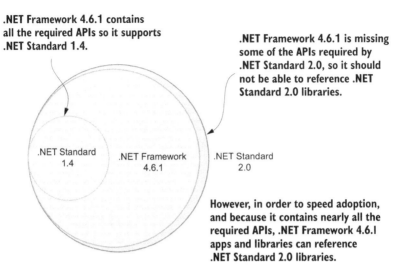

.NET Framework 4.6.1 contains all the required APIs so it supports .NET Standard 1.4.

.NET Framework 4.6.1 is missing some of the APIs required by .NET Standard 2.0, so it should not be able to reference .NET Standard 2.0 libraries.

.NET Standard 1.4

.NET Framework 4.6.1

.NET Standard 2.0

However, in order to speed adoption, and because it contains nearly all the required APIs, .NET Framework 4.6.1 apps and libraries can reference .NET Standard 2.0 libraries.

Figure A.6   NET Framework 4.6.1 doesn't contain the APIs required for .NET Standard 1.5, 1.6, or 2.0. But it contains *nearly* all the APIs required for .NET Standard 2.0. In order to speed up adoption and to make it easier to start using .NET Standard 2.0 libraries, you can reference .NET Standard 2.0 libraries for a .NET Framework 4.6.1 app.

To blur things even further, libraries compiled against .NET Framework 4.6.1 can be referenced by .NET Standard libraries through the use of a compatibility shim, as I describe in the next section.

A.2.3   *Fudging .NET Standard 2.0 support with the compatibility shim*

Microsoft's plan for .NET Standard 2.0 was to make it easier to build .NET Core apps. If users built libraries targeting .NET Standard 2.0, then they could still use them in their .NET Framework 4.6.1 apps, but they could also use the libraries in their .NET Core apps.

The problem was that when .NET Standard 2.0 was first released, no libraries (NuGet packages) would implement it yet. Given .NET Standard libraries can only reference other .NET Standard libraries, you'd have to wait for all of your dependencies to update to .NET Standard, who would have to wait for *their* dependencies first, and so on.

To speed things up, Microsoft created a compatibility shim. This shim allows a .NET Standard 2.0 library to *reference .NET Framework 4.6.1 libraries*. Ordinarily, this sort of reference wouldn't be possible; .NET Standard libraries can only reference .NET Standard libraries of an equal or lower version, as shown in figure A.7.[4]

By enabling this shim, suddenly .NET Core 2.0 apps can use any of the many .NET Framework 4.6.1 (or lower) NuGet libraries available. As long as the referenced

---

[4]   The process by which this magic is achieved is complicated. This article describes the process of assembly unification in detail: http://mng.bz/k1TR.

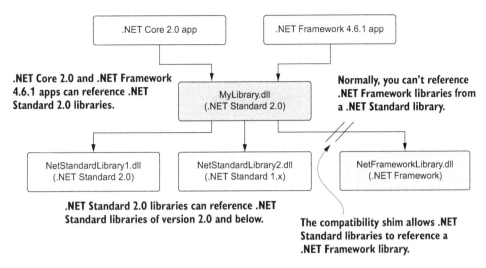

Figure A.7   By default, .NET Standard libraries can only reference other .NET Standard libraries, targeting the same .NET Standard version or lower. With the compatibility shim, .NET Standard libraries can also reference libraries compiled against .NET Framework 4.6.1.

library sticks to APIs which are part of .NET Standard 2.0, you'll be able to reference .NET Framework libraries in your .NET Core 2.0 app or .NET Standard 2.0 libraries, even if your app runs cross-platform on Linux or macOS.

> **WARNING**   If the library uses .NET Framework-specific APIs, you'll get an exception at runtime. There's no easy way of knowing whether a library is safe to use, short of examining the source code, so the .NET tooling will raise a warning every time you build. Be sure to thoroughly test your app if you rely on this shim.

If your head is spinning at this point, I don't blame you. We're at a particularly confusing point in the evolution of .NET Standard, in which rules are being bent to fit the current environment. This is already in the process of settling down, as .NET Framework 4.7.1 supports .NET Standard 2.0 without the caveats and hand-waving of .NET Framework 4.6.1.

   In section A.3, I provide guidelines you can apply to your apps when navigating this sea of .NET platforms and .NET Standard. Creating libraries for general consumption comes with some complexities, but for the most part, you should find these suggestions get you a long way.

A.3   *Choosing a target framework for your libraries and apps*

When you create an app or library, one of the first choices you need to make is which framework you're going to target: .NET Core 2.0, .NET Core 1.1, .NET Framework 4.6.1, or .NET Standard 1.3?

Which framework you should choose will vary depending on whether you're building an app, such as an ASP.NET Core app, or a library that you potentially want to reuse between multiple apps. If you're building an app, I'll assume it's ASP.NET Core, given you're reading this book!

A.3.1   *If you're building an ASP.NET Core app*

If you're building an application, you *can't* target .NET Standard. .NET Standard isn't a platform, it's a specification, so you can't run on it; there's nothing to run *on*! Instead, you must run an app on a platform implementation, such as the .NET Framework or .NET Core. The fact that these platforms implement .NET Standard means you can use .NET Standard libraries in your app, but you're still running on a platform.

> **WARNING**   An app must target a .NET platform implementation, such as .NET Core or the .NET Framework. It can't target .NET Standard.

Additionally, you must target a specific version of a .NET platform, so you must target .NET Core 1.0, .NET Core 2.0, or .NET Framework 4.7.1, for example. This book is about ASP.NET Core 2.0 specifically, and if you're building an ASP.NET Core 2.0 app, you must choose either .NET Core 2.0 (or later) or .NET Framework 4.6.1 (or later).

Personally, I recommend choosing .NET Core where possible, as it will give you greater flexibility in the long run. If you need to target the .NET Framework, I'd recommend choosing .NET Framework 4.7.1 where possible, as it avoids some of the workarounds I described in section A.2. .NET Framework 4.6.1 should work, but you may occasionally find issues when you consume .NET Standard 2.0 libraries.[5]

To set the target framework project for your app, use the `<TargetFramework>` element in your project's csproj file, along with your chosen framework's moniker.[6] For example, to target .NET Core 2.0, use

```
<TargetFramework>netcoreapp2.0</TargetFramework>
```

To target .NET Framework 4.7.1, use

```
<TargetFramework>net471</TargetFramework>
```

It's also possible to multi-target your app, so that you build it for more than one framework. You could, for example, target both .NET Core 2.0 and .NET Framework 4.7.1. Personally, I've never found multi-targeting *apps* in this way to be appealing or useful, but if you want to do so, you can use the `<TargetFrameworks>` element of your csproj, and separate the target framework monikers with a semicolon:

```
<TargetFrameworks>netcoreapp2.0;net471</TargetFrameworks>
```

---

[5] See https://github.com/dotnet/announcements/issues/31 for details and workarounds.
[6] For a list of all available monikers, see https://docs.microsoft.com/en-us/dotnet/standard/frameworks.

> **NOTE** When targeting a single framework, you use the `<TargetFramework>` element. When targeting multiple frameworks, you use the `<TargetFrameworks>` element (note the "s").

In general, I recommend your ASP.NET Core app targets .NET Core 2.0 or higher. If you're building libraries, I recommend taking a different approach, as described in section A.3.2.

A.3.2 *If you're building a shared library or NuGet package*

When you're building libraries, whether you're directly referencing a class library in the same solution or building a library to ultimately share on NuGet, I recommend using .NET Standard.

As I described in section A.2.2, .NET Standard lets you share code between multiple .NET platforms, so by targeting .NET Standard, you can reach the widest audience.

In addition, you should normally target the lowest version of .NET Standard that you can. The lower the version of .NET Standard you support, the more platforms will implement it, so the greater compatibility your library will have. The lower the version of .NET Standard, the fewer APIs you have available to you, so it's a tradeoff. Unfortunately, there's no automatic way to work out which version of .NET Standard provides all the APIs you need, so you'll need to use trial and error to find the version best for you.

> **TIP** For the largest compatibility, generally you should target the lowest version of .NET Standard that contains the APIs you need.

There's no reason you *must* target .NET Standard in your libraries; you can just as easily target specific platforms, for example .NET Core or the .NET Framework. But if you create a library that only targets a specific platform like .NET Core 2.0, then you'll *only* be able to use it in .NET Core 2.0 (or above) apps.

If you can get away with targeting .NET Standard 1.4 or below, then you'll be in a great position, as you'll be able to use your library on a wide range of platforms. If you need to go higher than that then take care; the workaround for .NET Framework 4.6.1 I described in section A.2.2 can lead to unexpected difficulties. I've found the following rules to be a good compromise:

- *If you need to target .NET Standard 1.4 or below*—No problems, your library can target .NET Standard 1.4 and you can reference it from .NET Core 1.x, .NET Core 2.0, and .NET Framework 4.6.1 apps without issues.
- *If you need to target .NET Standard 1.5 or 1.6*—These versions contain APIs that are found in .NET Core 1.x, but not in .NET Framework 4.6.1. If you need to target these APIs and not .NET Standard 1.4, then your library will likely fail on .NET Framework 4.6.1. The safest option is to target .NET Core directly.
- *If you need to target .NET Standard 2.0*—This will likely be the most common case. .NET Standard 2.0 includes thousands more APIs than 1.6. But because .NET

Framework 4.6.1 doesn't implement .NET Standard 2.0, I suggest you multi-target your libraries to .NET Standard 4.6.1 and .NET Standard 2.0.

The last of these options will likely be the most common, so I'll reiterate: if you're writing a library targeting .NET Standard 2.0 and there's any possibility you'll use it in apps targeting .NET Framework 4.6.1 - 4.7.0, then also target .NET Framework 4.6.1. This will reduce the possibility of referencing problems that can occur when referencing .NET Standard 2.0 libraries from .NET Framework 4.6.1.[7]

> **WARNING** If you're targeting a library to .NET Standard 2.0, and there's the possibility it will be used by an app or library targeting .NET Framework 4.6.1, then multi-target your library to .NET Standard 2.0 and .NET Framework 4.6.1.

If you can follow this advice, you should have a `<TargetFrameworks>` element in your library that looks like this:

```
<TargetFrameworks>netstandard2.0;net461</TargetFrameworks>
```

As .NET Framework 4.7.1 installations become more common, this problem should slowly disappear, and you can go back to targeting .NET Standard 2.0 alone. If you're definitely only targeting .NET Core, then you can already take this route.

   Hopefully, that clears up how to choose a target framework. If you stick to these guidelines, you shouldn't have any issues. There's one final practical issue I'd like to touch on in this appendix: the compatibility shim and whether you should use it.

A.3.3   *Referencing .NET Framework libraries from .NET Standard projects*

On the face of it, the compatibility shim, which allows .NET Standard libraries or .NET Core apps to reference .NET Framework libraries, sounds great. And for the most part, it is. But on occasion, it could cause you a world of pain. And the worst part is, you won't find out until runtime.

> **NOTE** As a disclaimer, I've never found any runtime issues with any libraries I've referenced. But that could be partly because it makes me nervous, so I avoid it as best I can!

If you reference a .NET Framework library from a .NET Standard 2.0 library or a .NET Core 2.0 app, you'll receive multiple warnings, as shown in figure A.8:

- Visual Studio will show a warning on the library reference in Solution Explorer.
- You'll get a warning every time you build.

All these warnings should make it clear you're living life in the danger zone. It's important you thoroughly test the behavior of the referenced library, or preferably

---

[7] I spent hours this week trying to rectify issues caused by referencing .NET Standard 2.0 in a large .NET Framework 4.6.1 app. For details, see this issue on GitHub: https://github.com/dotnet/standard/issues/481.

You can reference a .NET Framework library from a .NET Core app,
but you will see a warning in Solution Explorer.

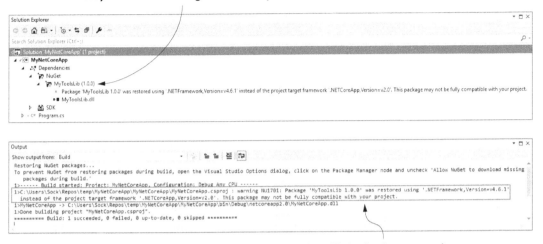

Figure A.8 The .NET Standard compatibility shim lets you reference .NET Framework libraries from .NET Standard or .NET Core apps. Although useful, this gives the potential for runtime errors, so a warning is displayed in the Dependencies node in Visual Studio, and every time you build the project.

verify that the source code doesn't contain any .NET Framework-specific API calls that would throw a `PlatformNotSupported` exception when used in your library.

Once you're happy with the referenced library, you can choose to ignore the warning, to keep you build log clean. You can do this by adding a `NoWarn="NU1701"` attribute to the `<PackageReference>` in your .csproj file, for example:

```
<PackageReference Include="MyToolsLib" Version="1.0.0" NoWarn="NU1701" />
```

Alternatively, if you're using Visual Studio, right-click the dependency in Solution Explorer and select Properties. In the Properties window, enter `NU1701` for `NoWarn`, as shown in figure A.9.

There's one final tool I've found useful for identifying cross-platform issues: the Roslyn API analyzer. You can install this NuGet package into your project and it will check your code for potentially problematic APIs. Add the Microsoft.DotNet.Analyzers.Compatibility package using the NuGet package manager, or add the reference to your .csproj file:

```
<PackageReference Include="Microsoft.DotNet.Analyzers.Compatibility"
    Version="0.1.2-alpha" PrivateAssets="All" />
```

If you call an API that isn't available on all platforms, the analyzer will add a build warning, and in Visual Studio you'll see a quick-action warning, as shown in figure

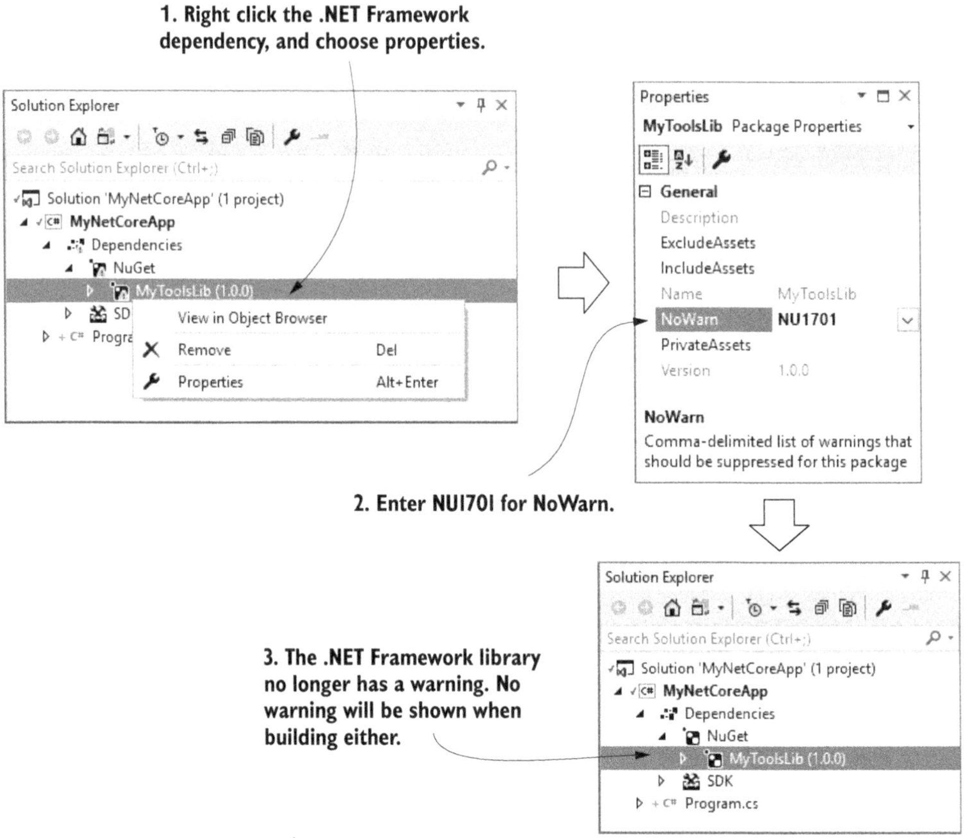

**1. Right click the .NET Framework
dependency, and choose properties.**

2. Enter NUI70I for NoWarn.

**3. The .NET Framework library
no longer has a warning. No
warning will be shown when
building either.**

**Figure A.9   This shows how to ignore the warning produced when referencing a .NET Framework library
from a .NET Standard or .NET Core app. With the `NoWarn` property set, you'll no longer get a visual
indicator in the Dependencies node, and you won't get warnings when you build your project.**

A.10. If you're not using Visual Studio, you'll still see the warning when building your
project, but you won't see the quick-action tool tip.

The API analyzer isn't only for cross-platform calls. It will also warn you if you're
using deprecated APIs, and, most importantly for my sanity, it will warn you if you're
using a .NET Standard API that isn't available on .NET Framework 4.6.1.

The analyzer has only recently been released, but I strongly recommend giving it a
try in your projects, especially if you're creating .NET Standard libraries. You can see
the announcement blog post and watch the analyzer in action here: http://mng
.bz/8Yl8.

```
static void Main(string[] args)
{
    Console.WindowWidth = 400;
    Console.Writ    ne    🔧 int Console.WindowWidth { get; set; }
                          Gets or sets the width of the console window.

                          Exceptions:
                          ArgumentOutOfRangeException
                          System.IO.IOException

                          Console.WindowWidth isn't supported on Linux, MacOSX

                          Show potential fixes (Alt+Enter or Ctrl+.)
}
```

Figure A.10   The quick-action warning for an API that isn't supported on all platforms. Even though the API is part of .NET Standard 2.0, on Linux and macOS it will throw an exception when called. The API analyzer adds warnings so you can find these issues at compile time, instead of at runtime.

Summary

- .NET has many different implementations, including the .NET Framework, Mono, and Unity. Each of these is a separate platform with separate Base Class Libraries (BCLs) and app models. .NET Core is another separate platform.

- Each platform has a BCL that provides fundamental .NET types and classes such as strings, file manipulation, and streams. Each platform has a slightly different BCL.

- Portable Class Libraries (PCLs) attempted to solve the problem of sharing code between platforms by allowing you to write code to the logical intersection of each platform's BCL. Each additional platform you targeted meant fewer BCL APIs in common.

- .NET Standard defines a standard set of APIs that are available across all platforms that support it. You can write libraries that target a specific version of .NET Standard and they'll be compatible with any platform that supports that version of .NET Standard.

- Each version of .NET Standard is a superset of the previous. For example, .NET Standard 1.2 includes all the APIs from .NET Standard 1.1, which in turn includes all the APIs from .NET Standard 1.0.

- Each version of a platform supports a specific version of .NET Standard. For example, .NET Framework 4.5.1 supports .NET Standard 1.2 (and hence also .NET Standard 1.1 and 1.0).

- .NET Framework 4.6.1 technically only supports .NET Standard 1.4. Thanks to a compatibility shim, you can reference .NET Standard 2.0 libraries from a .NET Framework 4.6.1 app. Similarly, you can reference a .NET Framework library from a .NET Standard 2.0 library, which wouldn't be possible without the shim.

- If you rely on the compatibility shim to reference a .NET Framework 4.6.1 library from a .NET Standard 2.0 library, and the referenced library uses .NET Framework-specific APIs, you'll get an exception at runtime.

- An app must target a .NET platform implementation, such as .NET Core or the .NET Framework. It can't target .NET Standard.

- I recommend targeting .NET Core 2.0 when writing apps or targeting .NET Framework 4.7.1 if you can't use .NET Core.

- When building shared libraries, for the largest compatibility you should target the lowest version of .NET Standard that contains the APIs you need. This will let you use your library on the largest number of .NET platforms.

- If you're targeting a library to .NET Standard 2.0 and there's the possibility it will be used by an app or library targeting .NET Framework 4.6.1 or below, multi-target your library to .NET Standard 2.0 and .NET Framework 4.6.1.

- When targeting a single framework, use the `<TargetFramework>` element. When targeting multiple frameworks, use the `<TargetFrameworks>` element (note the "s").

- Install the Microsoft.DotNet.Analyzers.Compatibility NuGet package to add a Roslyn analyzer to your project. If you call an API that isn't available on all platforms, the analyzer will add a build warning and in Visual Studio you'll see a quick-action warning.

appendix B
Useful references

In this appendix, I provide a number of links and references that I've found useful for learning about .NET Core, .NET Standard, and ASP.NET Core.

Relevant books

In this book, we touched on several topics and aspects of the .NET ecosystem that are somewhat peripheral to building ASP.NET Core applications. For a deeper understanding of those topics, I recommend the books in this section. They cover areas that you'll inevitably encounter when building ASP.NET Core applications:

- Metzgar, Dustin. *.NET Core in Action.* Manning, 2018. https://livebook .manning .com/#!/book/dotnet-core-in-action/. ASP.NET Core apps are typically built using .NET Core, and .NET Core in Action provides everything you need to know about running on the platform.
- Osherove, Roy. *The Art of Unit Testing, Second Edition.* Manning, 2013. http://mng.bz/79n2.
- In this book (*ASP.NET Core in Action*), I discuss the mechanics of unit testing ASP.NET Core applications. For a deeper discussion of how to create your tests, I recommend *The Art of Unit Testing.*
- Seemann, Mark. and Steven van Deursen, *Dependency Injection in .NET, Second Edition.* Manning, 2018. https://livebook.manning.com/#!/book/ dependency-injection-in-dot-net-second-edition/. Dependency injection is a core aspect of ASP.NET Core, so *Dependency Injection in .NET* is especially relevant now. It introduces the patterns and antipatterns of dependency injection in the context of .NET and the C# language.
- Smith, Jon P. *Entity Framework Core in Action.* Manning, 2018. https://livebook .manning.com/#!/book/entity-framework-core-in-action/. If you're using EF Core in your apps, I highly recommend *Entity Framework Core in Action.* It

covers all the features and pitfalls of EF Core, as well as how to tune your app for performance.

Announcement blog posts

When Microsoft releases a new version of ASP.NET Core or .NET Core, they typically write an announcement blog post. These posts provide a high-level overview of the topic, with many examples of new features. They're a great place to start if you want to quickly get acquainted with a topic:

- De la Torre, Cesar. "Web Applications with ASP.NET Core Architecture and Patterns guidance (Updated for .NET Core 2.0)," *.NET Blog* (blog), Microsoft, August 9, 2017, http://mng.bz/t415. Blog post introducing a free e-book on how to architecture modern web apps using ASP.NET Core and Azure.
- Fritz, Jeffrey T. "Announcing ASP.NET Core 2.0," *.NET Blog* (blog), Microsoft, August 14, 2017, http://mng.bz/0004. Announcement blog post for ASP.NET Core 2.0. Describes how to upgrade a project from 1.x to 2.0 and introduces some of the features specific to ASP.NET Core 2.0.
- Lander, Rich. "Announcing .NET Core 2.0," *.NET Blog* (blog), Microsoft, August 14, 2017, https://blogs.msdn.microsoft.com/dotnet/2017/08/14/announcing-net-core-2-0/. Announcement blog post for .NET Core 2.0, describing the new features compared to .NET Core 1.x.
- Landwerth, Immo. "Announcing .NET Standard 2.0," *.NET Blog* (blog), Microsoft, August 14, 2017, http://mng.bz/jH8Y. Announcement blog post for .NET Standard 2.0 and how it fits into the .NET ecosystem.
- Landwerth, Immo. ".NET Standard—Demystifying .NET Core and .NET Standard," *Microsoft Developer Network*, Microsoft, September, 2017, https://msdn.microsoft.com/en-us/magazine/mt842506.aspx. Long post explaining introducing .NET Core and explaining where .NET Standard fits in the .NET ecosystem.

Microsoft documentation

Historically, Microsoft documentation has been poor, but with ASP.NET Core there has been a massive push to ensure the docs are useful and current. You can find walkthroughs, targeted documentation for specific features, documentation for supported APIs, and even an in-browser C# compiler:

- Microsoft Docs, ".NET API Browser." Microsoft Docs. http://mng.bz/yT90. This is an API browser, which can be used to work out which .NET APIs are available on which .NET platforms.
- Miller, Rowan, Brice Lambson, Maria Wenzel, Diego Vega, and Martin Milan. "Entity Framework Core Quick Overview." Microsoft Docs. October 27, 2016. https://docs.microsoft.com/en-us/ef/core/. This is the official documentation for EF Core.

- Roth, Daniel, Rick Anderson, and Shaun Luttin. "Introduction to ASP.NET Core." Microsoft Docs. September 3, 2017. https://docs.microsoft.com/en-us/aspnet/core/. This is the official documentation for ASP.NET Core.
- Wenzel Maria, tompratt-AQ, and Luke Latham. ".NET Standard." Microsoft Docs. August 13, 2017. https://docs.microsoft.com/en-us/dotnet/standard/net-standard. This is the official documentation for .NET Standard.

Security-related links

Security is an important aspect of modern web development. This section contains some of the references I refer to regularly, which describe some best practices for web development, as well as practices to avoid:

- Allen, Brock, and Dominick Baier. "IdentityServer4 1.0.0 documentation." https://identityserver4.readthedocs.io. Documentation for IdentityServer, the OpenID Connect and OAuth 2.0 framework for ASP.NET Core 2.0.
- Baier, Dominick. *Dominick Baier on Identity & Access Control* (blog). https://leastprivilege.com/. The personal blog of Dominick Baier, co-author of IdentityServer. A great resource when working with authentication and authorization in ASP.NET Core.
- Doran, Barry. "ASP.NET Core Authorization Lab." https://github.com/blowdart/AspNetAuthorizationWorkshop. A workshop walking through adding authorization to an ASP.NET Core app.
- Helme, Scott. *Scott Helme* (blog). https://scotthelme.co.uk/. Scott Helme's blog, with advice on security standards, especially security headers you can add to your application.
- Helme, Scott. "SecurityHeaders.io—Analyse your HTTP response headers." https://securityheaders.io/. Test your website's security headers, and get advice on why and how you should add them to your app.
- Hunt, Troy. *Troy Hunt* (blog). https://www.troyhunt.com. Personal blog of Troy Hunt with security-related advice for web developers, particularly .NET developers.

ASP.NET Core GitHub repositories

ASP.NET Core is entirely open source and developed on GitHub. One of the best ways I've found to learn about the framework is to browse the source code itself. This section contains the main repositories for ASP.NET Core, .NET Core, and EF Core:

- .NET Foundation. ".NET Core Libraries (CoreFX)." .NET Core (framework libraries and documentation). https://github.com/dotnet/corefx.
- .NET Foundation. ".NET Core Common Language Runtime (CoreCLR)." .NET Core Runtime. https://github.com/dotnet/coreclr.
- .NET Foundation. ".NET Command Line Interface." .NET command line interface (CLI). https://github.com/dotnet/cli.

- Microsoft. "ASP.NET." The framework libraries that make up ASP.NET Core. https://github.com/aspnet.
- Microsoft. "Entity Framework Core." The EF Core library. https://github.com/aspnet/EntityFrameworkCore.

Tooling and services

This section contains links to tools and services you can use to build ASP.NET Core projects:

- .NET Core SDK: https://www.microsoft.com/net/download.
- Cloudflare is a global content delivery network you can use to add caching and HTTPS to your applications for free: https://www.cloudflare.com/.
- Gavrysh, Olia. "Introducing API Analyzer," *.NET Blog* (blog), Microsoft, October 31, 2017, http://mng.bz/8Yl8. The announcement blog post for the Roslyn API analyzer discussed in appendix A.
- Let's Encrypt is a free, automated, and open Certificate Authority. You can use it to obtain free SSL certificates to secure your application: https://letsencrypt.org/.
- Rehan Saeed, Muhammed. ".NET Boxed" https://github.com/Dotnet-Boxed/Templates. A comprehensive collection of templates to get started with ASP.NET Core, preconfigured with many best practices.
- Visual Studio, Visual Studio for Mac, and Visual Studio Code: https://www.visualstudio.com/.

ASP.NET Core blogs

This section contains blogs that focus on ASP.NET Core. Whether you're trying to get an overview of a general topic, or trying to solve a specific problem, it can be useful to have multiple viewpoints on a topic.

- .NET Team. *.NET Blog (blog).* Microsoft, https://blogs.msdn.microsoft.com/dotnet. The .NET team's blog, lots of great links.
- Alcock, Chris. *The Morning Brew (blog).* http://blog.cwa.me.uk/. A collection of .NET-related blog posts, curated daily.
- Boden, Damien. *Software Engineering (blog).* https://damienbod.com/. Excellent blog by Damien Boden on ASP.NET Core, lots of posts about ASP.NET Core with Angular.
- Brind, Mike. *Mikesdotnetting (blog).* https://www.mikesdotnetting.com/. Mike Brind has many posts on ASP.NET Core, especially on ASP.NET Core 2.0's Razor Pages feature.
- Hanselman, Scott. *Scott Hanselman (blog).* https://www.hanselman.com/blog/ Renowned speaker Scott Hanselman's personal blog. A highly diverse blog, focused predominantly on .NET.

- Lock, Andrew. *.NET Escapades (blog)*. https://andrewlock.net. My personal blog, focused on ASP.NET Core.

- Pine, David. *IEvangelist (blog)*. http://davidpine.net/. Personal blog of Microsoft MVP David Pine, with lots of posts on ASP.NET Core.

- Rehan Saeed, Muhammed. *Muhammed Rehan Saeed (blog)*. https://rehansaeed .com. Personal blog of Muhammad Rehan Saeed, Microsoft MVP and author of the .NET Boxed project (linked in section 2.6).

- Strahl, Rick. *Rick Strahl's Web Log (blog)*. https://weblog.west-wind.com/. Great blog by Rick Strahl covering a wide variety of ASP.NET Core topics.

- Wildermuth, Shawn. *Shawn Wildermuth's (blog)*. https://wildermuth.com. Blog primarily covering ASP.NET Core and Angular.

- Wojcieszyn, Filip. *StrathWeb (blog)*. https://www.strathweb.com. Lots of posts on ASP.NET Core and ASP.NET from Filip, a Microsoft MVP.

Video links

If you prefer video for learning a subject, I recommend checking out the links in this section. In particular, the ASP.NET Core community standup provides great insight into the changes we'll see in future ASP.NET Core versions, straight from the team building the framework.

- .NET Foundation. "ASP.NET Core Community Standup." https://live.asp.net/. Weekly videos with the ASP.NET Core team discussing development of the framework.

- Landwerth, Immo. ".NET Standard—Introduction." YouTube video, 10:16 minutes. Posted November 28, 2016. http://mng.bz/DY40. The first video in an excellent series on the .NET standard.

- Microsoft. "Channel 9: Videos for developers from the people building Microsoft products and services." https://channel9.msdn.com/. Microsoft's official video channel. Contains a huge number of videos on .NET and ASP.NET Core, among many others.

- Wildermuth, Shawn. "Building a Web App with ASP.NET Core, MVC, Entity Framework Core, Bootstrap, and Angular." Pluralsight course, 10:03 hours. Posted October 27, 2017. http://mng.bz/Z35G. Shawn Wildermuth's course on building an ASP.NET Core application.

index

.NET Core in Action

by Dustin Metzgar

ISBN: 9781617294273
275 pages
$44.99
June 2018

Entity Framework Core in Action

by Jon P Smith

ISBN: 9781617294563
470 pages
$49.99
May 2018

C# in Depth, Third Edition

by Jon Skeet

ISBN: 9781617291340
616 pages
$49.99
September 2013

For ordering information go to www.manning.com

Concurrency in .NET
Modern patterns of concurrent and
parallel programming
by Riccardo Terrell

ISBN: 9781617292996
528 pages
$59.99
May 2018

Get Programming with F#
A guide for .NET developers
by Isaac Abraham

ISBN: 9781617293993
448 pages
$44.99
February 2018

Metaprogramming in .NET
by Kevin Hazzard and Jason Bock

ISBN: 9781617290268
360 pages
$44.99
December 2012

For ordering information go to www.manning.com